SO VAST AND VARIOUS

CARLETON LIBRARY SERIES

The Carleton Library Series, funded by Carleton University under the general editorship of the dean of the School of Graduate Studies and Research, publishes books about Canadian economics, geography, history, politics, society, and related subjects. It includes important new works as well as reprints of classics in the fields. The editorial committee welcomes manuscripts and suggestions, which should be sent to the dean of the School of Graduate Studies and Research, Carleton University.

So Vast and Various

Interpreting Canada's Regions in the Nineteenth and Twentieth Centuries

EDITED BY

JOHN WARKENTIN

McGill-Queen's University Press
Montreal & Kingston • London • Ithaca

© McGill-Queen's University Press 2010

ISBN 978-0-7735-3719-4 (cloth)
ISBN 978-0-7735-3738-5 (paper)

Legal deposit fourth quarter 2010
Bibliothèque nationale du Québec

Printed in Canada on acid-free paper that is 100% ancient forest free
(100% post-consumer recycled), processed chlorine free

McGill-Queen's University Press acknowledges the support of the
Canada Council for the Arts for our publishing program. We also
acknowledge the financial support of the Government of Canada
through the Canada Book Fund for our publishing activities.

Library and Archives Canada Cataloguing in Publication Data

So vast and various : interpreting Canada's regions in the nineteenth
and twentieth centuries / edited by John Warkentin.

(Carleton library series ; 219)
Includes bibliographical references.
ISBN 978-0-7735-3719-4 (bound). – ISBN 978-0-7735-3738-5 (pbk.)

1. Canada – Historical geography. 2. Canada – Description and
travel. 3. Canada – History – 1841–. I. Warkentin, John, 1928–
II. Series: Carleton library ; 218.

FC179.S68 2010   917.1   C2010-902984-4

Typeset by Jay Tee Graphics Ltd. in 10.5/13 Sabon

Contents

Preface

My title, *So Vast and Various*, comes from George Parkin's 1895 introduction to his book on Canada: "It need scarcely be added that in regions so vast and various Nature is often seen in her most splendid and picturesque aspects" (*The Great Dominion*, 7). Every writer on the geography of Canada has to face up to its great regions, with their distinctive scenery, people, cultures, ways of making a living, communications, and settlements. This book allows us to see how seven authors, writing over a span of almost a century and a half, from 1831 to 1977, describe Canada's major regions and in so doing help elucidate the country. Both Canada and the ways of describing it changed over that long period, and through the authors' perceptions of regions at different times we get a deeper understanding of the regional nature of Canada and in turn of the country as a whole.

This project has its origins in an article I published in 1999 in *The Canadian Geographer* on the regional writing of five perceptive observers of Canada: Joseph Bouchette, a surveyor from Lower Canada who wrote on British North America in the early nineteenth century; George Parkin, an educator and journalist from New Brunswick who described the country in the late nineteenth century; J. D. Rogers, a British barrister, scholar and onetime fellow of University College, Oxford, and Harold Innis, an economic historian from Ontario, who both provided regional interpretations of Canada in the first quarter of the twentieth century; and Bruce Hutchison, a journalist from British Columbia who viewed Canada's regions through encounters with its men and women in the mid-twentieth century. All brought out the inherent regional differences within Canada in the time period in which they were writing. This article caught the eye of a member of the editorial board of

McGill-Queen's University Press, who suggested to his colleagues that I be asked to prepare a book of readings by these astute observers of Canada. Philip Cercone, director of the Press, persuaded me to submit an outline of what such a book might cover. The editorial board accepted my ideas in principle but suggested, correctly, that based on my selections there appeared to be little on the Canadian North in what these authors had to say. To remedy this, I added two sections on the North: an article of 1930 by R. C. Wallace, a Scottish-born geologist who became a leading educator in Canadian universities and had administrative experience in the North, and Thomas Berger, a lawyer and judge from British Columbia who in the 1970s presided over an important Royal Commission on northern development, which took full account of the indigenous peoples.

Over the century and a half in which these authors published their thoughts and interpretations various forces transformed Canada: these include immigration, re-settling of new parts of the country, new communications facilities, new technologies, new economies, and changing relations with the outside world. But despite all the changes the distinctiveness of the major regions has held fast, and distinctive they remain today. Bringing the contributions of the seven authors together into one volume allows us to compare directly their descriptions, ideas, and conceptions and thus gain a deeper insight into our country and the regional foundations on which it is built.

In the introduction I provide a brief account of the development of regional geographical writing in British North America and Canada. This provides a context for the writing included in this collection. The regional portrayals are arranged chronologically by author, and I provide short introductory essays for each and additional comments within the text where necessary. These are indicated by ᴥ at the beginning and end of my comments.

I want to thank Connie Ko, of the York University Department of Geography, for her assistance in scanning the books and printing various versions of the text as it was pruned to manageable size, and Joan McGilvray of McGill-Queen's University Press for her careful copyediting and astute, helpful comments. Also I wish to express my appreciation to the McGill-Queen's editorial board, and Philip Cercone in particular, for suggesting this project in the first place and supporting it through to final completion.

Excerpts in the book were taken from:

Joseph Bouchette, *The British Dominions in North America; or
a Topographical and Statistical Description of the Provinces of
Lower and Upper Canada, New Brunswick, Nova Scotia, The
Islands of Newfoundland, Prince Edward, and Cape Breton.
Including Considerations on Land-Granting and Emigration;
and a Topographical Dictionary of Lower Canada; to Which are
Annexed, Statistical Table and Tables of Distances, &c.* 2 volumes.
London: Longman, Rees, Orme, Brown, and Green, 1831
George R Parkin, *The Great Dominion: Studies of Canada.* London:
Macmillan and Co., 1895
J. D Rogers, *A Historical Geography of the British Colonies,* Volume
5, Part 3: *Canada, Geographical.* Oxford: The Clarendon Press,
1911
– *A Historical Geography of the British Colonies,* Volume 5, Part 4:
Newfoundland. Oxford: The Clarendon Press, 1931 (First edition
1911)
Harold A. Innis, *A History of the Canadian Pacific Railway.* London:
P.S. King; Toronto: McClelland and Stewart, 1923
R. C. Wallace, "The Canadian Northland," *The Book of Canada,*
edited by Chester Martin, W. Stewart Wallace, T. C. Routley.
Published by the Canadian Medical Association on the Occasion of
the Meeting of the British Medical Association in Winnipeg, August
1930, Toronto 1930, 77-82.
Bruce Hutchison, *The Unknown Country: Canada and Her People.*
New York: Coward-McCann, 1942; Toronto: Longmans, Green &
Co., 1943
– *Canada, Tomorrow's Giant.* Toronto: Longman Canada, 1957
[Thomas R. Berger] *Northern Frontier Northern Homeland: the
Report of the Mackenzie Valley Inquiry.* Ottawa: Minister of
Supplies and Services Canada, 1977. Reproduced with the permis-
sion of the Minister of Public Works and Government Services
Canada, 2009.

The editor and the Press are grateful to the previous publishers of works
still in copyright for allowing us to reprint the excerpts included here.

SO VAST AND VARIOUS

Recognizing Canada's Regions

When Canadians think of their country and its major sections, they commonly divide it into six regions: Atlantic Canada, Quebec, Ontario, the Prairies, British Columbia, and the North. Of course variations are numerous. For instance, Atlantic Canada may be further divided into the Maritimes and Newfoundland and Labrador, Quebec and Ontario together may be referred to as Central Canada, the term "the West" may be applied to the Prairies plus British Columbia, and the North is defined in various ways. But the broad pattern holds. How did these regional generalizations, these regional perceptions, come into being? How long have they been with us? What factors affected how these regions were perceived?

Our planet's shell – land, water, air, plants, animals, and humans – is an infinitely complex geographical reality. Within this world countless regional divisions have been devised, with numerous regions of various kinds shown on maps. Political regions such as countries may have boundaries marked on the ground, but basically regions exist in people's minds and in records such as maps, articles, and books. People conceive, define, and name regions for practical everyday purposes, to identify particular sections of the earth. Such regions are of any size and will have some dominating characteristics, which may be physical, human, or a combination of both, that have proved practical for identifying and differentiating them. Every child learns regional divisions of many kinds from parents, acquaintances, in school, and from reading newspapers and viewing television. Small regions in the immediate home area and local community will be known in particular detail, but regional divisions in the wider world are also quickly learned. It is part of the knowledge acquired in growing up and being in the world.

Before regional divisions could be conceived for an area as huge as northern North America, considerable comprehensive information on that part of the continent had to be acquired. Information had to somehow be brought together on the area that now is Canada. First Nations people had much local information, travelled long distances, and provided essential information and assistance to European "explorers" once they arrived and journeyed through their homelands, but the first comprehensive information on northern North America as a whole was only gradually and painstakingly compiled in metropolitan centres of western Europe. That is where reports brought back by explorers of various parts of the continent were published, information from many sources assembled and integrated, and maps prepared from increasingly accurate survey data. Essentially, the roster of explorers who recorded basic information on northern North America in their forays into the New World and then brought it to Europe is a roll call of the explorers of Canada taught about in Canadian schools. These explorers include Giovanni Caboto, Jacques Cartier, and Samuel de Champlain, who were active on the Atlantic Coast in the fifteenth and seventeenth centuries; Henry Kelsey, Pierre Gaultier de la Vérendrye, Anthony Henday, and David Thompson. who travelled in the interior in the sixteenth to nineteenth centuries; Martin Frobisher, Henry Hudson, Samuel Hearne, Alexander Mackenzie, William Parry, and Otto Sverdrup, who investigated the Arctic in the sixteenth to twentieth centuries; and James Cook, George Vancouver, and Alexander Mackenzie, who acquired information on the Pacific Coast in the eighteenth century. Through the efforts of these individuals and many others the general configuration, physical nature, and some knowledge of the human geography of northern North America became available in numerous reports and maps. This diverse information that had been gradually accumulated awaited writers on geography to bring it into focus, conceptualize regions, and prepare geographic descriptions and interpretations of northern North America.

European cartographers helped greatly. They waited eagerly for explorers to return to Europe and make known their latest findings on the outlines of the coasts, main rivers and lakes, and mountain ranges. Champlain was himself a mapmaker, but in most instances it was well-established cartographers resident in various countries who brought the information together into maps. These included Jacques Bellin and Philippe Buache in France, and Aaron and John Arrowsmith in England. Maps of North America were regularly revised as soon as new information made this practicable.

In addition to basic information on the physical configuration and main water features of northern North America on which broad regional divisions can be based, a second important element in such regionalization is territorial control. Before the sixteenth century this land was the home of First Nations and Inuit populations. In following centuries European countries cavalierly ignored the rights of these inhabitants, invaded their territories, and dispossessed the indigenous people. British, French, Spanish, Russian, and Norwegian governments claimed land; some established outposts, brought in colonists, overran established societies, and fought for territory amongst themselves. Particularly important for the future Canada was the lengthy contest for colonial supremacy between the British and the French on the Atlantic coast and in the interior of northern North America. Eventually the British won out, but a vital French North American population remained behind in what became Quebec. On the Pacific coast competing claims amongst British, Spanish, and Russian rivals had to be worked out, but in the end the British prevailed over an extensive mid-latitude section of the coast, now British Columbia, although the southern boundary with the United States was not finally determined until the mid-nineteenth century.

By 1763, the British were in control of what is present eastern and interior Canada. After the American Revolution the southern boundary with the new United States had to be established in eastern North America and subsequently, as the British and United States empires rapidly extended westward, the boundary between the two had to be drawn all the way to the Pacific Ocean. This was accomplished in three stages: in the east in 1783 the boundary was drawn south of present New Brunswick and Quebec and through the middle of the St. Lawrence River and four of the Great Lakes; in the western interior in 1818 the boundary was drawn across the plains along the 49th parallel to the Rocky Mountains; and, finally, in the far west in 1846 the boundary was continued along the same parallel across the western cordillera to the Pacific Ocean, bending south of Vancouver Island. These were lines on maps: the actual boundary marking on the ground came years later. In 1825 it was agreed between Great Britain and Russia that the northwestern boundary of British North America should be the 141st meridian, and when the United States acquired Alaska from Russia in 1867 that meridian became another boundary with the United States, although some details were not worked out until 1903. In the Arctic the British were the prime claimants, and Great Britain officially transferred the northern Archipelago to Canada in 1880. Norway

also claimed Arctic lands west of Greenland, mainly based on Otto
Sverdrup's explorations at the turn of the nineteenth century, and not
until well into the twentieth century, in 1930, for a pittance, did it graciously transfer its claim to Canada.

To organize this vast territory in northern North America, the British,
over the course of many years, established numerous separate colonial
jurisdictions, which were sometimes kept small for ease of local administration, especially at a time when communications were slow and,
particularly in winter, difficult. On the fragmented Atlantic coast five
colonies emerged, all relatively small: Newfoundland, Cape Breton (in
separate existence only for a short time), Nova Scotia, Prince Edward
Island, and New Brunswick. The Province of Canada, which extended
from the Gulf of St. Lawrence to Lake Superior, was divided in two in
1784: the mainly French-Canadian area along the St. Lawrence River
became Lower Canada and the peninsula thrust into the Lower Great
Lakes, together with the large area extending to the western watershed
of Lake Superior, became Upper Canada. These areas were united again
in 1842 to form the United Provinces of Canada, i.e. Canada East and
Canada West, only to be split at Confederation to become Quebec and
Ontario. In the Confederation of Canada in 1867 the original four
provinces were Nova Scotia, New Brunswick, Quebec, and Ontario.
Two areas remained apart in eastern North America: Prince Edward
Island did not join Confederation until 1873, and Newfoundland and
Labrador not until 1949. For many years the western interior was under
the jurisdiction of the Hudson's Bay Company, but in 1870, after the
Riel Resistance, that huge area was transferred to Canada; Manitoba
was created as a tiny province, and the North-West Territories was
established. Then in 1905 Saskatchewan and Alberta were separated
out from the North-West Territories and became provinces, and in
1912 Manitoba was extended to Hudson Bay and Ontario and Quebec
attained their present boundaries. On the Pacific coast, the British had
established Vancouver's Island and British Columbia as colonies. These
were united in 1866 and then became part of Canada in 1871 as the
province of British Columbia. In the North, the North-West Territories
were subdivided into internal administrative areas in various ways
over the decades, but there were two major changes: in 1898, after the
Klondike Gold Rush, the western part was severed and became Yukon
Territory, and in 1999 the eastern part also was severed and became
Nunavut Territory, leaving the central part as the Northwest Territory
of today.

Conceptually, the major regions that concern us here arose mainly out of combining the broad configuration of northern North America, the bordering oceans, and the British North American administrative units that came into being in the eighteenth and nineteenth centuries. It was natural to differentiate the major external regions fronting on the great oceans – the Atlantic, Pacific. and Arctic – and the extensive interior regions, with one of the greatest rivers of Canada, the St. Lawrence, a complicating factor in this simple scheme. As we will see in the next section, it took some time to combine the regional conceptions into the grand regional divisions of Canada we know today, but by the 1830s Joseph Bouchette had discerned the divisions clearly. Before we turn to the authors who described the regions, a very brief reminder of the nature of these regions will be helpful background.

Resources, ways of making a living, and trends in population and urban growth have varied greatly in the generally recognized major Canadian regions: the Atlantic, Great Lakes–St. Lawrence, Prairie, Pacific, and North. In the Atlantic area a combination of fish, forest, farming, coal, and ocean carrying-trade supported people. Both fish and coal have greatly declined in importance. Major urban organizing centres situated on the coast emerged at St. John's, Halifax, and Saint John and one interior centre, Moncton, grew later with the arrival of the railway. The population is predominantly of British and Acadian origin. Farming, forestry, and then increasingly manufacturing, communications, and the service industry characterize the lands along the St. Lawrence River and Lower Great Lakes. This is where Canada's great metropolitan centres, Montreal and Toronto, industrial cities such as Hamilton and Windsor, and capitals such as Ottawa and Quebec City have flourished. Until the 1960s the population in Quebec was mainly of French origin and in Ontario of British origin, but, as a result of large migrations from southern Europe, the Caribbean, Asia, and Oceania, the populations quickly became increasingly diverse. Agriculture and fossil fuels are economic mainstays on the Prairies, with some manufacturing. Urban growth followed the railways, with Winnipeg flourishing as the gateway trading centre, but, propelled by the oil industry, Calgary and Edmonton have now taken the lead. In the great period of immigration to Canada before World War I the region received a very diverse population, largely from Europe. On the Pacific, fish, forests, mining, and trade dominated the economy, and with the completion of the transcontinental Canadian Pacific Railway in 1885 one large city, Vancouver, quickly became prominent. The population, largely British in origin, was also given diversity through immigration from Asia. In the North, furs and forests were early resources and, once technological advances made exploitation possible, mining, hydroelectric, and pulp and paper developments became important in the southern sections. Native peoples continued to live in all these regions, Indians and Métis in southern and middle Canada, and Inuit in the Arctic. Their numbers declined most grievously after initial contact with Europeans, especially due to diseases to which they were not immune, but their population grew quickly in the twentieth century. Only in the North do indigenous people form the largest population, usually living on what is at the present stage of economic development a limited resource base.

WRITING THE GEOGRAPHY OF NORTHERN NORTH AMERICA

The stage is almost set to find out what observers of northern North America made of the information on land and people that had gradually accumulated in Europe in the sixteenth century and after. Cartographers, as noted above, generally made quick use of the spatial information flowing in and steadily up-dated their maps. For geographers, incorporating new geographical information into their accounts was not quite as straightforward, because the craft of writing regional geography was still maturing in Europe. Richard Hakluyt (c. 1552–1616) in Great Britain was assiduous in printing early explorers' narratives, but this was vital raw source material, not systematically organized geographical writing.

It was the Germans who set much of the pattern for writing regional geography after 1500. From the sixteenth to eighteenth centuries this material was rather dull geography, mainly narrative lists of physical features, cities, and towns and factual descriptive compilations, all arranged by political regional units in what has been called the political-statistical school of geographical writing. By the end of the eighteenth century some authors were beginning to use natural regional units, usually river basins, in describing and interrelating geographical features. Then in the early nineteenth century two master German geographers led the way in writing greatly improved regional geography. Alexander von Humboldt (1769–1859) produced an outstanding geographical synthesis of a New World colony in his *Essai Politique sur le Royaume de la Nouvelle-Espagne* (i.e. Mexico) (1811), including an acute interpretive analysis of economic and population geography, and Carl Ritter (1779–1859) published multi-volume regional geographies of Africa and

Asia, *Die Erdkunde im Verhaltniss zur Natur und zur Geschichte des Menschen*, (1822–59, 21 vols.), that relied on historical development to explain the human geography of the regions discussed. In the long run Humboldt and Ritter had a great impact on the evolution of geography as a discipline and on regional writing but, despite their example, the political-statistical approach remained supreme for many decades and was the model used by the first writers on the geography of what is now Canada, including the authors of school geography texts. Many years passed before regional geography became interpretive.

Regional writing on British North America and later Canada from the time of the first books in the mid-eighteenth century up to the third quarter of the twentieth century can be divided into three periods, identified here by the names of notable writers and contributions:

1750s–1832   Edmund Burke, Robert Rogers, and Joseph Bouchette
1832–1895   School Texts, Canada Legislative Assembly Debates, and G. R. Parkin
1895–1977   J. D. Rogers, Harold Innis, Bruce Hutchison, R. C. Wallace, and Thomas Berger.

Each period is briefly introduced below, with only the main contributors noted.

1750S TO 1832: EDMUND BURKE, ROBERT ROGERS, AND JOSEPH BOUCHETTE

In the mid-eighteenth century geographical knowledge of many parts of what is now Canada came from the published narratives of explorers and travellers, which provided descriptions of their expeditions, travels, and experiences. Fur traders and missionaries had also penetrated into distant areas, but their information was not widely disseminated. Most knowledge was local and remained with the people who lived in the different regions, including the First Nations and Inuit peoples and the early colonists. Nevertheless, the first simple descriptive geographical accounts of the known areas began to appear in Europe. Publishers were eager to provide the public with whatever information was available on the New World colonies. The first comprehensive geographical work is *An Account of the European Settlements in America* (2 vols.), published in London in 1757. It is usually attributed to the great British political theorist Edmund Burke (1729–1797), but is actually the result of the collaboration of Edmund and William Burke. (Apparently they were not related.) Written in the political-statistical tradition, Burke's descriptions proceed colony by colony from the southern tip of South America through two continents right to the territories of the Hudson's Bay Company, providing population, resource, and trade information on each colony as known in the 1750s. The approach is highly mercantilist: what does each colony possess that is of value to the mother country? The colonies and territories described in what is Canada today are discussed in the following order: the French possessions of Canada and Cape Breton, followed by the British possessions of Nova Scotia, Newfoundland, and Hudson's Bay. Interpretive comments are included in the general descriptions, as in this remark on the problem of supporting Nova Scotia, the British colony founded in 1749 in reply to the French fort at Louisbourg in Cape Breton:

> when the colony which in our days we have fixed there, if the support of the royal hand was withdrawn but for a moment, after all the immense sums which have been expended in it's establishment, would undoubtedly sink into nothing. It is with difficulty it subsists, even encouraged and supported as it is.   (Burke, 1757, Vol. 2: 267)

Major Robert Rogers (1731–1795) wrote the second geography that includes present-day Canada, published in 1765, also in London. The full title tells us the contents: *A Concise Account of North America: Containing A Description of the Several British Colonies on That Continent, Including the Islands of Newfoundland, Cape Breton, &c. As to Their Situation, Extent, Climate, Soil, Produce, Rise, Government, Religion, Present Boundaries, and the Number of Inhabitants Supposed to be in Each. Also of the Interior, or Westerly Parts of the Country, Upon the Rivers St. Laurence, the Mississipi, Christino, and the Great Lakes. To Which is Subjoined, An Account of the Several Nations and Tribes of Indians Residing in Those Parts, As to Their Customs, Manners, Government, Numbers, &c. Containing Many Useful and Entertaining Facts, Never Before Treated Of.* Rogers, born in Massachusetts, fought for the British against the French in North America in the Seven Years War. At the conclusion of fighting, in 1860 he travelled as far west as Detroit to accept the surrender of French outposts. On this assignment he tried without success, because of ice on the lake, to reach

Michilimacinac at the northwestern end of Lake Huron but he did meet First Nations people. Basically Rogers' book is also a political-statistical account, colony by colony, using these as his regional divisions, but he was also faced with the problem of referring to distant unknown interior areas within the continent. It is always difficult for authors to devise regional divisions for areas where information is extremely limited and where there is no established colonial administration. In those situations writers generally fall back on one of two expedients. One approach is to use assumed headwaters and divides of major rivers to create regional divisions; i.e. since there are no political boundaries they define regions by watersheds even though the upper courses of the rivers may not be mapped as yet. The other approach is to divide the largely unknown country abstractly, by means of lines of latitude and longitude. (Today in Canada we have both kinds of administrative boundary divisions. For example, the southern part of the boundary between Alberta and British Columbia is a watershed and the northern part is a line of longitude.) Rogers had no accurate information on the area west of Lake Superior, so he divided the interior into regions using the watersheds of three great rivers that he thought radiated from a common central high land – the St. Lawrence, the Mississippi, and the Christino (likely the Nelson River of today). Note that he lists them in his title.

Other books on the British overseas possessions continued to appear in Britain, mostly political-statistical in content. Changes had to be made when the United States split off as a separate country and as new British colonies were created. However, the geography continued to be described colony by colony, relying on government statistics for trade and population figures and using whatever general information was available, normally from travellers' or explorers' accounts. The main interest for us is what was done with fresh reports from the most distant and least known areas, such as the continental interior, the Pacific coast, and the Arctic, as each returning explorer brought new information back to Europe. Usually there was only room to incorporate a few lines on the remote parts of British North America into the geography texts. However, provocative sub-section headings do appear, such as in John Pinkerton, *Modern Geography* (1807), where the heading "Unconquered Countries," applied to northwestern North America, conjures up images of warfare with First Nations peoples. However the term turns out not to be as empire-building as appears at first sight. Pinkerton believed that prior discovery did not give a European country full possession of new lands. Rather, he suggests:

The first settlement seems however to be the most rational claim, and no such event having yet happened, the western coast of North America shall be arranged among the Unconquered Countries, which seems to be the most proper method, when the settlements are only a few detached factories, to which the natives profess no subjection. Hence the regions around Hudson's Bay, with Labrador and Greenland, are, from the intense severity of the climate, declared free by nature, and shall also be classed among the Unconquered Countries. (Pinkerton, Vol. 3: 273)

How far Pinkerton would have been prepared to carry his definition of Unconquered Countries into the geopolitical realm in lands under the nominal administration of the Hudson's Bay Company is not clear.

Two books by fur traders published in London provided important new information on distant parts of British North America. In 1795 Samuel Hearne published *A Journey from Prince of Wales's Fort in Hudson's Bay to the Northern Ocean. Undertaken by Order of the Hudson's Bay Company, for the Discovery of Copper Mines, a North West Passage, &c. In the years 1769, 1770, 1771, & 1772*, a description of his attempts to journey from what is today Churchill, Manitoba, to the Arctic coast at the mouth of the Coppermine River, travelling as the sole European with a group of Chipewyan. On his third try, in 1771–72, he succeeded in reaching the Arctic Ocean. For the first time mapmakers had an approximate astronomical fix on the limit of the northern mainland of North America, and Hearne's very fine narrative became a source of information on terrain and people for that part of the Arctic. Moreover, Hearne's track soon began to appear on maps published in Europe.

In 1801 Alexander Mackenzie published an account of his two great explorations, the first in 1789 to the Arctic Ocean by the river later named after him and the second, four years later, from Montreal via Lakes Winnipeg and Athabasca, and the Peace and Upper Fraser Rivers, to the Pacific Ocean. This was the first crossing of the North American continent north of the Spanish colonial possessions. The full title of the book is *Voyages from Montreal, on the River St. Laurence, Through the Continent of North America, to the Frozen and Pacific Oceans; In the Years 1789 and 1793. With a Preliminary Account of the Rise, Progress, and Present State of the Fur Trade of That Country*. Mackenzie confirmed Hearne's descriptions of the nature of northwestern British North America and also provided new information on the mountainous land that we know as the Canadian Cordilleran region, an area between the Great Plains and the Pacific Ocean previously unknown to Europeans. Mackenzie's last chapter, a history of the fur trade and a proposal for its expansion beyond North America to Asia, is full of geographical content and contains general remarks on the vegetation, watersheds, and terrain of British North America. Amongst other important generalizations, Mackenzie notes the distinctive rocks that extend from the east shore of Lake Winnipeg all the way to Labrador, the first recognition I have found of the great extent of the Canadian Shield within North America. For many decades Hearne and Mackenzie were the sole authorities that writers could turn to on the geography of northern British North America. Sadly, however, the concluding sections in Mackenzie's book mostly escaped notice, perhaps because its geographical power is most apparent when, pencil in hand, you map what Mackenzie has to say; only then do the great British North American geographical patterns he described leap out at you.

Published sources on other distant parts of British North America also became available, mainly on the rim of the continent and Hudson Bay. Already in the seventeenth century there were accounts of voyages to Baffin and Hudson Bays by William Baffin, Thomas James, and Luke Foxe. James Cook and George Vancouver explored the Pacific coast in the late eighteenth century. In the early nineteenth century Arctic explorations by canoe, boat, and on foot under John Franklin connected the points established on the Arctic mainland by Hearne and Mackenzie, and William E. Parry and James Ross, searching for a North West Passage, began the mapping of the Arctic Archipelago. All these accounts have often been discussed in histories of Canadian exploration.

Numerous general geographical books, including school textbooks published in Europe and the United States in the late eighteenth and early nineteenth century, included descriptions of British North America. The thin descriptive geographical content on the settled colonies does not differ greatly from one book to another. Information provided by Hearne and Mackenzie was used for northwestern North America, their routes drawn on maps as wavering lines, penetrating into homelands of First Nations and Inuit peoples previously unknown to Europeans. One of the better books was by Michael Smith, a preacher from the United States who migrated to Upper Canada in 1808. In an effort to induce United States citizens to migrate to Upper Canada he published *A Geographical View of the Province of Upper Canada, and Promiscuous Remarks Upon the Government* (1813), printed in Hartford, Connecticut. The next year he published a larger edition that included the other British colonies, *A Geographical View, of the British Possessions in North America: Comprehending Nova Scotia, New Brunswick, New Britain, Lower and Upper Canada, With All the Country to the Frozen Sea on the North, and Pacific Ocean on the West*, printed in Baltimore. The book is a much fuller account of the land than in other publications of this time, where British North America only warrants a small section, but Smith still proceeds colony to colony. He uses Mackenzie extensively as a source. Of particular interest for us is that the largely unknown interior, the North-West Land as he calls it, is nevertheless delimited by borders that Smith describes in the text. For the southern border he uses the 48th parallel as the international border, and from east to west the region extends from 95° West longitude (approximately the eastern boundary of Manitoba today) to 127° West longitude (approximately intersecting the Pacific Coast at 60° North latitude). To the north is the Frozen Sea. Smith's book shows not only the need to identify distant North-West Land but also to give it borders, since otherwise it would appear to be limitless.

Early school geographies used in British North America came from outside the colonies, including Jedidiah Morse's famous *The American Geography*, first printed in1789, which was widely used in U. S. schools and kept in print in numerous revised and enlarged editions for many years. School texts, whether from the United States or Great Britain, followed the political-statistical, state-by-state, colony-by-colony approach, presenting very short descriptions of each area's most dominant characteristics. Since few other sources were available on the geography of British North America, school texts provided a source of information about the land for others beside school children. British North American educators, as well as clergymen interested in improving education, were particularly dissatisfied with U.S. books, not just because of their brevity on British North America but because of their prejudicial remarks about British colonies. It took many years before this was corrected through texts written and published in British North America for local use.

In 1831 Joseph Bouchette (1774–1841), surveyor-general of Lower Canada, published his exceptional geography of British North America. Titled *The British Dominions in North America*(2 vols.), it is truly an astonishing book, head and shoulders over other geography books published at this time. Many decades passed before other books comparable in originality and quality to Bouchette's geography appeared, and his two volumes mark the end of the first period of regional geographical writing on Canada. Bouchette's work bears comparison with the regional writing of Humboldt and Ritter. Humboldt was more focussed and systematic in his analysis, for example in discussing trade and population, and Ritter was more penetrating in his historical explanations, but Bouchette's geography is a significant achievement in early nineteenth-century geographical writing.

Bouchette's greatest contribution is that the lineaments of the major regional divisions of British North America that are generally accepted today and are listed at the beginning of this essay are presented clearly and the topographic characteristics of the settled regions are described fully. One can discern the origins of the great regional divisions of Canada in Alexander Mackenzie's *Voyages from Montreal* but it is in Bouchette's volumes that the foundations of the major Canadian regional divisions are first firmly laid. Selections from this major work are printed in this collection.

Bouchette's two volumes became sources for other general books on British North America. R. Montgomery Martin, *History of the British Colonies: Possessions in North America,* Vol. 3 (1834) and Hugh Murray, *An Historical and Descriptive Account of British America,* 3 vols. (1839), for example, are heavily dependent on him. In some sections in those books much of the approach and content is based on Bouchette, and Martin at least does give credit to "Colonel Bouchette, the Surveyor-general of Lower Canada, to whose valuable observations I am so much indebted in this volume," (Martin, 1834, Vol.3: 42). Other writers in turn used Martin and Murray as sources and thus Bouchette's ideas and descriptions received wide, usually unacknowledged, circulation.

1832–1895: SCHOOL TEXTS, CANADA LEGISLATIVE ASSEMBLY DEBATES, AND G. R. PARKIN

After 1840, important new factors affected the kinds of information that was available for writing the geography of British North America. In 1842 the Geological Survey of Canada was founded and in future years it contributed substantial and absolutely essential basic information on the country, not only on geology but also on vegetation, wildlife, and ethnology. A second factor, a new force in the changing geography of British North America, was the steadily increasing interest in the resource potential of the area west of Lake Superior, especially the agricultural possibilities of the Great Plains and, after mid-nineteenth century, the gold and other resources of the Pacific colonies. As the better farmlands in Lower and Upper Canada were taken up, Canadians, especially Upper Canadians, began to look to those distant areas as lands where their young people might migrate and thus be diverted from heading to the factories of New England and the farmlands opening up in the U.S. Middle West. To appraise the agricultural potential of the North West and the feasibility of establishing connections across the difficult rock and lake terrain from Lake Superior to Red River Settlement, scientific exploring expeditions were dispatched from Great Britain and Canada in the late 1850s. Both the reports and maps of the Palliser exploring expedition, published in various forms by the British government from 1857 to 1865, and also those of the Canadian expeditions published from 1857 to 1859, which culminated in a well-illustrated book intended for the general public, *Narrative of the Canadian Red River Exploring Expedition of 1857 and of the Assiniboine and Saskatchewan Exploring Expedition of 1858* (1860) by the geologist on the expedition, H. Y. Hind, contain extensive descriptions of land and people and also generalizations on the areas considered fit for settlement on the Great Plains and those to be avoided.

A decade before these scientific exploring expeditions in the Great Plains, there was an unanticipated flurry of exploring activity in the Arctic. In 1845 Captain John Franklin led two ships and 128 men for one more search for the North West Passage. Within the next two years, in the greatest tragedy that has befallen Arctic exploration, all were dead: the ships were caught in the ice, and when the seamen attempted to walk southward out of the Arctic Archipelago to the main land they died of starvation and cold, hastened perhaps by food poisoning. In the course of the ensuing lengthy search – from 1848 to 1859 – intended at first to effect a rescue and then, when it became evident that was not to be, to find out what had happened to Franklin and his men, much mapping was accomplished. Only the far northern reaches of the Archipelago, where Franklin had not intended to venture, and which were therefore not searched, remained unknown.

During this period of scientific exploring and unsuccessful searching for a doomed expedition, one of the finest geographies ever written on any part of North America was prepared by the aging fur trader David Thompson (1770–1852). It was based on his travels and observations in the Great Plains and western cordillera before 1812. His great map of the North West, compiled in the early nineteenth century, was known in two manuscript copies, but his geographical narrative was not published until 1915 by the Champlain Society, edited by J. B. Tyrrell. The first volume of a new three-volume edition of Thompson's writing, edited by William Moreau, was published in 2009.

After 1930 geography textbooks finally began to be published in British North America. In 1835 Zadock Thompson (1796–1856), a Vermont naturalist and teacher, wrote *A Geography and History of Lower Canada,* a county-by-county description of the colony that was published in Stanstead and Sherbrooke, and in 1855 T. A. Gibson, a Montreal teacher, compiled a *Geography of Canada* that contains lists of facts and narrative descriptions of many districts in the Province of Canada and was published in Montreal. Both books are small in size (octavo) and only 116 and 126 pages respectively. The best of the new geography books is J. George Hodgins' (1821–1912) *The Geography and History of British America* (1857), which is slightly larger in format than the above two books and 128 pages. Hodgins was deputy superintendent of Education for Upper Canada. His view of the insidiousness of foreign texts – the U.S. in particular is meant in the quotation below – is clear:

> Until a very recent period, the pupils of our public and private schools were left, either to glean a scanty knowledge of their own and the sister Provinces through the often uncertain and inaccurate medium of an European geography, or to adopt the foreigner's unfriendly interpretation of our colonial institutions and laws.
>
> (Hodgins, 1857, i)

In future decades numerous Canadian authors of geography textbooks repeated such sentiments in similar words. Hodgin's book is still a compilation of data colony by colony but there is also considerable descriptive information. Moreover, inserted in fine print within the general text are extensive descriptions of geological features whose content is much too difficult for elementary pupils. These remarks on geology had received final correction from Canada's two leading geologists, Sir William Logan, head of the Geological Survey of Canada, and J. W. Dawson, principal of McGill College. Soon other British North American publishers were also producing geography books and the content improved as they spurred one another forward. However, the regional organization always remained a colony-by-colony description of British North America.

Pedestrian repetition of fact after fact, colony followed by the next colony, must have been ingrained in some inherent pedagogic consensus

as to what should be taught in school geography. This despite the fact
that many geography books, including the first one printed in British
North America, by Zadock Thompson, emphatically stated in their
introductions that geography teaching should begin with the pupil's own
neighbourhood and go onward from there. Thompson's first words in
his preface are:

> It is now generally admitted, that, in acquiring a knowledge of
> Geography, the pupil should begin at home, with his own neighbour-
> hood, and with those objects which are open to his personal observa-
> tion. The knowledge which he has at the outset, and that which is
> successively gained, then becomes continually, a stepping-stone to
> still greater advancement, and a standard by which his subsequent
> attainments are measured and arranged in their relative order.
> Without a standard of this kind, what the pupil commits to memory
> from his book and recites to his teacher, leaves no definite or durable
> impression upon his mind. The knowledge acquired is that of names
> and sounds, and perhaps of figures and lines on his maps, but not
> of countries and productions of the earth. It is verily believed that
> children have sometimes studied geography for months and perhaps
> years, whose thoughts have hardly extended beyond the paper and
> ink of which their geographies are composed. Confining their atten-
> tion to these, they have scarcely imagined that the things signified are
> objects of their concern.   (Thompson, 1835, iii)

Whatever their shortcomings, geography textbooks were given considerable respect in nineteenth-century Canada. Community leaders
regarded geography as a very important means of informing young
minds about their own country and they were ready to give attention to
the quality of the textbooks produced. This is clearly shown in *Lovell's
General Geography for the Use of Schools,* another book written by J.
George Hodgins, published in 1861. Proofs were sent out to educators,
churchmen, and many others in Canada for their comments; 88 persons
responded and their letters were printed in full in an appendix in the
book. The respondents included Mrs Susanna Moodie, Sir William Logan,
director of the Geological Survey of Canada, The Hon. D'Arcy McGee,
Rev. S. S. Nelles, the president of Victoria College, and many other distinguished persons. The comments were all highly positive, although there
was some criticism of the maps, mainly because the readers received
proofs that had not yet been hand-coloured so the maps were hard to

read. Mrs Susanna Moodie's remarks, in a letter dated Belleville, 29 April 1861, are illuminating on the textbooks available in Upper Canada. Note that she regards the geography text as a "national undertaking":

> The Geographies issued from the American press, are so hostile to the British Government that a child must close them with the impression that Britain is far inferior to the States in its social, political and commercial advantages.
>
> Such a work as the one before me was greatly needed in these Colonies, to remove these false opinions, and convince our young people of the importance of the glorious country who claims them for her subjects.
>
> The "General Geography" will, no doubt, become a valuable national work, and take its place as a standard book in our schools. It is superior to Parley's Geography [a U. S. text written by Samuel G. Goodrich, first published in 1844 and after that issued in numerous editions], containing many valuable statistics in which that very popular school-book is deficient, while it comprises all the modern discoveries made during the present century. It is sincerely to be hoped that it may banish these American works from our seminaries, and be favourably recognized as the best Geography extant in these Colonies.
>
> Wishing you success in your laudable and national undertaking, ...
>
> (Hodgins, 1861, appendix, 7)

We know that school texts could have been much improved, provided much more general information, described landscapes better, presented simple distribution patterns and provided reasons for them, explained why certain towns have grown, and established simple explanatory relationships because that is exactly the kind of information that was published in a few books printed in Canada at mid-century. In 1855 Canada mounted displays at the Paris Exposition and to augment the displays the Paris Exhibition Committee for Canada staged a contest with prizes for the best essays on Canada and its resources. The first and second prize essays, by J. Sheridan Hogan, *Canada: An Essay* (1855), and Alexander Morris, *Canada and Her Resources* (1855), were published. Each essay was over one hundred pages long and contained much more comprehensive and explanatory material than any previous geography schoolbook. Textbook writers must have been held back by pedagogic conventions, because the source material was obviously there, available to anyone.

A good diagnostic indicator of what was generally known about the geography of British North America in the last half of the nineteenth century, and how that huge area was already thought to be divided into regions, is to be found in the debates held in the United Province of Canada legislature in Quebec City in February and March of 1865, when Canadian legislators debated whether or not to federate with the colonies of New Brunswick, Nova Scotia, and Prince Edward Island (Warkentin, 2004). The legislators also looked into the future and considered whether Newfoundland, the North-West, and the colonies of Vancouver's Island and British Columbia on the Pacific should be added to Canada at some future time. They prepared well for the debates, making good use of sources available in the parliamentary library. Many of the debaters, including government leaders such as John A Macdonald and George Brown, were very clear in their statements about the existence of major sections or regions within British North America. The terms Lower or Atlantic Provinces were applied to the four colonies on the Atlantic; less frequently Maritime Provinces was the term used, which at that time also meant all four eastern colonies. The United Province of Canada was seen as one government entity, divided into Canada West and Canada East for many administrative purposes, but in the debates the terms Upper Canada and Lower Canada were invariably applied to what today are southern Ontario and Quebec. The common term for the area that included Red River Settlement and the Saskatchewan Country was the North-West, and the colonies of British Columbia and Vancouver's Island together comprised a distinct region on the Pacific, usually referred to by using the names of both colonies. The only part of British North America that was not given a clear designation was the North. The far northern reaches of British North America were implicitly recognized as distinctive, but those areas did not enter into the substance of the debate, apart from some rhetorical flourishes about British North America's northern character. A critical factor in this regard is that the Canadian Shield had not yet entered British North American consciousness, despite Alexander Mackenzie's recognition sixty-five years earlier that it was a distinctive area of great extent. It is clear that the United Province of Canada legislators, discussing the different sections of British North America during the Confederation debates of 1865, identified the same major regions that are generally used in Canada today.

Right after Confederation in 1867, when the awareness of creating a new country out of widely scattered colonies was still very much in the air, a few astute and concerned observers published books on

Canada and other parts of British North America that contain much geographical material. In 1869 Alexander J. Russell, former inspector of Crown Timber Agencies, Canada East and West, published *The Red River Country, Hudson's Bay & North-West Territories, Considered in Relation to Canada,* where he argued the case for adding Rupert's Land and British Columbia to the newly formed country. Of particular interest for us is that Russell identifies sixteen regions based on their dominant physical characteristics and describes these regions fully, based on the latest information from scientific explorations and travellers' accounts. Russell names and discusses the following regions in northern and western British North America: East Main, or the Peninsula of Labrador; South Hudson's Bay Territory; North Hudson's Bay Territory, or Barren Ground; North M'Kenzie Country; Pelly River and Mountain Country; Central Prairie Country, or Red River, Saskatchewan, and Peace River Territory; Central Prairie Country Continued – Lake and River Winnipeg, Lake of the Woods, Red River, and the Country Between Them; Central Prairie Country Continued – River Assiniboine – Infertile Region on Its Branches, The Souris, and Qu' Appelle; Central Prairie Country Continued – Fertile Region on the Assiniboine; Central Prairie Country Continued – Lakes Manitoba and Winepegoos, Red Deer and Swan River, Riding, Duck, and Porcupine Mountains; Central Prairie Country Continued – River Saskatchewan and Its Country; South Branch of the Saskatchewan; North Branch of the Saskatchewan; Central Prairie Country – North Half, Beaver River; River Athabasca and Country; Peace River; and Slave River, Hay River, and River of the Mountains. Here we see a regional division and nomenclature base mainly on rivers and lakes in the process of being worked out.

Russell thought geographically. Often in nineteenth-century books on geographical topics the reader has to disinter and define the regions based on what is written in the text. Not only does Russell define and discuss the above regions chapter by chapter, he also shows their boundaries on an accompanying map. The vast extent of the North-West is subdivided into geographical regions and the reports of scientific explorers such as Palliser and Hind come into full use as sources. Russell's prime strategic concerns were the potential for settlement in the Central Prairie Country, the possibility for exploitation of resources in the area between Lake Superior and Red River where a railway would have to be built, and the role of the northern mountain region, i.e., present-day northern British Columbia and Yukon, as a means of defence against possible U.S. encroachment from Alaska. However, there is little discussion of

British Columbia except to emphasize that it is a much-needed addition
to Canada as a Pacific outlet. Russell gives attention to the extent of the
Laurentian Range, or Laurentian Country as he also calls it, when he
considers and describes the South Hudson Bay Region, which sweeps out
of Labrador south of Hudson Bay, bounds the settled lands of Quebec
and Ontario, and continues onward into the Arctic west of Hudson Bay.
Clearly a conceptual basis and name for that vast area, which we now
know as the Canadian Shield, was still wanting. Even in the late 1860s,
as Russell was writing this book, s administrative arrangements were
rapidly changing because negotiations were underway to incorporate
the North-West and British Columbia into Canada. Russell notes this in
a footnote in the third, 1870, edition of his book.

Alexander Monro, a New Brunswick surveyor, also came to grips
with the major regions of Canada in his book *The United States and
the Dominion of Canada: Their Future*, published in 1879. Monro
argued that Canada must be incorporated into the United States. To
argue this position he appraised British North America's (both Canada
and Newfoundland are included in his study) settlement potential
from the Atlantic to the Pacific and analyzed the following regions:
Newfoundland, the Lower Provinces, Quebec, Ontario, the Country
Between Ottawa and Red River (i.e. the Shield), the Canadian Plains, and
British Columbia. Monro was merciless in critiquing the exaggerated
way Canadian resources were promoted. Given his acerbic wit, Monro's
appraisal was an especially useful antidote to the many over-blown statements, so characteristic of this period, on Canada's economic potential
and future population. He too was extreme, but on the negative side.

As good source material became increasingly available, and concepts
of what should be taught in geography broadened, school texts began
to improve. However, the regional divisions of Canada continued to be
administrative units. After Confederation the authors of school geographies simply proceeded across the land in their texts, describing the
country province by province. Quite apart from inhibiting generalizations, organizing the regional descriptions by province could lead to
startling spatial anomalies. In a Canadian textbook (Calkin, 1872) published in the years between Canadian Confederation and 1873, while
Prince Edward Island remained a separate colony, the Island was not
placed with Nova Scotia and New Brunswick as part of a Maritime
region but rather, many pages later, was described, with Newfoundland,
at the end of the entire long section on Canada. Administratively, of
course, this was correct but geographically it made little sense.

Even if there were improvements in content, it still remained difficult to write good geography books. Authors of geography texts and general geographical compendia tended to have problems devising effective approaches. Stanford's Compendium of Geography and Travel, a famous British geographical series, commissioned A. R. C. Selwyn (1824–1902), director of the Geological Survey of Canada, to prepare a geography of Canada, and Ferdinand V. Hayden (1829–87), director of the U. S. Geological Survey, to do the same for the United States; their two contributions were published in one volume, *North America,* in 1883. Selwyn divided Canada into regions using seacoasts and river basins as organizing units. This resulted in a very segmented treatment, with little coherence in discussions of the human aspects of the country and little interpretation.

At the end of the nineteenth century there was considerable progress in geographical writing on Canada. With the completion in 1876 of the Intercolonial Railway from Montreal to Halifax, and then in 1885 the Canadian Pacific Railway from Montreal to Vancouver, Canada finally could function efficiently across its southern domain, all the way from Nova Scotia to British Columbia. Assisted by easier travel Canada could more readily begin to know itself, and this increasing self-knowledge was soon reflected in a wide range of new books.

George M. Dawson (1849–1901), assistant director of the Geological Survey of Canada, made a much better job of describing the geography of Canada in *Elementary Geography of the British Colonies* (exclusive of India and Ceylon), co-authored in 1892 with Alexander Sutherland, a college teacher in Melbourne, Australia, than his superior A. R. C. Selwyn had managed nine years earlier. Dawson was responsible for Canada, the West Indies, and the southern part of the South Atlantic Ocean. Canada comprised almost half the book, and the physical and human geography of the provinces were skilfully portrayed in clear, succinct, flowing descriptive prose, unlike the staccato presentation of facts in the usual textbooks. Writing only seven years after the completion of the Canadian Pacific Railway, Dawson recognized the great significance the new east-west rails from the Atlantic to the Pacific would have for Canada's functioning, by connecting major sections across the country:

by means of the railway a free interchange of the products of all
parts of Canada has been rendered possible, and a community
of sentiments and interests otherwise impossible has begun to be
realised, which must increase and spread as more such highways are

opened and the population extends to wider areas. (Dawson and Sutherland, 1892, 58).

Writers with something interpretive to say about Canada, who made good use of regions in their analysis, wrote with much greater geographical insight and also much more interestingly than textbook writers or compilers of compendia because they provided much fuller explanations of Canadian human geography. Two outstanding interpretations of Canada appeared in the 1890s. In 1891, Goldwin Smith (1823–1910) published *Canada and the Canadian Question*. Like Monro, Smith's overriding question was whether Canada would not be better off in a union with the United States. In his opinion the answer was yes and he presented sharply expressed arguments for such a union. To Smith, Canada's major regions were fundamentally extensions northward of U.S. physical and economic regions. However, he also divided Canada into two major cultural zones, French and English. He then evaluated Canada's viability as a country by analyzing the characteristics of the country's major regions: first the French Province, i.e., Quebec, and then the British Provinces, i.e., Ontario, Lower Provinces, Manitoba and the North-West, and British Columbia. In evaluating the country's cohesiveness, Smith was particularly interested in relations between the different major regions of Canada. Although he did not describe the regions in detail, he provided succinct vignettes of each one as well as acute insights about regional contrasts across the country and power relationships. Northern Canada was not mentioned because Smith was primarily interested in the power of the settled Canadian regions as they existed at the end of the nineteenth century, but there was a passing dismissive reference to the "Arctic Wastes," which gives some idea of Smith's confident, incisive, terse style, aimed at carrying his argument forward sharply.

Three years after Smith's brilliant, opinionated dissection of Canada, another close student of the country, George Parkin (1846–1922), published his interpretation. This more rounded book is one of the finest geographies of Canada we possess, also with a point of view but a view that arises much more clearly out of the broad geographical character of the regions, not just out of power relationships, although those are there as well. At the end of the nineteenth century, Parkin's *The Great Dominion* (1895), is a fitting culmination to the attempts since 1832 to write a geography that provides a comprehensive understanding of Canada. Selections from the book are reproduced in this volume.

1895–1977 J. D. ROGERS, HAROLD INNIS, BRUCE HUTCHISON, R. C. WALLACE, AND THOMAS BERGER

In the early twentieth century a big national challenge was to fulfill the great promises envisaged in Canadian Confederation, especially the re-settlement of the Great Plains and industrial growth in Eastern Canada. A new and further challenge was the development of mineral and hydro-electric resources in the Canadian Shield, the vast ancient geological area that in 1883 finally received a name that stuck, bestowed by the Austrian geologist Eduard Suess in his famous book *Das Antlitz der Erde*, translated and published in English in 1904 as *The Face of the Earth*. The term "Shield" gradually worked its way into the Canadian consciousness. Various books record, with greater and lesser degrees of success, geographical changes across the country and in the different major regions that transformed the country.

The British Association for the Advancement of Science has met in Canada on four occasions, in 1884 in Montreal, in 1897 in Toronto, in 1909 in Winnipeg, and then in 1924 in Toronto again. For each meeting handbooks on the local area and on Canada were prepared for the dele-gates. These books contain some of the best distilled geographical infor-mation on Canada for each period, written by authorities on geology, climate, vegetation, population, agriculture, forestry, mining, manufac-turing, transportation, banking, and many other topics, thus presenting a good portrait of the country. Useful as these books are as surveys of many aspects of the geography of Canada, especially because they con-tain excellent maps, they are not interpretive regional presentations of Canada. In the bibliography I have listed these practical source books under the name British Association for the Advancement of Science.

By the last decade of the nineteenth century travellers moved easily across the country by rail, and a steady stream of books on Canada was published, especially in Great Britain, that describe the growth of the Dominion. Some were very good comprehensive descriptive accounts, providing vivid impressions of life in the different major regions, often with considerable insight. A. G. Bradley's book, *Canada in the Twentieth Century*(1903), is a particularly fine example of this popular genre.

Many writers in this period were bedazzled by the potential of the country and extravagant predictions were made on future growth. The height of absurdity was reached in a book by Reverend F. A. Wightman, *Our Canadian Heritage: Its Resources and Possibilities* (1905). Without

any consistent criteria for identifying regions except their location
within the country, he divided Canada into thirty regions and gave
many of them startling names. Outlined on the regional map in his
book (Wightman, 1905, 80) are regions with names such as Cresylvania
(where the Cree live in northern Manitoba), Centralia (at the mid-point
of the country at Thunder Bay), Slavonia (near Great Slave Lake), and
Translavonia (north of Great Slave Lake). Agreed, this nomenclature is
fun, but Wightman's book is a cautionary object lesson, demonstrating
that although regions can be any size, and can be defined by any pertin-
ent criteria related to the purpose for which the regions are intended,
there must, as a minimum criterion, be some correspondence and adher-
ence to geographical reality and regions should also serve a useful purpose in gaining an understanding of particular portions of the world.

Some distinctive idiosyncratic books, however, can be very useful in
advancing a further geographical understanding of a country. Such a
book is *A Historical Geography of the British Colonies – Canada – Part
III, Geographical* (1911), by J. D. Rogers (1857–1914) and selections
from it are reproduced in this volume. The book too has its oddities
in regional nomenclature, such as calling Quebec, "The Middle East,"
New Brunswick, "Links Between Far and Middle East," and so on,
but it is an innovative analysis of Canada, two generations ahead of
its time in the way it relates settlement and space. The main thrust of
the book is the history and spatial distribution of Canadian settlement.
The amount of detail Rogers provides on the occupation of the land
can be overwhelming, and his prose can be elliptical, but he makes one
look at the regions of Canada in a new way through examining spatial
interrelationships, and it is worth the effort to work one's way through
his often elusive thinking. Also in 1911, Rogers published a volume on
Newfoundland, *A Historical Geography of the British Colonies – Part
IV, Newfoundland,* which covers both the history and historical geography of Newfoundland.

In 1914, sound interpretive accounts of various aspects of Canadian
geography were published in *The Oxford Survey of the British Empire:
America,* edited by two highly regarded British geographers, A. J.
Herbertson and O. J. R. Howarth. Well-thought out, lucid essays on
important aspects of Canadian geography were prepared by Canadian
authorities, including A. P. Coleman, professor of geology, University of
Toronto, writing on physical geography and geology, Frederick Stupart,
director of the Dominion Meteorological Service, on climate, and James
Mavor, professor of political economy, University of Toronto, on the

economic geography of the major sections of Canada. J. D. Rogers wrote the essay on Newfoundland and Dr W. T. Grenfell, superintendent of the Labrador Medical Mission of the Royal National Mission to Deep Sea Fishermen, the one on Labrador. This was thematic geography, not a regional interpretation of all of Canada, but the essays were more comprehensive in scope than the shorter pieces that appeared in the Handbooks prepared for the British Association for the Advancement of Science referred to above, and Mavor's essays in particular give a good sense of the geographical characteristics of the different major parts of the country.

Turning once more to the schools, it was apparent after the First World War that there was a need to improve instruction in geography and that this endeavour would involve new textbooks. Ontario is a good example. A committee approved by the Ontario Department of Education (the members are not named) prepared a new geography text on Canada and the world, *Ontario Public School Geography*, for the province's public schools. It was first authorized for use in 1921/22. In this book, individual provinces remain the regional units across Canada, except for grouping the Prairie Provinces into one region. The content of the book is adequate, with sound descriptions of the physical and human geography of the major regions, even if pedestrian and with little interpretation. The shocking thing is that the text remained the same, except for occasional changes in a few words, illustrations, and new statistics as censuses came and went, until 1950/51, a span of almost thirty years. The book went through at least twenty-two printings and always contained exactly 256 pages. Thus this geography textbook, unimaginative in its basic regional divisions, was studied by a whole generation of Ontario pupils. However there were leavening factors. Good teachers supplemented the text with other books, particularly after the mid-1930s when social studies became more important in Canadian schools. The Ontario Department of Education also authorized a Teachers' Manual, simply titled *Geography*, to accompany the *Ontario Public School Geography*. Its anonymous authors were very conscious of the dangers of dull geography instruction and made many sensible suggestions to try and avoid rote teaching in the classroom. In the regional section the manual even stated that there should be some grouping of regions in order to avoid repetition:

It is better not to deal with each province separately; for in some cases it takes more than one province to make a natural unit. A great deal of what is said in teaching the geography of Manitoba will be repeated in dealing with Saskatchewan and Alberta. It is far wiser to deal with all the Maritimes Provinces as one unit, and all the Prairie Provinces as another unit. British Columbia, Ontario, and Quebec should be taken separately. (*Geography*, 1926, 162).

In this period between the two World Wars geography texts used in other Canadian provinces were little different from the books used in Ontario in their regional approach to Canada.

Geography was gradually making its way into the Canadian university curriculum, and in the long run this was to be of great importance in improving geography teaching in the schools. Right after the First World War Canada still had no university geography departments, although in some institutions geography courses were taught, usually in physical and economic geography. At the University of Toronto, topics that today are considered to be part of physical geography were taught in geology beginning in the 1850s (Warkentin, 2008). Political economist James Mavor (1854–1925) introduced an economic geography undergraduate course in the Department of Political Economy in 1906/07, where it soon became a required introductory course for both honours economics and commerce and finance students, and he taught it until 1922. Economic historian Harold Adams Innis (1894–1952) then took over the course and also introduced more advanced work in economic geography. In the Department of History, geography courses were offered for a few years after 1919–20, and then resumed in 1932–33. This geography instruction by economists and historians in the Departments of Political Economy and History continued until geographer Griffith Taylor was appointed to the university in 1935. However, geography teaching at the university level had lagged badly in Canada; geography was much further ahead in England, France, Germany, and the United States.

One outstanding college-level regional geography text on North America was produced in the 1920s in the United States. J. Russell Smith, professor of geography in Columbia University, published a thorough regional study of North America, *North America: Its People and the Resources, Development, and Prospects of the Continent as Agricultural, Industrial and Commercial Area* (1925), in which the regions, based on human economic activity, cut across international, provincial, and state boundaries, and Canada gets good coverage. The book effectively demonstrates what regional geography texts try to do – to bring out the significant interrelated physical and human characteristics of different parts of the earth, using regions as a means of accomplishing this effect-ively, and also to place the regions in wider context in their interrelation-ships with other parts of the world. Smith's book was written in a highly readable explanatory style, had substantial content, and is still useful today in explaining what the geography of North America was like in the early twentieth century. Few textbooks survive that kind of test.

In Canada some fine academic minds also were making use of regions in their studies of Canada. In his first book, *A History of the Canadian Pacific Railway* (1923), Harold Innis discusses in grand interpretive generalizations the civilizations that had developed in each of three major regions, the "Pacific Coast" (British Columbia), the "Hudson Bay Drainage Basin" (the Great Plains), and "On The St. Lawrence" (Eastern Canada), that the CPR was intended to unite. The evolving spatial and geopolitical interrelationships within these three regions are analyzed, as forces gradually emerged that would connect the regions by means of the first Canadian transcontinental railway. Innis anticipates the spatial interaction geography of the 1960s. In the manner of Goldwin Smith and George Parkin, this was also a study in power, investigating the eco-nomic strengths of the regions and the relations between them. Selections of what Innis had to say on these Canadian regions are printed here.

In seminal articles published in the 1920s and 1930s other Canadian social scientists and historians also made use of major Canadian regions in thinking about Canada. W. A. Mackintosh wrote about the signifi-cance of the Canadian Shield – the region that had been so hard to identify as a physical entity over many decades – in the development of Canada (Mackintosh, 1926), and R. G. Trotter considered the signifi-cance of the Appalachian barrier in Canadian history (Trotter, 1939). W. N Sage (1937) discussed the geographical and cultural aspects of the five Canadas: "The Maritime Provinces – Three Political Units – One Culture – Canada's New England; Quebec – The Two Races; Ontario – The First Melting Pot – British Traditions; The Prairies – The Wheat Belt and the Parklands; British Columbia – The West Beyond the West – Facing the Orient." In an essay on the importance of geography in Canadian history, A.R.M. Lower very briefly recognized similar major regions and in addition assessed the significance of the Appalachians and the Canadian Shield as barriers. His main interest, however, was the problem of establishing east-west connections in Canada across major north-south physical continental axes, the importance of the St. Lawrence River hinterland, and the emergence of the North, which he considered to be a highly distinctive environment (Lower, 1939).

Even though there was a serious lag in introducing a more interpretive approach into regional geography school textbooks, Canadian
educators increasingly recognized that geography teaching in schools
had to be improved and that universities must play a significant role
in achieving this. This is evident in editorials and articles published in
the journal issued by the Ontario College of Education, *The School*.
As early as 1918–19 George A. Cornish (1872–1960), an instructor in
natural science and geography at the Ontario College of Education in
Toronto, wrote an article on the teaching of geography in British and
American universities and made a strong plea to introduce geography
into Canadian universities so that Canadian high school geography
teachers would be better prepared (Cornish, 1918–19). Numerous articles appeared in *The School* on how to teach geography, the geography
of various Canadian regions, teaching particular geographical themes,
and where to find appropriate geographical source material for use in
the classroom. Cornish contributed many articles on those topics. In
1920–21 he prepared a review of books that could be added to school
libraries for use as high school geography reference books. There he suggested that a book by Taylor Griffith – actually Griffith Taylor – on
Australia could very well serve as a model for a similar book on Canada:

> We may also mention Taylor Griffith [the book is listed in Cornish's
> bibliography as Taylor Griffith: *Australia Physiographic and
> Economic*] as a model monography [*sic*] on the geography of
> Australia. It is hoped that we soon have a similar book on Canada.
> (Cornish, 1920–21, 362)

In 1935 Griffith Taylor was appointed to teach geography at the
University of Toronto and rapidly began laying the foundations for the
first Department of Geography in English-speaking Canada. In 1947,
Taylor published the first geography of Canada intended for university
level studies, *Canada: A Study of Cool Continental Environments and
Their Effect on British and French Settlement*. What Cornish had suggested twenty-six years before had actually happened. In 1940 Taylor
had published an advanced geography of Australia, in which he divided
the country into twenty natural regions for his regional discussion and
also explained the basis of this regional division (Taylor, 1940, 127–9).
In his Canada book Taylor airily states that in a book he had written on
the geography of Australia, twenty regions had been a useful number of
regions for studying that country and, since Canada was an analogous

case, he would use the same number of regions (Taylor, 1947, 113). And he did. Despite Taylor's cavalier statement on how the number of regions was selected, he actually is very analytical in identifying what he terms natural regions: similarly to what he had done in his Australia book, he devised a grid for identifying and classifying the regions. For Canada the grid is composed of three major vertical natural units – going from the Cordillera in the west, through the central plains and lowlands, to the Appalachians in the east – that are crossed by four east-west horizontal zones of settlement – going from the densely populated band along the U. S. to the less densely populated belts toward the north (Taylor, 1947, 113–15). Broad physical and population characteristics are related in this schematic model, which remains one of the most logical and methodological approaches to identifying regions in Canada devised by any author. The twenty natural regions placed within this grid going from south to north, and placed as appropriate in the Cordillera, plains and lowlands, and Appalachian columns, are A. *Populous Zone*, 1 Maritimes, 2 South Quebec, 3 South Ontario, 4 North of Superior, 5 Winnipeg, 6 Western Prairie, 7 Vancouver, 8 Selkirks, 9 Fraser, B. *Transition Zone*, 10 Newfoundland, 11 Claybelt, 12 Peace River; C. *Pioneer Zone*, 13 Labrador, 14 North Quebec, 15 Churchill, 16 Mackenzie, 17 Yukon, 18 North British Columbia; D. *Tundra Zone*, 19 Keewatin, 20 Archipelago.

After the Second World War geography had finally become established in many Canadian universities, and well-trained teachers were ready to respond. University teaching in geography had a pronounced impact on the way the subject was taught in schools, which were finally released from the rigid system of authorizing only a few geography textbooks that had prevailed in most Canadian school systems. Publishers took advantage and quickly recruited authors to write new texts. In Ontario, by far the largest market for schoolbooks in the country, the geography textbook approved in 1921/22 was replaced by numerous different kinds of geography books and fresh material rapidly entered the classrooms. Many approaches were used in teaching the geography of Canada, such as major regions based on economic and urban factors, or even by themes based on social groups or resources, and it was clear that the province-by-province approach was finally gone.

The general public also was finally served by some fine books on Canada and its major regions. Many observers and writers have attempted to present a portrait and understanding of Canada's regions. Nobody has been more successful in achieving this than the great Canadian journalist Bruce Hutchison (1901–1992). In 1942 he published

The Unknown Country: Canada and Her People, a view of the country
at the end of the Great Depression and the beginning of the Second
World War and fifteen years later, in 1957, just barely a decade after
the war, he appraised the country once more in *Canada: Tomorrow's
Giant.* These two books are at the pinnacle of regional geographical
writing on Canada, based on historical depth and acute personal observation, with much thought given to how the country functions as a total
entity yet is composed of many contrasting regions. Selections from
both of Hutchison's books are presented in this volume. What he had to
say about cities in these two books is combined in a separate section to
make comparisons easier.

None of the authors thus far selected for this book say much about
the North. To balance the region's absence, excerpts from two very different writers on that immense but thinly populated part of Canada
are included. One selection, from R. C. Wallace (1881–1955), a distinguished geologist and educator, provides an account of the North as
perceived in the early twentieth century, mainly as a potential natural
resource base for Southern Canada (Wallace, 1930). The other selection on the North is from Mr Justice Thomas Berger (1933–), writing
in Volume I of the report of the Royal Commission on the Mackenzie
Valley Pipeline, *Northern Frontier – Northern Homeland* (Berger 1977).
This document has opened the eyes of southern Canadians, as nothing
else has succeeded in doing, to the drastic impact that southern Canada
has made on northern Canada over many decades.

In the approximately two centuries from Edmund Burke's geography of
1757 to Thomas Berger's report of 1977, regional writing on Canada
has come a long way. Yet it is never easy to do it well. It started off with
compendia on colonies, based on limited data, and it is helpful to quote
Burke's cautionary remarks on what he was faced with in writing a
geographical account of the New World in the mid-eighteenth century:

> My principal view in treating of the several settlements, was
> to draw every thing towards their trade, which is the point that
> concerns us the most materially; for which reason I have but little
> considered their civil, and yet less their natural history, further than
> as they tended to throw some light upon the commerce of these
> countries; except where the matters were very curious, and served to
> diversify the work.

It is not to be expected that a performance of this kind can be written equally throughout. In some places the subject refuses all ornament, and the matter, dry itself, is by no art to be made otherwise: in some a contagion communicated from the dulness of materials, which yet were necessary to the work, may probably appear; in many, and perhaps the most blameable parts, the author alone must be answerable; however there are some errors of the press, especially towards the beginning, which are owing to the author's absence from it. (Burke, 1757, Vol. 1, Preface, n.p.)

A break-through in regional writing came with Joseph Bouchette's fine comprehensive geography of the 1830s, where he laid firm foundations for the major regions we know today within the huge area that extends from the Atlantic to the Pacific and on to the Arctic Ocean, although information was still scanty on much of British North America. Two kinds of books began to emerge in the mid-nineteenth century: on one hand, staid schoolbooks and geographical compendia and, on the other, occasional scintillating, sometimes idiosyncratic, geographical interpretations of the different regions of the country, exemplified by George Parkin, J. D. Rogers, and Harold Innis. Such writing culminates in two highly personal books by Bruce Hutchison that provide images of the major regions through the lives and ideas of the people who live there. In Hutchison's books the personalities of the regions emerge. Sparsely settled regions, such as the North, tend to be afterthoughts in many books on Canada, although the regions have been lived in for thousands of years. Selections from R. C. Wallace and Thomas Berger address this gap. Regions never exist alone, and Berger demonstrates this forcefully as he examines how powerfully outside cultural and economic forces affect the lives of Northerners, especially the indigenous peoples.

I hope this review of regional writing in British North America and Canada will stimulate readers to go to their local and university libraries and peruse some of the books mentioned. A few of the most acute observers are represented in this volume and provide a fresh appreciation of the nature of Canada and its major regions.

BIBLIOGRAPHY

[Berger, Thomas R.] *Northern Frontier Northern Homeland: the Report of the Mackenzie Valley Pipeline Inquiry,* Volume I. Ottawa: Department of

Indian Affairs and Northern Development, Ministry of Supplies and Services
Canada, 1977, 213 p.
– Volume 2, 1977, 268 p.
Bouchette, Joseph, *The British Dominions in North America; or a
Topographical and Statistical Description of the Provinces of Lower
and Upper Canada, New Brunswick, Nova Scotia, The Islands of
Newfoundland, Prince Edward, and Cape Breton. Including Considerations
on Land-Granting and Emigration; and a Topographical Dictionary of
Lower Canada; to Which are Annexed, Statistical Table and Tables of
Distances, &c.* 2 volumes. London: Longman, Rees, Orme, Brown, and
Green, 1831. 498 and 296 p. (Not including the unpaged Topographical
Dictionary.)
Bradley A. G., *Canada in the Twentieth Century*. Westminster: Constable,
1903, 428 p.
British Association for the Advancement of Science, *Hand-Book for the
Dominion of Canada, Montreal Meeting, 1884*, edited by S. E. Dawson.
Montreal: Dawson Brothers, 1884, 335 p.
– *Handbook of Canada, Toronto Meeting 1897*, edited by Ramsay Wright and
James Mavor. Toronto: Publication Committee, 1897, 425 p.
– *A Handbook to Winnipeg and the Province of Manitoba Prepared for
the 79th Annual Meeting 1909*, edited by C. N. Bell, W. Sanford Evans,
Matthew A. Parker, Swale Vincent. Winnipeg: W. Sanford Evans, 1909, 301
p.
– *Handbook of Canada, British Association for the Advancement of Science,
Toronto 1924*, edited by W. A. Parks, et al. Toronto: University of Toronto
Press, 1924, 449 p.
[Burke, Edmund], *An Account of the European Settlements in America. In
Six Parts ... 6 Of the English. Each Part contains An Accurate Description
of the Settlements in it, their Extent, Climate, Productions, Trade, Genius
and Disposition of their Inhabitants: the Interests of the several Powers
of Europe with Respect to those Settlements; and their Political and
Commercial Views with regard to each other.* 2 volumes. London: R. and J.
Dodsley, 1757, 312 and 300 p.
Calkin, J. B., *School Geography of the World*. Halifax: A. & W. Mackinlay,
1876, Revised edition, 164 p. (First edition 1872)
– *The World: An Introductory Geography*. Toronto: James Campbell and Son,
1878, 100 p.
Cornish, G. A., "A New Status for Geography," *The School* 7 (1918–19):
392–4.

- "Books in Geography for High School Teachers." *The School* 9 (1920–21): 362

Dawson, George M. and Alexander Sutherland, *Elementary Geography of the British Colonies.* London: Macmillan and Co., 1892, 330 p.

Geography Notes. Toronto: The Educational Publishing Co. Limited, 1906, 112 p.

Gibson, T. A., *Geography of Canada.* Montreal: Hew Ramsay, Toronto, A. H. Armour & Co., 1855, 126 p.

Hayden, F. V., and A.R.C. Selwyn, *North America.* London: E. Stanford, 1883, 652 p.

Hearne, Samuel, *A Journey from Prince of Wales's Fort in Hudson's Bay to the Northern Ocean. Undertaken by Order of the Hudson's Bay Company, for the Discovery of Copper Mines, a North West Passage, &c. In the Years 1769, 1770, 1771, & 1772.* London: A. Strahan and T. Cadell, 1795, 458 p.

Herbertson, A.J., and O.J.R. Howarth, editors, *The Oxford Survey of the British Empire: America.* Oxford, Clarendon Press, 1914, 511 p.

Hind, Henry Y., *Narrative of the Canadian Red River Exploring Expedition of 1857: and of the Assinniboine and Saskatchewan Exploring Expedition of 1858.* 2 volumes. London: Longman, Green, Longman, and Roberts, 1860, 494 and 472 p.

Hodgins, J. George, *The Geography and History of British America, and of the Other Colonies of the Empire; To Which is Added a Sketch of the Various Indian Tribes of Canada, . . ,* Toronto: Maclear & Co., 1857, 128 p.

- *Lovell's General Geograph, for the Use of Schools; With Numerous Maps, Illustrations, and Brief Tabular Views.* Montreal: John Lovell, Toronto, R. & A. Miller, 1861, 100 p. + 12 p. appendix.

Hogan, J. Sheridan, *Canada: An Essay: To Which was Awarded the First Prize by the Paris Exhibition Committee.* Montreal: John Lovell, 1855, 110 p.

Humboldt, Alexander von, *Essai Politique sur le Royaume de la Nouvelle-Espagne.* Paris, 1811, 350 p.

- *Political Essay on the Kingdom of New Spain.* New York, AMS Press, 1966 (Reprint of the translation by John Black published in London in 1811)

Hutchison, Bruce, *The Unknown Country: Canada and Her People.* New York: Coward-McCann, 1942; Toronto: Longmans, Green, 1943. Both editions are 386 p.

- *Canada, Tomorrow's Giant.* Toronto: Longmans, Green, 1957, 325 p.

- *The Far Side of the Street.* Toronto: Macmillan of Canada, 1976, 420 p.

Innis, Harold A., *A History of the Canadian Pacific Railway.* London: P.S. King; Toronto: McClelland and Stewart, 1923, 365 p.

Lower, A. R. M., "Geographical Determinants in Canadian History." In
    Ralph Flenley, editor, *Essays in Canadian History; Presented to George
    MacKinnon Wrong for His Eightieth Birthday.* Toronto: Macmillan of
    Canada, 1939, 229–52.
Mackenzie, Sir Alexander, *Voyages from Montreal, on the River St. Laurence,
    Through the Continent of North America, to the Frozen and Pacific Oceans;
    In the Years 1789 and 1793. With a Preliminary Account of the Rise,
    Progress, and Present State of the Fur Trade of That Country.* London: T.
    Cadell, W. Davies, Cobbett and Morgan, 1801. 412 p.
Mackintosh W. A., "The Laurentian Plateau in Canadian Economic
    Development," *Economic Geography* (1926): 537–49
Martin, R. Montgomery, *History of the British Colonies* 5 volumes. Volume 3:
    Possessions in North America. London: James Cochrane and Co., 1834, 604
    p.
Monro, Alexander, *The United States and the Dominion of Canada: Their
    Future.* Saint John: Barnes and Company, 1879, 192 p.
Morris, Alexander, *Canada and Her Resources: An Essay, To Which, Upon a
    Reference from the Paris Exhibition Committee of Canada, was Awarded ...
    the Second Prize.* Montreal: John Lovell, 1855, 156 p.
Murray, Hugh, *An Historical and Descriptive Account of British America.* 3
    volumes. Edinburgh: Oliver & Boyd, 1839
Ontario Public School Geography. Toronto: W. Gage & Co. Ltd., 1922, 256 p.
Ontario Teachers' Manuals, Geography. Toronto: The Ryerson Press, 1926,
    228 p.
Parkin, George R., *The Great Dominion: Studies of Canada.* London:
    Macmillan and Co., 1895, 251 p.
Pinkerton, John, *Modern Geography: A Description of the Empires, Kingdoms,
    States, and Colonies; with the Oceans, Seas, and Isles; in All Parts of the
    World: Including the Most Recent Discoveries, and Political Alterations,
    Digested on a New Plan.* 3 volumes. London: T. Cadell and W.Davies ... and
    Longman, Hurst, Rees, and Orme, 1807.
Province of Canada, *Parliamentary Debates on the Subject of the
    Confederation of the British North American Provinces, 1865, 3rd Session,
    8th Provincial Parliament of Canada,* Quebec: Hunter, Rose & Co., 1865,
    1032 p.
Ritter, Carl, *Die Erdkunde im Verhaltniss zur Natur und zur Geschichte des
    Menschen.* 21 vols. Berlin: G. Reimer, 1822–59
Rogers, J. D., *A Historical Geography of the British Colonies, Volume 5, Part3:
    Canada, Geographical.* Oxford: The Clarendon Press, 1911, 302 p.

– *A Historical Geography of the British Colonies, Volume 5, Part4: New-foundland*. Oxford: The Clarendon Press, 1931, 274 p. (First edition 1911)

Rogers, Major Robert, *A Concise Account of North America: Containing A Description of the Several British Colonies on That Continent, Including the Islands of Newfoundland, Cape Breton, &c. As to Their Situation, Extent, Climate, Soil, Produce, Rise, Government, Religion, Present Boundaries, and the Number of Inhabitants Supposed to be in Each. Also of the Interior, or Westerly Parts of the Country, Upon the Rivers St. Laurence, the Mississipi, Christino, and the Great Lakes. To Which is Subjoined, An Account of the Several Nations and Tribes of Indians Residing in Those Parts, As to Their Customs, Manners, Government, Numbers, &c. Containing Many Useful and Entertaining Facts, Never Before Treated Of*. London: Printed for the Author, and Sold by J. Millan, 1865. 264 p.

Russell, Alexander J., *The Red River Country, Hudson's Bay & North-West Territories, Considered in Relation to Canada*, Montreal: G. E. Desbarats, 1864, 202 p. Third edition.

– *The Red River Country, Hudson's Bay & North-West Territories, Considered in Relation to Canada*. Montreal: G. E. Desbarats, 1870, 187 p., Third edition

Sage W. N., "Geographical and Cultural Aspects of the Five Canadas," *Canadian Historical Association, Report of the Annual Meeting*16 [10?], No. 1(1937): 28–34).

Smith, Goldwin, *Canada and the Canadian Question*. Toronto: Hunter, Rose, 1891, 325 pp.

Smith, J. Russell, *North America: Its People and the Resources, Development, and Prospects of the Continent as an Agricultural, Industrial, and Commercial Area*. New York: Harcourt, Brace, 1925, 849 p.

Smith, Michael, *A Geographical View of the Province of Upper Canada, and Promiscuous Remarks Upon the Government*. Hartford: Printed for the Author, by Hale & Hosmer, 1813. 107 p.

– *A Geographical View, of the British Possessions in North America: Comprehending Nova Scotia, New Brunswick, New Britain, Lower and Upper Canada, With All the Country to the Frozen Sea on the North, and Pacific Ocean on the West, With an Appendix, Containing a Concise History of the War in Canada, To the Date of this Volume*. Baltimore: Printed by P. Mauro, for the Author, 1814. 288 p.

Suess, Eduard, The Face of the Earth (Das Antlitz der Erde) Translated by H.B.C. Sollas under the direction of W.J. Sollas. Oxford: Clarendon Press, 1904–24, 5 vols.

Taylor, Griffith, *Australia in Its Physiographic and Economic Aspects*. Oxford: Clarendon Press, 1911, 256 p.
– *Australia A Study of Warm Environments and Their Effect on British Settlement*. London: Methuen, 1940, 455 p.
– *Canada A Study of Cool Continental Environments and Their Effect on British and French Settlement*. London: Methuen, 1947, 524 p.
Thompson, David, *David Thompson's Narrative of His Explorations in Western America, 1784–1812*, edited by J. B. Tyrrell. Toronto: The Champlain Society, 1916, 582 p.
– *The Writings of David Thompson*, Volume I, *The Travels, 1850 Version*. Edited by William E. Moreau. Montreal & Kingston: McGill-Queen's University Press, University of Washington Press, and The Champlain Society, 2009, 359 p.
Thompson, Zadock, *A Geography and History of Lower Canada*. Stanstead and Sherbrooke, Walton & Gaylord, 1835, 116 p.
Trotter, Reginald G., "The Appalachian Barrier in Canadian History," *The Canadian Historical Association, Report of the Annual Meeting*. Toronto: 1939, 5–21.
Wallace, R. C., "The Canadian Northland," *The Book of Canada*, edited by Chester Martin, W. Stewart Wallace, T. C. Routley. Published by the Canadian Medical Association on the Occasion of the Meeting of the British Medical Association in Winnipeg, August 1930, Toronto 1930, 77–82.
Warkentin, John, "Canada and Its Major Regions: Bouchette, Parkin, Rogers, Innis, Hutchison," *The Canadian Geographer* 43 (1999): 244–68
– *Geography of Confederation*. Toronto: Department of Geography, York University, Discussion Paper No. 57, 2004, 47 p.
– "'Partially provided': Geography at the University of Toronto, 1844–1935," *The Canadian Geographer* 52 (2008) 380–400
Wightman, F. A., *Our Canadian Heritage: Its Resources and Possibilities*, Toronto: William Briggs, 1905, 287 p.

Joseph Bouchette, *The British Dominions in North America*, 1831

⌐ Joseph Bouchette (1774–1841) was surveyor-general of Lower Canada from 1804 to 1840, and he knew the colony intimately. Over his long career he participated in surveys in every British North American colony except Newfoundland. In Upper Canada in 1791/92, when a young man of eighteen, he prepared the first plan of York Harbour. In 1828 he led an exploring expedition from Quebec City into the Canadian Shield to Lake St. John, seeking land suited for settlement. He had personal knowledge of much of eastern British North America and because of his position could also readily draw on official information compiled for the colonies, especially data on trade. In 1831/32 Bouchette published *The British Dominions in North America,* printed in London, England in two volumes of 498 and 296 pages respectively. The volumes contain numerous illustrations, tables, and maps. Information on western and northern British North America was scanty and Bouchette relied on descriptions provided by explorers such as Alexander Mackenzie and John Franklin. Explorers of eastern British North America, such as Samuel de Champlain, had provided accounts of the land along the routes they followed and in later years travellers described the communities they visited, but Bouchette is the first person to provide an adequate topographic and comprehensive description of much of the land, particularly of Upper and Lower Canada. Bouchette's second important contribution is his cogent explanation of the reason for dividing the colonies into regions: to facilitate effective description. Most authors of geographical works fail to explain why they define and make use of particular regions. Bouchette, on the other hand, carefully defines different kinds of regions and explains why he uses them, thus demonstrating a thoughtful sophisticated approach to geography that is well ahead of its time. A third distinctive contribution is that Bouchette provides a separate chapter on the St. Lawrence River because of its critical role in Canada.

Bouchette gives no reason for starting his geography with the Indian Territories, including the North, the least-known parts of British North America and the most distant from where he was writing. At least one can say that his description of the North is not an afterthought, as it often seems to be in many books. Bouchette next goes on to Upper Canada and, working his way eastward, describes the St. Lawrence River and then gives very detailed attention to his own home area, Lower Canada. In Volume II the colonies of New Brunswick, Nova Scotia, Prince Edward Island, and Newfoundland are described in separate chapters and he ends with chapters on land granting, emigration and immigration, and general remarks on the colonies, especially trade and relations within the British Empire and with the United States.

From Bouchette we can get a general impression of the major regions of British North America as they were perceived in the early nineteenth century. The Indian Territories, i.e., the North East, North West, and North of British North America, is still a new world. People of European origin are beginning to know this homeland of aboriginal peoples, but it is not certain what its future within British North America will be. There is little firm information about potential agricultural possibilities. Upper Canada is recognized as an important area for agricultural, where transportation by water is very important and more land is waiting to be cleared. In Bouchette's exceptionally high praise of the agricultural advances in Upper Canada we can already see an essential component of Ontario's future powerful position within Canada. Lower Canada is a region of great internal diversity because of its mix of a central agricultural lowland, the Canadian Shield, the Appalachians, the St. Lawrence River, the lands on the Gulf of St. Lawrence, and the two founding European peoples, the French and British. Bouchette has a much fuller experience of Lower Canada than of the other regions, so provides a more complete sense of life in this region and of what is going on in the central settled area, in the towns, and on the margins of settlement. We get a picture of local activity in the early nineteenth century, and there is a Humboldtean sense of landscape, of the feelings that the land produces in people. Nova Scotia, including Cape Breton, is a land of many coastal communities dependent on the sea, small separated agricultural pockets, and an awareness of potential mineral resources. In New Brunswick the forest is overwhelming, with an agricultural future foreseen when the trees are finally cleared. In Prince Edward Island the trees have been cleared and agriculture is underway. Newfoundland is clearly dependent upon the sea and the seeming lack of timber resources and potential agricultural land contrasts with the other Atlantic colonies.

Occasionally, in discussing the population of various regions, Bouchette is much too facile in generalizing on the inherent nature of different peoples, something characteristic of many nineteenth-century writers. He does not hesitate to use the word barbarian, or even savage, typical nineteenth-century stereotypes, in referring to aboriginal peoples, because, in the view of the time, Europeans are bringing civilization to such groups., He does not recognize and respect the inherent civilizations of aboriginal cultures. His remarks, however, are not consistent. Where he knows aboriginal people least he is harshest, as with the Indians of the North-West and the Inuit, but he is not so dismissive when he refers to Indians of Upper Canada on the Grand River, or those near Montreal. Bouchette writes before Darwin, but there is still the feeling that the more fit are forcing out the weaker, i.e., the Indians. ☞

I INDIAN TERRITORIES

a) Geographical Situation – Boundaries

☞ Bouchette states that the distant parts British North America beyond the settled areas are generally called the Indian Territories. This designation also includes the lands under the jurisdiction of the Hudson's Bay Company. The Indian Territories are divided into five major regions: (i) Labrador, and (ii) the immense area between Hudson Bay and the Arctic and Pacific Oceans, which is divided into another four regions "for the greater convenience and aptness of description." Bouchette does not understand the role that the Indians play in the fur trade, nor does he give a sense of the widespread fur trade networks and the incredibly efficient ways these trading systems worked over long distances. He is bound by his topographic description. ☞

An obvious division of these extensive dominions presents itself, in that part of them is colonized under established local governments, and that which is not, or which is at least out of the pale of present civilization.

Referring, therefore, the consideration of the settled parts of the British dominions to ulterior chapters, we will now proceed to give of the
Indian countries, as correct an idea as may be formed, from the collective information arising out of the laborious surveys performed under
the direction of the Canadian North-west Company, in their trading
territories, the explorations of the interior by some of its members, and
the several expeditions that at different times, have penetrated over the
continent, to the shores of the Hyperborean seas, and the borders of the
Pacific Ocean.

By the NORTH-WEST TERRITORIES, is generally understood all that
portion of country extending from the head of lake Superior, westward
to the western shores of America, northward to the Frozen Ocean, and
northwestward to the *limits* of the territory granted under the Hudson's
Bay Company charter....

... The peninsula of Labrador will form part of this division; and,
for the greater convenience and aptness of description, all that tract
of country lying west of the bounds of Hudson's Bay will be divided
into four other sections, – the *first* being comprehended between the
49th degree of north latitude and the highlands north of the Saskatchawan and Beaver rivers, in the average latitude of 56° north; the *second*
extending from the latter bounds to the 65th degree of north latitude;
and the *third* from the 65th degree to the Polar Sea; the limits of these
three divisions on the west, being the Rocky Mountains. The *fourth*
division will embrace the whole extent of country belonging to Great
Britain, lying between the Rocky Mountains and the Pacific Ocean.

(Bouchette, *British Dominions*, 1831, I: 28–31)

b) Section I [Hudson's Bay, Labrador, and the Lands Around Hudson's Bay]

☞ After a few remarks on Hudson Bay Bouchette describes the land
that extends in a great horseshoe from Labrador through present
northern Ontario and Manitoba to the North West Territories and
Nunavut. For Labrador, Inuit, referred to as living in savage barbarism,
and a Moravian mission are mentioned. Rivers are the main physical
features described, and there is a wildly over-optimistic reference to
agricultural potential. Methye Portage was the vital portage connecting
the Hudson Bay and Arctic Ocean watersheds. The "primitive formation" refers to rocks of Precambrian age. ☜

The magnitude of Hudson's Bay, and its geographical inland situation, impart to it much more the character of a mediterranean sea than one of those deep indentations of the ocean called by the subordinate appellation of bays.... The coasts are generally high, rocky, and rugged, and sometimes precipitous. To the south-westward they are lower, and frequently exhibit extensive strands. The depth of water in the middle of the bay has been taken at one hundred and forty fathoms, but it is probably greater. Regular soundings have been found from Cape Churchill, towards the south, and, in that direction, the approach to the shore is shoal and flat. Northward, from the same point, soundings are very irregular, the bottom rocky, and, at low water, reefs of rocks, are in some parts uncovered....

The country on the west of both [Hudson's and James's] bays has been denominated New South Wales, and that on the east, East Main. The interior of the peninsula of Labrador, or New Britain, of which the latter may be considered to form a part, has been but very superficially explored, except by barbarian tribes of wandering Esquimaux, who are characterized as the inhabitants of wild, bleak, and inhospitable regions. That it is traversed by numerous rivers, diverging from the interior towards the Gulf of St. Lawrence, the Atlantic, the Strait of Hudson, and Hudson's Bay, appears indubitable from the number of outlets that have been discovered along the whole extent of its immense coasts....

At Nain, near Unity Bay, a Moravian settlement is established, where missionaries reside, under the direction of the Moravian Missionary Society in London, and the most laudable efforts appear to be made by that institution to reclaim the Esquimaux from the most savage barbarism, and inculcate the doctrine of revealed religion....

[Six rivers that flow into Hudson and James Bays, the East Main, Rupert's, Harricanaw, West, Moose and Albany, are briefly described.] The navigation of all these rivers is in many places interrupted by impetuous rapids, occasioning frequent portages; but, nevertheless, the long interstices of gentle current that are found between the impracticable cascades, render them extremely important as the highways of a wilderness.

Of the susceptibility of the soil, these rivers and their several branches seem to fertilise, to yield agricultural produce, little is known, or can be collected from the information of the traders, whose attention appears to have hitherto been confined to the beaver, the buffalo, and the other savage inhabitants of those wilds; but considering the geographical situation of this country, between 49° and 53° north latitude, and its vast extent, it is natural to presume, and the accounts of the natives, as far as they go, justify the presumption, that a considerable portion of it must be more or less arable, and will eventually be submitted to the plough.

New South Wales, or the western section of Hudson's Bay territory, extending from Severn river inclusive to the north-eastern head of the bay, has been, in some parts, tolerably well explored. It abounds with lakes, rivers, and creeks, which, like those already mentioned, offer to the traveller and the trader the most convenient means of communication in a wilderness, however hazardous, in general, from the frequency and violence of the rapids. [The chief rivers are listed, the Severn, Hill (the Hayes is an extension), Port Nelson, Pauk-a-thaukus-Kaw, Churchill, and Seal, and a few of these are described.] ...

... Five miles above the mouth of the Hayes river, on its west bank, stands York Factory, the head quarters of the Hudson's Bay Company within their territories, and the principal depot of their trade....

"The principal buildings are placed in the form of a square, having an octagonal court in the centre; they are two stories in height, and have flat roofs covered with lead. The officers dwell in on portion of this square, and in the other parts the articles of merchandise are kept: the workshops, storehouses for the furs, and the servants' houses are ranged on the outside of the square, and the whole is surrounded by a stockade twenty feet high. A platform is laid from the house to the pier on the bank for the convenience of transporting the stores and furs, which is the only promenade the residents have on this marshy spot during the summer season. The few Indians who now frequent this establishment belong to the *Swampy Crees**.*" *Franklin's Journey to Coppermine River, vol. I p. 37....

[A few rivers and lakes to the west of Hudson Bay are described.] Methye Lake is divided from Clear Water river, by a portage of twelve miles, carried over a range of hills, varying in height from sixty to one thousand feet, and chiefly consisting of clay and sand; the soil at their base, on both sides of Methye, Buffalo, and Clear Lakes, being a sandy alluvion. The country traversed by the Churchill river, between Isle à la Crosse and Frog Portage (which is three hundred and eighty yards long, and forms the division of the waters of the Churchill from those of the Saskatchawan) is generally flat, and exhibits all the appearances of primitive formation [i.e. Precambrian].

Trading posts are established at the Lakes Methye, Buffalo, and Isle à la Crosse; and at the latter is also found a North-West fort. These posts are stated to be frequented by Crees and Chipewyans, who supply them but inadequately with peltries, owing to the actual paucity of furred animals in those parts. The discouraging results of the chase have turned the attention of the Indians from the forests to the waters, which supply them with several varieties of fish, the chief means of their subsistence.

Deer Lake is the largest as yet known within the limits of the Hudson's Bay territories.... its length about ninety miles, and its width about five and twenty....

North of Seal river, between 60° and 65° of north latitude, a succession of lakes have been discovered, some of which are represented as equal in extent to Deer Lake; but, occupying a section of country not so much frequented, even by the Indians, as that just described, very little is known of them beyond what may be derived from the observations of Captain Hearne, who traversed that region in 1772, on his journey to the Polar Sea....

(Bouchette, *British Dominion*, 1831, 1:32–40)

c) Section II "between the 49th degree of north latitude and the highlands north of the Saskatchewan and Beaver Rivers, in the average latitude of 56° north" [Southern Great Plains and Adjacent Shield]

☞ From west to east this region extends from the Rocky Mountains into present western Ontario, and from the 49th parallel to just north of Lesser Slave Lake. Rivers are the prominent features that serve to organize Bouchette's description. The struggles between the Nor'Westers, Hudson's Bay Company, and the Selkirk settlers are gently alluded to in passing, but the existence of the Selkirk Settlement is barely noted. Floetz limestone refers to the Paleozoic sedimentary beds of the Great Plains. In the description of this region Bouchette provides barely an impression of the topography of the vast Great Plains, since his descriptions of Assiniboia and what is known today as the Red River Plain, near present-day Winnipeg, cover only the flat lands left by former glacial Lake Agassiz. ☞

The second section of the Indian territory comprises the country between 49° and 56° of north latitude, or the southern boundary of British America, in that part of the continent, on one side, and the highlands constituting the boundary of Hudson's Bay, according to Bennet's and Mitchell's maps, on the other; the Stony Mountains of the west, and the height of land dividing the waters of Lake Superior from Lake Winnepeg, on the east. Lake Winnepeg, though considerably to the east of the centre, may

still be considered the focus of this tract, and the most striking object
within it, whether from its magnitude, or the fact of its being the reservoir of the waters of numerous large streams flowing into it, from most
of the cardinal points of the compass....

The Saskatchawan is the largest river traversing this part of the country; and its many ramifications, taking their sources in the Rocky Mountains, blend their tributary waters to form two principal branches, one
called the north and the other the south, which meandering in a general
easterly direction, with a northern tendency, form a junction in longitude
about 105° 10' west, at the remote distance of four hundred and twenty
miles below their highest source, in a straight line, and two hundred and
ten miles above its mouth. Upon both branches are established several
trading posts ; those on the north branch, commencing from its head,
being Acton House, at the conflux of Clear river; Nelson, at the foot
of Beaver Hills; Edmonton, at the mouth of Tea river; all of which are
frequented by the Blood Indians and the Blackfort [sic]tribe, as are also
Buckingham, Manchester, and Carlton, and a north-west post stationed
opposite to the latter. On the south branch traders reside at two stations,
the one is Chesterfield House, near the discharge of Red Deer river, and
the other, South Branch House, nearly opposite to Carlton.

From the shores of Lake Winnepeg to Pine Island Lake, on the borders
of which are trading posts belonging to the respective companies, the
banks of the Saskatchawan consist of floetz limestone; they are low and
marshy, and covered with reeds and willows, amidst which very few forest
trees are to be seen. Above Cumberland House, the station on Pine Island,
up to Tobin's Falls, the banks of the river exhibit an alluvial mud, and
beyond it, laterally, are poplar forests, swamps, and extensive plains....

Fifty or sixty miles to the southward of Pine Island are the Basquiau
Hills, a short range of considerable elevation, the white faces of which
are occasionally contrasted with tufts of dense stunted pinery. They
are distinctly visible from Cumberland House, not withstanding their
remote distance; and have, therefore, been estimated by Mr. Hord [sic,
Hood] to be 4000 feet above the common level, and supposed to be the
highest points between the Atlantic Ocean and the Rocky Mountains.

The Assiniboine and Red rivers are next in magnitude to the Saskatchawan and its branches.... On the Assiniboine, and not very remote
from its sources, are four trading houses, Malboro, Carlton, Albany, and
Grants, that are within a few miles of each other; and at a considerable
distance lower down are Brandon and Pine Houses. Upon the Red river
are also several trading posts of importance, ...

The extensive tract of country sold by the Hudson's Bay Company to the Earl of Selkirk comprehends the whole course of the Red river, ... This territory, to which the name of Ossiniboia was given, is understood to compromise a superficies of about 116,000 square miles, one half of which has since fallen within the limits of the United States, according to the boundaries determined by the convention of 1818, between the American government and Great Britain. Its surface is generally level, presenting frequent expansive grassy plains, that yield subsistence to innumerable herds of buffalo. The aggregate of the soil is light, and inadequate to the growth of trees, either large or abundant; but the banks of the river often exhibit more promising alluvions, and have, when cultivated, produced very competent returns to the agriculturist.

(Bouchette, *British Dominions,* 1831, 1:40–4)

d) Section III *"country ... between 56° and 65° north latitude"* [Lesser Slave Lake to Great Bear Lake]

☞ Rivers and lakes traversed by explorers are described. Igneous and metamorphic rocks characteristic of the Shield, known to Bouchette in the nomenclature of the time as Primitive rocks, are mentioned. The ancient rocks of the Shield and more recent Paleozoic formations meet in this region. Sir Alexander Mackenzie had remarked on the bitumen along the banks of the Athabasca River below its Clearwater tributary, known today as oil sands, but Bouchette does not mention this. ☜

The next section of country coming under consideration, is situated between 56° and 65° north latitude, and is bounded, north by the range of hills dividing the heads of Coppermine, from those of Yellow Knife river; south, by highlands passing between Elk and Beaver rivers; east, by the west bounds of Hudson's Bay; and west, by the Rocky Mountains. This extensive tract may be considered a valley, having its lowest region occupied by Slave Lake, in which are united the waters of numerous large rivers, and their abundant tributaries, that descend to it from the verges of all parts of the valley, from whence they have but one outlet, by Mackenzie's river, which carries their waters to the Arctic seas.

The lakes most worthy of note as yet known within these limits are Slave, Athabasca, or the Lake of the Hills, Wollaston, Chisadawd, Methye, Martin, and Winter; but there are an infinite number of minor lakes at the sources of rivers, or formed by the broad and frequent expansion of their beds, which the scope of a general description will not permit us to particularise. Slave Lake, by far the largest and most important of them all, has considerably the superiority of either of the Lakes Erie and Ontario in point of magnitude.... Its north shore is skirted by well wooded hills that slope to the margin of the lake, their summits rising sometimes in naked rock above the forest. It abruptly recedes northward, and forms a very deep bay, on the western side of which is situated Fort Providence, ... Fort Resolution is built on the lake's southern shore, near the mouth of Slave river. A multitude of small gneiss and granitic islands, along its western sides, rise above the lake's surface, to an elevation of one and two hundred feet, the most conspicuous of which are the Red Deer Islands, and also Isle Caché and Big Island.

Of the numerous rivers that fall into Slave Lake, none have been properly explored, except those upon which trading posts have been established, or through which the various discovery-expeditions have passed, in their progress towards the pole....

Lake Athabasca, or the Lake of the Hills, is next to Slave Lake in superficies, and is situated about 180 miles south-west of it. It is an elongated body of water, nearly 200 miles in length, and fourteen to fifteen miles general width. Stone river issuing out of Lake Wollaston, a circular lake, forty-five miles in diameter, bearing W. S. W. of Athabasca, winds through several small lakes, between which it is sometimes called Porcupine river, and ultimately falls into the Lake of the Hills. The shores of Athabasca, to the northward, are high syenitic rock, just sufficiently covered with soil to sustain shrubs and mosses, and several species of the fir and poplar. Those to the southward opposite the forts are alluvial; but advancing eastwardly, they rise into barren sandy hills, perfectly divested of vegetable growth. As they approach the mouth of Stone river they become again rocky, and seem to belong to an extensive tract of primitive formation, extending many miles to the north and east of the lake [Canadian Shield]. Peace river rises far in the Rocky Mountains, at the stated distance of 317 yards from the waters of Fraser's river, exhibiting one of those singular, though familiar, features of nature by which the sources of large rivers, flowing hundreds of miles in contrary courses, are found in such near proximity, on heights of considerable elevation....

The Athabasca has also its sources in the Rocky Mountains, but they appear not to have been completely explored. Its general course is northerly, though sometimes due east; and as it winds through an extensive country, receives the waters of Lesser Slave Lake, by its outlet, Lesser

Slave river, Pembina, Red Deer, Clear Water, and Red Willow rivers. It falls into Lake of the Hills, some miles west of the old, and nearly opposite the actual N. W. Chipewyan and H. B. Fort Wedderburne.... Stony river, the principal outlet of Athabasca Lake, flows between marshy banks, and, at the distance of twelve or fourteen miles, mingles its waters with Peace river. The combined streams of both form Slave river, which varies in width from three quarters of a mile, to one mile and three quarters. About sixty miles below its head, its navigation is interrupted by a series of rapids, occasioning a succession of portages between Dog river and the rapid of the Drownd; after which the river becomes uninterruptedly navigable to the lake. The banks of the river, below the rapids, are almost unexceptionably low and alluvial, and the country on either side, and especially to the westward, appears to abound with pine, poplar, and larch, interspersed with the cypress and willow; the soil on that bank exhibiting a rich black mould, and on the other a yellow clay intermixed with gravel.

Yellow Knife river, which Sir John Franklin ascended on his route to the source of the Coppermine, rises in latitude 61° 4' 30", longitude 113° 36', and descends through numerous lakes, in a southerly course, to its influx into Great Slave Lake, one hundred and fifty-six statute miles from its sources. Its navigable reaches, or interstices, are little calculated for any description of conveyance larger than canoes, and the frequency of its rapids and cascades would render it of minor importance, as a means of facilitating commercial intercourse. Its banks exhibit no extraordinary appearances, are moderately high in general, and thinly clad with the poplar tree, the larch, and the willow. From the rocky nature of its bed, it appears to traverse a stony tract of country, which frequently indicates the characters of primitive formation. Numerous herds of rein-deer frequent the region it waters, during nine months in the year, between August and May.

(Bouchette, British Dominions, 1831, 1:44–7)

e) Section IV "from the 65th degree to the Polar Sea" [Great Bear Lake to the Arctic Ocean]

☞ Bouchette describes the sparser vegetation toward the North but does not generalize about what today is known as the tree line. The Inuit are once again referred to in much harsher words than Bouchette uses when discussing Indians, likely because they are the aboriginal peoples least known to him, but that is no excuse. ☜

Another section of the Indian countries, agreeably to the division adopted, includes the whole of that portion of the continent, eastward from Mackenzie's river inclusive, lying between the 65° of north latitude and the utmost limits to which the discoveries have extended towards the pole, or the 78° of latitude, the extreme point attained in this hemisphere by arctic explorers, in penetrating northward to the depth of Baffin's Bay. Of these inhospitable regions, the Siberia of the new world, nothing is known beyond what may be collected from the voyages by sea, and the journeys over-land, of the several explorers, whose zeal in extending the field of human observation, and the bounds of geographical knowledge, first led them to penetrate far within the vortex of the frozen zone. Limited, however, as are the means of information, relative to the precise geography of those parts, sufficient light has nevertheless been upon it by the voyages of Davis, Baffin, James and others, and, subsequently, by Mackenzie, Hearne, Parry, Ross, and Franklin, to enable us to form a very competent idea of the character of the polar regions, and to establish the certainty of the existence of a north-west passage.

The impression, hitherto so universally prevalent, that the *continent* of America extended much farther north than those of Europe or Asia, must now be completely removed; and the consequences inferred therefrom, as affecting the temperature and other meteorological phenomena of the American climate, stand likewise unsupported; whilst to other causes must be ascribed the frigidity of its atmosphere, compared with similar latitudes on the old continent. Indeed the discoveries of Franklin have gone far to prove, not only that continental America did not approach the arctic pole nearer than the European or Asiatic continents, but, on the contrary, that the latter extended by several degrees further north. The points attained by Mackenzie and Hearne, and afterwards by Franklin, are in the same general latitude, and in no instance beyond the sixty-ninth degree; and we have abundant reason to presume, from the verification of these facts, and from the bearing and general course of that portion of the coast explored by the latter discoverer, that the main shores of America, washed by the Frozen Ocean, do not stretch far to the north of the 70° of latitude. Northward from this parallel, the polar regions seem to consist of numerous large islands, or extensive peninsulas, dividing the polar seas into a profusion of channels, straits, inlets, and sounds, forming almost a labyrinth, the mazes of which have been as yet too partially explored to enable us to form any thing like a correct estimate of what proportion of these hyperborean realms is land,

and what, water, and whether many of the supposed islands are really insular, or connected with the continent, or (to venture upon one speculative assertion) form part of a polar continent, of which Greenland may be a projection to the south....

Of the interior of the country retiring from the coasts, two degrees south of the arctic circle, a tolerably correct conception may be formed from the familiar or scientific descriptions we possess of various sections of it that have been traversed by European explorers. The country through which flows Mackenzie's majestic river, the borders of the Coppermine, and the region obliquely traversed by Franklin, from Hood's river to Fort Enterprise, are described in a manner to afford very satisfactory data from whence to judge of the general characteristics of the country. It appears to be profusely watered by lakes and rivers with their numerous tributaries, judging from the frequency of the streams intersected by the arctic party in their diagonal journey across it; and it is a remarkable proof of this fact, that in no one instance, on so long a march, has (if recollection serve) a deficiency of water been once stated to have occurred....

As far as general terms may be applied to so large an extent of territory, it may be said, that its surface exhibits far more of the plain than of the mountain, that its hills never rise to very considerable heights, and that sterility is the predominant characteristic of its soil. The rivers that flow through it are, for the most part, rapid, and the lakes frequent and fantastic in their shapes. Of the limited variety of the trees, the pine, the poplar, the willow, and the larch are the most common. Lichens and mosses abundantly clothe the faces of some hills, or cover the surface of deep swamps: and the plains consisting in parts of clay flats or bottoms, and marshy meadows, and so frequently stony and utterly barren, are sometimes covered with arid grass, which yields a slender sustenance to the musk ox and the rein-deer; the hills, crags, and cliffs being the haunt of the black and white bear, and of the preying wolf.

Such is the home of the barbarian Esquimau, whose country ranges from the base of the Rocky Mountains, and perhaps from the very shores of the Pacific, to the coasts of the Atlantic Ocean, inhabiting, in his desultory and wandering mode of savage existence, the bleakest hyperborean regions of the globe. The copper Indians frequent the country to the southward of the Esquimaux lands east and west of Yellow Knife river.

(Bouchette, *British Dominions*, 1831, 1:47–54)

f) Section V "on the western side of the Rocky Mountains
[The Cordillera]

☞ Bouchette's book was published well before the international boundary along the 49th parallel from the Rocky Mountains to the Pacific
Ocean was decided in 1846. Thus the area between the Rockies and
the Pacific Ocean is described from sources that refer to mountain
ranges and valleys in both British North America and the United
States. The description of Salmon River and the three villages is based
on Sir Alexander Mackenzie. Salmon River is the Bella Coola River
by which Mackenzie reached the Pacific Ocean in 1793. The area of
mountain ridges and plateaus between the Coast Mountains and the
Rocky Mountains, about 600 km wide and known today as Interior
British Columbia, is referred to as a valley. Its topography still had
to be sorted out by future exploration. Bouchette foresees successful
colonization in both the interior and on the Pacific coast. He places
the cordillera in a South and North American perspective and ponders
whether the isolated northwest coast can be best reached by sailing
around Cape Horn, by finding and braving a North West Passage, or
by ship canal across Panama. Access to the Pacific Coast is thus considered in a global context. ☞

The fifth and last section of country remaining to be described is the
whole tract of British territory lying on the western side of the Rocky
Mountains. It occupies an extent of coast on the Pacific Ocean exceeding
twelve hundred miles, situated between Cape Blanco or Oxford on the
south-east, and Mount St. Elias on the north-west....

   The coasts are remarkably broken and indented by deep arms of the
ocean, leaving extensive insulated tracts, which form, numerous gulfs,
straits, inlets, and sounds. The islands most worthy of note, from their
magnitude are Quadra and Vancouver's, forming with the main the Gulf
of Georgia, and the Strait of Juan de Fuca, Princess Royal Islands, Queen
Charlotte, the Prince of Wales's Archipelago and George III Archipelago,
Admiralty and Revellagegeida Islands. The Oregan, or Columbia, and
Fraser's river, with their various branches, some of which form considerable streams of themselves, are the two rivers too which explorations
have hitherto been chiefly confined. The Columbia takes its source in
the Rocky Mountains in latitude 53° 30' north, and flowing out of a
lake that bears the name of the fruit (the cranberry) found abundantly
in its vicinity, descends to the Pacific Ocean, first directing its general

course to the southward, and afterwards to the westward, to its mouth, in latitude 124° 10' west....

Salmon river is not remarkable for its magnitude, but a variety of adventitious circumstances concur to render it worthy of particular notice. Its length is not more than forty-five or fifty miles, and its general breadth about fifty yards; it meanders in a deep ravine, and is navigable for canoes of the largest size. It abounds with salmon, which the natives take in the greatest profusion, by means of an ingenious "weir," dam, or snare set in the river; and it is from these fisheries that they almost exclusively derive subsistence throughout the year. The natives are effectually domiciled upon the banks of the river, and congregate in small villages, of which a lively description is given by Mackenzie. These little communities are three in number, and have been distinguished by names indicative of the cordiality or hostility that marked the reception of the explorer. Friendly Village is the highest on the river; the Village of Rascals is at its mouth, near Mackenzie's Outlet; and the Great Village, containing in 1792 upwards of 200 souls, is situated on the north side, about mid-way between the other two. Their habitations bore evident signs of their intercourse with Europeans when Mackenzie visited that coast; and they not unfrequently answered in good English, "No, no," to such of his proposals as they were disposed to negative.

The courses of the rivers discharging themselves into the sea have in most cases, a southern direction. Their streams are swift and often rapid; but they appear in general to be deep and navigable for considerable distances; subject, however, to occasional portages, rendered necessary by impracticable cascades. The lakes of which any knowledge is possessed are few in number, and of very inferior dimensions when compared with the expansive sheets of water found to the east of the Rocky Mountains; but several lakes of great magnitude are reported by Indians to exist in the interior, the locality and proportions of which are equally unknown.

The information extant with respect to the surface and soil of the country is quite as superficial and imperfect; yet we are not wholly without the means of forming some opinion upon the subject, from the observations and surveys of Vancouver, Mackenzie, Clark, Lewis, Franchere, &c. it appears that between the Rocky Mountains and the sea a subordinate but high range of hills, running nearly parallel to the continuation of the chain of the lofty Andes, skirts the coast from Admiralty Bay to the bottom of the Gulf of Georgia, and, extending along Puget's Sound, stretches S. S. E. across the Columbia, and loses itself among the

mountains of Mexico. Its altitude is conspicuous at many points, and
in some instances attains nearly the inferior limits of perpetual snow,
between the 52nd and 53 rd degree of latitude. It is in this range that
the peaks observed by Vancouver are to be found, which he respectively
named Mount Rainier, Mount St. Helen's, and Mount Hood.

The valley formed by this ridge and the Rocky Mountains does not
appear to correspond altogether with the extensive barren plain at
the base of the Rocky Mountains to the eastward. Judging from the
accounts of the tracts that have been explored, this valley may be said to
enjoy the advantage of a competent degree of fertility; it undulates into
bold swells, in the midst, however, of occasional plains, seldom wholly
divested of verdure and copses, and, generally speaking, yields an abundant growth of forest trees, the dimensions of which, and especially of
the cedar, the fir, and hemlock, increase to a prodigious magnitude in
approaching the coast.

The massive range of granitic mountains that constitute the eastern
face of the valley occupies of itself a vast surface, varying in breadth
from fifty to nearly one hundred miles. It rises into towering cones, high
rounded summits, and sometimes continued, sometimes broken ridges,
in the intervals of which or at the base of pinnacles are frequently found
broad valleys and flats of argillaceous deposits, possessing a high degree
of fertility. A great number of its peaks are exalted far into the regions
of perpetual snow, and are beheld at the distance of more than one hundred miles in approaching them at some points from the eastward. The
highest summits that have ascertained by trigonometrical admeasure-
ment are found to be about 8,500 feet above the water-table of the country, extending along the eastern base of the Rocky Mountains, which
is placed about 2700 feet above the "assumed" level of the ocean. The
altitude of this immense range seems to diminish towards the north; but
how and where it subsides has never yet been ascertained....

Returning to the consideration of the valley west of the Stony Mountains, it may safely be said, that between the southern boundary of this
portion of the British possessions, and the 52nd or 53rd degree of latitude, large tracts will be found to possess all the advantages requisite
for colonization, both as regards fertility of soil and congeniality of climate; and there can be no doubt that at some period, probably not very
remote, the civilizing arts of agriculture and commerce will extend their
social influence to the north-west coast of America, and flourish on the
shores of the North Pacific Ocean.

Then would the importance of a north passage become paramount, at least as far as the precarious and ephemeral navigation of icy seas could be rendered subservient to commercial intercourse, as it would materially abridge the length of voyage between the ports on the northwest coast of America and European markets. Whether the Cape of Good Hope or Cape Horn can be doubled, as must unavoidably be done at present, the voyage is equally long and circuitous; yet it would for two-thirds of the year be the only alternative left. The hazards and perils of arctic navigation, even during the summer months, would in all probability operate as a check on the frequency of passage by the northern seas, and in many instances render preferable the practiced and incomparably longer route to the southward.

The gigantic but feasible project for some time contemplated of opening a ship canal across the Isthmus of Panama, connecting the Bay of Mandinga with the Gulf of Panama, and therefore the waters of the Caribbean Sea or the Atlantic with those of the Pacific, would, if consummated, be an effort of human ingenuity and art which would incalculably facilitate the commercial relations of every part of the world. It would in a great measure supersede the expediency of the further discoveries of a northern passage, as regards at least the promotion of commerce; although they might still be prosecuted with invaluable advantages to mankind as a means of extending the boundaries of human knowledge. (Bouchette, *British Dominions*, 1831, 1:54–60)

2 UPPER CANADA

☞ According to Bouchette, heights of land and ridges are major topographical features in a flat land such as Upper Canada. The watershed he describes north of Lake Ontario is what we know today as the Oak Ridges moraine. At this time the Niagara Escarpment had not yet been conceived as running from Queenston on the Niagara River all the way to the Bruce Peninsula, and after the Escarpment rounds Hamilton Bouchette combines it with the Oak Ridges moraine, thus forming a great loop around the eastern end of Lake Ontario.

Once he has identified the major watersheds, Bouchette states his approach to regional geography. He will use "imaginary divisions," i.e., regions he has conceived and defined, that will be useful in describing the geography of Upper Canada. Three regions are defined: the Eastern Section, from Belleville to Bytown (Ottawa) and Cornwall; the Central

Section, from Belleville to Hamilton; and the Western Section, from Hamilton to present Windsor and Sarnia.

In his topographic description Bouchette, writing in 1830, presents a land that is being rapidly settled, particularly after the end of the War of 1812–14 only sixteen years earlier. Lakes and rivers are very important for transportation, and the rivers are also a source of motive power. The Trent River system, the Thames River, and the newly opened Welland Canal, and its impact on the portages around Niagara Falls, are described. Roads are abominable but a postal system is functioning. We see a land being organized at the beginning of the age of steam but before the railway arrived. The towns and cities that are emerging are small but the urban network is already there. Bouchette is still sensitive about the War of 1812–14. He considers York, i.e., Toronto, vulnerable to enemy attack and mentions alternative locations for a capital. Upper Canada is still largely forest-covered and the openings in the woods, called plains, stand out. Bouchette raves about the agricultural potential of western Upper Canada but says nothing of the hard life immigrants encounter in clearing trees. Districts where fruit is grown are noted. Scenic landscapes are described, including the Canadian Shield and waterfalls at Bytown and at the Niagara Escarpment at Queenston. Even in this generally flat land Bouchette looks for the picturesque and the sublime. Southwest Upper Canada is singled out as one of the outstanding parts of British North America, the magnitude of the forests and the adjacent lakes are elements of the sublime, and the fertile rural areas have the charms of the picturesque. A special section on the lands of the Canada Company is mainly promotional literature, but the importance of water communications in this period is apparent when Bouchette compares the potential of Goderich and Guelph. ⌒

a) Natural Divisions of the Province – Its Rivers, Roads, Soil, and Settlements Described in Three Sections

In attempting to give to the reader a view of so extensive and open a country as Upper Canada, no division or feature so naturally presents itself to the mind of a topographical describer, as the chains or ridges of high lands running through the country, in which the various rivers and streams take their sources, and dividing the head waters of those of such rivers as flow in one direction from those that take the opposite course. In a country generally level, abundantly watered by rivers of every dimension, from the broad, full-flowing, and majestic stream, the

impetuous roaring and resistless torrent, to the gentle meandering of a
purling brook, emptying themselves into spacious lakes, almost, claiming
the title of' seas, as is the case with the province now under notice; ....

The first of these ridges, or ranges of elevated or table-land, that presents itself to our notice is that which divides the waters falling into the
Ottawa, from those that are lost in the St. Lawrence....

From the Bay of Quinte another ridge of high lands runs in a westerly
direction along the northern shores of Lake Ontario, at a distance, in
some places, of not more than nine miles, which is the case at Hamilton, dividing the numerous streams and head-waters of rivers falling
into that lake from those descending northward into the river Trent,
Rice Lake, [and] Otanabee river, ... The ridge receding northward and
westerly from the lake to the distance of twenty-four miles from York,
there separates the waters of Holland river and other streams flowing
into Lake Simcoe and Lake Huron, from those discharging themselves
into Ontario. Thence, bending round the heads of the Toronto and its
tributary streams, dividing them from those of the Grand or Ouse river,
it pursues a south-easterly direction towards the head of the lake, merges
in the Burlington Heights, and runs along the shores of Burlington Bay
and the south side of Lake Ontario, at a distance not exceeding from
four to eight miles, to Queenstown Heights.... This ridge ... constitutes
a striking geological feature of that part of the country, which points it
out as the shores of the original basin of the lake.

Having thus given a preliminary description of the most prominent
features of the province, the surface of which is characterized by its general evenness, notwithstanding the table ridges of moderate elevation
we have traced, we will endeavour to convey a more definite and distinct idea of the face of the country, its soil, and its settlements, without,
nevertheless, entering into those minute details or descriptive elaborations that are inconsistent with the plan of the present work. To do so
the more efficiently it will be convenient to divide the province into three
imaginary divisions, within the circumscribed boundaries of which it
will be easier to travel in our description, and to dwell upon the particular points that may appear most deserving of paramount notice and
consideration, within their respective limits.

Adopting for this purpose the most obvious and natural division of so
extensive a territory that suggests itself, the province may be divided into
the three following sections:

The first or eastern section, embracing all that tract or tongue of land
between the Ottawa river and the St. Lawrence, bounded on the west

by the eastern line of Newcastle district and on the east by the western boundary of the province. It includes five districts; Eastern, Ottawa, Johnstown, Midland and Bathurst. [Cornwall/Ottawa to Belleville]

The second or central section will comprise the districts of Newcastle and Home, and extend from the bottom of the Bay of Quinté to the north-eastern limits of the district of Gore. [Belleville to Hamilton]

The third or western section, embracing the residue of the surveyed parts of the province westward, will consist, of the western, London, Niagara, and Gore districts. [Hamilton to Windsor and Sarnia]

b) I Eastern Section [Cornwall/Ottawa to Belleville]

Situated between two broad and navigable rivers, the Ottawa and the St. Lawrence, and centrally traversed in a diagonal course by an extensive and splendid sloop canal, connecting the waters of Lake Erie with those of Ontario, – this section of country evidently enjoys important geographical and local advantages. Its surface presents, almost unexceptionally, a table level of moderate elevation, with a very gentle and scarcely perceptible depression as it approaches the margin of the magnificent streams by which it is bounded to the northward and south-east.

The soil, though sometime too moist and marshy, is extremely rich and fertile in general, and chiefly consists of a brown clay and yellow loam, admirably adapted to the growth of wheat and every other species of grain. In the immediate vicinity of the Bay of Quinté and the shores of Ontario it is still ore clayey, and rests upon a substratum of bluish limestone, which appears to be co-extensive with the section of country we are describing, and sometimes penetrates through the soil above the surface. The forests abound with a variety of large and lofty trees; among which are profusely found white pine, white and red oak, maple, beech, hickory, basswood, ironwood, butternut, and poplar; ash, elm, and cedar are also found in the forests in considerable quantities, but are less frequented than those first enumerated.

It is intersected by numerous rivers, remarkable for the multitude of their branches and minor ramifications, and by frequent lakes and ponds, peculiarly irregular and fantastic in their shapes.... The streams .... besides fertilizing the lands through which they meander, and affording, in general, convenient inland water communications, turn numerous grist, carding, fulling, and saw mills....

The principal public roads by which it is traversed are, the main front road along the St. Lawrence, between Lower Canada and Kingston, passing through Cornwall and Lancaster, and the front road on the Ottawa, between Point Fortune and Plantagenet....

.... a number of by-roads afford a ready access to neighbouring or remote settlements; but as they often penetrate a wilderness, and have been opened within a comparatively recent period, they are indifferent at best, and often bad. Indeed, the generality of roads in Upper Canada necessarily suffer from the richness of the soil they traverse, and will always require the greatest attention and constant repair.

The population of this section of the province in 1824 amounted to 69,996 souls, and in 1828 to 85,105; giving an increase in four years of 15,109 souls.

The most populous and improved part of the colony is undoubtedly that from Pointe au Baudet to the head of the Bay of Quinté, a range of one hundred and seventy miles, in which are contained the towns of Kingston, Johnstown, and Cornwall, Port Wellington, the Mohawk Village, Brockville, and several smaller villages; besides a continuation of houses (many of them spacious and well built) and farms by the side of the main road, as well as the other roads that lead to the interior settlements. Great industry and attention to improvements are displayed upon most of the lands throughout this tract; the roads that were formerly made have been gradually rendered sound and good, and many new ones constructed; bridges have been thrown across the rivers, and various communications both by land and water opened to the interior; indeed, various indications of a flourishing and accelerated progress are apparent in almost every direction....

... A regular line of stage is daily run between .... [Prescott] and Montreal (Sundays excepted), and steamboats afford an easy communication between it and the different places on Lake Ontario.

The town of Kingston, the largest and most populous of the Upper Province, is very advantageously seated on the north side of the river St. Lawrence, or rather at the eastern extremity of Lake Ontario.... On the ground upon which it is built formerly stood Fort Frontenac, an old French post. Its foundation took place in 1783, and by natural increase it now presents a front of nearly three quarters of a mile, and in 1828 contained a population ascertained by census to amount to 3,528 inhabitants, exclusive of the troops in garrison: including the latter, and making due allowance for two years' increase, its population may now be computed at not less than 5,500 souls.

The streets are regularly planned, running at right angles with each other, but not paved. The number of houses may be estimated at about six hundred and twenty. Most of them are well built of stone; many of them spacious and commodious: but very few are remarkable for the taste or elegance of their structure....

This town has obtained considerable mercantile importance within the last twenty years: wharfs have been constructed, and many spacious warehouses erected, that are usually filled with merchandise: in fact, it is now become the main entrepôt between Montreal and all the settlements along the lake to the westward. From the commencement of spring until the latter end of autumn, great activity prevails; vessels of from eighty to nearly two hundred tons, employed in navigating the lake, are continually receiving and discharging their cargoes, as well as the bateaux used in the river; and the magnificent steam-boats that ply between Kingston, York, and Niagara, contribute largely to the lively animation of the scene. Its commercial importance must also be considerably enhanced by the opening of the Rideau canal, which will necessarily render it the emporium of the whole trade of the two provinces, whether carried on by the St. Lawrence or through the Ottawa....

By Town [Ottawa], in Nepean, is situated on the southern bank of the Ottawa, a little below the beautiful falls of the Chaudiere, and opposite the flourishing village of Hull in Lower Canada. It stands upon a high and bold eminence surrounding Canal Bay, and occupies both banks of the canal; that part lying to east being called the Lower, and that to the west from a superiority of local elevation the Upper Town. The streets are laid out with much regularity, and of a liberal width, that will hereafter contribute to the convenience, salubrity, and elegance of the place. The number of houses now built is not far short of one hundred and fifty, most of which are constructed of wood, frequently in a style of neatness and taste that reflects great credit upon the inhabitants. On the elevated banks of the bay, the hospital, an extensive stone building, and three stone barracks, stand conspicuous; and nearly on a level with them, and on the eastern side of the bay, is delightfully situated the residence of Colonel By, the commanding royal engineer on that station. From his veranda the most splendid view is beheld that the magnificent scenery of the Canadas affords. The bold eminence that embosoms Entrance Bay, the broken and wild shores opposite, beyond which are seen a part of the flourishing settlements and the church of Hull, the verdant and picturesque islands between both banks, and occasional canoes, barges, and rafts plying the broad surface of the Grand river, or descending its tumultuous stream, are the immediate objects that command the notice of the beholder. In remoter perspective the eye dwells upon a succession of varied and beautiful bridges, abutting upon precipitous and craggy rocks, and abrupt islands, between which the waters are urged with wonderful agitation and violence. Between them, and above their level, the glittering surface of the river is discovered in its descent through the broad and majestic rapid Des Chênes, until the waters are precipitated in immense volumes over the verge of the rock, forming the falls of the Great and Little Chaudière. From the abyss into which they are involved with terrific force, revolving columns of mist perpetually ascend in refulgent whiteness, and as they descend in spray beneath a glowing sunshine, frequently form a partial but bright iris, that seems triumphantly to overarch a section of the bridge.

c) II Central Section [Belleville to Hamilton]

This section of the province embraces the districts of Home and New-castle, which occupy a front of about one hundred and twenty miles upon Lake Ontario, extending from the head of the Bay of Quinté west-ward, to the line between Toronto and Trafalgar. Although less populous than the tract of country composing the first part of the division which we have adopted, this portion of the province does not yield to it in point of fertility, and is equally well watered by numerous lakes, broad and beautiful rivers, and innumerable rivulets and brooks.

The Trent, which is the largest river flowing through it, issues out of Rice Lake, and taking a winding and circuitous course of about one hundred miles falls into the Bay of Quinté, near the village of Sidney, after receiving the waters of the Marmora and numerous other tribu-taries. The Otanabee, discharging itself, from the northward, into Rice Lake, might be considered a continuation of the Trent. It is a full, broad stream, navigable, as well as the Trent, for boats; and a spot, since called Peterborough, in the township of Monaghan, was selected on its western bank, eighteen or twenty miles north of Rice Lake, for the location of 2024 settlers sent out by government in 1825. It communicates from its source, in Trout Lake, with a chain of lakes stretching westwardly towards Lake Simcoe. From Balsam Lake, the last of this chain, a short portage is made to the source of Talbot river falling into Simcoe, thus opening an almost continued interior water communication between the Bay of Quinté and Lake Huron. But the rapids and cascades by which the navigation of the Severn, connecting Lake Simcoe with Huron, is interrupted, operate, in some measure, against the advantages that might be derived from so singular a fact. The route is, nevertheless, practised by *voyageurs,* by means of portages at the most dangerous passages of the river, which render available this abridged distance into Lake Huron.

The Nottawasaga, descending northward to Nottawasaga Bay, Holland, Mukketehsebé, Beaver, Talbot, and Black rivers falling into Lake Simcoe, – Credit, Etobicoke, Humber, and Don rivers, flowing into Lake Ontario, are the most worthy of particular mention. They in general abound with excellent fish, and especially salmon, great quantities of which are annually speared in the river Credit for the supply of the western country. Besides these rivers, a great number of "creeks" of considerable importance discharge their streams into the lake, fertilizing the lands through which they flow, and generally furnishing hydraulic powers to work various descriptions of mills, chiefly applied at present to the purposes of grinding grain and sawing timber....

Lake Simcoe, situated in Home District, between Lakes Huron and Ontario, covers a surface of about 300 square miles, and is the most extensive interior lake of the Upper Province....

Rice Lake is about twenty-five miles long, and four or five miles. wide. It lies nearly south-west and north-east, in the district of Newcastle, and about fifteen miles from the shore of Ontario. The name it bears is derived from the wild rice growing upon its margin; the grain is not, however, restricted to its shores, but is indigenous to that part of the country, and is frequently found in marshes, and upon the borders of lakes. It yields abundant food to quantities of wild fowl, and is gathered by the Indians, who beat it in their canoes, and apply it to their own uses, or dispose of it to the inhabitants. The exposed situation of York has frequently suggested a removal of the seat of government to some more defensible spot, and Rice Lake has not injudiciously been mentioned as offering superior advantages under that aspect. Rice Lake could easily be connected by a ship canal with Lake Ontario, and the capital being thus removed from the immediate frontier, and covered by the rising ground between the two lakes, which might be made a very effectual secondary barrier of defence, would be less open to invasion, and therefore better calculated to be the depository of the public archives and records of the province. The lakes forming the chain, of which we have before spoken, are Balsam, Sturgeon, Pidgeon, Shemong, Shibauticon, and Trout....

In front of Newcastle district, on the borders of Lake Ontario, the soil consists of a rich black earth; but in the district of Home, the shores of the lake are of an inferior quality. The lands upon Yonge-street, which connects York with Lake Simcoe, are exceedingly fertile, but so destitute of stones to create some inconvenience to the settlers. A sandy plain, of some extent, exists some distance north of Ontario, towards Rice Lake; but saving this, and probably one or two more comparatively insignificant exceptions, the soil of this tract of country is extremely fertile, highly conducive to agriculture, and yields luxuriant crops of wheat, rye, maize, pease, barley, oats, buck wheat, &c.

The population of these two districts amounted, in 1824, to 25,901 souls, and had, in 1828, increased to 36,264 souls, being an accession of 10,363 inhabitants in four years, or an increase, in that period, of 40 per cent, which exceeds that of any other part of the province.

The front of all the townships from Kingston to York, are, with few exceptions, well settled; roads lead through them, from which, in many places, others branch off to the interior. At intervals, rather distant indeed from each other, there are a few small villages, the principal of which are Belleville, Coburg, Port Hope, Darlington, and Windsor; but single dwellings and farms are continually presenting themselves along the road, which is that followed by the mail. On the lands that are occupied great progress has been made in agriculture; the houses, generally speaking, are strong and well built; and the inhabitants appear to be possessed of all the necessaries as well as most of the comforts that a life of industry usually bestows.

The town of York, the infant capital of Upper Canada, is …. exceedingly well situated in the township of the same name, on the north side of an excellent harbour. In a military point of view, its position is weak and extremely vulnerable; yet, if judiciously fortified and competent works thrown up on the peninsulated beach in front, it might be capable of considerable resistance against an attack from the lake. It is very regularly laid out, with the streets running at right angles, and promises to become a very handsome town. The plot of ground marked out for it extends about a mile and a half along the harbour, but at present the number of houses does not greatly exceed four hundred and fifty, the greatest part of which are built of wood but there are however many very excellent ones of brick and stone, and most of the numerous dwelling-houses annually added to the town are of the latter description. The public edifices are a government-house, the house of assembly for the provincial parliament, a church, a court-house, and a gaol, with numerous stores and buildings for the various purposes of government.

The new college [Upper Canada] stands immediately opposite the government-house, and comprises five neat brick buildings of two stories high. The centre building, appropriated exclusively to collegiate instruction, is eighty-two feet in length by eighty-five in depth, and surmounted by an elegant ornamental dome. The buildings forming its wings are respectively forty-five feet square, and are dedicated to the use of the principals, professors, and masters of the college.... Such institutions are peculiarly interesting in a new country, and have long been among the *desiderata* of the province, they are, at the same time, a pledge that intellectual cultivation will go hand and hand with local improvements, and that whilst the industrious agriculturist and the enterprising trader are prosecuting their various meritorious pursuits and speculations, the youth of the colony will be receiving the benefits of collegiate education, the stepping-stone to eminence in the learned professions, and an advantage no less valuable to the philosopher, the statesman, and the gentleman.

The new parliament-house, the emigrant's asylum, the law-society hall, the Scots kirk, and a baptist chapel are also conspicuous in the list of the recent improvements of the town, and are evidence of much public spirit and prosperity....

No place in either province has made so rapid a progress as York. In the year 1793, the spot on which it stands presented only one solitary Indian wigwam; in the ensuing spring the ground for the future metropolis of Upper Canada was fixed upon, and the buildings commenced under the immediate superintendence of the late General Simcoe, then lieutenant-governor, whose liberal and enlarged plans of improvement have materially advanced the welfare and prosperity of the province. In the space of five or six years it became a respectable place, and rapidly increased to its present importance; it now contains a population of four thousand souls.

The parliament of the province annually holds its sittings here, as do all the courts of justice. Considerable advances have also been made in the commerce, general opulence, and consequent amelioration of its society. Being the residence of the chief officers of government, both civil and military, many of the conveniences and comforts of polished life are to be met with. Several newspapers are there printed weekly. The lands of the adjacent townships for several miles round are in a high state of cultivation, so that the market of the town is always well supplied....

Immediately in the rear of the town is a very good road, called Yonge-street, that leads to Gwillimbury, a small village thirty-two miles to the northward, and thence five miles more to Cook's Bay, from which by Lake Simcoe there is a communication to Lake Huron. This being a route of much importance was greatly improved by the North-west

Company, for the double purpose of shortening the distance to the Upper Lakes, and avoiding any contact with the American frontiers. The land on each side of it for a considerable depth is very fertile, and many settlements are already formed, where some of the farms are in a good state of cultivation.

d) III Western Section [Hamilton to Windsor/Sarnia]

The western division of the organized parts of Upper Canada comprises four districts – Niagara, Gore, London, and Western. In 1824 it contained a population of 55,200 inhabitants, and appears by the census of 1828 to have increased in four years to 64,157, thus giving a ratio of increase, of 16 1/4 per cent. during that period.

Situated between the parallels of 42° and 45° 30' north latitude, it has the advantage of extending further south than any other portion of the British North American possessions, and hence enjoys in an eminent degree a superior fertility of soil and milder temperature of climate. But a correct idea of its meteorology is not to be formed, however, from the analogy of similar latitudes on the old continent; and it is not exactly to be assumed that the atmosphere of this part of the Upper Province is possessed during winter of as moderate a degree of rigour as that of the places situated under the same circles of latitude in Italy, or any other part of Europe. The climate of America is indeed essentially different from that of any other quarter of the globe; but to what precise physical agency so wide a dissimilarity is ascribable has not yet, it is believed, been very satisfactorily discovered, although various causes have been already assigned for it....

... The surface it exhibits is uniformly level or slightly undulating, if we except a very few solitary eminences, and those parts of the districts of Gore and Niagara traversed by the ridge of elevated land traced in a previous chapter, the general altitude of which does not exceed one hundred feet, although at some points it may approach very near three hundred and fifty. It is not, therefore, in a country so little variegated by hill and dale, and so utterly a stranger to the towering grandeur of the mountain, that sublimity is to be sought: yet the immense extent, magnitude, and beauty of its forests, and the prodigious vastness of its waters, are no insignificant sources of the sublime; whilst the exuberant fertility of extensive plains, the luxuriance of orchards recumbent with the weight of their delicious fruits, the graceful meanderings of full flowing streams, or he soft murmurings of more humble rivulets, added to the busy scenes of rural and thriving industry, cannot be denied eminently to possess the most interesting charms of the picturesque....

.... The almost total absence of stones or gravel within the greatest arable depth is a peculiar feature of the generality of lands in the Upper Province, which has been felt as serious inconvenience by the inhabitants in the progress of their rural improvements, whatever may be its probable advantage as facilitating some of the operations of husbandry....

The forests are remarkable for the sturdy growth, the variety, and the rich foliage of their trees. Out of the long list of their different species, the following may be selected as being of most frequent occurrence: maple, beech, oak, basswood, ash, elm, pine, hickory, walnut, butternut, chestnut, cherry, birch, cedar, and pine, and their several varieties. The cedar and pine are much prized in consequence of their scarcity, particularly in the Western and London districts, where they are barely found in sufficient quantities to furnish materials for durable buildings and fencing enclosures. In the heart of these dense woods and on the borders of rivers, extensive plains suddenly present themselves, that lay open to view a beautiful area of natural meadow often expanding several thousand mile's [*sic:* likely feet] in extent, and delightfully relieved by occasional clumps lofty pine, white oak, and poplar, agreeably clustered in the various vistas of the plain. In the neighbourhood of Long Point and on the banks of the Grand river are situated the most extensive of these vast and often fertile plains, which are generally in a flourishing state of cultivation. In the townships of Burford, Stamford, Niagara Toronto, York, Dumfries, and Ancaster, broad and beautiful natural meadows are also to be found; but in general they are considered more prevalent in the London district than in any other section of the province.

These four districts are remarkably well watered by several large rivers and their various branches, intersecting the country in every direction, and generally affording exceedingly convenient means of internal conveyance, as they are for the most part navigable for small boats to very remote distances, and for river sloops and craft for several miles above their mouths. The rivers entitled to more particular consideration are the Thames, the Ouse or Grand river, the Welland or Chippewa, the Big Bear, and the Maitland.

The Thames, formerly called the Rivière à la Tranche, rises far in the interior, rather north of the township of Blandford; and after pursuing a serpentine course of about one hundred and fifty miles, in a direction nearly south-west, discharges itself into Lake St. Clair. It is navigable for large vessels as far up as Chatham, fifteen miles above its mouth, and for boats nearly to its source. A bar across its entrance is certainly some drawback; but as there is at all times sufficient water upon it to float small craft perfectly equipped, the resources of art would very easily pass those of a much larger burden. Camels [devices for adding buoyancy to boats] for instance, might be used; or even common lighters, dexterously managed, would, as it is believed experience already has shown, prove adequate to the service. The river winds through a fine level country, highly fertile, and rich in every requisite for new settlements. Its banks present many fine plains and excellent natural meadows. The soil is principally a sandy earth, intermixed with large quantities of loam, and sometimes marl, under which is a substratum of clay; and the flats of the river annually acquire much richness from the overflowing of its banks, by which rich alluvial deposits are made upon the surface. The oak, maple, walnut, beech, and pine growing in its vicinity are of very superior quality. There are roads opened along its course, and on each side of it numerous scattered settlements down to Lake St. Clair; but the roads are rather neglected, from the preference generally given to the use of the river as a highway. The Delaware Indian village, and another of Moravian settlers, are situated on it. The last is about thirty-five miles from the mouth of the river, and is under the superintendence of missionaries from the Society of Moravian United Brethren, who maintain a chapel here. There are many Indian converts residing in it, whose peaceable conduct and general demeanour show some of the benefits derived from civilization. The village is surrounded by thriving corn-fields, and tillage has made considerable progress in its neighbourhood.

About twenty miles further down the river is a small place called Chatham, very desirably seated at the junction of a large stream with the Thames: it is in a very centrical situation, and at the head of the ship navigation of the river. A dockyard might be advantageously established on the point of land formed by the confluence of the two streams, from whence vessels might be conveniently launched. London is situated in the township of the same name, on the banks of the main branch of the Thames, about ninety miles from the mouth of the river, and in a tolerably central position between the surrounding lakes. From the obvious analogy intended to be drawn between the local appellations of this part of the province and those of the mother country, it has been inferred that Governor Simcoe contemplated, at the time the surveys took place the possibility, that London might ultimately become the metropolis of the colony. However improbable or visionary such a change may now appear, there is no anticipating the changes that the progressive and rapid improvement of the province may dictate; especially when it is recollected that the present capital is considered by many as untenable whilst the interior position of London, and its numerous and improvable advantages, are admitted to give it a superiority under various aspects although deficient as a shipping port, in which particular it yields altogether to York.

The Grand river is next in magnitude to the Thames, and takes its source in the interior of the country towards Lake Huron. It flows in a general south-easterly course, with very serpentine windings, and traversing a tract of the highest degree of fertility, discharges itself into Lake Erie at Sherbrooke, between Point au Barbet and Grand river Point. At its mouth it is upwards of nine hundred yards wide; but its access to large vessels is rendered difficult by a sand bar stretching across the entrance that fluctuates in its elevation, but upon which is generally found eight feet of water. The river is navigable for schooners about twenty-five miles above its mouth, and considerably farther up for large boats. It offers one of the few harbours that the north shore of Lake Erie affords; and might, if judiciously fortified, be rendered very safe and secure. Its banks abound with gypsum, which may be easily obtained from copious beds, and conveyed to any part of the extensive region the river traverses, by the convenient means its navigation allows. The lands on both sides of this beautiful river were originally appropriated exclusively to the Indians of the Six Nations; but part of them have since been laid out into townships. Villages of the various tribes are dispersed along its picturesque banks; and in ascending the stream, we come first to the Senecas, and then in succession to the Delawares, Mississagas, Onondagas, Tuscaroras, and Cayugas. The Mohawks, although not one of Six United Nations, have also several settlements upon the Grand river, the largest of which contains about two hundred souls, and is situated about three miles below the ferry.

The Welland or Chippewa is a remarkably fine river, wholly unobstructed by falls, and flowing through the heart of the district of Niagara. Its source is in Binbrook, about fifty miles west of its junction with the Niagara river, nearly three miles above the stupendous falls of the latter river.... It is connected by elegant broad sloop canals, with Lake Ontario to the north and Lake Erie to the south, the canals being linked by a section of the river about ten miles in length, which is used as part of the communication, and forms one continued canal, from one lake into the other. This magnificent work of art and important commercial undertaking has but recently been completed, and in the early part of last August was thrown open for the ingress and egress of vessels. The Bull Frog, Lieutenant Jones, R.N., was the first vessel that passed down the canal. The towing was so effectually performed by one horse, that in sixteen hours she descended through that section of the canal lying between the Welland river and Lake Ontario, and met on her way, an American schooner bound upwards....

Considering the comparative infancy of the settlements of this section of Upper Canada, the numerous roads by which it is intersected, are evidence of the rapid improvement and prosperity of the country. Dundas Street, Talbot Road East, the Middle Road, Talbot Road East, Talbot Road North, and the road east from Port Talbot, along the shores of Lake Erie, along the Niagara, and the southern shore of Lake Ontario, to Dundas village, are the leading public roads, connecting the extremities of the settled parts of this section of the province. There are, besides upwards of fifty other main, bye, and cross roads, several of which are of considerable length; the principal of these being, the roads leading to Galt and Guelph; the new routes opened by the Canada company to the town of Godrich, on the shores of Lake Huron, those between Burford and Malahide; between Brantford and Charlotteville; between Grimsby and Rainham; and several others.

Dundas Street, styled a military route, traverses Gore and London districts centrally, commencing at the capital, York, passing through the villages of Neilson, Dundas, Oxford, and London, and joining the road north of the Thames, which is opened along the banks of the river, down to its mouth in Lake St. Clair. By this road the mail passes between York and Dundas; and from the latter place a branch or by-post is dispatched to the westward, by the Dundas route to Sandwich and Amherstburgh, and another to Galt and Guelph. The village of Dundas, about forty-five miles from York, is prettily situated at the head of Burlington Bay, near the spot known as Cootes' Paradise....

From Dundas the mail route lies through the village of Ancaster, the settlement at Stony Creek, and the villages of Grimsby and St. Catherine's, to Niagara. Ancaster contains a church, and about three hundred and fifty or four hundred inhabitants, and is most eligibly situated in the centre of a picturesque and champaign country, in a high state of cultivation. Indeed, the villages on this road generally are seated in one of the most diversified parts of the province, and are much relieved by some of those grateful varieties of surface that yield so many charms to the romantic scenery of more hilly regions....

Fort George, or Niagara, formerly Newark, but changed by law, in 1798, to its present appellation, occupies the west bank of Niagara river, opposite the old fort of the same name, on the American frontier. Its position, on the shores of Ontario, and at the mouth of the river, – that together from Mississaga Point, upon which a lighthouse has been erected, -is peculiarly advantageous; but its proximity to the frontier boundary lays it open to the depredations of foreign hostility, in the event of war. In December, 1813, at a period when the town seemed most flourishing, the American forces, under General M'Clure, of the New York militia, barbarously set it on fire in abandoning the fort, and it was totally burnt to the ground. Niagara has, however, risen from its ashes with astonishing rapidity, and is decidedly become one of the most thriving villages of the province. Its population in 1828 amounted to 1262 souls, and it will not now (1830) be overrated at 1500. It contains many neat houses, numerous shops, two or three respectable taverns, and has a market held once a week, to which the farmers of the surrounding country bring their various produce. Nor is it divested of the means of suggesting public improvements in print, or of discussing foreign politics; two weekly newspapers, published in so infant a town, are positive evidence of a laudable spirit of literary emulation, as well as general advancement. Its harbour is remarkably good, and exhibits the gay scene of frequent arrivals and departures of sloops, barges, and steamboats from and to every part of the lake and the St. Lawrence, as low down as Prescott....

Queenston, in the southern part of the township of Niagara, and distant seven miles from Fort George, is pleasantly situated at the base of the romantic heights to which the village gives its name, and at the northern extremity of the portage, from tne foot to the head of the Falls. The village contains a church, a court-house, and government stores, partly appropriated to the use of the Indian department, and a population of four or five hundred inhabitants. The lands around Queenston are in a very flourishing state of tillage; and the tame but highly beautiful aspect of the fertile fields the eye surveys, is agreeably contrasted with dense foliage of distant forests, and the bold ridge rising majestically to the southward of the village, and stretching west and east across the deep and toiling stream of the Niagara river. Several steam-boats, most elegantly fitted up and with excellent accommodations, run regularly between this place and York and Kingston....

Immediately opposite Kingston is the rival village of Lewiston, on the American bank of the Niagara river. Both places are similarly circum-

stanced, from the position they respectively occupy at the corresponding extremities of the portages on either side of the Falls of Niagara.
Queenston has hitherto enjoyed the advantage over Lewiston in its
growth and consequence, but it is believed that the opening of the Welland Canal will materially affect its prosperity, by transferring the carrying trade from the portage to the canal. Queenston, however, commands
many valuable advantages, independently of the one of which it has
been thus deprived: the fertility and beauty of the surrounding country,
the excellence of its harbour, if such the Niagara may here be called, and
the undiminished attractions of the splendid scenery in its vicinity, will
always secure to it an eminent degree of interest, and insure its progressive aggrandisement....

The village of Chippewa is ten miles from Queenston, at the southern
extremity of the portage, and occupies both banks of the Welland river
near the mouth of which, it is situated. It contains several neat houses,
and about two hundred inhabitants: near it is a small fort, and also
barracks for troops. The relative position of Chippewa, with regard to
Queenston, renders both villages, in some measure, dependent upon the
same causes of commercial prosperity, and both will inevitably be, to
a certain degree, influenced, in the rapidity of their improvements and
increase, by the changes that must take place in the direction of the trade,
by the opening of the Welland Canal. Chippewa will, however suffer the
least of the two from such a circumstance, owing to the advantage it
enjoys of being upon the banks of a navigable river, linked with, and, as
it were, forming part of the canal itself. The Welland is in fact used as an
eastern branch of the canal already, and is the channel through which
produce passes to and from Buffalo....

Before passing from the consideration of the district of Niagara to
the description of the settlements west of it, the peculiarly favourable
geographical position it enjoys should not go unnoticed. Forming nearly
an oblong square, bounded on three sides by navigable waters, and
traversed centrally by a splendid canal, the access to all parts of it, is
rendered extremely easy and inviting. The fertility of its soil and the
congeniality of its climate, are not excelled in any district of the province, unless it be, probably, by the Western. The choicest fruits seem
to be congenial to its soil; peaches, nectarines, and apples are richly
clustered on the branches of crowded orchards, and acquire a degree
of perfection, equaled only on the luxuriant banks of the Detroit river.
The sublimity of the views disclosed in the Niagara river, and the picturesque varieties of landscape produced by the Queenston heights,

and occasional inequalities of surface, give the scenery of this district a decided superiority, over that of any other in Upper Canada....

... Port Talbot is almost equidistant from the extremities of Lake Erie, and at the bottom of a sweeping bend of its northern shores, placing it at the broadest point of the lake. This was the spot selected in 1802 by Colonel Talbot, a member of the legislative council of the province, for the formation of a settlement which he had planned on a large scale, and has since, in a great measure, happily realized. Having obtained from his majesty's government a grant of one hundred thousand acres of crown land, under the specific condition of locating an actual settler to every two hundred acres of the tract, he courageously penetrated the dense forests of Canada, and at the above date laid the foundation of the colony which now bears his name. The Talbot settlement is spread over a considerable extent of country from the principle and policy that dictated the plan of its formation. With a view of opening a communication with the settlements of the Detroit and Niagara, the settlers were judiciously located to contiguous lands on the borders of two extensive roads, leading to the extremities of the lake, and upon another road leading into the back country, which has since been prolonged to Godrich, on the margin of Lake Huron.

The tract of country the settlement occupies is not excelled in fertility by any of equal extent in the province; and the inhabitants, emulating the example of their persevering leader, have industriously turned to account the advantages of their situation. Most of them have very good houses and barns, horses, horned cattle, hogs and sheep. In fact the settlement is populous, prosperous, and rapidly increasing, and is altogether a conspicuous example of success in the history of colonization, that cannot fail to reward the generous exertions of its intelligent, but eccentric founder and promoter....

Amherstburgh, in the township of Malden, about three miles up the eastern side of Detroit river, contains nearly two hundred houses, a church, court-house, and gaol, many good shops, and a population exceeding twelve hundred souls. It is decidedly one of the most delightful towns of the province; and, from the wealth and respectability of its inhabitants, is by no means a stranger to the pleasures of good society and the charms of social refinement.... Its situation is extremely picturesque; the country around perfectly exuberant with richness and fertility; and the climate most salubrious and invigorating, notwithstanding the intensity of the heat during some parts of the summer. Indeed, the banks of the Detroit river are altogether peculiarly favoured by nature: they stand unrivalled, if equalled, in Upper Canada, for the generous luxuriance of their soil, the crystalline beauty of the streams by which they are watered, the cerulean purity of the skies, and the deliciousness and delicacy of the fruits the orchards produce in the most abundant profusion. Peaches, pears, plums, apples, nectarines, and grapes are produced in the highest degree of perfection, and seem far more the spontaneous offsprings of a congenial earth and atmosphere, than the result of horticultural cultivation, which is, in general, rather neglected. The rivers abound with a variety of excellent fish, and the marshes and woods with a still greater diversity of game; whilst the numerous orchards, loaded with their impending treasures, and skirting the main road a short distance from the banks of the Detroit, re-echo with the shrill, sweet, and merry notes of thousands of wild warblers.

The settlements in this part of he Western District, the most remote of any in the province, originated when Canada was yet under the dominion of France, and are therefore composed chiefly of French Canadians. The distribution of the lands in narrow elongated slips, the consequent contiguity of the farms, the mode of cultivation, and the manners of the people are strongly contrasted with the same features in the other settled parts of Upper Canada ; but they bear so striking an analogy to the character of the seigniorial settlements in the sister province, that it would be easy to fancy ourselves in one of its many flourishing parishes, were it not for the superiority of the Detroit fruits that would dissipate the illusion.

Fourteen miles beyond Amherstburgh, pursuing the course of the river, stands the town of Sandwich [Windsor], containing 140 or 150 houses, a church, distinguished by the appellation of the Huron Church, a courthouse, and gaol. There are wharfs along the river side, where vessels may be safely moored during the winter. Opposite Sandwich is the American village of Detroit.... The lands on this lake are laid out onto townships, but not yet settled; however, they are not likely to be long uninhabited, as their establishment promises to be accelerated by the progressive extension of the settlements of the Canada Company on the shores of Lake Huron. Beyond these there is no cultivated land; and the northern shores of Huron and the borders of Lake Superior remain in their pristine state of wilderness, except where occupied by a straggling fur-trading post, established by the late North-West Company. Fort William, at the head of Lake Superior, is by far the most important of any of these posts, and the only one, on this side the height of land forming the boundary of Hudson's Bay territory, deserving particular notice.

e) General Statistical Summary

In taking a general and comprehensive view of Upper Canada, and glancing retrospectively to what it was fifteen years back, the accelerated march of its prosperity and improvement is remarkably striking. Within that period, the mass of the country has been surveyed, settlements formed in almost every township, and towns and villages have sprung up with extraordinary energy, in various directions. Canals of an elegance and utility, and of dimensions unrivalled, if equalled, on this continent, have been opened through the province. The Welland and the Rideau canals remove from the frontier, the internal communication by water, from the remotest British settlements of the St. Lawrence, to the sea. The Burlington and Desjardins canals afford important advantages to the fertile district in which they are situated.

The navigation of the lakes and rivers has undergone the greatest amelioration. Eight or ten steam-boats, some of them of great elegance, now form several complete and convenient lines of communication between the remote parts of the country. Manufactures and mechanics have also made considerable progress; coarse linens and woollen cloths are successfully manufactured for domestic use by most good farmers and manufactories of iron are established at Marmora and Charlotteville. Saw and grist mills (there are upwards of five hundred of them), distilleries and breweries, are to be found in all the settled parts of the province. The principal towns in most districts contain proper public buildings, such as churches, court-houses, gaols, warehouses, &c.

At York, a provincial bank is established under legislative authority, with branches at Kingston and Niagara. District schools, under the general superintendence of a board, and the immediate direction of trustees, are established throughout the province; and a college, upon the principle of similar institutions in England, has been founded and recently opened in the capital of the colony.

f) The Canada Company

... In the township of Godrich, a town has been laid out on the borders of Lake Huron, and at the mouth of the river Maitland, from which a road is opened to join Talbot Road North, and another has been traced, communicating eastward through Wilmot and Guelph, with the head of Ontario. The town is very judiciously planned, and peculiarly well situated, upon the elevated shores of the lake, and on the southern side of the harbour formed by Maitland river. This harbour is capable of affording safe shelter to vessels of two hundred tons' burden, and is well calculated to admit hereafter of the construction of quays, to facilitate the loading and unloading of produce and merchandise....

... Guelph enjoys most of the advantages of the Huron tract in respect of climate and fertility; but a nearer proximity to the older settlements of the province, give it probably a superiority of relative location.

Guelph and Godrich are decidedly rivals: each possesses certain advantages over the other which will for some time render their prosperity co-equal; but it is believed that the position of the latter on the shores of a great lake, accessible as it is to large vessels, and having a good harbour to protect them – superadded to the advantageous circumstance, of being at once made the focus of populous settlements, that will soon be flourishing around – will eventually give it the ascendancy.

The little town of Galt is seated on the banks of the Grand river, in the township of Dumfries, and about seventeen or eighteen miles from Guelph. It is another of the villages founded by the Company; and however its importance may be considered secondary, as compared with the other towns, its situation is peculiarly eligible, and cannot fail to attract many settlers of respectability and capital....

... It is probable, that, before the lapse of five years, lands that may now be obtained upon terms extremely moderate, even as sections of a forest, will cost treble what they now do, owing to the extraordinary demand that has been created for lands, by the encouragement held out by the government and Canada Company to emigrate to Upper Canada; and this increased value of the land is the more to be anticipated from the geographical position of that province. That section of it which is most desirable for settlement is by no means unlimited or exhaustless, and may probably be confined, northward, by a line drawn from the head of Lake Chaudière, on the Ottawa, to Matchedash Bay, on Lake Huron, which includes, to the southward, all the organized and surveyed parts of the province, so much of which has already been stated to belong to the Company. Thus circumscribed, with a population whose natural increase is great, and whose adventitious increase is far greater, every acre of ground must daily acquire a high degree of augmented appreciation. The growth of Upper Canada, we believe, is unprecedented for its rapidity, in the annals of colonization; but it must be considered, that few countries in the world can compete with it as a field for new settlement. Few sections of the earth are so especially endued by nature with richness, exuberance, and fertility, with bright and pure skies, a salubrious atmosphere, a climate calculated to ripen luxuriant fields, and mature delicious fruits; in fact, endowed with all the advantages that can render any spot eminently desirable as the abode of man, or rivet his affections to the soil.

(Bouchette, *The British Dominions*, 1831, 1:70–120)

3 THE RIVER ST. LAWRENCE – THE GREAT LAKES – THE GULF – CANALS

☞ Bouchette recognizes the special role that the St. Lawrence River–Great Lakes system has in North America because the waterway extends such a great distance into the heart of the continent. Various sections of the river system had different names then than they do today. Bouchette gives much attention to the Welland, Rideau, and Genville canals that had recently been constructed to improve movement of goods. He says that the St. Lawrence is the commercial outlet for an area extending almost to the Pacific Coast and also for adjacent parts of the United States. He envisages that a ship-canal along the St. Lawrence will eventually connect Kingston and Montreal, overcoming the violent rapids on stretches of the river. Most Europeans visiting North America sought to see Niagara Falls and their travel accounts vied in describing its overwhelming impact. As one can see from his emotional language, Bouchette valiantly enters this verbal contest. ☜

The St. Lawrence, originally called the Great River of Canada, or the Great River, to mark its pre-eminence, is the indelible link formed by nature between the Canadas, and the source at once of the wealth, beauty, and prosperity of both provinces. In passing, therefore, from the topography of Upper to that of Lower Canada, the description of that splendid river seems naturally to suggest itself as a typical illustration of that link. The introduction of it here, from the circumstance of its following the account of one province, and immediately preceding the description of the other, will at the same time enable the reader the more easily and intimately to associate the topographical features and characters of each province with the utility, magnificence, and grandeur of that gigantic stream.

The St. Lawrence, though not the longest river in the world, is certainly the largest in every other respect, if, as appears proper, its immense lakes be considered to form part of it. Under this aspect it will be found that the surface it covers, and the cubic mass of its waters, far exceed those of the Amazon or the Mississippi, but it probably does not carry to the ocean a greater volume of water than either of these two majestic streams....

... In different parts of its course it is known under different appellations: thus, as high up from the sea as Montreal, it is called St. Lawrence; from Montreal to Kingston in Upper Canada, it is called the Cataraqui, or Iroquois; between Lake Ontario and Lake Erie it is called Niagara river; between Lake Erie and Lake St. Clair, the Detroit; between Lake St. Clair and Lake Huron, the river St. Clair; and between Lake Huron and Lake Superior, the distance is called the Narrows, or the Falls of St. Mary.

Lake Superior

Lake Superior, without the aid of any great effort of imagination, may be considered as the inexhaustible spring from whence, through unnumbered ages, the St. Lawrence has continued to derive its ample stream.... Its surface is about six hundred and twenty-seven feet above the tidewater of the Atlantic; but the shores exhibit almost conclusive inditiae of its having been, in former ages, as much perhaps as forty or fifty feet higher than its present level. Various soundings have been taken, from eighty to one hundred and fathoms; but its greatest depth probably exceeds two hundred fathoms, thus demonstrating the bottom of the lake to be nearly six hundred feet *below* the level of the ocean....

Falls of Niagara

... It would be difficult to ascertain with certainty the exact measurement of the curvatures of the Horse Shoe, but it is computed, by geometrical process, to be seven hundred yards; and its altitude taken, with a plumb-line from the surface of the Table-rock, was found to be rather more than one hundred and forty-nine feet. The American Fall does not probably much exceed three hundred and seventy-five yards in curvelinear length; but its perpendicular height is one hundred and sixty-two feet, or thirteen feet higher than the top of the Great Fall. It is subdivided by a small island, cutting off a minor portion of the sheet of falling water, to which the name of Montmorency has been appropriated, either on account of the resemblance traced between it and that celebrated fall near Quebec, or the more strikingly to contrast its comparative insignificance with Niagara. The face of Goat Island, which intervenes between these awful cataracts, keeps them three hundred and thirty yards asunder, and perhaps adds greatly to their romantic effect and beauty, by destroying the sameness which one unbroken sheet of water would present, although the collective waters of the Niagara, thus hurled down *en masse,* might, if possible, be still more grand and astounding.

About half a mile above the cataract the river descends on a deeply inclined plane. Its surface begins to ripple a short distance below the entrance of Welland river; but soon accelerated in their career, the waters dash and foam with terrific violence, until they approach the head of Goat Island, when their convulsive agitation partially subsides; and they sweep on in a broad, ceaseless, and swift current, and are thus projected over the rock, forming a parabolic section in their appalling descent to the profound abyss into which they are ingulphed. This abyss is 200 feet deep, and about 1000 yards wide; but it soon becomes contracted to less than half that width, forming a dark, dread basin, bounded by rugged limestone and slate rock, rising perpendicularly from the surface of the waters below, or overhanging the foaming surge.

The shores of the Niagara immediately above the Falls are, perhaps, too tame in their aspect to bring forth the whole grandeur of so stupendous an object. Surrounded by towering Alpine cliffs, its overwhelming terrors could even be augmented, and its sublimity much enhanced. The islands and the eastern bank of the river are low and thickly covered with trees, whose autumnal foliage, decked "in ten thousand dies," alters the face of nature, and, by its gorgeous tints, imparts new interest and novelty to the scenery of the Falls The western shore is bolder: an horizontal ridge is formed along the margin of the rapids by the depression of the river, commencing from the Welland, and gradually increasing in elevation above the surface of the stream from eight to eighty feet, and even attains the altitude of one hundred. The Table-rock, so famous as the spot whence a very near view may be had of the cataract, lies at the foot of this ridge, nearly on a level with the summit of the Horse Shoe Fall; indeed it forms part of the ledge over which the torrent is precipitated. Its surface is flat, and, jutting out horizontally about fifty feet, overhangs the awful chasm beneath. The access to it is down a winding path, cut through the copses and shrubbery that cover the slope of the ridge we have just described. The rock is defaced by innumerable inscriptions carved by travellers, and intersected by many crevices and fissures, some of which are nearly an inch broad. The process of disintegration is perceptibly going on ; and there is little doubt that the Tablerock will eventually be hurled, section by section, into the depths of the cavern below. In the autumn of 1818 a large fragment suddenly gave way, and is now partly to be seen by the explorers of the lower region of the Falls....

Five miles from the Falls is the whirlpool; a phenomenon scarcely less appalling in its terrors, and probably involving more inevitable destruction to every thing coming within the pale of its attraction. It is occasioned by the stream, as it passes in heavy volumes from the cataract, and sweeps with impetuous violence round an abrupt bend of the river, producing so forcible a reaction as to form a stupendous vortex between the high perpendicular cliffs by which it is walled. By thus diverging from its forward direction, and being as it were embayed for a time, the velocity of the current is checked and subdued to a more tranquil course towards Lake Ontario. Nine miles lower down the Niagara emerges from the deep, rock-bound chasm of the Falls, and thence flows in a deep and gentle tide, between banks of more moderate elevation, to its discharge into the lake. Its mouth is .... between Fort George or the town of Niagara on the west, and the old French fort Niagara on the east.

That the Falls of Niagara, in ages now long past, and at the period, probably, of the formation of the great lakes, were situated much lower down, between the present villages of Queenston and Lewiston, appears almost indisputably true; and it is believed that all the geologists who have critically examined the locality concur in the assertion of the fact. It is not in the province of the topographer to speculate upon geological phenomena; but we would merely hazard a remark, which superior science may improve if correct, or reject if erroneous. The fact that the Falls have receded being admitted, might not the age of the lakes, at least of Erie and Ontario, as confined to their present basins, be ascertained with tolerable certainty? The waters of Ontario are supposed to have bathed the base of Queenston Heights – nay, the level of the lake is admitted generally to have once been co-equal with the summit of that range: if then, by a series of nice and long-continued observations, the ratio of disintegration in a given time were properly ascertained, the calculation could be carried retrospectively, with all the modifications that the breadth, depth, &c. of the water-worn chasm would dictate, until it would arrive at the period of the original formation of the cataract, and the gradual depression of the surface of Ontario to its present level. The calculation might, in the same way, be made prospectively, and afford a very curious result as affecting the great physical changes that future ages may work in the bed of the Niagara.

In taking leave of Niagara river, to proceed in our description of the other parts of the St. Lawrence, its lakes and canals, we feel how inadequately we have portrayed the grandeur and manifold sublimities of its unrivalled scenery; but, in truth, there are in nature objects that beggar description, and the cataract of Niagara belongs pre-eminently to that class. There are not wanting, however, faithful portraitures of its magnificence by far abler pens, and we might therefore have excused ourselves from the attempt here; but an account of the Niagara would have appeared to us very deficient, had it not contained such a sketch of the great Falls as accords with the topographical character of the present work.

Welland Canal

The cascades and cataracts of Niagara river throwing insuperable obstacles in the way of its navigation suggested some years ago the expediency of cutting a ship canal connecting Lake Erie with Lake Ontario, and an association was accordingly formed and incorporated in 1824, under the name of the WELLAND CANAL COMPANY....

This momentous work is now nearly completed, ...The total length of the canal is forty-two miles, consisting of three sections; the first extending from the Grand river to the Welland, sixteen miles; the second being part of the river Welland itself, ten miles; and the third lying between Welland river and Lake Ontario, sixteen miles. The entrance of the canal from Lake Erie is situated about two miles above the mouth of the Grand or Ouse river, where the cutting is carried through Wainfleet Marsh to the level of Welland river.... The level of Lake Erie is 330 feet above that of Ontario, and the step is performed by the intervention of thirty-seven locks, thirty-two of which form a successive series, descending from the summit to the base of the range of high grounds constituting the Queenston Heights. The locks are not, however, in immediate contiguity, but sufficiently remote from each other to admit the crossing in the intervening spaces of vessels bound in opposite directions, thus avoiding the tedious delays that would necessarily result from the situation of locks in proximate succession.

The canal is 56 feet wide at the surface of the water, 26 at bottom, and 8 1/2 feet deep. The chambers of the locks are 100 feet in length by 22 in breadth, and therefore amply large enough for vessels of 125 tons' burden, which is above the average tonnage of those employed in trade upon the lakes....

The two powerful rivals of the Welland Canal are, the Grand Erie and Ohio canals, the former opening an avenue to the Atlantic by the

Hudson river, the latter to the Gulf of Mexico by the Mississippi; but we apprehend that both these grand works will yield the palm to the other in the competition. The superior dimensions of the Welland Canal, that render inexpedient the delays and expense of repeated trans-shipments, – its shortness when compared with its rivals, and the consequent facility and despatch, besides the diminished expense with which it must be passed, – the link that it forms between the schooner navigation of two extensive lakes, and indeed between all the navigable waters above Lake Erie and those of Ontario, – are circumstances which of themselves would be sufficient to secure the patronage of a large proportion of the trade of the lakes, especially if the commercial regulations of both countries be framed upon such principles of liberal policy, as will leave it optional with the inhabitants of either, to adopt that route which their respective interests may dictate....

The Rideau Canal

... the Rideau Canal [is] an undertaking of stupendous magnitude and incalculable utility.

The Rideau Canal commences at Kingston, and, traversing the tract of country lying between the St. Lawrence and the Ottawa, strikes the latter river at the foot of the Falls of Chaudiere, and a short distance above those of the Rideau, situated at the mouth of that river. It is one hundred and thirty-five miles long, and perfectly unique of its kind in America, and, probably, in the world, being made up in its whole length by a chain of lakes, dams, and aqueducts, so connected by locks of large dimensions as to open a steam-boat navigation from Ontario to the Ottawa river. Rideau Lake, which is about twenty-four miles long, and six broad on an average, is the grand summit level of the canal: it is 283 feet above the waters of the Ottawa on one side, and 154 above the surface of Lake Ontario on the other, requiring in the rise and fall a total number of forty-seven locks, seventeen of which are on the Kingston side, and thirty between Rideau Lake and the Ottawa. These locks were originally planned upon a scale to correspond with those of the La Chine Canal, *i.e.* 100 feet by 20; but these dimensions were subsequently increased to 142 feet in length by 33 in width, the depth of water being 5 feet. There are twenty dams on the whole route, constructed with remarkable solidity and skill, which, by the reflux of the waters they produce, have strangely altered the natural appearances of the country. "In several instances, a dam not more than twenty-four feet high and one hundred and eighty feet wide will throw the rapids and rivers into a still sheet above it for a distance of more than twenty miles. The dams also back the waters up creeks, ravines, and valleys; and, instead of making one canal, they form numerous canals of various ramifications, which will all tend greatly to the improvement of a very fertile country. The land drowned by the raising of the dams is not worth mentioning, consisting chiefly of swampy wastes, the haunts of otters and beavers." [M'Taggart, vol. i] ...

... There can be little doubt that when the whole line of canal from Kingston to Montreal will be completed, and it is now nearly so, the great thoroughfare of the Canadas will be transferred from the frontier to the Rideau route, until a canal shall have been opened along the St. Lawrence. When sloops and steam-boats of from one hundred to one hundred and twenty-five tons' burden can pass without interruption from the remotest settlements of Upper Canada to Grenville on the Ottawa river, whence their cargoes can be transported with ease and safety through inferior canals to the port of Montreal, we believe that few will hesitate to forward their produce through that channel, even in times of profound peace with our neighbours; especially if the tolls that will be exacted by government on the Rideau and the Grenville canals be moderate, as in truth it is its interest and policy to make them....

The Grenville Canal consists of three sections: – one at the Long Sault, on the Ottawa, another at the Chûte à Bloudeau, and a third at the Carillon Rapids, opening into the lake of the Two Mountains, through which an uninterrupted navigation is practised by steam-boats to La Chine, nine miles above the city of Montreal. The dimensions of this canal are calculated to correspond with those of the canal of La Chine, which are 28 feet wide at bottom, 48 at the water-line, and 5 deep. It is unfortunate that its proportions should not have been originally planned upon a scale to admit of sloop and steam-boat navigation, and therefore corresponding with the Rideau, by which means no trans-shipments would have become necessary in the transport of produce from the remotest settlements of Upper Canada to La Chine, and the returnof goods from thence to the upper countries. The Grenville Canal is nevertheless a work of vast importance under every aspect. It is opened under military superintendence, and its expenses are defrayed by the imperial government.

The route by the Rideau Canal, the Ottawa, and the Grenville Canal is calculated to avoid, not only the frontier, ... but also the rapids of the St. Lawrence, between Lake Ontario and Montreal. From its discharge, out of Ontario, the St. Lawrence is also known under the names of the *Iroquois* and the *Cataraqui*. It issues from the lake in so broad and beautiful a stream, that it assumes the appearance of a lake for a distance of thirty-nine miles, which is so singularly studded with a multitude of islands, that it has been denominated the Lake of the Thousand Islands, or Mille Isles: but their number far exceeds this mere descriptive computation; the operations of the surveyors employed in establishing the boundary, under the 6th article of the Treaty of Ghent, having ascertained that there were one thousand six hundred and ninety-two, forming an inextricable labyrinth of islands varying in magnitude, shape, and aspect, and presenting the most extraordinary and pleasing vistas and perspectives, in which the rapid and magic combinations of the kaleidoscope seem naturally exhibited.

The St Lawrence Below Kingston

The distance between Kingston and Montreal is about one hundred and ninety miles. The banks of the river display a scene that cannot fail to excite surprise, when the years which have elapsed since the first settlement of this part of the country (in 1783) are considered. They embrace all the embellishments of a numerous population, fertility, and good cultivation. Well-constructed high roads, leading close to each side, with others branching from them into the interior, render communication both easy and expeditious; while the numerous loaded bateaux and rafts incessantly passing up and down from the beginning of spring until the latter end of autumn, and the steam-boats plying in the navigable interstices of the river, demonstrate unequivocally a very extensive commercial intercourse. The islands, the shoals, the rapids, with contrivances for passing them, form altogether a quick succession of novelties that gives pleasure while it creates astonishment....

[Scenery at Quebec City] From Cape Diamond, and from Point Levi on the south shore, one of the most striking panoramic views perhaps in the whole world offers itself to notice; the assemblage of objects is so grand, and though naturally, yet appear so artificially contrasted with each other, that they mingle surprise with the gratification of every beholder. The capital rising amphitheatrically to the summit of the cape, the river St. Charles flowing, in a serpentine course, for a great distance, through a fine valley, abounding in natural beauties, the falls of Montmorency, the island of Orleans, and the well cultivated settlements on all sides, form together a coup d'oeil that might enter into competition with the most romantic. At Quebec the St. Lawrence is 1314 yards wide, but the basin is two miles across, and three miles and three-quarters long: from the basin, the river continues increasing in breadth until it enters the gulf of the same name, where, from Cape Rosier to the Mingan settlement on the Labrador shore, it is very near one hundred and five miles wide....

With the powerful conviction upon our mind of the great estimation the river St. Lawrence ought to be held in, from presenting itself as the outlet designed as it were by nature to be the most convenient one for exporting the produce of these two extensive and improving provinces, the country stretching to the north-west nearly to the Pacific ocean, and even the adjacent parts of the United States, which, in defiance of prohibitory decrees, will find an exit by this channel, we have, it is feared, incurred the charge of prolixity in wishing to convey to others a clear conception of its importance; yet we must still trespass upon the patience of our readers long enough to mention that the observations hitherto made apply only to one part of the year; and also to notice that, from the beginning of December until the middle of April, the water communication is totally suspended by the frost. During this period, the river from Quebec to Kingston, and between the great lakes, except the Niagara and the Rapids, is wholly frozen over. The lakes themselves are never entirely covered with ice, but it usually shuts up all the bays and inlets, and extends many miles towards their centres: below Quebec it is not frozen over, but the force of the tides incessantly detaches the ice from the shores, and such immense masses are kept in continual agitation by the flux and reflux, that navigation is totally impracticable in these months.

But though the land and water are so nearly identified, during so long a winter, the utility of the river, if it be diminished, is far from being wholly destroyed, for its surface still offers the best route for land carriage (if the metaphor can be excused); and tracks are soon marked out by which a more expeditious intercourse is maintained by vehicles of transport of all descriptions, than it would be possible to do on the established roads, at this season so deeply covered with snow, and which are available until the approach of spring makes the ice porous, and warm springs, occasioning large flaws, render it unsafe. When this alteration takes place it soon breaks up, and, by the beginning of May, is either dissolved or carried off by the current.

(Bouchette, *The British Dominions*, 1831, 1:126–70)

4 LOWER CANADA

a) Face of the Country – Rivers – Roads – Soil – Settlements

☞ At the beginning of his discussion of Lower Canada Bouchette makes important conceptual distinctions in defining regions. He differentiates regions of "artificial creation," i.e., administrative units established by governments, from "natural divisions," i.e., those delimited by actual physical features and configurations. The "artificial" regions referred to in this section should not be confused with his earlier reference to "imaginary" regions in his discussion of Upper Canada. "Imaginary" regions are conceptual geographical regions that Bouchette himself devised to enable him to effectively and insightfully describe the physical and human geography of a particular area.

  To the north of Lower Canada is the Canadian Shield, the geological region that as yet did not have a widely accepted name, and to the south are the Appalachians and the United States border. The northern border of Lower Canada is the watershed with Hudson Bay. Within the "Great Valley," as he calls Lower Canada, there are six geographical regions, three north of the St. Lawrence and three south of the river, mostly delimited from one another by rivers flowing into the St. Lawrence. They are "imaginary regions," identified "in order to avoid too vague, unsatisfactory, and general description." ☞

The divisions of the province enumerated and described in the preceding chapter [i.e. Districts, Counties, Seigniories, & Townships] are those that owe their existence to artificial creation, and are such as were dictated with a view to the judicial, political, and social interests and convenience of the inhabitants. The *natural* divisions of the country are those bold and distinct lineaments traced on the face of Nature, forming and dividing extensive valleys by prominent highland ridges, and separating vast tracts of territory by large rivers and streams. In viewing the divisions of Lower Canada under the latter aspect, the St. Lawrence conspicuously presents itself as a leading feature in its physical geography, bisecting the province into two grand sections, the one lying to the north, the other to the south, of that great river. Emerging from Upper Canada at Point-au-Baudet, it flows exclusively through the Lower Province, traversing in a north-easterly course the grand valley which it drains in its broad career to the ocean. This valley is confined to the northward by a range of mountains commencing at Grenville on the Ottawa river, and stretching north-eastward across the country as it passes at various distances from the banks of the St. Lawrence, from which it recedes at some points about 40 miles, approaching at others to within 15 or 20, until it strikes the river at Cape Torment, 30 miles below Quebec. From this cape the mountainous character of the shores of the St. Lawrence may be properly said to commence, and especially to the northward, where they consist of bold and abrupt hills, rising to a general elevation of 3 and 400 feet, and in some instances attaining an altitude of nearly 2000. To the southward the Great Valley is bounded by a range of hills situated about the sources of the Connecticut river, and connecting to S. W. with the Green Mountains in the state of Vermont, and by them with the bold range of the Alleganies, which forms the grand geological division between the waters of the Atlantic and those of the St. Lawrence. The mountains at the heads of Connecticut in their progress north-eastward diverge into two different ramifications or spurs about the source of the St. John river: one directing its course centrally through the country, nearly parallel with the course of the St. Lawrence and the shores of the sea; the other diverging more to the north, and extending along the St. Lawrence to its mouth. Its distance from the borders of the river varies from thirty to thirteen miles, until it actually subsides on its banks and confines the bed of the waters. Seen from the northward it has a distinct outline, but it does not exhibit the appearance of a mountainous range when viewed from the southward, in consequence of the table elevation of the country on that side. Beyond the mountains that bound the valley of the St. Lawrence on the north, the common level of the land is marked by a considerable table elevation above the surface of the river, and is traversed by several ridges of no very conspicuous altitude till the bolder mountains rise to view, that bound the province to the north-west, and divide the waters of Hudson's Bay from those that descend in opposite courses to the St. Lawrence.

Having thus endeavoured to convey to the reader a general idea of the face of the country, or rather an outline of its most prominent natural divisions, it behoves us in the next place to afford him the means of forming as correct a conception of the roads, rivers, soil, and settlements of the province as the information we command may allow; and the more easily and efficiently to accomplish the task, it may appear proper to adopt separate sections of country, in order to avoid too vague, unsatisfactory, and general a description.

That grand division of the province lying north of the St. Lawrence may, for this purpose, be subdivided into *three sections:*

The *first* embracing the country between the *Ottawa* and the *St. Maurice;* the *second,* the country between the *St. Maurice* and the *Saguenay;* and the *third,* the residue of the territory east of the *Saguenay* to the extreme boundary of the province.

The grand division south of the St, Lawrence will also constitute *three subdivisions:* the *first* comprising all that part of Lower Canada west of the *river Chaudière,* the *second* the territories east of the *Chaudière* to the west bounds of Gaspé, and the *third* consisting of the district of Gaspé itself.

(Bouchette, *The British Dominions,* 1831, 1:185–6)

b) North of the St. Lawrence

I COUNTRY BETWEEN THE OTTAWA RIVER AND THE ST. MAURICE

☞ The settlement assault on the wilderness of the Canadian Shield is underway. Bouchette starts by describing the favourable land of the Ottawa River area and then continues eastward to the St. Maurice River. An exploration for agricultural land in the Shield is described. Contrary to the usual optimistic nature of such surveys, Bouchette accepts that agriculture is not possible in most of the tract north and east of the Ottawa Country extending to the St. Maurice. However, settlement is deemed possible in the wilderness at the rim of the Shield north of Montreal and Three Rivers, and he recommends that a road be built well to the north of the St. Lawrence River but parallel to it in order to attract settlers. Finally, Bouchette turns to the towns on the St. Lawrence: Three Rivers is stagnant but Montreal is thriving, and there is a long discussion of its urban landscape, institutions, transport, and commerce. ☜

The front this section of the province presents on the Ottawa river and on the St. Lawrence exceeds 450 miles; the whole of which distance, saving portages or carrying-places in remote parts of the Ottawa, is navigable for canoes and boats; upwards of 200 miles of it are navigable, at long interstices, for steam-vessels drawing from 4 to 15 feet water, and a section of 90 miles, or the distance between Montreal and Three Rivers, is actually navigated by square-rigged vessels of various burdens, from 100 tons to 600.

Issuing from Lake Temiscaming, upwards of 350 miles north-west of its junction with the St. Lawrence, and having its remotest sources nearly 100 miles beyond that lake, the Ottawa river flows majestically through a fine and fair country, as yet in a state of nature, although, generally speaking, remarkably well adapted to the purposes of agriculture and settlement. From the Falls and *Portage des Allumettes,* distant about 110 miles above Hull, the river becomes better known, as it is usually frequented thus far by timber contractors, who derive their valuable supplies of timber from those remote districts of the Ottawa. The fur traders extend their explorations considerably beyond this point, and a trading-post for that object is established on the shores of Lake Temiscaming....

... [About 90 km above Ottawa] is Bisset's *Chantier,* consisting of a log-house, a small clearing, and an area of one or two acres in culture. This romantic and interesting little spot is situated at the foot of the *Rapides du Fort,* and agreeably relieves the eye from the monotony of savage nature, whose characters, however beautiful or grand, are often gloomy. In traversing a wilderness, whether by land or water, the first appearances of domiciliation, however rude, have something extremely grateful in their associations; and it would not be an easy matter to describe the sensations produced by the curling column of smoke, when it is first discovered floating above the dense forests, from the bosom of which it is seen to emerge.

This small settlement is already very much frequented in winter by traders and voyagers, as a welcome asylum from the inclemency of the weather; it being chiefly during that rigorous season that speculators in furs and timber resort to the wilderness, the communications being then facilitated by the winter roads traced for hundreds of miles together on the ice.

At the foot of the Chenaux, opens to view the magnificent lake which derives its name from the *Rapides des Chats,* situated at its eastern extremity. In extreme length it is fifteen miles, and in mean breadth about one; but its northern shore is deeply indented by several sweeping bays, by which extensive points are formed, sometimes contracting the lake to a width of scarcely one mile, whilst at others it is nearly three. The surface of the waters is prettily studded with occasional islands, richly wooded, and so situated as to diversify most agreeably the natural beauties of the soft and sweet scenery of the lake. The calms of the Ottawa are peculiarly glassy and beautiful, and its waters are much esteemed for their softness....

... the Chaudière Falls ... are situated immediately in front of Wright's Village, in the township of Hull. Above the falls the river is about 500 yards wide, and its scenery is agreeably embellished by small grove-clad islets, rising here and there amidst the waters as they gently ripple by or rush on with more or less violence, to the vortex of the Great and Little Chaudière. The bed of the river is composed of horizontal strata of limestone, and the *chûte* is produced by its deep and sudden subsidence, forming broken, irregular, and extraordinary chasms, one of which is called the *Great,* and the other, the *Little Kettle* or *Chaudière.* The former derives its name from its semicircular form and the volume of water it involves; but the latter bears no similitude to justify its appellation, the waters being precipitated into a broad, elongated, and straight fissure, extending in an oblique position north-west of the Great Kettle, and being thus strikingly contrasted with it.

The principal falls are 60 feet high, and their width is measured by a chord of 212 feet. They are situated near the centre of the river, and attract by their forcible in draught a considerable proportion of the waters, which, strongly compressed by the circular shape of the rock that forms the boiling recipient, descend in heavy torrents, struggling violently to escape, and rising in spray-clouds which constantly conceal the lower half of the falls, and ascend at irregular intervals in revolving columns much above the summit of the cataract.

The Little Chaudière may without much difficulty be approached from the Lower Canada shore, and the spectator, standing on a level with the top of the fall and on the brink of the yawning gap into which the floods are headlong plunged, surveys the whole length of *chute* and the depths of the cavern. A considerable portion of the waters of the falls necessarily escapes subterraneously after their precipitation, as a much greater volume is impelled over the rock than finds a visible issue. Indeed this fact is not peculiar to the Little Chaudière, but is one of those curious characters of this part of the Ottawa of which other singular instances are observed; the waters in various places being swallowed by deep but narrow rents and fissures, leaving their natural bed almost dry, to dash on through some subterranean passage that defies the search of the explorer. There are in the Falls of the Chaudière materials for much geological speculation, and the mere admirer of Nature's scenic wonders and magnificence will derive great gratification and delight by the survey and contemplation of their manifold beauties.

The diversified chain of the Union Bridges has given much additional interest to the scenery of this section of the Ottawa, by combining with the greatest possible effect, ingenious works of art with objects of native grandeur and sublimity....

Below the Falls of Chaudière the Ottawa river is uninterruptedly navigable for steam-boats to Grenville, a distance of 60 miles. The current of the stream is gentle, and the banks of the river generally so low as to be flooded in spring to a considerable distance in the interior, especially on its northern bank, the opposite side of the river being almost uniformly higher and sometimes bold, and therefore not so liable to inundation. The scenery of this part of the Ottawa is indeed tame, yet always pleasing: the frequently varying widths of the river, its numerous islands, the luxuriant foliage of its banks – objects ever changing their perspective combinations as the steamer moves along – and an infant settlement appearing here and there on the skirts of the forest and the margin of the stream, are all in themselves possessed of sufficient interest to destroy the monotony of a trip upon this part of "Ottawa's tide."

The impetuous Long Sault, which commences at Grenville, is stemmed or descended but by *voyageurs* and raftsmen of experienced energy and skill. The river below it still continues, at intervals, rapid and unnavigable as far as Point Fortune, where it expands into the lake of the Two Mountains, and finally forms a junction with the St. Lawrence, below the cascades; but the waters of both streams do not immediately commingle, the line of contact being distinctly observable, by which the black hue of the waters of the Ottawa is strongly contrasted with the bluish-green colour of those of the St. Lawrence....

The face of the country is not generally marked by that boldness of feature that characterizes the eastern section of the province, but it is, nevertheless, in receding from the borders of the Ottawa, divided by hilly ridges, and formed into valleys, which, if we could allow fancy to represent as divested of their heavy forests, might exhibit the agreeable aspect of an undulating or rolling country, the picturesque diversity of plain, hill, and vale, and, if similarly cultivated, picture to the eye some of the most admired counties of England....

Beyond the first ridge that skirts the flats of the Ottawa, to the north, the country has not been surveyed, excepting to the depth of the townships, which, in general, may be said to be twelve miles from the borders of the river. Explorers, however, have gone much farther than this in the interior, ascending rivers sometimes to their sources, in the prosecution of divers speculations, which had chiefly for their objects furs and timber.

The lands on the Ottawa are in the aggregate remarkably fertile, consisting in front of rich alluvions, and more inland of gentle ridges and acclivities, adapted to the growth of plants requiring the drier soils. Natural meadows, affording rich and wholesome pasturage, are very common along the river, the islands and *presqu'îles* of which are also highly valuable as depasturing and grazing grounds....

The township of Hull ... is bounded in front by the Ottawa river, and traversed diagonally by the Gatineau, which is navigable for small steamboats and crafts as far up as six miles above its mouth. The position of Wright village must eventually render it a place of much commercial importance; it is at the head of the present steam-boat navigation of the Ottawa, on one of the direct lines of land and water communication with the eastern districts of Upper Canada, and will necessarily participate with By Town, which stands on the opposite bank of the river, in the great benefits that may naturally be expected to flow from the Rideau Canal. Besides these considerations, it will hereafter derive incalculable advantages from the fertility of the back country, and of the lands on the lakes Chaudière and Des Chats, which, as they become settled, will pour their produce into the stores of this growing town, which would thus become the place of transit, if not the emporium, of the trade of the extensive fertile tracts of territory above it. We apprehend, nevertheless, that a branch canal, such as is contemplated, connecting lake Chaudière with the Rideau Canal, would prejudicially influence the prosperity of Wright village, by diverting the produce of the upper districts of the Ottawa through that channel. Such an effect could only be counteracted by a canal on the Lower Canada side, or a rail-road, which would probably be less expensive from the locality, and quite as effectual.

Hull is sixty miles distant from Grenville, but the communication between both places is rendered easy and expeditious by means of steamers. The "Union of the Ottawa," the first steam-boat that plied upon this part of the river, was built in 1819, and formed an era in the history of the Ottawa settlements, from its contributing materially to their acceleration: a new vessel has since been launched, which is considerably larger, and affords very superior accommodations....

In the townships above Hull, the settlements are few, ...

The Ottawa country offers one of the most promising fields for colonization to be found in the province; but its settlement is materially retarded and embarrassed by old and unimproved grants. It is much to be lamented that such large tracts on the immediate banks of the river should be kept so long in a state of almost absolute wilderness by the proprietors of the soil....

Looking at the map of this interesting section of the province with an eye to its future settlement, the importance of a grand interior road, extending across the country from the north-east angle of the township of Wentworth to the Falls of the Grand Calumet, naturally suggests itself as the basis of a chain of settlements. This plan of opening in the outset great avenues through the wilderness was successfully practiced in Upper Canada; and a striking illustration of the encouragement it operates in the settling of new lands is found in the rapid growth and prosperity of the Talbot settlement in that province. Of the practicability, on a general principle, of such a route, little doubt can be entertained; and at a period when, from the large influx of emigration, comprehensive views of the settlement of the colony should be taken, the expediency of the measure appears to us a matter of paramount consideration.

The total population on the northern shore of the Ottawa river westward from the west bounds of Argenteuil does not now much exceed 5,369 inhabitants, and this population is very unequally spread, although the mass is confined to the townships of Hull, Chatham, and Grenville, and the seigniory of La Petite Nation. It is very heterogeneous in its origin, consisting of about equal proportion of Irish and Americans, some English, more Scots, and a few families of French Canadians.

The country north of the St. Lawrence, below the township of Chatham, extending eastward to the river St. Maurice .... makes up the residue of the north-western section of the province which we have undertaken to describe. The whole of the lands of this large tract lying along the navigable waters in front are taken up by seigniorial grants; in the rear of which, and contiguous to their rear lines, are situated the townships or soccage lands....

Excluding, for the present, from the description the islands of Montreal and Jesus, and the county of Vaudreuil, which lies south of the Lake of the Two Mountains, all of which will be more particularly noticed hereafter, a very important portion of the province will still remain under consideration, the surface of which, to a various depth of from five to fifteen miles from the banks of the Ottawa and the St. Lawrence, is generally level or slightly elevated into table ridges, with occasional short acclivities and descents. The interior of the country was partially explored in 1829 by a party consisting of a land-surveyor, a gentleman acting as geologist, and an assistant, with six men and three canoes. The expedition ascended the St. Maurice as far as Wimontichingue, whence they travelled south-westward, ascending first the Matawin river to its source: thence, after traversing a chain of lakes to come to the head-waters of the river Aux Lièvres, they came down that river to its mouth in the Ottawa, a direct distance of nearly 150 miles, but considerably more by the bends of the river....

Thus we have a circumnavigated tract of about 11,500 geographical square miles, lying between the river Aux Lièvres on the west, the St. Maurice on the east and north-east, the St. Lawrence and the Ottawa in front, and a chain of lakes in the rear. Numerous instances of similar facilities afforded by natural water-communications are met with in the Canadas, the face of the country being almost every-where checkered with lakes and intersected by rivers that spread into a multitude of ramifications.

The information that has resulted from this expedition is, we believe, confined to the objects that came under observation upon the immediate route, no offsets to any considerable distance in the interior having, it appears, been made collaterally, to ascertain the nature of the soil on the right and left of the track. We are therefore without any adequate means of knowing how far the interior of this tract of 11,500 square miles may be susceptible of culture; but judging from the reported character of the lands along the remote lakes and rivers that were explored, we are led to infer unfavourably of that section of country as a field for settlement.

The seigniories and townships situated between Argenteuil and the St. Maurice are abundantly watered by numerous rivers and streams, whose tortuous meanderings spread more broadly and beneficially their irrigating influence.... The navigation of the rivers .... is interrupted at intervals by rapids and falls, but the intermediate distances are generally navigable for boats and canoes; .... The borders of rivers in Canada, and indeed in most new countries, are invariably preferred and chosen for the formation of early settlements; and we therefore find these rivers assumed as the front of extensive ranges of connected flourishing settlements that extend to remote parts of seigniories, when in some instances lands of much nearer proximity to the villages and towns have been left uncultivated....

The town of Three Rivers is situated on the north-west side of the river St. Maurice, at its confluence with the St. Lawrence. It derives its name from the entrance into the former river being separated by two islands lying at the mouth, into three channels. The town plot covers nearly 400 acres, forming a front of rather more than 1,300 yards on the bank of the St. Lawrence. It stands on an exceeding light and sandy soil, which extends also over the environs. To the bank of the St. Maurice the ground rises very considerably, but in the opposite direction it sinks almost to the level of the river. Three Rivers ranks as the third town in the province, but bears no comparison with either Quebec or Montreal in population and importance. It contains about 400 houses and 3000 inhabitants, allowing for the increase since 1825, when its population by census was given at 2,453 souls....

In the year 1618 some of the French colonists began building this place, with a view of making it a depôt whence the fur-trade might be carried on with the Indians to the northward. Their plan in the outset exhibited many flattering indications of success; but after Montreal was founded, and had so increased as to be able to defend itself against the attacks of the natives, it was supposed to be a situation better suited to the improving traffic, and was consequently preferred. From that period Three Rivers, being greatly neglected, made but languid advances in prosperity or population. About the beginning of last century, a new era seemed to dawn for it, and hopes began to be entertained of its rising into some consequence by the opening of the iron mines at St. Maurice; but these hopes proved nearly as delusive as the former, and up to the present time its improvement has been upon a very moderate scale.

The trade carried on here is chiefly in British manufactured goods, that from hence are plentifully distributed through the middle district of the province. The exports consist of wheat, timber, though now not so much as formerly, and the produce of its iron foundery, added to that of the mines of St. Maurice. Peltry in small quantities still continues to be brought hither by the Indians from the northward, and which is received by the agents of the Hudson's Bay Company. Several pot and pearl ash manufactories, two or three breweries, and an extensive brick factory, considerably increase the general trade of the place. Many of the bark canoes used in the north-west voyages are built here, and of the same material a variety of ingenious and ornamental works and toys are made. As a shipping-port it is conveniently situated, there being a sufficient depth of water for ships of large tonnage to lie close to the wharfs, and receive or discharge their cargoes by a temporary stage from their gangways.

The town itself possesses but little to attract a stranger's notice: the streets are narrow and unpaved – ... The shops and storehouses are numerous, wherein may be had British goods of all denominations. Several inns afford to travellers very respectable accommodations....

... The prosperity of Three Rivers must materially depend upon the settlement of the extensive tracts of waste lands in its vicinity; until the back country is brought under cultivation, its growth can be but tardy, notwithstanding the advantages of its situation in the central district of the province.

From Three Rivers, westward, the north bank of the St. Lawrence and the river St. Jean or Jesus, exhibits one uninterrupted succession of flourishing settlements and gay villages, situated along the main road, at intervals of eight or nine miles. Several of these villages are of considerable importance, and vie with Three Rivers itself in the extent of their trade and commercial consequence....

... From the city of Montreal to the eastward the shores are from 15 to 20 feet above the level of the St. Lawrence: but in the opposite direction, towards La Chine, they are low: between the Coteau St. Pierre and the river the land is so flat, and particularly near the little lake St. Pierre so marshy as to induce a conjecture that it was once covered by water. Over this place a canal has been opened, by which a direct communication between the city and La Chine is formed, and the difficult passage of the rapid of St. Louis avoided.

The soil of the whole island, if a few insignificant tracts be overlooked, can scarcely be excelled in any country, and is highly productive in grain of every species, vegetables, and fruits of various kinds: there is hardly any part of it but what is in the most flourishing state of cultivation, and may justly claim the pre-eminence over any other of Lower Canada. Several roads running from north-east to south-west, nearly parallel to each other, are crossed by others at convenient distances, so as to form a complete and easy communication in every direction. There is a good turnpike-road from Montreal, almost in a straight line, to the village of La Chine, a distance of eight miles, by which the constant intercourse between these places is rendered easy: by this route all the commodities intended for Upper Canada were formerly conveyed to the place of embarkation; but the canal has superseded the turnpike, as regards, at least, the transport of heavy articles of trade. Between the city and the village there is a great variety of prospects, some of which are very romantic. A mile or two from the town, near the tanneries, the road ascends a steepish hill, and continues along a high ridge for more than three miles, commanding a beautiful view over the cultivated fields below, the rapid of St. Louis, the islands in the St. Lawrence, and the varied woodland scenery on the opposite shore; descending from the height, it passes over a flat country until it reaches La Chine.

The city of *Montreal* stands on the south side of the island, ... The second city of the province in point of importance, it is undoubtedly the first with respect to situation, local advantages, and superiority of climate; its form is a prolonged square, that, with the suburbs, covers about 1020 acres of ground, although within the walls of the old fortifications the contents of the area did not exceed 100 acres. A few houses, built close together, in the year 1640, on the site of the Indian village of Hochelaga, was the commencement of the city of Montreal, or, as it was first named, Villemarie; the situation being well chosen, and possessing many inducements for the colonists to associate themselves for the comforts and convenience of society, it very soon assumed the appearance of being built with some attention. to regularity and solidity of the dwellings; containing a population of 4000 inhabitants, its improvement and extension were rapid....

In its present state Montreal certainly merits the appellation of a handsome city. It is divided into the upper and lower town, although the elevation of one above the other is scarcely perceptible; these are again subdivided into wards. The streets are airy, and the new ones particularly, of a commodious width; some of them running the whole length of the town, parallel to the river, intersected by others at right angles. The houses are for the most part built of a greyish stone, many of them large, handsome, and in a modern style: sheet-iron or tin is the universal covering of the roofs....

Montreal, as it is at present, containing a population of about 30,000 souls, rivals the capital of Canada in many respects, and as a commercial emporium certainly surpasses it: seated near the confluence of several large rivers with the St. Lawrence, it receives by their means the productions of the best settled and also the most distant parts of the district, those of the fertile province of Upper Canada, as well as from the United States. Possessing these combined attractions, it is by no means unreasonable to infer that in the lapse of a few years it will become the most flourishing and prosperous city of the British North American dominions; .... To the northward of Notre Dame-street there is another street parallel to it, sixty feet wide, called St. James's-street, running from the Place d'Armes to the Haymarket; but it is contemplated to continue it through the whole length of the city, and to terminate it at the Quebec [northeast] suburbs by one of the same breadth, leading to the St. Lawrence suburbs. In this street is situated the: Montreal bank, a regular and elegant cut-stone edifice, ornamented in front with emblematical devices of Agriculture, Manufactures, Arts, and Commerce, executed in basso-relievo. Near the bank is the Wesleyan chapel, built in a good style of architecture, and quite an ornament to the street....

The new market-place, occupying the ground where formerly stood the college founded by Sieur Charron in 1719, and destroyed by fire many years back, is 36 yards wide, and reaches from Notre Dame-street to St. Paul-street; in the middle of it are ranges of stalls for butchers, covered in by a roof supported on wooden pillars: great care is taken to enforce the regulations to ensure cleanliness. On the two principal market-days in each week the market is well supplied with every neces-sary, and nearly every luxury for the table, in great abundance, at prices extremely moderate. The produce of the upper part of this fertile district is almost wholly brought hither for sale, besides a great quantity from the American states, particularly during the winter, when fish frequently comes from Boston and the adjacent parts....

The harbour of Montreal is not very large, but always secure for ship-ping during the time the navigation of the river is open. Vessels drawing fifteen feet water can lie close to the shore, near the Market-gate, to receive or discharge their cargoes; the general depth of water is from three to four and a half fathoms, with very good anchorage every where between the Market-gate Island and the shore; .... The greatest dis-advantage to this harbour is the rapid of St. Mary, about a mile below [the east end of the island] , whose current is so powerful, that, without a strong north-easterly wind, ships cannot stem it, and would sometimes be detained even for weeks about two miles only from the place where they are to deliver their freight, were it not for the application of tow-boats impelled by steam-engines of high power. In pursuing the grand scale of improvements it may probably be found practicable to remedy this evil by the formation of another short canal, or extension of that of La Chine; ships might then discharge their cargoes at their anchorage below the current into canal boats, by which they could be by such a communication conveyed immediately to the city.

The environs of Montreal exhibit as rich, as fertile, and as finely diversified a country as can well be imagined. At the distance of a mile and a half from the town, in a direction from S. W. to N. E., is a very picturesque height, whose most elevated point at the furthest extremity is about 550 feet above the level of the river; it gains a moderate height at first by a gradual ascent, which subsides again towards the middle, thence it assumes a broken and uneven form until it is terminated by a sudden elevation in shape of a cone. The slopes on the lower part are well cultivated, but the upper part is covered with wood. These forests,

however, are soon to give place to works of art, government having commenced the construction of fortifications upon this part of the mountain,
by which its sylvan appearance will necessarily undergo a total change.
From several springs that rise towards its top the town is plentifully and
conveniently supplied with water, which is conveyed to it under ground
by means of wooden pipes. The summit, to which there is a good road
of very easy ascent, commands a grand and most magnificent prospect,
including every variety that can embellish a landscape; the noble river St.
Lawrence, moving in all its majesty, is seen in many of the windings to
an immense distance; on the south side the view is bounded by the long
range of mountains in the state of New York, that is gradually lost in the
aerial perspective.

The space near the town, and all round the lower part of the mountain, is chiefly occupied by orchards and garden-grounds; the latter producing vegetables of every description, and excellent in quality, affording
a profuse supply for the consumption of the city. All the usual garden
fruits, as gooseberries, currants, strawberries, raspberries, peaches, apri-
cots, and plums are produced in plenty, and it may be asserted truly, in
as much, or even greater perfection than in many southern climates. The
orchards afford apples not surpassed in any country; .... On the skirts of
the mountain are many good country-houses belonging to the inhabitants of the city, delightfully situated, and possessing all the requisites of
desirable residences....

The county of Vaudreuil contains a population of 13,800 souls; but
a large portion of its inhabitants follows the pursuit of *voyageurs,* to
the material injury of the agricultural interests of that valuable tract of
country, and the evident demoralization of the people, from its inducing
those wandering habits that are incompatible with rural economy, and a
dissoluteness of morals which marks but too generally that class of men.
(Bouchette, *The British Dominions,* 1831, 1:187–236)

II COUNTRY BETWEEN THE ST. MAURICE AND THE SAGUENAY

☞ In discussing this region Bouchette takes the opportunity to describe
the seigneurial long-lot landscape, as seen below Quebec. At Quebec
he emphasizes the splendid physical setting: the great St. Lawrence
River dominates and the Canadian Shield is visible to the north and
the Appalachians to the south. The city has a critical place in the transportation system that extends from Lake Superior to the Atlantic and
steamboat communications between Quebec and Nova Scotia are being

established, thus perhaps envisaging a closer association amongst the British North American colonies. The Shield continues to beckon and Bouchette has a personal connection with this area because in 1828 he was on a reconnaissance expedition to Lake St. John and the Upper Saguenay River to assess the region's settlement potential. He quotes extensively from his report. After his lengthy remarks on the scenery of Quebec, it is surprising that he does not say more about the spectacular Saguenay Valley. ⌒

The population of the tract of country lying between the rivers Saguenay and St. Maurice amounts to about 70,000 souls, occupying the lands on the northern bank of the St. Lawrence to the average depth of three leagues from the margin of the river. The distance from the mouth of one river to the estuary of the other rather exceeds 190 miles, Quebec being situated in an intermediate and almost central position between them.

Of the two sections of country divided by the intervention of the capital of the province, that to the westward is by far the most populous, though perhaps not the most interesting under every other aspect. It is amply watered by the numerous tributaries and main branches of the rivers Jacques Cartier, Portneuf, St. Anne's, and Batiscan, which have their sources to the north and north-east of their mouths, and flow in the general direction of south-west to their respective junctions with the St. Lawrence. They all are frequently rapid, and consequently can offer but limited advantages from their navigation; yet some of them are effectually used in spring for the transport of rough timber, made solidly into cribs or small rafts, and floated down to mills, which are usually situated as near as possible to the waters of the St. Lawrence. They, nevertheless, generally admit of river craft ascending a few rods above their embouchures to convenient places of embarkation and loading. Several other inferior streams flow through the country, turning in their courses grist and saw mills, which are often, however, inoperative in summer, owing to the deficiency of water.

There are from three to four concessions or ranges of the seigniories and fiefs lying above Quebec, within the limits above mentioned, that are effectually settled, if the seigniories of Champlain and Cap la Magdeleine be alone excepted, the settlements whereof extend but partially to the second range. The concessions seem almost universally to be laid out to suit the convenience of the settlers, without regard to regularity, and for this purpose the course of rivers is, for the most part, adopted as a line of double ranges *(double concessions)*; and hence in many instances, as on the Batiscan, the St. Anne's, &c., the settlements are formed on both banks of the river to a remote distance from the St. Lawrence. A far greater quantity of land is in general conceded within the seigniories than what is actually cultivated, most of the inhabitants having, besides the farm they cultivate, another lot, from whence they derive supplies of building-timber and fuel.

The lands in the aggregate consist of a generous soil, which, however productive near the shores of the river, is stated to improve as it recedes from them – a circumstance tending to remove the prejudices existing against inland settlements....

Leaving Quebec by the upper road, either of Abra'm's Plains or St. Foy, the eye dwells with delight on the picturesque valley of the St. Charles, which meanders beautifully through fertile and luxuriant fields, amidst flourishing settlements, along the rear of which, bounding the horizon westward, extends a bold mountain range, whose majestic grandeur is displayed to singular advantage immediately after sunset, when its distinct and prominent outline is figured against the heavens, still glowing with the transparency and warmth of solar radiance....

Quebec

Some notice of Quebec has been taken already as a sea-port in the observations that have been made upon the river St. Lawrence, but it will perhaps be excused should the same points be again adverted to in giving a detailed description of the city. From the time that Cartier visited Canada, up to the period when the concerns of the colony came under the superintendence of Champlain (about seventy years), the French settlers and adventurers were dispersed over various parts of the sea-coast, or islands in the Gulf of St. Lawrence, as each, or a few together, discovered convenient places to fix their habitations in: during that time none of them had attempted to settle on or near the Great River.

The selection of a situation for building a town, wherein the benefits and habits of social life might be enjoyed, and from whence the management of the trading intercourse with the natives, and the government of the colony, could be more advantageously carried on than what they hitherto had been, was reserved for Samuel De Champlain, geographer to the King of France. Acting under a commission from the Sieur de Monts (who shortly before had obtained from the court of France the exclusive privilege of trading between Cape Raze in Newfoundland and the fortieth degree of north latitude), he in 1608 made choice of the site of an Indian village called Stadaconé, upon the promontory now named Cape Diamond, and there, in the month of July, laid the foundation of the metropolis of New France, which has through many vicissitudes risen into importance, and at the present day maintains a distinguished rank amongst the towns of the greatest consequence on the northern division of the new hemisphere....

The situation of Quebec, the capital of Lower Canada, and the residence of the governor-general of British North America, is unusually grand and majestic, in form of an amphitheatre. The city is seated on a promontory, on the N.W. side of the St. Lawrence, formed by that river and the St. Charles. The extremity of this headland is called Cape Diamond, whose highest point rises 845 feet above the level of the water. It is composed of a rock of gray granite mixed with quartz crystals (from which it obtains its name), and a species of dark-coloured slate. In many places it is absolutely perpendicular and bare; in others, where the acclivity is less abrupt, there are patches of brownish earth, or rather a decomposition of the softer parts of the stone, on which a few stunted pines and creeping shrubs are here and there seen; but. The general aspect of it is rugged and barren....

In 1825 the population of the city, suburbs, and banlieue, or limits of the town, amounted to 22,021, exclusive of the troops in garrison; but it is believed that the census taken that year fell considerably short in its results of the numerical strength of the people of Lower Canada, as well in the towns as in the country. At present Quebec would not probably be overrated at 30,000 inhabitants, and, during the shipping season, that number acquires an ephemeral increase, that, in a great measure, subsides at the close of the navigation, yet leaves in the town no inconsiderable accession, arising from the emigrants that remain in the capital with their families, out of the whole mass of those that are landed on the wharfs....

The communication between Quebec and Montreal has been rendered not only easy and expeditious, but even agreeable by the improvements that have, within late years, taken place in the construction of steamboats on the St. Lawrence. The first steam-boat that plied on the St. Lawrence was launched in the year 1812, which, from that circumstance, forms an epoch in the history of both towns, inasmuch as this application of the steam engine in that quarter gave quite a new and very vigorous impulse to the commercial relations and general intercourse of one place with the other, and in fact imparted additional energy to the whole of the mercantile and trading concerns of the country.... Steamers start almost every day from both cities, and perform the voyage up the river in from 36 to 40 hours, but they are several hours less in accomplishing the trip downwards, from the advantage of having a current setting in this direction as far as the Richelieu, where they meet with the tide....

... a vessel of large tonnage (stated at 700 or 800 tons) is now on the stocks at Quebec, and will soon be launched, destined to navigate as a steam packet between that capital and Halifax, Nova Scotia: such an event must conspicuously mark the period of its realization, from the powerful influence it will necessarily exercise upon the relations now subsisting betwixt the chief towns of both provinces. Thus will be formed an extensive line of steam vessel communication from the Atlantic sea coast to Amherstburgh, one of the remote settlements of Upper Canada, a distance exceeding 1500 statute miles, which we may expect soon to see extended to the head of Lake Huron, and eventually to the western extremity of Lake Superior, about 700 miles beyond Amherstburgh, yielding a grand total of nearly 2200 miles of internal steam navigation....

The navigation being closed in November, the intercourse between Quebec and Montreal is carried on in winter by stages that start regularly from each city thrice a week, and perform the journey in two days, the intervening night being devoted by the travellers to rest....

Between the city and Point Levi, on the opposite shore of the St. Lawrence, a steam ferry-boat plies regularly every half hour from six o'clock in the morning to eight in the evening, performing the trip across in from ten to fifteen minutes. There are also three horse-boats, to which the preference is generally given by the country people in bringing their produce to market....

... When the river *takes*, i. e. is frozen over from Quebec to Point Levi, which, of late years, has rarely happened, it is not only productive of much amusement, but of great advantage to the city, as well as to the inhabitants of the southern shore, who can at that time bring their produce to market in large quantities without inconvenience. Hay, fire-wood, and all bulky articles of consumption are furnished in abundance, and the consumers usually experience a great reduction in price in consequence of such an influx. As soon as the surface is deemed sufficiently solid, the road across it is immediately traced out, and continues under the inspection of the *Grand Voyer* of the district, who causes proper beacons to be set up on each side, and at intervals where they are required. When the river has *taken* in the north channel between the Island of Orleans and the Main (the southern channel is never frozen over), which is the case every year, the markets of the city never fail to feel the effect of it, as abundance of provisions of all kinds, the growth of that fruitful spot, which have been prepared for the approaching season, are immediately brought in: considerable supplies are drawn thence during the summer, but such as do not spoil by keeping are commonly retained, until this opportunity admits of their being sent with much less trouble and expense.

The summer scenery of the environs of Quebec may vie in exquisite beauty, variety, magnificence, sublimity, and the naturally harmonized combination of all these prominent features, with the most splendid that has yet been portrayed in Europe, or any other part of the world.... [Toward the north] the surrounding country every where [has] an appearance of fertility and good cultivation, upon which the eye of the spectator wanders with ceaseless delight. As the prospect recedes it is still interesting, the land rising in gradation, height over height, having the interval between succeeding elevations filled up with primeval forests, until the whole is terminated by a stupendous ridge of mountains, whose lofty forms are dimly seen through the aerial expanse....

... On the plains of Abraham, from the precipice that overlooks the timber-grounds, where an incessant round of activity prevails, the St. Lawrence is seen rolling its majestic wave, studded with many a sail, from the stately ship down to the humble fishing-boat; the opposite bank, extending up the river, is highly cultivated, and the houses, thickly strewed by the main road, from this height and distance, have the appearance of an almost uninterrupted village, as far as the eye can reach in that direction. The country to the southward rises by a very gentle ascent, and the whole view, which is richly embellished by alternations of water, woodland, and cultivation is bounded by remote and lofty mountains, softening shade by shade until they melt into air. Whoever views the environs of Quebec, with a mind and taste capable of receiving impressions through the medium of the eyes, will acknowledge, that. as a whole, the prospect is grand, harmonious, and magnificent; and that, if taken in detail, every part of it will please, by a gradual unfolding of its picturesque beauties upon a small scale.

North-eastward from the capital lie the counties Montmorenci and Saguenay, and part of Quebec, exhibiting in the outline by far the boldest features of any other part of the county. The strongly defined range of mountains that subsides on the Ottawa river in front of Grenville, stretching eastward across the angular tract of land formed by the St. Lawrence and the Ottawa river, skirts the flourishing settlements of Charlesbourg, Beauport, and the Cote de Beauprè, and finally strikes

the St. Lawrence at Cape Torment. This conspicuous mountain measures about 1890 feet in altitude, and from its romantic situation on the
borders of the St. Lawrence, has acquired much notoriety, although it
is seldom visited by travellers. It is also the first and highest of a succession of granitic mountains called "Les Caps," that rise in abrupt
slopes to a considerable elevation from the immediate level of the river.
The mountainous character of the northern shore of the St. Lawrence
may properly be said to commence at Cape Torment, although its banks
above Quebec are for many miles high, bold, and majestic. From Cape
Torment the ridge continues unbroken, except by the beds of rivers and
rivulets, until it effectually subsides 15 or 18 miles below the Saguenay,
in which quarter the boldness of the north shore sinks to a moderate
level, presenting a degree of flatness and equality of surface singularly
contrasted with the opposite shore, which now becomes mountainous,
rugged, and abrupt....

... [Of the numerous tributaries of the St. Lawrence River] the Saguenay is the only one known to be navigable to any extent, vessels of any
burden being able to ascend upwards of 75 miles above its estuary....

The river Montmorenci is remarkable, not only for the continued
rapidity of its course, but on account of the Falls, situated at its mouth,
which lie about nine miles N. E. of Quebec, and are celebrated for
their height, magnificence, and beauty. Violently projected over a
perpendicular rock into a precipice 240 feet deep, the waters of the
Montmorenci descend in a bright fleecy sheet, of snowy whiteness, to
the broad recipient beneath, which forms a deep bay, whose sides rise,
almost vertically from the foot of the Falls, to an altitude several feet
above their summit....

The communication by land with St. Paul's Bay and the settlements
lower down has hitherto suffered some impediment from the badness of
the road laid open in the interior along the highlands already mentioned,
called "Les Caps;" but a recent legislative provision, for the amelioration
of that route, will throw the Quebec markets open to the produce of
a rich and fertile tract of the district of Quebec. Below St. Paul's Bay,
whose settlements lie chiefly in the deep vale of the Rivière du Gouffre,
or on the slope of the lofty hills that bound the valley, the traveller is
oppressed with the aspect of a succession of steep and lengthy ascents
and descents, seldom relieved by the grateful aspect of the plain throughout the distance to Mal Bay, whose settlements are the last with which
a land communication is kept up on that shore of the St. Lawrence. To
compensate in some degree for the fatigues of so tedious a journey, the

traveller almost constantly beholds a scenery well calculated to inspire him with ideas of the sublime, and elicit his admiration. Exalted considerably above the St. Lawrence, he commands a magnificent view of the majestic stream before him, its diversified islands, and the flourishing settlements that adorn the southern shores; and most probably may be seen, no insignificant objects in the landscape, the cheering harbingers of news and commerce sailing up or down the river.

(Bouchette, *The British Dominions,* 1831, 1:237–81)

III INTERIOR OF THE COUNTRY LYING BETWEEN THE SAGUENAY AND THE ST. MAURICE, AS TAKEN FROM THE REPORT OF JOSEPH BOUCHETTE, JUN. ESQ., DEPUTY-SURVEYOR-GENERAL OF THE PROVINCE

⌁ The Canadian Shield between the Saguenay and St. Maurice Rivers had long been regarded as fur trading country. Was farming possible? In 1828 Bouchette had been part of an exploring expedition to Lac St. Jean to assess the potential for agriculture, and he quotes extensively from the report prepared by his son, also on the expedition. ⌁

It was reproachfully but correctly stated anteriorly to the performance of the exploring operations of 1828, that the country for ten leagues to the northward of the capital of British North America was as little or less known than the heart of Africa. The importance, however, of acquiring a competent knowledge of that portion of the vast wilds of this continent lying to the north of the St. Lawrence, and within the probable range of eventual settlement, had previously been felt by a learned and eminent member of the Assembly of Lower Canada, who, taking that characteristic and enlarged view of the subject which it deserved, laid the ground-work of those valuable explorations, that have since afforded so much valuable information relative to the Indian country ranging between the Ottawa river and the Saguenay. If on the whole the result did not prove altogether as favourable as had been desirable, the lands in the interior having been discovered to be, in the aggregate, characterized more for their barrenness than their fertility, the accession it has yielded to the geographical knowledge of the province, is nevertheless of the utmost importance; at the same time that the surveys, from the judicious combination of talent with which they were carried into effect, have tended to develope much of the geological character and other parts of the natural history of the country.

Under the French government there is no doubt that the interior of Canada was comparatively better known than it afterwards was up to the period of the late surveys, the religious zeal of missionary Jesuits having at the time led them to form establishments amongst the natives with a view of converting them to christianity, whilst the prospects of a lucrative fur trade, induced several individuals to push their discoveries to remote parts of the Canadian wilderness. The information, however, that had come down to us was but vague and very imperfect. Jean Du Lact, Champlain, and Charlesvoix all mention the Saguenay country, and describe it generally from the dicta of the Indians as mountainous and barren, covered with perpetual snows, and altogether forbidding in its aspect; but this unfavourable account, though partially true, was obviously coloured by the fears of the natives from whom it was derived, they being desirous of damping the zeal of explorers who might eventually usurp the possession of their hunting grounds. Motives something of a similar nature, it is probable, tinctured the narratives of traders, who felt loath to encourage either competition or settlement in those Indian countries, by communicating too exact a knowledge of them. We have, nevertheless, in Père Charlevoix's History of New France, a tolerable correct map of Lake St. John and the Saguenay, which, considering the early period when it was drawn, added to the vestiges of Jesuits' settlements found at Tadoussac, Chicoutimi, and Lake St. John, constitutes abundant proof that the French were not then ignorant of the geography of that section of the province, and that they looked upon it as not altogether unfit for colonization. It was left, however, to the present age to develope more satisfactorily the physical geography of those regions, and much it is admitted has already been done towards the promotion of that important object....

Of the country thus explored [in 1828], the following description is quoted from the Report of the deputy Surveyor-General:- "In taking a summary and collective view of the tract just described, it may be observed, that the territory lying between the St. Maurice at La Tuque, and Lake St. John, is generally covered by lakes and extensive swamps, occasionally traversed by chains of hills of no remarkable height or continuity, composed chiefly of primitive granite. The prevailing timber, that composes its forests, are spruce and tamarack, white birch and pine. Around some of the larger lakes, occasional tracts of cultivable land may be found, but their remote situation, and the consequent impracticability of throwing them open to actual settlement, must render this section of country a barren waste and wilderness for ages yet to come." ...

Lake St. John ... [in its] general shape is circular, and its circumference about 100 miles....

In describing the Lake St. John and Saguenay country, we shall borrow Mr. Bouchette's own language....

[The following description and evaluation of a small section of land on the south shore of Lake St. John is representative of the soil and vegetation surrounding the lake.] "From the King's Post Company's Establishment, at the mouth of the Metabetshuan, the land that borders the southern shore of the lake, to the foot of the hills that form a chain with the Ouiatshuan Hills, is generally of good quality, the soil of which is variously composed of an argillaceous and sandy loam, on which a rich vegetable mould has been deposited. The timber growing thereon consists of ash, black and yellow birch, basswood, elm, fir, balsam, cedar, and sprnce, intermixed with some red and white pine and maple."

"Near Point à la Traverse is a valuable limestone quarry, and the coast, from Metabetshuan to Ouiatshuan, occasionally bold, is chiefly composed of inclined strata of calcareous stone, on which specimens of marine shells and other organic remains, as also fragments of blocks of white and gray marble, are to be found, all of which are, more or less, indications of a fertile soil. It may therefore be said that, between these two last mentioned places, is offered a front of near twelve miles on the lake, by an average of four miles depth, forming a superficies of about, 30,000 acres of land susceptible to cultivation." ...

.... [After a summary statement on the potential of the Lake St. John area, Bouchette goes on to describe the country southeast of the lake at Chicoutimi, and along the Saguenay River.] [There is a] total of 340,000 acres, or thereabouts, adapted to the purposes of colonization.

The section of this country called the Peninsula, is situated between the Grande Décharge, Lake St. John, the Belle Riviere, Lakes Kinuagami and Kinuagomishish, Wiqui, Lac Vert and Chicoutimi river. It is about 38 miles long, by an average breadth of 17, and contains about 400,000 acres of land. Its position, from being almost surrounded by navigable waters, is very advantageous, and its general soil and timber such as hereafter to invite settlement.

Chicoutimi, the principal post, after Tadoussac, established by the King's Post Company, is situated almost intermediately between Lake St. John and the river St. Lawrence, being about 23 or 24 leagues distant from Tadoussac, and nearly the same distance from Metabetshuan. It is well calculated to become the focus of the trade of that part of the country, and commands momentous advantages from the excellence of its harbour, which, though not calculated for ships of heavy burthen, affords safe shelter and anchorage in one fathom and a half water.

The Saguenay is navigable for two leagues above Chicoutimi, but its width is more contracted. Below Cape St. Franyois, the stream increases in magnitude, and the banks gradually rise into greater and bolder altitude, particularly on the northern shore, where a prominent chain of mountains is seen stretching from the north coast, and thence bending its general direction with the course of the Saguenay. About five miles below Chicoutimi, the river assumes that boldness of character which it preserves to its discharge into the St. Lawrence, its rocky banks rising abruptly in barren hills, thinly clad with fir, spruce, birch, and cypress. The rocks composing the hills on the north shore are, in some places, strongly impregnated with magnetic iron ore, which produces such frequent aberrations in the compass as to render its use extremely deceptive.

The Bay des Has! is 60 miles above the mouth of the Saguenay. "This bay," says Mr. Bouchette, "appears to have been formed by nature, as the principal seat of the trade and commerce of all this portion of country. 1st. On account of the vast tracts of arable land that surround it, and extend to Lake Kinuagami and Chicoutimi. 2d. On account of its harbour, capable of affording shelter to the largest ships of the line, that can sail directly into the bay with the same wind that brought them up the river, and anchor in the second bay, which is formed into something like a basin, offering upon its shores, a fit site for the establishment of an extensive mart of trade. 3d. Because of the facility that is offered of opening a road to Chicoutimi, or direct to the head of Kinuagami; besides the practicability of opening a water communication with the lake, to avoid the intricate and circuitous route by Chicoutimi rIver."

"It is protected by Cap à L'Est, and the other prominent hills that form its entrance; the former, rising boldly in broken cliffs to an elevation of about 500 feet, commands a view of 12 or 13 promontories down the river, and guards the entrance to the upper parts of the Saguenay."

The post of Tadoussac is situated at the mouth of the Saguenay, ...

The land about Tadoussac is of very inferior quality, its soil is sandy, and the hills are barren and rocky.

(Bouchette, *The British Dominions*, 1831, 1:281–91)

IV TERRITORY EAST OF THE SAGUENAY, TO THE BOUNDARY OF THE PROVINCE

☞ The unknown always fascinates. Bouchette would like to have more information on this remote country along the north shore of the St.

Lawrence River, but he is very much aware that this home of native peoples is not suited to agriculture.

The last section of the province, north of the St. Lawrence, remaining to be noticed, is that which extends eastwardly from the Saguenay river, as far as Ance au Sablon, on the Labrador coast, from whence a line drawn due north to the 52d parallel of north latitude, forms the eastern limits of Lower Canada in that quarter. This section occupies a front of about 665 miles on the river St. Lawrence and the gulf, following the curvatures of the coast, which beyond Pointe des Monts, sweeps suddenly round in a deep segment, and imbosoms the island of Anticosti.

The knowledge we possess of this tract of territory is, in a great measure, confined to the coasts, which have been from time to time explored by individuals connected with the fur trade or the fisheries. Below the Saguenay, the mountainous boldness of the north shore gradually subsides in approaching the Bergeronnes, and sinks to a moderate elevation at Portneuf, a trading port .... situated about 40 miles below the Saguenay. The mountains below this river recede to the distance of 4 or 5 leagues from the immediate borders of the St. Lawrence, leaving a tract of gradual ascent at their base, which was at first supposed to be cultivable, from its exhibiting a rich vegetable border; but it was found upon penetrating into the interior that it consisted of a deep swamp, covered with moss to the depth of nearly 3 feet, and could therefore present no agricultural attractions....

The chief rivers discharging themselves in the river and gulf of St. Lawrence between the Saguenay and Ance Sablon, are the Grande and Petite Bergeronnes, the Portneuf, Missisiquinak, Betsiamites, Bustard, Manicougan, Ichimanipistick or Seven Islands, St. John, St. Austin's and Esquimaux. None of these rivers have been explored to any extent; and the interior of the country remains as yet the undisputed haunt of the prowling wolf and savage bear. It has, however, been traversed in various directions, by Esquimaux and Indians of other tribes, in the pursuit of the martin, the otter, and the beaver; but few facts of much importance have been gleaned from their narratives; and although it is probable, from the geographical situation of the country, and its unpromising appearance, that it is unfit for the purposes of settlement, it were still very desirable and satisfactory that a more accurate knowledge of its locality existed. The possibility of its leading to the discovery of minerals and mines, that might eventually prove of great advantage to the trade of the province, is by no means visionary, as fragments of coal were found in several rivers of that section of territory, by individuals connected with the Indian trade of Labrador.

As far as our information of the face of the country goes, as derived from the natives, it may be described as consisting of rocky cliffs, and rugged hills of no very considerable elevation, variously dispersed over barren plains or thick forests, studded with crooked and stunted pines, birch, firs and cedar. The valleys are generally coated with a thick moss, which usually extends beneath the woods, and is frequently overgrown with a variety of small shrubs, some of which bear quantities of berries; and the country is chequered with small lakes, that are sometimes formed by the melting of snow, and the accumulations of rain water.

There are no roads along the coast; and the only settlement of any consequence to be met with upon it, is that of Portneuf, which is composed of a chapel, 3 or 4 dwelling houses (the most conspicuous of these being the agent's house), and several stores. After traversing the gulf, and dwelling for some time upon the grand but gloomy range of prominent hills that bound the shores of the River St. Lawrence, the eye is agreeably relieved by the aspect of this solitary and picturesque little settlement, wholly unconnected with the civilized world excepting by water communication. It is one of the trading marts of the King's Posts Company, and has been many years established....

Along the coasts of Labrador, extensive fisheries are carried on that contribute to the supplies of the markets of the province, and also to the exports of fish and oil from Quebec. The fisheries of the Gulf are extremely productive, and it is the policy of the colonies to encourage them, as one of the exhaustless feeders of the trade of the country.

(Bouchette, *The British Dominions*, 1831, 1:292–5)

c) South Side of the St. Lawrence

1 COUNTRY WEST OF THE RIVER CHAUDIÈRE

☞ In this topographic description Bouchette starts with the seigneurial lands of the Chaudière valley near the St. Lawrence River, follows the course of the great river westward to the fertile plains south of Montreal, and then praises the highly attractive Appalachian landscapes of the Eastern Townships. The Beauce Country south of Quebec City already stands out as a flourishing area. The volcanic plugs of the Monteregian Hills are listed, except for Mount Royal itself, the volcanic remnant from which the line of hills received the name it has today. Poor roads make it difficult to reach the markets of the St. Lawrence River towns from the Eastern Townships. Bouchette draws a contrast between the British-influenced landscape of the Eastern Townships and that of the French Canadian landscapes and notes the influence of United States farming and building styles. ⌒

The highly valuable tract of country embraced in the present section, is bounded to the eastward by the River Chaudière, to the northward, in front, by the St. Lawrence, and in the rear, by the highlands of the Connecticut, and the parallel of the 45th degree of north latitude, which constitute the southern and south-eastern boundary of Lower Canada, dividing it, in that quarter, from the American states of New Hampshire, Vermont and New York.... It contains one town, numerous villages, and a total population of about 181,000 souls.

To give at once a collective and correct idea of the face and features of this extensive tract, it may be said that, receding from the St. Lawrence in the direction of east and south-east, after passing the almost uninterrupted level of the country, through which flow the rivers Richelieu and Yamaska, the land gradually swells into ridges, becomes progressively more hilly, and finally assumes a mountainous character towards lakes Memphramagog and St. Francis, the country beyond continuing to preserve, more or less, that boldness of aspect to the borders of the Chaudière and the height of land at the Connecticut's sources. The range of hills traversing Bolton, Orford, &c. appear to be a continuation of the Green Mountains, that form a conspicuous ridge running from south to west, through the state of Vermont. The uniform flatness of what might be called the valleys or plains of the Yamaska and Chambly (Richelieu), is agreeably relieved by the several isolated mountains that rise boldly and conspicuously above the surface, their soaring forms being distinctly seen, and giving by the various combinations of perspective, as they are viewed from different positions, considerable beauty and interest to the scenery. These mountains are distinguished by the names of Rouville or Beloeil, Yamaska, Boucherville, Chambly, Rougemont, and Mount Johnston. As might be expected in so wide an extent of territory, some variety of soil will occur and occasional swampy tracts be found; but the uncultivable tracts bear no proportion to the lands susceptible of a high degree of agricultural improvement. It is profusely watered by lakes, rivers, and rivulets winding through it in every direction. The principal rivers, besides the Chaudière, which bounds the tract to the eastward, are the Becancour, the two branches of the Nicolet, the St. Francis, the

Yamaska, the Richelieu or Chambly, the Chateauguay, and the Salmon. All these have their sources within the province, except the three last, whose waters flow from the other side of the boundary line, the one issuing from Lake Champlain, the others having their rise, as well as several of their branches, on the confines of the State of New York. Numerous other rivers and streams of inferior magnitude, with an innumerable class of tributary waters, also contribute to fertilize the soil, and are very useful to the farmers for various purposes of rural economy. The chief lakes are Memphramagog (which lies partly within our territory and partly within the dominions of the States), Scaswaninipus and Tomefobi, Lakes St. Francis, Nicolet, Pitt, William, and Trout, together with a number of others of inferior note.

Of the rivers, the Richelieu is the only one navigable for steamboats, the minor class of those vessels being able to ascend from Sorel to the basin at Chambly, provided, however, their draught of water do not exceed four feet, and even then there is a cessation of this description of navigation during the low waters about midsummer....

The feudal grants occupy a superficies of about 3,800 [square] miles, and circumscribe at all points, excepting to the southward, the tract known by the appellation of the eastern townships, having to the east and north-east the seigniories of Nouvelle Beauce, on the Chaudière, to the north and north-west those of the St. Lawrence, and to the westward the seigniories of the Yamaska and the Richelieu, and those composing the fertile tract of seigniorial lands lying between the Richelieu and the St. Lawrence, to St. Regis.

In glancing at the settlements of the circuit of country thus presenting itself, those of La Beauce will be found to possess considerable interest, whether we view their advanced and flourishing condition, or their advantageous geographical position, enjoying a climate somewhat milder than the seigniories on the St. Lawrence below Lake St. Peter, and situated on a direct communication with Boston, in the United States, by the Kennebec road, which was effectually completed last autumn (1830), and is already much frequented. By this important route the distance from Quebec to Boston is essentially abridged, and the markets of the capital consequently thrown more easily open to American produce. Through this route, large importations of live stock are made into this province, and the internal trade being otherwise great and increasing, a custom-house officer was appointed at St. Mary's, which is the largest and most flourishing village on the Chaudière.... The road along the Chaudière, upon the borders of which are the most improved and oldest settlements, is remarkably good, and presents various points of view extremely beautiful and picturesque.

At the mouth of the Chaudière, the banks of the St. Lawrence still retain the characteristic boldness, for which they are remarkable at Quebec and Point Levy; but proceeding westward, they gradually subside to a moderate elevation, till they sink into the flats of Baie du Febvre, and form the marshy shores of Lake St. Peter. Between the St. Francis and the Chaudière, the soil and settlements of the seigniories are of various degrees of excellence and prosperity. There are, generally speaking, much larger portions of them yet covered with impervious forests, than undergoing the operations of tillage; but such as are now under process of improvement, yield abundant harvests of every description of grain; and, from the prevailing depth of the soil, would not be unfit for the growth of hemp. Flax is already raised in small quantities for the use of domestic manufactures. A number of the villages are peculiarly well built and prettily situated on the river's banks, at intervals of 3 or 4 leagues, a bright tin-spired church, invariably figuring a pleasing and conspicuous object in the landscape of a Canadian village.

The villages more worthy of note are those of De Lotbiniere, Becancour, St. Gregoire, Nicolet, St. Antoine, and St. Francis....

The rich and luxuriant plain, lying between the Yamaska and the St. Lawrence, and traversed centrally by the Richelieu, completes the circuit of French grants, described as confining the eastern townships.... The exuberance of the crops raised in this fertile tract of country, justifies the appellation it bears as the granary of Lower Canada; since it not only affords subsistence to a dense and large population, but is the principal source whence the export wheat is derived for the British markets. The most prevalent quality of soil, is a deep rich mould, consisting chiefly of clay, in some places combined with a black earth and marl. The lighter soil is generally to be found along the rivers Chambly and Yamaska, and bordering the St. Lawrence. If any degrees of fertility, can properly be distinguished in one section of this valuable tract, over another, the seigniories in the vicinity of the basin at Chambly, seem entitled to the superiority: such are Chambly, Blairfindie, and Longueuil, that enjoy a climate several degrees milder than the seigniories on the St. Lawrence, and even sensibly milder than the fruitful country lying below them, on the Richelieu river. The main roads, following the banks of the several rivers, are very good in general; but the stage routes from St. John's, through Blairfindie, to La Prairie, or by Chambly to Longueuil, are exceedingly bad, and the latter in particular, when traversing the swamp between the villages of St. Joseph and Longueuil. By these two roads is kept up the communication with the United States, the intercourse with which is carried on, without cessation, at all seasons, rendering Chambly, Blairfindie, and La Prairie, great thoroughfares; and largely contributing to the encouragement of trade and business, and a consequent increase of the settlement and population of those places, and others situated on that route. The village of La Prairie on the north [*sic, south*] shore of the St. Lawrence, about 8 miles from the city of Montreal, has the advantage of any other village of the province, as regards the extent of its trade and population. The streets are more defined, the buildings more contiguous, and not unfrequently two stories high, and many of them covered in tin; tradesmen of every order, mechanics and shopkeepers, are to be seen in every direction, and much activity appears to prevail every where. The constant arrival and departure of steam boats and stages, contribute to enliven the place, and produce an almost ceaseless bustle and novelty of scene, occasioned by the coming and going of strangers, from the States, or from Canada....

If the scenery about Quebec command our admiration for its boldness, sublimity, and grandeur, that of the Richelieu will no less do so for its champaign and picturesque beauties. The eye here dwells with peculiar delight, on the frequent succession of rich and fruitful fields, luxuriant meadows, neat and flourishing settlements, and gay villages dispersed over this beautiful plain, and adorning the banks of the Richelieu, the Yamaska, and the St. Lawrence; whilst the towering mountains of Rouville and Chambly, Rougemont, Mount Johnson, and Boucherville, are seen soaring majestically above the common level, the monarchs of the vale. The Table Rock, at the summit of the cone, or *Pin de Sucre* of Rouville mountain, has been established to be 1,100 feet above the level of the river. Its access is extremely tedious and difficult; but none will look back to their fatigues with regret, when they behold from its exalted pinnacle, the most enchanting panoramic view, and the most extensive scope of country, that can be embraced at once from any spot in Lower Canada. Beneath the spectator, lies the magnificent valley from which the mountain rises; and winding amidst its numerous beauties, he can trace the Richelieu from its outlet from Lake Champlain, to its confluence with the St. Lawrence, which is also discovered at various points, till its surface is distinctly disclosed opposite Montreal. The city and mountain of Montreal are very clearly seen to the westward. To the eastward, the prospect is partially intercepted by one of the hills forming the group collectively called the Rouville mountain. With the aid of a telescope, the town of Three Rivers can be descried, in clear weather, to the N.E., and to the southward the settlements of Burlington, on Lake Champlain, in the state of Vermont, at the respective distances of about 60 and 70 miles from the spectator....

Labouring under the weighty disadvantage of the want of good and convenient roads communicating with the principal market-towns of the province, the prosperity of the eastern townships can only be attributed to the enterprise, industry, and perseverance of the inhabitants, who, considering merely the mildness of the climate, the advantages of the soil, and the locality, boldly entered the wilderness originally, and have now the gratification of seeing around them, corn-fields of unrivalled luxuriance, thriving farms, and flourishing villages. The town of Sherbrooke contains about 50 dwelling-houses; it occupies a high position on both banks of the River Magog, at the forks of the St. Francis, and its settlements are connected by a bridge; the old court-house and jail are on the Ascot side. As the seat of jurisdiction of the district of St. Francis, it is a place of general resort; besides being, as it were, the emporium of the township trade, or rather (as the head of the present navigation of the St. Francis), the place of transit through which the chief part of the township produce is conveyed to the market-towns, or elsewhere. The chief articles of trade are grain, pot and pearl ashes, and likewise horses, horned cattle, sheep, and other live stock....

Stanstead village is the next in the scale of consequence, although in point of neatness it takes precedence of Sherbrooke. The buildings are generally more regular and tasty, many of them two stories high, and several are built of brick. The style of building throughout the townships, is very different from that followed in the French settlements of the province, and borders considerably, if it is not absolutely similar, to the American style, in the adjoining state of Vermont. Indeed, when we come to contrast the system of agriculture, as well as the plan of building, pursued in the townships, with those adopted in the seigniories by Canadian farmers, we find a striking dissimilarity, and can easily trace the analogy of appearance that prevails between the township settlements and those of the American frontier. That the American agricultural system has the advantage of the Canadian, is, we believe, generally admitted, and to this the superior produce of the township lands seems to bear abundant testimony. The domestic cleanliness usually to be met with in the houses of the inhabitants is such as to characterise them for that virtue; whilst domestic manufactures of every description, introduced in the country, such as homespun cloths and linens, diaper, &c., are evidence of their industry: some of the cloths and linens are of a tissue and texture, not much inferior to the common description of imported British cloths and Irish linens....

In dismissing the consideration of this part of the country, we would remark the broad and conspicuous distinction existing between two classes of the people of the same province, in a small comparative extent of territory, as betwixt the inhabitants of the seigneurial settlements and those of the townships, differing as they do in their language, their religion, their habits, their systems of agriculture, the tenure of their lands, and partially in their laws. The prevalent language in the townships is English, the tenure of the lands, free and common soccage, and the laws by which lands descend by inheritance, are English. The French idiom is universal in the seigniories, the tenure of the lands, feudal, and the law of descent by which property is governed, is prescribed by the custom of Paris.

(Bouchette, *The British Dominions*, 1831, 1:297–311)

II COUNTRY EAST OF THE RIVER CHAUDIÈRE TO THE WEST BOUNDS OF THE DISTRICT OF GASPÉ [TO STE. ANNES DES MONTS]

This region includes the face of the Appalachian Range along the St. Lawrence River. The front along the great river is settled in a few places, but settlement thins out eastward into long stretches of empty land, with communication confined to a beach trail. Bouchette considers this an area where settlement should be encouraged. Quebec is a market for some produce, and Kamarouska is already a watering place. Difficult portage routes to New Brunswick cross this region and increased settlement on those routes would lead to improved connecting roads.

This section of Lower Canada is bounded to the north-west by the St. Lawrence, which forms an extensive front of 257 miles, and to the south-east by the highlands dividing the British from the American territories in that quarter. These highlands are situated, at their nearest point, 62 miles, perpendicular distance from the St. Lawrence; but, in approaching the river Chaudière, they diverge southerly, to the sources of the Connecticut. The superficial extent of this tract of country is about 18,802 square statute miles, and its population about 65,430 souls, chiefly occupying the borders of the St. Lawrence to the lateral depth of 9 miles, and the banks of the river Chaudière....

The face of the country, though abounding with extensive valleys and flats, is decidedly hilly; but it is neither so bold or so mountainous as the country on the opposite banks of the St. Lawrence. The land generally rises in irregular ridges from the borders of the river, towards the rear, and attains, in general, a considerable elevation at the distance of 10, 15, and 20 miles from the front, forming at its height the verge of a broad and extended tract of table-land of gentle descent towards the River St. John, beyond which it reascends again, and acquires a superior degree of altitude, towards the sources of the Allegash, merging in the range of highlands that are a continuation of the Connecticut range, stretching eastwardly, and winding round the sources of the rivers falling into the Atlantic, and those flowing into the St. Lawrence, and the St. John, in the opposite direction.

This vast tract of territory is very well watered by numerous rivers and lakes, and their tributary waters, that flow through the soil in multifarious ramifications. Of the rivers, the largest are the St. John and its principal branches, the Madawaska, Etchemin, Du Sud, Le Bras (a branch of the Du Sud), Ste. Anne, OueUe, Du Loup, the Green River, Trois Pistolles, Rimouski, and the Great Mitis and Matane rivers. The chief lakes are those of Metapediac, Mitis, Temiscouata, Long Lake, and the Eagle Lakes; but others of inferior magnitude are frequent, and these in general, as well as the larger lakes, abound with a variety of excellent fish.

From the high grounds of Lauzon, opposite Cape Diamond, a general and gradual declivity eastward is perceptible along the St. Lawrence as far as the River du Sud, beyond which the immediate banks of the river are moderately elevated for a considerable distance down. The River du Sud takes its source in the hills to the S. W., and winding in a general north-easterly course for about 30 miles, through a level, rich, and fruitful plain, discharges itself into the St. Lawrence 35 miles below Quebec. The richness of the harvests in the luxuriant valley it traverses had long acquired to it a reputation as the granary of Lower Canada, but it is now supposed to yield in fertility to the lands on the Richelieu river. Its scenery is soft and beautiful in the extreme. The village of St. Thomas [today Montmagny] stands on the N. W. shore of the River du Sud, near its junction with the St. Lawrence. Viewed from Chapel Hill, which lies about 5 miles to the S.W., it appears to great advantage, a conspicuous object in one of the most enchanting prospects to be seen in the province. From the insulated altitude of the rock, the spectator commands a beautiful panoramic view of the surrounding champaign country, which is in a high state of cultivation, and chequered with frequent farmhouses and extensive barns, whose dazzling whiteness is agreeably contrasted with the rich verdure or maturer hue of the field, and the luxuriant foliage of the elm. To the N. and N.E. the broad stream of the St. Lawrence is displayed in all its grandeur, the eye being able from this one point to survey its expanded surface above and below for a total distance of nearly 40 miles. The villages above St. Thomas, and particularly St. Michel and St. Vallier, are remarkably picturesque, and their locality peculiarly advantageous, as they are seated on the banks of the St. Lawrence, upon some agreeable eminence, and on the borders of an excellent road.

At Ste. Anne's, 24 leagues below Quebec, are first to be met with those insulated cliffs which characterize the scenery about Kamouraska. They are composed of granite, and generally rise in abrupt slopes, presenting rugged faces, thinly clad with dwarf trees. The highest of these hills is Montagne Ste. Anne, which from its towering elevation, not much unlike that of Rouville Mountain, peers above the fine country at its base....

... The parishes above Bic, or from Cacona inclusive, are very populous, the farms in a good state of cultivation, the soil generally excellent in its varieties, and the inhabitants in every respect easy and comfortable. One principal road, running along the river's bank, connects the whole line of flourishing settlements; whilst others, called *routes,* lead to the interior concessions and parishes, and are intersected by other front roads running parallel to the main road on the St. Lawrence's border....

River Ouelle and Kamouraska are the most populous villages below Ste. Anne's; and of these two Kamouraska enjoys a superiority in point of magnitude as well as situation. Both villages contain several very neat dwelling-houses, the residences of the principal inhabitants of the respective places; a few shops, and two or three good taverns. At River Ouelle is established at the mouth of the river a very productive porpoise fishery, held by several individuals in shares. Kamouraska, 90 miles distant from Quebec, is celebrated in the province for the remarkable salubrity of its atmosphere, which enjoys all the invigorating properties of sea air, arising from the breadth of the St. Lawrence, which is here upwards of 6 leagues, and the perfect sea salt of the waters. Kamouraska is now the chief watering-place in Lower Canada; and, as such, is the resort of numerous visiters, of the first rank and respectability, during the summer months....

The seigniory is wholly settled, and indeed the redundant population occupies part of the waste lands in its depth. The front, which is generally low, abounds in those rich natural meadows to be met with in some of the parishes above, affording abundant wholesome pasturage, and enabling the farmer to produce large quantities of butter, much esteemed for its excellence in the Quebec market. The islands in front, besides embellishing the landscape, are used as the sites of extensive fisheries, the chief of which is that of the herring. Between these islands and the main shore, schooners find a safe strand at low water.

East of Kamouraska, the country continues for some distance singularly diversified, by abrupt and insulated hills, whose craggy and almost barren faces are usually contrasted with well cultivated fields....

The portage of Temiscouata is 12 leagues long, and traverses the country from the shores of the St. Lawrence to Lake Temiscouata. Through this communication lies the mail route to Frederickton, St. John's, and Halifax; and hence may be formed an opinion of its importance, and of the consequent expediency of improving it, to render the intercourse more easy and expeditious between the eastern and the western parts of the British colonies. It was first opened in 1783, but has since undergone, from time to time, considerable repairs; .... The road penetrates a wilderness, and is irregular and winding in its course, in order to avoid, as often as practicable, the hills that present themselves on the direct route. There is a good bridge across River du Loup, and small bridges over the minor streams, so that waggons may now pass through without interruption....

The parishes of Cacona, Isle Verte, and Trois Pistolles present themselves next in order after River du Loup. Their settlements do not extend far beyond the river or front range, which exhibits neat farmhouses, large barns, and extensive enclosures that bear evidence of a good soil and industrious cultivation. After traversing these seigniories, we come to that part of the road called the Rimouski or Nine-league Portage. It is but partially settled, and the rugged aspect of the rocky ridges to the north and south of it render it a gloomy section of the road. These ridges form a valley whose breadth at its western entrance is nearly 2 miles; but tapering towards its eastern extremity, its width is contracted to not more than 800 yards. It is 27 miles long, and comes out over the bold and broken mountains of Bic, where it becomes excessively hilly, presents a series of abrupt cliffs and craggy hills, from the aspect of which, the eye is much relieved by dwelling on the mellowed landscape that offers itself in the well-dispersed settlements of Rimouski. After passing the steep and broken high grounds of Bic, the banks of the St. Lawrence become of a moderate varying elevation, excepting at Grand Mitis, where they rise abruptly about *Anse aux Snelles*. The public road is not open beyond *Anse au Coq*, a distance of 4 leagues below the church of Rimouski, and follows in its bearings the sinuosities of the river, having on its borders comfortable farmhouses and well-cultivated fields. It passes at Father Point, a spot of much beauty, remarkable as the place of residence of most of the pilots of the St. Lawrence, several of whom are in affluent circumstances. Below *Anse au Coq* no proper road exists; but the beach is frequented as such, and the communication kept up with Mitis and Matane by that medium. The locality admits of the opening of an excellent road at trifling expense; and there is no doubt that the making of such a road would be an important encouragement to the settlements of that section of the province....

From Grand to Little Mitis, the distance is only 6 miles; but there is no regular road connecting both places, the communication being kept open merely over the beach, along which a proper road might easily be traced. The banks of the river are of a moderate elevation, rising in slopes by no means too precipitous for tillage, and possessing a light but fertile soil. The chief settlements of the seigniory of Mitis are situated at Little Mitis Bay, upon a rocky point, having to the N. W. the St. Lawrence, and to the S. E. the deep bay which receives the waters of Little Mitis River. The lands in the vicinity of the bay consist of a light but good soil, whose properties are improved by the sea-weed which abounds along the shores, and is profitably used as manure. Extensive salmon and herring fisheries are set up in the bay S. E. of the point, which yield an abundance of both articles for the Quebec market, where they generally meet with ready sale.... The opening of Kempt Road from Grand Mitis to Lake Metapediac, and thence to Ristigouche, was an undertaking of great moment to that part of the province; and at the same time that it will add to the means of communicating with New Brunswick and Gaspé, it will give an additional impulse to the settlements in the lower section of the district of Quebec.

The parish of Matane lies about 30 miles below Mitis, from which it is separated by a total wilderness. The intercourse between both places is kept by water only, or sometimes, but with considerable difficulty, by the beach. The banks of the river are almost uniformly low, and the surface of the country so level, as to offer combined facilities in making a road to connect the settlements. The timber, consisting chiefly of evergreen woods, is generally diminutive upon the skirts of the forest; but, receding from the river, the trees increase in magnitude, and the rising grounds are clothed with a more sturdy growth of hard woods. The tract of country lying between Mitis and Matane possesses all the advantages necessary to render it fit for the reception of a large colony of emigrants, and from its situation is peculiarly adapted to that purpose. The soil is sandy towards the front, but it becomes richer in the interior, if the quality of the timber be a faithful indication of the character of the land....

.... There being no regular road along the front of the seigniory, the beach, a beautiful firm sand, is used as the highway at low water, the accumulation of drifted timber above high-water mark, rendering the communication by land impracticable at any other time. A few wretched habitations are scattered along the beach as far as the eastern extremity of the seigniory, below which are the settlements of Cape Chat and St. Anne's, at the respective distances of 27 and 36 miles from Matane.

(Bouchette, *The British Dominions*, 1831, 1:311–23)

III DISTRICT OF GASPÉ

☞ This is a distinctive region within Lower Canada where the sea, fishing, and the lumber trade are important. Bouchette is misinformed about the interior elevated valley. Most settlement is on the Bay of Chaleur. Loyalists had settled on the Bay, as indicated by some place names. This was an area of both British and French settlement, but Bouchette does not mention this. Already there is evidence of over-fishing as regulations on open seasons are defied. ☜

The district of Gaspé is the only section of Lower Canada of which a general description remains to be given. The peninsulated tract of country so called .... is bounded by the River St. Lawrence to the north, by the Gulf to the east, south by the Bay of Chaleurs, and by the district line dividing it from Quebec to the westward. It therefore enjoys the advantage of an extensive coast, which, including the shores of the numerous bays that indent it, may be about 350 miles, extending from Cape Chat round to the head of Ristigouche Bay. Its greatest width, from north to south, is about 90 miles.

The imperfect knowledge of the natural divisions of this district existing some years antecedently to the present period had led to the belief that it was traversed centrally by a ridge of mountains terminating at Cape Rosier; but it would appear, upon further and more accurate observation, that the central parts of the peninsula exhibit the aspect of an elevated valley, having to the north a range of hills skirting the St. Lawrence, and another to the south, at no very remote distance from the shores of the Ristigouche River and the Bay of Chaleurs....

The face of the country is, generally speaking, uneven; in some parts it is decidedly mountainous, and the valleys, which are often irregular and broken, are occasionally intersected by deep ravines; but the mass of the lands is nevertheless perfectly adapted to agriculture. With the exception of some of the higher hills, that are thinly clad with a diminutive growth of timber, the country is very well wooded, the forests chiefly consisting of maple, beech, birch, pine, larch, white cedar, spruce, and hemlock; but there is a scarcity of oak, and what there is of it is inferior in size and quality.

From Port Daniel to Maria, a distance exceeding fifty miles, along the Bay of Chaleurs, the land, to the depth of about ten miles from the shores, is composed of a friable red clay soil, covered with a thick coating of vegetable mould, easy of cultivation, and producing the finest crops. This description of soil appears, as far as observation goes, to predominate in the district; excepting on the River Ristigouche, where the lands are marked by a superior degree of richness. There are on the Ristigouche many valuable spots of excellent meadow and interval land, and several good tracts on the shores of the Gulf, at Pabos, Grand and Little River, L'Anse au Beaufils, Mal Bay, Douglas Town, and Gaspé Bay....

There are numerous lakes in the interior; but that part of the country being only very superficially explored, their exact position is not known. It is ascertained, however, that they, as well as the rivers, abound with a variety of fish, and that salmon, at one period very abundant in the rivers, has since several years become almost extinct.

The roads in the district of Gaspé are few and very bad, and indeed the various settlements would be wholly without the means of intercommunication but for *bridle* roads – that is, such as may be travelled on horseback – or the beach, which is in many places used as the highway. From River Novel to Port Daniel, where the country is most thickly settled, a tolerably good road of that description is opened, that may be travelled part of the way by wheel-carriages. Beyond Port Daniel the road has been traced and opened to Percé, and, although traversing a thinly settled country, is, together with other roads of the district, about being materially improved out of the funds appropriated for that object by the legislature of the province....

The population of the district, by the census of 1825, was given at about 5000 souls; and it may at present be computed, from correct data of increase, at 7,677. This population is chiefly situated between Point Mackarel and Ristigouche, and on the borders of Gaspé Bay. There are besides about 400 Indians of the Micmac tribe domiciliated at Ristigouche and Cascapediac, who are not included in the above statement.

The principal and indeed the only villages are those of Carlisle and Percé, at each of which there is a jail and a court-house, where the provincial courts and courts of general sessions of the peace are held. The courts are also held at Carleton and at Douglas Town.

The inhabitants of this district, during the earlier period of its settlements, chiefly derived their subsistence by fishing and hunting; but these resources having in some measure failed, they have more generally turned their attention to agriculture, and have succeeded so well, that they now stand in little need of those supplies they were accustomed to import. Their lands yield good harvests of wheat, barley, pease, oats, and potatoes; excellent green crops, such as turnips, carrots, &c.; and the meadows produce hay in great abundance. The usual time for sowing is May, and the reaping-season September. The Canadian breed of cattle is that most generally raised by the farmers, but its condition had for a long time been neglected, in the pursuit of other objects foreign to rural economy, and the various species had degenerated. Some enterprising individuals have, however, imported superior kinds from the United States, New Brunswick, and even from Europe, and a stimulus has thus been given that has since produced a very perceptible improvement in the department of stock-farming....

The staples of the trade of the district are fish, oil, timber and furs; and of these the two former are by far the most abundant articles of export. Of the fisheries the cod is the most extensive. It commences in May, and terminates in October, and is chiefly carried on in open barges of 18 feet keel, manned by two fishermen, who daily put out about 3 or 4 miles from shore to cast their lines. The cod fishery likewise employs small craft that venture out to greater distances than the barges, and fish for several days together on the neighbouring banks. There are about 15 vessels of this description belonging to the district managed by a complement of from 6 to 10 men each, thus employed for about 2 months in the summer season. Of the first-mentioned class of fishing boats or barges, there were in 1820, 680; but this number is now much augmented. The cod fisheries of Gaspé employ about 1800 persons of both sexes, of whom about 500 are men who go thither for the season, from the parishes in the neighbourhood and below Quebec. The whole product of the cod fishery may be estimated at about 50,000 quintals of dried, and 10,000 quintals of green fish, with about 20,000 gallons of cod oil, which are exported to Quebec. The herring and salmon fisheries are the next in degree of importance, or at least produce. About 4,000t barrels of the former, smoked as well as pickled, are annually shipped to Quebec, and about 2,000 of the latter, which is a considerable diminution upon the produce of former years, attributable to the deficiency of proper regulations, restricting the time of fishing to certain seasons, and otherwise regulating the mode of taking the salmon. This fishery is carried on by persons practically unconnected with the cod fishery, and its supplies are exported to Quebec, Halifax, and the West Indies.

The whale fishery gives employment to 5 or 6 large schooners, manned by from 8 to 10 men each, who are extensively engaged in this branch of the fisheries during the summer months. The produce is from 18,000 to 20,000 gallons of oil, which are chiefly exported to Quebec; and the total number of persons occupied in the fishery, whether in taking the whales or preparing the oil, amounts to nearly 200. The whale fishery particularly merits the attention of the legislature. By encouraging bounties to secure the adventurer against the serious loss consequent upon an unsuccessful voyage, the number of vessels employed would soon be considerably increased, and this important branch of trade so effectually carried on by the hardy inhabitants of Gaspé district as to compete, in some degree at least, if not rival, that of our American neighbours, who are now almost in the exclusive enjoyment of it, and carry on their enterprising fisheries at the very mouths of our bays and harbours.

Upwards of sixteen square-rigged vessels are annually employed in the export of dried fish to the south of Europe. Most of these vessels are built in the district, and are of the first class of merchants' ships. Upwards of fifty small vessels are constantly, during the summer months, employed in the coasting trade, and from thence to Quebec, Halifax, and the West Indies.

The lumber trade of the district has only commenced since 1815 or 1816. In 1818, four vessels sailed from thence, laden with timber. In 1819 and 1820 this number had much increased; and in the years 1825 and 1826, about 60 sail of vessels were engaged in the trade, and carried away about 750,000 feet of pine timber. The vast quantities of pine timber growing in certain parts of the district render this branch of trade susceptible of great augmentation. It is carried on to a far greater extent on the opposite shore of the bay of Chaleurs that lies within the province of New Brunswick; and indeed frequent instances are found of inhabitants of that province coasting over to the Gaspé side, and carrying away, in defiance of the authorities of the district, large quantities of pine of great value. The prosecution of the timber trade is attended with a variety of advantages to a certain class of the people of the district, inasmuch as it gives them employment during the suspension of the fisheries in winter, at which season the Chantiers are always opened, and the timber prepared for market the following spring....,

The Magdalen islands, in the Gulf of St. Lawrence, are annexed to the district and county of Gaspé. They contain a population of nearly 1,000 souls, chiefly French Accadians and Catholics. Eleven English and five Irish families are settled among them, all of whom derive their principal subsistence from the fisheries. Beyond the cultivation of potatoe gardens, agriculture seems wholly unknown on the islands; but natural meadows and pasturing grounds are common, and afford wholesome sustenance to a tolerable proportion of live stock.

(Bouchette, The British Dominions, 1831, 1:323–32)

5 NOVA SCOTIA

☞ The topographic description of Nova Scotia is organized county-by-county. Bouchette begins with Halifax County, goes on to the eastern part of the colony to Chedabucto Bay, and then ends with the counties in the western part of Nova Scotia. Settlement is on the coast, mainly dependent upon fishing, but pockets of good arable soil have been searched out in what is generally a difficult land for agriculture. Districts that possess a range of usable soils, including dyked marshland, interval land (flood plains of rivers), and upland are considered ideal. The Annapolis-Cornwallis Valley is barely mentioned. Much of the description is by villages and towns, all located on or close to the coast. Each community is a small shipping centre, handling the trade of its neighbourhood and connected by water to its markets, often in far-away places. Early French settlements are mentioned, as is the Acadian expulsion and the subsequent re-settlement by New Englanders, Germans, Loyalists, and then later Scots and English immigrants, all with varying degrees of success. ☞

a) General Face of the Country

Nova Scotia was the name formerly given to all that immense tract of country bounded on the north by Lower Canada, on the east by the Bay of Chaleurs and the Gulf of St. Lawrence, including the Island of St. John, Cape Breton, and all the other islands on the coast, and on the west by the then New England provinces, and contained what has since been divided into the separate provinces or colonies of New Brunswick, Prince Edward's Island, Cape Breton, and Nova Scotia.

The province of Nova Scotia is an extensive peninsula, connected with the continent of North America by a narrow isthmus of only eight miles in width, between Bay Verte, in the Straits of Northumberland, and Cumberland Basin, at the eastern extremity of the Bay of Fundy....

The face of the country is agreeably diversified with hill and dale, but is nowhere mountainous, the highest hills not exceeding 600 feet. The highlands generally run north and south, branching off in all directions, terminating in some instances in bold cliffs on the coast, the most remarkable of which is Aspotagoen, between Mahone and Margaret's Bay, and is about 500 feet high. Ardoise Hill, between Halifax and Windsor, is the highest land in the province. The Horton mountains run nearly north and south; and the north mountains, which are washed by the Minas basin, terminate in Cape Blomidon, whose head may be often seen above the clouds by which it is sometimes encircled. The highlands which lie in the interior of the counties of Annapolis, Shelburn and Queen's, are called the Blue Mountains, and are said to retain traces of volcanic eruption.

This province contains numerous lakes, which are scattered over it in every direction, many of them of considerable extent, and forming in several places almost a continued chain of water communication from sea to sea....

The rivers that intersect, beautify, and enrich the country are far too numerous even to be named. Perhaps there is no country in the world better watered, nor any of equal extent containing so many rivers capable of navigation. The principal are, the Annapolis, running parallel with the Bay of Fundy from the township of Cornwallis, in King's county, and discharging itself into Annapolis Bay, navigable for small craft and boats the greater part of its course; the Shubenacadie, running from the Grand Lake, in the county of Halifax, dividing that county from Hants county, and falling into Cobequid Bay, receiving the tides, and navigable for upwards of thirty miles; the Avon, which receives the waters of the rivers St. Croix, Kermescook, and several others, discharges itself into the Bay of Minas, and is navigable for a considerable distance; the La Have, having its source in a chain of lakes that also feeds the Gaspereaux river, in the county of Hants, traverses the whole county of Lunenburg, and, after a course of about sixty miles, discharges itself into the harbour of La Have; the Mersey, winding from Lake Rosignol through the Queen's county, and discharging in Liverpool Harbour; the Medway, commencing in a chain of extensive lakes in the northern part of the Queen's county, and discharging itself into the noble harbour of Port Medway ; the Shelburne, discharged from a chain of lakes in the northern part of that county (contiguous to the sources of the river Hubert in the county of Annapolis), and extending to within fifteen miles of the town of Shelburne, where it forms the noble harbour of that name; the Clyde which rises upwards of forty miles in the interior in an extensive chain of lakes, and is deemed one of the most beautiful rivers in Nova Scotia; the Tusket, with its numerous branches, many of which expand into lakes, the principal rising in the Blue Mountains, is navigable for shipping about ten miles, and for boats above thirty; and the St. Mary, the principal branch of which rises in College Lake, within a very short distance of the Antigonish river, and, crossing nearly the whole county of Sydney, from north to south, forms the harbour of St. Mary, where it becomes navigable for the largest vessels for about ten miles. Besides these rivers, there are several others of nearly equal magnitude and importance in all parts of the province, particularly those that run into Pictou Harbour, Cumberland Basin, and the north-eastern coast of the county of Cumberland. These several lakes and rivers beautify the scenery, enrich the soil, and afford singular facilities for internal communication.

Anteriorly to 1748 so little had been done towards the local improvement of the colony, that the whole province exhibited at that late date but a dense forest; and although the proportion of land still unreclaimed from its wilds is indeed very considerable, yet there are districts in which the arts of agriculture, guided by industry, have effected extensive ameliorations in the condition of the country. Some tracts of the province consist of extensive barrens, interspersed here and there among the forests, which forests are generally composed of large and lofty timber.

(Bouchette, The British Dominions, 1831, 2:1–9)

b) Division of the Province into Counties, Districts and Townships

I HALIFAX COUNTY

The county of Halifax is the largest in the province, and stretches quite across it, from the Atlantic Ocean to Cumberland Straits.... All the southern part of the county, which lies upon the Atlantic, is high, broken, rocky land, interspersed here and there with some good strips, but in general barren and unfit for cultivation. The same remark applies also to all that extensive tract of country surrounding the Great Lake, and extending several miles both east and west. But the country extending from the Great Lake northward to the head of the Minas Basin, and on both its shores, is altogether of a different quality. The land is low and fertile, adapted to agricultural purposes, filled with limestone and gypsum, and affording indications of extensive beds of coal and other minerals. This character applies to the country extending along and for several miles to the east and west of the Shubenacadie River. Again, that part of the county bordering on Northumberland Straits, and the whole district of Pictou, is every where diversified with hill and dale, intersected by streams and brooks, which form several rivers. The soil is generally rich and capable of high cultivation, and this district is in fact one of the best cultivated in the province. About half way between Halifax and the Minas Basin occurs an extensive chain of lakes, the principal of which is called the Great Lake....

The harbour of Halifax is one of the finest in America. A thousandSalmon vessels may ride in it in safety. It is accessible at all seasons of the year, and easy of approach....

The town of Halifax is, in point of extent and population, the third town in British North America. It was founded, upon the first permanent settlement of the English in this province, by Governor Cornwallis in 1749. It is situated on the western side of the harbour, on the declivity of a hill 240 feet above the level of the sea. There are eight streets running through the town, intersected by fifteen others, laid out with regularity, some of them paved, and the others macadamized. The town and suburbs are upwards of two miles in length, and about half a mile in width. It has been very much improved within the last five years. There are meat, vegetable, and fish markets, all extremely well supplied. The fish, in point of quality, variety, and cheapness, may vie with any in the world.... Amongst the public buildings is the Government-house, built of freestone, situate at the south end of the town, and occupied by the lieu-

tenant-governor of the province for the time being. The province building is the best-built and handsomest edifice in North America. It is built
of freestone, ... Dalhousie College, established in 1820, is a spacious and
handsome structure, situate at the end of the old military parade.

Halifax has been always the principal naval station of British North
America; and here is a king's dock-yard, which is enclosed towards the
town by a high stone wall, and contains within it all the requisite workshops, warehouses, and stores, besides commodious residences for the
officers and servants belonging to the yard; it is on a more extensive
footing than any in America.... There are also a residence for the, military commandant, two barracks, and a military hospital....

Halifax contained, in 1790, 700 houses and 4000 inhabitants; in
1828, 1580 houses and 14,439 inhabitants. It is the seat of government,
the principal emporium of the trade of the province, and returns two
members to the House of Assembly. Besides Dalhousie College, there
are a grammar-school, with an endowment of 200*l* from the province,
three large schools on the national and Lancasterian plan, and several
common schools. There are no fewer than six weekly newspapers published, and it has several charitable institutions. The manufactures carried on in Halifax are still in an imperfect state: they consist of a sugar
refinery; distilleries of rum, gin, and whiskey; breweries of porter and
ale; and factories of soap, candles, leather, flour, and cordage, and a few
other minor articles.... Nearly the whole of the import and better than
one-half of the export trade of the province are carried on at Halifax.
There were owned at Halifax in 1828 seventy-three square-rigged vessels and seventy-seven schooners; of which seventy were employed in
the West India trade, four between Halifax and Great Britain, six in the
trade with foreign Europe and Brazil, and the remainder in the fishery.
There is a respectable private banking-establishment at Halifax, and
the Falmouth packet regularly arrives with the mails once a month.
The situation of Halifax is very beautiful. The noble harbour in front,
Bedford Basin beyond, and the north-west arm in the rear, with the
extensive forests in the background, unite in exciting the admiration of
every beholder.

The township of Halifax extends westward to the boundary line
between this county and Lunenburg county. The land is of the worst
description in the province, being both naked and barren; but the coast
is almost one uninterrupted succession of harbors....

... The town of Dartmouth lies opposite to Halifax, on the eastern
side of the harbour, which is here about a mile wide; it considerably

increased in size, population, and wealth during the late war, but has not since been so flourishing. A steam-boat constantly plies between Dartmouth and Halifax for the accommodation of passengers....

The township of Preston is situated on the east of the township of Dartmouth, and on the north and in the rear of Lawrence Town. It was laid out and granted in 1784 to 388 proprietors-loyalists, disbanded soldiers, and free negroes. The negro settlers were industrious and thrifty, but some agents of the African Company induced them to remove to Sierra Leone. The land in this township is inferior and stony, but its proximity to Halifax gives it a value it would not otherwise possess....
There are few finer agricultural tracts than the country to the eastward of the river Shubenacadie, which composes the district of Colchester....

... [Truro] township was originally settled by the French, who were forcibly expelled in 1755. It was subsequently granted, in 1765, to some Irish emigrants, several of whom came to this province, under a Colonel M'Nutt, who found the remains of the French improvements, a quantity of diked marsh land orchards, &c. in a state of tolerable preservation. The township contains 50,000 acres, and abounds with gypsum and limestone. The upland soil is good, well cultivated, and fruitful; and there is a considerable quantity of marsh and interval land of extreme fertility. The town of Truro is situated on the south side of Cobequid Bay, near its head, and contains about 100 houses....

... Truro, Onslow, and Londonderry, with the several settlements Economy, Stewiack, Tatmagouche, Salmon River, &c., comprise a tract of country which, for richness of soil, mineral productions, local convenience, and beauty of scenery, is quite equal to any in this province. Cobequid Bay, around which they are all situate, is easily navigable on its northern shore by vessels of any magnitude, and on its southern by vessels of 150 tons, abounds with fish, and has several small harbours and inlets. The produce is carried to Halifax market, and exported to St. John's, New Brunswick; cargoes are also assorted for the West Indies, and lumber, in some quantities, exported to Europe: it is, in short, one of the best-circumstanced, most fruitful, populous, and best-cultivated districts in Nova Scotia....

That part of the county of Halifax called the district of Pictou contains the three townships of Pictou, Egerton, and Maxwelton. It is a diversified county of hill and dale, well watered by numerous streams and rivers. The soil is very good, and it has been as well cultivated and is as productive as any in the province. It abounds with coal, iron ore, copper, freestone, and lime. The great coal field of this district is very extensive, and the coal is of the very best quality, and is now being worked by the lessees of His late Royal Highness the Duke of York, Messrs. Rundell and Bridge, of London. It has several good harbours, the principal of which are Pictou, Merigomish, Carriboo, and Tatmagouche, in all of which the Shore and Labrador fisheries are carried on to a great extent. The timber of this district is also of a superior kind, particularly the birch, which is considered the best in America. This district, though one of the last settled, is the most important part of the province; in fertility of soil, abundance and value of its mineral productions, proximity to the fishery, and facilities for carrying it on, it has the advantage of every other part of Nova Scotia....

The principal town of this district is Pictou; it is situated on the harbour of that name, about three miles from the entrance. Although not very regularly laid out, the houses are generally better than in any of the other provincial towns; many of them are built of stone. It contains four places of worship – an episcopal, a Roman catholic, and two presbyterian chapels. There are also the Pictou Academy, a grammar-school, court-house, and public library. The population in 1828 was nearly 1500 souls, and it has since very rapidly increased; it cannot now be less than between 2500 and 3000. Pictou has been declared a *free warehousing port,* and its trade is very considerable in lumber, coal, and the fishery. Coasters from all parts of the Gulf of St. Lawrence resort to Pictou, and its exports have amounted to *100,000l.* in a single year. One hundred vessels have been loaded here with timber for Great Britain, and its exports to the West Indies were not less extensive and important.

II SYDNEY COUNTY

The county of Sydney is the most easterly part of the province: .... The soil of the northern and eastern part of this county – interval, alluvial, and upland – is equal to any in the province. The agricultural produce is very considerable, and large quantities are exported. The lumber trade is extensively carried on, and the fisheries are the best in the province. It is exceedingly well watered, abounding with lakes and rivers, and no part of the province affords so many fine harbour....

The township of Dorchester, or Antigonish, is situate on and about the bay of that name. The first settlement made by the English was in 1784, and it was materially increased in 1795 by emigrants from Scotland. Dorchester, or Antigonish, is the shire town of the district. It is situated about a mile above the navigation on Antigonish River. It has but one

principal street, and contains a court-house, a Roman catholic, a presbyterian, and a baptist church. It is a very pretty village, and is the principal
trading place in the district....

... The land of [Guysborough] township is extremely good, but the
fisheries afford such lucrative employment that very little more land is
cultivated than is sufficient for internal supply; but great quantities of
horses, black cattle, and sheep are reared, and several cargoes are annually exported to Newfoundland, together with considerable quantities
of butter....

... The town of Guysborough is situate at the western side, near the
entrance of the lower basin, and commands a full view of Chedabucto
Bay and its southern shore as far as Canseau, and few places possess
more beautiful natural scenery. It contains a court-house, an episcopal,
a Roman catholic, and a methodist church, besides several chapels scattered through the township. The land on both sides the harbour is very
good, and has been long since cleared of timber, now affording extensive
natural meadows and pastures....

... The fisheries of [Chedabucto Bay] are as productive as any in the
known world. The inhabitants are all engaged in them, and the quantities of cod, herring, and mackerel taken are immense.

Canseau is situate at the southern extremity of the county. The greater
part of this district is a barren naked rock, with a few hills of good
land. The town-plot, called Wilmot, is situate on the southwestern side
of Canseau Harbour. It has lately been much improved. The harbour
of Canseau is a very excellent one, accessible at all seasons of the year.
The strait is called Little Canseau, and is navigable for the largest ships,
affording safe and commodious anchorage. During the prevalence of
westerly gales, all the vessels to and from the Gulf of St. Lawrence
anchor here, and wait for a favourable wind; and it is a great resort for
the fishing-craft in the season...

... Sherbrooke is situate at the extreme head of the navigation of the
river, and is accessible to vessels of 50 to 100 tons. A very considerable
lumber trade has been and is carried on from this place.

III CUMBERLAND COUNTY

The settlement of Fort Lawrence adjoins the boundary line [between
Nova Scotia and New Brunswick], lying between the rivers Missiguash
and La Planche. It consists principally of dike land, and is one of the
most productive in Nova Scotia. Vast quantities of hay are raised, and

herds of cattle fed, upon these lands, and the farmers are generally wealthy and independent.

The township of Amherst contains 26,750 acres, of which a considerable quantity is dike land, and the remainder interval, upland, and wood. Meadow and grazing are the principal agricultural pursuits, and beef and butter are raised and exported to a large amount. The little town or rather village of Amherst is in a flourishing condition. It is situate near the narrow isthmus which here separates the Bay of Fundy from Northumberland Straits; it is therefore connected with the navigation of both, and can with the same facility avail itself of the markets of St. John and Miramichi....

The settlements on the Maccan, the Nappan, and the Hibbert River, and at Minudie, consist principally of the same quality of dike land as Amherst, and are cultivated in the same manner, meadow and grazing. The settlement at Minudie consists of Acadians, the descendants of those who escaped the general expulsion of that people in 1755. They are a temperate, industrious people, forming a little distinct community, and pursuing their own customs, language, and religion with remarkable pertinacity....

... Pugwash settlement is situated on Pugwash Bay, the best harbour in the county. The shore is so bold, that vessels of 500 tons may lie with safety, at all times, within twenty yards of it. Above the channel, which is not more than a quarter of a mile wide, it becomes a beautiful basin, into which the river Pugwash, which rises in a chain of lakes about seven miles distant, discharges itself. The land on the harbour and river is of superior quality, although not very populous. The, river Philip, which is a union of several others rising in the interior of the county, also discharges itself into the sea near Pugwash Harbour. This river is remarkable for the quality and size of its salmon and trout, and gaspereux and shad are also abundant....

West Chester is situated on the summit of the Cobequid highlands, in the centre of the county. It was settled by loyalists from New York. The soil is naturally good, but the local situation is much against it, and the settlement is on the decline.

The county of Cumberland is well intersected by roads in all directions. The great road from Halifax to Quebec runs quite through it. Although containing some of the richest, and the greatest quantity of dike and other valuable land, of any county in the province, agriculture, with the exception of meadow and grazing, is not as extensively followed as it might be. Little grain is exported from this county, but the export of beef and butter is considerable. The grazing farmers in the districts bordering on the Bay of Fundy are as wealthy and independent as any in Nova Scotia; but the same remark will not apply to the settlements on the Gulf shore, where the inhabitants are principally engaged in the lumber trade, to the neglect of their rich and valuable lands.

IV HANTS COUNTY

The county of Hants is bounded on the north by the Minas Basin, on the east by the Shubenacadie river, which divides it from Halifax county, on the south by Halifax county, and on the west by the King's county and the county of Lunenburg. It contains six townships: Windsor, Falmouth, Newport, Rawdon, Kempt, and Douglas. The county returns two members to the provincial parliament, and the townships of Windsor, Falmouth, and Newport, each one. The greater part of this county was originally settled by the French, who enclosed the dikes and marsh lands, and brought them into a state of cultivation and improvement, so as to enable them, before their expulsion from the province in 1755, to export wheat and other grain to Boston. After their expulsion their farms and improvements were laid waste and abandoned, until within about the last twenty-five years, when the English became aware of the value of these tracts, and they were granted in extensive lots to the then members of Council, and others.

Windsor township was originally settled by the French, as before mentioned. It is an agreeably diversified county of hill, dale, and lawn. It contains a considerable quantity of marsh and interval land. The climate is considered warmer than either to the north or south of it, and it is well adapted for the growth of wheat and other grain. The orchards originally planted by the French have been improved and extended, and fruit is abundant and good. There is abundance of gypsum found in this township, and it forms a very considerable article of export to the United States. The local scenery is very beautiful, and coming from Halifax, the contrast to the general character of the southern part of that county is striking and remarkable. The river Avon receives the Kennetcook, St. Croix, and Cockmagon, and conducts them to the Minas Basin. The rise and fall of the tide at Windsor is thirty feet, and the bed of the river is at times entirely exposed. The extreme breadth of the river here is about 1000 feet, and it is intended to erect a bridge over it. Windsor town is the shire town of the county. It is situate at the confluence of the St. Croix, and the Avon rises forty-five miles from Halifax; the great mail-road from that place to Annapolis running through it. Windsor contains an university (King's College), an academy, episcopal, Roman catholic, presbyterian, baptist, and methodist churches, a court-house, and county jail. Packets ply between Windsor and St. John's, New Brunswick, and also to Parrsborough, across the Minas Basin, and the mail-coach runs to Halifax and Annapolis three times a week. Windsor is the only town in the county of Hants; there being nothing like a town in any of the other townships.

V KING'S COUNTY

The township of Horton was originally settled by the French, and in it was situated the French village of Minas, of which no traces are now to be seen, except the cellars of the houses, a few old orchards, and the constant appendage of an Acadian settlement, scattered groups of willows. It contains 100,000 acres, and was settled by the English in 1760, with emigrants from New England, who found the dikes much dilapidated, and the meadows under water. After considerable difficulty, delay, and expense, the tide was at length shut out from all the old enclosed lands, by means of embankments. This township has about 4000 acres of diked land, besides interval and salt marshes; and the upland, the hilly and broken, is mostly good tillage land. The only village in the township is Kentville, on the borders of Cornwallis. It contains several good private houses, a court-house, a jail, and a good grammar school. There are one episcopalian, one presbyterian, two baptist, and two methodist churches, in the township, eleven grist mills, two oat-mills, five saw-mills, one flax, and three fulling-mills, and two carding machines. The river Gaspereaux, which flows through the entire township, abounds with salmon, trout, smelts, and the fish called gaspereux.

Cornwallis township lies between Horton and Aylesford, along the Minas Basin and Bay of Fundy. It was settled at the same time with Horton by emigrants from Connecticut. This township is well watered by several rivers, and the land throughout is of the very best quality, every farm having a proportion of dike, meadow, and upland, whereby the farmers are enabled to keep large stocks of cattle. There are numerous and productive orchards; and this township, from its extraordinary fertility, has been styled the garden of the province....

The Minas basin is a large reservoir that receives the waters of nineteen rivers, some of very considerable magnitude, and communicates with the Bay of Fundy by a strait between Partridge Island and Cape Blomedon. The tides rise in this basin higher than in any part of America, and rushing in with extraordinary velocity from the Bay of Fundy, deposit vast quantities of alluvial matter on the shore, whereby those tracts of rich dike and marsh land have been formed, which render the districts surrounding it the most productive, best settled, and populous in Nova Scotia.

VI LUNENBURG COUNTY

The township of Chester was laid out in 1760, and first settled by emigrants from New England, to whom were subsequently added several German families. The land is, in general, covered with spruce and fir timber, well watered, and capable of cultivation.... The principal harbour is Mahone Bay, which is very extensive, and affords secure anchorage inside its numerous islands, to vessels of the greatest magnitude. Chester town is situated on the north side of the bay, about nine miles from its mouth, upon a snug and commodious harbour. It is a very thriving town, and carries on a very considerable lumber trade and fishery. There are seven saw-mills, two grist-mills, and a fulling-mill, in this township, and an episcopal and a baptist church.

Lunenburg township is, next to Halifax, the oldest formed by the English in this province. It was settled in 1753, by 400 families of Dutch and Germans, who were brought out at the expense of the British government, and who received very liberal encouragement and assistance. The settlement continued to prosper, more or less, and in 1791 the population amounted to 3247 souls; since when it has increased both in population and wealth. The harbour of Lunenburg is small but easy of access, and is well sheltered by Cross Island; vessels can lie alongside the wharfs in fourteen feet water. The town of Lunenburg is constructed on a regular plan; it is the shire town, and contains about 250 dwelling-houses, stores, &c. There are a court-house and jail, and four churches, Episcopalian, Lutheran, Calvinist, and Methodist. There is an extensive trade carried on here with the West Indies, Newfoundland and Quebec. Lunenburg is one of the flourishing townships of the province, and although the land is nowhere rich, yet its contiguity to the Halifax market enables the settlers to raise and dispose of any article of produce with advantage.

VII QUEEN'S COUNTY

... The interior of this county is stony, and generally incapable of cultivation. On the sea board it is somewhat better; there are, however, several tracts of better soil, and several thriving settlements.

Liverpool is the shire town of the county. It is surrounded by hills, well watered, and enjoys a pure air. It contains about 250 houses, stores, &c.; a court-house, jail, and three churches, episcopalian, congregational, and methodist; a school-house and block-house. It is one of the best built and most regular county towns in the province, and there is a handsome drawbridge, 1100 feet in length, over the river Mersey. The trade of the place is very flourishing, consisting of the lumber trade and fishery, both Shore and Labrador, and carried on with Europe and the West Indies. The harbour was called by the French Rosignol.

VIII ANNAPOLIS COUNTY

... The first European settlements in Nova Scotia were established by the French in this county, who made some very extensive improvements. After the expulsion of the Acadians, their lands became an object of attention to the people of the British colonies, a considerable number of whom removed thither in 1764, and obtained a grant of the township of Annapolis. This township contains a considerable quantity of valuable dike land; and the upland, though stony, is generally good. Annapolis is the county town. It was founded by the French, who called it Port Royale, and was the capital of the province while in their possession. It was also the seat of the British government until 1750, when it was superseded as such by Halifax. The town is built upon a peninsula, which projecting into the river, forms two beautiful basins, one above and one below the town. It has not much increased in size or population since the conquest of the province, but it is still a respectable town. It contains a government house, a court house, an episcopalian and methodist church, an academy, commodious barracks, and several handsome private buildings. The military works erected at various times for its defence are now in a state of decay. There are several good roads leading to all parts of the province; a stage coach runs through Granville, Wilmot, Aylesford, Cornwallis, Windsor, and Newport, to Halifax; and a steam packet plies constantly to St. John's, New Brunswick. The trade of this town is comparatively insignificant to what it formerly was, business being removed to other more convenient and better circumstanced settlements.

Granville and Wilmot townships comprehend, for 46 miles, the peninsula formed by the river Annapolis, running parallel to the Bay of Fundy. They were granted in 1764 to several New England settlers who came here. The land is of a very superior quality, consisting of dike, salt marle, interval, and upland. The river Annapolis rises in the King's county, and, keeping its course parallel to the Bay of Fundy, runs into and from the harbour of Annapolis, and is navigable up to Bridgetown, in Granville district. This thriving village is situated just at the head of the navigation of the river, and is the place of shipment for the produce of these districts. It contains an episcopalian, a methodist, and a baptist church, some good dwelling-houses, and several stores and shops.... The farms in these townships are in general well cultivated and productive; most of them have orchards; and the cider and cheese made here are equal, if not superior to any in the province....

... The town of Digby is situated on the Basin of Annapolis. It contains about 200 houses, a court-house, and spacious church. The air is salubrious, and the situation agreeable; and it is much frequented in the summer by company from St. John's, to which a steam-packet runs three times a week. The inhabitants of this town and neighbourhood are largely engaged in the cod and mackerel fishery along the coast....

The township of Clare, including the settlement of New Edinburgh, lies between Digby and Yarmouth, in Shelburne county. It is almost exclusively settled by Acadians, the descendants of those who were expelled from this province in 1755, and allowed to return after the peace of 1763; and here those people preserve their distinctive character and customs more especially than any where else in Nova Scotia. This township is in a flourishing condition. Farming, lumber, and the fishery are industriously and extensively carried on. There are several small vessels owned by the inhabitants; they have erected between thirty and forty saw-mills and several grist mills. The whole township forms one parish, and contains two Roman catholic chapels, one of which is a very spacious, handsome place of worship....

The navigation of the Bay of Fundy has been represented as difficult and dangerous; but the experience of years has proved the reverse: for in fact fewer vessels have been lost in it than in any other equal portion of the seas of North America. The tide rises to a great height, sometimes seventy feet, in the bay, and it flows with great rapidity, running at the entrance at the rate of about three miles an hour, and increasing as it advances to more than seven, and at length rushing with impetuosity into the Minas Basin and Chignecto Bay. This rise and flow of the tide considerably aids the navigation both in and out of the bay. On the Nova Scotia side there are few or no ports from Minas Basin to Annapolis; but from thence to the entrance, and round to the Atlantic, there are several places affording anchorage and shelter.

IX SHELBURNE COUNTY

... The whole of the interior of this county remains, with few exceptions, in a wilderness state. In some places it is well wooded, and the soil of a good quality. The whole population is settled on the sea coast, where the best land is found....

... [Shelburne township] was subsequently [after a failed attempt c. 1764] settled by American loyalists, 500 families of whom: arrived here in 1783, and the number was subsequently very much increased. They erected the extensive town of Shelburne, on the harbour of that name. This town arose with astonishing rapidity, and in the course of a year its population was not less than 12,000. Its decline was almost as rapid: owing to many and insurmountable combining circumstances, it began immediately to decay, and now is in a most deserted and dilapidated state. The harbour of Shelburne is esteemed one of the best in America; it is twelve miles in length, easy of access, and perfectly secure, affording anchorage for ships of the heaviest burthen....

... The Acadians had several small settlements in [Yarmouth Township]; after their expulsion the township was granted, in 1767, to settlers from New England. It has always maintained a steady state of improvement, and promises, from its various local advantages, to become a place of considerable importance. The inhabitants are industrious and enterprising, and carry on a trade of some consequence both with England and the West Indies. There are in the township a court-house and a jail, four churches of several denominations, eighteen small school-houses, fourteen grist-mills, and upwards of 700 dwelling-houses. Yarmouth village and Melton are classed among the towns of the province. Yarmouth contains about 100 dwelling-houses, and there are nine trading establishments. Melton contains about thirty houses....

... [Shelburne is] the only county in the province in which the population has not increased [between 1817 and 1827]; a circumstance attributable, not to the want of a due natural increase in the resident population, but to be ascribed to emigration, the greater part of the settlers in and about the town of Shelburne having removed from that place.
(Bouchette, *The British Dominions* 1831, 2:11–42)

c) Isle of Sable

Sable Island, or *Isle aux Sables,* although distant eighty-five miles from Nova Scotia, is considered as belonging to that province.... it is about

thirty miles in length and fifteen in breadth. It consists entirely of an
accumulation of loose white sand, utterly barren, producing neither tree
nor shrub. It lies in the direct track of vessels hound to and from Europe,
and upon it very many have been wrecked, and numerous lives lost. An
establishment was formed in 1804 upon this island for the purpose of
assisting persons wrecked: it consists of a superintendant and about ten
assistants, who constantly reside on the island, and have in charge a competent supply of such articles as would be useful in cases of shipwreck.
The establishment was maintained by the province of Nova Scotia from
1804 to 1827 at an annual expense of about 500*l.*; but in the latter year
the British government undertook to add a further sum equal to that
voted by the province, whereby the establishment has been enlarged, and
its usefulness very much increased. The superintendant and his assistants
continually perambulate the island. There are several signal-posts and
flag-staffs to direct vessels, and huts to shelter the sufferers. The island
is regularly visited to convey supplies, and bring away those who may
have been thrown upon its shores. The supply of stores and provisions
is always abundant, so that 300 persons at once upon the island have
been liberally subsisted and supplied with all necessaries. There never
were any inhabitants on the island but those connected with the establishment. The only native animals to be met with are some wild horses,
whose flesh has been occasionally found a providential substitute for
better food; a few seals are caught upon the shore. The coast is exceedingly dangerous, and almost every where surrounded with breakers.

(Bouchette, *The British Dominions* 1831, 2:54–67, 72)

6 CAPE BRETON

⌐ Cape Breton was a separate colony until 1820, when it was joined
to Nova Scotia for reasons of administrative economy. Bouchette
describes it by itself. ⌐

a) Situation – Extent – Divisions – Harbours – Soil – Settlements

The island of Cape Breton constitutes a county of the province of Nova
Scotia. Its extent is equal to about one-fourth of that of Nova Scotia
Proper.... It is distant from the south-western extremity of Newfound-
land about sixteen leagues, and is divided from Nova Scotia by St.
George's Bay and the Gut of Canseau, twenty-one miles in length, and
varying from one mile to one and a half in width. Its shape is nearly

triangular, indented with many deep bays, and nearly separated by the waters of the Bras d'Or into two natural divisions; the one to the north being high, bold, and steep; the other to the south, low, and intersected by water; diversified with moderate elevations, and gradually rising from the interior shore of the Bras d'Or, until it presents abrupt cliffs towards the ocean. There are not any mountains, properly so called, in the island; the highest ridges in the southern division do not perhaps exceed an altitude of 600 feet. The highlands in the northern division are more elevated, bolder, and continuous; but even there the supposed highest point, Smoky Cape, does not probably exceed five hundred yards....

The Bras d'Or is a vast internal sea, occupying a considerable portion of the area of Cape Breton, intersecting with its numerous arms every part of it, and dividing it almost into two islands.... From the entrance of the Great Bras d'Or to the head of the Great Lake at St. Peter's is above fifty miles in a straight course, and its greatest width about twenty miles. The depth varies from twelve to sixty fathoms, and it is every where secure and navigable. This extensive sheet of internal waters is of peculiar advantage to the island, for, exclusive of the fishery, which is carried on there to a considerable extent, it spreads out into such an extensive and ramified navigation, as to afford every part of the island the benefit of water communication, and enables every district, almost every farm, to ship its own produce without the intervention of land carriage.

The Isthmus of St. Peter, which divides the waters of the Bras d'Or from the Atlantic Ocean at St. Peter's Bay, is so narrow that a canal could be easily made between the two waters for ship navigation. The ground has been examined and surveyed by an eminent engineer, who has reported upon the complete practicability of such a work, and has estimated the expense at no more than 17,150*l*. The whole length of the canal required would not exceed 3,000 feet. The principal part of the expense would be the necessary works at the points of communication with both seas.

The soil of Cape Breton is considered quite equal to that of Nova Scotia, or any of the neighbouring countries. There is no dike land, such as is found in Nova Scotia, but the upland is of an excellent quality, and very productive....

Sydney is the shire town and capital of the island, and a free port. It is situated on the harbour of that name, on the eastern coast of the southern division of the island. The courts of justice and public offices are kept here, and here also the principal officers of the island reside. It contains about sixty houses, besides a government-house, government stores and barracks, a court-house; likewise episcopal, Roman catholic, and dissenting churches. The streets are regularly laid out, the houses tolerably good, and the grounds in the vicinity cultivated with some taste, so that on the whole it presents a pleasing appearance. The population is about 500 souls.... The surrounding country is one of the finest agricultural tracts in the island: the advantages for carrying on the fishery are excellent. The principal coal-works are carried on in the neighbourhood, where useful timber abounds. The vicinity of these works must eventually render Sydney a place of considerable importance.

All the settlements in Cape Breton have been made on the shores of the Atlantic, of the Gulf, and of the Bras do'Or. None have as yet been made to any considerable distance in the interior; and all the points on those shores fit for settlement are occupied. The line of coast from the Bras d'Or to Cow Bay may be called the coal coast, the whole range being faced with cliffs streaked lvith veins of that mineral....

... The once famed harbour of Louisburg is utterly deserted; although capacious and secure, no settlement has been made upon it since the destruction of the town; and what was once, if not the largest, certainly the most splendid town of La Nouvelle France, is now without an inhabitant....

The Isle Madame, separated from the main land of Cape Breton by St. Peter's Bay and Lennox Passage, is about sixteen miles in length and five in breadth, indented with numerous harbours, and possessing a tolerably good soil. It is situated near to the Atlantic side of the Gut of Canseau, and peculiarly calculated for prosecuting the fishery. The principal port is Arichat, now, and for many years past, the seat and centre of the fishing establishments of the Jersey merchants, who export their produce hence to the West Indies, the Mediterranean, and the Brazils. It is a fine harbour, accessible at all times. The town is situate on the harbour, and is fast increasing in size, appearance, and population, and is the most important commercial port of Cape Breton.

The Bras d'Or shore of the southern division of the island is settled more or less along its whole length, commencing at that part of the Grand Lake called St. George's Channel, and bending round to St. Peter's; there are settlements every where, principally composed of Scottish highlanders, formed at various periods since 1800; ...

The northern natural division of the island commences at Ship Harbour, on the Gut of Canseau, from which to Port Hood there is no considerable harbour, although there are several inlets. The land on the whole of this coast is good, and thickly settled by Scottish emigrants, who have extended themselves four or five miles inland all the way, and are employed in agriculture. Port Hood is a spacious, safe harbour, fit for the largest vessels, and is the most important place in the northern division. The courts, &c. are held here, and it carries on a considerable trade in agricultural produce to Newfoundland. From Port Hood to Marguerite, on the Gulf Shore, the same line of Scottish agricultural settlements continues upwards of thirty miles along shore, and extends some distance back towards the interior. These form the largest series of continued settlements in the island. The coast is high and bold; there are no harbours except that of Mabou, which admits only small vessels. Lake Marguerite lies between the Gulf Shore and the Bras d'Or, from which Salmon River runs into Port Marguerite. The land on both sides of this river for several miles, and along the coast northward for sixteen miles more, as far as Chetecan, the most northern settlement on this shore, is entirely settled by Acadians. These people, although necessarily agricultural, still devote much attention to the fishery. There is a considerable village at Marguerite, and the Jersey markets have an establishment at Chetican, in both of which places a considerable trade is carried on....

The island of Cape Breton, forming the eastern barrier of the gulf of St. Lawrence, commands the usual, and indeed (with the exception of the circuitous route of the Straits of Belleisle) the only access from the Atlantic by the Gut of Canseau on the south, and the passage 'between this island and Newfoundland on the north. It is, in fact, from its relative situation, the key of the Gulf of St. Lawrence; and being provided with excellent harbours, the naval power in possession of it will be the arbiters of the commerce of the Canadas, Prince Edward Island, and all the coast bounding that gulf.

(Bouchette, *The British Dominion*, 1831, 2:73–81)

b) Mines – Resources – Population

The coal found in Cape Breton is of the best quality; a specimen has been carefully analysed, and found to contain only three-quarters of an unit per cent. of extraneous substance. Coal is traced in the western part of the island, on Inhabitants River, at Port Hood, and at Mabou. This field has never been worked or examined, but the indications are decided and numerous. The eastern, or Sydney coal field, is very extensive: it commences at Miray Bay, and follows the course of the shore all round to the Great Bras d'Or, being in length about forty miles, and averaging five miles in width. From a minute calculation, after deducting harbours, bays, and all other interpositions, it appears that there are 120 square miles of land containing available veins of coal. It is supposed the veins in many places run out into the sea ten miles from the shore. There are fourteen distinct veins, one over another, varying from three to eleven feet in thickness; and there are extensive works now carried on at Sydney Harbour and at Lingan by the lessees of the late Duke of York, Messrs. Rundell and Bridge....

The natural riches of this island seem to consist preeminently in its fisheries. There is no place along the coasts of America, with the exception of Newfoundland, where the fish is so abundant and so good, or which is so well adapted for taking and curing it. The fish, consisting of those varieties taken in Newfoundland-cod, herrings, mackarel, &c. swarm on the whole coast, and in all the harbours, exterior and interior. In fact, every farmer and settler in Cape Breton may, and in general does, become as much a fisherman as an agriculturist, uniting the two profitable occupations, drawing wealth alike from the land and the ocean....

... The number of the inhabitants has been lately estimated as high as 30,000: in 1814 it was, upon a census taken that year, rated at 8,000: it therefore appears to have more than trebled itself in about sixteen years.

(Bouchette, *The British Dominions*, 1831, 2:83–5)

7 NEW BRUNSWICK

Bouchette states that natural features, particularly linear ridges, have been useful in devising regional divisions in British North America but not in New Brunswick. In this colony, major rivers and coastlines will be used to organize the description of settlement and development.

Right from the start Bouchette's language in extolling resources is extravagant. He begins his regional description with the Saint John River, following the stream from its headwaters down to the city of Saint John. In descending the river he notes a transition in landscape from the sublime to the picturesque. Bouchette then describes the districts behind the Fundy coast to the west and east of Saint John. The Bend, located on the Peticodiac River, is now the city of Moncton. In describing northern and eastern New Brunswick, Bouchette says it will not be necessary to adhere to administrative divisions, once more indicating his acute awareness of the problem of devising effective regional divisions for geographical study. To Bouchette New Brunswick's forests comprise a vast "almost inexhaustible" resource.

*a) The Territory on the Banks of St. John's – Madawaska Settlements
– York – Sunbury – Queen's County – King's – St. John's City and
County – Harbours, Roads*

In surveying this extensive and important portion of the British dominions, we are not guided by any of those continuous ridges of elevated
land, by which nature itself separates one district from another, and
which have divided and regulated some of our former descriptions. It is
not less remarkable for all those grand features which stamp and characterize the operations of nature in this quarter of the globe, amongst them
comprising many towering heights and precipitous elevations, but these
being isolated and detached, rather claim our attention as they occur in
following another species of division, than of themselves direct us in our
general view of the province....

In common with every portion of those regions, the province enjoys
that grand advantage and distinguishing feature, abundant irrigation and
water communication; not a section of it but is traversed and intersected
by almost innumerable streams, whilst the greater rivers form accessible
channels of intercourse from its heart to its extremities, and into the
interior of the adjacent provinces; and bounded almost on two-thirds of
its circumference by the ocean, it invites the commerce of the world. Vast
plains, principally covered by immense forests of timber trees, forming
in the early stages of colonization an important article of commerce,
and indicating the richness and fertility of the soil, occupy the intervals
between the scattered settlements; whilst the prosperous and flourishing appearance of the latter seem prodigal inducements to colonists to
occupy the tracts of valuable land courting their acceptance.

The general face of the country may be described as composed of bold
undulations, sometimes swelling into the height of mountains, and again
subsiding to vale and lowlands, principally covered by noble forests,
not so dense as to be inaccessible, diversified by occasional swamps,
and tracts of level, settled, and cultivated country. The banks of the
larger rivers for the most part disclose a country of the latter description, though in some places they are enclosed by lofty and precipitous
rocks; whilst the abundance of inferior streams produces frequent slips
or spaces of what is termed interval, which, overflowed by these during
the wet season, become, at stated intervals, distinguished by extreme
fertility. The borders of the rivers and the islets with which they abound
furnishing extensive tracts of pasture, and flourishing crops of Indian
and European corn, attest on multitudinous chosen spots the diligence

of the husbandman, the general adaptation of the soil to the most profitable uses of agriculture....

As the principal settlements of this province are on the banks of the
great rivers, and as, of these, the St. John's in every respect claims the
pre-eminence, we shall, in our further account, trace the course of this
river, noticing in succession the counties through which it flows, the
towns, villages, and settlements on its banks, with all the other par-
ticulars of such counties as claim attention, and afterwards proceed to
describe every other noticeable feature of the province, and the parts not
comprised in our view of this most important tract.

This river intersects the province in or near latitude 47° north, and
winds through it in something like a regular semicircle of about 220
miles in length, falling into the Bay of Fundy, in lat. 45° 20' north....

Beginning then at the north-western extremity of the province, ...

The Madawaska settlement is chiefly composed of French Acadians,
formerly settled in the neighbourhood of Frederickton, whither they had
been located by the British Government; but the tenure of their lands
being little better than sufferance, when it became desirable to locate the
American loyalists and the disbanded soldiers of the American war, they
were dispossessed by the government of Nova Scotia; and after the separation of the provinces, invested by the government of New Brunswick
with the lands they now hold at Madawaska, as a compensation. This
settlement, though considered within the boundary of Lower Canada,
has always been subject to the jurisdiction of the government of New
Brunswick, being contiguous to the latter province, whilst it was, till
lately, separated by an almost impenetrable barrier of wilderness from
the former. The land on both sides of the river here is exceedingly fertile,
and well adapted to the growth of wheat, which is assiduously cultivated
by the inhabitants, who, after grinding it into flour, send considerable
quantities to the market of Frederickton, where it meets with a ready
sale, at an abundantly remunerating price.

Continuing its south-easterly course, the St. John's receives, a few
miles below this settlement, the waters of the Grand River, which flows
from the northern extremity of the county of York; and at the distance
of about forty miles below this settlement are the Grand Falls. A sudden
turn of the river, forming a little bay a few rods above the cataract, offers
a safe and commodious landing-place for boats; immediately below this
the river rushes with great fury over. a rocky bed, till it is suddenly narrowed by the projection of the rocks.; from the western side it rolls with
irresistible impetuosity over their ledges, and is precipitated in a perpen-

dicular line forty-five feet into a narrow basin of pointed rocks, amidst which it foams and rages till it escapes through a narrow rocky channel, over a series of declivities half a mile in continuance, enclosed on each side by craggy cliffs, overhanging its course, and almost completely intercepting the view. Below the whole series of cascades is another small bay, in which are collected such timbers as have been committed to the falls; for though the trees are sometimes ground to powder in the whirling abyss, or are sometimes tapered to a point, and frequently broken, yet the great saving of labour induces many to incur this risk, rather than drag their weighty commodities over a distance of 100 rods of hilly portage. This bay is the station where all boats proceeding up the river stop and commence the portage. From St. John's. to this place flat-bottomed boats of twenty tons burden ascend, but above the falls no craft larger than canoes is used. A mile below this landing-place commences a succession of rapids, whirling in a narrow bed amidst craggy rocks.

The river then takes a course, with some involutions, nearly due south, bounded on either side by precipitous eminences or dense forests, whose solemn gloom has not yet been cheered by the busy hand of man. Here is an abundant and inviting field for new settlements to an immense extent; for whilst the growth of timber proves the fertility of the land, the vicinity of the river affords a ready intercourse with the capital of the province, and the situation being on the direct road from St. John's to Quebec renders a constant communication through it inevitable – advantages which are constantly attracting new settlers, and hence tending to a rapidly progressive amelioration.

About ten miles below the falls, on the eastern side, is the mouth of the Salmon River, and twenty miles lower still that of the Tobique River, which extending by a chain of lakes and inferior streams from the immediate neighbourhood of the source of the south-west branch of the Miramichi, to which there is a portage, constitutes a communication entirely across the breadth of the province from west to east, from the St. John's to the Gulf of St. Lawrence. The whole of the banks of this river are composed of good land, producing great quantities of the red pine, and affording fine slips of interval, whilst the islets in the river are most favourable for agriculture. A little above the mouth of the Tobique, on the opposite or western side, the St. John's receives the waters of the Ristook or Aroostook River, flowing from the interior of the state of Maine. The whole course of this river is considered to fall within the United States; there are, nevertheless, many British settlers on its banks, who are not restrained by this consideration from felling the timber....

We now reach Woodstock on the western bank.... It is here that the more grand and sublime features of the scenery of the St. John soften into the beautiful and the picturesque. The towering and abrupt eminences, the precipitous crags, the darksome and unpenetrated forests here open into smiling plains and cultivated farms; and the numerous beauties which nature has lavished on the scene, heightened by the hand of art, enrich the landscape with the cheering prospect of human comfort and prosperity. The land on both sides of the river is here well cultivated, whilst the numerous islands that stud its surface yield large quantities of hay. From this place to St. John's the river is navigable for rafts of all kinds of timber, here produced in almost inexhaustible profusion; and though the rapids may occasion some little addition to the labour, they offer no danger either to rafts or boats going down to the sea....

Although the present settlements are principally confined to the banks of the river – a situation invariably chosen by early settlers – they comprise a vast extent of country stretching westward and northward to the American line, the whole of which has been ascertained by explorers, as well from the quality of the timber it produces, as from other circumstances, to be equal in quality of soil to that already cultivated. The woods are open and easily traversable....

We have now arrived at Frederickton, the seat of government and capital of the province, situated on the west side of the river, which again takes a more southerly direction, in latitude 45° 57' north, 66° 46' longitude west, and eighty-five miles distant from the sea-coast at St. John's. The situation of the town is peculiarly favourable, being on a flat fronting the river, which is here three-quarters of a mile wide, and, making an elbow, encloses the town on two sides, whilst on the land side the plain is likewise enclosed by a chain of hills, and opposite to it the Nashwak rolls its broad stream into the St. John's. To this point the river is navigable for vessels of fifty tons, and the town hence becomes the chief entrepôt of commerce with the interior, receiving and distributing large quantities of British merchandise, whilst the timber and lumber from the upper district are here collected before they are floated down to St. John's for exportation. The town is laid out in blocks of a quarter of an acre square, of which there are eighteen. The streets are disposed rectangularly, some of them being a mile in length, and for the most part continuously built, though the houses are chiefly of wood and of very irregular heights. The public buildings consist of the province hall, where the Provincial Assembly and Courts of Justice assemble; the offices of the surveyor-general and secretary of the province; the barracks, with adjacent storehouses; the county court-house, which is also the market; one church; three chapels for baptists, methodists, and catholics; a gaol; and a meeting-house of the kirk of Scotland. 'fo these have recently been added a handsome college.... The public institutions of Frederickton are a public library, a savings' bank, the Frederickton Emigrant Society, the New Brunswick Agricultural and Emigrant Society, a branch of the Society for promoting Christian Knowledge, the Bible Association of the city and its vicinity, and a branch of the Methodist Missionary Society.

The town is surrounded by a level plot of lowland extending over a surface of about four miles by two, on the sides not immediately bordering upon the river. It was founded by Sir Guy Carleton in 1785, shortly after the erection of New Brunswick in to a separate province. It forms an admirable central depot for military stores, being eighty-five miles from St. John's, ninety from St. Andrew's, about as distant from Northumberland, 140 west of Fort Cumberland in Westmoreland, and from the upper settlement at Madawaska, about the same distance....

The Grand Lake, a conspicuous feature of this district, is situated in the parish of Waterborough; it is about thirty miles long and three miles broad, and its entrance lies at Jemseg, opposite to Gagetown. At this port is a depot of provisions for the accommodation of troops passing betwixt Frederickton and Fort Cumberland. On this lake and on the two creeks, named respectively Coal Creek and Newcastle, both emptying themselves into its basin, are extensive veins of coal, lying a few feet above the level of the water, and running horizontally and parallel thereto; they are worked by mines, and considerable quantities consumed by blacksmiths and other manufacturers, but they are not found to burn well in grates....

... [Farther south, located on the north-east side of the St. John River, are the parishes of Sussex, Norton, and Hampton]: the two former are traversed in their whole length by the Kennebecasis, which takes its source amidst the highlands that bound Sussex Vale, in the immediate neighbourhood of the source of the Petcondiac. Hampton is likewise intersected by the Hammond River and its various branches, till it loses itself in Darling Lake, communicating with the spacious estuary of the Kennebecasis. But perhaps no part of this tract of country has exhibited a more rapid improvement, or can boast a more substantial degree of prosperity, than the parish of Sussex. A few years back, and it was the most forlorn and dreary part of a vast desert, exhibiting no other marks of the hand of man but the trunks of enormous pines encumbering the ground, blackened by fire, and lying in heaps: persevering and active industry have now transformed it into a lovely and luxuriant valley, smiling with abundant harvests and rich pastures; numerous houses, barns, and other domestic establishments attest the prosperity of the inhabitants, whilst their roads, bridges, and public works evince their public spirit. At Sussex Vale is a decent church, erected by the inhabitants without any assistance from government; also a handsome academy for the purpose of civilizing and educating a certain number of Indians. The River Kennebecasisis navigable twenty miles for vessels of any burden, thirty miles for vessels drawing seven feet water, and thirty miles more for flat-bottomed boats....

The city of St. John is situated on a peninsula projecting into the harbour, at the mouth of the river of the same name.... It stands on rugged, rocky, and uneven plots of ground, the general character of that in its vicinity, and contains about 700 houses. The streets are laid out at right angles, and in many parts display fine ranges of building, which are now principally of brick. Considerable pains have also been taken to level and smooth the rugged rocky surface, so that there is now a good carriage road through most parts of the city, though it occasionally is carried up rather steep ascents. The city is divided into what are called the upper and lower coves by a projecting rock, the latter of which is the more backward in improvement; government however, by building a new range of barracks on the point, have materially contributed to better its appearance. The principal of the wharfs and warehouses are situated in the upper part of the city, where consequently the traffic is most considerable....

"A square near York Point, reserved for a market, has an old building in the centre, the upper part of which has served for many years as a court-house, and the under part as a flesh-market; a fish and vegetable market having been lately built contiguous to it, at the edge of high-water mark, and a handsome flesh-market in the lower cove, which are well supplied. King's-square is situated on the height of land in King-street, and is reserved for public use. It is a very pleasant situation, commanding a fine view of the city and harbour. It is in contemplation to erect a court-house on the east side of this square, on a liberal scale. Queen's-square is situated in Duke's Ward, and is also reserved for public purposes." ...

"The corporation have at their disposal an annual revenue of about £2000 for the improvement of the city. It must, however, be observed, that no great. attention has yet been paid to ornamenting the city. A few seats have, however, lately been begun on the marsh near the city, which will soon make an alteration in the appearance of the suburbs [Quoted from "Sketches of New Brunswick, &c. By an Inhabitant of the Province. St. John, 1825."]

The port of St. John, the principal harbour in this county, and indeed on the whole line of coast, is convenient and safe, and sufficiently deep and spacious to accommodate a considerable number of vessels.... The ebb and flow of the tide in this harbour is from sixteen to twenty-four feet perpendicular; and one of its most important advantages is, that in the most severe winter it is free from the encumbrance of ice.

The imports into this city consist chiefly of British manufactures and colonial produce; the exports, lumber, fish, furs, lime, with which the rock forming the basis of the town abounds, masts, spars, and other timber, in such proportions as are pointed out in another part of our account of the province....

... The city of St. John's is plentifully supplied from the adjacent counties with all kinds of butchers' meat, vegetables, fruit, poultry, and wood during the summer months, and before the formation of the ice, and whilst it is sufficiently formed to afford a means of communication; during the spring months the supply is less abundant. Fish is generally rather scarce....

Abundant as are the water communications throughout the vast tract of country we have now traced, viz. the whole course of the St. John's from Lower Canada to the Bay of Fundy, there are likewise roads wherever a chain of settlements has shown the expediency of communication between one place and another. It cannot be said, however, that these roads are continually efficient, or can be calculated on as a constant practicable mode of conveyance. Few of them are passable for carriages for any continuous distances, and at many seasons of the year they are totally untraversable. The principal causes of these deficiencies are the facilities of water-carriage; but the roadways are cleared and the foundations laid, and as the population of the settlements increases, they must, for mutual accommodation, be progressively perfected. The most important of these, perhaps, is the post road from Nova Scotia to Canada, which traverses this province diagonally from the city of St. John, and nearly parallel to the river. This road, which runs on the western side of the river, is passable for carriages as far as fourteen miles above Frederickton, to which place the distance is eighty-two and a half miles: but it is only in summer that it is practicable; in spring and autumn it is very wet, and in winter the only mode of communication is by the ice on the river. From Frederickton to the Great Falls is passable only for foot-passengers....

Almost all the great streams have, in like manner, a road running near and nearly parallel to them, which usually joins with the road of the nearest river on any great line of communication. Such is that which, running side by side with the Nashwak River, joins the road of the south-west branch of the Miramichi, thus forming a line of communication from Frederickton to Miramichi Bay in the Gulf of St. Lawrence; also that which, skirting the Kennebecasis in its whole course, communicates with that which accompanies the channel of the Petcondiac. A like road attends the course of the Oromocto; and in fact there is no chain of settlements in any part of this tract which has not a similar mode of communication, accompanying and supplying the deficiencies of those water channels, which are a preferable medium for the transportation of heavy merchandise.

(Bouchette, *The British Dominion*, 1831, 2:93–122)

b) *Charlotte County – Campo Bello – Grand Manan and Deer Islands – Westmoreland, and the remaining Counties*

Turning to the westward from the St. John, on the southern boundary of the province, we come to Charlotte County, which is bounded .... south by the Bay of Fundy and Passamaquoddy Bay, and west by the St. Croix, which separates it from the United States.... St. Andrew's .... is the shire town. It is situated at the north-eastern extremity of Passamaquoddy Bay, on a narrow slip of lowland fronting on the bay, at the distance of sixty miles from St. John's, and three from the American shores. In its rear rises a range of highlands; its two principal streets run parallel to each other the whole length of the town on its water front, and are intersected by several others crossing them at right angles. They are almost entirely built up with substantial houses of decent appearance. It has a church of the regular establishment, and one of the kirk of Scotland, ... There are also a court-house, a gaol, a grammar-school, and many handsome private buildings. There is a chamber of commerce, an Agricultural and Emigrant Society for the county, a savings' bank, and a Bible Society; also barracks and commissariat stores.... It is conveniently situated for commerce, and especially for the fishing-trade, which is carried on here to a large extent, for which the neighbouring islands afford many facilities, and abundant supplies of cod, haddock, &c. are yielded by the adjacent waters. The lumber trade is also actively prosecuted here, and ship-building carried on to a considerable extent....

[Westmoreland County, east of the St. John River] was originally settled by French Acadians, whose descendants are still numerous, strongly reinforced by steady and industrious settlers from England, who apply to farming with perseverance and intelligence. The produce in corn is very considerable, as likewise in hay; but the most profitable product of the county is the rearing of stock, for which the extensive tracts of diked salt marsh afford immense advantage. Very considerable quantities of butter and cheese are produced here and exported, and during the American war from 800 to 900 head of fat cattle, and above 800 firkins of butter, were annually sent to Halifax. The River Petcondiac, rising at the-western extremity of the county, traverses about one half of its extent eastward, then making almost a right angle, flows in a course nearly southerly till it empties itself into Shepody Bay, an indentation from the Bay of Chignecto, thus flowing through the very heart of the county. The land on both sides of this river, especially on the northern and eastern sides, in the district termed the Bend, has been reported by Colonel Cockburn to the emigration committee of the House of Commons to be fit for the highest and most profitable purposes of agriculture.

"The land about the Bend in Petcondiac River (for so the place is called) was for a long time considered of inferior quality, and was thereby prevented from being settled as soon and as thickly as might have been expected. The importance of the situation, however, at last brought it into repute, and the soil now proves to be as productive as any in the province. The number of houses that have lately been erected give it the appearance of a town [Moncton]; and although no regular village has been laid out, there is already some difficulty and much expense in procuring a space sufficient for a building-lot. This place stands on an isthmus through which place the land communication between Nova Scotia and all parts of New Brunswick and the Canadas does and must continue to pass. The distance from it to the Gulf of St. Lawrence, at Shediac, is only sixteen miles; to the Bay of Fundy, either by land or water, twenty; the river being navigable so far up for schooners of the largest class, and the road to Halifax good for any description of carriages the whole way. With such advantages of situation, the settlements at the Bend of Petcondiac cannot fail of rapidly increasing in population and importance." ...

... Besides its agricultural produce, one part of the wealth of this county arises from the immense supply of grindstones furnished by some of the rocky districts, especially the Shepody mountains, near the shores of the Bay of Fundy, of which as many as 20,000 have been exported in one year to the United States. There is little of the bustle of trade in this county, but it is steadily progressing to prosperity by the certain though slower advance of agricultural improvement.

The harbours are not numerous, and the coast on the Bay of Fundy is for the most part rocky. The tide of the Bay of Fundy towards its head is remarked by that peculiar phenomenon termed the Roar, by which the receded waters seem to accumulate without advancing, till the waves attain a considerable perpendicular height, when they rush forward with an incredible velocity and irresistible force, their roaring noise striking terror even in the animals near the shore, who fly to the highlands in awe.

Along the whole extent of coast, from Fort Cumberland to Cape Chignecto. and thence to Cape Enrage, the spring tides rise from forty-five to fifty-five feet, whilst in Bay Verte, on the other side the isthmus, the common tides are from eight to ten feet perpendicular only. At a place called the Joggin, about fifteen miles from Fort Cumberland, is found abundance of coals. The breed of horses and cattle has been most sedulously improved by numerous settlers from Yorkshire in England....

Turning now to the more northerly region of this extensive province, we have to contemplate the tract hitherto composing the county of Northumberland, which embraces more than one third of the whole province.... In contemplating this vast section of the province, exceeding in the aggregate 10,300 square miles, the mind is struck no less by its extent than by the number and grandeur of the rivers by which it is watered, and the length of coast it occupies. Of the rivers, the Miramichi, opening into a spacious bay of the Gulf of St. Lawrence, and stretching through the county to its south-western extremity, and communicating by easy portages with the St. John, is the most remarkable.... It is navigable for large ships for more than thirty miles.... Near the sea the land is low, and covered only with dwarf trees; but as we advance into the country, we soon find tracts of heavy timber....

... The whole tract abounds with timber of the most valuable description – white and red pine, birch, spruce, hemlock; and maple, which the numerous streams afford the most easy and commodious means of forwarding to the market the seaboard. The soil, as is attested by the quality of the timber; is of the best description, and the frequency of the streams leaves. numerous valuable slips of interval; yet, not withstanding these advantages, these counties are the thinnest settled and the worst cultivated in the whole province. There is scarcely any collection of houses worthy the name of a town in any of them; the port of Miramichi, the settlement of Chatham on the southern side of the river, and that of Newcastle on the north, are the principal.... Though many wealthy merchants are settled at both these places, and each possesses a church, court-house, gaol, &c., there is nothing that can accord with the expectations that would naturally be formed from the immense resources of the country. The whole of this desolation is probably accounted for by the temptation which the lumber and timber trades furnish to the new settler, especially if possessed of any capital. These counties produce in profusion the finest timber of America, and the convenience of transportation operates as a further inducement to settlers to confine their cares to this branch of labour and commerce; and there is no doubt but the preference given to this pursuit has materially retarded the improvement of the province generally. Originally the Americans were permitted to act at pleasure in the forests of the Miramichi – the privilege has since been confined to British subjects; but the consequence is that the finest of the timber has been destroyed, and the persons so engaged maintaining no interest in the country have wholly neglected to take any steps towards its improvement. The prospect of an immediate return still attracts persons of small capital to embark in the lumber trade, but many have been ruined by that trade in the province of New Brunswick, whilst hundreds have been gradually advancing to certain independence and prosperity by a steady attention to agriculture. The quantities of timber that have been felled, squared, and exported from this part of the colony are enormous, and yet no one presents so few symptoms of improvement. The pursuit of lumbering (perhaps a necessary evil in colonizing a wilderness) seems indeed of a demoralizing tendency, sometimes depriving its followers of the inclination and even capability for consistent and steady industry....

At Caraquette, near the western [*sic*, eastern] extremity of the Bay of Chaleurs, (so named by the French navigator Cartier, from the excessive heat he experienced there), there is a pleasant village, with a church, the inhabitants of which are descendants of the Acadians, with some admixture of Indian alloy. The land about it is good, but their principal subsistence is fishing. Along the eastern shore from Miramichi north to the Bay, the land is low, and but thinly settled, and ill cultivated, the inhabitants dividing their attention between agriculture, fishing, and hewing timber. The same remark will apply pretty generally to the whole northern shore of the province along the Bay of Chaleurs, and the Ristigouche. The small settlements along their banks having been formerly principally engaged in fishing, but which they now seem disposed to abandon, for the sake of the timber trade.

An improvement which has been long in contemplation, which was strenuously urged by Colonel Cockburn, and is now in active progress, cannot but very materially assist the advancement of this county. This is the new road from Halifax to Canada, along the eastern portion of the province, from the head of the Bay of Fundy, through Westmoreland, on the bank of the Peticoudiac River, through the county of Northumberland to Chatham, across the smaller branch of the Miramichi, and thence by Newcastle and Bathurst, on the banks of the Ristigouche, till it joins the Kempt road at Matapediac, most desirable in every point of view, both as a shorter and safer communication between Halifax and Canada, and as establishing a line of communication through a chain of the most fertile settlements in the province of New Brunswick. There is not the slightest doubt that this important advantage will more than any thing contribute to the rapid improvement of the hitherto too much neglected county of Northumberland.

(Bouchette, *The British Dominions*, 1831, 2:123–38)

c) General Remarks

Having thus cursorily traversed the several departments of this province in detail, we will proceed to a few general remarks on its resources and capabilities. We use the term cursorily, because, when all the information we have given is compared with the immense extent of the domain, it may appear meager and unsatisfactory; but throughout this vast expanse of territory, the resting places (if we may use the term), or particular points requiring local description are comparatively so few, as to give to any account of it a vague and sketchy appearance. Great as is its extent, and almost incalculable as are its resources, so small a portion of the former has been appropriated, and so little of the latter called into action, that it may almost yet be termed a vast wilderness. Enough however has been seen, and done, and acted on, to convince us of its immense value as a possession, of the advantages it enjoys as a field of colonization, and the probabilities of its becoming as fruitful, populous, wealthy, and happy a portion of the British Empire, as any that art, perseverance, industry, and policy have rescued from the dominion of desolation and barbarism. New Brunswick, after all that has been hitherto done towards reclaiming and settling it, may still be considered as a vast forest; but then it is a forest possessing such advantages, its present wild luxuriance bearing such strong testimony to its fertility, its great extent of coast and abundance of harbours so inviting to commerce, its multiplicity of navigable streams affording ready access to its very heart, furnishing such facilities of intercourse, and its intersection in every direction by chains of settlement and civilization, giving at once an earnest of what may be done and an assistance to the doing of it, as may convince all those who have the hardihood to tax the productiveness of nature for subsistence, and to subdue her ruggedness to the sagacity and industry of man, that nowhere can a more profuse reward, a more certain and profitable result, be promised to their perseverance. The immense tracts of country covered by forest trees may, to those who have been used to the beaten paths of society and civilization, convey an appalling idea of gloomy desolation, but yet they possess such features of romantic grandeur and picturesque beauty, as cannot fail to raise in every mind at all tinctured with the love of Nature's charms, emotions of the liveliest admiration and delight....

... These very forests too furnish the first and most practicable source of wealth to the settler; for though they must needs be felled before he can apply himself to the only certain and permanent source of subsistence, the actual tillage of the ground, the valuable timber they afford, is the most tempting, because the earliest available fund of remuneration. It has another recommendation too, it is a fund almost inexhaustible; for centuries has the axe of the woodman pursued its prostrating course in the woods of America, and for ages it may yet do so, and millions, yet unborn, carry on the work before these worlds of timber shall be removed, or even thinned.

(Bouchette, *The British Dominions*, 1831, 2:139)

8 PRINCE EDWARD ISLAND

☞ Prince Edward Island, according to Bouchette, has no absolutely flat country, nor does it rise into mountains. We now know that the highest elevation is 142 m above sea level. The New London area, where Cavendish is mentioned, became the setting for L. M. Montgomery's *Anne of Green Gables,* published in 1908. Prince Edward Island's small size makes it possible for Bouchette to describe the distribution of ethnic settlements more effectively than in the other colonies. However, national stereotypes colour his accounts of the ethnic populations. ☜

Geographical Position – History – General Surface – Harbours –
Settlements – Climate – Soil Produce – Agriculture – Population –
Trade – Society

This island is situated in the Gulf of St. Lawrence, in a kind of bay or recess, lying between Cape Breton, Nova Scotia, and New Brunswick. It ranges in somewhat of a crescent form, between 46° and 47° 7' north latitude, and 62° and 64° 27' longitude west, from Greenwich. Its length, traced in this direction, is 135 miles; and its breadth in the widest part, which is from Beacon Point to East Point, towards its eastern extremity, thirty-four miles. Its form, however, is exceedingly irregular, being in some places indented with deep harbours on both sides, making its width insignificant, and at others stretching boldly into the sea in projecting promontories and spacious headlands, swelling its breadth to the extent we have mentioned. It lies conveniently near to the provinces before named, the distance from West Cape to Richibuctoo being eleven miles, from Cape Traverse to Nova Scotia, across the Strait of Northumberland, nine miles, and from East Point to Cape Breton twenty-seven miles. From the nearest point of Newfoundland it is 125 miles....

The general appearance of Prince Edward Island is picturesque and attractive, destitute of those bold romantic features which form the characteristic of most parts of the adjacent continent; it presents a surface naturally, where it is not artificially, fertile, swelling in gentle undulations, and clothed with verdure to the water's edge. There is no continued tract of absolutely flat country, nor does it any where reach the elevations of mountains. The principal high lands are a chain of hills, traversing the country nearly north and south from De Sable to Grenville Bay: with this exception, the land has few inequalities which interfere with the ordinary pursuit of agriculture.

The island is so indented and intersected by numerous bays, creeks, and inlets, there is scarcely any part of it more than eight miles distant from tide water. From this circumstance the coast furnishes several convenient harbours. The principal of these is that of Charlotte Town, situated on the south-west side of the island, at the bottom of Hillsborough Bay, and at the confluence of the three rivers, Hillsborough, York, and Elliott....

Prince's County forms the north-western division of the island.... The entire vicinity of Richmond Bay is well settled, comprising the villages of Ship-Yard, Indian River, St. Eleanor, Bentick River, Grand River, and a considerable village on the banks of Goodwood Cove, in township

No. 13. Near the North Cape is the settlement of Tigniche, in which the land has been found productive of wheat, barley, and potatoes to a very satisfactory extent. The shore from North Cape to West Cape is perhaps the least thickly settled of any part of the island; but it boasts a rich soil, covered with lofty trees, and abounds with streams and ponds of water. The whole line of coast is without a harbour; but it is practicable for landing in boats, and no doubt its many advantages will quickly attract an adequate population. At Cape Egmont there is a settlement of Acadian French....

... The principal settlement in [Queen's] county is Charlotte Town, the seat of government and metropolis, if it may be so termed, of the island. The situation of this town, as mentioned in our account of the harbour, is at the confluence of the Hillsborougb, York, and Elliott Rivers; the two former of which bound two of its sides, the first on the north-east, the second on the south-west sides. It stands nearly in the centre of the island, with all parts of which it has ready communication, either by water or good roads. The ground on which it is built rises with a gentle slope from the river's edge to a moderate height; the streets are regularly laid out in rectangles, in building lots of 80 feet frontage and 160 depth, with vacancies at chosen intervals for squares; the number of houses already built amounts to nearly 400, several of the more recent being of very handsome appearance. The public buildings are the court-house, in which the legislative assembly and the courts of chancery and judicature hold their sittings, the episcopal church, the new Scotch church, a catholic and a methodist chapel, and the new market. The barracks are situated near the water. The aspect of Charlotte Town from the water is peculiarly pleasing, rising in an amphitheatrical ascent from the water's edge, composed of gay and lively buildings, separated from each other by groves and gardens, whilst the quantity of land assigned to each house gives it the appearance of nearly twice its actual size....

On the northern shore of this county is the settlement of New London, in the district of Grenville Bay, including a very interesting new settlement called Cavendish. This district includes Elizabeth Town, Campel Town, and the whole chain of settlements round the bay and on the borders of the Stanley, Hope, and other rivers that fall into it, the whole of which are cultivated and thriving. At Rustico, on the same shore, are two Acadian French villages; and the banks of Hunter's and Whately Rivers are thickly settled, principally by emigrants from Scotland. Between this and Stanhope Cove, Breckly Point presents a pleasantly situated and flourishing settlement, whilst, at Little Rustico, the extensive and well cultivated farms afford the most cheering and inviting prospects. Along the coast to Bedford Bay, and thence to Savage Harbour, the land is pretty well settled, chiefly by highlanders. On the southern shore of this county, and on the eastern side of Hillsborough Bay, we have the district of Belfast, including the villages of Great and Little Belfast, Orwell, Pownall's, Perth, Flap River, and Belle Creek, and indeed the whole eastern and northern shore of the bay, from the estuary of the river to Beacon's Point, is thickly settled and in most flourishing circumstances. This part of the island was originally peopled by about 800 emigrants from Scotland, brought by the Earl of Selkirk, in 1803, who, together with their descendants, are now as prosperous as any inhabitants of the island. The soil is favourable, agriculture well attended to, and crops are raised which furnish exports to New Brunswick Nova Scotia, and Newfoundland.

King's County comprises the eastern division of the island, ... The town plot for George Town has been laid out ... at the confluence of the Cardigan, Montague, and Brudenelle Rivers: but little progress has as yet been made in the erection of buildings. The banks of the rivers in the vicinity are, however, tolerably well settled, and ship-building and exportation of timber are carried on to some extent at the port. On the northern shore of this county, adjacent to Savage Harbour, and stretching thence to St. Peter's Bay, is a pleasant line of settlement, with good farms, fronting on a small lake, and thence termed the lake settlements. The borders of St. Peter's Bay and the banks of the River Morel are also thrivingly settled, and in rapid advancement towards improvement.... On a peninsula, enclosing the bay from the gulf, is a very pleasant settlement called Greenwich. The whole line of coast thence, to the east point is cleared, settled, and cultivated by Scotch farmers, whose husbandry is greatly assisted by the quantity of marine productions thrown on shore, affording valuable manure. Colville, Fortune, How, and Boughton Rivers, stretching from the eastern shore deep into the land, are settled on both their banks, principally by Acadian French and Highlanders. The county is on the whole so thickly settled, and the villages lie so near to each other, that where water-carriage does not afford a complete and convenient communication, good roads have been established, and are kept in constant repair.

Though situated in the Gulf of St. Lawrence and surrounded by Canada, Nova Scotia, Labrador, and Newfoundland, the climate of Prince Edward Island is by many degrees more mild and favourable than that of either of those colonies....

... There are very few portions of land throughout the island not applicable to agriculture, the soil being mostly light, of easy tillage, and remarkably free from stones. The deviation from this general character is found in the swamps and bogs, which, when drained, form good meadow land; there are indeed some tracts termed barrens, but these bear a very insignificant proportion to the good land, nor are there any of them but what good management might reclaim. The marshes on the sea-board, which are occasionally covered by the tide, produce a strong grass, which is consumed by the cattle in winter, and when they are enclosed and drained become either excellent meadows, or, if ploughed, afford good grain crops. The land has, for the most part, been cleared of its heavy timber, which has been an important article of export to Great Britain....

The nearly level surface of the ground through the greater part of the island, the quality of the soil, and the favourable nature of the climate, are peculiarly calculated to invite the settlers to a steady pursuit of agriculture. The timber trade and the fishery have here, however, as in other colonies, seduced the short-sighted and those eager for rapid returns, to their apparently more productive employments; but the timber is now so far cleared, and the prosperity of the consistent agriculturist so palpable, that the cultivation of the earth seems from this time forward likely to be looked to as the most certain and profitable occupation of time, labour, and capital. Wheat thrives well here, and has furnished not only an abundant supply for the consumption of the inhabitants, but also for exportation to Nova Scotia. As agriculture improves, no doubt the quantity produced will increase, and the West Indies afford a ready market for any quantity that may be raised. Rye, oats, and barley also succeed. Beans and peas are not cultivated to any extent, but generally yield average crops. Indian corn does not seem to thrive in this soil. Flax is raised for domestic purposes, and the success that attends its culture seems to promise well for its growth as an article of exportation: hemp does not succeed so well.... The farms are usually laid out in 100 acre lots, of 10 chains frontage by 100 depth, and wherever it is practicable, fronting on a river, creek, bay, or road. The agricultural system pursued here, however, is defective in the last degree, and were not the soil by nature exceedingly productive, the little skill employed on it would afford but small assistance. The farmers are exceedingly negligent in applying manure, though that of the most efficacious kind abounds in all directions. Great quantities of sea-weed are constantly thrown on shore, which is an excellent manure; and in all the bays and creeks may be collected, to an incalculable extent, that composition of mud, decayed vegetable and animal substances, shells, &c. called muscle-mud, remarkable for its efficacy as a manure. The introduction of some intelligent farmers from Yorkshire and the southern parts of Scotland, has, within these few years, done much towards improving the usual mode of cultivation....

The trade of this island is inconsiderable. During the time it was in the possession of the French, their jealousy on behalf of Louisburg prevented them from at all cultivating it. The locality of the place seems as well to adapt it for a fishing station as Newfoundland, and the facility with which supplies are raised would seem to offer a temptation greater than any which that island possesses; nevertheless the curing of fish for exportation has never been carried on here to any great extent. A good market is afforded at home for the consumption of cured fish by the timber and ship-building trades. In all new wilderness countries the timber trade is the first object of attraction; but the quantity that has been felled, and the small proportion of uncleared land that remains, have reduced the timber trade of this colony to a trifling amount. Ship-building is still a branch of trade of some moment; and the vessels built here have a good reputation for trim and durability. Numbers of vessels, from 150 to 600 tons, are readily disposed of in the British market; and to this may be added a large number constantly constructed for the Newfoundland fisheries; a considerable supply of live stock, provisions, corn, and vegetables is also uniformly forwarded to that country, from which West India produce is received in return. Large exportations of agricultural produce also take place to Nova Scotia and New Brunswick, and of provisions of every description to the Bermudas....

The population of the island, by the census of 1827, was taken at 36,000, but since that time the increase has been so considerable, that it may now be estimated at about 50,000. Society, which has here advanced rapidly, is not distinguished from the society in the other colonies by any peculiar features, and its different classes are very similarly divided. A decided aristocracy is of course wanting, but the members of the council, the employes of government, the superior classes of the military, merchants, and traders of all sorts, who have attained a tolerable degree of affluence, constitute here an upper class, who are by no means backwards in cultivating the amusements and refinements of civilized life. Charlotte Town is the only place where people are sufficiently congregated to form any thing that can be termed society, and, this being the capital, possesses of course persons of every class. Those who are received at the castle, or government-house, being deemed the superiors, have assemblies, balls, dinners amongst themselves, and sometimes amateur theatricals. Others indulge in pic nic [sic], or what in England would be termed gipsy parties, in making country excursions, and each taking his own provisions. As almost every housekeeper is the owner of a horse and a carriole, or winter sledge-carriage, they are readily able to procure such indulgencies. The farmers and husbandmen comprise every class – American loyalists, Acadian French, and emigrants from England, Scotland, and Ireland, whose manners, even in this distant but desirable exile, are in a great measure influenced by their national characteristics and peculiarities. English settlers are distinguished by the cleanliness, neatness, and propriety of their establishments; Scotchmen by their patient endurance of the hardships incidental to early settlement, and their persevering pursuit of wealth and substance, with much more neglect of what we term – comfort; and the Irish by a more eager desire to secure temporary advantages and the means of present indulgence. All those occupied in husbandry and farming, to which many join some share in the fishery, timber, and ship-building trades (though the advantage of such a multiplicity of pursuits is somewhat more than equivocal) find abundant employment during the year, without seeking to share the amusements of the town, or substituting others of a more rural description. The amassing of money, it may be here observed, and the remark applies equally to all the American colonies, is absolutely impracticable. From nothing a man may rise to independence; he may find the means of comfortable subsistence assured to all his family and their future generations, but the realization of sums of money is not to be accomplished. The American settlers. peaceable and industrious, are remarkable for the variety of occupations which each individual unites in his own person. The facility of obtaining ardent spirits. and the free use made of them, operates. here, as in all our other colonies, as a serious drawback on the morality and prosperity of the colonists.

The French Acadians, probably about 4,000 in number, and settled principally along the coasts, retain much of their primitive simplicity in dress, manners, and pursuits. A round jacket and trousers is the usual habit of the men, any instance of departing from which would be treated with the utmost ridicule; and the women exhibit an appearance very similar to that of the Bavarian broom-girls so commonly seen in this country. They are rather looked down upon by the European settlers, but are nevertheless perfectly inoffensive, and for industry they are not to be surpassed. They, however, apply this virtue to such a diversity of pursuits, – those who live on the coast following ship-building, lumbering, fishing, and farming-that they seldom advance in wealth so much as those who steadily follow anyone of those occupations singly. The women, as housewives, are perfect patterns, and such is their activity, that they have seldom to go beyond the precinct of their own establishment for any necessary whatever, the whole of their clothes and other articles for home use being the product of domestic manufacture.

(Bouchette, *The British Dominions*, 1831, 2:158–78)

9 NEWFOUNDLAND

☞ Bouchette does not possess the topographic knowledge of Newfoundland that he has of the other British North American colonies and is perhaps overly dismissive of St. John's. To Bouchette's consternation, Newfoundland has not attained the degree of local administration that the other British North American colonies enjoy. ☞

The island of Newfoundland lies on the north-eastern side of the entrance into the Gulf of St. Lawrence, ... Its form is somewhat triangular, but without any approach to regularity, each of its sides being broken by numerous harbours, bays, creeks, and estuaries.... From the sea it has a wild and rugged appearance, which is any thing rather than inviting. Its interior has been very imperfectly explored, and is therefore but little understood. In 1823, a Mr. M'Cormach succeeded in traversing its breadth from Conception Bay on its east to St. George's Bay on its western side; and, from his account, it appears, that this district is much intersected with lakes and rivers, is poorly wooded, and of a rocky and barren soil. Newfoundland, in this respect, thus differs amazingly from the other American colonies, producing little timber but what is dwarf and stunted, except on the margins of bays and rivers, where spruce, birch, and poplar sometimes grow to a considerable size....

For a long series of years the colony existed merely as a fishing settlement, the fisheries being carried on entirely by merchants residing in Great Britain. These considered the small and insignificant number of planters resident in the colony as persons by no means entitled to interfere with their interests or dispute their pleasure, and therefore always resisted any measures for the amelioration of the situation of a body of people whom they treated as subservient to themselves; the increase of the population however, now amounting to not less probably than 75,000 souls, and the advance of agriculture and commercial pursuits amongst the residents, render them entitled to be placed a little above the caprices of the body of traders, however the interests of the last, duly considered, are identified with those of the British empire at large. It is stoutly contended on the behalf of the fisheries, that they are utterly incapable of submitting to any burthen or contributing to any expensive form of government for the colony; and their vast importance as a nursery for British seamen, and a source of employment for British shipping, renders their situation a subject of anxious attention to the British legislature, which must, however, keep on its guard against the representation of that ruthless selfishness which is but too frequently the characteristic of those absorbed in a commercial speculation.

As all the importance attached to this colony has arisen exclusively from its fisheries, little has been done on shore to claim our attention. The different settlements amount to about sixty or seventy in number, and are scattered on the shores of the eastern and southern sides of the island, but principally the former; there are indeed some inhabitants on the western shore, near its southern extremity, but they do not extend northward of St. George's Bay, though the vicinity of that bay has proved extremely fertile. Both the eastern and southern shores are broken by several deep bays; on the former, the principal are Hare Bay, very near the northern extremity; and proceeding southerly, White Bay, Bay of Notre Dame, Bay of Exploits, Bay of Bonavista, Trinity Bay, and Conception Bay; on the southern shore are Trepassey Bay, Placentia Bay, St. Mary's Bay, and Fortune Bay. It is about the heads of these bays that the settlements are found. On the whole shore of Conception Bay, thence to St. John's, and southward to Cape Race, the settlements are numerous and populous; the principal are, besides St. John's, the Bay of Bulls, Brigus, Cape Broyle Harbour, Ferryland, Fermore, and Renowes; but there is little in any of these settlements to demand particular attention. Ferryland is the first that was ever brought into cultivation and importance, by the early settlement of Lord Baltimore; and even now there is a greater extent of land under tillage there than at any settlement on that coast.

St. John's is the principal settlement, and only town in the island; it is the seat of government, and chief harbour for our vessels....

[St. John's] is situated about seventy miles to the north of Cape Race, and about 120 south of Twillingate Island, in the Bay of Exploits, our most northerly settlement on the island. The town forms one long straggling street, extending nearly parallel to the shore on the north side of the port, from which branch out several narrow lines of houses, which will bear no designation superior to lanes. The houses are built chiefly of wood, though diversified by some of brick, and a few of stone, but they are most irregularly placed, in consequence of an act of the British legislature, passed in 1820, after the great fires, and which directs, that where the houses are built of stone, the street shall be forty feet in width, and where of wood fifty, so that all the stone houses project ten feet into the street. The principal feature of the town is its multitude of wharfs and fishing stages, which entirely line the shore. The government wharf is a fine broad quay, open to the accommodation or the public. The number of taverns and public-houses seems very disproportionate to the place. The roadway of the main street is very rugged and irregular, and in wet weather scarcely passable for mud and filth. The general appearance of the town indicates exactly what it is – a mere fishing station.

It is difficult to calculate the population of a town which varies so constantly. At the height of the fishing season it is perfectly crowded, but the greater part of this population returns with the vessels to Europe. The resident population may be fairly rated at about 11,000.... There are places of public worship of various denominations at St. John's, and two school-houses, one established by Lord Gambier, in 1802, for children of both the protestant and Roman creeds, who attend to the number of 300, and another, erected by the efforts of the Benevolent Irish Society, the benefits of which are extended to 700 or 800 children. There are three weekly newspapers published, and a book society has been established.

Since several merchants, deeply engaged in the trade, have settled here, and many industrious inhabitants have by their consistent efforts raised themselves to comparative wealth, and since the administration of justice has been placed on a more permanent and certain footing than formerly, the state of society has continued rapidly advancing in respectability and civilization, and is now better than could be expected from a fishing station, the internal improvement of which has been so uniformly discouraged. The settlements continue almost continuously along the southern shore, as far as Fortune Bay, and at most of the harbours there are places of worship. The settlement at St. George's Bay is perhaps more agricultural than any other on the island....

The climate is severe and the winter long, but it has generally been represented more unfavourably than strict truth will warrant. The excess of humidity and constant visitation of dense fog, which have been commonly ascribed to these coasts, is by no means a continual visitation; the sea winds often bring a considerable quantity of vapour to the southern and eastern coasts, but it is only when the wind blows from the sea that this inconvenience is felt....

The population of the island has greatly increased of late years. The census of 1827 gave 36,000 as the gross amount; it has been recently rated as high as 90,000, but truth will perhaps be more strictly consulted in fixing the number at 75,000. There are no good roads in the island but those in the immediate vicinity of St. John's. As has been before remarked, the fisheries are the chief business of the island, agriculture being pursued to an amount far from sufficient to supply the wants of the inhabitants. The number of vessels employed in the fisheries in the year 1830 was 700, ...

... Application has been recently made to the British parliament for the institution of an independent colonial legislature. This, like every other attempt to improve the colony, is resisted by those principally engaged in the fisheries; but as neither parties nor jealousies can, at the present day, be expected to influence the inquiries or decisions of the British legislature, there is no doubt that all will be done which the welfare of the colony requires. If the parliament does not go the length of granting an independent legislature, the institution of a corporate body in St. John's might in some measure supply the deficiency, and it seems one to which the advanced wealth, number, and intelligence of its inhabitants entitle them.

(Bouchette, *The British Dominions*, 1831, 2:180–9)

2

George R. Parkin, *The Great Dominion: Studies of Canada*, 1895

☞ George R. Parkin, in *The Great Dominion,* published in 1895, describes Canada at an exciting time when the country was just beginning to be knit together effectively on the ground. Canada was at a critical stage in its geographical development: the Canadian Pacific Railway had been in operation for almost a decade, the Intercolonial Railway for almost two, so the continent-wide country could at last function with new, amazing proficiency. Trains revolutionized the country: people and goods moved at marvelous speeds relative to earlier times, finally linking the various regions serviceably. Paradoxically, the new rapid connections brought out Canadian regional differences more clearly than ever. Parkin visited each of the major regions and had the acumen to search out the forces, the processes, that underlay the life of each region. Each region seemingly was at a nascent stage, and Parkin was able to catch and describe this vital period in Canada's development.

Parkin, born in New Brunswick in 1846, grew up on a backwoods farm, became a schoolteacher, a common route of advancement for bright young men of the time, and attended the University of New Brunswick. In 1885, while headmaster of the Collegiate School in Fredericton, he became a member of the Imperial Federation League when the first branch was established in Canada and soon became a very active advocate of imperial federation. An eloquent speaker, Parkin toured New Zealand and Australia on behalf of the League in 1889 and then stayed in England until 1895, eking out a living by journalism and lecturing and writing for the League. From 1895 to 1902 Parkin was headmaster of Upper Canada College in Toronto and then returned to England when he was appointed the founding administrator of the Rhodes Trust, where he organized its scholarship system. Parkin was knighted in 1920 and died in England two years later.

In the autumn and winter of 1892–93 Parkin, age forty-six, went across Canada to lecture on Imperial Federation. His rail fare was covered by the Canadian Pacific Railway and *The Times* of London commissioned long articles on the state of the country. Parkin returned in the summer of 1894 to check some matters and collect more material, and the revised articles were collected and published the following year as *The Great Dominion*. Parkin was well equipped to write the essays. With good contacts and entrée to leading people in most parts of Canada, curious and possessed of a perceptive eye, and with a global perspective as an advocate of federation within the British Empire, he was in a solid position to delve into the character of the various major Canadian regions on the threshold of the twentieth century. The Prairies were ready to receive settlement, the resources of British Columbia awaited development, Ontario was on the brink of industry and wealth, Quebec's population and aspirations were distinctive within the country, the Maritimes were lagging, and the North was an enigma. Parkin provides us with a late-nineteenth-century benchmark, a set of processes, a platform, a point of departure, to which we can relate what actually has happened in a regional sense to Canada over the last century. The chapters follow Parkin's organization. ☞

I INTRODUCTORY

☞ Parkin views recent changes in Canada as significant new factors within the British Empire. An Old and a New Canada exist and there is a hint of environmental determinism in his reference to Canada's northern vigour. ☞

Many of the problems connected with the present condition and future development of the Dominion of Canada have a profound interest for the people of the United Kingdom and of the empire at large. In these problems are involved matters deeply affecting maritime position, imperial defence and communications, food and coal supply, trade relations, emigration, and many other questions which, from a national point of view, are of the first importance.

The study of these questions seems more necessary now than ever before. While the growth of population in the Dominion has not been so great during the last two decades as was expected, events have

nevertheless moved fast. Advances in political and physical consolidation have been made which greatly change Canada's relation to the
empire and to the world. This movement is one which, in the very nature
of things, must have far reaching national consequences.

It does not seem an exaggeration to say that the course which affairs
take in Canada during the next few years may have a decisive influence upon the direction of British History. The primary reason for this
impression is obvious. Canada is the first of the great colonies which
has formed a political combination which gives her a position closely
akin to that of a nation. Her territory comprises nearly 40 per cent. of
the whole empire, and covers half of the North American continent. It is
only within the last few years that Canadians themselves have become
fully conscious of the vast possibilities of this largely undeveloped area.
Facing upon the two greatest oceans of the globe, the country is now
brought into easy commercial communication and international relation with the rest of the world. Across the breadth of the continent it
borders upon, and therefore has more or less intimate relations with,
the United States. Thus, though Canada has not a nation's franchise,
her people and statesmen have been forced to consider in many ways
the interests of a nation. By the mere compulsion of circumstances her
statesmen are fast becoming statesmen of the empire. Already more than
once their advice has been essential to the wise conduct of the most difficult imperial negotiations. It is facts like these which give such extreme
national significance to her present position. In what direction will point
the interests and aspirations of a great colony which has reached this
stage of growth? How far do these interests and aspirations coincide
with those of British people generally? These are large questions which
cannot be answered off-hand. That they must be answered sooner or
later invites or almost compels the careful study of Canadian conditions.

For gaining a due sense of proportion in such study some glance at the
main geographical facts is a necessary preliminary....

When we consider the country from east to west some remarkable
features are to be observed. Old or Eastern Canada extends from the
Atlantic to Lakes Huron and Superior. The fact which here most of all
arrests attention is that even to the heart of the continent Eastern Canada has a position essentially maritime....

New Canada lies westward of Lake Superior. "Taking a line drawn
north and south in the longitude of the Red River Valley, which is, as
nearly as may be, the centre of Canada from east to west, it may confidently be stated that by far the larger part of the country in which
agricultural settlement is possible lies to the west, while the great bulk of

the actual population lies to the east of this line" [Dr. G. M. Dawson, of the Canadian Geological Survey]....

Such, in broadest outline, are the geographical features which must dominate the development of Canada; which will mainly influence the industries, the character, and the tendencies of its people. They open up a large field for study and speculation.

It need scarcely be added that in regions so vast and various Nature is often seen in her most splendid and picturesque aspects. The traveller who has penetrated the Selkirk and Rocky ranges of British Columbia; who has explored the magnificent surroundings of the National Park at Banff; who has crossed the thousand miles of North-Western prairie; who has traversed the expanse of the great inland lakes; who has stood beside the Horseshoe Fall at Niagara and traced the course of the mighty gorge below; who has sailed amid the Thousand Isles and through the swirling rapids of the St. Lawrence; who has looked down from the heights of the Mountain at Montreal; from the promontory on which stand the Parliament Buildings at Ottawa; and from the lofty terrace of historic Quebec, has seen some of the most striking and impressive scenery of the world. Doubtless such surroundings may have a profound influence in moulding the character of a people. Canada is a country which certainly stirs the imagination of her children which begets in them an intense love of the soil. If the front which nature sometimes presents to them is severe, it is also noble and impressive. In the breadth of its spaces, the headlong rush of its floods, the majesty of its mountain heights and canon depths, and the striking contrasts of its seasons in their march through the fervid warmth of summer, the glory of autumnal colouring, and the dazzling splendour of a snow-covered land to the sudden burst of new and radiant life in spring – in all these, Canada has characteristics unique among the many lands under the British flag. There are those who believe that it is a country peculiarly fitted to rear a people whose northern vigour will give them weight in the world, and will add strength and character to the nation of which they form a part. But it is with the practical facts of Canadian life, rather than its ideals, that we have now chiefly to deal.

(Parkin, *The Great Dominion*, 1895, 1–9)

2   THE NORTH-WEST

☞ Parkin begins *The Great Dominion* in the North-West, since what is happening in this region is the most significant force in bringing about change in Canada. Bouchette did not know what to make of

the North-West, but sixty-four years later Parkin takes us through
the formative years of this great agricultural region. With the recent
completion of the Canadian Pacific Railway the region has just been
opened up for viable commercial agriculture, a great area of highly
inviting arable land for thousands of potential settlers. The thrust of
Parkin's analysis of the North-West is settlement opportunity and
migration, particularly for people coming from Great Britain, but also
from elsewhere. The North-West is the engine of Canadian growth,
and we get a good picture of development processes on the prairies
in a period when immigration was just beginning to gear up. A prime
point Parkin stresses is that the North-West is a poor man's country,
although, as is true in bringing any new area into cultivation, life will
be hard for some years. He discusses problems that wheat farmers face
in the southern prairies. Frost is a hazard, especially since hybrid Mar-
quis wheat seed with a shorter growing season was not widely available before 1911. ☞

Among the Canadian problems which may fairly be regarded as of
national interest, I am disposed to place foremost those connected with
the growth and settlement of the vast provinces of the North-West. These
provinces are sure, sooner or later, to be filled with a population of many
millions of people, English-speaking, and for the most part of British
blood. To emigrants from the United Kingdom they now offer the most
readily accessible areas in the Empire where homestead lands can still be
easily acquired. They equally offer abundant lands to those foreign emigrants who are willing to add to the strength of the Empire by adopting
British citizenship. The extent to which this process of assimilating energetic and useful material from other races is being carried on in Canada,
as in the other colonies, may be strikingly shown by a single illustration.
Within the last few years Manitoba and the North-West have absorbed
nearly 10,000 of the industrious and intelligent inhabitants of Iceland,
who have voluntarily become most useful, loyal, and satisfactory British
subjects. This migration is still going on, and It seems not unlikely that a
considerable proportion of the population of that interesting island will
ultimately be transferred to British soil.

Increasing population in these vacant areas means increased powers of
production in directions which intimately concern British consumers. It
is only eight or nine years since railway communication was fully established with the North-West, but already wheat from Manitoba farms
and cattle from Alberta ranches are finding their way to the English mar-

ket in increasing volume. Anyone who studies existing conditions, who sees how comparatively small is the area as yet occupied, who observes the facility with which production may be increased, will, I think, be convinced that the Great Lakes, the St. Lawrence, and Canadian railway systems will soon be the channels for an immense outflow of food products directed towards Britain. The inevitable pressure of consumption upon production in the United States, hitherto the chief source of British importation, gives peculiar interest to this question of Canadian food supply, the filling up, moreover, of these vast territories with an adequate population is almost essential to the complete consolidation of that remarkable, but as yet not fully appreciated, maritime position which is secured to the Empire by the fact that the Dominion rests with commanding outlook upon both the Atlantic and the Pacific, where these oceans respectively furnish the shortest and easiest access from the American continent to Europe and Asia. Just as the middle and western States bind New England and the east to the Pacific States, so the filling up of the North-West will complete the cohesion between the Atlantic and the Pacific provinces of Canada.

Wishing to form an estimate of the progress and prospects of the North-West, of its food-producing capacity, and of the conditions of settlement, I elected to visit the country at a season not usually considered favourable. Friends in England and Canada alike reproached me for not planning to reach the prairies in time to see the wonderful prospect afforded by the wide stretches of waving grain. But we know that in all countries not only the promise of spring verdure and of summer growth, but also of early autumn ripening, may be blighted by rain or drought or frost, and so I preferred to visit the North-West in the late autumn and early winter, when the farmer had got down to the bed rock of reality; when his stacks had been threshed and the grain measured or sold; when he was preparing to face the winter and was carrying on the operations necessary to make the work of the spring most effective. If such a time for studying a country lacks some elements of the picturesque, it has interest equal to any other, and perhaps more of instruction.

A new and strange sense of vastness grows upon the mind as one travels day after day over the prairies, with the distant sky-line as the chief object which fixes the eye. The impression is different from that produced by wide space at sea, for the imagination at once begins to fill up these enormous areas with homes and busy inhabitants. At first sight it seems only necessary to pour out population over these vast spaces in any direction. This is soon found to be a mistake. There are lands good, bad, and middling. Some districts are more subject to frost than others. There are areas where the soil is excellent, but where at some seasons water in sufficient abundance is wanting. There is alkali land in the far West, where the great American desert pushes northward a considerable offshoot. One limited district there is where, from some peculiar configuration of the country, hail is an almost annual infliction, and where, as in Dakota, the hail insurance companies build up a business. All this is in the midst of an extent of good farming land well nigh incalculable. In such circumstances the first, second, and third duty of those who would settle the country is manifestly to reduce the business of land selection as closely as may be to an exact science. To allow any settler in the North-West to go upon land which is not the best available is a gross mistake. The railway companies and the Government. are beginning to realize this too long neglected truth. Lands are now carefully surveyed and their characteristics noted. Skilled pioneers are invited to precede parties of emigrants and make careful choice. The Canadian Pacific Railway Company challenges investigations of its lands and gives free passes to those who wish to examine them with a view to settlement. It sends put experienced agents to assist the individual settler in making a choice. All this is having a good effect, and is correcting the mistakes of earlier days. The trouble taken will be well repaid, for of all emigration agents the contented settler is by far the best. It is from him that the North-West is now getting its best impulse. The steamship in which I crossed the Atlantic was carrying many emigrants, chiefly Scottish, to Manitoba and the Territories. It was satisfactory to find that in most cases they were going on the recommendation of friends who had preceded them. Often in the Far West I met with men and women who were saving their money to bring out relatives, or even, in some cases, going home to induce them to come out. Emigration effected in this way is of the healthiest kind, and is the best recommendation that a country can have.

While the rush of emigration has not been so great as the sanguine hopes of the early settlers led them to anticipate, the progress made seems to the ordinary observer, very great. It is, as I have already said, only eight or nine years since the main railway line across the continent was completed. A glance at a good railway map shows how rapidly branch lines have been pushed for many hundred miles in various directions, as settlement justified their construction. What the traveller sees in a journey over some of these branch lines furnishes the best proof of the progress of the country. From Winnipeg I went over the Southern Manitoba road to Estevan, the point to which it was at that time completed, and thence back to rejoin the main line at Brandon, in all a distance of nearly 500 miles. At intervals of ten or twelve miles over nearly all this distance prosperous little towns are springing up, each equipped with two, three, or four elevators to deal with the grain raised in the surrounding districts. Wheat was being shipped rapidly at the time, and these elevators were usually surrounded by teams waiting to deliver their loads. Huge stacks of straw, soon to be burned for want of any better use, showed where the grain had been threshed in the fields where it was grown.... A man with two yoke of oxen and a gang plough breaks up a quarter section (160 acres) during five spring and summer months, and the whole expense per acre is less than three dollars (12s. 6d). The rapidity and cheapness of preparation strike the observer forcibly after he has watched the slow processes by which farms are made in the forests of Eastern Canada or British Columbia, in New Zealand bush, among Tasmanian and Australian gum trees, or by reclaiming waste lands in England or Scotland. Manifestly any considerable application of capital or a large inflow of farming population might, under such conditions, increase the wheat output very rapidly....

Instances occur here and there through Manitoba and the territories of men who have begun in the small way on a quarter or half section, and with increasing prosperity and enlarged experience have gradually widened their operations till they were farming on a great scale.... Whether by large proprietors or small, however, the north-western prairies have a capacity for rapid increase of production which might speedily become very great under any exigency of demand.

I pause here to guard against a possible misapprehension. It must not be thought that the rapid increase of wheat production in the North-West has hitherto meant a correspondingly large surplus for export from Canada as a whole. As the output of the newly opened western areas has increased, that of the eastern provinces, where cereals are not produced without careful culture, has diminished. Quebec and all the maritime provinces make a heavy demand, for their own consumption, upon the surplus product of the West. Ontario, as the result of the drop in wheat prices, is gradually changing from a wheat-producing to a dairying country. Thus, though Manitoba and the territories show a large increase of production, Canada's export as a whole does not enlarge with corresponding rapidity.

Only a large addition to population in the West can make it do this. But given this inflow of population, and such a rise in price as makes wheat growing profitable, and there is scarcely any limit to the possibility of production in the Dominion. The area of Manitoba and the territories of Assiniboia, Alberta and Saskatchewan is 360,000 square miles, or 230,000,000 acres. It has been estimated, and, I think, not unfairly, that one-half of this is either good or workable wheat land. Yet of all this vast area little more than a million acres are now under actual cultivation for wheat.

The extent of land which the small farmer can profitably hold and cultivate is a question of some interest.

In travelling through Eastern Canada the impression constantly left upon the mind is that the average farmer clears up more land than is necessary and is wrestling with a larger area than he can properly till. If eastern experience be taken as a guide, then for the man of the West an ordinary quarter section, which contains 160 acres, is quite enough for a single holding, and this is the amount usually taken up.

But it is maintained by some that for the most successful farming in the North-West it is necessary to work two sets of fields, and for this two quarter sections, or 320 acres, are required.

Senator Perley, who for many years has made a close practical study of North-Western farming, stated to me the arguments for this course. The first object is to get abundant opportunity for summer fallowing, which, he holds, is better than fall ploughing, inasmuch as it not only clears the land of weeds, but rests it; can be done when the farmer has more time, and from peculiar conditions about the retention of moisture ensures a better crop. Of this ideal farm of 320 acres, 200 acres should be arable, one-half being kept under crop, and the other half under summer fallow. The remaining 120 acres will suffice for pasturage and hay. Senator Perley believes that the 160 acre farm now commonly taken up will, as the country gets more settled, prove insufficient. Free pasturage on unoccupied land makes it appear enough now, but this condition will change rapidly. Even now the ordinary farmer is far from anxious that settlers should take up the blocks adjoining to himself, since, through exclusion from pasturage, he at once feels the pressure. The question is one that the intending settler should take into careful consideration, since a false start is not always easily remedied.

The North-Western farmer has his special difficulties to contend with. Here, as elsewhere, man learns by slow degrees to wrestle successfully with the problems of nature, and he does so by studying them and adapting himself to new conditions. The key to successful farming in the North-West consists in knowing how to meet the dangers of frost. To this end the farmer must prepare during the autumn for the work of the spring. Abundance of fall ploughing is a necessity of the country. The moment the harvest is off the fields the plough is turned on, and it must be kept at work until stopped by the freezing of the ground. Then with the earliest April warmth seeding may begin at once. Nowhere does the first fortnight of spring count for so much. Farmers once thought it necessary, as in other climates, to wait till the frost was out of the ground to begin sowing. Now they sow when barely an inch or two of ground is thawed, sufficient to allow the seed to be covered. After that the lack of spring showers, very common in the West, makes no difference, for the frost as it thaws furnishes moisture to the roots, while the hot inland sun forces on growth with great rapidity. Thus the frost which threatens the wheat becomes also its salvation. It is under such conditions that the No. 1 hard Manitoba wheat, pronounced by experts to be the best in the world, is grown.

Still, after all that the farmer can do, allowance must always be made in the North-West for a proportion of frozen wheat, though the quantity will decrease, as experience shows, with the cultivation of the country, the drainage of lands, and the increase of skill in farming. But the term "frozen wheat," which suggests to most minds the entire destruction of the crop as a mercantile commodity, means nothing like this to the North-Western farmer. Slightly frosted wheat is reduced for flour-making purposes perhaps 30 per cent in value, what is called frozen wheat 50 per cent. Both are freely used by millers to make a cheaper kind of flour. But many experiments have now proved that they are open to a much more profitable use. It has been shown that frozen wheat, fed to pigs and cattle, is worth much more than when sold for milling purposes....

But the North-Western farmer takes to mixed farming slowly and reluctantly. For this there is at present more than one reason. Labour is often scarce and expensive, and the attention to detail required in mixed farming is therefore rendered difficult. Fencing is necessary with a variety of stock, and fencing in some parts of the treeless prairie country is expensive. On the other hand, there is something of the temptation of gambling in wheat raising. With a good season, large crops, and a favourable price, the profits from a few hundred acres of wheat land are very large. As far as one could learn from rather extensive inquiry, the production varies all the way from fifteen to forty bushels per acre, according to the nature of the soil and season. The price, too, has varied in different years from 55c. to $1 per bushel for the best grade of grain. In such circumstances the temptation to speculate on the chances of the year is very great. As long, however, as the farmers of the North-West

stake so much upon a single product, so long must they be prepared for
great fluctuations of prosperity. Wheat, in sympathy with prices all over
the world, has never been so low as during the last two years. I found
many a farmer in Manitoba who was getting only 55c. a bushel for his
wheat, paying at the same time high prices for pork, beef, butter, and
other necessary articles of food, brought from Ontario and the United
States. That this is bad farming, for which there can be no sufficient
excuse, is a lesson which is being slowly but certainly learned. When it
has been thoroughly learned – when mixed farming is the rule rather
than the exception – I believe that the permanent prosperity of the North-
Western farming interest is assured.... It is scarcely too much to say that
if the depression in the price of wheat during the last three years, sore
as is the strain which it has put on the North-Western farmer, drive him
into making the most of farming opportunities outside of wheat-raising,
a healthier condition of things will have been brought about in the country. The risk from frost, if faced with far-sighted energy, does not seem to
me so great as the risk from drought in Australia – scarcely greater than
the risk from a prolonged wet season in Great Britain. Hence I believe
that this vast country will gradually be filled up with a prosperous farming population. The cold winter is not seriously dreaded by the people,
and the other seasons give great climatic compensations. During the
whole month of October, while I was going westward over the prairies,
there was not a drop of rain, while the perfect sunshine which prevailed
week after week furnished a striking contrast to the reports of storm and
wet and cold which came from England. As I journeyed eastward some
weeks later winter was settling down on the land, and at Winnipeg the
thermometer had already been at 20 degrees below zero. But there were
the same bright sky and sunshine, and the clear cold seemed to give an
added activity to people's steps and a buoyancy to their spirits.

(Parkin, *The Great Dominion*, 1895, 9–25)

3 THE NORTH-WEST-CONTINUED

⌒ There is more to the prairies than wheat farming. Parkin discusses
mixed farming in the park country, the push to the Peace River country,
and ranching in the more arid areas. He describes the beginning of
an urban system, based on serving an agricultural population that is
growing rapidly. Parkin is reassuring: Canadian prairie towns provide
secure pioneer institutions, unlike some other frontier societies. He
notes the wide range of nationalities that are establishing settlements

on the prairies and is especially concerned about what kinds of people are particularly suited to pioneering in this region, revealing a prejudice against southern European immigrants. Parkin is critical of the English remittance man but extols the role of the Englishwoman, "a centre of wholesome and refining influence." It is of particular interest that experienced American farmers are beginning to come, since good homestead lands in the United States have all been taken up and Frederick Jackson Turner's frontier is closed. Indeed, Parkin quotes one migrant from the United States: "Land is getting to be land on this continent." In the two chapters on the North-West Parkin is very positive on the potential for farming in the region, but in a later chapter he allows that if he had a personal choice as an immigrant he would purchase an established farm in Eastern Canada rather than go through the hardships of pioneer farming on the prairies.

This is the age of coal. Parkin discusses coal in a separate chapter, and I have moved his remarks on coal in the Rocky Mountains and in the plains to this section. He describes various places in the North-West where coal is already mined and notes its importance for settlers on the treeless plains. ◠

What has been said in the previous chapter about the North-West had reference chiefly to the comparatively treeless prairie country which has hitherto been the principal area of wheat culture. It would be a great mistake, however, to suppose that North-Western Canada consists exclusively of level prairie. Westward from Manitoba along the Qu'Appelle, northward on the Saskatchewan, and all along the eastern slope of the Rocky Mountains are vast regions of a partly wooded, partly grass-covered country, park-like in appearance, undulating for the most part, and with striking variations of scenery formed by the grouping of mountain, hill, lake, and river.

Country of this kind will always have for many settlers attractions which they do not find in the absolutely level prairie-attractions for which no richness of soil or ease of culture can compensate. Parts of these regions, while admirably suited for ranching, are, without irrigation, less fitted for agriculture. This is true of considerable districts in the vicinity of Calgary, where, however, the opportunities for irrigation are excellent, and only await the application of capital and skill.

Altogether the area of the semi-arid country where irrigation is occasionally necessary, or would give greater security to agriculture year by year, has been estimated to extend between 300 and 400 miles east and

west, and more than a hundred miles north and south. Large as this area
seems it is a mere bagatelle in the vast spaces of the North-West, and is,
in reality, only a small spur of the corresponding area in the United States,
wholly or partly arid; an area which has been estimated to cover more
than a million square miles. Settlers in this district have been rather slow to
admit to themselves that their part of the country labours under any farming disability, or is liable to peculiar risks. But it is better to face facts, and
there is much reason to think that the lands of this region will be among
the very best and the most profitable to work when irrigation has been
secured. This has been American experience in California, Utah, Nevada,
Colorado, and many other states where similar conditions prevail. One
large district has already been selected for settlement by immigrants from
Utah, accustomed in that state to deal with similar difficulties. The land
department of the Canadian Pacific Railway is preparing to irrigate from
the Bow River a plateau of about 1,000,000 acres near Medicine Hat, and
steps of a like kind are being taken by smaller companies....

Other parts seem suited alike for grazing and agriculture. It is difficult to speak with anything short of enthusiasm of the appearance and
apparent possibilities of one vast region which is now attracting much
attention and to which a very considerable stream of settlers has already
set in. The railway lately opened for a distance of about 200 miles from
Calgary to Edmonton gives easy access to one part of this country; the
line between Regina and Prince Albert to another. Between these points
and both north and south of the Saskatchewan are areas which nature
seems to have specially adapted for that mixed farming which I have
mentioned as being the most reliable and satisfactory. There are numerous streams, large and small, of excellent water. The nutritious native
grasses, once the only food of millions of buffalo, turn naturally into
good hay as they stand, and, as in the purely ranching districts, give
winter as well as summer food to horses, which are accustomed to paw-
ing away the snow, and to cattle as well, when the snow is not deep on
the ground. Abundant shelter for cattle is furnished by the valleys and
woodland bluffs, and the latter supply also material for fencing and fuel.
Of other abundant fuel I shall have occasion to speak when considering
the coal supplies of the Dominion....

... I cannot but think that this whole range of country offers great and
varied inducements to hardy settlers, and would yield a rich reward to
those who brought industry and intelligence to the work of farming. It
is sure to be filled ultimately with a prosperous population, whether the
process of settlement goes on slowly or rapidly.

Of the extent of territory capable of successful settlement still further north, in the direction of the Peace River, no one as yet even attempted to form an estimate. There is already abundant evidence to show that the deep northward bend of the isothermal lines which occurs as we approach the Rocky Mountains upsets entirely all calculations based on the idea that latitude alone determines climate. How far this fact enlarges the supposed scope of agricultural settlement in Canada is one of the interesting problems of the future. Our present concern, however, is with lands actually in the process of settlement.

Turning from the farming to the grazing districts, we find that the ranching industry, in Alberta especially, has in a few years grown to large dimensions. It is carried on chiefly by the aid of English capital and under English direction. At Calgary I found an interesting experiment being carried out with a view of reaching distant markets rapidly and effectually. Large numbers of cattle from the Cochrane Ranch were being killed in *abattoirs* at Calgary, and the chilled beef was being sent to the cities of Eastern Canada in cars specially arranged for the purpose. The meat was received at Montreal and Ottawa in perfect condition, competing successfully with the best that local markets could supply. It is claimed that, with improved transport arrangements, this is by far the best way in which to carry the products of the ranches to English markets as well. Some ardent believers in the system think that the scheduling of Canadian cattle, by compelling the use of new methods, may prove to the Canadian farmer a blessing in disguise. In 1872 Canada had exported no meat, live or dead, to Great Britain. The numbers of live cattle sent had already risen in 1891 beyond a hundred thousand annually, and yet this does not represent more than a fifth of what the British market absorbs. A special class of ships has been designed to meet the wants of this great trade, which has become a considerable factor in the prosperity of several British ports as well as Canadian, and in the success of steamship and railway systems. Horses have not as yet been exported in large numbers to Britain, but the stock on the ranches has increased rapidly, and the wants of the British market are now being carefully studied. Lately an experiment has been made in transferring numbers of choice horses from the ranches to Ontario farms, whence, after being thoroughly broken, they are brought to England for sale. That it only pays to bring to the English market horses of the best quality is a point now well understood.

The ranching of the North-West, like its farming, has had its entire development within the last ten years. Experience has been painfully acquired: the ranchman has had many fluctuations of prosperity, and has felt his way slowly towards success. The best accessible information indicates that the industry is now established on a permanent and fairly satisfactory basis. Between Western ranches and Eastern farms it seems clear that Canada will more and more become a chief source of meat supply for the United Kingdom.

The clear, cool climate of the Dominion has proved exceptionally favourable to the health of cattle, and the scheduling which has been enforced for some time rests upon evidence so doubtful that the order will probably soon be withdrawn. The Alberta ranches, however, do not depend entirely upon the British market or that of Eastern Canada. They contribute to the supply of the mining regions of the Rocky Mountains, and this promises to be an outlet of increasing importance.

What has now been said shows to how great an extent the Canadian North-West depends upon its agricultural interests. Alike in the areas principally devoted to wheat culture, in those where from the first mixed farming predominates, and in the ranching districts, the present and pro-spective prosperity of the country will consist in finding an adequate market for a large surplus of food products. This broad fact should be kept constantly in mind, since it cannot but exercise a decisive influence on the future policy of the Dominion.

I have as yet said nothing about the towns of the North-West. These must always furnish some index to the general prosperity of the country around them. Winnipeg, as is well known, after springing up with won-derful rapidity in the first years of settlement, suffered a violent reaction as the result of over speculation in business, and especially in real estate. The truth is that the inflow of farming population never matched the expectations of those who first went to Manitoba; the city increased in size beyond the necessities of the province, and so was compelled to wait some years for the latter to overtake it. Now the period of stagna-tion is past, and Winnipeg is making a steady and healthy growth. The constantly-increasing mileage of railway lines which centre at the city mark out for it an assured and large future. Not such a future, however, as Toronto or Montreal, for Winnipeg is without their immediate access to navigation, the key to great development, but still to stand at the gateway of the North-West, and to become its commercial, social and educational capital is no mean outlook. Brandon, too, is becoming a con-siderable railway centre; much building is going on, and the smaller town is anxious to secure from the railway companies the same advantages as a wholesale distributing point which Winnipeg now enjoys. From both

Regina and Calgary railway systems extend north and south, and both have a prevailing air of substantial prosperity. I have before referred to the numerous small but flourishing towns which spring up along every new line of railway. None of these depends upon manufactures; all owe their existence to the increasing wealth of the surrounding agricultural country, and furnish the most conclusive proof of its producing capacity. One remark about all North-Western towns should not be omitted. In them life is as safe, property as secure, and the ordinary supremacy of law as complete as in the old towns of Eastern Canada, or in the country towns and villages of England and Scotland. This advantage over the western towns of the United States the country owes in part to the greater slowness of growth which is so often complained of, and to the natural selection of population effected by a northern climate – partly, no doubt, to superiority of judicial and social institutions. It is no small thing that the North-West can offer to every immigrant all the social security to which he has been accustomed in the oldest communities.

A larger population is unquestionably the greatest need of the country. While, however, there is at present a strong popular demand for a vigorous immigration policy on the part of the Government, I have found that this demand is always qualified by the opinion that numbers should not be purchased at the expense of quality. Should restraints be placed upon undesirable immigration by the United States, Canada will scarcely welcome what her neighbours refuse. But there are strong reasons for thinking that the North-West has now gained a stage of development and established for itself a name which will draw to it a steady and sufficient inflow of the most desirable population.

What are the classes of settlers who succeed and seem best fitted for the North-West? On the whole one is inclined to describe it as essentially a country for the poor man or the man with a moderate amount of means. Alberta, with its ranches, and some of the prairie districts, such as the Qu' Appelle Valley, with opportunities for farms on a large scale, furnish openings for the successful use of larger capital; but men who themselves work the land are what the country chiefly requires, and to them it will prove most satisfactory. Among these the advantage certainly lies with immigrants who have had some previous practical acquaintance with the farming conditions of the Canadian climate, or of a climate similar to it. They begin at once to make crops grow, which the unskilled immigrant rarely does. Settlers from the Eastern Provinces or from the more Northern States easily adapt themselves to the conditions of the country; so on the whole does the Scottish labourer. The English and Irish farm hand has less flexibility for change, but he, too, succeeds by dint of pluck and industry. Among foreigners the Icelander easily takes the first place, in virtue of his sobriety, industry, and frugality. The Scandinavian does well, and the plodding German. The North-West will never be a congenial home for the Italian and other Latin races. These naturally gravitate towards the warm southern and middle portions of the United States or towards South America. I heard very grave doubts expressed about the success of one or two colonies of Russian Jews. The difficulty in this case was attributed to inherent disinclination to agricultural pursuits. It may have been quite as much due to the fact that as emigrants they had too much assistance. The experience of the North-West shows that extraordinary care is required to make a success of assisted emigration. Lord Brassey has discussed in the columns of *The Times* the comparative failure of his first efforts to make easy the path of the emigrant on the colonization estate in which he is concerned. It was interesting to find that most of the men who appear to have been discontented, if not idle, when receiving aid, have become comparatively successful when thrown entirely upon their own resources and compelled to work in their own way....

To speak broadly, it must be said that the young Englishman of the better classes sent out to the North-West to be a farmer is not a success....

Often it is not the strongest fibre which is sent out from the better class of English homes, the market for all that is excellent being best at home.... A good deal of the loafing around hotels and bar-rooms in the North-West is done by young Englishmen, and the term "remittance man" tends to become an expression of contempt. If these men must come out, let the extra ladies of the family come to exercise their better influence over them. They will be as well employed as in slumming or parish work at home, and they will be giving what the North-West wants – something of England's best to leaven social life. One never meets in the West an Englishwoman who is not a centre of wholesome and refining influence. It would, indeed, be a boon to the country if the same were true of every son of an English gentleman who goes to it....

In addition to the settlers from the older provinces of the Dominion, and from England, Ireland, and Scotland, there are being formed at some points in the North-West a curious variety of small colonies of different nationalities, mostly northern-Danes, Swedes, Norwegians, Belgians, Bavarians, Alsatians, Icelanders, and many others. A small band of settlers comes at first under some special impulse, and gradually attracts to itself recruits from the home centre. The numbers are sufficient to give a degree of cohesion to these small communities and some vitality to the languages they speak. A more complete intermixture with the prevailing English-speaking population would facilitate the work of assimilation. On the other hand, the emigrant finds himself at once among friends, and so does not feel so keenly the change from the old to the new land. It is difficult as yet to judge how far this method of settlement will extend. It can in any case only temporarily lengthen out the process of amalgamation.

A new and highly interesting factor has lately appeared in the settlement of the North-West. The United States have become an important recruiting ground for immigrants. In the Eastern Provinces I had heard of a movement northward from the Western States towards the Alberta and Saskatchewan districts. On inquiry at the land office at Winnipeg I was shown long lists of receipts for first payments on lands in the Prince Albert districts made by farmers in Dakota, Nebraska, Washington, and even as far south as Kansas. These men had already moved into the country, or were preparing to do so in the coming spring....

In conversation with the immigrants it was easy to discover the explanation of this new and unexpected movement of population. "Land is getting to be land on this continent," one of them remarked to me in Western idiom. The rush into a newly-opened district, such as that which took place at Oklahoma a few years ago, illustrates the extent to which land hunger is already felt in the United States. Guided by an instinct almost like that which directed the buffalo to the fertile feeding grounds of the Saskatchewan, the tide of population which filled up the older Western States and flowed on to the less fertile regions of Dakota, or to the mountain districts with their limited farming lands, seems now to have taken a bend northward. If the expectations of its pioneers are fulfilled, it seems probable that this movement will become very considerable during the next few years.... These immigrants are of a class which the North-West most of all wants. Many are Canadians returning after trying their fortunes in the United States. Most seemed to be bringing with them money, horses, cattle, and household equipment. Best of all, they bring skill in pioneering work and acquaintance with its conditions, in these points having an infinite superiority over the emigrant direct from Europe. It was striking to observe the confidence and reliance upon their own resources with which these men, accompanied by their wives and children, faced the task of finding homes for themselves north of the Saskatchewan in the months of October and November, when the long, severe winter was all before them. They were doing it in order to be ready for a good spring's work.

Once more, in Southern Alberta I found that a group of Mormons – an offshoot from Salt Lake – had purchased to the south and east of Lethbridge more than 500,000 acres of land from the Alberta Coal and Mining Company. About 500 settlers have already entered this country, and preparations are being made for a continued influx from Utah, where land has become scarce. Other immigrants are freely accepted, as there is not, I believe, any wish to form a distinct Mormon colony. The capitalists who have undertaken this enterprise expect to repeat here the process of irrigation by which the Salt Lake Valley was changed from a semi-desert to a richly productive country. It is proposed to divert the waters of the St. Mary's river through a canal which will make a large area as well suited for agricultural as it now is for pastoral purposes.

The North-West is thus being approached from various points, and by many classes of immigrants. A great rush of population, such as marked the settlement of some of the Western States, is neither to be expected nor desired. But everything now points to a steady and healthy growth, such as is required for the fuller consolidation of the Dominion.

Coal

An important coal area has lately been opened up in the Rocky Mountain district. A few miles from Banff, and scarcely a hundred yards from the line of the Canadian Pacific Railway, a mine of anthracite coal is being worked....

At Canmore, only ten miles distant from the anthracite mine, the Rocky Mountain deposits furnish a coal of a different quality. The mines have not long been opened, and their extent has not yet been fully determined, but the coal has been found to be almost smokeless, and has the further quality of coking well. Both these facts are of the utmost interest, as the one suggests the possibility of our ships of war in the Pacific being supplied near at hand with the smokeless coal at present obtained from Wales, while the silver mines now opening up in the Kootenay districts, as well as those on the other side of the national boundary, create a large demand for coke to be used in smelting.

Further south along the range of the Rockies, once more, at the Crow's Nest Pass, other outcrops of a remarkable thickness and good quality have been discovered. As there is at present no railway connection to this point, and as the country around is comparatively unsettled, there has been no inducement to work these deposits, which await the advance of civilization. But it is through the Crow's Nest Pass that an easier access to the Kootenay country will ultimately be sought, and the Canadian Pacific Railway is even now feeling its way in this direction, having made surveys with a view to the early construction of a line.

Thus the coal mines of the Rocky Mountains promise to supply what is lacking in the quality of those of the Pacific coast and those of the prairies.... Of the coal areas of the prairies, however, I have not as yet spoken.

In a country mainly treeless and with a cold winter season the existence of coal decides the question of settlement, or at least of dense settlement. This consideration for some time seemed to hold the destiny of the Canadian North-West in the balance. Along the river beds and in the rougher undulating country there was wood sufficient for the purposes of the early settlers, but it was evident that any increase of population on the plains would soon exhaust these limited supplies. In many districts it has already done so. Coal, therefore, has always been essential to the permanent success of the North-West. Fortunately, vast beds have been discovered, equal apparently to any necessities of future population. It is of varying quality. The Galt mines at Lethbridge are the most important of those yet opened. The product is a good bituminous coal, excellent for railway use, and giving the farmer a not too expensive fuel....

Eastward from Lethbridge, and reaching along the American boundary to the borders of Manitoba, are coal measures which have been estimated by Dr. Dawson to cover 15,000 square miles. The coal hitherto obtained is not of the best quality, and many of the seams consist mainly of lignite. They lie quite near the surface and are easily worked. In special localities the quality may improve. I visited the newly-opened mines at Estevan, about 325 miles from Winnipeg. The early product of the mines was not very satisfactory, as the coal, which looked well when it came out of the mine, crumbled after exposure to the air. Deeper mining is expected to produce better results. At the worst, however, Southern Manitoba and Assiniboia are assured of an abundance of cheap fuel, which will meet the necessities of the farming population. Outcrops are met with in many places, and as railways are pushed forward new mines will be opened.

When we go northward to the Saskatchewan a striking illustration of the abundance of coal in this district is furnished by the thick seams which are visible all along the banks of that river in the vicinity of Edmonton. A serviceable domestic coal is delivered in Edmonton and at most points in the country around for about 10s. per ton.

(Parkin, *The Great Dominion,* 1895, 26–42, 82–7)

4 EASTERN CANADA – ONTARIO

☞ A bountiful agricultural area and also the Canadian region where manufacturing industry has benefited most from protective tariffs, Ontario, Parkin says, will remain a centre of power in Canada for a long time to come, despite the changes taking place in the North-West. He notes, as did other writers before the First World War, that lighter machine goods, compared to the ponderous goods of British manufacture, are made in Canadian and American factories, providing an international competitive advantage. Parkin writes at a time before the automobile industry expanded in nearby Detroit and before Niagara hydroelectric power became an important industrial asset in Ontario. In this period of recent growth Toronto is beginning to rival Montreal. ☞

I began these studies of Canada by consideration of the North-West, as presenting one of the most interesting and critical problems in the development of the Dominion. But it must constantly be remembered that, after all, the brains and pith and marrow of the country are still in the Eastern Provinces; that these are still the centre of political force, of the country's progress, wealth, and culture, of those decisive characteristics which have given Canada its strong individuality, and will, for many years to come, chiefly mould its future; that, in fact, the North-West is but a yesterday's offshoot and creation of the sturdy life which has been steadily growing up for a long time in the East. It would therefore leave quite a wrong impression on readers in other parts of the Empire to lay the emphasis, in discussing Canada's affairs, on the West, to the exclusion of the East. A precisely opposite course would at the present moment be more just. The great possibilities of the prairie country have impressed the imagination of people at a distance, and have made it, during the last few years, rather unduly overshadow the older provinces of which I am now to speak. As far as political and social power go these latter still constitute by far the greater part of Canada....

Nor must it be thought that the developments of the future belong to the West alone. All the Eastern Provinces still have large unoccupied areas, while their resources are much more varied than those of the somewhat monotonous West. Eastern Canada is a country of seacoast, islands, peninsulas, great rivers, and lakes; of splendid fisheries; of varied scenery and climate; of coal, timber, iron, and gold; precisely that combination of condition and resources which history has proved most favourable to human progress.

Of the provinces, Ontario is by far the greatest and wealthiest, at present containing well nigh one half the population of the whole Dominion, and with great possibilities of future growth. Bounded by three great lakes, Ontario, Erie, and Huron, and by three great rivers, the St. Lawrence, Detroit, and Ottawa, so that its position, though in the middle of the continent, is almost insular; equipped with a most complete railway system; having a climate which favours the growth in abundance of grapes, peaches, melons, maize and similar products in the south, and is singularly suited for wheat, barley, and all the hardier cereals further north; with petroleum and salt areas in the west, timber areas on Lake Huron, mineral deposits of great variety and extent on Lake Superior, the province seems almost unique in situation and resources for production and commerce of all kinds. Its future must be very great indeed, and whatever may be the growth of the West, Ontario will assuredly remain for a long time the centre of political and commercial energy in the Dominion. At least, if there is any lack of prosperity and influence, it will lie in the people themselves, not in their stars....

... as late as 1835 the population, now nearly two millions and a half, numbered only three hundred thousand.

When it is remembered also that this growth of little more than half a century has not been made on a prairie soil, but that everyone of its 25,000,000 cleared acres has involved hewing down a heavily wooded forest, the progress made seems surprising, and explains why the province has reared a hardy race of men.

The truth is that the southern and western districts of Ontario – those which lie between the St. Lawrence and the Ottawa, and those which are enclosed by the lakes Ontario, Erie and Huron – have almost everything that could recommend them as a place in which to make a home – a fertile soil, variety of production, a plentiful water supply, and a salubrious climate. I doubt if any mainly agricultural area of equal size in the world gives evidence of more uniform prosperity among the mass of the people than do the older portions of Ontario....

Speaking generally, agricultural employment and products in Ontario are not unlike those of the United Kingdom; a warmer summer and drier autumn giving, in comparison, advantages in ripening fruit and harvesting grain; a colder winter presenting drawbacks in the feeding of stock and for outdoor farm work. But there are districts with characteristics worthy of special note.

A visit to the Niagara Peninsula of Ontario, for instance, upsets many preconceived ideas about the Canadian climate and the range of Canadian production. It is the greatest fruit district of the Dominion. Could Louis the Fifteenth have seen it as it is to-day he would have understood that instead of the "few arpents of snow" which he thought, or affected to think, he was signing away when he ceded Canada to Britain, he was really handing over to English people one district, at least, which compared not unfavourably in soil and climate with the richest and sunniest parts of France. Grapes, peaches, melons, and tomatoes, which in England are ripened with difficulty when not under glass, are here raised in the greatest profusion in the open air....

The fruit growing industry of the Niagara district is already important, but a steadily widening market seems likely to give it a great expansion. Few parts of Canada illustrate more fully the advantage which has come from the extension of the railway system of the Dominion.

The prairies of the North-West produce little or no fruit, and are never likely to minister much to their own wants in this respect.

Already many hundred tons of grapes, pears, tomatoes, &c., are shipped yearly from the country between Hamilton and Niagara to Winnipeg, whence it is distributed as far west as the Rocky Mountains. The growth of Western population will steadily increase the importance of this market. Eastward a market is found as far as Prince Edward Island and Nova Scotia, the latter of which, though an excellent apple region, does not favour the growth of grapes and peaches. Special daily fruit trains are run regularly during the autumn to Toronto and Montreal, and fruit transport forms at this season an important item in the receipts of the Grand Trunk and other lines.... One would think that with good appliances for cold storage, grapes and tomatoes, at least, could be cheaply and profitably placed upon the English market.

I had heard that hopes were entertained of the Peninsula becoming a large wine producing area. There are; of course, many difficulties involved in producing wines of the best quality to compete with those of Europe, and, in addition to this, I was told by one of the largest growers that it only paid to use the grapes for making wine when the price had fallen to what seemed a ridiculously low point; I think below a cent per pound. Under these conditions the growing demand for the grapes as a fruit must, one would think, check for a long time any attempts at wine production on a large scale.

Still a good deal of wine has already been made, and there are growers, who take a much more hopeful view of the industry than that here stated....

In other districts of the province there are the best opportunities for mixed farming. Stock raising and dairying have of late years steadily taken the place of wheat growing, once the farmer's chief reliance....

The farmer of Ontario is beginning to find out that in producing wheat only he commits himself to the chances of competition not merely with the easily tilled expanses of the fertile prairie, but also with the poorly paid and poorly fed peasant of India, Russia, and South America. The higher form of product demands greater intelligence and expenditure of thought, but gives a larger and more reliable return.

Ontario supplies much the larger proportion of the cheese and live cattle which the Dominion sends to England, and now aims at increasing its output of butter, especially during the winter season, in alternation with the cheese making of the summer.

Ontario is the province also which has benefited most largely by the protective policy; manufactures of great importance have sprung up at many points. In agricultural implements, pianos and cabinet organs, sewing machines, carriages, furniture, and railway plant, the people of Ontario could now probably hold their own in the markets of the world without protection. Large shipments of farming tools are now being made to Australia, the British manufacturer not yet having sufficiently learned the art, common to American and Canadian, of making tools which combine a maximum of strength with a minimum of weight, the special requirement of warm countries. The coarser forms of cotton manufacture have also advanced rapidly in Canada, but this centres chiefly in Montreal and the Lower Provinces, where the French population furnishes a cheap and steady supply of factory labour. The same is true of the sugar-refining industry, which has made immense strides under the national policy....

Among the cities of Ontario, Toronto, the capital, tends to become the literary and intellectual centre of the Dominion, and almost the rival of Montreal in commercial prestige. Its population is close upon 200,000. The largest and most influential daily newspapers of the Dominion are published here; those of the larger city of Montreal being somewhat handicapped by appearing in the midst of a bi-lingual population. The state-supported University and the well-endowed collegiate institutions of several religious bodies adorn Toronto with groups of fine buildings, and give it a considerable learned society.

The situation of the city immediately upon Lake Ontario mitigates the severity of inland summer heat. Boating clubs and yachting clubs around the harbour illustrate the tastes and amusements of the people,

and explain the aquatic reputation of the place. By means of good steam-
boat connection across the lake, and of the electric railway, Niagara has
been brought within the limit of a day's pleasant outing. On summer
afternoons and evenings the populace streams across in cheap ferryboats
to the Island which fronts the harbour, to enjoy the fresh breezes of
the lake. In default of the sea shore, fashionable Toronto escapes, for
outdoor life in holiday time, to the charming Muskoka Lake district, a
hundred miles to the north, the numerous islands of which are becoming
dotted with the huts, cottages or villas of its summer visitors.

Altogether Toronto has advantages which make it, among the cities of
the Empire, a distinctly pleasant place in which to live....

In sentiment Toronto is intensely British. The foundation of the place
by United Empire Loyalists after the American Revolution, and the part
which it has taken in various crises of Canadian history since that time,
sufficiently account for the peculiar strength of this feeling. The remark
applies equally to much of Southern Ontario, which owes its early settlement chiefly to the Loyalist migration. In the war of 1812 its borders
formed the chief line of attack and defence. Along them are found the
battle-fields on which aggression was resisted, and security won for
Canadian territory. Noble tradition has thus been added to original
sentiment to form a persistent and active force which still profoundly
influences the whole community.

Hamilton, beautifully situated on a bay at the head of Lake Ontario,
with London and Woodstock further inland, are other towns of the
province which derive a very marked prosperity chiefly from being the
centres of splendid agricultural districts. Kingston, at the foot of Lake
Ontario, has a history dating back to the early days of French occupation, and is now the seat of a flourishing University, and of the Military
College of the Dominion.

Ottawa, the political capital of the Dominion, is also in Ontario.
When selected in 1858 to be the seat of government, it was a remote
and unimportant lumbering village, chosen as a compromise between
the rival claims of Montreal, Quebec and Toronto. Since that time it has
grown rapidly and has now 50,000 inhabitants.... Ottawa continues
to be the centre of an extensive lumbering industry, and the saw-mills
along the river, with the pulp-mills which utilise the refuse wood, are
the main dependence of the labouring population. The outskirts of the
city still indicate its recent origin, or perhaps the inability of municipal
government to keep pace with the wants of a rapidly growing community. Possibly the perfection of the tram system which reaches out

in all directions, driven, lighted, and in winter warmed with electricity obtained by utilising the Chaudière Falls, makes attention to suburban streets a secondary question. Many think that the American plan of making the seat of the general government an area exclusively under federal control might have been adopted with advantage at Ottawa.

(Parkin, *The Great Dominion*, 1895, 90–101)

5 EASTERN CANADA – THE MARITIME PROVINCES

☞ The great promise that Bouchette saw in the Maritimes has not been fulfilled by the time Parkin writes, more than eight decades later. With the growth of Ontario, and then the opening of the prairies to agricultural settlement, this region feels left behind. In part this is because of a two-fold blow: the decline of the wooden sailing ship and the rise of rival areas, including the United States. A son of New Brunswick, Parkin is frank about economic stagnation in the Maritimes and out-migration. He is highly critical of the fact that Maritimers have not shown initiative and energy. Because of "business fatalism," the area has not kept up with Ontario and Montreal. He hastens to add that this lag is compensated for by the "higher glory of moral influence and intellectual power" and cites the names of Maritimers who have made good and achieved positions of leadership elsewhere. Parkin says there is great scope for agricultural improvement and suggests forest lands should be cleared to make farms. While writing this, no doubt sitting at his desk in relative comfort, he does not hesitate to recommend such difficult lands to immigrants who are willing to work fourteen to fifteen hours a day in summer, balanced by more leisure time in winter.

The remarks on coal have been moved from the chapter on that commodity to this section. Parkin views Nova Scotia's great coal reserves as essential assets that can be used to maintain strategic coaling stations for defence of the British Empire and for industrial and commercial use within eastern Canada. ☜

Passing by the Province of Quebec for the present, as requiring individual treatment, I go on to the Maritime Provinces – New Brunswick, Nova Scotia, and Prince Edward Island – where the population is practically homogeneous with that of Ontario. One geographical fact makes the relation of these provinces to the Dominion and to the Empire of the utmost significance. They contain the only good ports on the eastern coast of Canada open to navigation in all seasons of the year. As a harbour Halifax ranks among the best in the world, as a naval station among the most important in the Empire. The whole British navy could float, with room to spare, at the splendid anchorage in Bedford Basin. The harbour is strongly fortified, the length and narrowness of the entrance channel making it singularly adapted to defence. When two or three more guns of the heaviest metal and most modern type have been placed in the casemates prepared for them, when a complete search-light system has been installed, and telegraphic and telephonic communication completed between the various forts and batteries, Halifax harbour will be practically unassailable. Those whose professional opinion is entitled to great weight complain of an incredible hesitation on the part of the authorities in adding these final touches which are necessary to give full effect to a. position already so nearly impregnable....

St. John, on the Bay of Fundy, stands next in importance to Halifax. As a commercial port it has the advantage over the latter of saving two or three hundred miles of land carriage to the Western Provinces. The harbour has often been represented as difficult of access on account of fog, but reliable statistics seem to prove that there is no real ground for this opinion. St. John has an important commerce, and is likely to have more, but it is practically undefended. I know of no place of equal importance in any part of the empire which would in time of war be so entirely at the mercy of anyone who chose to attack it....

The industrial position in the Maritime Provinces during the last fifteen or twenty years has been very peculiar. For a long time the chief industries, those which occupied the great mass of the population, were lumbering, shipbuilding, and fishing. The finest pine timber has now become partially exhausted. Spruce timber, which at present constitutes the principal export, grows on soil not very well suited for agriculture, reproduces itself rapidly if the forests are protected from fire, and will therefore remain a permanent industry, though not one capable of maintaining a large population. Besides, the timber trade is very uncertain, and subject to serious fluctuations from variation of snowfall and flood, as well as from ordinary commercial competition.

The substitution of iron for wood in shipbuilding has had a disastrous effect upon several formerly prosperous communities. Places like St. John and Yarmouth, which twenty-five years ago had more tonnage afloat in proportion to population than any places of equal size in the world, have seen the carrying trade which brought them wealth gradually slipping away without the chance of recovery, and in the effort to maintain an almost hopeless contest many large shipping firms have come to grief....

... Once more, the opening of the prairies of the North-West has not only had the effect of carrying the tide of immigration almost entirely westward past Nova Scotia and New Brunswick, but has also drained away a proportion of the young and enterprising population.... But there has been a lack, among the mass of the people, even of such energy and adaptability to changing conditions as might fairly have been expected. This is perfectly manifest to the observer who has the opportunity of making comparison with other communities, but would require too much space to discuss fully here. Partly a business fatalism, the offspring, I think, of long subjection to the incalculable chances of the lumber and fishing industries; partly careless habits of farm work induced by the same employments; partly the hope constantly indulged of help from some god's hand thrust out from the political machine; this, perhaps, embodies in the fewest possible words what one wishes to express. Surely nowhere in our wide British Empire, or in any other country, have so much talent, effort, and time been spent in trying to squeeze public and private prosperity out of politics as in the Maritime Provinces of Canada. The attempt has not succeeded; the provinces by the sea, though with most varied resources, remain comparatively poor, while Ontario grows increasingly rich, and Montreal begins to add up its long lists of millionaires. A high average of comfort widely prevails, but there are few examples of the great business success often achieved in other parts of the Dominion.

But it must not be thought that the poorer provinces are without their compensations for the present or their hopes for the future. I am not sure that both are not such as fairly to balance the situation. If these provinces have not the prestige of wealth, they have the severer and, as some may think, the higher glory of moral influence and intellectual power. One of the most remarkable facts connected with the growth of federated Canada has been the influence – quite disproportionate to population – of the public men of the Maritime Provinces in the Councils of the Dominion. Ontario owed to Scotland Sir John Macdonald, George Brown, Alexander Mackenzie, and Sir Alexander Galt. Montreal also has drawn its merchant princes and organizers of industry chiefly from Scotland and England. The smaller provinces have bred their own men, and they need not be ashamed of the type. No doubt it was Sir John Macdonald's mind, with its Imperial turn of thought, which first fully grasped the idea of a United Canada as a part of a United Empire, but no one who knows the prejudices and problems he had to face believes that he could ever have realized his dream without having had at his back the political fighting energy of Sir Charles Tupper and the remarkable financial prudence and ability of Sir Leonard Tilley, the one a son of Nova Scotia, the other of New Brunswick. When the veteran Premier died, the first and, second choice for a successor, after the temporary leadership of Sir John Abbott was from among Maritime Province men....

This range of influence is not confined to politics and law. Very singular it is to observe how these comparatively poor provinces, with their simple and sometimes rigorous conditions of life, are furnishing brains to other parts of the continent. Sir William Dawson. the distinguished scientist and head of M'Gill College, Montreal; Principal Grant, of Queen's University, Kingston; Dr. Rand, President of the new M'Master University at Toronto; Dr. Bourinot, of Ottawa, the keen analyst and exponent of Federal Government; Dr. Schurman, President of Cornell University, New York; Professor Simon Newcomb, of the Washington Observatory, admittedly one of the foremost astronomers of the world; Archbishop O'Brien, the most conspicuous figure of the Roman Catholic Church in Eastern Canada, are all from the same provinces. So are Charles Roberts and Bliss Carman, whose names as poets, well known in Canada and the United States, are also beginning to be known in England, and who, whatever estimate critics may ultimately put upon their work, are certainly genuine outgrowths of their native soil, and catch their inspirations from the conditions amid which they live. Professorships, editorial chairs, and the pulpits of all denominations, not only across the breadth of the Dominion from Quebec to Vancouver, but through the Eastern and Western States, are in a singularly large proportion supplied from the same source....

This is a long list, but it is worth going over. It is not at all clear that in the longer judgments of history the people of Nova Scotia, New Brunswick, and Prince Edward Island will be thought to have sufficient reason for envying the material prosperity of Ontario and the millionaires of Montreal.

But to me the business possibilities of these provinces in the future, given well-directed energy, enterprise, and thought, seem in the highest degree promising. Fisheries, coal mines, forests, gold-bearing quartz reefs, iron, gypsum, and lime deposits are all large and fairly remunerative fields of industry....

There was a prevalent opinion in the early days of Confederation that the Maritime Provinces were to become in manufacturing to the rest of

Canada what New England has been to the West of the United States. That expectation has not been realized, and may be still remote. But there are other opportunities. The farming resources of these. provinces have only as yet been tapped. Let the earnestness and common effort so long turned upon party politics be bent more fully upon agricultural improvement; let something better be substituted for the present careless, rough-and-ready methods of farming and marketing; let cheese and butter factories be established everywhere at intervals of a few miles, as in Ontario, over which the provinces have the greatest possible advantage in pasturage; let a thoroughly organized means of rapid transit with cold storage be provided to England; let rigid inspection and grading of all products before shipping-apples, hay, butter, cheese, fish, poultry, eggs, &c. – be provided, and the people of the Maritime Provinces will awake to find out that they hold an almost unequalled position with relation to external markets....

As a fruit-growing country Nova Scotia stands only second to Ontario. The orchards of the Annapolis and Cornwallis valleys are famed far and wide, and the export of apples to both Britain and the United States has already grown to large proportions....

Of the Maritime Provinces generally it may be said that the climatic conditions are singularly favourable. Nearness to the sea mitigates alike the heat of summer and the cold of winter. The tide of tourist travel is now turning this way, and the Gulf of St. Lawrence and Bay of Fundy, with their cool breezes and beautiful scenery, promise to become one of the chief summer resorts of dwellers in the heated inland regions of America.

Although manufactures have increased much in the Dominion, agriculture is still, and will be, the mainstay of general prosperity in Eastern as well as Western Canada, in Ontario as well as in the Maritime Provinces. It still offers a sufficient opening for emigrants, but under very different circumstances from those of the West. The attraction of the prairies, the facility with which farms are created there, have during late years diverted emigration from the wooded Eastern Provinces. But a wooded farm has its very distinct advantages, although involving more preliminary labour. Plenty of timber for building and fencing, abundance of fuel close at hand, occupation during the winter season, shelter from the extreme severity of winter – all these are weighty considerations in fixing a home. Hardy working men, especially those accustomed to the use of an axe, or willing to acquire it, not afraid of a fourteen or fifteen hours day during the summer, balanced by the hope of greater leisure in the winter, still have, in my opinion, an excellent opportunity to make comfortable homes for themselves and provide a healthy life for their families by taking up the unsettled woodland districts of Eastern Canada, where ungranted lands of excellent quality can still be obtained on easy terms. Railways have been so extensively built in all the provinces that nowhere will the settler be far removed from ready access to markets and civilization, and the severe privations and the isolation of the early pioneers of the country need not be undergone.

Such things are largely a matter of personal inclination, but I must confess, after much observation of the two sides of Canadian life, that the East would have for me the greater attraction. The nearness of the sea, the varied scenery and range of industry, the easier access to the best educational advantages, or to European and American markets and social centres, weigh heavily against what is the supreme advantage of the West – facility in the immediate creation of a farm....

Coal

It has been pointed out before, but cannot be pointed out too often, that the coal deposits of Canada make her relation to the maritime position of the Empire one of extraordinary interest. This is true, whether we have regard to the needs of commerce or to the maintenance of naval power. When a large proportion of the world's trade is carried in steamships, and when every effective ship of war that defends trade is propelled by steam, easy access to coal at essential points becomes a matter of the first consequence. This is true in times of peace, but infinitely more so in times of war, when coal for naval purposes can be obtained by belligerents only in ports under their own flag. It is generally admitted that in any future struggle for maritime supremacy an immense advantage would lie with the Power which can retain the widest control of bases of coal supply. It is this idea which prompts our large national expenditure on coaling stations; it is, perhaps, less thought of in connexion with territories possessing coal deposits.

Certainly the points at which Canada's great coalfields are found may be spoken of emphatically as essential. Eastward and westward, on the Atlantic and on the Pacific, their location is striking enough.

Nova Scotia projects far out into the Atlantic, and there, at the most northern port on the continent which is open both summer and winter, we have fixed the great naval station of Halifax, which in time of war would necessarily be our chief base for defending what has become the greatest food route of the United Kingdom. Immediately behind Halifax and closely connected with it by rail are the Pictou and other Nova Scotian coal mines, which already turn out about a million tons of coal per annum. Further north is the island of Cape Breton. A century and a half ago, long before steam came into use, the keen eye of French soldiers fixed upon Louisburg in Cape Breton as the point from which the road to the St. Lawrence could best be guarded and French commercial interests maintained upon the mainland. The strong fortress is gone, but around the fine harbours of the island are numerous mines far more useful than was the fortress for the prosecution of commerce or, in case of emergency, for its defence. From these mines, again, are raised yearly about a million tons of coal of excellent quality for steaming and other purposes. The mouths of the pits are in some cases close to the shore, and as the mines are carried far out under the ocean a ship may be loading directly over the spot from which the coal is obtained. Nature could scarcely have done more to give an advantageous position.

Great activity has been given to mining operations in Cape Breton by the formation in 1892–3 of a powerful syndicate of American and Canadian capitalists to work one of the largest and most important groups of mines. The predominant influence in the company is American, and the action of the Nova Scotian provincial government in granting a ninety years' lease of the coaling privileges to a body chiefly composed of foreigners was at first subjected to a good deal of criticism from a national point of view.

It now seems to be clear that the transaction had no political significance, and that the combination was made entirely as a commercial speculation.

The application of abundant capital under the vigorous direction of the syndicate is an unmixed good, while the existence of other mines in the Sydney district uncontrolled by the new company will probably act as a permanent hindrance to the creation of a dangerous monopoly....

The full significance of these coal resources to a great maritime Power can only be fully understood when we reflect – first, that the importance of the St. Lawrence as a food route is fast increasing; and, secondly, that, with the exception of what might be temporarily stored at Bermuda and the West India stations, these are the only coal supplies to which British ships would have the national right of access in time of war along the whole Atlantic coast of America. As things now stand, Britain is the only Power which has adequate bases of coal supply on both sides of the Atlantic.

These supplies are, of course, as useful for inland traffic as for ocean service. Nova Scotian coal finds its way in large quantities several hundred miles westward from the Atlantic coast, and supplies the provinces of New Brunswick and Quebec with the greater part of what they consume. During the summer it has a water route up the St. Lawrence, and it is also carried by the Intercolonial Railway at exceptionally low rates, in accordance. with the Government policy of giving all possible encouragement to inter-provincial trade....

... New Brunswick also has bituminous coal, but the only seam yet discovered of sufficient thickness to work is one at Grand Lake, which gives a supply for local consumption, but does not add greatly to the product of the country. An attempt is now being made to enlarge the output, and to use the coal for smelting purposes....

(Parkin, *The Great Dominion*, 1895, 101–15, 73–8)

6 EASTERN CANADA – QUEBEC

☞ The question of French Canadian nationalism, and how Quebec relates to other parts of Canada and North America, is at the heart of Parkin's discussion. The effort he puts into this chapter reflects the importance of Quebec's place in Canada. In particular Parkin analyzes Quebec's role as a French-speaking province in the Dominion. He is very much aware of French Canada's sense of place and rootedness, and of the strong spirit of nationalism. Sympathetic as he may be to French Canadian desires to remain a distinctive people within North America, Parkin assumes that, to attain greater positions of power, French Canadians will have to adapt, even if only so slightly, to what he considers the broader Canadian culture. The concept of complete equality between cultures is not evident in Parkin's position. He says the right things about equality of citizenship in Canada, but his remarks on acculturation in the North-West, and the need for adaptation he expresses in his consideration of Quebec, contradict this. He makes the obvious, but nevertheless penetrating, observation that the history of Canada would have been very different if the migration of French Canadians to New England had been diverted to the North-West, a theme Canadian scholars have studied in recent years. The French Canadian migration to New England, and also in many instances their return to Canada, is described and Parkin notes the population movement to cities rather than, for instance, to the "newly opened West." Because of broader Canadian immigration trends, i.e., European immigrants in large numbers going to other parts of Canada, Parkin concludes that the proportion of French Canadians in Canada will decline.

French Canadian nationalism is described, using the term race and stressing the importance of religion and of Roman Catholic church leaders. It is not clear what Parkin means by race, but he seems to refer to what we now know as ethnicity. In discussing the French language he treads a very delicate line. He recognizes the fundamental importance of the French language for French Canadians, laments that more English-speakers don't learn French, yet acknowledges that French Canadians have to learn English to attain the highest positions in Canada. In analyzing class, French Canadians are stereotyped, and Parkin even refers to "racial inertia." Briefly mentioned are French Canadians in parts of Canada other than Quebec and the Acadians. He recognizes Montreal's primary role in Canada. Parkin is at greater ease in discussing Montreal and Quebec City than in discussing the equivalent Ontario cities, especially in discussions of where the power of the Quebec cities rests. There is a frank linking of British capital, and the power it implies, with a docile French Canadian labour force, with no comment on what internal stresses this causes for French Canadians. In some ways this is a very astute analysis of Quebec, in other aspects quite obtuse. It is surprising that Louis Riel is not mentioned, even though the Riel Rebellion occurred a mere ten years earlier. ☞

The French Canadian question is the crux of politics in the Dominion. It does not present so many difficulties or arouse such bitter animosities as does the Irish question in Britain; it is not so impracticable as the race and colour questions which are clouding the national horizon in the United States; it does not even seem to me so perplexing as the questions which the contact of a temperate and tropical climate, and therefore of strong and weak races, is beginning to produce in Australia, but still it is difficult, and for a good while to come will test the temper, the tact, and the patriotism of the Canadian people, whether French or English.

In some of its aspects, however, there has been of late a tendency to exaggerate the magnitude of the question. People in England were so accustomed less than a generation ago to think of Canada as a country chiefly inhabited by Frenchmen, they were so conscious of the fact that the presence of a French element dominated all questions of Canadian. policy, that the impression has scarcely yet died away. It is well, therefore, to form an accurate idea of the place which Quebec and the French Canadian hold and are likely to hold in the Dominion....

Out of the whole population of the Dominion, which was 4,833,237 in 1891, 1,404,974 were French-speaking; of these 1,186,346 were in the Province of Quebec. These proportions, it will be seen, are weighty, but not dominant.

So much for the present. In forecasting the future one or two main points must be kept in view. The first is that the French population of Canada is not reinforced from without. France, with her declining population, now sends very few emigrants abroad, and she sends them least of all to Quebec....

On the other hand, the French Canadian has himself become an emigrant from his native country. In an article in the *Forum,* Louis Frechette, the French Canadian writer, estimates the number of his compatriots in the United States at between eleven and twelve hundred thousand. This estimate appears to be much exaggerated, but the number is certainly very great. An American estimate places the numbers in the six New England States alone at something over 300,000.

One qualifying feature of this exodus to New England is, however, to be noted. Numbers of the people do not go to remain. The Commissioner for the census of 1891 pointed out to me at Ottawa the remarkable fact that in the returns Quebec was often given as the birthplace of the elder children of a large French family, the United States as the birthplace of a succeeding group, to be followed again by others born in Quebec. The migration, therefore, is in part temporary, and the present inclination of the *habitant* is to gravitate back to his native soil.

This exodus is almost exclusively confined to the poorer and less educated population of the province; for the able, educated, and ambitious French Canadian the best field is still found at home among his own. people and under the Canadian system, where he has a far better opportunity to win political, professional, or literary success. In the United States he could only succeed by using the English language and becoming entirely Americanized; in Canada he can succeed even while remaining a Frenchman; a moderate adaptation to English ideas opens freely to him all the avenues to power.

But, whatever qualification we give to it, a migration which has already advanced so far must profoundly affect the future of the French race in Canada, unless some change of industrial circumstances or of race feeling – and neither is impossible – should result in a refluent wave of movement on a corresponding scale. The tendency of the French Canadian both in Canada and the United States to drift into the cities and to become a factory operative, instead of the hardy and adventurous pioneer of Western civilization, such as he once was, is another element in the question; it is almost as significant as the change which has made France cease to be a colonizing power in the true sense of the expression, Had the whole tide of migration from Quebec been directed to the newly opened West instead of to New England the results must have been very considerable....

There are apparently few things which give to the *habitant* of Quebec such unalloyed satisfaction as to see himself surrounded by a numerous offspring, whatever the degree of comfort in which he may be able to maintain them. In this feeling he has, curiously enough, public support.

Three or four years ago the government of the province, reverting to the policy of the French Kings in the early days of Canadian colonization, instituted a system of premiums on large families, by offering to give a grant of a hundred acres of land to all heads of families who had twelve or more children. This grant has already been made in nearly 2,000 cases, and applications are said to be still flowing in. Families of twenty children are common; families of twenty-five or more are not unknown. But in spite of special facts like these the last Canadian census proved that the advantage in the natural rate of increase of Quebec over the other provinces was comparatively slight – in the case of Ontario it amounted to scarcely more than 1 per cent.

A higher death-rate, possibly arising from lower conditions of life, in part neutralizes the higher birthrate.

There is a still more important point to keep in mind. While Quebec is not reinforced from without, all the rest of Canada is being strengthened by a steady stream of people who, even when they come from the German, Scandinavian, and Latin countries of Europe, hasten to learn the English language, and within a generation or two become thoroughly Anglicised. In a previous chapter I have referred to a movement of pioneers from some districts of the United States towards the North-west of Canada. This migration alone, under the pressure of land hunger in the Western States, might easily grow to proportions which would add to the English speaking population of the North-West as much as is subtracted from that of Quebec by the exodus to New England....

All these facts – and they are mentioned only as facts – go to show that the relative weight of French Canada in the Dominion must steadily and perhaps rapidly decline. But though Quebec is thus becoming a secondary factor in Canadian development it presents problems which, as I have said, are perplexing.

To understand the situation, it must, in the first place, always be remembered that the Frenchman, so far from being an alien in the country, is a Canadian of the Canadians. The love of the soil is burned into his very soul. He looks back to a long period in the early occupation of the country which the brilliant pen of Parkman has shown to present not merely the most picturesque page in the history of America, but one of the most picturesque in the history of the world. He underwent the greatest hardships in settling the country; he suffered and fought and died to keep it under the French flag. Since he was abandoned by France he has fought with even greater intrepidity and has died as heroically to keep his country under the British flag.

The many thousands of French Canadians who go to work in the mills and factories of New England the American looks upon as aliens – just as he looks upon the Italian or the Polish Jew – almost as he looks upon the Chinaman. A limited naturalization, which has made the French Canadian vote count in elections, may suggest modification of this statement; but it is still, in the main, true. In Canada, on the other hand, and, above all, in Quebec, the French Canadian is on his native heath. No sense or right of citizenship is stronger than his. His English fellow-subjects not only freely acknowledge this perfect equality of citizenship, but they even look upon him as a fellow-citizen who has special claims upon their consideration, in view of the anomalous position which he has so long held – that of a loyal citizen of an Empire to which he is not tied by either race or religion....

... With all their most responsible and reflective men, loyalty to the British connection has long been a first tenet. Sir George Cartier described himself as an Englishman speaking French. Sir Etienne Taché emphasized the loyalty of his people by affirming that in any national conflict, it would be a French Canadian who would fire the last shot in defence of the British flag in America. At Winnipeg, the late Archbishop Taché quoted to me his relative's words with the warmest approval and satisfaction. Throughout nearly the whole of the present century, the clergy of Quebec have uniformly looked upon British connection as the best guarantee of the secure position of themselves, their church, and their people. Their highest representatives have not hesitated to state this in formal ecclesiastical declarations.

English Canadians have certainly met these indications of a common loyalty with goodwill. If they have had at times some difficulty in working harmoniously with Englishmen speaking French, they are quite prepared, under favourable conditions, to go far with Frenchmen speaking English, or reasonably in sympathy with English ideas....

And this, perhaps, brings us to the point where the line of difficulty and dangerous friction may be most clearly discerned. Unfortunately, not all French Canadian leaders are responsible and moderate men. The Frenchman is a Canadian of the Canadians, but the Canada of to-day is not, as he sometimes seems to think, the Canada of Louis XV. Within the past few years, however, a persistent attempt has been made to narrow the French Canadian's patriotism to Quebec; to fill him with the idea that it is possible to create on the banks of the St. Lawrence something which, as pictured to him, is practically a separate French nationality in Canada; a nationality, too, which belongs to a past century rather than to the present....

... One of the most prominent of their public men once said to me that, as a matter of fact, a majority of French Canadians look forward to an exclusiveness on the American continent as complete both in race and religion as was ever that of the Hebrews. No one familiar with Quebec will doubt that the statement has in it much truth. My informant was not himself in sympathy with this feeling, and he referred to it with regret. His own influence has been used to bring his people more freely into the general tide of Anglo-Saxon movement on the continent. But he preaches to comparatively deaf ears. Amalgamation was never, perhaps, to be expected. It makes as little progress among the scattered Acadians of the maritime provinces as in the concentrated population of the province of Quebec; as little in the United States as in Canada. Does the obstacle lie in race, language, or religion? The strong objection of the Roman Catholic Church to mixed marriages does not altogether account for it, since amalgamation with Irish Roman Catholics, who are numerous in Montreal, is almost as uncommon as with the English or Scottish Protestants. It is, therefore, probably in large part a matter of race, and, in a less degree, of language, and must be accepted as a permanent condition.

But there may be a broad national sympathy, unity of public effort and aim, a reasonable yielding to the will of the majority, and a delicate respect for the constitutional rights of others without amalgamation, as we see from the example, say, of Switzerland, where cantons which differ in race, religion, and language act with the most patriotic unanimity. Should Quebec push provincial rights to the utmost in her own case, and yet use all her political influence to interfere with the right of majorities in the other provinces to deal freely, within the limits of the Constitution, even with educational questions, she will awaken a profound distrust in the English provinces. If she pursue a policy of studied race isolation she will become more and more fossilized amid all the progress and activities of a strenuous continent, and will destroy her own just weight in the councils of the Dominion. If any impression is created that French Canadians sympathize with a policy of national disintegration in any form, they will find themselves face to face with a wall of adamant in the consolidating national purposes of the rest of the Dominion.

These are the warnings which all prudent and impartial thinkers in the Dominion express openly or have in their minds when they consider the position of the French Canadian. They are warnings which are needed, though they are meant more for a few of the leaders, political and ecclesiastical, than for the body of the people. The *habitans* are a simple and docile people, far from aggressive or discontented if left to themselves, but with a Parisian facility for being stirred to sudden and what seems to colder-blooded men unreasoning effervescence. They are what their teachers and leaders make them to a degree almost beyond parallel. It is upon the moderation and self-restraint of these leaders, lay and clerical, more than upon anything else, that freedom from serious friction in the government of the Dominion must depend.

These leaders must say, too, whether French Canada is to be narrow, bigoted, and isolated, or liberal, progressive, and with a legitimate influence constantly increasing. French dominance on the American continent received its death-blow a century and a half ago from a policy which sought to make Canada and Louisiana a close preserve for a single set of ideas and a single type of Frenchman; a like policy pursued now would mean in the long-run the certain weakening of French influence in the Dominion.

Outside the province of Quebec the French question has no very important bearings. Of 1,404,974 French-speaking people in Canada, all but 218,628 are in Quebec. Those in Manitoba and the North-West only number about 13,000, and can now never form more than a very small fraction of the increasing population. The overflow from Quebec into the counties of Ontario which lie along the Ottawa gave a population in 1891 of 101,123....

... Doubtless the French language will have to struggle for its existence on a continent where all other races tend at once to become Anglicized in tongue. That it has withstood the effects of its environment so successfully for a full century indicates a singular and, in its way, admirable ten-

acity of purpose and habit in the French people. Perhaps it is more due
to isolation than to any set purpose. Now that the *habitant* goes abroad
from the province more freely, indications are not wanting that even in
language he cannot altogether resist the influence of his surroundings.
The operative in the mills of New England, and the lumberman in the
woods of Michigan, when he returns to Quebec has had his native *patois*
interlarded with numerous expressions which are certainly not French,
though but doubtfully English....

... When I landed in Quebec I found that the French papers, both of
the ancient capital and of Montreal, were vigorously discussing how far
importations of English words were affecting the purity of the French
tongue as spoken throughout the province. There seemed a consensus of
opinion that nothing but a vigorous resistance would give security to the
French language. The limits to which that resistance should be pressed
bring up a nice question for the French Canadian. No one can doubt for
a moment that the man on the American continent who does not know
the English language is handicapped in the race for success of any kind.
If the French Canadian chooses to isolate himself in this respect, he does
it at his own expense; he loses opportunity and influence. It is a heavy
price to pay for the maintenance of a sentiment. He can see for himself
that his most successful men are those who have mastered the prevailing
tongue of the continent.

"Why," one asks, "in the face of facts so manifest, does he not, like the
great German communities of the Western States, the Icelanders of the
North-West, the people of all races who come to America, hasten to learn
the language which they all find is the readiest key to the opportunities
of the continent? Why do not the clergy and public men of Quebec, who
would gladly see their people prosper and grow in power and influence,
insist that English shall be well and carefully taught in every school?"

There can be but one answer. Devotion to the French tongue has
become associated in the minds of the clergy with devotion to religion.
The *habitant* has had this lesson inculcated till it has become well nigh
an instinct in his nature, and to-day we find him controlled by a feeling
precisely opposite to that which influences every other race which has
settled in America. He prefers, on the whole, not to learn English.

To the Anglo-Saxon the theory that religion needs support of this kind
seems absurd; the French pastor, whose personal hold might be weakened by the change, gauges his people by a different standard....

While the industrial position of the *habitant* would be greatly improved
by a knowledge of English, as is the political position of his leaders, no

one would wish to see him give up entirely the tongue which has for him such a wealth of association. Rather is it to be regretted that more of the people of the English provinces do not make themselves familiar with French. Such a knowledge, especially among public men, would create a very real bond of sympathy which does not now exist.

Occasionally one hears regrets expressed in Canada that the French language was ever given any official status in the Federal Parliament. The objections to its employment are manifest, but superficial. The argument on which its permissive use rests is fundamental. Sir Henry de Villiers, when pointing out, during the Colonial Conference, to a French Canadian audience at Quebec, that he could not speak French because the language of his French ancestors had been crushed out under the Dutch rule at the Cape, added that a man or a people "can be all the more loyal when they are able to express their loyalty in their own language." Such a remark as this embodies the pith of the whole matter.

It is the glory of British government in Canada that it has cheerfully accepted the inconveniences arising from the use of mixed languages that it may give unmixed liberty to the French people of Quebec....

One has no hesitation in discussing frankly this question of race inertia in Quebec. The most clear-sighted men of the province admit and deplore it.

Doubtless it has been due in part to unavoidable circumstances. Cut off from easy contact with the higher standards of France, and not yet in sympathy with those of British people, the difficulty of maintaining social and intellectual activity over a thinly settled country during a large part of this century can easily be understood. But a supreme effort should be made to change these conditions. Something like an attitude of helplessness in face of the immobility of the *habitant* seemed to me to prevail among able and earnest Frenchmen who were thinking much on the question.

A most intelligent priest spoke to me of one form which this immobility took. "A young man in our French villages," he said, " has little encouragement to work his way up to that social distinction of which you speak. If he begins to acquire the culture and adopt the habits of refined society, there is a disposition to look upon him askance, as one who is willing to forsake his own people and their ways for alien forms of life and thought."

Such a feeling as this, if correctly stated, must be a great barrier to progress. It does not represent the aspiring spirit of the France from which the *habitant* sprang, nor that of the Britain with which he is now associated.

Whether the future of the French Canadian is to be a growing or diminishing one seems to me to be hanging just now more than ever before in doubtful balance, and he himself holds the scales, or, to be more precise, a few of his leaders do so.... The larger hope of Quebec lies in the unconditional acceptance of her Canadian destiny. In any attempt to pursue an individual course without reference to the sentiment of the whole Dominion the French Canadian will make shipwreck of his fortunes.

If a gospel of moderation and liberality must be preached to some classes of French Canadians, one of patience and generous consideration must equally be preached to certain sections of their English-speaking fellow-citizens. The average Frenchman of Canada can no more be calm than the Frenchman, of France: under excitement he is apt to lose his head, and to say far more than he means. The stolid Saxon rarely says as much as he means, and makes little allowance for a contrary temperament. This latter he must learn to do. There is no sufficient reason why the Orangeman of Ontario should treat so seriously as he does every sign of temporary effervescence in Quebec. Perhaps he too has a strain of Celtic blood. If so, then the mass of reasonable Canadian opinion must restrain the excesses of both alike, ...

... for mutual respect there is abundant ground. The Frenchman may well reflect how just and considerate, on the whole, has been the dominant Briton. The Englishman should equally think how loyal, on the whole, has been the French Canadian under peculiar circumstances. If there cannot be in Canada the same mingling of blood which followed the Norman Conquest of England, and made the characteristics of both races the common heritage of all their descendants in England to-day, there can at least be hearty recognition of the better qualities in each, mutual toleration of constitutional differences, common and sympathetic effort for the general good.

The Acadians of the Maritime provinces number about 100,000. Many circumstances have conspired to make this interesting people far from homogeneous with the *habitans* of Quebec, and more in touch with the English among whom they live. Not long since, in one of the maritime provinces, an Acadian Frenchman was for the first time raised to a seat on the bench of the Supreme Court. In political life he had filled with great credit important administrative posts, and had won a high reputation among English as well as French constituents for integrity of character, honesty of purpose, and painstaking care in the management of public affairs. The Acadians are now an extremely contented people – almost too contented, some think, with their comparatively humble lot;

and one of the greatest merits of the new judge is the energy with which he has always pointed out to his compatriots that under the constitution of the country in which they live all positions are freely open to them, provided they take the trouble to place themselves on an intellectual equality with their English fellow-citizens and competitors. His example might with advantage be followed throughout French Canada....

Not much can be said about the opportunities offered by Quebec to emigrants from the United Kingdom. It should be pointed out that in all the old provinces of the Dominion the ungranted and unsettled crown lands are under the control, not of the Dominion Parliament, as in the North-West, but of the Provincial Legislatures, the policy of which is directed by local considerations. Quebec has still large unoccupied areas, but the prevailing inclination seems to be to fill them with a native French-speaking population rather than from outside. Of late years a very vigorous effort has been made by a colonization and repatriation society, working under clerical supervision, but with the aid of the provincial government, to colonize new districts with young men taken from the older settlements, or others drawn back to the soil from the factories of the United States. The period of depression through which the latter country lately passed has greatly favoured this movement, and the number of those returning to take up homesteads in new districts has been large.

South of the St. Lawrence, in what are known as the Eastern townships, a very flourishing English population has long been established in a good agricultural country. Sherbrooke is the principal town of this portion of the province, and is a centre of manufacturing as well as agricultural industry. Mines of asbestos give employment to a large body of workmen. There are also marble quarries and deposits of copper. A college and a public school on the English model near by at Lennoxville give exceptional opportunities for education.

This is one of the districts to which the attention of settlers with some capital, wishing to obtain partly improved farms, within reach of English and American, as well as Canadian markets, can be with some confidence directed.

In fisheries and timber the resources of the province are very great, and the *habitant* is singularly expert both as fisherman and lumberman. He is, however, a bad farmer – the worst in Canada – partly, perhaps, because he tries to combine farming with fishing and lumbering, but chiefly from ignorance. In travelling through the purely French portions of the province, one is everywhere struck by the manifest exhaustion of the soil from lack of intelligent cultivation, both in the past and at present; by the inferiority of the stock to that in the other provinces; and by the apparent content of the people with primitive and long obsolete methods and implements of agriculture. Steps are now being taken by the Church as well as by the civil authorities to remedy this state of things. The bishops of the Roman Catholic Church have issued a pastoral letter calling the special attention of their flocks to the importance of improved methods of farming....

Montreal is the greatest city of Quebec and of the Dominion. If the St. Lawrence were not frozen in winter, it would be the commercial rival of New York, and probably one of the greatest cities of the world. Even as it is Montreal's future must be very great, standing as the city does at the meeting-place of ocean navigation and of an astonishing inland water system, at a point where immense combinations of railways tend more and more to focus themselves. The Canadian Pacific, controlling about nine thousand miles of railway in the United States and Canada, the Grand Trunk, controlling four or five thousand more, both have their chief offices and termini here. So have the great inland and ocean navigation companies. The city is in close railway connexion with St. John and Halifax, Portland, Boston, and New York, all of which it uses as convenience determines for winter ports. Every considerable expansion of Canada's exporting and importing capacity must mean extending business for Montreal. The completion of the canal system seems likely to bring it a share of the export business of the Western States as well. It is the chief point for Canadian wheat, timber, cattle, pork, cheese, butter, and fruit export; it is the greatest wholesale distributing centre for manufactured goods. Not very far from one half of the whole import and export trade of the Dominion passes through Montreal. The largest business firms of the Dominion, the most powerful banking houses, the greatest organizers of industry, of the carrying trade, of railway construction, are here. Among the monetary institutions of the world, very few stand higher than the Bank of Montreal. The finer streets of the city indicate clearly that it is the home of merchant princes, and the centre of much realized wealth. A vast amount of business capacity, chiefly imported from Scotland and England, has gone to build up Montreal, deepen its harbour, open the way to the sea, establish steamship lines, create industries, and organize railway connexion with all parts of the continent.

Montreal is also the meeting-place of the two nationalities of Eastern Canada. The two sides of the city are in striking contrast, yet each is the industrial complement of the other; one the home of capital and business energy, the other of a crowded population distinguished by patient and, on the whole, contented industry.

English Montreal complains that, as compared with Toronto, it is handicapped by French inertia, and that it has to pay heavy penalties in the shape of taxation for being connected with a province and municipality where vast accumulations of Church property are free from civic burdens, where the French vote prevails, and French politicians are sometimes extravagant at the expense of their richer neighbours. It freely utilizes the French voter, however, as a workman, and grows wealthy in the process. An excellent workman he is too – not over-strenuous, but intelligent. "A born carpenter" was the phrase by which a large employer of labour described him. Industry in Montreal has enjoyed a singular immunity from disastrous strikes, and the fact should be remembered to the credit of the artisan class. An organised effort to improve municipal government gives promise of good results.

Montreal refines sugar, spins cotton, and manufactures tobacco on a large scale. In these and minor industries, as well as in its great export and import trade, its railway and steamboat lines, its financial institutions, and, above all, its geographical position, the city has the foundations of a prosperity more solid and enduring, in the opinion of good judges, than that of any city of its size on the American continent.

The prosperity of Montreal has to some extent been secured at the expense of the ancient capital, Quebec, where shipping has decreased since the deepening of the St. Lawrence, where the timber trade has fallen off, and from which the vigorous English business element seems to have in part withdrawn.... With an abundance of cheap labour, for its French population numbers nearly 60,000, and a situation well adapted for commerce, it is a little difficult to see why the city does not become more of an industrial centre than it is. It manufactures boots and shoes, but not even these to an extent commensurate with its available working population, which ought to make it the Lowell or Birmingham of Canada.

The bridging of the St. Lawrence near the city, which has been contemplated and is believed to be quite practicable to modern engineering, has been thought of as a means to renew the commercial importance of the place. It is claimed, too, that as the export of wheat from the St. Lawrence increases, through the development of the North-West and the completion of the canal system, the climatic advantages offered by Quebec as a point of storage, and in other ways as a point of shipment, may revive its fortunes....

But no industrial change can take away from the historic interest of a spot which was for so long one of the pivots of the world's history, or from the picturesque grandeur of the massive fortress as it towers over the ancient city. More and more the St. Lawrence becomes one of the greatest routes of American and Canadian tourist travel, and Quebec is the central feature of enduring interest. A splendid hotel has lately been completed on the terrace beneath the Citadel, to meet this increasing volume of travel. From its windows the traveller looks out upon one of the noblest prospects that his eye is ever likely to meet the broad St. Lawrence, stretching away in gleaming brightness between the blue hills which rise on either side; ...

In its wealth of picturesque association Quebec is by far the most interesting city on the American continent. So long as the memory of great deeds moves the human heart, it will continue to be a place of pilgrimage.

But as one studies the French Canadian province he becomes convinced that what it most needs is some great awakening of the people to the splendid opportunities which lie before them if they would but throw themselves more heartily into the tide of Canadian progress. (Parkin, *The Great Dominion*, 1895, 127–56)

7 BRITISH COLUMBIA

☞ Parkin stresses the grand, impressive scenery of British Columbia, mountain, coast, and forest, and the great natural resources. We sense that the Canadian Pacific Railway has just been completed and feel the fresh energy of Canadian federation as the far-away Pacific Ocean goal is finally achieved. This is a breathless account of the strategic reasons for constructing the transcontinental railway, set within the spatial context of the British Empire and Canada. Building the railway was "a great common [unifying] task" for all of Canada. The interrelations of location, commodities, special technology, skilled labour, the need for capital, and the problem of distant markets in developing the resources of British Columbia are analyzed. Capital must go in first to develop resources, labour follows; this is contrasted with the way the prairies are being developed. Again there is a contrast of the management practices of British and American capitalists. Parkin recognizes the contributions of Chinese workers in building the CPR, but he reveals an incredible blindness with respect to their rights as citizens, and he expresses an equally incredible class distinction when he says they are doing "good work for the country" in menial jobs. The Vancouver Island coal deposits on the Pacific match those of Cape Breton on the Atlantic for the strategic purposes of the British Navy and the Empire; Parkin's discussion on coal is added to this section. ☞

To learn the price Canada was ready to pay for confederation and for a pathway from ocean to ocean, the traveller must climb by rail up from the prairies at Calgary through the gorges of the Rocky Mountains to the summit of the Kicking Horse Pass, and then sweep down through the defiles and valleys of the opposite slope, across the Selkirk and Coast ranges, and past the canons of the Fraser and Thompson Rivers, till he has reached the Pacific.... he must look out for two or three days continuously on the marvelous succession of mountain peak and range and gorge and embattled cliff guarding the long narrow valleys, all of which go to make up the impressive and magnificent scenery of the greater part of British Columbia....

... And for what purpose was this mighty barrier of the Rockies and Selkirks, 600 miles wide, to be crossed?

Not to unite two great communities striving for closer intercourse, as was the case when the 40,000,000 people of the Eastern and Western States, already advanced far beyond the Mississippi, made the first American line across a narrower range of mountains to get in touch with San Francisco and the large population of the Pacific States, which was also pressing up to the base of the Rockies. In Eastern Canada there were only 4,000,000 people; in British Columbia there were less than 50,000 white people – the population of a small English manufacturing town – and few of these on the mainland, when the railroad was undertaken. It was to complete and round off a national conception; to prepare the way for commercial and political advantages as yet far remote, and by many deemed imaginary, that the work was faced. British Columbia, insignificant in population, was significant enough in position and in some of its resources. It fronted on the Pacific; it had splendid harbours and abundant coal; it supplied a new base of sea power and commercial influence; it suggested a new and short pathway to the Orient and Australasia. The statesmen at Ottawa who in 1867 began to look over the Rockies to continents beyond the Pacific were not wanting in imagination; many claimed that their imagination outran their reason; but in the rapid course of events their dreams have already been more than justified.

They were, perhaps, building even better than they knew. When Japanese and Australian mail and trade routes are already accomplished facts, when Pacific cable schemes are being discussed, and when the docks and fortifications of Esquimalt are being completed jointly by Britain and Canada, we can see clearly that they were supplying the missing joints and fastening the rivets of empire. While they were doing this they were also giving political consolidation to the older provinces of Canada. Common aspirations and a great common task, with the stirring of enthusiasm which followed on the sudden widening of the Canadian horizon, did more than anything else to draw those provinces out of their own narrow circles and give them the sense of a larger citizenship.

So, though British Columbia made no great addition to the population of Canada, its absorption into the Dominion some years after confederation, and the pledge of a transcontinental railway which was the condition of that absorption, marked a great turning-point in Canadian history. It also added new and interesting features to the already manifold conditions of Canadian life.

It gave the Dominion a new climate, or, one might rather say, a variety of new climates, for between the summit of the Rockies and the shore of the Pacific there are gradations of temperature and climatic effect for both summer and winter as marked as between Norway and northern Italy. It gave a Pacific seaboard many hundreds of miles in length, as rich in the wealth of the ocean as that of the Atlantic, and wonderfully picturesque in its mingling of gulf, inlet, sound, and fiord. It opened up new and diversified fields for enterprise.

I have shown how much the problems of the North-West differ from those in Eastern Canada; those of British Columbia have an individuality quite as marked, and distinct from both of the others. This might be inferred from the nature of the country. British Columbians are somewhat inclined to object to the phrase "a sea of mountains" by which their province has been described, probably thinking it likely to deter those in search of new homes. Yet the phrase expresses accurately the chief impression left upon the mind of a visitor, and it furnishes the best starting-point from which to discuss the capabilities and limitations of the province.

British Columbia is not, and can never be in any large way, an agricultural country. The people will have reason to congratulate themselves when the production of food fully matches the consumption. This is not the case now, though it ought to become so in respect of many products within a few years. On the coast and islands, along the streams and in mountain valleys, there are considerable patches of good alluvial soil. A moist and warm climate makes it most productive. There are other areas less fertile, but well fitted for pasturage. In many cases they require irrigation, but for this the numerous unfailing mountain streams give abundant opportunity. Northward, as the mountains sink down towards the Peace River, there is said to be a wide extent of pastoral land, but this is still inaccessible, and ranching is now confined to more southern valleys.

Here is obviously a new set of conditions. In writing of the North-West I described it as especially a country for the poor man; one might have added, a country which gave even the unskilled labourer a chance. Something very nearly the opposite of this must be said of British Columbia. No province of Canada so little admits of indiscriminate immigration. The good farming land is limited in quantity, and, compared with that in other provinces, expensive. The vast deep-sea fisheries of the coast, on account of their distance from markets, can only be developed by degrees, or else by some great organization of collecting and distributing agencies involving the use of much capital. The plans for such an organization have been devised and submitted to the Legislature, in connexion with a scheme for settling Scotch fishermen along the coast, but the practicability of the scheme has yet to be established. The salmon fisheries and tinning establishments of the rivers require comparatively little labour, and even then employment is intermittent. Mines can only be worked with capital, and capital which does not demand a very quick return. The same is true of timber industries, and in this case, even if abundant capital were forthcoming, the difficulty of access to adequate markets hinders the full and rapid development of enterprise in dealing with a bulky material of commerce. In short, the capacity of British Columbia to receive immigrants is strictly, dependent upon the previous influx of capital, which, courageously and yet intelligently applied to the development of the resources of the country, will gradually draw in its train the skilled and general labour required for its operations. Labourers should not go to the province on the mere chance of finding employment, as they may without excessive risk go to some parts of Canada. If this is clearly understood, much disappointment will be avoided. But for men with capital, energy, and common-sense in business: men not afraid to risk something in the hope of large gains: men who can afford to wait, study the country, and watch for opportunities, the openings are varied and most promising.

In the depths of these great mountain ranges are vast stores of mineral wealth. The gold mines of the Fraser and Carriboo districts, the silver and copper mines of the Kootenay, the coal of Canmore, Anthracite, and the Crow's Nest, are only suggestions, but striking ones, of what lies behind. Fifty million dollars' worth of gold was taken in a few years after the first discovery from the rich Fraser and Carriboo alluvial deposits. The almost insuperable obstacles to the transport of heavy machinery to these districts are being gradually overcome, so that hydraulic operations and quartz-crushing are now being substituted for the old placer mining....

The richness of the silver deposit of the Kootenay districts has been fully established by the discoveries of the last two years. Making due allowance for the usual exaggerations of prospectors and company promoters, it seems clear that the district will ultimately prove to be one of the most important areas of silver production on the continent. Still its development will probably be for some time slow. The present difficulty of access, the heavy import duty on lead and on silver ores entering the United States, which furnish the nearest smelting furnaces, and the depreciation of silver during the past two years have all contributed to delay operations. So has the exaggerated price at which silver claims are held by men or small companies not able to work them. The Canadian Pacific Railway appears to be feeling its way past Fort M'Leod towards the Crow's Nest Pass as a means of access to the Kootenay country. Great deposits of coal are also found in this pass, some of which make good coke, so that the means of transportation and the material for smelting may soon be within easy reach....

American much more than British capital is at present seizing the opportunities offered by the Kootenay silver deposits. The truth is that much experience in Nevada and Montana has made the American an expert, beyond all others, in silver, and in the methods of dealing with it. Besides, he goes to new fields of enterprise not merely to invest his money, but to look personally after his investments, as the British capitalist seldom does.

One peculiarity of the industry should be mentioned. Veins of silver ore are singularly uncertain and variable. I found an agreement of opinion that they can be most successfully dealt with by large companies taking up numbers of claims, and so able to balance successes and disappointments over considerable areas. This is the prevailing American system, and it should be adopted by British capitalists if they seek a footing here.

The resources of the mountainous interior are supplemented by those of the coast. The seal fisheries, in spite of restrictions, are still of considerable value. More than 70,000 skins were taken in 1893. The abundance of fish in the rivers and in the coast waters is probably without parallel in the world. The export of tinned salmon alone amounts annually to nearly three million dollars. Of the whole output, the markets of the United Kingdom absorb about five sixths; the rest goes to Eastern Canada and Australia. The Fraser River is the centre of the salmon-packing industry, and this stream also abounds in sturgeon, which have lately become an article of commerce. Halibut and black cod are found in the greatest abundance off the Island of Vancouver, but the development of a large fishery is hindered by the difficulty of access to adequate markets. The splendid pine of the province is in demand all round the Pacific. It goes to San Francisco, to South America, to China, to Japan, and to Australia....

The Douglas pine is also exported to the Eastern States, where for many purposes it is preferred to Southern pine, to Cape Colony, and to England. A cargo has quite recently been sent to Egypt. I believe that it can be obtained of greater lengths, squaring to a larger size, than any other wood of equal quality. Cedar also is abundant, and of astonishing size. It is used chiefly in the manufacture of shingles, which on account of their excellence find their way far across the continent. Three hundred feet is not an uncommon height for both pines and cedars. The girth of the trunks is proportionate....

There is still a great extent of unexhausted timberland. One of the largest operators told me that with a widened market and more capital his firm could, from the land it had actually under lease, as easily turn out 100,000,000 feet of timber as the 30,000,000 feet which represented its present annual output. Considering the rapid exhaustion of forest going on in the United States, the value of the best timber on the American Continent must increase rapidly, and the present limitation of output in British Columbia is perhaps not entirely a subject for regret.

Nowhere in the world can more impressive forest scenery be met with than along this Pacific coast of the Dominion. Even where the heavier timber has been cut out, the thickly growing pine-trees which remain, with their clean trunks, straight and lofty as palm-trees, and crowned by dark-green foliage, form a striking picture, which remains long in the memory. Often the heaviest growth is found on soil of comparatively poor quality, suggesting that the nourishment of these forest giants is derived as much from the atmosphere as from the earth. The fact also suggests the possibility of a continuity of forest products in British Columbia, since the soil is often unfitted for agriculture or pasturage. In the Government reservation of Stanley Park, at Vancouver, the traveller can see, with little trouble, an excellent example of British Columbian forests, with specimens of the great trees, fifteen or twenty feet in diameter, which once covered the site of the town. It is much to be desired that this fine remnant of the original forest may be guarded with jealous care.

Of the extensive coal-measures of Vancouver Island and of their national importance I have written in a previous chapter. [These remarks are inserted here.]

When we cross the continent to the Pacific coast we find, in connexion with the coal of British Columbia, a group of facts scarcely less striking than those to which reference has already been made. Along the whole Pacific coast of South America no coal is found suited for steaming purposes. There is none along the coast of North America until we come to Puget Sound. At different points on the Sound mines are being worked on American territory, but the coal is all of a distinctly inferior quality. It is only when we cross the boundary line into Canadian territory that in Vancouver Island, the site of Britain's only naval station on the western coast of America, we meet with large deposits of good steaming coal.... The annual output of the mines at Nanaimo and Wellington has now risen beyond a million tons. At Nanaimo the principal mine is directly upon the shore, and the galleries are being run out far under the arm of the sea which divides Vancouver Island from the mainland, so that here, as at Cape Breton, ships of heavy tonnage take in coal while moored immediately over the place from which it is obtained.... [End of insertion on coal.]

... Tasmania has not a better climate than parts of British Columbia for the production of all the ordinary fruits. Many species of fruit, like the trees of the country, grow to an unusual size. Hops promise to be an important product, and are grown in great perfection.

It will be noticed that the prevailing industries are such as require special skill even among the workmen. A green hand does not easily fit into the work of the saw mills and lumber woods. Hop-growing and fruit-raising are occupations which require special knowledge. So are cattle-raising and dairying, which, in the dry inland valleys, have often to be carried on by the aid of irrigation. The coal miner and fisherman must grow up to their business. Gold and silver prospecting and mining in America tend more and more to drift into the hands of specialists, men to whom it becomes well-nigh an instinct to detect the "colour" of gold and estimate the value of ores.

For small farmers who have some money to invest in good lands within marketing distance of the towns, and skill to work them when bought, there is an excellent chance, perhaps the best in Canada. The province still imports much of its food, and prices are high. As the population increases, good farming land, which is scarce, is sure to improve in value. But it is a country for small, not large farming....

Among the towns, Victoria, though not on the mainland, still holds the foremost place. Originally a Hudson Bay trading post, it sprang into importance when gold was discovered on the Fraser River. The wealth then gained has been increased by the mining, sealing, and fishing industries, and by its being the chief centre of wholesale supply for the province. In this last particular it still holds its own against the rivalry of Vancouver. The immediate vicinity of Esquimalt, with which it is connected by tramway, makes Victoria practically our naval base for the North Pacific. As Esquimalt has the only British graving dock on the Pacific coast of America, the defences of the place, which are now being pushed on rapidly, have not been begun too soon. The docking facilities must soon be increased.... Victoria has a distinctly English look. With a climate like that of the warmest parts of Devonshire, and picturesque surroundings, it attracts numbers of holiday visitors from San Francisco....

Here we see the Far West begin to merge into the Far East. At Victoria we meet with the advanced guard of that Chinese host which many believe only steady resistance can prevent from revolutionizing the industrial condition of America. To the Chinaman, however, Canada, and particularly British Columbia, owe a debt of gratitude. Without the army of 15,000 or 20,000 Chinese labourers who assaulted the western slope of the Rockies, the railway across the mountains could scarcely have been built, or only at disastrous cost. The Chinaman has received his reward in kinder treatment than he has met with in the United States or in Australia. The restrictions placed upon his coming are not severe; he is safe under the protection of the laws, though not admitted to all the rights of citizenship. He is doing good work for the country as a domestic servant, gardener, or laundryman in the towns; far up in the mountains, as a gold miner, winning the precious metal from old washings where others could not make a living.

Vancouver, the terminus of the Canadian Pacific Railway, and one of the termini of the Northern Pacific, furnishes an illustration of the magical change that can in modern times be quickly wrought by the application of capital in combination with science and labour. Eight years ago its site was entirely occupied by a dense forest of the magnificent pines and cedars of the Pacific coast; now it has nearly twenty thousand inhabitants, enjoying all the comforts and most of the luxuries of civilization. The signs of rapid growth are already disappearing; dynamite has blown out the stumps; fire has burnt up the wood; massive blocks of buildings are seen on all sides; the telephone is everywhere; electricity lights the streets, the hotels, even the private houses; it works the excellent tram system which connects Vancouver with the beautiful and flourishing town of New Westminster, ten miles away. The people, coming chiefly from Eastern Canada and England, have retained their eastern and English habits. On Sunday the place has an aspect of quiet respectability like that of an English cathedral town. In spite of its rapid growth it has never known anything of the roughness of new towns across the border. The site of the city is admirable. A moderate elevation gives it an air of dignity; the eye looks down upon the broad and placid waters of the harbour, beyond which are noble ranges of mist-covered hills. Close at hand is Stanley Park, a splendid reservation of primeval forest, covering many hundred acres. Already intersected by pleasant walks and surrounded by a carriage drive which winds along the cliffs and bays of the peninsula, giving wonderful panoramic glimpses of land and sea, the whole forms a recreation ground for this community, born but yesterday, that the proudest and most ancient capitals of Europe might envy....

... An air of commercial activity pervades the place, and is an augury of further growth.

(Parkin, *The Great Dominion,* 1895, 157–72, 78–9)

8 NORTHERN CANADA – THE GREAT FUR COUNTRY

☞ "Belts" is a term often favoured in Canada in discussing the settlement potential of large new tracts of land and Parkin starts by comparing the settled belt across southern Canada with a second thinly settled belt farther north and then with the Arctic beyond. Much of Northern Canada, he tells us, remains unexplored for resource purposes. However Parkin makes good use of what has since become a forgotten government resource survey of the Mackenzie Basin and notes that it is known that coal deposits and extensive oil sands exist in the North West. Regional names such as "Barren Grounds" are in use. The fur trade remains the great commercial enterprise of the North and its transport operations have been modernized. Parkin recognizes that

there may be a need for conservation in the fur enterprise. Discussion
has started about a possible railway to Hudson Bay for shipping prairie
grain to Europe. The great investments in northern pulp and paper
and mining enterprises are in the future, as we know today, but nickel
mines have begun operating in Sudbury. Nowhere are the local inhabitants, the indigenous peoples, mentioned. ⌒

I have said before that climatic conditions will always keep the bulk
of Canada's population within a belt which has, speaking roughly, a
breadth varying from 300 to 500 miles, and which stretches all the way
across the continent. It is of this belt alone that I have hitherto spoken. It
includes the old provinces and those western regions out of which new
provinces are being gradually carved, where fifty or a hundred millions
of people could manifestly find the same opportunities of comfortable
existence as does the present population of five millions.

But this belt represents barely one-third of the whole land area of
the Dominion. North of it is another with features of great interest. In
parts the limit of possible wheat culture runs far to the north; in other
parts the hardier crops, such as barley, rye, hemp, and flax, together
with rapidly-maturing vegetables, can be successfully cultivated. This
belt is known to contain large sections where the soil has all, the natural fertility which characterizes the more southern lands hitherto
referred to.

Regions similarly situated in respect of climate, and lands inferior in
point of fertility, maintain considerable populations in the north of Europe, and furnish much and varied material for commerce. In Canada
their settlement for agricultural purposes will no doubt be slow, and
dependent to some extent upon the occupation of the more favourable
lands to the south. But settlers will meanwhile be attracted for other
industrial purposes, and it is clearly impossible to form a just conception
of what the Dominion really is, or is likely to become, without taking
them into consideration.

In the past this second belt, itself a fur-producing country, has been
associated almost exclusively in people's minds, even in Canada, with
the still more northern regions, also vast in extent, where agriculture is
yet more difficult or impossible, where even timber is in places wanting,
and where furs furnish practically the whole material of commerce and
industry. But this association of thought is a very misleading one. Information is still very incomplete, but enough has been obtained to lead to
important conclusions.

A committee of the Canadian Senate was appointed in 1887–8 to inquire into the resources of Northern Canada, and particularly those of the great Mackenzie Basin. The field of inquiry covered the regions which lie between Hudson's Bay and the Rocky Mountains, and from the watershed of the Saskatchewan northward to the Arctic Ocean. After hearing and comparing the evidence of fur traders, missionary bishops and clergy, geological experts and travellers, the Committee reported that of this region 274,000 square miles could be considered good arable land; that the climate permitted wheat to mature over 316,000 square miles, barley over 407,000, the potato over 656,000 square miles, and that the area suitable for pasturage was even greater. It was shown that the deep northern inclination of the summer isotherms brought it about that spring flowers and buds appeared as early north of the Great Slave Lake as at Winnipeg, Kingston, or Ottawa, while the length of the northern summer days was singularly favourable to the rapid growth of cereals. Along the Peace, Liard and other western affluents of the Mackenzie River spring came still earlier, and here, under the influence of warm south-westerly winds, the summer weather resembled that of Ontario, and the growth of nutritious native grasses was especially luxuriant.

While the heavier timber of Eastern Canada and British Columbia is wanting, the supply of smaller timber suitable for house and ship building, for railway, mining, and other like purposes was found to be practically inexhaustible, and likely to prove of great value in supplying the needs of the treeless regions of Canada and the United States further south. The lakes and rivers yield fresh-water fish of various kinds and of excellent quality in extraordinary abundance. The auriferous region at the head of the Peace, Liard, and Peel Rivers is large, while mineral deposits of various kinds are found in sufficient number in the vast mountain districts especially to justify the expectation that the country will not prove inferior on the average in mineral production to other areas of like extent.

Along the valleys of the Athabasca and Mackenzie Rivers deposits of coal occur at frequent intervals, and the existence of a very remarkable petroleum field has been established. For a great distance along these rivers the sandy soil is saturated to a depth sometimes of a hundred feet with tar or asphalt, and this is believed by geologists to have its origin in petroleum oozing from the Devonian rocks beneath. Oil has already been observed at several points, but the difficulty of introducing the necessary machinery into the country has hitherto prevented sufficient tests of the value of the field being made by boring. The recommendation of the Committee that parliament should reserve from sale a tract of about 40,000 square miles in order to include this petroleum area, furnishes some suggestion of its supposed extent.

While these are among the general conclusions arrived at by the Committee, it must be borne in mind that they were based, not on detailed knowledge of the whole districts under consideration, but on the evidence of observers at widely separated points. Fur traders, missionaries and explorers have hitherto followed for the most part the great watercourses of the country, and have made observations extending over the whole year only at a comparatively few stations. The spaces still left between for fuller exploration are therefore very large. Dr. G. M. Dawson, in a careful study of the question, enumerates no less than sixteen different areas, varying in size from 7,500 to 289,000 square miles, none of which has been subjected to intelligent and adequate examination. He sums up by saying that, "while the entire area of the Dominion is computed at 3,470,257 square miles, about 954,000 square miles of the continent alone, exclusive of the inhospitable detached Arctic portions, is for all practicable purposes entirely unknown."

Part of this almost unexplored country consists of the "Barren Grounds," which are chiefly known as the home of the musk ox, and as being frequented by astonishing herds of caribou, which migrate southward during the depth of winter, and return to the shores of the Arctic Ocean during the breeding season. These "Barren Grounds" have not, probably, much to yield to investigation. But there are other parts, such as the great Labrador peninsula, which give distinct promise of rewarding the adventurous explorer by mineral and other discoveries.

Dreary as much of this vast northern region is, however, severe as are the conditions of life which its more remote parts offer, the extent to which its products of one kind have long ministered to the comfort and luxury of mankind is very striking. It supplies furs in larger numbers, of finer quality and of greater value than any other part of the world. For more than two centuries the fur trade has been vigorously prosecuted, and still the supply, save in the case of two or three varieties of animals, shows no signs of exhaustion. The furs are, in the first instance, brought almost exclusively to the London market....

Northern Canada has therefore been rightly called "the last great fur preserve of the world." This character it is likely to retain. The buffalo, whose hide was once an important article of commerce, has disappeared before the advance of civilization. The limits over which the beaver is found have steadily narrowed, and this animal, too, can apparently only be saved from extinction by the reservation of areas where it can multiply undisturbed for fixed periods, and by limitations put upon the catch. With these exceptions, there seems to be no reason why the furs of Northern Canada may not remain a permanent element in the industry and commerce of the country....

... There is still a great extent of territory over which the old methods of transport by canoe and portage obtain. But much of the goods once sent to the remote north by way of York Factory and Moose Factory on Hudson Bay are now despatched by rail from Montreal to Winnipeg, which is the chief distributing centre for the northern districts. A steamer plies on the Saskatchewan in the summer for the transport of goods and furs, and another on Lake Winnipeg. On the Athabasca and Mackenzie Rivers three steamers are employed for the delivery of outfits and for bringing back the furs which have been collected. There are thus at present fully two thousand miles of steam navigation where the paddle and pole of the *voyageur* were once the only dependence.

There is still the regular annual despatch from England of ships to Fort Churchill and Moose Factory, and the return cargo consists not only of furs, but also of the oil and salted salmon which have been collected at the various posts of the company along the Labrador coast.

It will thus be seen that the Hudson's Bay Company continues to hold a most important relation to the industry and development of Northern Canada.

There remains for mention one problem connected with Hudson's Bay itself, the solution of which may profoundly affect the future of some parts of the Dominion.

Many practical men believe firmly in the possibility of successfully establishing a route by way of Hudson's Bay for the transport to Europe of the products of the North-West. The practicability and safety of the navigation for four if not five months of the year for vessels partially prepared to deal with ice, seems to be fairly well established.... Fort Churchill furnishes an excellent harbour, though it is the only one on the western coast of the Bay, for the largest sea-going ships. Five or six hundred miles of railway would put Fort Churchill in close connection with existing lines of communication which extend over the great wheat and cattle region of the North-West. Such a line would be expected to tap the products of the Western States as well. Transport by a route so much shorter than those now used by Montreal and New York would mean a saving in time and expense so considerable as to distinctly modify the conditions of farming in the western regions of Canada. This saving has been estimated at £3 per head for cattle and five shillings per quarter for wheat. Though the difficulties are considerable, the inducements to the establishment of such a line are therefore great. The question of construction will probably be decided by the extent to which production in the North-West presses upon the means of transportation. That again will depend in part on the completeness of the water carriage established from the head of Lake Superior to the sea.

Nickel

... I visited the mines of nickel ore at Sudbury, in Ontario, which surpass anything yet found in the world. It is difficult to obtain accurate information about these deposits, since, in the uncertainty as to the future of the metal, both the English and Canadian companies which have works here are exceedingly reticent about the extent and value of their possessions. But the reports of Canadian geologists and of experts sent by the American Government to institute inquiries make it clear that the supply of nickel in the districts is practically inexhaustible. At present a considerable quantity of ore is smelted, and shipped chiefly to South Wales and the United States. The output could easily be increased, but it is fixed by the comparatively limited application of the metal in the arts. If nickel realizes the expectations conceived about it, and becomes a necessary ingredient in amour-plating, it will no doubt seek the English centres where armour-plating is chiefly manufactured.

(Parkin, *The Great Dominion*, 1895, 173–83, 193)

9 LABOUR, CLIMATIC DETERMINISM AND MIGRATION

☞ Parkin discusses labour agitation in Canada and the movement of workers. Following his interest in the British Empire, he compares labour in Canada and Australia and also brings in the United States. Climate is introduced as a factor in labour migration and in building a hardy vigorous people, in the simplistic deterministic fashion characteristic of geographers and other writers in the nineteenth and early twentieth centuries. Such views have long since been discredited, but still occasionally appear today. ☜

Curiously enough, although strenuous work is ... the distinctive note of Canadian life, one may yet travel for months through the country without hearing the subject of labour discontent specially referred to. Labour problems as they are known in England and Australia, for instance, do not fill any large place in people's thoughts. The reasons for this contrast are not hard to discover.

In the first place, the country is not crowded.

Canada's prime characteristic is the abundance of land which is easily accessible and which gives a fair and speedy return to individual labour with a comparatively slight expenditure of capital. There is no desert interior, as in Australia, to limit the range of settlement, and the people are free to spread over the whole country from the Atlantic to the Pacific. The prevailing occupations are agricultural, and as a rule each farmer owns the land he works. A man who is hurrying to get through with his fall ploughing before the frost comes on, or to make the most of the first fortnight's seeding in spring, or is trying to get the greatest possible amount of his own work squeezed into the short summer, or the autumn which presses so closely upon it, has not much leisure to think over the eight hours' question, or to spend time on labour agitations. Not how many hours he ought to work, but how much work he can put through in a day, is the paramount question. This applies to the warmer seasons. In the lumber woods and on the farms in winter labour has a natural limitation in the shortness of the northern day. There is then much time for recreation or self-improvement. When a man is his own master and retains the profits of his industry, the labour problem takes on new aspects for him. Fortunately for Canada the majority of workers are their own masters. The natural conditions of the Dominion thus appear to relegate serious labour problems to a very remote future.

In the next place, the winter climate squeezes out for a part of the year the "tramp" and" swagger" class – the incorrigible loafer who takes no pains to provide a roof for himself, and who poses as unemployed while really unwilling to work. For nine months of the year, in most parts of Australia, a man of this type can sleep without discomfort under the open sky; there are nearly nine months in Canada when some provision for shelter is a necessity. The advantages of a mild climate are doubtless many, and one is more conscious of the luxury of easy living in Australia; a climate like that of Canada, severe for lengthened periods even while it is exhilarating, has merits which, though less obvious, are far-reaching in their influence on national character. It drives men back on home life and on work; it teaches foresight; it cures or kills the shiftless and improvident; history shows that in the long run it has made strong races. It certainly saves Canada from a class which everywhere does harm to genuine industrial improvement. The Canadian winter exercises upon the tramp a silent but well-nigh irresistible persuasion to shift to a warmer latitude. It is a permanent barrier to the influx of weaker races. It is a fundamental political and social advantage which the Dominion enjoys over the United States, where the gradual and inevitable spread of a black zone across the South, and the increasing attraction of the warm Middle States for the races of Southern Europe, infinitely complicate the processes of national development, and qualify the undoubted industrial advantage of varied production.

In what has been said one speaks chiefly of the country, but even in the towns there has hitherto been little labour agitation. The inclination to drift from country to city life is noticeable in Canada as elsewhere, but unhealthy pressure towards the centres has not as yet become serious, and there is little sympathy with an unemployed class created by such a tendency. Till a man has tried what he can do on the land, he is not, even in the cities, thought to have much right to grumble or demand help from private charity or from the State.

Canada has a still further safeguard against labour troubles in the neighbourhood of the United States. If a man is not suited with the work and wages he gets in his own country, he can go to another close at hand. The extent to which the French Canadian of Quebec thus migrates in order to find a market for his labour as a factory hand has been before referred to.

While the States in this way serve as a safety-valve for labour questions to the Dominion, it must be confessed that they have in past years drawn from Eastern Canada a great deal of material which it would gladly have retained. This so-called "exodus" has undoubtedly retarded the growth of the Dominion, and has been a fiercely discussed question in Canadian politics. One of the chief grounds on which protection, or, as it was called, the "national policy," won favour in Canada was the belief that the development of manufactures, by creating a variety of industry, would retain in the country many who were going away. This, to a certain extent, it has done. The opening up of the North West has also contributed to divert this flow of population westward, and will do so more in the future. Still, a limited migration to the States goes on, and is likely to do so. It is the natural penalty which Canada pays for being a northern country with those rigorous conditions of life which develop a strong type of character and physique. She is, in fact, repeating the experience of Scotland and New England. A climate which tends to produce a hardy race, a Puritan turn of mind which gives moral strenuousness, good schools, the leisure of winter for thought and study – all these tend to produce men likely to go abroad to win their way by their wits.

(Parkin, *The Great Dominion*, 1895, 212–15)

3

J. D. Rogers, *A Historical Geography of the British Colonies, Canada – Geographical*, 1911

☞ This book is part of a multi-volume series on the history and geography of the British Empire published at the beginning of the twentieth century, to which J. D. Rogers (1857–1914) contributed four volumes. Preparatory to writing *The Great Dominion*, George Parkin travelled widely within Canada and interviewed numerous people, but Rogers does not say whether he had ever visited Canada. It is very apparent, however, that he had spent many hours studying in libraries and archives, gleaning material on the progress of Canadian settlement, and then put this information together in a narrative that describes the European settlement of the land within an evolving transportation system.

To Rogers the historical geography of Canada is the occupying of the country by Europeans. First Nations peoples are barely mentioned and are certainly not a thread of the story. According to Rogers, once new colonists are in place historical geography stops: at that point, he says, other approaches to geography take over and do not concern him. That, of course, is an eccentric view of historical geography, particularly as the subject developed in universities in the mid-twentieth century.

Useful as Rogers' settlement history is in its own right, his significant geographical contribution actually lies elsewhere, in his spatial interpretation of Canadian regions. For each of Canada's major regions, except the Far North, Rogers describes and explains emerging spatial population patterns as the filling in of land by Europeans progresses. He does this in the context of the physical geography of each region and takes particular account of changing means of transportation. It is a story of European settlement streams feeling their way forward, region by region, into what to the participants are new lands. Rogers works very close to the local ground, i.e., to the special geographical circumstances in each region and to the source material. This results in very distinctive approaches to Canada's different major regions, bringing out great contrasts across the country. Each region is seen in its own geometric form and characteristic spatial infrastructure and spatial interactions.

The distinctive regional nomenclature reflects Rogers' spatial approach. In the Arctic (*The Far North-Land*) Rogers does not go beyond a record of exploration, with little awareness of a local population; in Nova Scotia (*The Far East*) two centres, Louisbourg and Halifax, contend to organize the region during a period of European rivalry; New Brunswick (*Links Between Far and Middle East*) has two cross-linked belts of settlement and itself is a national link; the Canadian Shield (*The Core of Canada and the Middle East*) in its southern limits is developing a new spatial geometry closely connected with the Middle East (Rogers' term for southern Quebec and southern Ontario) through the forces of new transport and industrial technologies; Quebec (*The Middle East, or the Province of Two Nations and One River*) has a linear geometry and its growth evolved in the course of rivalry amongst three main centres striving to establish connections nationally and internationally; Ontario (*The Middle East, One Nation on Three St. Lawrence Valleys and Beyond*) is a great fertile triangle where vulnerable separate settlement nuclei had to coalesce; the Prairies region (*The Middle West*) is a great oblong where waterways gave way to railways as the creative force in establishing a new settlement geometry in the face, and perils, of easy spatial connections to the United States; in British Columbia and Yukon (*The Far West and North-West, or the Land of Mountains*) threads of resource and national development drove linkages through fragmented terrain. In summing up, Rogers sees Canada as a whole as a vital link in a globe-girdling empire, very much as Parkin did.

Rogers' work is a study in spatial interaction. His brisk energy, always forging ahead, is devoted to describing the location of settlements in each region and the geographical forces that influenced that settlement. At first the vocabulary, the distinctive phrases, frequent allusions to comparisons distant in time and space, and ubiquitous, quite startling generalizations can be distracting and jar and dislocate, but they make one reflect and see things in a new way. Once one gets used to Rogers' unique style one can appreciate a highly unusual quirky geographical mind, working with the nitty-gritty of a settlement geography focussed directly on the land, district by district, informed and organized by a regional spatial geography. Rogers should be read in two ways: as a straightforward narrator of progress of settlement and, simultaneously, as a scholar writing in the early twentieth century who anticipates modern day conceptual concerns in geography, but whose ideas are expressed in a highly individualistic style and vocabulary.

Rogers' book has summary side-notes throughout, which have occasionally been quoted to provide succinct excerpts. They are indicated as side-notes. ☞

I THE FAR NORTH-LAND AND ITS HEROES

☞ Rogers views the North not as a home of a people, the Inuit, but as an arena for British explorers and their heroic endeavors. To him it is a "dead or half-dead region." Essentially this chapter is a roll call of British expeditions in the Arctic, with a bow to Otto Sverdrup and another to Roald Amundsen. Cockburn Land was the name given to a northern part of Baffin Island before it was known that it was a section of the huge island, and Grant Land was the name given to northern Ellesmere Island during the years the High Arctic was being explored. Rogers argues that the British action of searching for Franklin is a prime reason for making the northern archipelago part of Canada. Note how he ends with a ringing list of the resounding names of ships involved in Arctic exploration. The 283 years mentioned by Rogers is the run of time from Martin Frobisher (1576) to the year Captain William McLintock confirmed Sir John Franklin's fate (1859). The region Rogers describes is more and more in the news, as climate warming makes it easier to navigate the Northwest Passage. ☞

One glance at the map suggests that nature and nature alone made the northern boundary [of Canada]; that on the east but for the colony of Newfoundland and on the west but for Alaska the same artificer was at work; but that the frontiers of Newfoundland colony and Alaska, and all the southern frontiers, were the work of men's hands. If the inference were drawn that these natural frontiers were first-created, self-created, and created without human sacrifices, the inference would be a truism in one sense and the reverse of true in another sense. The coast of America and its islands existed before white men existed, but did not exist as frontiers until white men knew of their existence; and this knowledge was obtained after the last man-made boundary had been settled by war, treaty, or Act of Parliament, and was obtained by a deadly war against nature which lasted 283 years. The names of the men who waged this war or directed it from afar still consecrate its shores, and brave men's blood proved once more the only possible cement of the walls of empire. Although some of these warriors still live, they belong in spirit to the heroic age; for they fought not against human foes but, like Thor, against the frost giants; they displayed "one equal temper of heroic hearts", and their doings and sufferings were on an heroic scale. Their aim was to discover a north-west passage from, the Atlantic to the Pacific. Their results were to ascertain the northern shores of the American continent and northern frontiers of Canada. It is now known that the north-west passages, for there are more than one, are too icy to be used for trading with Japan, China, India, or any other country, and that all the northern shore of America which lies west of Hudson's Bay lies within the Arctic circle, while Hudson Strait, though situated in the latitude of the Shetlands and Faroes, is closed by ice for eight or nine months in the year, and Hudson Bay, though touching the latitude of Bristol, touches also the Arctic circle and is chilled all the year round by stores of never-melted ice which pour southward and eastward from Fox Channel. The north-west passages are all but unnavigable, the northern shores are all but uninhabitable; but great names and memories live in this dead or half-dead region, and here at all events geographers tread on holy ground, and geography if not history has proved itself synonymous with the biography of great men....

It is sometimes asked why the archipelago of islands to the north of continental Canada are considered part of Canada. The answer is that the differences between straits and isthmuses and between islands like Southampton, King William and North Somerset Islands, and peninsulas like Melville and Boothia Peninsulas, are infinitesimally small, that the last crowning discovery which was made on the northern coast was the discovery that what was thought a promontory was really an island, and that the discoveries of these tiny differences cost the greatest amount of suffering and. deaths. Even now maps are not agreed as to whether Cockburn Land is an island or a part of Baffin Land. Men sailed or walked round every foot of every island coast – except some northern islands recently discovered by Otto Sverdrup (1898–1902), except too the greater part of Grant Land, and except a small strip of Victoria Land on the west coast of McClintock Channel, which was examined by Amundsen – before the real continental coast was ascertained, and in order that it might be ascertained.... But the principal tie is the human interest of the tragedy associated with Sir John Franklin, who explored on foot, in boats, and in ships of the Royal Navy, the continental barrens and shores and the islands and their shores, and perished in the fulfilment of a mission which equally concerned the waterways amid the northern islands and the delineation of the northern frontier of the American continent. The Dominion Government sends a steamer from time to time to control or save the whalers of Lancaster Sound and Barrow Strait; and Herschel Island, a little west of the mouth of the Mackenzie, is a rendezvous of American whalers from Bering Strait and of representatives of the North-West Mounted Police, who also frequent the islands of Hudson Bay; otherwise these arctic islands and this arctic coast have once more resumed their primeval desolation; nor are they destined to become the theatre of history or the home of any one white man, and the only history of which they are or will be the theatre is contained in catalogues of names of kings, queens, princes, admirals, officials, men of commerce and explorers of a bygone age, names which mark their dates and illustrate their characteristic features in a way which resembles the mute records of the past furnished by geology. But the resemblance is not complete; for the names which are written on these shores are human names, and names which speak from spirit to spirit and eloquently perpetuate no mere succession of events, but an heroic tragedy in which Intrepid and Resolute Investigators pursued Discovery through regions of Sunshine, but also of Erebus and Terror and Fury, until their Enterprise and Resolution were rewarded with Victory.

(Rogers, *Historical Geography – Canada*, 1911, 1–28)

2 THE FAR EAST: NOVA SCOTIA, THE TWO ISLANDS AND THEIR PEOPLE

☞ Rogers sees the Far East – Nova Scotia, Cape Breton, and Prince Edward Island – as geographically organized by significant urban centres, or capitals as he calls them. Here we see direct imperialism at work: local inhabitants are largely ignored and emphasis is placed on the relations between European antagonists, i.e., the French and the English, as they play out their geopolitical stratagems on North American shores. Two main organizing centres, Louisbourg and Halifax, emerge as focal places in the fight between the French and the British for supremacy in the region, and the relations of these centres to settlement and the hinterlands that support them is discussed. In the French period Louisbourg started as a fishing centre in the late sixteenth century and then became a capital and was fortified. Rogers describes how its influence was more than local. Halifax, the chief centre of the British period, did not have an immediate hinterland, so the importance of the cross-peninsula link to the Annapolis Valley is emphasized and so, of course, is its role as major military base. By 1830 the settlement pattern of the Far East was roughly in place, but Rogers does note the new factors of coal, industry, railways, and the connections with Quebec. ☞

We must now leave the Arctic solitudes for the hum of the market-place....

The four Maritime Provinces, all or some of which the French called Acadia, are the eastern vestibule of Canada. Three of the Maritime Provinces, Cape Breton Island, Nova Scotia, and New Brunswick, occupy the curving coast along the south shore of the Gulf of St. Lawrence, and the west shore of the Atlantic Ocean; and the fourth, Prince Edward Island, is an island in the Gulf, shaped like a new moon and mimicking the Gulf shores off which it lies....

... the prevailing littleness of the Maritime provinces is veiled by the vast American forest, which clothes them throughout – except in very stony or very marshy places – with a coat of many colours; and their human geography is instinct with interest, variety, and sometimes tragic depths, presenting as it does a moving picture of great political Powers, and of still greater social forces, combining, dividing, and recombining, filling, emptying, and refilling large tracts, and of Acadians, New Englanders, Germans, British Americans, Ulstermen, Yorkshiremen, Highlanders, Lowlanders, Irishmen, and Englishmen supplanting or supplementing one another, and the writer who describes it inevitably lapses into narrative.

Nova Scotia, which is the central object in the narrative, was once possessed – and parts of it are still possessed – by the Acadians, who, like the French Canadians, came from the apple-growing, cider-drinking districts of France, but were unlike, and were not of the same stock as the French Canadians, who came from a different part of France, at a time when France was not yet one....

Louisbourg, or Havre à l'Anglais, is a harbour on the Atlantic coast of Cape Breton Island, and in 1597 French Basques went there to fish, and men of Olonne in La Vendée wintered there in order to fish on the Grand Banks of Newfoundland. To-day there are two conspicuous objects in Louisbourg Harbour: one, the old ruined fort, coiled like a green dragon upon a low grassy slope; the other, a brand-new elevated pier for loading ships with Sydney coal in winter, for Louisbourg Harbour is ice-free when Sydney Harbour is ice-bound. Beneath both pier and fort fisher-folk may be seen drying cod on flakes in the same fashion as they still do at outports in Newfoundland and did at Louisbourg in 1597.... But the great fort galvanized adjacent French fishing-villages, from Sydney (Spanish Harbour) to St. Esprit, into life; ... But the influence of Louisbourg was more than local. Three thousand soldiers clamoured for bread and meat, yet no land was cleared in the vicinity. A few imported Germans at Mire Bay, twelve miles north, and when the St. Peter's-Louisbourg road, which is still known as French Road, was built, the inhabitants of St. Peter's, sixty miles south-west, sent supplies; but the cry was still for more. It was heard in far-off Mines [Minas], Truro, and Chignecto ; and a military road from Beausejour to Baie Verte, and cattle-tracts [tracks?] from Windsor to Truro, and from Truro to Tatamagouche and Wallace Bay (Remsheg), were constructed. This was the first northward Acadian trek. The isthmus was crossed, and the first ports were opened on the Gulf coast of Nova Scotia in order to send meat and bread to Louisbourg. At the same time Port Hood (Just-au-Corps) (Cape Breton Island) was occupied by Acadians in order to supply it with stone.

... [Louisbourg, a new capital, i.e centre] faced Europe; so that it was a link not between Canada and Nova Scotia, but between Canada and France. Moreover, it tapped Nova Scotia, and ports were occupied on English as well as on disputed territory, on the Gulf as well as on the Bay of Fundy, through which the wealth and manhood of Nova Scotia began to drain away to a power at war with Nova Scotia. Or, to change the metaphor, what had been meant as a clasp was used as a wedge.

Then Louisbourg fell twice (1745, 1758), ... When Louisbourg fell first, those French colonists of Cape Breton Island who were caught were sent to France, but the Acadian trek towards the Gulf instead of being arrested was accelerated. The loss of Louisbourg meant the loss of a market; and amongst other causes economic distress drove 2,200 Acadians in 1749 from Chignecto to Prince Edward Island and Cape Breton Island, but chiefly to Prince Edward Island, at which we must now glance.

Prince Edward Island had been occupied in 1719 by two Norman families and in 1720 by 135 Frenchmen, and in 1745 there were some 800 persons in the Island, some of them Acadians. In 1751, owing to the inflow of Acadians, the population probably exceeded 2,000; and Acadians were still swarming in in 1752.... The Acadian trek from Chignecto made the coast line of Prince Edward Island overwhelmingly Acadian between 1751 and 1755. But the failure of the Louisbourg market was only temporary, and it was compensated, though inadequately compensated, by the creation of a new market at Halifax. Until the expulsion of the Acadians for political causes, the newly-created capital produced economic demands which checked the Acadian trek, and kept the Acadians in their old homes.

Halifax, or the port of Chebucto, on the Atlantic coast of Nova Scotia, was the British counterblast to Louisbourg. Halifax was built in 1749: the port is one of the best ports in North America; and the city, like St. John, is a city on a rock; indeed, from the east it looks like a rocky island engarlanded with houses, except on its bare brow, on which a fort rests like a crown; but its rear is really connected by a rocky ridge with the mainland, nine miles away, at the head of Bedford Basin. It is distinguished from every other first-rate Canadian town by the absence of a river, and therefore of mills, cultivations, and trade routes behind it. It was midway between useful sea and useless land, or would have been but for two things. In the first place, on the opposite side of Bedford Basin, one mile away by ferry and twenty-six by rail, a supplementary town was founded at Dartmouth; and the series of lakes which all but connect Dartmouth with the Shubenacadie and with Truro begin half a mile behind Dartmouth.... Almost every first-rate Anglo-Canadian town has its supplementary town, which is usually a *vis-à-vis* town, and the reason for the reduplication is sometimes mysterious, but in this case was too obvious for words. Dartmouth was called into existence in order to correct the barrenness and isolation of Halifax.

In the second place, although there was no waterway, there was already a cattle trail to Windsor, ... Colonel Cornwallis immediately proceeded to make the trail into a road, which was continued to Annapolis. In 1784 this road from Halifax to Windsor and Annapolis was the only carriage road in Nova Scotia. The road to Windsor is forty-six miles long, and passes through a sterile region, which only becomes fertile about nine miles from Windsor. It was built, with the help of Acadians and soldiers, not along any valley, nor in order to open up the interior to settlers, but in order to save Halifax from extinction. When Dartmouth failed, this road was a matter of life or death to Halifax. Without it Halifax which grew nothing would have been cut off from the Acadia where Acadians dwelt and grew everything; with it Halifax united the Acadians of Acadia with the English of England, although it was built too late to save Acadia for the Acadians.

And Halifax was more than a port, a rock of defence, and a possible inlet of Acadian wealth into England and of English wealth into Acadia. It was the first city ever built on the east coast of Nova Scotia, and it was built midway between Cape Sable and Cape Canso and their respective cod-fisheries. It brought these two places of resort under one control for the first time in history. Before then the Atlantic coast of Nova Scotia was dominated from its two ends, which never met; and it almost seemed as though the Bay of Fundy represented an alien civilization. Halifax tied these three threads into a single knot.... Louisbourg disunited Nova Scotia while uniting Canada to France. The harmony had in it a discordant note. Halifax united Nova Scotia with itself and to England, and was a harmony through and through.

The new colonists who arrived in Halifax (1749–52) were the first colonists who were not French, but it would be a mistake to infer that they were all of them from the United Kingdom.... [The settlement of Nova Scotia and Prince Edward Island is summarized in the following succinct side notes] The new colonists comprised (1) soldiers, sailors, &c. of British origin: (2) German Protestant; (3) New Englanders; (The Germans founding Lunenburg, and the New Englanders supplanting the Acadians) (4) Ulstermen; (5) Highland Roman Catholic ex-soldiers, &c. who supplanted Acadians in Prince Edward Island; (6) Highland Presbyterians, &c., who colonized Pictou; where class (5) joined them and went on to Cape Breton Island; (Scotch immigration being due to economic causes); (7) Yorkshire Methodists at Chignecto; (8) restored Acadians, whom Jerseymen attracted towards [the Gulf Coast and Cape Breton]; (9) Loyalists filled up intervals on coasts, and replaced or supplemented New Englanders, and settled on roads along with others. Immigrants re-immigrated inland. In Prince Edward Island Loyalists filled up intervals and went to the capital. In Cape Breton Islands Loyalists founded Sydney: and Sydney became a coal and steel centre....

A man might walk from end to end of Cape Breton Island and Nova Scotia, using Haliburton's *History* (1829) as guide-book, and without finding anything except what he expected to find. He would shake hands with a great-grandson of an 82nd Highlander at Pictou Landing, and would learn from Haliburton that that spot was granted to the 82nd Highlanders in 1784; he would find Antigonish Highland, New Glasgow Scotch, Clementsport and Lunenburg rather German, and the Annapolis and Windsor valleys very English. He would know exactly where to find Acadians and men from Cape Cod, and would recognize them at a glance....

The supremacy of Halifax over other towns is unchallenged, and it accounts for two-fifths of the town life but for only one-ninth of the whole life of Nova Scotia, for Nova Scotia is rural in its habits....

Except local branch-lines a few miles in length, and some ten miles of main line west of Mulgrave, every Nova Scotian railroad follows the chief main roads more or less. No line has been built between Halifax and Guysborough, and the lines to and through Windsor became less important than the lines to and through Truro owing to the political decay of Annapolis, the economic progress of the coal districts, and the completion of the through line to Quebec, which promoted Halifax from the position of Nova Scotian capital to that of winter-port of Canada. But for these additions, omissions, and changes, the old main roads which make the Atlantic Gulf and Bay towns of Nova Scotia one on Haliburton's map (1828), and the new railways, when they are shown upon a small scale, seem replicas. There has been a duplication of functions. Consequently Halifax, which is the one head, has grown out of all proportion; although Yarmouth, the junction, so to speak, for Boston, Truro, the junction for Quebec and Sydney, and minor ganglionic rail-and-road centres like Kentville and Bridgewater, have also benefited.

(Rogers, Historical *Geography – Canada*, 1911, 31–69)

3 LINKS BETWEEN FAR AND MIDDLE EAST: NEW BRUNSWICK AND ITS PEOPLE

☛ Rogers' emphasis on spatial relationships is particularly apparent in his separation of New Brunswick from the other Maritime Provinces for special consideration because of its strategic position and role as a vital link in a spatial connection reaching from the St. Lawrence River across the Appalachians to the Atlantic Ocean. Within the region he describes how cross-country routes based on river connections join the Gulf coast and the Saint John River. At the junctions, or trysting points as he calls them, towns have grown. Rogers recognizes and stresses that the indigenous people had used the same cross routes. (Joseph Bouchette also noted the importance of New Brunswick's rivers in linking different parts of the colony.) Rogers ends this chapter with resounding metaphors about New Brunswick, stating that it consists of two corridors between Quebec and the Atlantic Ocean, surely the ultimate in defining a region as a spatial link. In effect, to Rogers New Brunswick becomes a grotesque model of connections without a body. However, he clearly recognizes two "lines of life" – the St. John River and the Gulf of St. Lawrence coast. ☞

Lines of communication of river, road, and railway double and doubly intensify one another in Nova Scotia, but triple and triply intensify one another in New Brunswick, which is only a little more than a double line of communication between the Atlantic or Nova Scotia and Quebec; and the influence of Quebec being nearer is increased in proportion to its nearness. Even those parts of New Brunswick which adjoin the isthmus of Chignecto, and are geographically a part of Nova Scotia, became more famous as resting and starting places for the north than as places to live and die in....

... Denys's colonists [of the 1650s and '60s] had probably died out: if so, Acadians from Nova Scotia were the first fruitful seed sown along the eastern and northern shores of New Brunswick, and they are still there. They dotted two sides of New Brunswick with a succession of connected settlements for the first time in history. But they founded villages not towns, and the work of peopling these two sides was done a second time by men, of a different race and of a later generation, who founded towns. Thus Campbellton (pop. 2,652), Dalhousie (pop. 862), Bathurst (pop. 2,500), and Caraquet (pop. 773) on Bay Châleurs; Newcastle (pop. 2,507), Douglastown (pop. 481), Nelson (pop. 377), and Chatham (pop. 4,868) on either side of the estuary of the Miramichi; and the towns of Richibucto (pop. 760) and Shediac (pop. 1,075) are the fruits of Scotch seed which was sown twenty or thirty years later, and of which more anon. Of these towns Shediac is the Gulf by-port of Moncton (pop. 9,026), which is on the bend of the Petitcodiac; therefore it may be said that the only Gulf towns are the ports or port towns of the Miramichi, Richibucto, and Petitcodiac, which are the only rivers affording easy access from the Gulf to the St. John. Similarly Bay Châleurs and the Restigouche also point to the St. John. The Acadian villages and Scotch towns are termini of crossways leading to one great river. Of all these crossways the two valleys, which seem like one valley formed by the Upper Petitcodiac and Kennebecasis, constitute the easiest and straightest way, and were first furnished by British colonists with a main road past Petitcodiac, Sussex (pop. 1,398) and Hampton (pop. 650) to St. John (pop. 40,711) [1901 populations].

St. John owes its position as the commercial capital of New Brunswick to its fine harbour and situation at the mouth of the St. John. The harbour does not freeze in winter, and the city proper is on two rocks on the left bank of the river-mouth below the falls, but its suburbs extend above the falls and to the right bank, at West End. The river itself is one of the great river-routes into the interior of North America....

After Gagetown the river bends westward through flooded flats and more continuous settlements, past the *vis-à-vis* towns of Maugerville (north) and Oromocto (south), at the mouth of the Oromocto (south), to the low-lying, leafy city of Fredericton (pop. 7,117) (south), which is the political capital and University city of New Brunswick, and presents a striking contrast to its supplementary lumber-towns of Marysville (pop. 1,892) and Gibson (pop. 764) [1901 populations], on the opposite or north bank. Though eighty-four miles from the sea, the river is still tidal, half a mile wide, and thatched with lumber rafts, like Groby's Pool with pancakes. It is here that the Nashwaak penetrates towards the sources of the Miramichi, and presents a waterway to the Gulf, only inferior in importance to the waterway from St. John to Moncton.... The river now runs north and south for 112 miles past Perth (east) and Andover (west), which are twin towns near the mouths of the Tobique (east) and the Aroostook (west), past Grand Falls (pop. 644), where there is a miniature Niagara, 124 feet high, and past Grand River, where the Grand River flows in from the east, to Edmundston (pop. 444), where the river, which is now flowing west and east, is joined from the north by the Madawaska, a river one third its size and depth, and leading to Temiscouata Lake and Portage on the Appalachian Range, and so to Rivière du Loup, 81 miles away, on the St. Lawrence. The St. John, Madawaska, and Rivière du Loup are the natural highway through the 341 miles of impenetrable forest which separate the Bay of Fundy from the St, Lawrence River. Along this highway there are trifling interruptions formed by falls, rapids, and one low watershed, and towns have been built as trysting-places wherever and only where two or more similar highways meet; for instance, at St. John, Gagetown, Fredericton, Woodstock, and Edmundston. Even Westfield and Oromocto are at the ends of a pair of waterways which cut off a sharp corner of the St. John; and Petitcodiac and Sussex are and have been starting-places for short cuts to the Belleisle, Washademoak, and Salmon River crossways. But this rule has two exceptions. Grand Falls has its town, and, although it is a compulsory resting-place on the old main river-route, it is not the starting-point of a new crossway; and although the Grand River furnishes the only practicable crossway from the St. John to the Restigouche and Bay Chaleurs it has no town, unless Edmundston, twenty miles away, serves that purpose. These exceptions, or possible exceptions, occur where boundary disputes retarded natural development.

Hardly less important than the side-passages, so to speak, from the great river to the eastern gulf are its two back-stair passages to Passamaquoddy Bay, one from Woodstock up the Eel River and down the St. Croix , and the other up the Oromocto and down the Magaguadavic: the first leading to Milltown (pop. 2,044), St. Stephen (pop. 2,840), and St. Andrews (pop. 1,066), and the second leading to St. George (pop. 2,892) [1901 populations], all of which are on Passamaquoddy Bay. The towns on the west side of the St. Croix are rather larger than those on the east, but belong to the United States: for by the sport of Fate the frontier between British America and the United States is the St. Croix, and Fate as usual has been capricious in its choice....

Hence New Brunswick has an eastern and western line of life [side note].... New Brunswick is divided longitudinally into a Gulf-Coast-strip held together by a State road and rail: and a St. John River-strip held together by river, and at a later date by private roads and railways: the first strip being extended to include Bay Châleurs and Moncton, and the second strip being extended to include Passamaquoddy Bay. Dusty parchments drawn by London scriveners at the behest of a crowned pedant and unique historical complications produced this arbitrary dichotomy. But was it arbitrary?

Long before history began, Indians adopted these very same divisions: and the St. John River, including Passamaquoddy Bay, was the domain of the Maliceet, while the Gulf coast, including Bay Châleurs and the Petitcodiac, was the domain of the Micmac. To them New Brunswick was not one but two: and the ways between the two were the same as those which have been described between St. John and Moncton, between Gagetown and Richibucto, between Fredericton and Miramichi, and between Grand River and the Restigouche to-day; even the back entrance to the St. John from Passamaquoddy Bay and the short cuts were the same. The very trysting and council places of the Indians' at St. John, Fredericton, St. Andrews and Woodstock – not to mention lesser or later posts at St. George, Westfield, Oromocto and Edmundston, were at the same corners in Indian times as the principal places were under the French and English régimes.

The French régime was the Indian régime with a European veneer. In 1620 a Recollet missionary of Nipisiguit descended the St. John; and *coureurs des bois* from Quebec followed him; but in political geography these men were mere pupils of those whom they went to teach....

During this period two great intercolonial roads were completed to Quebec, one from Fredericton and Woodstock and the other from Moncton. These roads overshadowed every other road, and the second which continued to Halifax overshadowed the first. The first was indirectly due to war, and the second was directly due to apprehensions of war.

Before 1783 there was wilderness, and nothing but wilderness, between Woodstock and the St. Lawrence. In 1783 Sir Frederick Haldimand began to build, between Rivière du Loup and Lake Temiscouata, a road which in 1833 was from six to nine feet wide, with old tree-stumps on its dry patches, and rotting timber strewn corduroy-fashion on its wet patches....

The Kempt or Gulf road from Moncton to Newcastle, Bathurst, Lake Matapedia, and Métis on the St. Lawrence River doubled the sea-route to Quebec, and rarely followed either river or any other natural course. It was artificial, and was built chiefly as a military precaution, but partly also in order to induce settlement; ...

The whole history of this period was a history of roads; and the political effect of the two most important roads was to people, enrich, and unify the province by diminishing the importance of its capital. The great gulf road did not pass Fredericton or St. John; and the great river road had two branches from Woodstock, one to St. Andrews, which did not pass Fredericton, and the other to St. John, on which Fredericton resembled a beautiful wayside inn.

After the Fifties immigration almost ceased; roads played little part, ... It was a period of railroads, which shadowed the two intercolonial roads, and the main provincial roads from Moncton to St. John and from Fredericton to Chatham or Newcastle. The great intercolonial railroad, being political, shadowed the Kempt road, which is far from the frontier; and the railroads near the St. John were left to private enterprise. The Gulf settlements and St. John River settlements, so to speak, were united with themselves and the St. Lawrence by two vertical steel jambs, the left jamb dividing into two below Woodstock, and by two steel crossbars with each other. Fredericton sank to the material level of Moncton; and the extreme points at Halifax, St. John, and Passamaquoddy Bay were strengthened at the expense of intermediate towns. Of these towns Halifax, being the terminus of the Intercolonial Railway, profited more than St. John, which is, however, the terminus of a branch-line from Moncton, and of a concatenation of small private lines down the St. John valley. Perhaps the completion of the National Transcontinental Railway, which is meant to go across country from Grand Falls by Chipman to

Moncton, with branches to Fredericton and St. John, will readjust the scales; but its principal effect will be to open up new districts to settlement. At present the country away from the main railways and roads is very lonely. There has been extension by old settlers up Eel River, Tobique River, and the like, and by old and new settlers elsewhere, but always, more or less, in the neighbourhood of the new railway lines.... the face of the country and character of the population have hardly changed since the Fifties, when it attained some sort of finality.

The population has increased 50 per cent. during the last fifty years and was 331,120 in 1901, of which one-third was "English" (including British American), one-fourth Irish, one-fourth Acadian, one-seventh Scotch, and the minute residue comprised 1,368 negroes (who settled at Otnabog (1812) and Willow Grove (1817), and 1,309 native Indians (for whom twenty-five reserves have been set apart at the mouths of the Tobique, Richibucto, and elsewhere).

Geographically, if unimportant details are omitted, the Indian, French, and British civilizations, and the rivers, coast-lines, roads, and railways, resemble one another on the map. But the resemblance would be misleading, because it ignores the human element.

New Brunswick is still an oblong exhibiting a different type of civilization on its two longer sides – Military and Loyalist on the west, Scotch and Acadian on the East; but the nature, causes, and effects of its incurable dualism are not now what they were in old time. Thus the two types still meet along well-worn routes by river, road, and rail; but these cross-routes, which once were mere points of casual contact, are now means by which the two civilizations are indissolubly welded together.

The reader may be weary of seeing rivers and coasts, referred to as lines of development, and lines of development described by architectural and mechanical metaphors such as passages, props, bands, bonds, and the like; but these metaphors recur irresistibly to those who realize that if there is one essential truth which has persisted through the ages, it is that New Brunswick is the province with two corridors to Quebec Province, two bands and bonds between the St. Lawrence and the Atlantic, two props or pillars upon which Quebec Province rests, and must rest during half the year, unless it is to depend upon the United States. It was so when New Brunswick was dual and divided; and the more self-contained and united New Brunswick has become, the more irrefutably has it shown that its mission in the history of the world is to connect Quebec Province with the far Eastern provinces and with Europe.

(Rogers, *Historical Geography – Canada*, 1911, 73–88)

4   OTHER LINKS BETWEEN FAR AND MIDDLE EAST: PENINSULAS AND ISLANDS OF THE GULF

☞ Other Links comprise the Gaspé Peninsula, the Magdalene and Anticosti Islands, and Labrador. In the Gaspé, Rogers notes the mix of French and British Canadian settlement, something that Bouchette had overlooked. Labrador is thinly populated along the coast and there are few inland residents. In his inimitable way, and revealing that agriculture and the introduction of capital represent civilization to him, Rogers says that "the Saguenay has long since been rescued from Labradorism, and handed over to civilization." ☜

The north side of Bay Châleurs, although situated in the province of Quebec, reflects the civilization of its south side. No one lives there except upon the coast, behind which the wooded tableland of Gaspé Peninsula (c. 1,500 feet), crowned by the Shickshock Mountains (c. 4,000 feet), bring the long line of the Appalachian range of Eastern America to a fitting end, and prohibit settlements inland....

... New Carlisle was founded in 1784 by Loyalist Englishmen from New York State and a few disbanded soldiers, is still two-thirds English, and is the county town; Port Daniel and Hopetown are two-thirds French in origin and Paspébiac is six-sevenths French in origin and the head-quarters of the Jersey fish-merchants, who began their mission of industry and reconciliation here upon the green-sward below the purple mountains and above the low red rocks on the shore in 1767.... New Richmond being the second town of the county and half Scotch. West of New Richmond, Carleton (pop. 1,06 1) is wholly, Nouvelle Bay three-fourths, and Matapedia five-sixths French in origin; but elsewhere the British, chiefly the Scotch element, prevails, except in the historic settlement of Micmac Indians (pop. 422) [1901 populations] at Cross Point opposite Campbellton. The French mission to these Indians is nearly three centuries old; but the Church preceded the state, and there were no white settlers here, until Acadian refugees and some thousand sailors, who on their defeat by Commodore Byron (1758) fled to the woods, formed the stock from which the present French-speaking inhabitants of the Bay are derived....

... Gaspé Bay is the most populous place upon the coast; it was here that Cartier set up a cross (1534), and fishermen from Quebec used to live here in the summer, so that General Wolfe raided it (1758) in order to deprive Quebec of its principal fish supply. But there was no

permanent settlement here until the conquest. An Irishman, F. O'Hara
(1765), was the first agricultural settler; and its first town was Douglastown (pop. 1098), which was laid out for the Loyalists in 1784, and is
now four-fifths Irish, while the other settlements in Gaspé Bay are three-
fourths British. South of the Bay French influences are in the ascendant
at the settlements opposite Champlain's Pierced Rock and elsewhere;
and north of the Bay the atmosphere is French, but not decisively French
until the corner is rounded and we reach Magdalen River, St. Anne, and
Cape Chat. Here we are face to face with French Canada in its pur-
est form. There is no Acadian tinge, and the British element is almost
effaced; indeed, it is only one per cent. at Cape Chat.... In any case. Cape
Chat and everything west of it is Quebec in spirit; while Cape Rosiers
and everything south of it is a replica of the north shore, which is a replica of the south shore of Bay Châleurs....

Halfway between the Pierced Rock and Newfoundland (c. 120 miles),
and equidistant from Cape Breton Island and Prince Edward Island (c.
60 miles), or from the Gut of Canso and Anticosti (c. 90 miles), are the
Magdalen Islands, with ninety square miles of sandspits, on which the
inhabitants dry cod; of sandstone rocks, on which sea-birds breed as
they did in Cartier's day; of sandstone hills five hundred and fifty feet
high, and of red soil as in Prince Edward Island. The principal island is
composite, consisting of several islets known as Amherst, Grindstone,
Wolf, Grosse, Coffin, and Alright. Wolf Islet has been compared to a
"sesamoid bone in the middle of a muscle of sand nearly twenty-four
miles long", and the others are either joined by low sand-bars or disjoined by shallow salt-lagoons. On the south-east, Entry Island, and on
the north-east Brion and Bird Islets are wholly detached from these semi-
detached units. Like Anticosti, the islands lie in the mid-stream and are
strewn with wrecks.... Fishing and sealing are the principal pursuits of
the inhabitants, who now number 6,000 [1901 population], live mostly
on the compound island or islet-group, and of whom five-sixths are
Acadian or French, and the rest British in origin. The type of civilization
is essentially characteristic of the south side of the Gulf.

Anticosti Island, the other obstruction in the fair way of ships sailing
from Europe to Quebec, belongs geologically and historically, in body
and soul, to the north shore of the Gulf, which is the south shore of
Labrador. It is seven hundred feet high in parts, almost harbourless, and
2,600 square miles in size, or a little larger than Prince Edward Island,
and nearly as large as Cape Breton Island....

... Anticosti was a howling wilderness haunted by wrecked sailors, who turned cannibals, by lighthouse keepers, who were there to save sailors from wreck, and by philanthropists or monomaniacs in charge of food stores to save wrecked sailors from cannibalism. Then an Anticosti Company was formed and introduced settlers (1871); and the island reached its zenith in 1881, when it had 676 inhabitants, of whom 160 were English Newfoundlanders and the rest Canadian French, all the inhabitants living either in the westernmost or in the easternmost corner of the island. Then began the decline and fall of what seemed to be an incipient province, the inhabitants dwindling to 253 (1891). Then the province was bought at a public auction by M. Menier, of Paris, with the proceeds of the sale of chocolate (1895); and he has built a pier 1,200 yards long at Ellis Bay in the west end, where there is the nearest approach to a harbour along the smooth undented coast-lines of this inhospitable island. The east-enders have gone; the westenders number about 500; and a few wild beasts have been introduced in order to enliven the unromantic swamps and forests of the interior.

Anticosti is an outlier of Labrador, ... [Labrador's] only inland residents are a handful of white men, who occupy one Hudson Bay Company trading post at Lake Nichicun and another at Lake Mistassini; and perhaps 2,000 Montagnais or Nascaupi Cree-Indians who are Algonquins. The huge husk is twice the size of Germany and all but empty within; and its exterior is hardly more populous.

After the amalgamation of the North-West Company of Montreal with the Hudson Bay Company of London (1821) the latter invaded northern, southern, and eastern Labrador from east, west, and north, by sea and by land.... Various posts and forts on the north coast of the Gulf of St. Lawrence and up to and along the Saguenay had already been leased to the North-West Company and others, and were gradually absorbed by the Hudson Bay Company. Thus they ran a girdle round the Peninsula, which still holds, but with two differences: the Saguenay has long since been rescued from Labradorism, and handed over to civilization; and the trading posts are often doubled, so that a French-Canadian faces a London-Scottish post, not in rival war, as in the wild north-west before 1821, but in friendly competition.... On the east coast of Labrador there are Moravian missionaries who preach to and trade for some 1,000 or 2,000 Eskimos at Makkovik, Hopedale, Nain, Okkak, Hebron, Rama, and Killinek; and south of these missions some 3,000 Newfoundland fishermen have settled.

Resident fishermen, traders, and missionaries between the Saguenay and Blanc Sablon are now 8,000, of whom 4,000 are on the river shore west of Egg Island, and are almost all French Canadians, and 4,000 are on the gulf shore, where French Canadians are to British as three to two, and most of the British are English Newfoundlanders living east of Cape Whittle. French Canadians on the north shore of the Gulf include Acadians from the south shore, and the Magdalens, who, between 1857 and 1861, squatted at the mouth of the Natashquan, and in the neighbourhood of Cartier's Port Brest (Eskimo Point). Settlers have come from west, east, and south. The Gulf coast, which was never thoroughly French, is now parti-coloured. It is only when we enter the river that the French star shines alone, or almost alone, on its north as well as on its south bank.

(Rogers, *Historical Geography – Canada*, 1911, 91–9)

5 THE CORE OF CANADA AND THE MIDDLE EAST

☞ Bouchette devoted an entire chapter to discussing the importance of the St. Lawrence River to British North America. In this chapter Rogers gives his spatial imagination free rein as he speculates on the importance of the Canadian Shield and the St. Lawrence River to Canada, especially in relation to southern Quebec and southern Ontario, the "Middle East." The Shield, or Archean Canada as he calls it, is the "Core of Canada." He mentions the mineral resources that are being developed in the Shield and its oases, i.e., clay belts. Rogers takes pleasure in describing the boundaries of the Shield, leaping hundreds of kilometres from place to place, and tells us about the many low watersheds in the Shield that part south and north flowing waters. It is as if his imagination is caught up in this enormous natural section of North American terrain and he revels in exploring its spaciousness and special character, also reminding us that this region is not truly mountainous. It is strange that Rogers describes rocks and terrain in the Shield, yet not once does he mention glaciation. He ends by reflecting on the role that this vast land has had in Quebec and Ontario, and concludes that history was made not in the Shield but in the narrow sedimentary confines to the south. Like many other writers of this period, Rogers says nothing about the indigenous people and their role in the fur trade in the Shield.

After discussing the Canadian Shield, Rogers' spatial approach and sense of geometry take over more and more as he argues that southern

Quebec is linear and southern Ontario a triangle and alludes to how those spaces were filled in by settlers. Once again spatial restlessness dominates and he jumps from the course of the St. Lawrence River all the way to Lake Superior, the 49th parallel, and the Pacific Ocean. The "line of life" is the track of settlement along westward leading routes. Here too we have an example of the spatial thinking of the early twentieth century during the third great railway building era in Canada, as the National Transcontinental and Canadian Northern are constructed (both shortly became bankrupt and were combined to form the Canadian National). The National Transcontinental is another "line of life" and the base of an "immense triangle" that will give the Middle East breadth. This chapter is Rogers at his most imaginative, like a 1960s geographer thrilled with the new-found idea of spatial interaction. ⌒

Labrador is vast and desolate because it is a part of Archaean Canada [Canadian Shield]; and Archaean Canada, or the Canada where Archaean rocks are the only rocks, has been ever since the world began, before life began, and before the rest of America or any other continent rose from the deep. It is the core of the American continent and of Canada. It represents the prelude to the geological trilogy. It is the ground floor of the earth, on which upper stories have been built elsewhere, but on which nothing has been built here, for it is what and where and as it always has been, and its shape shows no trace of change. In Archaean countries distances in space count for as little as aeons in time, and the reader must now seat himself on the magic cloth of Jonathas and transport himself a few thousand miles to the north-west.... [Rogers then describes the very long boundary of the Shield.]

Broadly speaking, the whole Archaean area is stone, hill, and forest. The characteristic Archaean stone is hard, bossy gneiss; therefore the hills are low, rounded knolls, and the valleys high and three parts lake or river; and the soil is thin and sandy, so that the stones break through it like the rib-bones of a starved horse....

In the Archean area ... the rocks are not all gneiss and granite, but mineral rocks and rich clay belts have been discovered. What are called Huronian rocks are also Archean in age, but contain dolerite or diabase, and the copper and unique nickel of Sudbury (Ontario), the silver and unique cobalt of Cobalt (Ontario), the silver of Thunder Bay (Lake Superior), the copper of Michipicoten (Lake Superior), and of Wabigoon and Manitou (between Lakes Superior and Winnipeg), and probably all minerals east of the Rockies are found in Huronan strata. Nor is the soil always thin, deep deposits of clay being found on the shores of lakes and long stretches between lake and lake; and the history of Lake St. Jean, which is an expansion of the Saguenay one hundred miles from its mouth in the very heart of the Archean country, may be taken as a parable and a precedent....

... Tadoussac and the Saguenay were epitomes of Labrador; therefore civilization shunned them and clave to the St. Lawrence, so that the Saguenay and its Lake were never more than the home of a few traders and missionaries until Joseph Bouchette and others explored the lake from Quebec (1827–8).... He urged the colonization of the Lake shores and of the river banks to Chicoutimi, or a little further. In 1851 over 5,000, in 1901 nearly 50,000 colonists had responded to his call; and the St. Jean and Upper Saguenay district, with its capitals, Chicoutimi (pop. 5,796), Héberttville (pop. 2,580) and Roberval (pop. 2,593) is a fine example of French-Canadian enterprise under the British regime. This new district is an oasis redeemed from the wilderness and connected with the St. Lawrence and civilization by 190 miles of lonely railway, or seventy miles of the deep still waters of the lonely Saguenay.

Some four hundred miles due west of Lake St. Jean, between Lake Abitibi and Lake Timiskaming inclusively, there is a larger and richer clay belt which is now being reclaimed. Lake Timiskaming is an expansion of the upper Ottawa, ... and it was a mere passage with a wayside inn, until rich cobalt and silver mines were discovered at Cobalt (November, 1903), and gold mines at Larder Lake close by.... [By 1908] machinery crushed quartz, and there was a gold "city" on its shore.

For these reasons Lake Timiskaming has a railroad one hundred miles long to North Bay Junction (on Lake Nipissing], and so into the civilized parts of Ontario; and the railway has now been continued another hundred miles northward to Matheson close by Lake Abitibi; that is to say right through the clay belt. At Porcupine Lake, near Matheson, important discoveries of gold were announced in 1909.

The development of Lake St. Jean belongs to the past, that of Lake Abitibi and its neighbourhood to the present; and one hundred or two hundred miles west of Lake Abitibi there is a somewhat similar patch on the Archaean skirt, where a surveyor in 1907 discovered a lake fifty miles long, surrounded by rich clay, and unmarked on any map; and similar discoveries are being made from time to time in the heart of the forest, which intervenes between the outer and inner limits of the Archaean wilderness. These districts belong to the future; and it is hoped that all these oases will ultimately hang together like beads upon a string by means of the National Transcontinental Railway which is in course of construction.

These tracts, where rocks and lakes produce wealth recall that "good land of brooks, of waters, of fountains and depths that spring out of valleys and hills, of wheat and barley, ... whose stones are iron, and out of whose hills thou mayest dig brass"; and whether the lakes and rivers do or do not deposit soil, they are the natural roadways along which wealth is exchanged. As Pascal wrote, "Les rivieres sont des chemins qui marchent," but rivers are the highways of Canada in a peculiar sense. Eternal forest makes other roads impossible or difficult; Canadian waters are as innumerable as the stars, and unless very deep or swift, freeze in winter. Archaean Canada is a labyrinth of waters; lakes lie on almost every watershed, and full-grown rivers start from the lakes on journeys many hundred miles in length towards every point of the compass....

[Rogers goes on to discuss water transportation, travelling by canoe from lake to lake over low watersheds in the Shield.] Moreover in Canada the highest heights of land rarely exceed 2,000 feet s.m., and the highest mountains are hardly higher. But are they mountains?

A tourist who looks at Mount St. Anne (2,620 feet s.m.) behind Cap Tourmente (1,874 feet s.m.), or at Les Éboulements (2,551 feet s.m.), from a steamer on the St. Lawrence, or at Trembling Mountain (2,380 feet s.m.) in the Montreal District, looks at some of the loftiest heights from the lowest depths in Archaean Canada]; yet he is never conscious of the presence of mountains like Snowdon, partly because forests invest them from foot to blue rounded summit, and partly because the summits are mimicked and shadowed by numberless other blue, wavy, fretted summits of almost equal height. This country is no more mountainous than the Atlantic in a storm. These are not mountains, but the buttresses of an undulating plateau. The scenery here is comparatively bold, not because the hills are higher, but because the valleys are lower than usual. An equally bold descent marks the end of the Archaean system on the north shores of Lakes Huron and Superior. The plateau resembles some old fort, with bastions and lunettes on its outline, guarded by abattis of living trees and moats of running water....

... [The St. Lawrence-Great Lakes water system is never far from the Canadian Shield in Quebec and Ontario, and Rogers discusses how the historical development of those provinces, i.e. the Middle East, occurred in the lowlands south of the Shield boundary.] But those parts of Quebec and Ontario Provinces in which history was made lie between narrow confines. All their historical events took place in the valley of the St. Lawrence. There their colonies and towns were built, their battles fought, and their industrial successes won. In former times the river was called Canada; and what was once called Canada, and is now called the Middle East of Canada, is essentially the country of the River St. Lawrence. What the Nile is to Egypt and the Soudan, the St. Lawrence is to Quebec and Ontario. But the St. Lawrence is purer and straighter than the Nile. It has infinite islands but no mud islands or deltas, not even at its mouth, and for its last thousand miles, from Detroit to Pointe des Monts, the distances by air, land, or water differ but little. As the Nile above Khartum is the White and Blue Nile, so the St. Lawrence above Montreal is the Ottawa and the St. Lawrence; so that the Upper Province is the Province of Two Rivers. Quebec Province is bounded on the south partly by the boundary-line which has already been described, then by the Appalachian range, then by the 45th parallel of latitude until it strikes the St. Lawrence at St. Regis opposite Cornwall. Parts of the Appalachian range within Maine, Vermont, and New York States may be seen on a clear day from any hill-top between Montreal and Quebec, and on the north of the river the crowded hill-tops of Archaean Canada loom near at hand. All that is of interest in old Canadian history took place within these narrow limits. The figure described within these limits represents from time to time enclosed spaces, of small size in Quebec Province and of large size in Ontario, but French civilization might be typified by the straight line of the St. Lawrence, upon which miniature circles and triangles were sometimes described on its islands or at the confluence of its principal tributaries. No serious effort was made to fill the whole enclosed space until the very end of the eighteenth century. Above Cornwall, the southern limit of Ontario – for we are already in Ontario – lies in the present bed of the St. Lawrence and its inland seas, until Pigeon River on the west coast of Lake Superior is reached. Thence it continues up the old river route from Grand Portage on Pigeon River to the 49th parallel of latitude, which is the international boundary of the middle and extreme west of Canada as far as the Pacific. Rivers have never been boundaries for long, either in Asia, Africa, or Europe, and parallels and meridians have only been effective boundaries between "spheres of influence" in barbaric countries or between British provinces. The immediate palpable effect of these arbitrary lines was that in Ontario new towns sprang up at Niagara, Detroit River, and Sault St. Marie, opposite American towns or vice versa; and that the starting-point on Lake Superior for the middle west and north-west was shifted from Grand Portage to Fort William, forty miles north (1803), the old and new ways meeting rather more than one hundred miles west of the two starting-points. Ontario, south of the most ancient possible course of the St. Lawrence to Georgian Bay, is sometimes nicknamed old Ontario; it too has narrow confines, but it was always thought of as a triangle which colonists tried to fill. Nevertheless nearly all its principal towns lie on one of the three ways to the west, and on a Silurian or Devonian, not on an Archaean, foundation. The civilization of the middle east abhorred granite, and its line of life was thin-spun and single, except where the St. Lawrence seemed to go or to have gone two or three ways, and there it too became double or triple, and tried to cover the interval between the threads. West of French River the line is once more frail and single, and is symbolized by the Canadian Pacific Railway as it runs along or near the north shore of the first and second seas of the St. Lawrence as far as Fort William, which shines with the reflected glory of the middle west. After Fort William there are forty miles of the old water-system, 350 miles of a new water-system with the old wilderness, and then a new country.

But we must return to the middle east, which suggests three reflections. First, because it is the country of one great river, because that river is a pre-eminent example of "Les chemins qui marchent" and because all its main railways and roadways double or treble the course or courses of the great river, there is an incessant stream, not only of water but of men and things perpetually moving along the western way. Secondly, from end to end of the middle east there is not one rock later than rocks of Devonian age, which rocks precede Carboniferous rocks in the geological scale; consequently there is no coal. Thirdly, the middle west is often called the north-west because its southern limit is 49° lat. or two degrees north of Quebec City, and it is proposed that the National Transcontinental Railway shall connect it with Quebec by a straight line. When this is complete it is thought that the single thread with knots, networks, and tangles here and there, which is the emblem of Canadian destiny, will be changed into an immense triangle with a base 1,200 miles long; the middle east will no longer be length without breadth, and a new era will dawn. The St. Lawrence, which has hitherto been the only "Leit-Faden" [Leading-Thread] of the middle east, will be left at Quebec, and the track will plunge at once into the primeval forest, catching up cross threads here and there, like that at Abitibi, but without emerging until its journey is at an end. A more familiar metaphor is often used. It is said that hitherto the middle east has been like a row of one-storied houses in

Quebec Province, and of two-storied houses in Old Ontario, with two or three scaffolds and ladders erected to an unbuilt upper storey, and that the time has now come to build a still higher storey all along the upper ends of the scaffolds and ladders. The metaphor is not quite exact, for it can hardly be expected that the living places along the new track will be continuous with themselves and with the old track. Along the old track nothing is so striking as the continuous civilization which lines the valley of the St. Lawrence up to Lake Superior; but the continuity was attained by different methods and processes and with different results in the provinces of Quebec and Ontario.

(Rogers, *Historical Geography – Canada*, 1911, 100–16)

6 THE MIDDLE EAST: QUEBEC, OR THE PROVINCE OF TWO NATIONS AND ONE RIVER

☞ Thinking strategically, Rogers examines the French colonization of Quebec through the following themes: the three capitals, i.e., urban centres, of Quebec City, Three Rivers, and Montreal, all on the north bank of the St. Lawrence River; the conflicts with the First Nations peoples; the connections with Europe, particularly important for Quebec City; and the connections with the interior, particularly important for Three Rivers and Montreal. The interrelations with the First Nations peoples are considered in their spatial dimensions and the expansion of French settlement in seigneuries along the St. Lawrence is analyzed in its relationship to the three capitals. Rogers' descriptions of this colonization are too detailed for inclusion here, except for examples of settlement just east of Quebec City and west of Montreal, including some speculation on the nearby fringe of settlement occupied by Native Peoples. Rogers devotes much attention to the settlement of the Eastern Townships during the early British regime and to the changing proportions of people of French and British origin in particular districts in that region south of the St. Lawrence. Many new towns were established in the townships. Then he discusses urbanization in Quebec in the early twentieth century, including the Montreal "maelstrom" as the city grew rapidly. ☞

Quebec is the Province of two nations – Old French and New English – the former underlying the latter, and having the first choice of place, but both mingling and alternating in the centres of most disturbance, like successive geological strata. Both cleave to the St. Lawrence, but the French, who were there first, cleave most closely. The cities which were chosen by the French were on critical points on the great river, and are therefore most altered. In the chief cities as well as in the country districts the French are still first.

Under the French regime there were only three cities in Canada: Quebec, Three Rivers, and Montreal, which were founded in 1608, 1634, and 1641 respectively. These three places are all north of the St. Lawrence, and were in 1535 the chief places of the Indians, who lived on the St. Lawrence and spoke Iroquois, and may have been Hurons or Mohawks for aught we know, and were wiped clean out before 1608, when their vacant seats were filled by Frenchmen, who for awhile shunned the south shore as though it were plague stricken....

... The three sites had different advantages.

Quebec is a city on a hill – strong, fair, and opportune.... [It] became the port for the European vessels upon whose annual arrival the trade, safety, and existence of Canada depended....

Three Rivers never had direct dealings with Europe, and Europeans scarcely knew of it except as a half-way house between Quebec and Montreal; but it was the first base of the western fur-trade and the first goal of the western Indians.... Three Rivers had a long reach inland; which Quebec never had.... It also had a relentless foe across the water who rarely wrought havoc in the neighbourhood of Quebec, but incessantly attacked Three Rivers. This foe was the Iroquois.

The Iroquois, who spread death along the south shore of – the St. Lawrence, and dread from James Bay to the Atlantic, were the Five Nations; and the Mohawks who more especially menaced the Lower St. Lawrence, ... The Mohawks lived west of [Lake Champlain], on the Mohawk, a western tributary of the Upper Hudson, and the rest of the Five Nations lived still further west. The four Western Nations menaced the St. Lawrence from above Montreal to the west end of Lake Erie; and the Mohawks shot down the Richelieu to Sorel like arrows from a bow.... As a take-off for Europe Quebec was alone, but as a take-off for the west Three Rivers had a younger rival in Montreal. In 1656 the race between Three Rivers and Montreal began in earnest: when La Salle's explorations of Lake Ontario and the south-west began (1669), Montreal was his only base, and after that date Three Rivers was more or less eclipsed.... The Iroquois, so long as they commanded the river, threatened Montreal from every side. Montreal was Castle Dangerous. Down to 1665 the Iroquois made the existence of Montreal hang in the balance; after that date counter attacks were organized, and Montreal was comparatively secure. The power of the Iroquois was broken, and the Iroquois gradually, ceased to be a political force of first-rate importance. Then Montreal asserted its geographical superiority over Three Rivers, and fur-traders for the west and friendly Indians from the west gradually began to prefer Montreal to Three Rivers, as base, goal and meeting place.

The best defence of the French colonists was expansion, and expansion was from the same three centres, and was both on the north and on the south side of the river; for in the history of civilization the country which tries to keep one river-bank invariably gains or loses both....

... [Rogers gives examples of French settlement.]The island of Orleans was ... more populous than its capital in 1667; and from that date it and Beaupré have changed but little down to to-day. Nor has Beauport changed much along the shore line.

The Seignory or Lordship or Manor of Beauport was three miles long and four miles deep, and of Beaupré forty-eight miles long and eighteen miles deep: the "long" side being along the St. Lawrence, which served as road, till roads were built, and the "deep" side being uninhabited and uncultivated, except for a short distance from its long side. The building of roads and the clearing of the forest, of which the whole valley of the St. Lawrence consisted, was usually the duty of the lords of the manor or seigneurs, but invariably the act of the habitants or copyholders whom their lords imported and planted. In order to build roads across their front the habitants required narrow and contiguous fronts. The first holdings of the habitants in Beauport were from ten to seventeen-fold, and of those in Beaupré forty-fold deeper than wide. Roads crept on from front to front, and clearances crept on from front to rear; and the rearmost depths were often forfeited, because they had not been reclaimed, or even used, by their nominal possessors. Sometimes whole seignories deserved or incurred the same fate....

On the west of Montreal a tiny triangle between the St. Lawrence and Ottawa was marked off into seignories, and sparsely colonized at the eleventh hour of the French dominion; and it belongs for that reason to the Province of Quebec, although geographically it seems a part of Ontario; while opposite it, on the north, there was the Lake of Two Mountains, with a settlement of Algonquins and Iroquois, and on the south there were settlements of Iroquois at Caughnawaga and St. Regis, but for which the south bank of the St. Lawrence above Montreal was all but empty. At one time an Indian fringe hung along exposed parts of the frontier with a seriousness and system which suggests that the authors of the policy deemed Canada a province more like East India than what we usually call a colony. Indian reservations may still be seen a New Lorette, Bécancour, St. Francis, Caughnawaga, St. Regis, and the Lake of Two Mountains; and some people point to them as the ruined remnants of a wall of red men which was once meant to run round and protect what once was Canada; others compare them to pounds for deer, decoys for wild birds, kennels for the dogs of war, industrial schools, or labour colonies. But perhaps they were the outcome of mixed motives, and never had one *raison d'être*....

... [Rogers describes township settlement.] Townships appealed to American Loyalists, but most of them had settled or starved before the first Eastern township was designed. Many Loyalists had entered Canada by the Richelieu, some of whom lingered near the frontier, where a seigneur sold them land discharged from its mediaeval incidents; while others lingered at St. John's, Chambly, and Sorel, where the Government bought the seignory and laid out the present town of Sorel opposite Berthier (1785). Berthier was, and still is, a one-streeted town, and Sorel was from the first a square-shaped town like the towns in the townships. Nevertheless Sorel and the Richelieu were in the seignories, and for this reason many of their British occupants drifted away to the townships. Most of the pioneers of the frontier came, axe and compass in hand, from New Hampshire, Vermont, and New York State, direct to their new homes; amongst whom many were sons or relatives of Loyalists, and most were loyal as well as brave men; but a very few, in Hereford and elsewhere, were refugees from justice. After the frontier was well settled, and for the most part settled well, by British-Americans, the intermediate region began to be filled, but not with Loyalists; for the Eastern townships were too late to catch the Loyalist flood when the tide was coming in. Land was often given to Canadian militiamen as rewards; ... Nor did the mainstream of European immigrants fertilize the townships.... [British] immigrants, as a rule, used Quebec Province as a conduit pipe to Ontario, ... But there were exceptions.... in 1830 large numbers of Irishmen were sent into the townships to make roads and to stay; and it was by these exceptions from the general rule, by this residue of the westward-moving multitude, that the townships were peopled. There was never any British rush to the townships, although a Land Company was proposed (1823–4) in order to organize such a rush.... Though belated, the Land Company added new elements. The

Highland settlers of Compton County were first introduced by the Company in 1841....

... In 1821–5 questions were sent round to most of the parishes in Quebec Province asking if the young men went to the town-ships. The answers were unanimous not a single French-Canadian went near them. When at the end of the Twenties the uncultivated Clergy patches, and during the Thirties the uncultivated Crown patches, began to melt away, the French-Canadians began to appear and when during the Forties the uncultivated Crown-and-Clergy patches disappeared like snow in spring, floods of French-Canadians poured into the townships. Before 1830 or thereabouts it seemed as though the old wine of old France were destined to be kept in an old bottle, and the new British wine in a new bottle but now the two wines mixed in the new bottle, and every substantial difference between bottle and bottle was removed by the legislation which converted seignories into the similitude of modern estates in fee simple (1854). The central block of the Eastern Townships is now British-French, the British being the first comers and having the first choice of place; but it must begin west, not of the River Du Loup, but of Beauce County, and south of Bagot County; for these two counties are almost wholly French-Canadian. The eastern wing, too, is as French-Canadian as the oldest adjoining seignories, with which they should now be classed. The western wing, although it contains some converted seignories, resembles the central block more or less. It is significant that the only counties which show a majority of British origin are the frontier counties of Stanstead, Brome, Missisquoi, and Huntingdon, and that an English origin prevails in all these counties except Huntingdon, which is Irish. Next to the frontier, the townships and towns of the St. Francis are most British; and in. this case, too, British means English. No townships or towns on the Nicolet show a British majority, ... Where the British element is in the ascendant in Quebec Province it is never exclusive, as the French element often is. Where, amongst the British elements, the English element is in the ascendant, the immigration was probably early and through the United States. Irish ascendancy indicates immigration from Ireland, not before 1815, and usually in or after 1830. Scotch Highlanders, as a rule, came still later, under the auspices of the Land Company. All, or practically all, the Canadians of French origin came from France before 1759, if not before 1672.

The Eastern Townships put new life into that part of Quebec Province which lies south of the St. Lawrence. Formerly the south side was an insignificant addition to the north side, where the power and might of French Canada was concentrated. Between 1825 and the close of the century the southern half excelled the northern half in numbers but the race was always close, and before 1901 the phenomenal increase of Montreal tilted the balance, so that the northern half again excels the southern half. In French times there were no towns in the southern half, which is now honeycombed with small-sized towns, not only in the Eastern Townships but elsewhere. Of the towns in the townships, Sherbrooke (pop. 11,765), Granby (pop. 3,773), Magog (pop. 3,516), Kingsville (pop. 3,256), and Farnham (pop. 6,280) are the largest. Kingsville is the principal centre of the recent unique asbestos mines at Thetford, on the watershed between the Bécancour and St. Francis, and is the only mineral centre of any importance in the Province. The rest are industrial country towns, Sherbrooke being financial centre. The largest towns elsewhere fall into three classes. The first class consists of towns adjoining and resembling the township towns like Valleyfield (pop. 11,055), St. Hyacinthe (pop. 9,210), and St, John's (pop. 4,030, or, including Iberville, its vis-à-vis town, 5,542). The second class is Riviere du Loup (pop. 4,5691) in the far east; and the third class of towns are *vis-à-vis* the northern capitals and resemble them. Thus the two (pop. 11,999) or five (pop. 17,098) more or less confluent towns known as Levis are opposite Quebec; and Longueuil, St. Lambert, and Laprairie (pop. 5,648), which will doubtless coalesce some day, are opposite Montreal. It used to be said that Bécancour (pop. 1,992) was the *vis-à-vis* of Three Rivers, and Sorel (pop. 7,057) of Berthier (pop. 1,364) [1901 populations]; but of these towns Bécancour and Berthier have become stars of inferior magnitude, and Sorel and Three Rivers alone survive. Yet, all these districts, compared with districts of equal size and prosperity elsewhere, are essentially rural....

... [Population tables for 1881 and 1901 show] how the maelstrom of Montreal is sucking in people from the neighbouring counties; how steadily and surely French-Canadians are gaining ground upon British Canadians, and how insignificant immigration from the United States and France has been.

We must now cross the St. Lawrence, remembering, however, that rivers are the bonds, not the barriers of history, even although this river has not yet been bridged and is still a physical barrier below Montreal; and here at first blush the conditions seem similar. Quebec Province is still the arena of two national forces which compete but do not conflict with one another; furthest east and (if we except the addendum) furthest west are most alike in the results, and the French-Canadians increase more rapidly than the British. As a maelstrom Montreal is more potent than any other town or centre. A British-French element exists, but it exists in connexion with the capitals. The capitals, moreover, are towns quite unlike any towns on the right bank of the St. Lawrence.

Quebec (pop. 68,840), the capital of the Province, is not merely great in its memories, but for more than a quarter of a century it has been more populous than all Canada was in 1763. A railway bridge is now being constructed from Cap Rouge ... to the mouth of the Chaudière, which will stimulate its American commerce; and the National Trans-continental Railway, for which the bridge is being built, will bring it into direct contact with prairieland. Hitherto it has never had any intercourse with the far west except through Three Rivers or Montreal; now, for the first time in history, it will be able to combine the functions of an empor-ium of European and west-Canadian trade. The halo of its romantic past will hover round the prosaic crown of a prosperous future. Three Rivers (pop. 10,739) is squeezed between its big neighbours, but derives an importance of its own from the St. Maurice River, which penetrates a district with much lumber and some bog-iron. Montreal (pop. 346,927) [1901 population] is the commercial capital of Canada, but not even the capital of its Province.... Finance and railways centre in Montreal. It faces two ways: towards New York and Boston, and towards Que-bec and England. The deepening of the channel between Quebec and Montreal, and the invention of steamers, makes Montreal a port which communicates with Europe direct as well as with the far west; and it has a double function, just as Quebec will have a double function when the new railway is built. As a port for European goods, Quebec is wicket-keep, Montreal long-stop – if the metaphor may be allowed. Its British inhabitants are mostly English and are one-third of the whole, which is rather more than the present ratio in the township counties. The Scotch-men of Montreal, though fewest, are foremost.

(Rogers, *Historical Geography – Canada*, 1911, 119–47)

7 THE MIDDLE EAST: ONTARIO, ONE NATION ON THREE ST. LAWRENCE VALLEYS AND BEYOND

☞ In southern Ontario Rogers' spatial approach really comes into its own, as he carefully interrelates points of early colonization, forces at work, expansion of settlement, transportation, and growth of towns, all in a flowing energetic interpretation. Here he has the opportunity to describe the progress of settlement in a fairly large area, with diffusion outward from various bridgeheads. His discussion is directly linked to Lieutenant Governor Simcoe's early settlement plans, particularly with respect to the strategic planning of roads and the selection of a site for the administrative capital. Many factors are thus at work. Rogers analyzes the problem of choosing a capital, London vs. Toronto, and discusses the significance of selecting Toronto and some factors behind the growth of that city. Basic to Roger's conception of Ontario settlement is the latent danger that the widely separated points of settlement might lead to the area fragmenting into separate colonies, hence his emphasis on infilling and coalescing through the continuing diffusion of settlers and on Simcoe's critical role in fostering this. Rogers notes the "spiritual," i.e., symbolic, importance of the founding of Toronto (York at the time): it is the government's guarantee of the imagined future unified colony. Three forces behind the coalescing of the scattered settlements were the migrations in the early nineteenth century based on individual initiative, systematic emigration assisted by the British government, and the stimulus of canal building.

Rogers describes the spread of settlement in the Ontario triangle as fusing Middle and Lower Ontario, thus achieving "unity within itself," or as he also puts it elsewhere, "to complete the continuous civilization of the Peninsula." In the course of the first half of the nineteenth century the one remaining settlement gap in the arable lands of Old Ontario was in western Ontario, and this was filled by the Canada Company, as we have already seen in Bouchette. After this new spatial forces came into play. Rogers is excellent on the development of railways and the beginning of the great axis that we know today as the "401 corridor" from Windsor to Montreal, and on how railways stimulated cities. The railways, Rogers explains, cemented the union of settlements within Old Ontario; he refers to some of the railways as "cross-lines" since "British colonization was never content to run in one direction at a time."

New factors that came into play during Ontario's penetration of the Shield in the railway era trigger stream-of-consciousness digressions in Rogers' analysis and these remarks provide some of his most penetrating comments on settlement forces and geography. He generalizes on the forces that created Old Quebec and Old Ontario, and defines historical geography. (The civil war referred to in discussing Old Ontario is the American Revolution.) In the Ontario Shield Rogers paints a picture of how the steam railway, copper and nickel discoveries, and the introduction of a steel blast furnace created a new geography. He emphasizes the location of Keewatin and Kenora on "Canada's line of life, which runs east and west." Rogers says they are mill seats, but does not clarify that the flour mill at Keewatin ground wheat from the prairies for shipment to markets farther east and does not mention the pulp mill at Kenora. ⌒

At Montreal the St. Lawrence valley splits into the Ottawa, and the St. Lawrence valleys; at the Bay of Quinte, into the Trent valley and the valley of the inland seas; but all three valleys re-unite in Georgian Bay, which is part of the inland sea named Lake Huron. The first task of Ontarians was to fill and unite these valleys and river-banks and shore-lines. Afterwards Ontario overflowed and its inhabitants reached the Upper St. Lawrence and its sea, and the Upper Ottawa, and then passed beyond the watershed of the St. Lawrence to the Lake of the Woods, and beyond the watershed of the Ottawa to Lake Abitibi; – the Lake of the Woods, Lake Abitibi, and the hill-tops north of Lake Superior belonging to Hudson Bay.

Ontario without its overflow – that is to say, the great triangle between the meeting-place of the St. Lawrence and Ottawa, which serves as apex, the mouth of Georgian Bay, and the angle formed by Lake Erie and Detroit River – is sometimes called Old Ontario; and the overflow of Ontario is sometimes called New Ontario. Old Ontario was built up first, and the first stone which the builders laid was nearest the apex; and it was literally as well as metaphorically the corner-stone of Ontario. It was only not in the innermost niche of the apex, because that niche was already filled by representatives, and formed part, of Quebec Province.

The successive provinces of Canada lie in a line, and the preface of one province is the appendix to the last. It was so in Tantramar Marsh and Bay Châleurs; and it is so in the tiny triangle of seignories (Quebec Province) which fit wedge-like into the notch formed by the junction of the Ottawa and the St. Lawrence, and which seem to the outward eye a part of Ontario, but are in essence Canadian French. Conversely, Chateauguay, Huntingdon, and Argenteuil, on the borderland between Quebec Province and Ontario, though physically a part of Quebec Province, are a spiritual anticipation of Ontario; and Scotchmen, though rare elsewhere in Quebec Province, are numerous here. As soon as we cross the line from Quebec Province to Ontario, the whole atmosphere is Highland Scotch, and always has been Highland Scotch ever since 1781, when the history of Ontario began....

[In the side notes Rogers summarizes the Loyalist settlement of southern Ontario. Loyalists colonized four widely separated places, and it is these "living units" that had to be united to form a viable Ontario] (1)The east of Old Ontario ... was peopled along the St. Lawrence by Highland soldiers (like the Maritime Provinces); 1781–4, other Loyalists came to Cornwall, Prescott, and Brockville; and other Loyalists settled at Kingston and west to the Bay of Quinté, 1783–4, and movement inland towards the Rideau began. 1793, 1799. (2) Loyalists went to Niagara, 1776, 1782, and spread thence to Burlington Bay, 1781. (3) Long Point was a sub-colony from Niagara, 1795. (4) Amherstburg was a detached military colony....

Each detached centre almost formed a colony by itself and was fringed by friendly Indians, Iroquois on Grand River from source to mouth, Delawares, at Moraviantown on the Thames, Hurons on Lake St. Clair, Mississaguas on Credit and Trent Rivers, and Iroquois again in a small reserve on Quinté Bay; on each and all of whom tight control was kept; indeed, the Iroquois, Hurons, and Delawares were as much exiles and victims of civil war as the Loyalists themselves. Nevertheless, the settlements at Niagara, Long Point, and Sandwich were separate and remote from one another, and still more separate and remote from the settlements near Kingston and on the St. Lawrence. The Loyalist movement did not by itself create Ontario, but only created four living units which afterwards grew into Ontario. How were these units unified? Partly by far-seeing rulers, partly by isolated adventurers, and partly by co-operative schemes, which had their head and source in England.

Simcoe's specific for unifying the units was fourfold: soldiers, towns, a through road, and a central capital. Soldiers would create towns: for "towns", he said, "will spring up where troops are stationed"; soldiers, too, would build the road on which the towns would grow, and he used the Queen's Rangers, of which he was colonel, as road-makers. The road was to go from Amherstburg by Chatham (pop. 9,068), London (pop. 37,981), Woodstock (pop. 8,833), Dundas (pop. 3, 173) [1901 populations], and Toronto, all of which were as yet mere names but would some day be towns, to Kingston and Montreal; with branch-roads leading from Dundas (or Ancaster), east to Niagara, and south to the intended arsenal near Long Point. Simcoe's plan was realized, but not by the instruments of his choice; thus the road from Kingston to Dundas was finished by an American contractor (1798–1801), and the road from Dundas to the Thames by the earliest Loyalist settlers. The

roads were built and coaches soon ran between Montreal and Kingston
(1808), Kingston and Toronto (1817), Toronto and Niagara (1816), and
Ancaster and Detroit River (1828). The new through road shadowed
and shortened the waterway from Montreal to Detroit, leaving the old
capital at Niagara on one side. A new capital was required. Simcoe fixed
on an inland capital at London, and if this plan had been executed,
the peninsula between Niagara, Lake Erie, and Lake Huron might have
solidified earlier than it did; and it probably would have solidified into
a separate Province or foreign state. But Lord Dorchester, who had at
first chosen Kingston, now chose Toronto as the capital; Toronto (pop.
208,040) [1901] being midway between his first choice and Simcoe's
first choice, and midway between the beginning and end of the new
through road.

When Bouchette surveyed the new capital one wigwam was the only
sign of human habitation, and that was one more sign than London had
at the same date (1793). After Toronto had been the capital for four
years it boasted of twelve houses (1798). Its value was not material so
much as spiritual, and it served as a guarantee – so far as Government
could give a guarantee that, come what may, the Peninsula of Ontario
and the Ontario of Kingston should not be allowed to fall asunder.

Simcoe, who had no fancy for mere river-and-lake-side capitals,
immediately found a new use for the new capital. Toronto was thirty-
five miles by water north of Niagara portage, and thirty five miles by
land south of Lake Simcoe, which flows by Lake Couchiching and
Matchedash River into Matschedash – that is to say, into Georgian Bay.
Why should not Toronto become half-way house, not only between east
and west, but between north and south? Why should it not become the
one and only Canadian city of the crossways? Accordingly he set his
soldiers to build Yonge Street to Lake Simcoe, laid out lots on each side
of it, and opened it in 1796. Moreover, north of Lake Simcoe the River
Matschedash has many rapids, to avoid which, sequels to Yonge Street
were built from Lake Couchiching, and in later times from Barrie (pop.
5,949) to Penetang (pop. 2,422) [1901 populations]. The latter sequel
was the best, and was built partly by Dr. Dunlop during the war (1812–
14), and partly by the North-west Company, which recognized at an early
date the utility of this new-old route as a highway of trade. Penetang, the
goal to which both sequels led, was selected as naval arsenal and depot
by Simcoe (1793), and was used as such during the War (1812–14) and
for many years after 1829. Simcoe's revival of these disused routes was a
stroke of genius to which Toronto owed its subsequent commercial pros-

perity. And it had other results. Yonge Street was soon lined by farmers some were re-emigrants from Nova Scotia and the West Indies, and in later times from Lord Selkirk's Red River Colony, but most of the early settlers belonged to very different categories. In 1794 a large consignment of Germans was drafted by an adventurer named William Berczy into Genesee valley (New York State), where inadequate preparations were made for their reception. Sixty families wandered on to Niagara in Canada, and Simcoe re-planted them inland east of Yonge Street in a township of one hundred square miles named Markham, where they still remain. A little further north, close by the watershed, many French Royalists settled in 1799, but few remained. Beyond them again were Pennsylvanian Quakers, then Dutch Mennonites, then an American sect called the Children of Peace. Luck threw these odds and ends in Simcoe's way at the very nick of time.... A fifth detached colony [i.e. the settlers mentioned above], between the Kingston settlements and the settlements on the peninsula, was already in being. But before this date other forces had come into play and were beginning to blend the five colonies into that single finished colony, which Loyalist and Highland soldiers, strong rulers, stray settlers, and luck were vainly conspiring to create.

The first of these forces was that pure spirit of indomitable enterprise which began to pervade the New World, and to drive men out into the lonely wilderness, towards the close of the eighteenth century. [Rogers gives the examples of Philemon Wright and others developing the timber resources of the Ottawa River area, and Colonel Thomas Talbot bringing settlers to the Lake Erie north shore, both in the early nineteenth century.] ...

The systematic emigration of weavers, Lowlanders, Celtic and Ulster Irishmen, Englishmen, and ex-soldiers was the second great force which filled Ontario. This force only began to work when the Napoleonic wars were over. In 1815 the British Government issued a paper proclamation offering free passage, rations, tools, and land to intending settlers in Canada; and the proclamation, though not backed by cash, was widely circulated in the Lowlands, where emigration societies were formed. In 1826, 4,653 Renfrewshiremen, and about 8,500 Lanarkshiremen, asked aid to emigrate; and all, or almost all, were handloom-weavers, who occupied their leisure on farm-work. They were starving minute by minute at home. "I remember," said the son of an emigrant weaver, "often waking in the middle of the night and seeing my father working still at the loom as if he would never give over.... I remember I was always hungry then – always." British agony was

Canada's opportunity, and the dying men went to live again in a land where "almost every farmer ... has a loom in his house, and their wives and daughters not only spin the yarn but weave the cloth".... Some of the emigration societies which now spread from end to end of the old country were friendly self-helping societies, others owed their existence to the benevolent landlord; ...

Individualism was chiefly American, social energy was chiefly British, and the third force which directed the stream of immigrants hither and thither was wielded by the American, Canadian, and British Governments alike. It may be summed up in the one word – Canals. A great canal was being made between the Hudson River and Lake Erie by the Americans (1818–25), who almost persuaded themselves and their rivals, that traffic from the West would leave the St. Lawrence for the Hudson. The Canadians responded by canals, not from watershed to watershed, but from smooth water to smooth water on their great river. The first small Canadian canals of this kind had been made in the early days of the English regime on the St. Lawrence (1779–83), and at Sault St. Marie (1797) but now a line of canals began to be constructed past every rapid between Montreal and Lake Ontario. Of these canals the Lachine Canal, which is immediately above Montreal and holds the key both of the Ottawa and the St. Lawrence, was made by the Government of Lower Canada (1821–5); canals on the St. Lawrence above Lachine were made by local effort, and the Welland Canal between Lakes Ontario and Erie was made by private companies (1824–9). The Welland Canal made Port Dalhousie (pop. 1,125), St. Catharine (pop. 9,946), and Port Colborne (pop. 1,253) [1901 populations] into towns; and as at Niagara, a few miles east, the inland town derived most benefit. It was thus that Canada was saved from the commercial ruin which Canadian pessimists and American optimists foretold. Canal fever infected the British Government, which regarded the matter from a military and naval point of view, and built canals at the rapids of Carillon and the Long Sault on the Ottawa between Lachine and Hull, and up the Rideau, across the watershed, and down the Cataraqui between Ottawa and Kingston (1827–31), at the Imperial cost. Its object was to provide a way between Montreal, which is the last ocean port, and Kingston, which is the first fresh-sea port of Canada, by which stores and ships of light burden might penetrate inland out of range of American guns in case of war. Safety was its object, not trade.... The completion of the St. Lawrence Canals was the response by Canada to the United States, and the Ottawa and Rideau Canals were the British postscript to the Canadian response....

Ontario was united [side note]. In the early Forties lines drawn between Goderich, Guelph, Toronto, Barrie, Penetang, Orillia, the Lakes of the Trent and Mississippi, and the mouths of the Madawaska and Ottawa, roughly marked the northern limits of Ontarian civilization. Above it was the wilderness; below it a series of mutually connected settlements. Then new forces came into play.

The Forties were the decade of great railway plans, and the Fifties were the decade of great railway completions. Trains ran from Montreal to Toronto in 1856, and in 1858 two railroads led from Toronto to Sarnia, one by Stratford (pop. 9,959) and the other by Hamilton. Trains already ran from Hamilton to Niagara Falls and to Sandwich (1854), so that Ontario was knitted together from end to end in a way which more than realized Simcoe's wish. But British colonization was never content to run in one direction at a time; and Simcoe's crossroads were now represented by two railroads, ending respectively at Goderich (pop. 4,158), of which no one had heard before 1827, and at Collingwood (pop. 5,755), which Sir R. Bonnycastle described as "forest in the midst of unending impenetrable forest" (1842). The Toronto-Barrie-Collingwood cross-line was begun in 1849 and finished in 1854; and the Goderich-Seaforth-Stratford-Fort Erie cross-line was opened in 1858. The lines to Midland (pop. 3,174), Penetang (pop. 2,422), Meaford (pop. 1,916), Owen Sound (pop. 8,776), Colpoys Bay (pop. 2,443), Southampton (pop. 1,636), and Kincardine (pop. 2,077) [1901 population figures],were only later amplifications of these original and historic cross-lines.

This railway development doubled or trebled the great through waterway of the St. Lawrence, and Simcoe's great through roadway from Montreal to Windsor and Sarnia, and introduced variants of old short cuts between Lakes Erie, Ontario, and Huron, and Georgian Bay, these lakes being themselves parts of the St. Lawrence. The St. Lawrence was still the presiding genius of Ontarian development. These railways also doubled or trebled the importance not only of Windsor or Sarnia, but of Hamilton, Toronto, Stratford, Collingwood, Goderich, and London, all of which dominated the short cuts between the St. Lawrence under one of its names with the St. Lawrence under another of its names.

In the Sixties petroleum was obtained in the neighbourhood of Petrolea (pop. 4,135) [1901], ten to twenty miles from Sarnia, and salt between

Seaforth and Goderich and Southampton on Lake Huron. Natural gases
were afterwards discovered in these neighbourhoods; ...

   The Archaean region of what I have called Old Ontario was invaded
by settlers after 1868, when free land-grants were offered to immigrants
in Muskoka and Parry Sound Districts, which figure in the 1871census
for the first time. The southern gate-way of this region is "the granite
notch", a few miles north of the limestones of Orillia (pop. 4,907), and
101 miles north of Toronto; and its northern gateway is North Bay on
Lake Nipissing, 110 miles further north. In 1859 there was "no European town or village from Orillia to the north pole". In the Seventies
the first rail way passed north of the granite notch to Gravenhurst (pop.
2,146); but many years were destined to elapse before it reached North
Bay and linked Ontario and its capital to the Canadian Pacific Railway.
At present this district is largely dedicated to sportsmen and tourists;
though many a farmer finds good soil here and there on the shores of
some lake, and Parry Sound is a considerable lumber-port. Gravenhurst
(pop. 2,146), Bracebridge (pop. 2,419), and Huntsville (pop. 2,152)
[1901 populations], on the avenue between the two gateways, are its
tourist capitals. Memories of another kind linger round Lake Nipissing, which is on the old Indian water-route up the Ottawa, and down
French River, to Georgian Bay. French River and the Archaean parts of
Georgian Bay are the north-western borders of the Archaean region of
Old Ontario; and the Ottawa lies near its north-eastern border, which
is vague. While settlers came in by twos and threes through its southern
gateway, lumberers were stealing towards it up a tributary of the Ottawa
named the Bonnechere, north-west of the settlement of the MacNab
and lonely wayside farmers dotted the Musk Rat Portage of the Ottawa,
which was still further north-west, as early as 1830. Before the advent
of railways there were 850 settlers in Ontario near Lake Timiskaming
and Lake Nipissing (1811), and rapid progress came with the railways,
which led from Ottawa to Lake Nipissing and beyond in the Eighties
(Canadian Pacific Railway), and which also led from Ottawa to Parry
Sound (pop. 2,884) in the Nineties (Grand Trunk Railway), thanks to
which Renfrew (pop. 3,153) on the Bonnechere, Pembroke (pop. 5,156)
on Musk Rat Portage, and North Bay (pop. 2,530) [1901 populations],
on Lake Nipissing, became important towns. A railway from Toronto
to Sudbury was built in the first decade of this century as a companion to the railway which had been finished long ago from Toronto to
North Bay. The pace was accelerated, and Muskoka, Parry Sound, and

the railway lines through and round these lakelands, though populous compared to what they were, are desolate indeed, compared to the civilized districts of Old Ontario, around which we have been lingering so disproportionately long, as some may think.

As in Quebec, so in Ontario, the historical geographer must have two standard measures – one a foot-rule and the other a sextant. Parts of the country are crowded, and these parts were first entered in Old Quebec by members of some family, and in Old Ontario by some social group, inch by inch, district by district; so that their history is written on genealogical trees or tombstones or parochial registers. The chief difference between Old Quebec and Old Ontario was that civil war ... did for Ontario what religious fervour did for Quebec Province; and that while the founders of Quebec Province crept along the banks of a single river, spreading slowly up and down in one dimension from three points, the founders of Ontario overspread intervals as broad as long between two or three rivers and three or more fresh seas, like a multitude of distinct cloudlets which coalesced at last into a single complicated pattern, so that the entire earth was overcast. When that process was complete, when the outline was apparently filled in and intelligible, historical geography stops; for subsequent elaborations and permutations belong to history or some other kindred science. Thus far the student goes as with leaded cowl through some small dense country like a larger Scotland or a lesser England. The comparison is not unjust; for Old Ontario, excluding the Parry Sound and Muskoka District, is exactly the same size as Newfoundland and has only 40,000 square miles, some of which just trench [touch?] upon the Archaean region, and what is now called the Parry Sound and Muskoka District only adds another 5,000 square miles or so.

When we pass northward through the granite notch, we are in a country of big distances and little history, and our progress should be at astronomical, or at any rate railway speed. Indeed, we are in a country where, as a rule, railways preceded roads, and were the only events, or almost the only events, of history; and the railways were built, partly, it is true, for the purpose of colonizing the lean country through which they passed, but partly too for the sake of developing fat far-off countries, and partly for purely political purposes. The Parry Sound Railway opened up a new port for the far west, and the other railways to North Bay and Sudbury were feeders of the great through line of the Canadian Pacific Railway Company.

North Bay is the railway junction for several mineral districts; Cobalt, of which we have spoken, Sudbury, Bruce Mines, and Michipicoten, and of these Cobalt and Sudbury are already of world-wide significance.

'The town of Sudbury' (pop. 2,027) "is a creation of the Canadian Pacific Railway" (1882), being on the main line 80 miles west of North Bay, and the starting-point of a branch line 182 miles long to Sault St. Marie (pop. 7,169) [1901 populations]....

In 1886 a Canadian Copper Company started work in the neighbourhood; in 1889 MacNaughton's Bethel became Murray Mine, and Sudbury began to experience the chances and changes to which copper industry is invariably exposed. Meanwhile bicycles, and the invention of nickel steel (1888), and the new treatment of nickel ores (1891) supplied a more secure foundation for its prosperity (1891 et seq.), and thanks to the railways from North Bay to Toronto, and from Sudbury to Sault St. Marie, help came from far, and Power and Refining Companies at Sault St. Marie and Hamilton (1899) assisted the nickel-miners of Sudbury, who now supply the world with most of the nickel which it more and more greedily consumes.

Sault St. Marie (pop. 7,169) [1901] was, until recent railways were built, as much isolated from the rest of Ontario as the Bosphorus was in classical times from Hellas. It was the strait gate to the innermost inland sea; and there have been missions, trade "forts", or military forts there on and off since 1640, or long before similar posts occupied those other wicket-gates between its sister seas at Detroit and Niagara. In English times it gradually grew into a lumber and mill town; some copper-mining was done at Bruce Mines (1846–76), thirty-five miles to the east; and these mines were re-opened (1901) after the whole of the Sault-and-Sudbury branch line was opened. Sault St. Marie is now connected by a bridge with its *vis-à-vis* rival in Michigan (United States); and besides being a fresh seaport is one of the three land-channels by which Canadian produce passes to Chicago (United States); Sarnia (with its tunnel) and Windsor (with its steam-ferry) being the other two. Sault St. Marie has copper to west of it as well as copper to east of it; and Michipicoten Island, which is one hundred miles west of it, has been of romantic interest, as the starting-point of a canoe route up the Michipicoten and down the Missinaibi and Moose Rivers, to James Bay; ... In 1901 the Helen Mine, near Michipicoten river-mouth, began to yield iron under the direction of a Power Company at Sault St. Marie; and immediately the production of iron in Ontario leapt up from 25,000 to 272,538 tons a year. Blast-furnaces have been, or are being, erected at Sault St. Marie and

Collingwood, and a railway has been pushed on from Sault St. Marie to Michipicoten Harbour, which is no longer a mere distant isolated port upon an uninhabited coast. Two hundred miles beyond Michipicoten the River Nipigon flows into Lake Superior, and near its mouth is Fort Nipigon, which was the westernmost outpost of the French fur-traders, until Duluth went seventy miles further along the shore to Fort Kaministiquia, which was built in 1678 and rebuilt in 1717, and has since 1801 been represented by Fort William. Here, however, we enter upon a new arena; and the west shore of Lake Superior owes its inspiration to a changed country lying far away towards the west....

Fort William (pop. 3,997) and Port Arthur (pop. 3,214) are twin towns, three miles apart, but rapidly growing together into a joint town (pop, 7,211) [1901 populations]; and their gigantic elevators for storing the grains of the far west are, since 1885, the outward and visible reasons of their being....

... Like Sault St. Marie and Michipicoten, Fort William and Port Arthur were and are to some extent mining centres. But they were and are the one and only fresh-sea port for the produce of the far west....

... Then the Canadian Pacific Railway came (1885), and its way from Fort William lay ... to the north shore of Lake of the Woods. Here Kenora (pop. 5,202) and its twin Keewatin (pop. 1,156) [1901 populations], on the other side of the outlet of the Lake of the Woods, became railway towns, were united by a bridge, and became the principal mill seats not only for that district, but for the far west. East of Kenora we have seen twin town and *vis-à-vis* towns innumerable, and a few bridge-towns; but they have always cut Canada's line of life, which runs east and west, at right angles, and have been the outcome of emulation, imitation, or opposition. Kenora-Keewatin are the first but not the last looking-glass places, both of which the Canadian passes through rather than abides in; for in Canada movement east and west, west and east, rather than rest, is the first law of life....

In the preceding paragraphs special allusions are made to towns, because towns of a certain size and number are characteristic of Ontario as distinguished from Quebec Province. Toronto (pop. 208,040) is a lesser Montreal (pop. 350,000), Ottawa (pop. 60,000) a lesser Quebec (pop. 69,000), Kingston (pop. 18,000) a larger Levis (pop. 17,0001), and Windsor (pop. 12,000) a lesser Hull (pop. 14,000); but there are no towns like Hamilton (pop. 53,000) and London (pop. 38,000) in Quebec Province; towns of 11,000 inhabitants are only represented by Sherbrooke and Valleyfield in Quebec Province, but by Windsor, Guelph,

Peterborough, and St. Thomas, in Ontario; and towns of less than 11,000 and more than 8,000 inhabitants by Three Rivers and St. Hyacinthe in Québec Province, but by Stratford, Berlin, Chatham, Woodstock, Brockville, Belleville, and Owen Sound in Ontario; and if we lower the standard to 2,500 inhabitants the proportionate number of towns in Quebec to towns in Ontario is five to twelve [all population figures for 1901]. Town life is more energetic in Ontario; although, like the elder province, Ontario is essentially agricultural, and the people are and have been yeomen from the beginning. At the very moment when English writers began to bewail vanished yeomen who never existed, Englishmen were deliberately founding colonies of yeomen for the first time in history.

The towns which grew up in Ontario were the symptoms and results of agricultural success. Rural industries, as time went on, were able to spare more and more of their devotees to manufacturing industries, and the country created the towns. The same process has gone on in Quebec Province, but with less vigour. Perhaps Ontario is more fertile, and the peach-growing peninsula of Ontario is certainly more fertile than any part of Quebec Province; or perhaps the difference is due to the different nationalities of the provinces. By nationality ultimate European origin is meant. In this sense three nationalities are universally conspicuous in Ontario, – British, French, and German (including Dutch), – but British is vastly superior to its rivals, and the ratio of the rivals differs widely in different census districts.

(Rogers, *Historical Geography – Canada*, 1911, 151–88)

8 THE MIDDLE WEST: PRAIRIE-LAND

☞ In this chapter Rogers gives his fullest depiction of the physical geography of a Canadian region. His tendency to examine a concept in many variations is shown in his analysis of the word "prairie." He appears to know of continental glaciation, but were he more knowledgeable about it his discussion of terrain would have been made easier, although what we lose in crisp explanation we gain in imaginative description. This is a new and different country within Canada. Referring to the process of colonization, Rogers distinguishes between movement by river and lake, which he considers Canadian, and the very different movement by land that is possible on the prairies. Briefly, in a deterministic way, Rogers compares how settlement developed in Quebec, Ontario, and the prairies, symbolized geometrically by a single line, by a triangle bounded by water, and by oblongs and squares. He notes that development is proceeding quickly on the prairies. There are enthusiastic descriptions of the Peace River Country, the Mackenzie Valley, "a land of hope," and of mineral resources, including coal, gas and the potential for oil. Rogers says that Alberta will not attain the population of the two provinces to the east, clearly basing this on the future of agriculture as it relates to the relative aridity of the region. (That economic situation changed dramatically after mid-century with oil and gas discoveries in Alberta.) For once First Nations peoples are given systematic attention, and Rogers describes the spatial dynamism of various groups.

Somewhere on the threshold of Manitoba woods vanish, rough places are made smooth, the earth is a level lawn, lakes and rivers are not what they were, and the horizon widens. To the east an infinite series of wooded hills, watery hollows, lakes, swamps, and rocks, cramps while it diversifies the scenery, and perplexes while it enchants the imagination; and as we move westward the maze becomes more intricate and stone-strewn or wet up to a point, beyond which there is an utter change; but the point is not definite nor is the change sudden. The lovely, well-named, many-islanded Lake of the Woods is the last west lake which is a true lake, so that the point of change is west of this lake. The east frontier of Manitoba is a mere line of longitude drawn due north from the north-west angle of the lake; and henceforth provinces, like parallelograms enclosed by four straight lines of longitude and latitude, and sub-divided into square townships six miles by six, begin to disfigure the map as though we had reached a region destitute of geographical outline. But the dividing line between woodland and plain is west of the provincial frontier, and is the first of several real lines which now begin to straggle and stray across the map from south-east to north-west. It may be discerned by the traveller from the east somewhere near Whitemouth, forty miles or so north-east of Winnipeg; or, if he travels to Winnipeg by the Dawson road from the north-west angle of the Lake of the Woods, somewhere near St. Anne des Chenes, forty miles or so south-east of Winnipeg. There he sees his first plain. For 1,700 miles east of him, right to the Atlantic, there is nothing like this, except perhaps in miniature on the Acadian salt-marshes; and for 900 miles west of him, right to the Rockies, there is hardly anything but this. Here, well to the east of Winnipeg (pop. 95,300) [1906], which is the provincial capital of Manitoba and the commercial capital of prairie land, prairie-land begins, and there in the Rockies prairie-land ends.

But prairie-land is not all prairie, and the prairies are of several sorts. What, then, are the Canadian prairies? It is easier to say what they are not, than what they are.

A Canadian, when asked before a Royal Commission, "Are there no tracts of land" such as the Americans call prairies in Canada?' replied, "None in the Canadas" (1826), for the Canadas meant nothing to him but the old forest provinces where water is the only level surface. The old provinces were the very antithesis of prairie, which is dry, level, and bare. Again, the mossy, treeless marsh-lands and stone-lands of Arctic Canada between Great Bear Lake, Great Slave Lake, Fort Churchill, and the northern seas, are called in Canada "barrens", and in Lapland and Northern Siberia "tundras", and are sometimes flat; and early travellers mistook "prairies" for "barrens"; but "barrens" are the parodies of prairies, which are smooth, grassy, and dry, like our English Downs. Prairies are barer than barrens, flatter than downs, and better than the best parts of the forest provinces. But prairies do not monopolise prairie-land, and the parts of prairie-land which are not prairie are the most characteristic parts of prairie-land, and differ widely in three tracts, which lie side by side between Eastern Manitoba and the Rockies. As these tracts are at different levels – 700 to 950 feet s.m. in the east, 1,250 feet to 1,950 feet s.m. in the middle, and 2,200 to 4,000 or 5,000 feet s.m. in the west – they are called steppes, like the steppes of Western Asia and Southern Russia, which also lie on almost the same parallel of latitude.

A steppe is a table-land; but the first, that is to say the easternmost, of the Canadian steppes, though it looks like a flat table, is really a concave basin between two rims. The eastern rim is the impalpable watershed between the Red River and the Lake of the Woods, which watershed is 1,100 to 1,200 feet s.m. The western rim is a very palpable scarp, 360 to 400 feet high, which runs 300 to 400 miles north north-west, from Pembina Mountain on the frontier (49° N. lat.) to the River Saskatchewan at a point somewhere nearer Fort La Corne than Cumberland House. The wooded heights of Pembina, Riding, Duck, and Thunder "Mountains", and Porcupine and Pasquia "Hills", serve as successive towers, and countless hillocks serve as turrets to the scarp; but, as in the Great Wall of China, its towers and turrets are not much higher than its top. From the foot of the scarp the basin slopes insensibly some 200 feet down to Red River and Lake Winnipeg, which are mere dents in its middle, and so up again to the eastern rim.

The basin is now divided into three tracts – lake, marsh, and dry land – which were once one; for the lakes and marshes are relics of the past, and the dry land of to-day is the marsh of yesterday and the lake of the day before. Long before history began, somewhere in the Post-Tertiary Age, one lake – to which geologists have given the fancy name of Lake Agassiz – is said to have filled the whole basin between rim and rim. The lake bottom planed itself into curves so gradual as to resemble flats, and the black lake silt left by the receding waters is the most fertile soil in the world....

The area of possible future prairie-land is bounded on the north by the region of Archaean Gneiss, which extends from a little north of Lake Winnipeg, and of the north bank of the Saskatchewan, towards Hudson Bay and the Arctics. So far as is known the uselessness of this Archaean tract is irremediable. Its very rivers are unfit for navigation. Thus Nelson River, which conducts the waters of Lake Winnipeg into Hudson Bay, is so shallow and rocky, that it is avoided even by canoes. The most primitive forces of the earth and of history still fashion the hinterland of Inter-Lake-Land [between Lakes Winnipeg and Manitoba], which is and remains, what God made it, and the Hudson Bay Company made of it.

South of Lakes Winnipeg and Manitoba prairies stretch from the eastern border of prairie-land to the western rim of the first steppe, and right down to the frontier, more or less. The qualification "more or less" is necessary because, as a rule, the banks of rivers are clothed with trees, and tree clumps may be seen on the level land like sails on a still sea; so that on a clear day isolated trees of sorts are said to be always discernible from the highest Manitoban house-tops or elevators. This narrow strip is thickly peopled, for it contains all the prairies, which contain all the famous wheat fields, which Manitoba ever had, or was ever thought likely to have.

There are only two principal rivers of the Manitoban prairies, the Red River and its affluent the Assiniboine. The Red River flows north from its source-close by the source of the Mississippi, far within the border of the United States; and the Assiniboine flows east in so far as its course threads the first steppe for it comes from far, and belongs more to the second than to the first steppe. Both wind, for they are characteristic prairie rivers, and the rich soil makes Red River tawnier than the Tiber, or than any river between Red River and the marshlands of the Bay of Fundy. Similarly, Lake Winnipeg, which means "muddy water" – because, as the Crees say, a bad god was once so pelted with filth by womenfolk that in trying to clean himself in the lake he only muddied it – is a characteristic prairie lake, if it may be called lake, and points north more or less; while the Saskatchewan, turbid amongst other things with prairie mud, meets it at its north corner after coming from furthest west; but the Saskatchewan belongs more to the second than to the first, and more to the third than to the second steppe. Widely sundered river-lines run eastward, and widely sundered lines of river, lake, and hill run northward or north-north-westward. If, then, geography determines development, it might be expected that the first steppe would develop, not like Quebec Province along a single line, nor like Old Ontario within triangles bounded by water, but as an oblong. And this is what happened; but it must be remembered that development in Inter-Lake-Land presented a very different problem [that of drainage] to the problem of development on the compact continuous prairies to the south.

The second steppe begins with the scarp with which the first steppe ends, and may be described as an extension of the scarp-top three hundred miles to the west. The scarp is innocent of rocks, and consists of shale, sand, clay, and marl of Cretaceous, that is to say, of the uppermost Secondary Age....

The middle steppe slopes gradually upward towards its western boundary, which is a scarp, sometimes woody and: – sometimes not, known as the Côteau du Missouri, and of about the same apparent height as the scarp between the first and second steppes. Geographically this scarp is the eastern edge of the third steppe; geologically it is a moraine, formed of boulder-drift and earthy materials belonging to the lowest Tertiary Age; and it is the easternmost tract of Canada where tertiary formations prevail, if we except fragments of itself which are scattered along the middle steppe. This scarp runs north-west 350 miles or so just west of the Estevan-Moose Creek Railroad, or of Moose Jaw Creek and Long Creek, reaching the South Saskatchewan near Swift Current, resuming further north as Bad Hills and Eagle Hills, and perhaps (north of the North Saskatchewan) as Thickwood Hills. In the middle of the middle, steppe there is a disconnected series of tree-crowned flat-topped hills, a few hundred feet high, but sometimes with declivities fourteen miles long, known successively as Turtle and Moose Mountains, and Wolfe, Brandon, File, Pheasant, Little Touchwood, Touchwood, and perhaps Lumpy and Birch Hills, which lie parallel with and seem to mock the Côteau. These ten mild "mountains" and "hills" are also composed of boulder-drift, and also point north-west. Between the mock and the real Côteau the second steppe exhibits its longest stretches of pure prairie, and vivid descriptions of some of these stretches, which figured in books of forty or fifty years ago, used to pass as typical of all prairie land. A thin belt of salt-plain connects Long Lake and Quill Lake north-west of Touchwood Hill; from Birch Hill Thomas Simpson saw, as he gazed along (not across) this stretch of prairie, "barren hills and hollows like a petrified sea – said to extend to the Missouri". John Macoun, too, crossed forty-five miles of fissured, shrubless plain, between Moose Mountain and the Côteau. Observers noticed the vices and exceptions before the virtues. What seemed limitless prairie is common enough on the second steppe, but it is rarely hummocky or saline or fissured (except by the plough); and trees or hills are almost always near at hand....

[The rivers of the second steppe] are shallow, sinuous, devious shadows of what they once were. Absence of rock makes them meander aimlessly; the high, dry air of the plateau has shrivelled them, and accident has turned them awry. If the Assiniboine is followed up past its affluents, the Souris and Qu' Appelle, to its source, the differences between the rivers of the plain and the rivers of Eastern Canada are apparent. The Souris seems to come from, and to beckon wanderers towards the regions of the Missouri and Yellowstone in the far south-west; but the Côteau in Canada is its real source, and between Melita and Alameda it takes 180 miles to accomplish what the modern train accomplishes in 60 miles. The Jordan is not more tortuous....

The rivers are the playthings of chance; although the presence of definite river-valleys and banks, like those of the Qu' Appelle, suggests that they were once comparatively straight and deep. The North and Main Saskatchewan is the only river which has held its course consistently and persistently through the ages. It is by far the straightest river in prairie-land.... It is a great river and has played a great part in history; but it is quite unlike the St. Lawrence or Ottawa. The lucid waters of the old provinces were always the only, and often the nearest way between point and point; but the discoloured waters of prairie-land were never the only, and were always the longest, way between point and point. In prairie-land landways were direct and unobstructed, and waterways circuitous and sometimes obstructed, the converse being the case down east. On the second steppe it was possible to move in any direction, and to settle anywhere between five degrees of latitude, and in some places seven degrees of longitude, so that not triangles but oblongs once more symbolized progress. But the civilized oblongs on the first and second steppes differed in size as well as in character. Manitoba resembles a long low building – every inch of it alive with men, busy, and rich, with towers and spires shooting upward here and there, – the highest and most solid on its west where it touches the second steppe; the civilized parts of Saskatchewan resemble a square – like the great square of Pegasus – not quite so full as the living-rooms, but far higher than the highest pinnacles of its eastern neighbour, and with the same inevitable wastes above it.

The third steppe consists of those drifts and earths of the Côteau, which are superimposed upon those earths and shales of the second steppe, which are superimposed upon those limestones, which lurk underneath the first steppe. It is higher, drier, barer, and hillier than its fellows. The highest altitude on its west is more than 2,000 feet higher than the highest altitude on its east, and seems, when looked at from above, the uptilted end of a rolling plain, and, when looked at from below, a platform upon which mountains stand. It is really both; for the Rocky Mountains are rocks and glaciers piled up abruptly and confusedly upon the western extremity of prairie-land....

... The railway traveller of to-day enters the ... arid zone at Moose Jaw and leaves it at Gleichen, between which he sometimes sees "hard, white, sun-cracked clay", with scarce, tufty buffalo-grass, or even sage-brush, and sometimes a sand-dune or two, and sometimes an old dry river-bed littered with quartzite stones, smooth as pebbles on a sea-beach; and the ponds by the wayside are rarely fresh, as their white crystals and crimson salicornea show. The extent of this arid zone was once wildly exaggerated. Professor Hind, who was an optimist in his day (1860), described it as beginning at Pembina Mountain on the frontier and curving upward along the Assiniboine to Touchwood Hills on the mock Côteau (50° N. lat.), running straight thence to where Red Deer is now, and redescending abruptly from Red Deer to the frontier near the sources of the Belly; within which rude arch lay what he called desert, and above which lay what he called the Rainbow of the West. Modern authorities trace the upward curve along the real Côteau, and describe the land inside the curve as pastoral land, with patches of agricultural and patches of barren land, much of the latter being easily reclaimable. Indeed, on its borders the Alberta Railway and Irrigation Company drew water from the St. Mary River, and made the Lethbridge district into a beet-garden; and the Canadian Pacific Irrigation and Colonization Company drew water from the Bow, and reclaimed large tracts east of Calgary. These efforts began in the Nineties, and similar efforts are in process of being made near the junction of the Bow with the Belly and elsewhere. What drainage is doing for the northern parts of the first steppe [i.e. Inter-Lake-Land], irrigation is doing for that southern fraction of the third steppe, which reflects on a small scale and in a mild degree the characteristics of the so-called Central American deserts of the United States. Clearly the civilized oblong of Alberta has disadvantages from which its eastern neighbours are free, and which suggest that it will never be quite so full and busy as they are. [As we know today, a great misjudgment because of oil and gas.] But there is another side to the picture, and Alberta enjoys advantages which they do not enjoy.

A strip between the dry tract and the Rockies is influenced by warm winds from the Pacific. In mid-winter, thaws disperse the snow from time to time, and cattle fatten out of doors, but the re-freezing of the exposed earth injures its crops. A little north-west of the northernmost latitude of the dry tract, alternate ridged and swampy forests encompass the head-waters of the Athabasca beyond Lake St. Anne (near Edmonton), and all traces of prairie-land are effaced; but prairie-land recurs further north in the Peace River District, or that district through which the Peace River and its southern affluents flow, and which includes Lesser Slave Lake on the east, but excludes the mountain gorges of the west and the Arctic lands north of Fort Vermilion, or thereabouts.... These open tracts to the north of the shut tracts of the Upper Athabasca are to prairie-land what real is to Indian summer, or aftermath is to harvest. The Peace and Athabasca flow north into the Mackenzie, and the North and South Saskatchewan east into Lake Winnipeg; yet here, at all events, prairie-land ignores watersheds. This strip of prairie-land has no natural boundaries on its north and shoots up indefinitely towards the Arctics, or merges in the valley of the Mackenzie.

The whole valley of the Mackenzie from Athabasca Landing to the Arctics is also a land of hope. Edmonton is now the one and only gate-way to the Mackenzie. A portage, one hundred miles long, which is now a coach-road and will soon be a rail-road, leads from Edmonton to Athabasca Landing on the Athabasca River, which having risen in the south-west henceforth flows north and north-west, merging successively in Lake Athabasca, Great Slave River and Lake, and Mackenzie River, and reaching the Arctic Ocean nearly two thousand miles from the Landing. Athabasca Landing has two or more competing stores – the principal competitors being the Hudson Bay Company and Révillons Frères – a French Roman Catholic and an English Protestant mission; and these two trading and proselytising establishments face or alternate with one another from end to end of the Great River, reproducing in the oddest and friendliest way the piebald uncivilization of the Red River Colony of nearly a century ago, or the piebald civilization of the Quebec

Province of today. The line of life is very frail, and keeps strictly to
the river banks. The trade and mission stations on the river are always
more than a house and less than a village, are on the average one hundred miles apart, and, usually command, as the old forts on the St.
Lawrence once commanded some rapid, some affluent, or some inland
sea.... The barest minimum of white-man's civilization penetrates along
this favoured channel without one break from the crowded centres of
the western steppe into that desolate uninhabitable region, with which
the first chapter of this book dealt. It would almost seem as though
we had wheeled round again to the solitudes of the starting-place. But
there is nothing cyclical about the shape or destiny of Canada; and if,
as is probable, the Mackenzie basin and Peace River District, instead of
having only a few hundred white men – as is the case now – becomes as
populous as the analogous Russian Province upon the Lower Ob and
Irtish – where there are already a million and a half free Russians – that
result will be due partly to the fertility of the strip between Athabasca
Landing and the Arctic region, but partly too to the fact that the courses
of the Athabasca, Peace, Liard, and Peel lure men across the western
mountains; for Canada has always been and still is racing westward.

The strip between the dry lands and Rockies is of peculiar interest as
the approach to the mountain passes, of which thirteen are well-known
and six are famous in Canadian history.... These passes are given [in an
accompanying table] ... in their geographical order from north to south,
and the order of their discovery so far as it is known is not very different from their geographical order [Peace River, 1793; Pine River, later;
Smoky River, later; Yellowhead, shortly before 1827; Athabasca, 1809;
Howse, 1800; Kicking Horse, 1858; Vermilion, 1858; Simpson; White
Man; Kananaskis; Crow's Nest, 1858; N. Kootenay, 1858]

The steppes have their special minerals and coal. The lowest tertiary,
and possibly the highest secondary beds of the third steppe yield coal
at Estevan on the frontier; at Frank and Fernie on Crow's Nest Pass; at
Canmore, near Kicking Horse Pass, and Pembina River west of Edmonton; and lignite or coal are visible at Red Deer River (52° 19' N. lat.),
Edmonton, Dunvegan on the Upper Peace, and elsewhere on the third
steppe, and even in the far north, a little below Fort Macmurray and a
little above Fort Norman. East of the third steppe or its outliers, there
is an interval of 1,600 or 1,700 miles without actual or possible coal,
for the earth here is too old for coal. As in south-westernmost Ontario,
so along the railway lines between Medicine Hat and Calgary, natural
gases well up from Devonian depths; there is near Pincher Creek in the

south, and Fort Macmurray in the north, oil as well as gas; and the bitumen of Athabasca River, and the salt-springs worked since 1819 on the south-west shore of Lake Winnipegosis and at Swan Lake, are also Devonian.

The second steppe is without minerals, but bricks are made at Moose Jaw, Regina, and Sidney.

Bison, miscalled buffaloes, are the characteristic animals of prairie-land. They were seen by Kelsey (1691–92), La Vérendrye (1732 et seq.), and Hendry (1754–55), madly careering over the three steppes. Hearne saw them on the south shore of Great Slave Lake (1772), and Mackenzie heard of them there, and on the Liard, north-west of that lake. They still existed on the Liard in a wild state in 1872. Millions roamed over the prairies, ...

When bison waned the Indians of the prairie dwindled; and now the former are in preserves and the latter in reserves.

East of the Rockies, south of the Saskatchewan, or of 54° N. lat., and north of the frontier, Chippeways dwelt near the Lake of the Woods, Crees on the first, Assiniboines on the second, and the Blackfoot Confederacy on the third steppe. All, with two exceptions, were Algonquins and akin to all the Indians of Eastern Canada, except to the Hurons. The two exceptions were the Assiniboines and Sarsis. The Assiniboines were offshoots of the Sioux, who dwelt in Dakota (United States) and were not Algonquin; and the Assiniboines allied themselves to the Crees, and were to the Sioux what the Hurons of Quebec Province were in old times to the Iroquois of New York State. The Sioux, too, were waging war in 1680, 1731, and 1854, and probably in all the intermediate years, against the Chippeways, who for a similar reason became the allies of the Crees. The Sarsis were offshoots of the Chipewyan stock, which frequented the River Churchhill, and every river lying north of 54° N. lat. and leading to the Arctic Ocean, but the Sarsis seceded from their kith and kin of the River Peace in order to join the Blackfoot Confederacy. Horses and guns changed Indian boundaries, but did not change Indian alliances. In 1738–39 the horse seems to have been unknown in prairie-land; in 1742–43, "Gens des Chevaux" are mentioned in the far west, somewhere south of the frontier; Anthony Hendry (1754–55) called the Blackfoot Confederacy of the third steppe "Equestrian Indians", because they were the only mounted Indians; finally in Henry the Younger's time (1799 et seq.) all prairie Indians were mounted, and the Assiniboines used to steal horses from their western neighbours and sell them to their eastern neighbours for guns. The Blackfeet were the first to get horses, and the Crees were the first to get guns. As the horse stole,

or was stolen, into prairie-land from southwest and west, Frenchmen
and Englishmen brought their more deadly gifts from east and north-
east. The Assiniboines got both swiftness and strength at second-hand,
and were squeezed between friends and foes; and the Crees, with the
Chippeways at their heels, enlarged their range at the expense of the
Assiniboines, Blackfeet, and Chipewyans, but especially the defence-
less Chipewyans. Thus in the eighteenth century they invaded the Peace
River District, enslaved and made peace with the Chipewyan natives,
– hence the words Slave River and Peace River – and now reach along
the valley of the Mackenzie to Lake Athabasca. Horses and guns accelerated the doom of the bison, nor did the self-dependence of the Indians
survive the bison, which had hitherto been their clothes, houses, bridles,
saddles, bags, boats, weapons, fuel, meat, and very life.

(Rogers, *Historical Geography – Canada*, 1911, 197–216)

9 THE MANY NATIONS OF PRAIRIE-LAND

☞ To Rogers the Canadian prairie is a great spatial, oblong canvas.
On the east the oblong is bounded by lake and forest, on the north by
the North Saskatchewan River, on the west by the Rockies, and on the
south by the 49th parallel. As in Ontario, Rogers sees grand spatial
powers at work, preparing for, and guiding, prairie settlement, and he
emphasizes the openness and freedom to move in any direction during the re-settlement period on the prairies. He discusses the vulner-
ability of the international boundary during the first three-quarters
of the nineteenth century, especially given any geopolitical interest
the powerful United States might have had in the relatively weak and
thinly settled British North American (later Canadian) prairie. During
that time the region was mainly dependent upon the United States for
access, because of the relatively easy movement across the fourth side
of the oblong. However in the 1870s and 1880s new events and spatial
forces entered the picture: the arrival of the military force to end the
Riel Resistance and then the North-West Mounted Police, and the coming of settlers and the railway. The revolutionary role of the Canadian
Pacific Railway is described: "The new power was creative, conjuring
up towns from nothing, and scattering men from nowhere in its wake."
Even Rogers is overwhelmed by the widespread distribution of diverse
peoples on the prairies. His remarks on cosmopolitanism reflect the
assimilationist tenor of the times, and the maxims on placing colonists

from various countries on the prairies are his own generalizations, in part true, in part dubious. ☞

Down to 1870, Europeans invaded prairie-land from two sides – Hudson Bay, Nelson River, and Hayes River on the north-east; and Canada, Lake Superior, and Lake of the Woods on the east – and they reached its threshold in canoes. In 1691–92 Henry Kelsey explored the second steppe, and in 1754–55 Anthony Hendry explored the third steppe; both came from Hudson Bay, both journeys were on foot, and both were isolated; for in those days the Company, which they served, received but never returned Indians' visits.

Meanwhile La Vérendrye and his sons came from Canada and explored Lake Winnipeg (1732), Winnipeg (1734), and Portage La Prairie on the Assiniboine (1737) where they planted forts at confluences and portages in the usual Canadian style. From Portage a flying visit was paid to the Missouri (1738–9) and the spurs of the Rockies (1742–43) in the United States.... These were the first dashes across dry land in Canadian history....

... Only one route was used across the whole of prairie-land from east to west, and that was the water-route by the Saskatchewan and North Saskatchewan. Canadian instincts, which clave to one long water-way, with many short cuts, preferred this route and made it supreme, at all events until 1870. Before that date men thought exclusively in water; thus the east of prairie-land seemed spacious to them because it presented an uninterrupted water-base 300 miles long from north to south; and, west of the large lakes, lines of movement seemed narrowing and tapering towards the North Saskatchewan. Capitals were water-capitals. At the lower end of the base, Winnipeg, being a ganglion of waterways and portages to the north, east, south, and west, was important; and at the apex, Edmonton, being a similar ganglion for Athabasca Landing, Peace River (via Lesser Slave Lake, 1799), and the sources of the Athabasca and of both Saskatchewans, rivalled Cumberland as a water-junction. Le Pas, Prince Albert, and Battleford were not only water-junctions, but fords for horses; and horses supplemented boats in a way unknown in Eastern Canada. Posts, where men exchanged boats for horses, became even more important than fords; and Prince Albert, Carlton House, and Battleford became starting-points and goals for short cuts – or, rather, long rides – either across the bed of the North Saskatchewan, or in later times from the Saskatchewan, to the Swan River, Assiniboine, and

Qu'Appelle, at Forts Pelly, Ellice, and Qu'Appelle. These long rides over treeless levels often exceeded two hundred miles, and must not be confused with the portage roads of Eastern Canada, which seldom exceeded ten miles, and were always artificially cleared, although the effects produced on history were similar.

The belief that the development of prairie-land must proceed along rivers and lakes and their banks affected history. The permanent settlement of prairie-land by men who were not hunters began in 1871, but for twelve years or more dawn had been visible, and sixty years ago there had been a false dawn. The settlements of the real settlers, like those of the hunters, concentrated on the river-banks near Winnipeg; but there were also the germs of settlements on the Saskatchewan and North Saskatchewan. The first real settlers were Lord Selkirk's colonists, isolated "freemen" and the immigrants of the Seventies....

Then two other currents set in from the eastern and northern waterways, and bore "freemen" to Winnipeg. French-Canadians, after serving in prairie-land with Canadian masters (1732 et seq.), used to marry Indian wives and beget half-breeds, and settle where there was fish, fowl, fun, and salt, and not further than could be helped from bison. As in the seventeenth and eighteenth centuries, Newfoundlanders touched at Waterford, and hired cheap indentured Irish servants, of whom they had a monopoly; even so, after 1711, Hudson Bay factors touched at the Orkneys and indentured and monopolized cheap Scotch servants, and when the Hudson Bay Company invaded prairie-land, the Orkneymen did what the French-Canadian servants did, when their indentures expired, after Lord Selkirk had shown the way. All these freemen farmed or pretended to farm along the banks of the Red River for a few miles – Scotchmen west and French-Canadians east, and the banks of the lower Assiniboine – Scotchmen north and French-Canadians south. The farms were wretched, were twenty times as deep as broad, and after 1870 were replaced, ... Houses straggled with long gaps as far as Portage la Prairie, fifty-six miles west of Winnipeg (c. 1850); Portage was regarded in 1860 as the most westerly limit of civilization, and "the last house" lay ten miles west of it in 1872.... After 1859, a few traders settled at Winnipeg from the United States.

From 1859 to 1871 newspapers (1859), mails (1864), the first Governor (1869), steamers (1870), Commissioners (1870), Sir William Butler (though a member of the Red River Expedition) (1870), Fenians, food, travellers, telegraphs, (1871), Hudson Bay Company's stores, everything came from the United States to Winnipeg. Commercially Winnipeg was an appanage of the United States and owed its growth in the Seventies to this fact..

In these longitudes the Americans of the United States were a quarter of a century ahead of the Canadians, and the latter sometimes shone with the reflected prosperity of the former.... In 1870, and even afterwards, St. Paul's was the rich uncle and patron, Winnipeg the lonely orphan. Civilization at Winnipeg was composed of many opposing types, which met there beneath the shadow of many churches, and looked for material help exclusively to the United States.

Freemen had not only cathedrals and churches at Winnipeg, but mission churches at Lac la Biche, Lac St. Anne, and Victoria, which are over fifty miles north, west, and east of Edmonton respectively; afterwards at St. Albert, nine miles north of Edmonton (1859), and lastly at Edmonton (1872), which became their chief resort. There were also freemen at Prince Albert, whither Scotch and English missions attracted them in the Sixties. Nor were missions mere concentration camps; but the missioners did for prairie-land what the monks did for mediaeval Europe by teaching cultivation of the soil. As in the south-east corner, so in the north-west corner of the great oblong of prairie-land, economic dependence upon the United States began and grew. Fort Benton on the Missouri (United States) had a steam-service to the Mississippi in 1857. In 1863 miners reached Bow River from the west, and while prospecting were refreshed from Fort Benton. In 1870 Edmonton sent fur thither; and whisky sellers came thence to the Belly, where they built "Fort Hamilton" near Lethbridge. Before 1875 a Fort Benton firm began to trade at what was afterwards Calgary, midway between Edmonton and Lethbridge. Thus Americans began to trace the third line of the oblong and to open a new trade route along it; and Fort Benton became the back door, just as St. Paul's was the front door of the Canadian prairie-land.

Shortly before 1870 predictions were rife as to the channels along which population would flow to and between these fixed points. Palliser (and Hind) held that there were "no means of access" to the Red River, "save those via the United States" – that is to say, via the Red River; George [*sic*, Samuel E.] Dawson ... held that civilization would after reaching Winnipeg flow down the Red River Valley and up the Saskatchewan and North Saskatchewan to its sources beyond Edmonton, to which there would also be access by the American trade-route from the south; and Hind and Blakiston urged the superior attractions of an alternative route from Winnipeg up the Assiniboine, down the Swan, up the Red Deer, and down the Carrot Rivers to the Saskatchewan.

All believed in water, few in the Qu'Appelle, fewer in the South Saskatchewan, and no one in the open prairie, as the line of progress. They accounted for three external sides of the oblong, but not for the fourth side, which is dry land and follows the frontier. Their gods were gods of river and woodland, and they were sure that the prairie would be skirted on the north, east, and west, and scouted except for pastoral purposes.

Then four events occurred which turned these predictions awry, or fulfilled them with a difference. These four events were the Red River Expedition (1870), the establishment of the Royal North-West Mounted Police (1874), the arrival of the colonists of the Seventies, and the Railways of the Eighties.

In 1870 Lord Wolseley proved that the route between Lake Superior and Winnipeg which Dawson championed was feasible for an army; and after him, Governors (1870) and bodies of immigrants from Eastern Canada (1872) came that way. Prairie-land was weaned from the United States and restored to its natural mother. In the Seventies Winnipeg once more turned its face eastward, and faced two ways, eastward and southward equally.

Military intervention was temporary, but the Royal North-West Mounted Police, which was largely recruited from Lord Wolseley's officers and soldiers, was a permanent influence. The first feat of the new military police was to ride eight hundred miles from Emerson on the Red River, along the frontier, to Forts Hamilton and Macleod near the Rockies. They went boldly across the prairie, without regard to watercourses and with compass as guide. To some extent the International Frontier Commission anticipated them; but it did not keep to Canada as the police did. The police were the true white pioneers of the fourth side of the oblong, … it was a characteristic Canadian maxim that soldiers should be or should precede immigrants. They were meant to be, and were, the advanced guard of civilization. They proved that on the prairies there were no definite lines by which bodies of men must go, and that Geography imposed no limits. They too asserted Canadian supremacy and self-reliance; though it sounds odd that the expedition of the new Police force came to Emerson through Chicago, and on reaching Fort Macleod, which they created, drew supplies from Fort Benton....

Meanwhile new colonists came in flocks and crept from point to point. First came the Mennonites, or disciples of a Frisian named Menno or Menno Simons (c. 1536), who preached doctrines similar to those of the Baptists and Quakers of to-day. War against war made them flit from country to country; some wandering to America (1661–62) and others to Prussia (1670), thence to the Lower Dnieper, the Molotchna, and the Lower Volga (1786), and thence to Manitoba (1874), where they settled in compact masses between the Red River and Pembina Mountain in the footprints of the Royal North-West Mounted Police; but some loitered by the way and settled in Nebraska and Kansas (United States). They preserved their native language, which was Frisian, German, or Flemish, but never Russian, and reproduced the old German village, with its run-dale agriculture and pastoral communism; but these survivals of the past are dying out, as they have already died out among the Mennonites of Ontario. Recently they numbered upwards of 15,000 [1901 population] in Manitoba; and they still crowd the frontier, chiefly on the west, but also on the east of the Red River. Religion made them fly from conscription like the plague, and they became collective emigrants, almost by profession.

In 1876 a similar large body of Icelanders arrived, after shedding some of their members in North Dakota (United States), ... From Winnipeg they went down stream by boat to Gimli – which in Icelandic means heaven – on the west coast of Lake Winnipeg. There they cut down trees – though most of them now saw trees for the first time – minded cattle and sheep, and fished, and there are still 3,000 Icelanders near Gimli, all or nearly all of whom are bilingual and speak better English than any other foreigners in Canada; but most of the Icelanders have scattered throughout Manitoba, some northward to the Grassy Narrows of Lake Winnipeg, and others westward to the west shore and Narrows (1888) of Manitoba Lake; some near the frontier at Grunde (1881 et seq.) learned and taught agriculture to their fellow countrymen at Gimli (before 1895); and the intellectuals leavened the cosmopolitan city of Winnipeg.

National colonies, composed of Scandinavians or Germans, were already common on the American prairies, and there were massed Mennonites in Ontario; but an exclusive Icelandic settlement was a complete novelty. The Icelanders are still in the van of real settlers on the west coast of Lake Winnipeg, and they who flew first flew furthest down the Red River Valley. The Mennonite settlements on the frontier were, on the other hand, but a beginning of westward expansion, which left Pembina Mountain behind it in 1876, and lined Rock Lake and the edge of the Souris Plain in 1878–9, French-Canadians from the United States (1878) and Icelanders (1881) carrying on where German Mennonites left off.

The main stream of development lay north of the colonists of the frontier and south of the colonists of the large lakes. West of Portage La Prairie, Rapid City (1877), which was colonized direct from England,

Birtle (1879), Odanah, Minnedosa (1879–80), Shell River (1879–80), – half-way between Forts Ellice and Pelly – and Red Deer River (1879–80) near Carrot River, marked the direction; and it was the same direction which Hind and Blakiston foretold.

Then three towns were built which proved that a new force had appeared whose workings had not been foretold. Emerson (1875) on the frontier was the first pure railway town, attaining its zenith in 1879, when the first Manitoban railway was completed between Winnipeg and St. Paul's (United States). It was the gateway from the South. Selkirk (1875) was the second pure railway town, and would have been the gateway from the east, had not Winnipeg, fearing eclipse, offered to build a railway bridge over the Red River (1879), and so lured the Canadian Pacific Railway to Winnipeg, although Winnipeg is out of the direct way to its far western goal. By means of this bridge Winnipeg supplanted Selkirk as the gateway between east and west. Then a third railway town sprang into life. In 1879 it was decided that the Canadian Pacific Railway should pass south of Lake Manitoba (instead of across its Narrows), and so to Edmonton. Two years later plans were re-shuffled; and its present course, which is a long way south of Edmonton, was resolved upon. Immediately Brandon was transformed from an empty meadow to a town (1881). Brandon was the crucial example. But for the railway there was no reason for the existence of Brandon; and men knew now that the railway could go wherever it would in prairie-land, and that men and towns would follow, in the same way as effect follows cause, or noon sunrise.

From Brandon westward to Calgary the Canadian Pacific Railway (1881–82) pursued a course as original as that pursued by Sir George French and his police, and equally momentous. Brandon is on the Assiniboine, but a little west of Brandon the railway takes to the open prairie until it reaches Medicine Hat, on the South Saskatchewan, more than four hundred miles away, and almost on the same minute of latitude. Its course is not an air-line, for it wanders north as though it would shadow the Qu'Appelle, and then south as though it would shadow the South Saskatchewan; and it seems to strike a compromise between the route by these two rivers and the plain prairie route on its south. As it swept westward, Moosomin, Indian Head, and Regina (1882) rose from the dust and became markets for settlers on the Qu'Appelle; and Regina, Moose Jaw, Swift Current, Maple Creek Town, and Medicine Hat, when they were founded (1882–3), drew the Police northward from their hill-stations on the frontier, and became centres. Between Medicine Hat and

Calgary the railway followed from afar or abbreviated the long-neg-
lected course of the South Saskatchewan. The new power was creative,
conjuring up towns from nothing, and scattering men from nowhere in
its wake.

Meanwhile water exercised its old magnetic power to guide civilization. Steamers ascended the main and North Saskatchewan to Edmonton
(1875), and the Assiniboine to Fort Ellice (1879); Prince Albert boasted
of a steam saw-mill (1875) and attracted the half-breeds, who sold their
so-called farms near Winnipeg, and settled on what they called farms,
sixteen times as long as wide, between where the prongs of the South
and North Saskatchewan diverge (1875)....

Then Riel's rebellion broke out, and war cast its searchlight over the
problems of prairie-land. The puzzle was how to get to the Mesopo-
tamia of the half-breeds, and what should be base, rest-camp, or goal,
and whether to go there by steamer, railway, or horse; and this was how
the puzzle was solved....

... Reliance was placed on the new railway, the older rides across the
plains, and the oldest waterways; but amongst the latter, thanks to the
new railway, the South Saskatchewan for the first time took its rightful
place. All three methods were used in harmony with one another, and
each made for Canadian unity, the railway on a large, the river on a
medium, and the open prairie on a small scale – if the scale of a hundred miles to an inch may be applied. This war was the third national
movement which knit prairie-land to itself and to Canada; and it was
even more national than the war of 1870, and the police movements
of 1874. Nevertheless, the Canadian general in command reached Winnipeg by way of Chicago. The foster-mother was still just visible in the
background behind the real mother.

Since 1885 lines of development, except in Inter-Lake-Land, follow,
unless they are followed by, a railway. The line is always from east to
west except in the far west and centre where cross lines run north and
south. Lines of development may therefore be learned from railway
lines; [Rogers briefly describes the routes of six east-west railway lines
that became primary lines of development, and two cross lines.] ...

The one obvious characteristic feature of prairie-land, namely, its capacity to develop in any direction whatever, was unexpected; and its less
obvious capacity to attract and accommodate settlers from everywhere
was equally unexpected. Nowadays the former characteristic seems self-
evident, but the latter still seems a paradox. Instead, then, of tracing
the progress of population along the railroads, where people grew like

primroses by a pathway in spring, or of tabulating results which would be out of date while these pages are passing through the press, I will note a few of the motley national groups which are scattered along the various lines of advance, and which distinguish prairie-land from the rest of Canada. Associated families, Presbyterian, Baptist, and Roman Catholic congregations, Regiments, and other social groups in eastern Canada were usually British or American, and there were two or three instances of American-German groups in Ontario; but there is nothing like the large quantity and diversity of "colonies" composed almost exclusively of persons speaking the same language and following the same social and religious customs which permeates prairie-land throughout.... The lists [of group settlements, omitted here], too, are as arbitrary and eclectic as the lists of a vagrant collector of insects or butterflies. In omitting the British element, which advanced silently and seldom in groups, the hero and more than half the story is omitted, ...

The colonization of prairie-land differs from that of Eastern Canada in the absence of soldier and sailor settlers, and of a war or of an industrial revolution at home; in the presence of returned emigrants from the United States, and in the wider area from which groups of associated families are drawn. In prairie-land, Icelanders and Scandinavians, as well as Highlanders and Islanders, represent the clan; Americans from the Western as well as the Eastern States represent the neighbourhood guild; Germans, who lived in the Palatinate two centuries ago, South Russian Germans, Doukhobors, Galicians, Finns, Jews, and others from Eastern Europe represent foreign victims of political and religious intolerance. Persecution enriched the New World with those denizens of the Old World, who did not agree with their environment, and North America proved the safety valve of European discontents. Prairie-land is an epitome of the modern history of all Europe, except the centre and the south; and is the result of a free trade in men, of which no European nation or thinker has ever dreamed, since the days of the Roman Empire. Cosmopolitanism originated in Pennsylvania, and is now the characteristic creed of the United States. But American cosmopolitanism has an English bias; and it is this kind of cosmopolitanism which is moulding the destinies of prairie-land.

In applying cosmopolitanism to prairie-land three maxims have been observed. First, extreme types of one kind are planted near extreme types of different kinds, in order that alkalis may neutralize acids, and something which is neither may result, and become the salt of the earth. Secondly, colonists, though introduced in groups, are planted as indi-

vidual yeomen – each on his free 160-acre homestead – so that before
treatment the compound is resolved, as far as may be, into colourless,
self-subsisting atoms. Thirdly, Britons are superior in numbers, all-per-
vasive, and hold the keys of the commercial situation; so that foreigners
are compelled to be bilingual, the second language being always English.
It is believed that numerical, commercial, and linguistic predominance
will create a new British type, like and yet unlike the Cymric, Gael, Erse,
Huguenot and Danish types of the old United Kingdom; and that the
thousand and one nationalities will fuse themselves in a single crucible,
and will emerge British, not exactly in the sense which we know, but in
a sense very like the sense which we know.

(Rogers, *Historical Geography – Canada*, 1911, 217–44)

10 THE FAR WEST AND NORTH-WEST, OR THE LAND OF MOUNTAINS

☞ Rogers spends much space separating out the various mountain
ranges in British Columbia and Yukon, and follows the great loops of
the major rivers, but there is not room here to provide extensive quotations from his descriptions. He notes the magnitude of the forests and
the range of climates from wet to dry and gives special attention to the
many First Nations of the Far West. ☜

East of the Rockies and west of the Appalachians there are no mountains
in Canada, and even the wooded Appalachians are only tamer Apen-
nines, so that the first glimpse of the wild white crowded summits of
the Rockies from the east is like the revelation of a new world. They are
a range, but are not like other ranges. They lie parallel with the coast.
Their eastern side is gradual, and part of their gradual side consists, as
we have seen, of three inclined plains 800 miles long, descending from
west to east, from dais to dais, upon the topmost of which rude rocks,
sharp ice peaks, and smooth snow domes, high as the Rothhorn and of
every shape and hue, tower like a row of ruins. On this side the range
has two great rivers; the Athabasca-Slave-Mackenzie, which follows
in bold wide curves along the feet of the mountains from 100 miles
above Edmonton for 1,500 miles or so right into the Arctic Ocean; and
the Saskatchewan, which writhes and wriggles away from the range
for 800 miles or so to the east and then makes for Hudson Bay. The
western slope is steep, and western rivers, whether they belong, like
the Columbia and Fraser, wholly, or like the upper Peace and Liard,

partly, to the west, cling close to the skirts of the mountain for many hundreds of miles before they double back and make for the Ocean, whither they are bound. The eastern are unlike the western slopes and rivers; yet the Rockies do not form a true watershed like the Caucasus Pyrenees or Alps.

As we follow the Rockies to the north, rivers which are eastward-bound rise more and more to the west of the ideal line which geographers identify with the true range; the South Saskatchewan rising before, the North Saskatchewan; within, the Athabasca further within, and the Peace behind the range, and the Liard behind a range behind the range. Strangely enough, the rim which bounds the plains and big lakes of Manitoba on their west, and which lies parallel with the great range as though it were some distant shadow or projection of the range, has the same characteristic, its more northerly streams rising further and further behind it. Northerly waterways went furthest west; therefore adventurers first went westward from the Peace which feeds the Mackenzie, then from the North Saskatchewan, and lastly from the South Saskatchewan....

West of the Rockies there are nothing but high mountains in whose shadows mountain valleys hide. The mountains rise in *echelon,* like the Himalayas and Trans-Himalayas, and are parallel with one another and with their deep dividing valleys. They may be classed as five ranges or ideal lines, although the actual lines often exceed five in number: – The Rockies; an intermittent range of which the Selkirk, Babine, and Cassiar mountains are the most conspicuous examples; "a sea of mountains", composed of waves, so to speak, from the ranges immediately on its east and west, and which narrows at one place to the Gold Range, and to the familiar Eagle Pass between Revelstoke and Sicamous; the Coast Range, which defends the coast between New Westminster and the mountains of St. Elias; and the fragmentary ridges which penetrate Vancouver, Queen Charlotte, Texada, and other islands along their longer axis, making them fish-shaped. Each of these ranges is associated with a special type of country, and each yields minerals; the gold mountains of Cariboo, and the copper and gold of Rossland, Grand Forks, Boundary and Trail Creeks belonging to the third class; the silver-lead of Moyie, Kimberley, and the Slocan, and the silver and gold of Nelson and the Lardeau belonging to the second class; the gold of Hedley to the fourth class, the iron of Texada to the fifth class, and the copper of the inlets and the islands to the fourth and fifth class respectively. Coal of Cretaceous Age and excellent quality makes Crow's Nest Pass in the Rockies, and Nanaimo, Wellington, and Comox, on the east of Vancouver Island, rival Cape Breton Island; while Tertiary coal is found on uplands of the fourth type near Nicola....

In this western land the scenery is always bold, and mountains are visible everywhere barring the way; therefore valleys are, or should be, to British Columbia what they are to Switzerland, Tirol, and Scotland.

The valleys are threaded by rivers which expand into lakes, and the lakes are real deep lochs, and as unlike Lake Winnipeg as unlike can be; thus Shuswap Lake is almost as deep as Lake Ontario, and its sister lake, Lake Adam, is deeper than Lake Superior; and the great rivers are navigable from source to mouth, except where they rush through gorges, often many miles in length....

... If rivers of one country may be compared with those of another, the St. Lawrence recalls the Nile, the Mackenzie recalls the Ob, or Yenisei; and the rivers of British Columbia combine the longitudinal parallelism of the Salween, Mekhong, and Dichu, with the bendingness of the Yellow, Congo, or Niger; but perhaps there are no true parallels in geographical contours any more than there are in historical events....

British Columbia possesses not only mountains, rivers, and valleys, but also trees different from those of the rest of Canada. The Douglas Fir is sometimes as high as the North Tower of the Crystal Palace, and its lowest branches are higher than the Crystal Palace roof; within the trunk of a red cedar a whole family might live in comfort; and the hemlock – which is the particular glory of Queen Charlotte Islands – and the white spruce are akin to the Douglas Fir, and the yellow cedar is akin to the red cedar. The Douglas Fir, like the black pine, overlaps the Rockies from the Yellowhead Pass to the south, but none of these trees exists far north; except the black pine, which flourishes beside Frances Lake, and on the left bank of the Yukon at Selkirk. The forests are as dense as splendid.... The British Columbian trees, mountains, valleys, and rivers, are on a grand scale. Prairieland is the world's greatest cornland, British Columbia is one of its two or three greatest tree-lands.

Climate; of course, affects plants. In Yukon, Fort Cudahy barracks were built by the North-West Police on two feet of moss; Dawson was a marsh, and miners find the earth frozen at four foot deep. Nevertheless the wild rose blooms at Dawson, and early pioneers found grass and pasture for their horses on the sunny side of the river-banks. The climate is dry, and glacial traces are few. In the far south of British Columbia there is a strange alternation from wet to dry land. The coast is wet. In one year there were 64 inches of rain on the Lower Fraser, and 71 inches at Port Simpson; behind the Coast Range there were 8 inches at Kamloops, and 8 at Barkerville; the Selkirks were very wet indeed, and behind them again there were 10 inches only on the Upper Kootenay. These dry strips surprise the traveller with the spectacle so common in Europe, and so strange in Canada, of hills which are thinly dotted with hardy trees, or are wholly bare, not because they are too high, but because they are too dry. On the westernmost dry strip, which extends from Kamloops up to Stuart Lake more or less, and down by Okanagan to the frontier, the hopes of graziers, farmers, and fruiterers are fixed; or rather on those parts of the strip where there are valleys or where the sea of mountains is comparatively calm....

There are far more Indians of different stock in British Columbia than elsewhere in the whole of Canada. Everything north of Nelson River in Hudson Bay, the Yellowhead Pass, and the headwaters of the Chilcotin affluent of the Fraser, belongs to the Chipewyan Athapascan or Dene race, if recent Cree invaders between Edmonton and the Peace, still more recent Iroquois colonists at the Yellow head, and the occupants of the coast are excepted. Eskimos occupy the coast from Churchill (Hudson Bay), by the Arctic and North Pacific Oceans, to St. Elias (Yukon). On the coast line south or east of St. Elias, Eskimos are succeeded by Tlinkits near Bennett, by Haidas on Queen Charlotte Islands, by Tsimpseans near Port Simpson and the Skeena, by Kwakiutl-Nootkas from Gardner Canal to Bute Inlet (except at Bella Coola and Dean inlets) and on Vancouver Island (except near Victoria), and by Salish near Victoria, and on Bella Coola and Dean inlets. Salish also occupy the Lower Fraser, the Middle Fraser, the North Thompson, the South Thompson and the Middle Columbia, and Kootenays occupy the Upper Columbia and Kootenay. Probably these six nations are as different from one another as Algonquins are from Chipewyans; yet these two nations cover vast masses of land over two-sevenths of the earth's circumference; and those six nations are crammed into the western coast, and along the southern frontier of a single British province.

Mountains and fiords split the Indians into isolated fragments. Not that the fragments were ever sedentary. Thus the Haidas periodically visited the mainlands, and the Shuswaps the Yellowhead. But their area and their ideas of movement were "cabin'd, cribbed, confined" by the grandeur of their mountains and the intricacy of their shore line.

(Rogers, *Historical Geography – Canada*, 1911, 247–61)

11 THE PEOPLING AND CIVILIZATION OF THE FAR WEST

⌒ Forces and impulses affecting resettlement in the Far West include
the locations of fur posts either on the coast or in the interior and the
routes connecting them; the effects of international boundary lines;
the impact of amalgamating colonies; stimulation of local development and improved communications through gold and other mineral
discoveries; and railway systems constructed for idealistic and national
purposes or piecemeal to reach scattered mineral resources. The mix
of population is evident: people have come from eastern Canada, the
United States, Britain, and Asia. Two factors loom in British Columbia's
future: first, the impact of the Pacific Ocean, including the awakening
of China and the opening of the Panama Canal; second, in the spirit of
pre-World War I British colonial expansion Rogers ponders whether
British people can cope with settling a mountain area such as British Columbia, a nineteenth- and early twentieth-century imperialistic
psychological problem. ⌒

The white men who first landed in British Columbia, brought with them
the memories of Siberia, Spain, France, the Pacific Islands, India, China,
and every country except Canada.... Then Captain Vancouver was sent
out from England, by the Cape of Good Hope and Australia, to dis-
pel these ghosts of a dead past; sailed between Vancouver Island and
the mainland (1792); explored and named the creeks and islands of the
coast, and amongst others Burke Channel and Bentinck Arm (May and
June, 1793). Exactly one month later Canada flashed upon the scene in
the person of Sir A. Mackenzie. His route was up the Peace River, over
the Peace River Pass, up the Parsnip, down the Fraser to Alexandria,
back to the Blackwater affluent of the Fraser, up the banks of the Blackwater, over the Coast Range, and down the Bella Coola to Bentinck Arm
and Burke Channel.

The Scotchman travelling westward across one-third of the world, and
the Englishman, sailing eastward over the other two-thirds, all but met
in this lonely fiord. Both men were idealists, but there was no common
plan; each went about his own business, and between them they ran a
girdle round the earth. The so-called all-red route of to-day is an echo of
the Vancouver-Mackenzie route of 120 years ago.

Forts or trading-posts followed in Mackenzie's footsteps but slowly.
Simon Fraser, while discovering and exploring the Nechaco affluent of the

Fraser, built McLeod's fort for the Sikanni, St. James, Fraser (1806), and George Fort (1807) for the Carriers; and thence discovered the mouth of the Fraser from inland (1808), even as the mouths of the Niger and Murray were discovered. These four fur-forts ruled the country of the Fraser from inland and from the north. [Rogers then describes the exploratory journeys of the fur traders, and notes the forts established.] ...

The coast and the coast-tribes seem to have been forgotten since Mackenzie and Fraser; for the valleys drove men north and south, and the Coast Range and coast-tribes checked the white inlanders. Ultimately the coast was reached by fur-forts, but not from the interior. Fort Alexandria (1821), – which eclipsed Fort George, – and the short-lived Fort Chilcotin (after 1826), were founded lower down on or near the Fraser; but the Lower Fraser was not reached from this side. Then settling traders sailed north from the Columbia and founded Forts Langley (1827) on the Lower Fraser, Forts Simpson (1831, 1833) and Essington (1835) on the mouth of the Skeena, Fort McLaughlin (1833), just north of Fitzhugh Sound, and Forts Rupert (1835) and Victoria (1842) on the north-east and south-west respectively of Vancouver Island.

Meanwhile exploring traders pushed north from the four forts to Forts Babine on Lake Babine (1822), and Fort Connolly (1829) on the uppermost Skeena; but these inland forts were as unconnected with the forts on the mouth of the Skeena as the four forts were with Fort Langley. It was easier apparently to get from the inland forts to the Atlantic or Hudson Bay, than to the Pacific coast of Canada....

... Forts were founded on Dease Lake (1838) and the Upper Pelly (1842), and Fort Selkirk was built at the junction of the Yukon and Pelly (1848). The Peel-Porcupine-Yukon route was explored between 1842 and 1846, when Fort Yukon was built at the junction of the Porcupine and Yukon in Alaska, and the Yukon was navigated between Forts Selkirk and Yukon. The earliest news of these remote forts on what was then a new unknown water-system reached England from searchers engaged in the Franklin Relief Expedition so that the last chapter leads back to the first chapter of this book, as though the narrative ran in a circle. The four forts of the Fraser were now connected with the Liard, the Stikine, the Mackenzie, and the Yukon, but not with the Pacific on Canadian soil.

The impulse communicated by the fur-traders of one great company to historical geography had now reached its grand climacteric, and a new force came into play which was single, world-wide, and purely political in its character.

In 1846 the Anglo-American frontier was fixed at 49° N. lat., but gave Vancouver Island to England, although part of it is south of 49° N. lat. Immediately the scattered posts upon the coast, and the long-drawn lines in the interior, drew together, and one capital for both was selected upon the Pacific.

The Hudson Bay Company, which now governed Vancouver Island, made Victoria the seat of government. Esquimault, which is the twin city of Victoria, became until 1905 the principal British naval station on the Pacific, being as it is the only first-rate Pacific port south of 49° N. lat., except San Francisco (United States) and Acapulco (Mexico). Consequently, whalers and sealers bound for Alaska used Victoria as a dépôt from the first, and fish and lumber began to be exported thence even to the Hawaii Islands. Salmon was exported in barrels from Victoria as early as 1853; and eight British settlers arrived from England at Sooke Harbour twenty miles west of Victoria, in 1849. Coal was worked temporarily at Fort Rupert (1849), then permanently at Nanaimo (1851), which is seventy-three miles north of Victoria, and Victoria soon became to the East Pacific what one Sydney is to the North-west Atlantic, and another Sydney is to the South-west Pacific. These crude facts almost contain a complete epitome of the industrial geography of the island. The canned-salmon trade began to prosper in 1876; the Wellington coal-mines, five miles beyond Nanaimo, in 1871; the Comox coal-mines, sixty miles beyond Nanaimo, in 1888; and Malcolm Islet, opposite old Fort Rupert, yielded coal in 1908. A line of settlements connect Victoria with Wellington, and the sixteen-mile Saanich peninsula north-east of Victoria is fertile and inhabited throughout. Agriculture flourishes round the coal-mines. Otherwise settlements are discontinuous, and consist largely of fishermen and lumberers, who are scattered on many streams, and in many islets....

On the mainland the concentration produced by political events feebly united the Middle and Lower Fraser. In 1846 A. C. Anderson discovered what are now known as the Seton-Anderson-Lillooet route and the Hope-Nicola-Kamloops route between Alexandria on the Middle and Langley on the Lower Fraser, and the first loose links were forged between the coast and the interior. Fraser (1808) and Simpson (1828) had shot through the gorge; but the gorge was impracticable for ordinary purposes, and until 1846 white traders did not cross the Coast Range anywhere. Forts Hope and Yale were then built at or near the lower end of the gorge (1848), in order to bind the uplands with the sea-shore....

... But strange things were happening in 1859, because gold, which can remove mountains, was already in the air....

Gold not only found out new ways, but transformed British Columbia from a network of trade-centres into "a living colony"; and its advent was the signal for new developments. It swept like a storm up the American banks of the Columbia from the south, and there were rumours of its coming down the Thompson from the north in April, 1856. In 1857 gold gleaned from the Thompson was minted at San Francisco. In 1858 one red-shirted, armed Californian crowd struggled up overland by the Okanagan to Kamloops, and another sailed into Victoria, where quiet people took them for pirates, and up the Fraser to Hope, near which they winnowed gold-dust from the river in the forbidding gorges of the Fraser. One miner strayed upstream to the Chilcotin far beyond the gorge, heard from Indians of Horsefly Lake, somewhere out east under the arch of the Great Bend of the Fraser, and found gold there (1858). In 1859 Quesnel River, to the north of Horsefly Lake, and in 1860 Antler Creek, still further north, were found to be auriferous; and Lightning Creek and William (Dietz's) Creek, which are near Antler Creek, and on which Barkerville stands, came as a climax in 1861. Antler on Antler's Creek, and Keighley near the forks of the Quesnel, became towns in 1861, and Barkerville was in 1865, and still is capital of the Cariboo District, as these three new far-off gold-fields were called. Placer gold is still strained there, but since 1893 (c.) by hydraulic machinery, which has superseded individual sieves, and sometimes fails owing to the scanty rainfall.

In 1859 there were less sensational discoveries near Lillooet on the Middle Fraser, on the Similkameen, sixty miles east by south of Hope, and at Rock Creek – 119° W. longitude – 50 miles east by south of Hope, and just within the frontier.... The madding crowd rushed from Hope to Rock Creek through the valley of the Similkameen in 1860.

These events riveted the Middle to the Lower Fraser. The way between Harrison River and Lillooet was perfected, a good coach-road being built over thirty miles of portage before 1862. Simcoe's Yonge Street was also a good coach-road over thirty miles of portage, but that portage was very different to this. Then a coach-road was built from Hope through the great gorge between the Lower and Middle Fraser, past Lytton and Clinton – where another coach-road from Lillooet met it – to Quesnel, Alexandria (1863), and Barkerville (1865), which is 370 miles from Hope. Once more we recall Dundas Street, but there is no analogy east of the Rockies to the country which this great new road subdued. Parts of it were built by the Royal Engineers, parts by miners, but most by Chinese labourers. Fate strewed its potent gold-bait in the most impossible and important spot, and the greatest obstacle was converted into the greatest aid to development from the coast, whence all immigrants now came except casual Americans, who from time to time drifted in from the south – except, too, those 193 Ontarians whom the fame of the Cariboo mines drew from their homes 3,000 miles away, overland by the Yellowhead Pass, and down the Upper Fraser or the North Thompson to Quesnel and Kamloops (1862). These Ontarians were the first overlanders from Canada, and they came to stay. Indeed, most who came to mine stayed as farmers in the country or traders in the towns. Barkerville, Lillooet, and Kamloops became farming centres and general markets; and the Lower Fraser became what it is to-day – a series of farms, orchards, and fruit-gardens. Langley, Hope, Yale, Lytton, Douglas, Lillooet, and Clinton were described as towns in 1862, all of which lay along the great road; and New Westminster had been built in 1858–9 at the lodge-gate of this long avenue to the gold-fields. Nor was the Hope-Similkameen-Rock Creek trail neglected, over which in 1861 the Governor rode from end to end. Trails as well as roads converged on the Lower Fraser, and the Lower Fraser led to New Westminster, which was provincial capital during the short time that the mainland was detached from Vancouver Island. These trails and roads, for which the gold rush was responsible, are the A.B.C. of British Columbian history, as well as of its geography. They made the dwellers on and beyond the Middle Fraser and its affluents live, and lead one life, and draw breath, so to speak, through one tube from one source, the tube being the Lower Fraser and the source being the Pacific Ocean.

The trail to the Similkameen and Rock Creek also united the Lower Fraser to outliers of the water-system of the Columbia on or near the American frontier. And that was only the first link in a long chain....
[Rogers describes mineral discoveries in the southern interior plateau and the Kootenays.]

Meanwhile the coal of Fernie – near Crow's Nest Pass and fifty miles east of Fort Steele – which geologists described as "little known" in 1889, and as "phenomenal" in 1891, attracted its railway from the east. Passing west from Fernie (pop. 1,540) there were already nine stepping-stones of solid rock-hewn gold, silver, and copper at Cranbrook (pop. 1,196), Moyie (pop. 582), Nelson (pop. 5,273), Trail (pop. 1,350), Rossland (pop. 6,159), Grand Forks (pop. 1,012), Greenwood (pop. 1,359), Osoyoos, and Princeton (pop. 316) [1901 populations]; and Princeton was on the way to the coal-district of Nicola. The fact that each of these towns is near the frontier would suggest to a European a strategic road or railway. A road has been, and a railway is being built, but it is as little strategic as natural; and it is certainly not natural, for it cuts straight across the grain, hitting more than nine rivers and many more mountains at right angles. The roads and railways – for both were built piecemeal – were purely mineral. The section of railway, which was available in 1898 between Crow's Nest Pass and Kootenay Lake, followed more or less a trail, most of which was used by miners in the Sixties, and by Sullivan and David Thompson long ago. The Nelson-Greenwood- Midway section is complete; and a further section to Osoyoos, Princeton, and Yale, or to Spence Bridge via Nicola, or to some other point on the Lower Fraser, will be probably ready before this book. If so, a second through railway will zigzag from the tidal waters of the west, certainly to Alberta, possibly to Red River, always within fifty miles of the frontier, attesting the triumph not of political idealism, nor of strategy, but solely of gold, silver, copper, and coal over Nature.

The first through-railway was built long before; but its origin was political, and the mineral-thread must be followed further afield before politics are broached.... [Rogers turns to the search for gold in northern British Columbia.]

The mineral history of Yukon began in 1880. Stewart River, sixty miles above Dawson, on the east of the Yukon, was worked in 1885; Forty Mile Creek, below Dawson, on the west of the Yukon, in 1886; and Sixty-Mile Creek, between the Stewart and Dawson, on the west of the Yukon, in 1893. The Klondike, whose river-mouth is at Dawson, was being gradually approached; and its gold was discovered late in 1896. Immediately Canadian gold rose to equality with that of South Africa and Australia. During seven years the output of gold from the Yukon was nearly worth three millions a year; while the annual output of British Columbia, then at its zenith, exceeded one million for the first time in 1901, and was £1,126,108 in 1906. British Columbia nowadays just surpasses Yukon in its annual production of gold, Yukon producing £1,120,000 in 1906; moreover, British Columbian gold is more than three-fourths rock-gold, and is therefore permanent, while Yukon gold is wholly gravel or placer gold, and is therefore of doubtful permanence. The usual mob flowed and ebbed from creek to creek of the Klondike, and plied the usual tools, with simple devices for thawing buried river-beds; and, as might be expected, hydraulic machinery superseded the work of men's hands before 1908. Meanwhile, Yukon began to resemble a province. Dawson was founded in 1897, and in 1901 had over

9,000 inhabitants. The Royal North-West Mounted Police arrived there among the first; in consequence of which, pistols, locks, and keys are scarce, because useless, although the riff-raff of the wild west often drifts thither from Alaska. Horses were plentiful there in 1899, and motors in 1908, for the roads are good. In 1897 the first Canadian overlander arrived via the Mackenzie, Peel, and Porcupine; and in 1898 via the Liard and Pelly. In 1900 the Governor-General paid his first visit, coming by Lynn's Canal, the new White Pass Railway, and the river steamers of the Yukon....

... The mineral thread has now been retraced from the extreme north – not indeed to the very spot, but to the very parallel where its progress to the north was interrupted. In its progress east and west along the southern frontier of British Columbia agricultural invariably accompanied mineral development. This has hardly been the case, except on a very humble scale, north of Barkerville.

The final impulse towards development came from idealists, whose idealism, mad as it once seemed, proved to be sober sense, and their faith to be wisdom in disguise. When its godmother named British Columbia, and gave her name to its capital, she expressed her "hopes that this new colony might be but one step ... by which ... her dominions might ultimately be peopled in an unbroken chain from the Atlantic to the Pacific by a loyal and industrious population." Echoes of the Psalms and a sense of British greatness brooded over its birth, and a spirit of national rivalry stimulated its growth. Alfred Waddington complained in 1868 that the new colony was "entirely indebted to the United States" for the carriage of its letters and immigrants, and even its food; others too wrote in the same strain. In 1871 the new colony joined the Dominion, in order that it might lean on the east rather than on the south, and stipulated for a through-railway to the Atlantic, like that which San Francisco had already. The railway was to be a symbol and instrument of union with Eastern Canada, and for this purpose was to pass through two thousand miles or more of solitude. A passionate desire for the union of Canada with itself made Canadians run risks of what seemed certain material ruin.

Two of the proposed routes for this railroad, which visionaries set to work to build through vacancy, may be recalled. Its first proposed course lay through the Yellowhead Pass, by the Upper Fraser, Forts George and Fraser, the Bulkley Valley, and Hazelton to Port Simpson; with variants or tentacles from the Upper to the Middle Fraser, and so either to Gardner Canal, Dean Channel, or Bute Inlet, up which last Waddington built

a road at his own expense in 1864. All these routes are natural routes ...
but were rejected on the ground that they led no whither. The inlets to
which they led were as vacant as the great spaces which were traversed.
A further proposal to build a bridge across the archipelago from Bute
Inlet to Vancouver Island, and so reach the capital, was too expensive
to be adopted. The second, which is the actual route of the Canadian
Pacific Railway, crosses the Kicking Horse Pass over the Rockies, and
Rogers' Pass over the Selkirks, which passes resemble two Brenner
Passes in quick succession; and a third easy pass over the Gold Range
called the Eagle Pass; after which it passes through the broad lovely
Thompson Valley, which is comparatively civilized, through the narrow
gloomy Fraser Gorge, which a road already traversed, and through the
fertile levels of the Lower Fraser to the neighbourhood of New Westminster, where Burrard's Inlet was the terminus. At Burrard's Inlet there
was nothing but high thick trees and deep still water, when the railway
reached it. Immediately after it was reached, Vancouver City sprang up
like the prophet's gourd, and in 1901 was more populous (26,133), and
is now far more populous, than Victoria (20,816) (1901 populations],
although Victoria is the prettiest and oldest town in western Canada,
and has gained by whatever has happened in the province during sixty
years or more.

On the railway-track Golden (pop. 705), Revelstoke (pop. 1,600),
Kamloops (pop. 1,594), and Ashcroft (pop. 475); and south of it, Vernon
(pop. 802) on Lake Okanagan, Arrowhead, on Lake Arrow, Kaslo (pop.
1,680) [1901 populations] on Lake Kootenay, and Gerrard, on Trout
Lake, owed their growth to the railway or its branches, but Vancouver
City owed its very existence to the railway. The biggest town in the colony was created by a railway out of nothing in a moment.

Why, it was asked, could not this miracle be repeated? The Grand
Trunk Pacific Railway, which is now being built over what I have
described as the first projected course for the first main railway, is the
answer to the question. Prince Rupert, its proposed terminus near Port
Simpson, was vacant in 1907, and had 4,000 inhabitants in 1909. There
are farmers already in the Bulkley Valley, and some copper and coal.
Opposite Prince Rupert are the Queen Charlotte Islands, Graham Island
in the north, Moresby Island in the south, like Corsica and Sardinia
halved in size.... The climate is mild, and everything except mankind
abundant. The new through-railway is already beginning to galvanize
these islands, and many an inlet on the mainland into life.

One inlet began to be civilized long after it was known that the Canadian Pacific Railway would send no branches that way, and long before the Grand Trunk Pacific Railway existed. This was Bella Coola Inlet. A group of Norwegians, who had formerly settled in Minnesota (United States), began to hanker after mountains and seas, like those in the home of their fathers. Accordingly, under the leadership of their pastor, seventy-five went north in October, 1894, furnished themselves with supplies in Winnipeg, which became their base of operations, and took the train for Vancouver. Thence they sailed to Bella Coola Inlet, where Vancouver and Mackenzie just failed to meet a century ago, and formed a nucleus around which their kith and kin from afar clustered. In 1906 wagon-roads penetrated twenty-two miles, and settlers occupied seventy-five miles of the valley, and were still pushing towards the Middle Fraser. If, as is probable, a third railway is built along the Middle Fraser between the Upper and Lower Fraser, it will be partly a junction-line between the two great political lines, partly a mineral line for the Cariboo and Lillooet Districts; and if, as is also probable, it should some day send out a spur to Bella Coola, this spur will be wholly due to the agricultural enterprize of these pioneers, and will be unique in British Columbia, where railways have usually been the cause, not the effect, of agriculture, and where colonizing communities are as rare as lumber-camps, canneries, and Indian villages – served by a trader and a missionary in true Pacific fashion – are common on its coastal indentations. The story of the peopling of Bella Coola recalls the Icelanders of Gimli, and reads like a distant recollection of Prairie-land....

Emigration from Eastern Canada is the chief feature in ... [explaining the origin of the population], although Emigration from Great Britain has also left traces more deep than numerous. Chinese and Japanese immigrants are conspicuous here, as they are, or have been, in every Pacific Dominion and colony. The Far East of Asia casts its shadow over the Far West of Canada; but not, to an appreciable extent, over Central or Eastern Canada. Although Chinamen wash linen from Louisbourg to Victoria, nearly thirteen out of every fourteen Chinese residents in Canada resided in British Columbia in 1901, and the disproportion has increased since then.

British Columbia and the provinces of Prairie-land are the newest provinces of the Dominion of Canada. All of them are totally unlike the rest of the Dominion; and British Columbia is the very antithesis of Prairie-land. British Columbia is all mountain and the prairie is dead

level. The dead levels are being peopled at lightning speed; the mountain province, though covering an area equal to Austria and the United
Kingdom, has far less inhabitants than square miles. In discussing its
population we are discussing its future; and its future depends on two
unknown factors.

First, what will happen in China, Japan, and the Pacific? Will China
awaken? Will Japan trade more and more with Europeans? Will the Panama Canal and Western America make the Pacific as busy, or anything
like as busy, as the Atlantic? After all, the Atlantic was as lifeless a few
centuries ago as the Pacific was a few decades ago; and in human history
centuries count for little.

Secondly, will British enterprise be as successful among the mountains,
as it has been among the bare plains and interminable forests of Eastern
and Central Canada, and among the park-lands of Australia? British
colonists have rarely, if they have ever, grappled with mountains. Mountains are a comparatively new factor in British history, and in European
history symbolize slow progress and secluded lives. Statistics of size and
pace must not dazzle us; small numbers multiply with delusive rapidity,
especially under the stimulus of mineral wealth, and colonists must not
be expected on mountain-tops.

On the other hand, British Columbia is in many respects the greatest,
as it is the grandest, of the provinces; and into it its eastern neighbours
are still draining their superfluous numbers and riches, a process which
is likely to grow more and more common. Their future is assured, and it
is their residuary legatee.

(Rogers, *Historical Geography – Canada*, 1911, 262–81)

☞ GEOPOLITICAL CONCLUSION

In the few paragraphs that conclude the volume, placed at the end
of this chapter, Rogers thinks very much in terms of linkages and the
whole British Empire, continues his discourse on space, and places British Columbia and Canada in the context of the worldwide Empire. He
is not concerned with the nexus of economic and naval power, of Canada and the Empire, that was George Parkin's interest. To Rogers, the
creation of the worldwide chain of empire appears to be the result of
a mystical destiny. He foresees a closer bonding of the British Empire,
though he does not use the phrase Imperial Federation that was in
the air at this time; at the same time he recognizes that the British

world-girdling bond does not exist in isolation but is part of the world around it. ⌐

What was said in every chapter of this book holds of British Columbia. Nova Scotia Province is the link with Europe, New Brunswick with Quebec *plus* Ontario; Ontario at all events out west, is a mere link with the provinces of Prairie-land; and British Columbia is also a link between what is east and west of it, between continent, and ocean, and what is beyond the ocean, and its future depends wholly upon the next links on its east and west. Looked at by itself, its development ran along its valleys or coasts, which lie north, and south, or north-west and south-east, contrasting in this respect with that of every other province of Canada. Looked at as a part of Canada, it is the end of a series and depends solely on its eastern sister-provinces. But Canada itself resembles a link in a larger chain, a word in the middle of a sentence, or a hyphen between two half-words. The whole, of which it is an essential part, is the British Empire, which seems working towards unity in a way which our ancestors never contemplated. The unity is due to geographical facts, the most important of which are that the provinces of Canada lie in this order, east and west, and that Great Britain is the only European Power, except Russia, which holds continents or half-continents on the western side of the Pacific. Purely political ideals welded these provinces together; and it is possible that purely political ideals will weld these continents and half-continents together. Vast economic results have ensued from what political idealism has already achieved; but economics have not supplied the motives of the process. The series of provinces points from the Atlantic to the Pacific; and the continuation of the series across the Atlantic points to England, and the continuation of the series across the Pacific points to Australia and India, and thence by South Africa and an island chain respectively to England. The chain which is being run round the earth is not exclusive; indeed, in all its links it touches some other European power; and in North America, which contains its most important series of continuous links, every part of every link is continuous with the United States of America for many thousands of miles.

Nor has it any prospect of proving to be an exclusive chain even in the least of its links; but it has a far better prospect of proving to be a complete chain than any which any other Power upon the surface of the earth possesses. The dumb consciousness of this paramount mission has been the mainspring, economic and material factors have only been wheels within wheels, carrying on the British race irresistibly towards their common destiny.

The processes are very complex, and work sometimes in obedience to, and sometimes in spite of design, sometimes like automata and sometimes like an unspoken instinct, but work in harmony; and the harmonious working of different tendencies is the greatest driving force, just as sane idealism is the greatest ruling force in history.

(Rogers, *Historical Geography – Canada*, 1911, 281–3)

4

J. D. Rogers, *A Historical Geography of the British Colonies – Newfoundland,* 1911 (1931)

☞ For reasons explained in his preface, quoted here, J.D. Rogers wrote a separate volume in 1911 on the history and historical geography of Newfoundland. In the preface he recognizes the colony's individuality. Rogers died in 1922 but a new edition of his book on Newfoundland was published in 1931. There the new general editor, Sir C. Alexander Harris, explains that the only changes were made are to correct a few misprints or slips, and that some figures are brought up to date. Harris also comments on Rogers' writing:

> No attempt has been made to interfere with the individuality of the original writing. Rogers often had a quaint way of regarding things and expressing himself. But one tribute to him is demanded. His writing is the result of peculiarly wide and painstaking reading; he is conscious of being saturated with his subject to such an extent that he assumes that the reader must be fully aware of words or matters which to the ordinary man require a certain explanation. (Rogers, 1931, iii)

Most of the book on Newfoundland is not so much a discussion of land and settlement as it is a history of European exploration and colonial enterprise, relations with the Beothuk and Micmac, conflicts, treaties, settlement policies, administrative changes, and the introduction of institutions. Historical geographic discussions of the advance of settlement and enterprise are only inserted where appropriate.

The tragic contact between Europeans and Beothuk and Micmac in Newfoundland, and with Inuit of Labrador, is discussed and the exploration of the interior of the island is described, especially William

Cormack's famous walk across Newfoundland. As in his book on Canada, Rogers introduces spatial generalizations. The relationship between the Beothuk and Micmac is interpreted mainly in spatial terms, and that between the Micmac and English is in part inferred through the ways that individuals from the two cultures travelled. The Micmac stayed within the interior of the island and the English moved along the coastal rim, so that: "Englishmen, as they revolved in the outer circle, were in complete ignorance of the Micmac, who were revolving in an inner circle." Rogers' contrast of the Micmac nomadic way of life with the English practice of establishing outposts on the coast, and the implications of this, is far too simple and abstract. It is an inadequate spatial model of how two peoples of very different power interact. But as Rogers says in the last lines of his preface: "I write as a pure impressionist" (Rogers, 1931, x).

Advances in cultivation, railway building, and investments in pulp and paper mills are summarized here by excerpts from the side-notes. Information in the last two side-notes is updated in the 1931 edition. Rogers notes Newfoundland's recurring financial problems, including the bank crash of 1894–95. He describes how, although there was a fear of riots and even concern that Newfoundland might become part of Canada, all that happened was a transfer of "financial supremacy" from Great Britain to Canada. He uses the financial crisis to develop his sense of the "soul of the national life of Newfoundland." All the while he has been somewhat teasingly holding off discussing "Fish," but he finally does so in the last two chapters and also presents his conclusions on the importance of fish to Newfoundland. ☞

I PREFACE

When this series was projected it seemed likely that before its completion Newfoundland would have been absorbed into the Dominion of Canada; and in 1896 the second edition of Judge Prowse's well-known history of Newfoundland assumed that this fate was imminent. Had these forecasts been fulfilled this volume would have been reduced to a size a little larger than that which has been allotted to those chapters of the Fifth [Canada] Volume which deal with Nova Scotia. But Newfoundland has not been absorbed, and still remains *sui generis* and an exception to the rule in the British Empire; – therefore this book will also be an exception to the other books in this series, and is framed on somewhat different lines and on a rather larger scale.

I do not wish to suggest that the apartness of Newfoundland will continue. Some people think that the island of the United Kingdom which lies nearest to America is destined to draw furthest away from its European sister-realms, and that similarly the island of America which lies nearest to Europe is destined to draw furthest away from its sister Dominions on the continent of America; while other people think that the centrifugal forces of to-day will be succeeded by the cohesive forces of to-morrow, and that present tendencies are due to passing whims. I do not think at all about these things, but take facts as they are. The apartness of Newfoundland from the rest of British America has persisted for a long time, and its history has for many centuries contrasted with the history of other colonies in two or three essential characteristics, each of which, strange to say, alternately daunts and fascinates the student.

In the first place there is an immobility in the history of Newfoundland, and a fixity of character in the Newfoundlander, which is unique in colonial history. Somersetshire, Devonshire, and Irish peasants are there and have been there from the first or almost from the first, preserving their ancient types, partly it is true by constant movements between their old and new homes, but partly also from other causes. These things presage monotony. On the other hand, Newfoundland has lived a continuous life and has kept its identity inviolate for more than 300 years. Its earliest years were surrounded by the thrilling incidents of the heroic age of European history, its middle years were disturbed by the din of the three Anglo-French duels, and even its latest years enshrine bygone prejudices, which it requires some historical imagination to reconstruct. There is always interest in a long life; and the long life which is a doubtful and a threatened life, and over which swords hang by threads, is doubly interesting. The uncertainty of its fate is the second characteristic which distinguishes the history of Newfoundland from that of other colonies.

For three hundred years, that is to say, during the whole of its colonial life, the colony has been menaced complete or partial extinction; not by force but by incessantly reiterated arguments. From the very beginning until the very end of its life clever people proved over and over again almost to demonstration that the colony ought not to exist; and vital controversies raged from 1611 to 1817 between settlers and non-settlers, from 1662 to 1714 between French and English, from 1763 to 1904 once more between French and English, from 1783 to September 1910 – when this book was in page-proof – between American citizens and the colonial or Imperial authorities; ...

(Rogers, *Historical Geography – Newfoundland*, 1911, iv–vi)

2 THE BEGINNINGS OF PERMANENCE

... [Rogers discusses European contact with Beothuks (which he spells Beothics) in Newfoundland and Inuit in Labrador.] In 1768 Lieutenant John Cartwright, R.N., accompanied by his brother Captain George Cartwright, by a settler, and by some seamen, undertook the most important upland journey which had hitherto been undertaken, and ascended the Exploits River as far as Red Indian Lake, which they were the first white men to see. The river was guarded for some thirty miles by fences for impounding deer, while on their way from their summer haunts in the wild woody north to their winter haunts on the wilder woodless barrens in the middle south. The pounds belonged to the Beothics, who were themselves migratory, living partly by the inland lake on venison, partly by the shore on birds and eggs, and partly by the river-banks on venison. A few years later two salmon fishers on the Exploits repeated this expedition, in order to destroy these salmon-like migrants in their uppermost haunts, reached their winter villages by the lake, shot or drove off the inhabitants, and burnt the houses, with the approval of their fellow-countrymen. In September, 1803, a Beothic woman was brought by an Englishman to the Governor, who loaded her with gifts, ... , and sent her back, vainly expecting to make the rich-returned lady an ambassadress of peace. In 1810 Captain Buchan, R.N., left two marines for a few hours with the Beothics of Exploits Bay as pledges of peace; and the marines were duly welcomed and decapitated. Haie and Whitbourne observed long ago that the redskins had fled northward and westward before the white men. Guy [John Guy, the first Governor, 1610–14] parleyed with them in Trinity Bay, but they too were scared and fled next summer. Then for a century and a half history was silent or gave dark hints as to the doings and sufferings of this shy persecuting but persecuted people. And now in these latter days, when northern extension brought Englishmen near their last lairs, the Beothics flitted fitfully once more across the tragic stage, were still the same treacherous fugitive phantoms, but fewer and more implacable than of yore, were last seen in their wild state in 1823, and then vanished for ever, even as the white bears and great auks, which early travellers saw, have vanished from Newfoundland, and for the same reason as the Tasmanians vanished from Tasmania. Continental aborigines, white savages, and consumption, which is a white man's malady, accelerated their doom; but how could they fish where white men hauled the seine? or hunt without dogs or guns; where white men and Micmacs hunted with dogs and guns? They could not dig, and to beg they were ashamed. There was nothing for them to do but die. In 1827 W. E. Cormack, fired with the enthusiasm of humanity, founded an Institute at St. John's for civilizing the Beothics; but in 1827 there was only one Beothic in the world, and she was a poor captive, who was dying of consumption in the hospital at St. John's; and was it really worth while to found an Institute in order to civilize her? Moreover, she died in 1829, and with her died the last of the Beothics. But the Institute flourished more and more....

Except for the natives, the experiences both of residents and visitors in Labrador were replicas of former experiences in Newfoundland. There had been hardly any barter between white men and Beothics, and in Labrador the ways of the English traders were partly smoothed by Frenchmen, who had been in those parts since Cartier's time, had foregathered at or near Bradore Bay in the seventeenth century, had had some sort of fort there in the eighteenth century, and had made friends with the Mountaineer Indians. In making friends with the Indians, they made foes of the Eskimos, who in the times of Le Clercq and La Hontan still frequented the north coasts of the Gulf of St. Lawrence, as far west as the Islands of Mingan, opposite Anticosti. The Indians of Labrador dwelt inland, but used to visit French ships, from which they received guns and ammunition in exchange for furs and skins. There had been hereditary war between the Indians and Eskimos from time immemorial, and fire-arms turned the scale in favour of the Indians, who gradually extirpated the Eskimos of the Gulf. While this war was in progress, the Eskimos frequently crossed Belle Isle Strait and attacked the Breton fishermen in the peninsula of Petit Nord, and on one occasion slew some straggling Frenchmen in the neighbourhood of Petit Maître (Croc), clothed themselves in the clothing of the slain, and thus secured twenty-one more victims. The last of the Eskimos of Belle Isle Strait continued after 1763 to cross over to Newfoundland, where they were met at Quirpon Island (1764) and were at last reconciled to Europeans by Moravian missionaries, who settled by their side, trading for them and converting them, first in Château Bay (1765), then far north of Cartwright's furthest in Nain (1771), Okkak (1775), and Hopedale (1782). Frenchmen won the hearts of the Indians; Moravians won the hearts of the Eskimos; tactful Englishmen, who came into Labrador after 1763, amongst whom Captain George Cartwright and his partner Lieutenant Francis Lucas were pre-eminent, addressed

themselves with equal success both to the Indians and Eskimos, and
the eternal feuds of savages began to fade away in the dawn of the
white man's civilization.

(Rogers, *Historical Geography – Newfoundland*, 1911, 141–6)

3 PROGRESS BY LAND DURING THE LAST PERIOD, 1818–1910

At the beginning of this period Newfoundland, with the exception of
the Peninsula of Avalon, must have seemed to its inhabitants a husk
without a kernel. Midnight wrapt once more the mysterious country, on
which the Cartwrights had shed a momentary ray of light. The Peninsula of Avalon was already known from end to end, but outside Avalon
nothing was known of the inner world, except what could be seen from
the sea or from the Lower Exploits River, or what the Cartwrights were
rumoured to have seen when they peeped behind the veil. So in 1822
W. E. Cormack [1796–1868], fresh from his new-made colony at New
Glasgow, in Prince Edward Island, resolved to take a new prolonged
look behind the veil and to make a final exploration of the unknown
interior. He had heard that some of the rivers which flowed south were
short and steep, and that the Exploits River, which flowed northeast,
was gradual and long; he had seen the charts; and he inferred from these
meagre data that an open, high, and dry route would be found along a
line to the north of the southerly, and to the south of the north-easterly
rivers; so he started with knapsack and rifle from Smith's Sound, near
Random Island, in Trinity Bay, and after nine weeks' tramp emerged in
St. George Bay, 210 miles due west of his starting-point. His was the
first long walk in Newfoundland, and it was almost the last. It seemed
to prove nothing and to lead to nothing. It was wholly unlike anything
that had hitherto occurred in the colony, and men had to think long
before they could quite make out what they had learned from it. The
only thing that was clear was that they had learned a very barren geographical lesson about a very barren region.

After piercing through a rising forest fringe for twenty miles, Cormack reached"green plains marbled with woods and lakes," or yellow-
green with reindeer moss, berry-bushes, and thin sedgy grass; and the
plains, which were 700 to 800 feet above the sea, were studded with
rocky knolls some 700 to 800 feet above the plains. Spruce-beds three
feet high with interlacing boughs, marshes and moss-beds three feet
deep, over which the caribou alone amongst the larger mammals could

travel, lakes like beads upon many strings, and the daily need for venison, more than trebled the distance which he had to go; and when he was twenty miles from his goal he crossed the granite ridge, some 2,000 feet high, which runs through the whole island from Cape Ray to Belle Isle Strait, and he reached once more a region of steep hills and wooded coastline. Geographically the journey was a success.

But in addition to geographical curiosity Cormack was inspired by two political aims, in both of which he failed. In the first place, being a colonizing enthusiast, he dedicated himself to the service of his fellow-countrymen, and dreamed of some future trunk road, which should lure men inland and forge living links between the lonely dwellers on the west, east, and south coasts, and that was one reason why he chose a high and dry way where bridges might be dispensed with. But the dream proved illusion, although at one time it seemed about to materialize into a telegraph or railway line. Ultimately the telegraph-line, which was built in 1856 from Heart's Content in Trinity Bay to Port-aux-Basques, passed on its winding way from creek-head to creek-head far south of Cormack's trail; and although, when the first big railway scheme was mooted in 1875, Sir Sandford Fleming, the famous Canadian surveyor, selected a northern variant of Cormack's trail as his route, this route was soon discarded, not because of its difficulty, but because of its utter uselessness. The whole district which Cormack traversed was wilderness in 1822, was wilderness in 1875, and seemed likely to be wilderness for ever and ever. Such a railway would have consisted merely of two termini. The route was the route of least resistance, but it was also the route of least attraction. Nor has it even been utilized, like the Pilgrim's Way along the English North Downs, as a bridle-path; for it is supposed that horses would not thrive on the scanty wiry grass or marsh plants, and could not cross the forest-belts or marshes. Nor has it been followed by pedestrians. Cormack noted serpentine rocks, with which minerals are often associated in Canada, and gazed on myriads of Caribou, or tracks of Caribou wending their way from their summer woodland retreats towards the open moor in autumn, but geologists like Jukes (1839–40), Murray, and Howley (1864 et seq.), miners like Willis and Guzman, and sportsmen like Dashwood, Selous, and Millais, who have entered those wilds since Cormack's time, have invariably adhered to the better plan, which is the Indian plan, of moving on the wet instead of on the dry, and of following watercourses instead of watersheds. Cormack's geographical discoveries did not open up new country or new roads or even new routes to the white colonists.

In the second place, Cormack was a philanthropist, and wished to do something for the Beothics. But he discovered to his surprise that, except at King George IV Lake, he was never within ten miles of their haunts. He heard for the first time of a great war in the long long ago, in which Micmac riflemen shot down Beothic archers and their wives and children; since which, the Beothics had shunned the haunts of the Micmacs, and had confined themselves more and more to their capital on Red Indian Lake in the middle reaches of the Exploits. Thence they ranged as far as King George IV Lake near the sources of the Exploits, and as far as the mouth of the Exploits, in Notre Dame Bay, and the mouths of lesser streams, which empty themselves into Notre Dame Bay between the Exploits estuary and Hall Bay, and which may in past ages have been subsidiary mouths of the Exploits. They were river-spirits, and the river which they haunted was the Exploits. They touched neither the western nor the southern coast, nor even the feet of Petit Nord Peninsula. They were limited to a single river. Accordingly, in 1828, Cormack, on renewing his quest, made straight for the dwelling places of the Beothics – pack on back and rifle in hand – searched the whole country between the Exploits estuary and Hall Bay, between Hall Hay and Red Indian Lake, and between Red Indian Lake and the estuary of the Exploits, and searched in vain. The objects of his search eluded his grasp, for they were all dead. He might as well have searched for the ghosts of prehistoric man. There never lived a man who more signally failed to do what he wanted to do by travelling than Cormack. Nevertheless, Cormack's geographical success was not without historical result.

While searching for Beothics he found Micmacs and made an historical as well as an ethnological discovery. In 1822 his only companion was a Micmac, and to his amazement he met two or three parties of two or three Micmacs, who did not know a time when they or their forefathers did not know the unknown district which he was traversing. There was also a Montagnais Indian living in the western wilds, who had come from Labrador and married a Micmac woman. Cormack's historical discovery – unexpected by him and unsuspected by historians – was that during a century or more, while Englishmen were gazing out seawards with their backs turned to the land, Micmacs with their backs turned towards the sea were hurrying to and fro from end to end of the land that lay south of Petit Nord – sometimes darting at, more often eddying round and avoiding its centre – and unlocking its mysteries with their Indian key. The Indian key – if the metaphor may be allowed – is a paddle. They paddled upstream from Cabot Strait or its neighbourhood, hunted all over Cormack's plateau, carried their canoes across short flat "portages", and paddled downstream into the Gulf of St. Lawrence, or more rarely into the waters of the Atlantic. Thanks to the paddle, their topographical knowledge was a good century a-head of the Englishmen's knowledge, and the paddle was an emblem of power as well as an instrument of knowledge. Except in the Beothic sphere of influence, they, and they only, possessed the land. Their methods were European but European with a difference, and the English ignorance of what they had been doing was due not to any difference between Indian and European methods, but to the abandonment by Englishmen of European methods in colonizing Newfoundland.

All the Micmacs were Roman Catholic Indians from Cape Breton Island or Nova Scotia, and, like the white men, came spontaneously from overseas, first as visitors, then as settlers; but they came to hunt, and until they had a firm footing in the land they avoided Englishmen.

Indians and Englishmen went different way although their methods were sometimes superficially similar. Like the white colonists, the Micmacs looked to their old home across the seas where the chief-chief resided, and resides to this day, in St. Anne's Harbour, Cape Breton Island; and, like Englishmen in every English island of the world except Newfoundland, they used to go overland from a principal fixed base on one coast to distant goals where less important bases had been established on other coasts. As with their English neighbours, their principal fixed base was and is on the part of the coast nearest to the land of their fathers. In Cormack's time there were two principal Micmac bases – on Conne River in the east arm of D'Espolr Bay, and at Little Barachois close by White Bear Bay. But they abandoned Little Barachois when Burgeo became populous, and concentrated themselves on Conne River, where they still enjoy their primaeval isolation more or less.

In early times the Micmacs used their settlements on the Southern shore as war bases against the Beothics. The date of their earliest coming to these settlements is unknown; but they probably had had long-standing causes of strife against the Beothics, before Frenchmen added fuel to the flames, for Indians have never yet attacked their kith and kin at the mere bidding of white men. Under French instigation, and "because", we are told, "the French offered a reward for the head of every Beothic" and the Micmacs went about earning the reward, the Beothics invited some Micmacs to a feast, found scalps in their possession and slew all the guests. Then the Micmacs, who were apparently familiar already with the inmost recesses of the country, undertook a war of revenge, marched down"Shannoc Brook" to the middle Exploits, and being armed with European weapons almost exterminated their opponents. Cormack's date for these events was 1680 or thereabouts, and as they took place at a time when the French still feared the Beothics, they must have taken place before the Treaty of Utrecht (1713) and not at the date usually assigned. We do not know when the Micmacs first came, nor are we sure of the date at which the visitors matured into settlers – except in the case of St. George Bay (1783), which probably preceded permanent settlement at Conne Bay by a quarter of a century; but long before Cormack's time, and probably long before their great war of revenge, they lived there off and on and looked on the land or on parts of it as their very own.

The result of this war was that the hunters of the rival nations avoided one another, the Beothics keeping to the centre, and the Micmacs to the south coast and its neighbourhood, The actual coast was only used as a starting-point for those hunting grounds, from which the Beothics were now completely excluded, and of which the white men were as yet completely ignorant....

Their [i.e. the Micmacs] many ways led up, down, across, and athwart the body of the island, always by fresh water and never round its coast. English colonists went from all these bays to all these bays, but always by salt water and round the coast; so that English progress outside the Peninsula of Avalon was exclusively marine. Micmac methods of progression in the same region were by rivers and lakes, exclusively inland, and in early times, when the Beothics held the centre, almost as circuitous as the English methods. Cormack's discovery was that the Micmacs had so completely monopolized, and Englishmen had so completely eschewed fresh water and land, that Englishmen as they revolved in the outer circle, were in complete ignorance of the Micmacs, who were revolving in an inner circle. And yet "overlanding" is an essentially English instinct, and it would seem odd to find Londoners who thought that their only way to Bristol or Liverpool was by sea.

On the other hand, there was a difference between the overlanding of Micmacs in Newfoundland and the overlanding of the English colonists in other climes. English overlanding always meant the creation and maintenance of land-links between the extremities; Indians invariably kept the intervals empty. The English process led to progress and fullness; the Indian process led to stagnation and inanition, for Diana, whom the Indians worship under another name, is not the goddess of population. Consequently in 1822, 150 Micmacs and a few dying Beothics filled all that part of Newfoundland, which does not consist of peninsula and coast-line; in 1842 there were no Beothics, the Micmacs were 200, and but for them the body of Newfoundland was like an empty skin; in 1872 the Micmacs were under 200; and less than 200 Micmacs, along with railwaymen and lumbermen still occupy – or rather pervade – the land. But for them the frame is without a picture. Indian colonization is the antithesis of solid progress, and like some gas keeps small particles of itself in vast spaces for centuries at a time. English colonization is also wont to pass through the hunting and travelling stage; but the hunter and traveller have invariably ushered in men of another type who have peopled the land....

[Rogers' side notes summarize colonization and development, mainly in the nineteenth century.] Farming began seriously when Cochrane [Governor, 1825–34] introduced roads, which introduced horses which introduced oats and hat and replaced dogs. Settlers now began agriculture here and there; geological reasons preventing it from being general, except e.g. in the south-west, where there were farms in early times; and in the Exploits and other valleys where lumberers (1) worked near the sea and built ships; (2) did the same on a larger scale as capitalists, and began to go inland; (3) worked further inland under pulp concessions to Companies (this new departure being connected with railway development); (4) or worked wholly inland under pulp concessions to mammoth development companies. Railways were also connected with mineral development; which again is suggesting new railways. All these developments combined with bounties, have promoted agriculture, and manufacturing, but only on a small scale. The Bank crash, 1894–5, produced a fear of riots and many other expectations, but only transferred financial supremacy to Canada....

Everything was threatened [after the bank crash of 1894–95] – solvency, revenue, thrift, the entire currency, and perhaps peace. Rumours were rife that Newfoundland was about to become a Province of the Dominion of Canada. The Colonial Government telegraphed home for a loan of £200,000 and a warship in case of disturbances. In response to this demand a civil servant, named Sir H. Murray, was sent out with £20,000. The plague was stayed, and the history of the money affairs of Newfoundland turned over a new leaf. Specie to the extent of £190,000 was imported; the Banks of Montreal, of Nova Scotia, and the Royal Bank of Canada, became the three paramount banks, and the financial sceptre passed to Canada. But Newfoundland remained as far off as she ever was from political union with Canada. Capitalistic enterprises of a terrestrial character concentrated in Canadian hands. But the destinies of Newfoundland are little influenced by terrestrial considerations. World-wide tendencies are sweeping scattered units into large compact masses; but Newfoundland is old, very old as colonies go, has been during its long life impervious to worldwide tendencies, and has been living its own life, in its own way, which is not the way of other states or colonies.

This chapter might be entitled Much Ado About Little, for Newfoundland from within only reveals a fraction of its nature. Its heart is on its outside; there its pulse beats, and whatever is alive inside its exoskeleton is alive by accident. The sea clothes the island as with a garment, and that garment contains the vital principle and soul of the national life of Newfoundland. With the Greeks, Ocean was a synonym for barrenness, land alone being lifegiving, and the thankless task of ploughing the sands between land and ocean brought but scanty profit to Faust himself. To the Newfoundlander the land is a forest or a "barren", the ocean a mine or harvest-field, and on the foreshore the yield of the ocean is prepared for market. Briefly, this chapter is unreal and unilluminating. because it has totally abstained, and probably it is the only chapter in any book on Newfoundland, which has totally abstained, from the word which heads the next chapter.

(Rogers, *Historical Geography – Newfoundland*, 1911, 159–90)

4 FISH

Newfoundlanders are men of one idea, and that idea is fish. Their lives are devoted to the sea and its produce, and their language mirrors their lives; thus the chief streets in their chief towns are named Water Street, guides are called pilots, and visits cruises. Conversely, land-words have sea meanings, and "a planter", which meant in the eighteenth century a fishing settler as opposed to a fishing visitor, meant in the nineteenth century – when fishing visitors ceased to come from England – a shipowner or skipper. The very animals catch the infection, and dogs, cows, and bears eat fish. Fish manures the fields. Fish, too, is the mainspring of the history of Newfoundland, and split and dried fish, or what was called in the fifteenth century stock-fish, has always been its staple. And in Newfoundland fish means cod.

Newfoundland is as rich in coves, where cod-ships or boats may shelter, as it is poor in beaches where cod can be split and dried, and their place is supplied by "stages", or small wooden piers on wooden piles and with wooden roofs. The cod-fish are brought by boats to the piers, and are split and temporarily cured under the roofs upon the piers; as may be seen on the fiords of Norway. The final process of drying cod in the sun takes place in wooden erections called flakes, which resemble the pergole of southern Europe, but on whose roof instead of roses the hardly less odorous dead and split cod basks. A few years before this period began, most streets were flakes, beneath whose shadows young men and women walked,

"whispering murmurs of love at even".

Sir Richard Keats purged the north shore of St. John's Harbour, but sixty years ago the south shore of St. John's was still decorated with flakes, and even today flakes still lend their peculiar poetry and fragrance to Quidi Vidi and the smaller out-ports. Cod-fish, alive or dead, wet or dry, have exercised an all-pervading influence over the destiny of Newfoundland.

Until lately cod-fish were never caught in winter, but the whole "unsown harvest of the sea" was reaped and gathered in between May and October. If, then, all Newfoundlanders were codders, why should not they learn a lesson from the cod, and absent themselves from an island where they were not wanted for six months in the year? This was the unanswerable question which was asked again and again by advocates of the old English policy, which encouraged a fishing-fleet to ply between Newfoundland and England every year. Again, if residents never did anything seriously except fish for cod, were they not like fish out of water in winter? Might they not become idlers, drinkers, or paupers? At all events, they would be happier and better employed in England. This view was at the bottom of the old policy which discouraged residents. The political ideal of keeping England provided with hosts of men and ocean sailors, and with wooden walls, like those which repelled the Spanish Armada, only reinforced a position which was after all founded upon a study of man and cod.

But common sense replied to these arguments of common sense by arguments which were conclusive as far as they went, although they did not go far.

Ever since Cabot and his successors caught cod by letting down hampers from their decks into the sea, all cod, including those that were caught on the high seas, were caught in rowing-boats. It would be the height of absurdity to bring the same boats from England or to build new boats in Newfoundland each year, but boats could not be left in the island without some one to mind and mend them. Ever since the time of Guy residents have minded and mended boats. Similarly, in the principal harbours, except in Placentia and a very few other favoured places, "Nature has denied (the principal harbours) favourable beaches for drying the fish, and thus expensive establishments of curing houses, stages, and ways have to be kept up," or, as in old time, to be created and destroyed every year. Resident caretakers were required for flakes and stages as well as for boats, in order to prevent waste, and those fared best who recognized this necessity. But caretaking could scarcely be described as work, and the idleness of winter became the curse, just as the energy of summer became the blessing, which Providence, impersonated by the cod, bestowed upon the country; and the only reason why idleness did not lead to starvation was because the capitalist came to the rescue and persuaded the residents to rely during winter on credit for their daily bread. The remedy had its drawbacks, but the only alternative remedies were pauper relief, which would have been worse, or thrift, which was not available. The cod made its pursuers half-timers; and palliatives, but not cures, for periodic unemployment were furnished by resident caretakers, and by capitalism on an inchoate and tentative scale. In spite of these palliatives, winter pauperism was the baneful influence with which the cod afflicted its devotees, and in the Sixties it happened once that one-fourth of the entire public revenue was spent on pauper relief. The conditions of the cod-fishery indirectly modified the evils which it directly created; but these evils were only removable by things which had nothing to do with cod-fish. Antidotes were furnished in the early history of the colony by trapping and boat-building, then by seal and salmon, and in this century partly by ... incipient land industries ... , but mainly by subsidiary marine industries, which have already attained considerable importance. Seals, salmon, herring, lobsters, and whales began to counteract the bad example set by the cod, for the horoscope of the island was evidently cast in the constellation Pisces, with Gadus . Morrhua as its presiding but not its only star....

There is no civilized nation in the world which is so marine in its character as Newfoundland. The sea has asserted its sway over Newfoundlanders; they are wedded with the sea and "'their children's eyes change colour with the sea". Cod, seals, herrings, whales, and the clownish lobsters mould their destiny, and their pathway to reality lies through a life dedicated to the sea.

It is sometimes hard to distinguish causes from effects in history, for effects mesmerize men's souls, which are the media through which causes operate, so that effects react on causes. But if anything in history can be considered a pure unadulterated cause, the sea – with its bays

and products is the first cause of the life, character, industry, government, and history of Newfoundland. The chief places are bays like Conception Bay, creeks like St. John's, or islets like Greenspond, Fogo, and
Twillingate; and its institutions were only outward and visible signs of
abiding geographical influences. Old-fashioned theories about population, sea-power, and economics, which were neither right nor wrong but
only suitable, co-operated with the conditions imposed by nature until
the nineteenth century. Then facts were too many for the theorists, and
settlers won their fishing victory over visitors, and in the hour, perhaps
because of their victory, these old-fashioned theories became unsuitable
and crumbled in the dust. In the last century, without any help from
theories, the old geographical facts began once more to produce the old
historical effects and Burin became a second St. John's, St. George Bay
a second Conception Bay, and Burgeo a second Twillingate. It is true
that in this last century Treaties had a little to do, just as theories once
had much to do, with the process; yet Treaties like theories were only
symbols and expressions of the idea men had of the situation, and their
idea was not invented but was a mere reflection of geographical facts.
Laws, Treaties, and theories had not much more to do with the history
of Newfoundland than its froth has to do with the rapids of Great Rat-
tling Brook.

What distinguishes Newfoundland from other countries is that after
four centuries of history it has no town or settlement of any importance – except that of Grand Falls [site of a pulp and paper mill, built
1905–09] – so far from the sea as Athens, Rome, or London, and all
its coves are occupied by what once were, and in many cases still are,
family settlements. Moreover, although fresh-water influences have
been present in its history for at least two centuries, not a single seaside
town is on a river of importance, unless it be Curling above the Bay
of Islands, though Cornerbrook as a pulpwood centre may some day
become a big town.

(Rogers, *Historical Gegraphy – Newfoundland*, 1911, 192–5, 236–8)

5

Harold A. Innis, *A History of the Canadian Pacific Railway*, 1923

⌐ In 1895 George Parkin said the fortunes of Canada and the Canadian Pacific Railway were "closely intertwined," and in 1911 J.D. Rogers stated that the railway was based on "idealism," a vital component of Canada's east-west "line of life." In 1923 Harold A. Innis published an entire book on the CPR, *A History of the Canadian Pacific Railway*. It is a history, but Innis devotes the first seventy-four pages to describing the character of three major Canadian regions, including the forces that fought for control within the regions and the forces that led the regions to Canadian union. He does this because he regards the CPR as a transforming agent, spreading civilization over northern North America. Before the CPR, he argues, civilization, meaning in a broad sense human activity, was confined to three major areas in what is today Canada: the Pacific Ocean drainage basin, the Arctic Ocean/Hudson Bay drainage basin, and the St. Lawrence River drainage basin. In describing the civilization and regional development in each basin Innis also examines the march toward Confederation and the underlying need for a transcontinental railway. In a marvelously laconic understatement, he writes that after the North-West Territories were united politically to Canada, "geographically there remained a discrepancy." The new railway spanned the three basins and was testimony that the civilizations in the basins would now be able to communicate and interact with one another. At the end of his discussion of the three civilizations/regions Innis says that they are the pillars, the abutments, on which the CPR is built. He seeks to provide some understanding of the nature, needs, and aspirations of the regions that will be crossed and served by the CPR, regions that will inevitably themselves be transformed, both internally and in their external relationships, once the railway is in operation. In some ways Innis' approach, emphasizing interacting forces and movement, anticipates studies in spatial inter-action characteristic of geographical research in the 1960s.

Born in 1894 in Otterville, Ontario, Innis was just under thirty when this book, his Ph.D. thesis, was published. In the succeeding twenty-nine years, until his death in 1952, he was to become Canada's leading social scientist and an internationally recognized communica-tions theorist. One wonders what the examiners made of the way the Ph.D. candidate presented his research. In it we already see the brilliant generalizations that characterize his later work. Seemingly disparate factors are brought together in a single sentence to explain far reaching geopolitical forces and then he rushes headlong into the next gener-alization. Echoes of Rogers' writing style abound, but Innis' content is based on an amazingly concentrated interpretation of where power rests in the Canadian political economy, presented in a spatial/regional reading, whereas Rogers' interpretation is a brilliant connecting of settlement location and routes as perceived in his mental map of Canada. Innis writes with a staccato, rapid, and powerful thrust in succinct punchy sentences, but this is counter-balanced by exceedingly long explanatory footnotes full of statistics and long quotations, not printed here.

Innis ignores the First Nations peoples except insofar as they are a vital element in the fur trade or enter into conflicts. He is very clear that "the influence of geographic features" is of particular significance in determining the development of a distinctive civilization in each region, but this is not simple-minded environmental determinism. Geo-graphic features are only one prominent conditioning set of elements in the complex process of development that concerns Innis. ⌒

INTRODUCTION

Though almost two centuries and a half elapsed between the date of the earliest attempt to discover the North-West Passage and the completion of the Canadian Pacific Railway in 1885, both occasions were landmarks in the spread of Western civilization over the northern half of North America. This spread of civilization was dependent on the geographic characteristics of the area and on the character and institutions of the people involved. The rapidity and direction of the growth of civilization were largely dominated by the physical characteristics, the geological formations, the climate, the topographical features, and the consequent flora and fauna which these conditions produced. Topographical features which determined to a large extent the character of the drainage basins, and consequently of the rivers, were of primary importance. The largest basin is drained by rivers flowing into Hudson Bay – the Nelson River, the Churchill River and the Saskatchewan rivers extending westward from 1,000 to 1,500 miles and draining practically the whole of the central plains of Canada. The next largest basin is drained by rivers flowing into the Arctic Ocean – the MacKenzie River extending over 2,000 miles. The St. Lawrence River and the Great Lakes drain the southern portion of Canada as far west as the head of Lake Superior. Territory west of the Rocky Mountains is drained by several short rivers flowing into the Pacific Ocean.... Early civilization was confined by these limits to three distinct areas. The Canadian Pacific Railroad was tangible evidence of the growth of civilization beyond these boundaries.

Within each area geographic characteristics important with respect to the spread of civilization differed widely. In the St. Lawrence drainage basin, with the exception of territory along the north shore of the river and of Lake Ontario and Lake Erie, the geological formation is chiefly Laurentian, consisting of granite and granite gneiss.... The northern drainage basin with the exception of territory in the more immediate vicinity of Hudson Bay which is largely dominated by Laurentian formation, consists of a vast tract of fertile territory gradually rising as it approaches the Rocky Mountains.... On the Pacific coast, the cordillera ranges are dominant.... It was with these regions that early explorers searching for a new route to the Orient came in contact. Settlements came in the wake of exploration and, taking root, grew up and flourished to no small extent under the influence of the particular characteristics of the areas involved.

(Innis, *History of the Canadian Pacific Railway,* 1923, 1–3)

a) The Pacific Coast

⌒ In discussing the Pacific Coast, Innis essentially analyzes regional resource development and associated spatial interactions over time. In some ways this is similar to Rogers' attempt to understand the threads and forces of the European exploitation of British Columbia. Looking at the period from the time of James Cook's explorations in the 1770s to the planning of the CPR a century later, Innis examines the struggle to gain administrative control of the Pacific Coast as a sequence of resources was exploited. He stresses the attempts to establish connections between the coast and the interior; the interrelationships of fur trade, gold, settlement, and agriculture; and the importance of river routes and the contribution of roads. Innis moves swiftly through time as fur companies and different political powers interact in an area where the international border between British North America and the United States was not established until the Treaty of Oregon in 1846. Distant governments in London, Washington, and on the St. Lawrence River were involved. At the end what interests Innis is the "character of civilization which developed in British Columbia," and the region's attitude toward building a railway. ☞

Encouraged by the offer of a government reward to the finder of a north-west passage from the west, Captain James Cook discovered Vancouver Island in 1778. The account of the voyages, published in 1784, was of significance in the emphasis placed on the fur trade as well as on the geographic discoveries. Following the publication of the account came a scramble of interests to share in the profits. Englishmen from China and India, and later from England, were followed by representatives of other nations....

The direction of the attention of various nations towards new territory was not the only result of such competition. Of more immediate importance was the beginning of settlement which accompanied the establishment of posts by the traders and which became essential in connexion with the long ocean voyages. The history of the early settlement was closely bound up with the fur trade. Nootka Sound, because it offered "greater facilities for obtaining water and provisions as well as for repairs than any other harbour in that part of the ocean," was the earliest centre of importance. But the dependence of Nootka on the fur trade was a source of weakness as well as a source of strength. Under the pressure of competition new areas more strategic for the conduct of the fur trade were found and Nootka disappeared.

Following the achievement of Alexander MacKenzie in crossing the Rockies and reaching the Pacific in 1793, increased competition came from the east.... Determination of the North-West Company to secure a larger share of the fur trade of the district occasioned the dispatch of Simon Fraser in 1806. The territory acquired by this invasion of interests coming overland from the east was consolidated by the establishment of posts and the beginnings of settlement at the heads of lakes and the forks of streams where furs could be collected most advantageously and where supplies of such food as fish and agricultural produce could be obtained most easily. Such vigorous prosecution of the fur trade necessitated an outlet on the Pacific coast. This explained the race between the North-West Company and the Pacific Fur Company, representing the Astor interest, for the occupation of the mouth of Columbia River....

Nor did the effects on settlement of the competition of the fur trade cease after the victory of the North-West Company in 1813, or after the amalgamation of that company with the Hudson Bay Company in 1821. Imperialism became aggressive....

The development of agriculture prepared the way for immigration and in turn was encouraged by immigration. The truce of joint occupancy involved in the indefinite compromise reached between Great Britain and the United States was an incentive to American immigration. An increase in American population strengthened the position of the United States in the final division of the area and at the same time hastened the date of division. Growth of the fur trade meant increased attention to agriculture for supply purposes, and routes of the fur traders were blazed trails for the earliest settlers. With the opening of routes by fur companies immigration was inevitable. Following the prosecution of trade by the early American companies, missionaries first came with the expedition of Nathaniel Wyeth, in 1834....

The treaty of 1846, which gave to United States territory south of the 49th parallel, was only a landmark in the inevitable progress of settlement, and decline of the fur trade. The forces responsible for growth of settlement in Oregon continued, indeed became more powerful in the growth of settlement in British Columbia....

New posts, whether devoted to fur trading and yet engaged in production of supplies, or devoted wholly to production of supplies to meet the demands of expanding trade, were, as ever, promoters of settlement. The increased attention to agriculture, and the growth of shipping resulting from the expansion of the fur trade along the northern coast led to a search for a new centre farther north from Fort Vancouver. The site chosen was Camosun Harbour on Vancouver Island, and in 1843 Fort Victoria was established.

Growth of settlement in British Columbia as in Oregon involved the attention of the home authorities.... The growth of settlement, with the consequent disappearance of the fur trade, was the force underlying the growing interest of the British authorities.

The Oregon treaty served to consolidate the victory of settlement over the fur trade, and in narrowing the arena of the struggle prepared the way for further conquest. The Hudson Bay Company was obliged to limit activities to British territory, and Fort Victoria, the new head-quarters, received additional stimulus. Columbia River, no longer a highway through British territory over which supplies and furs were carried from interior posts, was gradually abandoned, and surveys and new roads were made to the interior by way of the lower Fraser River. These changes also made necessary increased shipping facilities which gave greater incentive to the search for coal and stimulated the mining industry....

... Progress of the fur trade in the development of transportation routes to the interior was a stimulus to further settlement.... As in Oregon, so it was in Vancouver Island and in British Columbia – the fur trade had paved the way for settlement, and for its own disappearance.

The direction and progress of settlement were greatly influenced by the gold rush to the tableland between the Upper Columbia and the Thompson and Fraser Rivers, known as the Coteau region. The Fraser River route from the coast to this territory being shorter than the Columbia River route was generally followed, and demand for improvements on the route was consequently great.... The mining industry stimulated, and was stimulated by, construction and improvement of roads. The accessibility of the upper Fraser and the disappearance of claims in the older regions led to a northerly search, and to the discoveries along the Quesnel River in 1859, and in the Cariboo territory in 1860 and 1861. There followed the construction of a main road from Lillooet to Clinton in 1861, to Alexandria in 1863, and from Yale to Clinton in the same year, as well as the opening of trails to neighbouring districts....

Development of transportation facilities incidental to expansion of the fur trade hastened, and was rapidly hastened by, the gold rush. The interaction was evident in every phase of economic development. The gold discoveries and the continued output magically increased settlement. Immigrants, made enthusiastic by glowing accounts, came in thousands. Agriculture was stimulated. Foreign trade rapidly increased. Shipping consequently flourished. Coal-mining received a decided impetus. The direction and strength of economic activity was shown in the growth of Victoria opposite the mouth of the Fraser River, and. in the development of towns along transportation routes to the interior.

With the gold discoveries, and the rapid development of the country which they occasioned, renewed interest was given to the search for a shorter route between British Columbia and the older countries than by Cape Horn, by the Isthmus of Panama, or overland by San Francisco. The construction of roads in the interior became links in an ultimate overland route through British territory, and the home authorities, aware of the advantages of such a route, gave encouragement.... Formal encouragement was limited to moral support.

Canada, the eastern terminus of the proposed route, was more vitally concerned. The interest in British Columbia, aroused by the gold discoveries, became more pronounced with the later developments. The Overland expedition organized in Canada crossed the continent by way of St. Paul, Fort Gary [Garry], Fort Edmonton and Tête Jaune Cache in 1862. Additional zeal on the part of Canada for an overland route was occasioned by the possibilities of American aggression.... The purchase of Alaska in 1867, and the Northern Pacific project gave further cause for anxiety. Canada was generally interested.

The rapid development of British Columbia, the resulting encouragement of the British authorities, and Canadian interest in the proposed route, made possible a definite project. The depression which followed the exhaustion of the more important mines, its peculiar effects on the character of immigrants attracted by the gold rush, and the dissatisfaction of the people of Vancouver Island, with the increasing prominence of the mainland, and with the union of the two colonies in 1866 all were additional factors explaining the importance attached to a road to Canada. On March 18, 1867, a resolution was unanimously adopted by the Legislative Council asking Governor Seymour "to take measures without delay to secure the admission of British Columbia into the Canadian Confederacy." ... With further encouragement of the home authorities, a delegation was dispatched to Ottawa to arrange the terms of union. Canadian enthusiasm aroused by the agitation of Waddington for the construction of a transcontinental road generally sanctioned the terms proposed, and Canada was pledged to the commencement of the construction of a railway within two years and to its completion within ten years.

The character of civilization which developed in British Columbia was therefore an important factor in determining the character of the terms of union. Geographic features were of particular significance. The navigability of the Columbia River determined the direction of the routes of the early fur traders. The early trading posts and the inevitable beginnings of settlement were located at the junctions of rivers and the heads of lakes. Growth of settlement at the mouth of the Columbia River, due to the expansion of the fur trade in the interior, aroused national jealousies, and led to the controversy which was settled by the cession of Oregon to the United States. Moreover, it drove back the fur trade. With the new boundary line it became necessary to find new routes to the interior and to explore the lower Fraser. With new routes, Victoria and settlements along the Fraser came into prominence. Of more importance, came the discovery of gold, the rush of immigration, the changes in government, the hectic economic development, the construction of roads and the discovery of other routes along the lakes and rivers, the renewed interest of Canada and Great Britain, and the entry of British Columbia into the union. The direction, the extent, and the character of the development of civilization in British Columbia, were determining factors in the attitude of British Columbia toward the terms of union, just as they were determining factors in her attitude toward the fulfilment of those terms.

(Innis, *History of the Canadian Pacific Railway*, 1923, 3–21)

b) The Hudson Bay Drainage Basin

☞ For Rogers, space itself was the dominant factor that affected the development of the Great Plains, with the geographic forces playing out within the region's spatial circumstances. In Innis the balance shifts: space remains significant, but whoever possesses geopolitical power gains the upper hand. First there are the early fur trade rivalries of the companies operating from London and Hudson Bay versus those from the St. Lawrence River, a period that includes the establishment of the Selkirk settlement at Red River. By the early nineteenth century the dominating power of the Hudson's Bay Company is clear and then the chief problems to be worked out concern whether the Company's monopoly control will continue, the fundamental battle between fur trade and settlement, and the increasing interest of the United Province of Canada, in the context of potential United States imperialism, to wrest control of the interior lands from the Company. First Nations peoples and Louis Riel play critical roles in this process, although barely mentioned in Innis' examination of the interplay of wider underlying forces that determine who will gain control of the area. In this region the growth of civilization before 1870 was fundamentally characterized by the battle over whether agriculture, under Canadian guidance exercised at a great distance, would prevail over the fur trade. ☞

The growth of civilization in the great central plain east of the Rocky Mountains to which Hudson Bay affords access, was also important as a condition leading to union. In an effort to discover a north-west passage from the east, benefiting by knowledge gained in the voyage of Frobisher in 1578, and in the voyages of Davis in 1585 and later years, Henry Hudson entered Hudson Strait and sailed into Hudson Bay in 1610. Immediately, attempts were made to find a passage westward out of the bay. With these attempts came beginnings of trade in furs. In 1670, partly in compensation for the failure of the attempts, and partly as evidence of the growing importance of the fur trade on the North American continent, a charter was granted to the "Governor and Company of Adventurers of England trading into Hudson Bay."

The beginning of settlement in the great central plain known as the North-West was dominated, therefore, as in Oregon and British Columbia, by demands of fur trade. Vessels sailing under the auspices of the Hudson Bay Company followed the eastern coast of Hudson Bay to the southern extremity, and, later, turned northward along the western coast establishing posts at the mouths of rivers giving access to the interior. Establishment of posts at the mouths of rivers as strategic points for prosecution of the fur trade, and consequent development of trade with the interior, occasioned the competition of the French, who attempted to divert furs to the St. Lawrence. As a result of this competition, forts were constructed at important points, and harried attacks were made on Hudson Bay Company posts, which only ceased with the Treaty of Utrecht. Persistence of the French and penetration, largely under the direction of La Verendrye, of the great central plain as far as the Rocky Mountains by Lake Superior and the Winnipeg River, or the southern gateway, was accompanied by the construction of forts at the heads of lakes, the mouths of rivers; and along waterways giving access to the interior. This effective control of the fur trade on the part of the French made necessary the construction of posts and the undertaking of journeys to the interior on the part of the Hudson Bay Company

After the conquest of Canada, English traders followed the routes to central Canada discovered by the French. The disastrous effects resulting from aggressiveness of these individual traders led to establishment of the North-West Company in 1783. Competition from this company, increased in 1794 by the Jay Treaty, which restricted territory of the North-West Company by transferring several of its posts to the United States, and necessitated the adoption of more northerly routes, was a further stimulus to the efforts of the Hudson Bay Company from the north and occasioned an increase in the number of posts by both companies at competitive points and in more remote regions. Rapid expansion of the fur trade occasioned by such competition led to improvement of the shortest possible routes and to the growth of settlement at strategic points for the handling of furs and supplies....

The necessity of increasing settlement to furnish supplies and to handle traffic – considerations involved in expanding trade – was a factor favourable to the grant of land by the Hudson Bay Company to Lord Selkirk for colonization purposes, and to the establishment of settlement at the Forks of Red River. On the other hand, severity of competition, more pronounced because the step appeared to be a direct blow at the North-West Company, made settlement almost impossible. But difficult as such attempts at settlement were, the demands of the situation were ultimately such as to favour a permanent establishment, and the very ferocity of competition, making amalgamation necessary, unavoidably involved an increase in population.

Increase in population left settlement none the less subject to exigencies of the fur trade. Amalgamation of the companies brought the decline of Fort Alexander (Bas de la Riviere) and Fort William, formerly important, because they were situated on the main route of communication of the North-West Company, and the growth of Fort Douglas at the confluence of the Red and Assiniboine Rivers, the centre of the southern fur territory....

Friction between the company and the settlers was the natural result of such regulations. Of necessity the breach widened with increase in population and particularly with increase in the number of half-breeds – the larger and more unsettled portion. The consequent increase in agricultural products and in the returns of the annual buffalo chase began to exceed the company's demand, and there arose the cry of the settlers for a wider market....

... Increase in settlement and its demands for a wider market, and growth of trade with the United States – results of the accessibility of the route by way of the Red River to St. Paul – made this dissatisfaction more pronounced. Although the Red River Settlement had suffered from the neglect of the British Government, it had not entirely escaped notice, and with the signs of American imperialism, more serious in view of the rapid western development of the United States, a more active interest was assumed.

The fact that the fur trade and the company's monopoly were irrevocably opposed to settlement, ... began to be appreciated. Propaganda which had been carried on by imperialistic writers in the insistence on the benefits of a transcontinental road also had its effect. The necessity of renewing to the Hudson's Bay Company, the grant which expired in 1859, offered an opportunity to investigate the whole situation, and finally the Select Committee of 1857 was appointed, and at the same time, Captain Palliser was dispatched to explore the territory in question.

Prospect of relief of Red River Settlement from the monopoly of the company as a result of these activities was much more promising. Although Captain Palliser pointed out the difficulties of establishing communication between Canada and the settlement, he strongly favoured the formation of a British colony extending from the Red River to British Columbia, and in this other members of the expedition substantially concurred.

Canada was even more seriously concerned than Great Britain with the possibilities of American imperialism, and with the growth of trade between Red River Settlement and the United States. [Canada sent out expeditions to explore routes to Red River west of Lake Superior, and to investigate the potential of the land for settlement.] ...

The primary issue was the claim of the Hudson's Bay Company to the North-West territory which was in substance a question of fur trade or settlement....

The aggressiveness of Canada continued. Further negotiations with the Imperial Government led to the visit of Hon. George Brown in 1864, and settlement of the North-West territories was a feature included in the programme of the Confederation delegates in the following year. Evidences of American Imperialism, as shown particularly in the offer of Anglo-American capitalists to purchase the territory of the Hudson's Bay Company, proved a decided stimulus to further activity. The British North America Act included provisions for the annexation of the North-West territory and the first Parliament on December 12, 1867, adopted resolutions strongly advising transference of the jurisdiction and control of the region to Canada, and presented an address embodying these resolutions to the Imperial authorities....

The Hudson's Bay Company had ample reason to protest against Canadian activity.... after a long series of proposals and counter-proposals both Canada and the company agreed to accept the terms proposed by the Imperial authorities as a solution to the apparent deadlock. With minor adjustments, these terms were finally incorporated in a deed of surrender, signed November 19, 1869.

The continual and protracted struggle of settlement against the fur trade had apparently ended. Actually it became more violent....

On July 10, 1869, Col. J.S. Dennis was dispatched by the Minister of Public Works for Canada, to survey the territory preparatory to transfer. Trouble with the half-breeds was anticipated, but surveys were prosecuted until they were ordered to stop by a party under Louis Riel on October 11.

Faced with opposition Canada immediately notified the Imperial authorities, and placed upon them the responsibility of securing order. Although the Imperial authorities declined to accept these views and the argument continued, the Canadian Government took active measures to meet the situation. Mr. D. A. Smith was dispatched as a special commissioner with sufficiently elastic instructions to handle the questions involved, as were also, though with less authority, Mr. Thibault and Colonel de Salabery. At a late date Bishop Taché was added to the list. The success of these measures was evident in the growth of a feeling of unity in the settlement, and in the dispatch on March 22, 1870, of delegates by Red River Settlers to Ottawa to present their demands. The Canadian Government in response passed the Manitoba Act, which was accepted by the settlement, and which brought difficulties to an end. After a long controversy, payment was made to the Hudson's Bay Company, and with later adjustments the Province of Manitoba was formally admitted to the Dominion of Canada....

The entrance of the province of Manitoba into the Dominion of Canada, marked another victory of settlement over fur trade. The settlement which grew up, dominated in character and in location by demands of the fur trade, and which increased under the favourable conditions peculiar to the Red River Territory, after a long struggle, broke the bonds of monopoly of the trade which had given it birth. The establishment of posts at points geographically and technically strategic for the handling of furs and supplies, as shown in the growth of Fort Alexander, of Fort William (as well as in their subsequent decline with the amalgamation of the companies and the abandoning of the Lake Superior route), and of Fort Gary, was a tribute to the influence of geographic features, as was also the growth of trade between the Red River Settlement, and the United States by the Red River. The physical characteristics which conditioned the growth of trade with America, and which gave to the development of the United States a more threatening character were responsible simultaneously for the development of interest on the part of Canada and of Great Britain and for the consequent activities which led to the purchase of the North-west territories by Canada. Politically the

North-west Territories were united to Canada but geographically there remained a discrepancy to measure the seriousness of which requires a study of the position of Eastern Canada.

(Innis, History of the Canadian Pacific Railway, 1923, 21–52)

c) On The St. Lawrence

☞ This section foreshadows Innis' famous major works on the Canadian fur trade and cod fisheries. The St. Lawrence region is the entire area from Lake Superior to the Atlantic. The great rivalries between France and Great Britain for vast parts of North America and then the conflicts between Great Britain and the United States after the American Revolution are examined in the context of the role of the magnificent St. Lawrence River as an entry into the North American continent and how they relate to the impulse to construct a railway to the Pacific Ocean. Again it is a study of power relations, but this time related to the spatial connections of the St. Lawrence. Innis was so absorbed in the larger play of geopolitical factors that the nature of the Canadian Shield does not even enter the discussion, though, of course, the Shield was an exceedingly difficult barrier. This section tends toward an abstract analysis of spatial relationships, with Innis analyzing spatial connections along the lines explored by Joseph Bouchette and Rogers. Once more the section ends with a succinct summary, a listing of the essential factors at work. Here Innis introduces another regional characterization, saying that the three major civilizations or regions serve as great "abutments" or "pillars" that support the CPR in the Canadian regional constellation. Later in the book, in a statement that concludes his chapter on constructing the CPR, he returns to the three civilizations and says that with this new technology the civilizations, dynamic regions that they are, will change and become "more closely a part of a civilization narrowly described as Canadian, and typically, western." This idea also returns us to the beginning of the book, which Innis opened with a statement on the spread of Western civilization. ☜

Acceptance of the terms of union by Eastern Canada implied a pronounced development of civilization in the St. Lawrence drainage basin. It remains to examine more closely the character of that development in order to understand the difficulties involved in fulfilment of the terms. Discoveries of Columbus, in search of a short cut to the Orient, had turned the attention of Europe westward. As a result Cabot sailing from

England reached the northeast coast of the North American continent in 1496 [*sic*, 1497]. The discovery of the Newfoundland fisheries on this voyage, and the profitableness of this trade led to a race of fishermen of various nationalities to the new field. Effective prosecution of the fishing trade necessitated arrangements and accommodation on the shore for winter residents, as well as for the conduct of operations characteristic of dry fishing. Need for suitable harbours for these purposes brought about the establishment of posts at St. John's, and at other points along the coast of Newfoundland. Beginnings of settlement on the shore stimulated the growth of trade with the Indians, and these settlements served as bases for extension of fishing and discovery of new territory. The incentive supplied by the scramble for territory, and for the North-west passage, resulted in the success of Cartier in distinguishing the straits of Belle Isle from the maze of inlets characteristic of the eastern Newfoundland coast, in discovering the mouth of the St. Lawrence, and in penetrating the interior as far as Hochelaga (Montreal).

Biscayan whaling expeditions and fur traders followed the route opened by this voyage, and began to found a settlement at Tadousac, a point strategically located at the mouth of the Saguenay River on the St. Lawrence. Movement toward the interior continued slowly, partly because of climatic difficulties evident in the unsuccessful attempt at colonization of M. de Roberval.... It was not until the establishment of a colony at Quebec, in 1608, by Champlain, at a point on the St. Lawrence particularly well-fortified and strategically located for the conduct of the fur trade, that settlement gained a continuous foothold in Eastern Canada. Accessibility of the St. Lawrence made the establishment of posts in the interior largely unnecessary....

But eventually the expansion of the fur trade and the penetration to the interior which it involved occasioned a demand for the establishment of posts farther up the river....

The expansion of settlement in the interior brought difficulties. Proximity of the St. Lawrence River and its southern tributaries to the sources of the Hudson River brought the fur trade of the French into competition with the trade of the Dutch and later with that of the English, conducted from Albany.... As a result the French were seriously hampered and restricted in the conduct of the fur trade to the territory north and north-west of the St. Lawrence. The energies of settlement were necessarily directed toward defence....

More strenuous efforts were necessary if the country was to be held in the face of the increasing competition characteristic of the mainland,

and of the interior. More direct control of the colony was assumed and measures taken to increase the size of the settlement. Troops were dispatched, forts were constructed at strategic localities, and attacks made on Iroquois and English territory. The trade of the Iroquois was cut off by the establishment of strategic posts. North and north-west, such aggressiveness was equally in evidence. The English and the Iroquois retaliated with raids upon French settlements, with destruction of forts and a constant warfare on the French fur trade.

These activities and the accessibility of the St. Lawrence drainage basin explained the rapidity of the French discoveries to the south-west, as shown in the exploration of the Mississippi followed by the establishment of posts from the mouth of the St. Lawrence to the mouth of the Mississippi. This expansion tended to direct the energies of settlement toward the fur trade and consequently French civilization in North America was characterized by a lack of concentration other than at points strategic for the conduct of that trade. On the other hand, the inaccessibility of the interior because of the Alleghany Mountains and the lack of advantageous water-routes explained the relative neglect of western exploration on the part of the English colonies. The English pressing north-west around the Alleghany Mountains were directly opposed by the French pressing south-west by the Great Lakes and the Mississippi River and later by the Ohio River. With increasing national and commercial competition on the outlying coast, and with increasing competition arising from the expansion of the English colonies north-west along the Hudson, a struggle for supremacy was inevitable. The struggle proved the weakness of the French position. The English broke the long line of communication between French establishments in the capture of Fort Frontenac and occasioned the fall of posts to the west. The strength of a concentrated force brought about the downfall of the flanks at Louisburg and of the centre at Quebec.

Cession of Canada to England in 1760 closed a chapter in the history of colonial expansion. Settlement in the New England colonies previously barred by the Alleghany Mountains and the national ambitions of France moved steadily forward with the conclusion of the struggle. English fur traders, long held back by strategic posts of the French, pushed rapidly into new territory. The Indian wars in the struggle with Pontiac, though in part an aftermath of the concluded struggle, were also a phase of continued westward expansion.

Growth of settlement, of which the cession of Canada and the conquest of the Indians were results and of which they were in turn causes occasioned an increasing antagonism to regulations of the English colonial policy which eventually terminated in the American revolution.... The treaty of Versailles of September 13, 1783, concluded the struggle of the colonies for the removal of barriers restricting westward expansion.

The westward movement gained in momentum with the removal of political barriers. It spread north of the St. Lawrence valley, and particularly with the United Empire Loyalists' settlements began to appear in the territory north of Lake Ontario and Lake Erie. Anxious as to the outcome of this movement in the United States, Great Britain in addition adopted measures to encourage the settlement of that area. Meanwhile settlement in the lower St. Lawrence valley necessarily hampered by conflicts characteristic of the long struggle was at last favoured by peace.

But peace was of short duration. With continued westward expansion in the United States the St. Lawrence valley became increasingly coveted as an outlet to the sea. Among a number of other causes the advantages of its possession led to the war of 1812. The growth of settlement in Upper Canada and in Lower Canada and the effectiveness of British naval supremacy which was evident in earlier struggles, proved sufficient to frustrate the effort of the Americans to loosen British control.

The conclusion of peace was favourable to the expansion of settlement in Upper Canada and in the Western states. This expansion, which had been largely determined by the waterways and particularly by the St. Lawrence system, occasioned the further development of trade and commerce which necessitated the improvement of those waterways by the construction of canals. Activity in this direction was increased by national and commercial rivalry. Settlement also had its effect upon the development of other means of communication and these in turn promoted settlement.

Increased trade of Upper Canada occasioned further demand for improvements on the St. Lawrence....

... The work was stimulated by growing recognition of the value of the river as a highway for increasing trade of the rapidly expanding western states and of its possibilities as a link in a chain of waterways extending even to the Pacific and was vigorously prosecuted. The result of these exertions and of encouraging legislation was a rapid increase in the trade of the lakes.

Unfortunately abolition of the preference to Canadian products in Great Britain resulting from the repeal of the Corn Laws occasioned the diversion of trade by Oswego on Lake Ontario to New York and the

Atlantic coast. This diversion of trade stimulated and was stimulated by the agitation which culminated in the Reciprocity Treaty of 1854.

These disappointing results of this diversion, particularly to Montreal and Quebec, led, with the continually increasing traffic and constantly growing recognition of the possibilities of a route to the Pacific, to the encouragement and vigorous projection of geographically strategic railroads. Results were scarcely more promising, and the shorter distance to the Atlantic coast by Oswego continued to prove effective. In addition traffic was drawn by the Great Western and American roads through Niagara peninsula. The Grand Trunk to Portland and Rivière du Loup was in difficulty.

These failures to divert the increasing traffic of the western states and of Upper Canada through Canadian territory occasioned further activity in the renewal of an agitation for access to a Canadian port on the Atlantic open to winter navigation. Arousal of nationalistic anxiety consequent to American expansion, increasing recognition of the possibilities of a route to the Pacific, and development of the maritime provinces gave strength to the agitation, which bore fruit in Confederation and in construction of the Intercolonial railway. Largely in retaliation to the activity evident in these measures and in further legislative efforts tending to divert the increasing traffic of Canada and of the western states through Canadian channels, the reciprocity treaty was abrogated by the United States in r866. The abrogation gave further stimulus to intercolonial trade and to union and in turn to development of communication with the North-West bespoken in the purchase of the Hudson Bay Territory and in the admission of British Columbia and Manitoba to the Dominion.

(Innis, *History of the Canadian Pacific Railway,* 1923, 52–72)

[Innis has no separate heading in what follows directly on the above, but in this short conclusion he provides a brilliant summation of his general argument on transcontinental communications, beginning with Newfoundland and ending with British Columbia.]

A study of the events following the admission of British Columbia to the Dominion which involved the acceptance of terms obligating Canada to the construction of a road to the Pacific within ten years is facilitated by a review of the developments leading to the assumption of the obligation and an estimate of the strength of the third and last abutment of a Canadian transcontinental bridge.

Wealth of fisheries in the territory adjacent to the Banks of Newfoundland occasioned the early establishment of settlement, but national and commercial competition incidental to such wealth seriously hampered its growth. The maze of rivers and inlets characteristic of the region facilitated the beginnings of settlement but delayed exploration and discovery of the St. Lawrence River and the interior. Accessibility of the St. Lawrence to the interior to a large extent conditioned the rapidity of exploration of the St. Lawrence basin, of the Ohio River and of the Mississippi by the French, and together with its climatic severity determined the importance of the fur trade and consequently the slow growth of settlement. Relative inaccessibility of the area south of the St. Lawrence retarded exploration and led to the growth of settlement along the coast. The southwesterly direction of the St. Lawrence basin and the northerly direction of the Hudson River and the routes to the interior leading around the Alleghany Mountains provoked the conflict between English and French, the result of which was determined by the consolidation and superiority of the English settlements and the accessibility of the St. Lawrence which gave effectiveness to British naval supremacy. Steady growth of English settlements conflicted with the restrictive policy of British control of the St. Lawrence as it had with the French. Maintenance of British control on the St. Lawrence because of naval supremacy, and success of the colonies on land because of the ineffectiveness of naval supremacy in less accessible territory were the results of this struggle. Westward expansion; successful in the removal of barriers interposed by the French and the British, gaining access to the rivers characteristic of the middle of the continent, proceeded rapidly, and contributed to the development of Upper Canada and of the western states. Trade resulting from this expansion increased pressure upon the St. Lawrence, in which the question of control became a contributing cause of the war of 1812, and which necessitated the improvement of transportation facilities to the Atlantic coast. In the competitive struggle for this trade, Canada's handicap of distance to the coast, and the disastrous results, compelled improved facilities. The nationalistic dangers of western expansion contributed to the force of this factor and there followed the Intercolonial, Confederation and the admission of British Columbia to the Dominion.

The apparent weakness of Canada as the important abutment to a transcontinental bridge was not offset by the strength of the remaining abutments. The hectic and relatively slight growth of British Columbia and the relative unimportance of the Red River settlement could not avail in a task of such immensity. In each of the three areas roughly included in the drainage basins concerned, civilization had developed almost alone. It had grown and expanded beyond the boundaries set by topographical features. Politically these sections were united but economically the barriers proved to be of a character which tested severely and almost to the breaking-point the union which had been consummated. Political union rested upon pillars the weakness of which bespoke difficulties before the economic obligation essential to such union could be fulfilled. [Thus ends the Introduction.]

(Innis, *History of the Canadian Pacific Railway,* 1923, 72–4)

[Later in the book, at end of the chapter "Fulfilment of the Contract," Innis once more sums up his thoughts on the growth of civilization in three distinctive Canadian regions, and how they in turn changed as a result of new transportation technology.]

The fulfilment of the contract in the completion of the main line of the road was a significant landmark in the spread of civilization throughout Canada. It was significant of the strength and character of the growth of civilization within the boundaries of three distinct areas which served as buttresses for this transcontinental bridge. With this addition to technological equipment, the civilization of these areas changed in its character, and its extent, and became more closely a part of a civilization narrowly described as Canadian, and typically, western. These changes are recorded to some extent in the history of the Canadian Pacific Railroad and the history of Canada.

(Innis, *History of the Canadian Pacific Railway,* 1923, 128)

6

R. C. Wallace, *The Canadian Northland,*
1930

☞ R. C. Wallace (1881–1955), a distinguished geologist, professor of
Geology, University of Manitoba, 1912–28, commissioner of Northern
Manitoba, 1918–21, president of the University of Alberta, 1928–38,
and principal of Queen's University, 1936–51, wrote this article for *The
Book on Canada,* published by the Canadian Medical Association "On
the Occasion of the Meeting of the British Medical Association in Winnipeg, August 1930." It reveals how a British-born southern Canadian
who became a renowned academic views the North primarily for its
resources. That attitude was entirely characteristic of the period. Native
peoples or other northern inhabitants are not mentioned once. A note
of romance does appear, just as there was in J. D. Rogers when he
wrote about the Land of Heroes, but here it is related to the challenge
of northern resource development.

The recent use of the airplane for mapping, exploring for minerals,
and assisting in the initial development of ore bodies is stressed, as is
the importance of university-trained men in developing such resources.
That the North can serve as a link between east and west in Canada
is recognized and Wallace sees the role of the new "northern pioneer"
as helping to unify the country. Wallace seems to have had a vision of
northern industrial development and to have proclaimed that endeavour to be a unifying force. An overlooked and critical factor in the
actual overall situation is that northern Canada is the home of a large
proportion of Canada's First Nations people and the Inuit and their
welfare in a distinctive northern environment and resource base is an
essential aspect of Canada. An understanding of that situation is not
seen here.

At the time Wallace wrote, the North's role as a powerful national symbol was being expressed and established by the Group of Seven painters, but he does not refer to that. The article takes a masculine-only, southern Canadian approach to northern Canada, the kind of thinking that was replied to forty-seven years later by Thomas Berger in his report, *Northern Frontier: Northern Homeland*, which we will see later. ⌒

In the early days of exploration and trade, interest was focussed in the territory which we are now accustomed to call the Canadian Northland. The Hudson's Bay Company established itself in 1670 on the shores of Hudson Bay, though not for a century did that company seek to build posts inland. It did so then, however, because the fur-trade, through independent traders, had found its way to Montreal by way of the Great Lakes. The great achievements in travel and exploration – the journey of the boy Kelsey far into the buffalo plains, the expeditions of La Vérendrye and his sons up the Saskatchewan River, Samuel Hearne's epoch-making journeys across country in search of the Coppermine River, Alexander Mackenzie's voyages down the great river that bears his name, Franklin's trips across to the Coppermine River and along the Arctic coast, and the great search for the northwest passage, in which Franklin is the central figure – all this background of stirring achievement rests on the territory which we now call the Canadian Northland. And until after this period of exploration, there was little of interest in the south country west of the Great Lakes. Even as late as 1875 the intention of the sponsors of the Canadian Pacific Railway was to build across the Rockies by the northern route – the Yellowhead Pass – through which the Canadian National Railways now passes, and there were not lacking those who strongly urged the claims of the Peace River route two hundred and fifty miles further north than the Yellowhead Pass. That fact reveals the north-mindedness of Canada even as late as sixty years ago.

With the advent of the railway into the western prairies there came the period of agricultural expansion of Canada, the carving out of the western provinces and the elevation of Canada to the important position she now occupies as a wheat-producing country. During this period the Northland has been of lesser significance. Attention has been concentrated on the problems of the plains, and they have been all-absorbing. The tide of immigration which flowed into Canada from the time of the completion of the Canadian Pacific Railway until 1913 flooded the prairies, but did not move northward. The trapper continued to pursue his calling, the fur companies to supply the needs of northern peoples and to purchase the furs which were almost the only inducement to northern endeavour. A great chapter was being written in Canadian economic history, and the energies and interests of the population of central Canada were absorbed in establishing western agriculture and eastern industry to meet in part the needs of the growing West.

But the pendulum of time again swings northwards in matters Canadian. The settling of agricultural spaces will still go on for many years, and the process will call for sound statesmanship and able administration. The knitting together of agricultural progress with industrial development will be Canada's major task for the next half-century. But the youth of Canada listen for the call of romance, nurtured as they are on Canada's romantic history. There has been a new note in those last few years which has had in it, for young people, something of the discriminating appeal of the call of the pied piper. Mr. Stefansson, the Arctic explorer, has shown us that the so-called barren lands are capable of supporting immense numbers of reindeer which may add material contributions to Canada's meat supply, and already steps have been taken to introduce the European reindeer into the lower Mackenzie valley. Ontario has now a history of twenty-five years of remarkably successful conquest of northern territory in the mining of nickel, copper, silver, and gold from the unyielding Precambrian rock; and the example of Ontario has fired the enthusiasm of Quebec, Manitoba, Saskatchewan, and the North West Territories north of Alberta to similar endeavour with very tangible results. The boundaries are being pushed back from the south, not from the north as in the early days, and the conquest of Canada's last unknown territory is proceeding apace. The conquest is proceeding, in point of fact, at a rate which fifteen years ago was not considered possible by those who were engaged in mapping and exploring northern territory by the laborious method of canoe travel. The aeroplane has conquered distance and has provided the means of mapping territory with amazing accuracy where mapping was heretofore slow, difficult, and inadequate. At the present rate of progress, northern Canada could be completely mapped in the next fifty years if it were considered advisable so to do. By the methods in vogue fifteen years ago, it would have taken many centuries to map the Canadian Northland, and there would have been little hope of ever presenting a completely accurate map of the topography of northern Canada. The journey from Churchill to the Coppermine River, which Samuel Hearne reached with such difficulty after two unsuccessful attempts a hundred years after the Hudson's Bay

Company had established itself on Hudson Bay, can now be made in two days by aeroplane, and at any time of the year except when the ice is making or breaking in the inland lakes. When faced with the aeroplane, the vast distances of the Northland have shrivelled into insignificance, as did Alice before the rabbit hole when on her voyage of exploration into territory hitherto unknown.

In the minds of the people of Canada, the Northland is synonymous with the Canadian shield of Precambrian rock which flanks Hudson Bay to the east, south, and west, and stretches southwards into Lake Superior and beyond the confines of Canada into northern Michigan, northern Wisconsin, and northern Minnesota. While the Precambrian shield is not the whole of the Northland – for the lower Mackenzie valley is beyond its confines, and the islands of the Arctic are of later age – and while much territory belongs to the southern edge of the shield, which cannot be strictly called Canadian North, yet this geological unit presents such strongly defined characteristics, which are so typically northern, that for practical purposes it may with reason be thought of as the Canadian Northland. It is the early continent, the oldest rock system in North America, and through all the vicissitudes of geological history remained for the most part above sea level, while from time to time the greater part of the continental area was submerged. During the long years since its formation, it has been deeply denuded by atmospheric forces, and in late geological times was swept bare by the ice sheets that moved southwards over its surface. The smooth hummocky expanses of granite and gneiss which stud the whole Precambrian area bear many traces of the movement of those ice-sheets. The rivers spill from rock basin to rock basin. The jack pine has a precarious foothold on the almost bare rock surface and on the sand ridges, while in clay-covered areas spruce and poplar flourish; and in the undrained, swamps and muskegs tamarack and black spruce may find satisfactory conditions for growth. Deep though the erosion has been through the geological ages, there are still to be found the roots of some of the ore-bodies which were formed during the periods of intense volcanic activity which characterized the Precambrian area. The search for these ore bodies has been the driving force behind the new attack on the fastnesses of northern Canada. The movement began with the discovery of the Cobalt silver camp in 1905, and was followed by the discovery of the Porcupine goldfields in 1909. Since that time has come the development of the Kirkland Lake gold area in Ontario, the Rouyn copper-zinc area of northern Quebec, the Flin Flon-Sherrit-Gordon copper-zinc area of northern Manitoba arid Saskatchewan, and the new discoveries of copper and zinc in the Sudbury field of Ontario, famous since the eighties of last century as an outstanding nickel deposit of the world. To these ore-bodies railway transportation has been made available, and communities of considerable size have been established in the mining and refining of the ore-bodies, in the raising of garden products for the new populations, and in the carrying on of general business. New discoveries are being tested out in many areas, and the aeroplane is made use of to explore territory far removed from present railway facilities. Mining machinery for exploration purposes has been accommodated to the new conditions, so that it may be taken down and transported in parts by aeroplane to any desired locality. There will still have to be faced the problem of providing some low-cost form of transportation to deposits, when "proved up," at distances from present railway facilities so great that the provision of railway communications would be unjustifiable.

Power development and the pulp industry have followed the mining industry northwards, and, particularly in Quebec and the eastern part of northern Ontario, these two phases of northern development have made a very significant contribution to Canada's economic welfare. With power has come in Quebec as well the establishing of chemical manufactures, which have transformed part of northern Quebec from wilderness into hives of modern industry. In many parts of northern Canada progress will go forward under most satisfactory conditions, if the development of power is associated not only with mining, but with pulp manufacture as well. The other possible industries of the north, fishing and the fur business, are accessory to the three major industries already discussed. There are many lakes where fish are abundant. The amount of annual catch must be carefully restricted in order that the supply of fish be not depleted. The fur industry cannot be maintained as settlement moves northwards. To an ever increasing degree, as time goes on, fur-farming will be engaged in to supplement the natural catch which will undoubtedly diminish as settlement proceeds.

The traveller from eastern to western Canada is invariably impressed by what appears to be the barren waste of territory north of Lake Superior and westwards to Winnipeg. It is in territory of that type that the industries which have been here described are making progress. A definite contribution is being made to Canada's economic welfare in areas which seemed inhospitable to economic treatment. But there is another phase of the situation which should be stressed. Eastern Canada. and Western Canada are separated by this Precambrian rocky country, which has not been favourable to settlement. There is a great wedge driven deep into Canada from the north, which has pushed apart the eastern and western people. Economic philosophies have developed from different backgrounds and environments; political conceptions have been at variance; and there has been serious concern to those who have looked forward to a national consciousness which would represent a reasonably united viewpoint on fundamental economic principles. There is now developing throughout the northland a consciousness which will provide the uniting link between East and West. The northern pioneer, whether he be trapper, lumberman, or miner, is of one type from Quebec to the North West Territories. His outlook is the same, his method of approach to his own problems is the same, and his contribution is the same. His is an industrial outlook, but closely knit to the raw materials with which he has to deal. There is nowhere in Canada a more united consciousness than that which is possessed by the newer population in Canada's Northland. It is a link of the finest kind and will play a part of which many Canadians are as yet but dimly conscious, in uniting the separate populations of the far-spread Dominion. And there is another factor which gives encouragement. The development of northern industries calls for very high scientific, technical, and engineering skill. There are now to be found in every newer settlement throughout the north young men of university training, skilled, resourceful, and thoroughly competent to handle themselves under northern conditions. They have the conservative attitude of the scientist, and the vision of the northern pioneer. The contribution which this army of young men will make to Canada's welfare in the next sixty years will be greater than even an optimist would dare to forecast.

(Wallace, "The Canadian Northland,"
The Book of Canada, 1930, 77–82)

7

Bruce Hutchison, *The Unknown Country: Canada and Her People*, 1942

It was wartime, 1941, when Bruce Hutchison (1901–1992), one of Canada's leading journalists, travelled from Nova Scotia to British Columbia by bus, train, car, and even by snowmobile to explore the character of Canada as seen in and through its major regions. On impulse an editor at Coward-McCann, a New York City publisher, had commissioned him to write a book on Canada. Hutchison was not certain what kind of book he should write; he was discovering the country himself, so the title of the eventual book was appropriate.

Hutchison, a British Columbian, had been based in Ottawa for many years as a national newspaper reporter and journalist and had completed assignments in the United States as well. He had good contacts in many parts of Canada, related well to people, and spoke easily with individuals in all walks of life, so the book includes much first-hand reporting on local areas. He had a sound knowledge of Canadian history and, as a journalist concerned with national affairs, a keen insight into government and the Canadian political economy, and for this commission did further research in the Parliamentary Library in Ottawa. Thirty-five years later in his autobiography Hutchison wrote: "I painted my own primitive picture of Canada when my eyes were innocent, my mind uninformed but still pliant, the world as yet unspoiled" (Hutchison, 1976, 163). It is that freshness that makes the book so interesting, together with its deep insight into the life of different parts of Canada. *The Unknown Country* was written quickly in the midst of other work, composed in what Hutchison calls disjointed fragments. That is part of the power of the book, because each region is approached from its own situation and characteristics, and each portrait rings true. Published in 1942 in the United States, and the following year in Canada, the book had gone through twelve Canadian printings by 1964, and remained in print in hardcover until 1977, and in paperback until 1985. Canadians still turn to it today for insights into their country.

Geographers used to speak about the personality of a region, a very difficult thing to portray effectively. Hutchison's book immediately caught on with the public and lasted because he unerringly presents the personality of each of the major Canadian regions, usually through portraying the experiences and feeling of the inhabitants themselves. Often he takes his theme on the character of a region from a conversation, perhaps with someone he meets on the street, or perhaps with a leading politician.

Most of *The Unknown Country* is presented from the position that Canada has until recently been a British colony, or at least under British influence, but that in the 1940s the United States looms large in our national, cultural, and economic existence. Indeed, in his Foreword Hutchison writes:

[This book] is written in the belief, reinforced by much traveling among them, that Canadians and Americans really know very little about Canada; that Canada is among the important nations of the world, the least known in its real content; that the future relations between Canada and the United States will inevitably form one of the basic factors of world politics; and that these relations are widely misunderstood and often misrepresented.

In the selections below I follow Hutchison's sequence, going major region by major region. He starts with Quebec, goes on to Ontario and the Maritimes, and then ends with the Prairies and British Columbia. I have taken out his descriptions of major cities and for comparative purposes placed them in a separate chapter, together with selections on many of the same cities from his second book, *Canada: Tomorrow's Giant,* published fifteen years later, which is considered in the next chapter. In this second book Hutchison visits different local areas than those covered in the first work, smaller places where possible, so there is little point in making similar side by side regional comparisons as I do with cities.

In *The Unknown Country* Hutchison illuminates what he considers the fundamental characteristics of each major section of the country: Quebec's continuing influence by the Roman Catholic Church and its cultural (often, in the terminology of the time, called racial) distinct-iveness; Ontario's industrial strength because of tariff protection that is detrimental to other sections of Canada; the Maritimes' lagging staples economy, especially as compared to Central Canada; the Prairies' ethnic diversity and dependence upon agricultural commodities vulnerable to world markets; and British Columbia's quality of being a perpetually new country with outsize natural features and resources, great geographical variety, and much wilderness. Canada in the early 1940s has just passed through a great economic depression and parts of the country that had not benefited from the rapid industrialization associated with the First World War still show the shabbiness of hard times. Hutchison also sees considerable sectional strains arising from protecting industry with tariffs. These gave industrialized Central Canada sheltered Canadian markets, while other parts of the country, such as the Maritimes and the Prairies, were dependent on selling their commodities into world markets with their fluctuating prices. The excerpts follow the order of the chapters in the book. ☞

I CHEZ GARNEAU, QUEBEC

☞ The duality of Canada, with its two founding peoples from Europe, the French and the British, is one of Hutchison's central themes in discovering Canada. He wrote in the period before recognition of the importance of the First Nations people and ethnic groups other than French and British in the life and power structure of Canada. To penetrate the French Canadian character Hutchison begins at the village of St. Pierre, on Île d'Orleans opposite Quebec City, where he stays with a family and also talks with the local priest. ☞

Canada is not English – that is the first thing to understand. Half of it has no British blood. A third of it speaks French. It is a North American country, its people a North American people, as old on this continent as the people who are called Americans. Two great races are here. One came from France but has been separated from its first homeland for nearly two centuries and knows no land but this. The other came from England but not until it had lived for several generations in the American colonies and become part of the New World. It is because these blood streams have not yet merged, because their cultures have remained so well balanced and each so vigorous, that Canada is still a dual personality – a country not fully formed, not crystallized yet into final shape and substance, young and awkward but with youth's strength in its lanky body, youth's restlessness and uncertainty and love of life in its heart. No guidebooks have pictured it, no historian has told its story, no poet has sung its song. To the world it is unknown; to itself, like the mind of young manhood, still a mystery....

[Hutchison stays with a French farmer, M. Garneau, in St. Pierre on the Île d' Orleans] We went out on the porch and looked down the street. The village clung to this narrow road, every house grasping it for support and comfort – the oblong, hip-roofed houses of Quebec, with fat, comfortable chimneys at each end and a little porch in front, the true Canadian architecture, brought from France but so deeply rooted in our soil as to be almost native. Like a Christmas card it looked, the village of St. Pierre, with its double line of gaily painted houses laughing at the snow....

... Here was a mixture of lusty worldliness and unquestioning faith that we tortured Anglo-Saxons can never understand. And they are wealthy, too, in real wealth, independent, lacking nothing of real value on an income that we would consider penury.

These are the things that distinguish the French Canadian from the rest of America – his grip on things, on the earth, on reality, where we have come to accept shadow for substance, radio jokes for the simple, profound humors of the day's work, desiccated breakfast powders for bread, and the synthetic celluloid fornications of the screen for life....

[Hutchison visits the local priest.] The curé closed the door to [the front] room and led me into another at the right of the hall. He sat down at his desk and quietly filled his pipe, waiting for me to speak. Unhappily, he knew no English but he listened patiently to my bad French and replied as simply as he could, asking me eagerly about Western Canada, the outer immensities of his country that he never hoped to see, for his flock was here, old men called on him in the night, and he would never leave. Here, in his black robes, this priest of a tiny village represented the undying power of the Roman Catholic Church in Quebec, the church's most faithful child. Nothing can prevail against the curé. He is the center of life in the village as his church is the gateway of life and death. Just such men as this young man before me had come out to New France with the first white soldiers, carried their little wooden crosses and beads on foot and by canoe into the forests, into the west, down the Mississippi, lived with the Indians, died of their diseases, suffered their torture, their filth and their obscenities....

We talked there for about an hour, of Quebec, and the war, and of the Island, and almost pathetically he kept asking me about those other countries that he would never see, nodding thoughtfully as I tried to tell him, smiling politely at my jokes. I left him at his door, a tall, solemn figure in his black robes, a young man who might have known wealth, luxury, women. I waded through the snow and he went back to his parishioner, the troubled old man who needed his comfort.

Next morning Madame Garneau had us up early to catch the snowmobile for Quebec City. It came along just as we were finishing breakfast, and M. Garneau, sighting it through the window, rushed out wildly in his shirt sleeves, and hailed it from the porch. We bundled aboard this contraption which has skis in front and caterpillar treads behind, the only mechanical device which can travel the island roads in winter. It was already full of farmers bound for town, and Amelie, Madame's niece (superbly turned out, painted and perfumed), sat on my knee and I didn't mind.

M. Garneau piled our grips in, talking fast. He was very proud of the snowmobile. It seemed to represent progress on the Island. It was part of the mysterious process of change which he had glimpsed vaguely – part of the revolution which long ago had shaken the world and now penetrated even here. But Madame stood on the porch of the house, hands folded in front of her, calm, immovable, her placid face watching us. She waved once and nodded gravely. Not for her the new machines, the new ideas. She stood there unshaken and unafraid, strong as Quebec itself, part of the past, rooted deep in the soil that Frenchmen have tilled here for three hundred years, part of the warp and woof of countless looms in countless little white houses like this. But a grim, sad figure after all, a childless woman – *"pas des enfants."*

The snowmobile started. Madame raised her hand slowly. Her husband waved and shouted and grinned after us. The machine heaved and lurched through the snow and everybody inside began to talk and laugh in an atmosphere stifling with the smoke of *tabac.* Yes, they will mechanize these people some day, with machines like this, bring them our civilization, teach them our clever ways, and our vague disease of glut and surplus and satiety.

(Hutchison, *The Unknown Country,* 1942, 8–19)

2 THE ROCK, QUEBEC CITY

☞ In Quebec City, which he calls The Rock, Hutchison continues his quest for the French Canadian character by talking to leading citizens about the French Canadian outlook on life. ☜

Politics they take very seriously in Quebec. These people have been brought up to politics, to law, to the classics. Every well-to-do farmer or tradesman wants his son to be an *avocat*, a doctor, or a priest. Most of the old aristocratic families are heard of no more; a lusty middle class, a comfortable and earthy bourgeois class, has risen to rule Quebec, and a poor country lawyer is the leader of the race, but still the classical tradition persists, and young French-Canadians find that they cannot compete in the crudities of modern industry with the young men of the English-speaking provinces. Yet, beside an educated French-Canadian, with his exquisite speech, his courtly manners, his fluid gestures and mobile face, the flowing cadence of his speech, any other North American must feel like a barbarian.

M. Langlois, a gorgeous old lad with white mane of hair, explained it to me with a sigh. "Our education, our life," said he, "is based on the premise that religion is the center of man's existence. Therefore, religious education comes first. Idealism is ahead of materialism. But our young man, trained in the classics, in the humanities, in religion, competes with a fellow who has studied engineering and business. Naturally, he is outdone. But we are learning."

Yes, learning our ways, learning business and industry, studying in technical schools. But will it mean the loss of something much more valuable? You wonder. Meanwhile the French-Canadian feels a sense of inferiority, and every so often a shrill cry of race is heard in these parliament buildings. A mountebank appears, carries the old torch among the villages, tells the habitants that the English are ruining them, that the English have all the best jobs, the capital and the power, and for a little while there is wild talk of an independent Quebec, a free French nation on the shores of the St. Lawrence. It is sure-fire, but never lasts.

Your French-Canadian is too shrewd not to know on what side his bread is buttered. By a law of 1774 the English, wiser than they were in the Thirteen Colonies, guaranteed the French-Canadian's religion, his language, his laws; and he knows they would be safe under no other flag. No state of the Union would ever enjoy such freedom and privileges as Canada has granted Quebec.

The two chief races of Canada have lived apart, seldom intermarrying, but they have learned to live in peace in a common country; and, though they were divided as never before by the first World War (which the French never considered their business) they are more united than ever by the second – a fact seldom noted by foreign journalists who visit Montreal for a day, talk to a few discredited politicians, and announce a deep schism in Canada. At this writing no schism has appeared, but the contrary. Yet if Canada should adopt a policy of complete military conscription and Quebec should oppose it as before, the old trouble might recur....

Old M. Langlois sighed. Why, he asked, cannot the French remain the cultured, religious people, the protectors of the classics, the artists and dreamers while the English build the factories, work the machines? It is a pleasant fancy, but the modern world drives the French-Canadian out of his study, his classical university courses. Ah yes, it is true, says M. Langlois, the young no longer honor even the church as they should, but it is of no significance really. These young agnostics of twenty will be faithful sons of the church at forty, when they have sons of their own. Of course, there are "movements" in Quebec, some labor talk, but the labor unions are led by priests. What harm can come of them? A few priests may have "tendencies" but, if so, can be moved by the bishop to another parish.

The French-Canadian calls himself generally a Liberal in politics. He is the chief surviving Tory of the world.

(Hutchison, *The Unknown Country*, 1942, 36–9)

3 THE WOOD CHOPPERS, QUEBEC

☞ Hutchison visits the village of St. Féréol, 42 km below Quebec City, just north of the St. Lawrence River, located in an area where industrialization has appeared. Change is coming to Quebec. ☜

[Hutchison is in a hotel in St. Féréol.] ... we sat in the parlor which declared itself above, with a stuffed white owl, a gigantic waterfowl, unidentified, a colored print of King George V made when he was under forty, a reproduction of "The Angelus," and a radio. Always a radio, in the smallest cottage, with French coming over it from Montreal. Ideas are flowing in here, into the towns and smallest villages. What these ideas are doing to Quebec, how they are changing the old values and the old virtues, how much they are helping to unite the two races of Canada and break down old barriers – this is one of the great imponderables and unknowables of Canadian life.

A couple of young French-Canadians were living at Morel's – engineers from the big paper mill down the road. They talked, in flawless English, about the mill, about their work, about costs, markets, methods of manufacture. Here was the basic change that sweeps the old French province – young men learning to compete with the English-speaking Canadians in their own business, in manufacturing, in modern technics.

All up and down the St. Lawrence the smoke of English-speaking capital billows up beside the French church spires, hard by the little narrow farms which, cut and re-cut, handed from father to son, all run down to the river edge. Back in the hills the streams and rivers are dammed for power by English-speaking corporations. Quebec, which was agricultural, peasant, as simple as St. Féréol, is being industrialized by the enterprisers of the other provinces. French people leave their farms to live in the new industrial towns and cities, and there they find that life is not what they used to think. It is infinitely more complex and difficult and glittering. There are pleasures they never heard of, and economic problems, class problems, wage problems unknown back in the village, where the curé could settle anything, from birth to death. Instead of the curé there are here agitators who stir them up against the owning class and against the English-speaking Canadians. Soon Quebec begins to develop a self-conscious proletariat, where it had once only a carefree peasantry.

The church grows worried. Some of the people in the towns are skeptical and question the old teachings. The ruling classes are worried also. The politicians find all sorts of new pressures, new cries, and new notions. An attempted New Deal by a group of charlatans, fattening on this blind new urge, has plunged the thrifty province into debt.

What is happening to Quebec, the most conservative, peaceful, innocent part of the whole New World? Civilization is coming to Quebec, that is all. The civilization of machines. From the window we would see the dark smokestacks of the mill and hear its whistle. Up and down the river, and back into the vast wooded interior, whistles are blowing and men are herding together as they have herded in every other aging civilization, as they herded into Rome....

But Quebec will change. It is changing. The machine is coming to Quebec, and the thing we call civilization. Yet still the bells peal along the river, above the whistle of the mill.

(Hutchison, *The Unknown Country*, 1942, 49–59)

4 ST. LAWRENCE RIVER: THE READY WAY TO CANADA

⌐ Joseph Bouchette, J.D. Rogers, and Harold Innis all sang the praises of the St. Lawrence, but none approaches Hutchison's lyrical description of the great river and its central role in Canada's life. This is one of the many highly personal meditations or causeries that Hutchison inserts between each major chapter: they capture deep-felt, often romantic aspects of Canada. The italics are his. ⌒

The statesmen made a treaty. They signed it in the gloomy East Block of Ottawa on a cold spring morning. In the silence of an historic moment the cameras clicked and the pens scratched. They would tame the River to men's uses.

Did the River hear the faint scratching of the pens? Was the sound of cameras perceptible beside the falls of Niagara, in the whirlpools, eddies, and rapids? No, the River only smiled that morning and went about its spring business of breaking the winter's ice, for it knew men would never tame it. They might use it, grasp a little of its power for themselves, build cities at its sides, and launch their ships upon its current, but nothing could alter by more than a few yards the irresistible current of the St. Lawrence or curb its yearning towards the sea.

How often the River had seen men calculate its future and measure its value! "And the said men did, moreover, certify unto us," wrote Cartier, "that there was the way and beginning of the great river of Hochelaga, and ready way to Canada, which river the farther it went the narrower it came, even unto Canada, and that then there was fresh water which went so far upwards that they had never heard of any man who had gone to the head of it."

So Cartier, sailing into a bay at the River's mouth on August 10, 1535, the feast day of St. Lawrence, named the ready way to Canada after that holy man....

Sir John A. Macdonald, a lad fresh out of Scotland, saw the blue water over the side of the ship – wee lad, did he hope then to rule this land beside the river and make it a nation? Laurier, his successor, saw the gray Ottawa join the blue St. Lawrence and both flow in bands of separate color like the two races of Canada, their difference clearly marked, but in perfect unity.

The ready way to Canada, and the statesmen sign their treaty, the engineers dream their dreams, and the St. Lawrence rolls on, draining the interior of the continent, bearing outward the loaded ships as easily as it bears the fine earth, the silt, the rain, the ice – rolls on, knowing that it will bear races of men yet unborn and still roll after all races of men have gone. Will roll as long as rain falls in America and water seeks the ocean.

(Hutchison, *The Unknown Country,* 1942, 129–31)

5 THE WEDGE, ONTARIO

☞ In the phrase, "The Wedge," Hutchison catches the great good fortune of southern Ontario: it is a highly productive agricultural tract
or wedge thrust into a strategic location between great lakes, in the
industrial heart of the continent. The wedge is Rogers' triangle. In
Ontario Hutchison did not have to seek out the subtle hidden forces
and feelings that affected land and people as he had to do in Quebec;
the forces were imposed upon him as a "businessman" drove him
by car from Toronto to Niagara. In Quebec Hutchison meets people
whom he names and who have substance; in Ontario he travels with
an anonymous businessman, the "Man from Toronto," whom he probably contrives as a caricature of the industrial ferment that is shaking
Ontario. Today, seventy years later, it is industry that is suffering in the
early twenty-first century because of new global competitive forces.
Giving his nostalgia free play, Hutchison builds up an extreme contrast
between the beautiful countryside and the "suppurating sores of modern industry."

Hutchison spends little time describing the Canadian Shield; it is part
of the immensity of Ontario. However, he does reveal why a man who
grew up in British Columbia cannot feel at home in the Shield. ☞

Between Lake Huron on the west, Lakes Erie and Ontario on the south,
and the Ottawa River system on the north, a ragged Canadian wedge
juts southward, across the forty-ninth parallel of latitude, deep into the
United States.

It is physically almost an island, surrounded by lake and river. Economically it is still more insular behind, a Chinese wall of tariffs. Spiritually it is isolated from the rest of Canada. Yet it is the very core and hub
of Canada.

Here beats its great industrial heart, with the steady beat of forges, factories, and arsenals. Here breathes steadily its lung, sucking commerce
through river and canal. Here also is the stomach, absorbing nourishment from the rest of the country with ravenous appetite. Here is the
chief nerve ganglion of electrical power. At the top of the wedge is the
nation's brain in Ottawa.

To this vital organic region, you might almost say, the rest of Canada
forms but the extremities, supplying the food, digesting the products. Cut
the wedge out of Canada, run the boundary straight along the forty-ninth
parallel, and Canada's heart stops beating, it suffocates and collapses.

In economic power, in money, in politics, in population, the wedge of Ontario is the true center of Canada. Yet in some ways it is the least typical part of the country. Most of us in the west came from there originally and scattered everywhere, but we can never return. Our birthplace is forever a stranger to us and its people not of our ways. Why, we do not rightly understand. We only know that these eastern people are different from us so that a westerner – or a French-Canadian or a Maritimer for that matter – does not feel at home here.

This is more than envy of Ontario's power and prosperity, or jealousy of its tariff, which costs us so dear. Urban Quebec around Montreal is economically part of the same wedge, and shares its fortunes, but in outlook is far removed from it. No, it is the life of industrial Ontario which baffles us, the feeling, the attitude. We take our goods from there, we take our politics largely from there, our business management, but we do not take our ideas. We feel, we who have gone from there and spread across the nation, like the son returning in middle age to his father's house, which he loves and sighs for, but cannot live in any more.... [Hutchison has more to say on this theme in his discussion of Toronto, printed in chapter nine.]

Something deep is stirring here. The old values are in flux. You cannot mistake that from the current character of Ontario politics. As this is written there presides at Queen's Park, in the wrinkled old legislative buildings, an important phenomenon of Canadian life, Mr. Mitchell Hepburn, whose memory, if not his person, will long outlast these present stirrings. That the Family Compact, within a century, could have heaved up such a successor must surely puzzle historians....

... Hepburn's only importance [is] as a symptom of a changing Ontario, the end of something and the beginning of something else which nobody yet understands. You can call him merely the cracker-barrel prophet of Hog Town, but this old conservative province, this province of gentility and of aristocratic tradition, of imperialism and, above all, of respectability, elects and re-elects the brawling antithesis of its supposed character.

That character must be in ferment. The ferment is deep indeed and more hopeful than we had thought, when Wendell Willkie, an American, is mobbed by cheering crowds in the Toronto streets and the Stars and Stripes flies in the legislature. Perhaps the wedge has changed far more than we have suspected. Perhaps it was never quite what we thought. Perhaps all we have been saying of it, all our painful analyses, are out of date, are shadows only of a thing which is quietly disappearing.

So much for speculation, which never can reach any goal. Toronto is not Ontario any more than New York is the United States, and you feel that as soon as you drive out of the city into the pleasant Ontario countryside.

Here you are in the region of the little towns again, with their remaining flavor of the old days, the smell of quiet and contentment – the old farms and the old roads where soldiers and rebels used to march. No other part of Canada is like this. It is the only part with sufficient population and density of towns, villages and industries to be compared with the industrial regions of the United States. Here – a spectacle unknown in most parts of our country – you may see furnace flame against the darkness at night and smoke against the daylight sky. Here you may feel the regular pulse of industry, which is strange to most of us. Yet a garden, outside the factory gate, and the only district of Canada so well tilled, tended, and beloved that you can see in it a touch of the English countryside, which has taken ten centuries to make – orchards in the Niagara Peninsula; clusters of apple and peach trees and long fields of grapes; old brick farmhouses under immemorial elms; fat barns reeling drunkenly homeward over the hills; cool lanes and rambling country roads; and always behind them the hard and glittering sheet of Lake Ontario.

I wanted to go to Niagara again as I had first gone, long ago, on a little steamer from Toronto. I still remembered the trees along the river, the fluid and ever changing flow of green down the steep hillsides, the trilliums in May so thick that you could not put your foot between them. I want to go on the absurd trolley which used to run in endless rattle up and down the river canyon between the autumn smolder of red maple leaves. But the Man from Toronto said we must drive this time by the new highways. He was a kindly man, but with a hard tongue, logical brain, and a face of native flint, and he wanted to show me that the old turnpikes of Ontario had been made as broad and smooth as the superhighways of the United States. I saw that they were, but it didn't interest me.

Like any Canadian from the outlands I could not keep my eyes off the great estates, mansions, gardens, and wealth of the homes along the lake shore. We do not have them in other parts of Canada – a few estates, maybe, the odd country home of the rich man, but never the concentrated, heaped-up riches of the Toronto suburbs, palace after palace, in broad grounds, too perfectly tended....

What surprises the outlander most is the stone house of Ontario. We are largely a nation of wood houses or, at best, of brick. Few Canadians ever live behind stone walls, but here in Ontario they have stone, some of the best in the world, and they know how to use it out of long experience. Still, as I said to my hard Toronto friend, we have no house architecture in Canada. We have originated nothing, unless it be the Quebec farm house, low and clinging to the soil, with deep eaves and vast chimneys at each end, a clean, simple, and good design. But it came in the first place out of Europe. Perhaps the old Ontario house, the oblong stone house with green shutters, is our best Canadian attempt, if a pretty literal copy of the Georgian can be called ours....

... Why, even on our Pacific Coast, where grows the finest building wood out of doors, we have never yet invented a form to capture and use it, a Canadian design natural to our Canadian materials, as the cuckoo-clock houses are to Switzerland, the white colonial houses to New England; and though I could see along the Niagara road how much the modern architect has improved on the red-brick era, it is theft only, of English designs mostly, and occasionally out of American modernism....

... Here in this Ontario country you could see what appeared to be the perfect balance between land and machine the finely tilled farms with their walls of field stones, gathered through the years out of the soil, and then, a few miles apart, the pleasant little towns built around their factories. Lively towns, streets crammed with cars, stores crowded, indistinguishable from the main streets of any manufacturing town in America. Perfect balance, yes, but so vulnerable.

How many of these people in the little towns understood, I asked, that they lived not on their own resources but on the resources of the sprawling, empty nation around them – on the ability of the prairie farmer to sell his wheat in the world and buy his machinery, tools, binder twine, clothes, shoes, automobile, breakfast food here in Ontario? Too busy, my friend repeated. Too busy indeed. Never realizing that this great wedge of industry is an artificial creation largely, made by the tariff which forces Canada to buy Canadian-made products even at a high price.

What marvelous growth in this wedge, despite all natural obstacles! The wedge has no iron of its own and can buy its supplies more cheaply from the Mesabi Range of Minnesota than from any source in Canada, though new iron deposits are being opened up now along the north shore of Lake Superior. Yet, bringing its raw materials so far, the wedge makes most of Canada's steel products, all its automobiles, nearly all its machinery.

The wedge also lacks that other basic ingredient, coal. This must come from the United States, or, in smaller quantities, from Nova Scotia or

Alberta, at artificial cost and government subsidy to cover the long haul, or from Britain. Oil was discovered in the wedge more than eighty years ago, but it is a small trickle now and present supplies must come from the United States or overseas. Yet so strategic is the location of the wedge, by geography and by tariff arrangement, that it can take these outside ingredients and mold them into more than half of all Canada's industrial output.

If Canada lacks iron, coal, and oil where they are most needed, it can buy them with exports of other minerals, for it produces a tenth of the world's gold, most of it in Ontario, 90 per cent of the nickel, 12 per cent of the copper and lead, 10 per cent of the zinc, half of the platinum metals, and more asbestos than any other country. Specialization is the secret of Canadian industry – concentrating on the things we have and trading them for what we lack. That is why we are vulnerable. Let our outside markets fail and we cannot import the lacking essentials.

The wedge of Ontario has advantages possessed by no other part of the country. It is the center of population and domestic markets, but, more than that, it is really a huge inland port, a thousand miles from the sea. Men made it a port with the work of their hands....

... Four canals have been built to join Lake Ontario and Lake Erie, to carry ships up and down the single great step of Niagara Falls. As long ago as 1829 they built the first canal here with four crude wooden locks, using every little local stream to save digging, but only boats of eight-foot draft could use this channel. Sixteen years later they built again, and still again in 1887 with twenty-five locks. We could see some of them now, with walls of field stone, weathered, overgrown, like the locks of England, and the lazy channels, which only needed a bulbous barge boat, with pots of red geraniums and a stout woman knitting at the tiller, to look like the canals of France. Now we could see the fourth channel – the Welland Canal, which has revolutionized the geography, economics, transportation, and defense of the whole continent....

... This is indeed the breathing lung of Canada. Without its first beginnings we could not have built our country. Without the larger ditch and the giant mechanism of locks, we could not exist in our present form. Steadily the lung breathes, carrying commerce into our arteries and remote veins, far into the inner regions of Canada, expelling our goods, our wheat, our minerals, taking cheap freight in and out of our inland seas, making the wedge an ocean port.

De La Moths' vision [of 1710 to build a canal] is not yet complete. It had to wait more than two centuries until the St. Lawrence Seaway was projected jointly by Canada and the United States. This scheme will circumvent the rapids that lie in the river system below the Welland Canal, so that the great freighters may come up, uninterrupted from the sea. Canada contributed to this inland route the channel between Lake Ontario and Lake Erie and built it to carry these ocean vessels, for Canada was looking ahead. At present the larger grain ships can only move from the Lake Head down to Lake Ontario and transfer their cargoes to smaller craft, which move by the smaller lower canals to the ocean, but the completed Seaway will make this transfer unnecessary.

The Great Lakes system will carry cheap freight into the middle of the continent, create naval shipbuilding yards far from possible attack, alter the whole economic balance of America. Of that project the Welland Canal, the product of Canadian engineering, Canadian money, and Canadian imagination, is the key. It is the route around the most difficult barrier of all, the portage of the Onghiaras.

The Seaway is only one of a series of titanic changes in a region always selected for events....

... Here they have utilized the entire height of Niagara Falls and the rapids below it to. develop electrical power in a swarming den of dynamos that used to be the largest in the world before the Americans built their new western dams.

From a roaring inferno, where the dynamos sit like spinning taps, fat and solemn in their long line, the power goes out to serve the industries of the Ontario wedge. In a central room like a movie set a couple of young engineers, by watching the red and green lights flash, can direct this energy all over the country, to city and remote hamlet. Now we could see why the wedge had become the heart of Canada. It has the power. The falls of the Onghiaras, which used to be the chief obstacle to Canada's development, have became one of its chief servants and, with the canal, have formed a combination of energy and transportation which keeps the heart beating.

Hundreds of thousands of people, Americans and Canadians, pass this way, catching a glimpse of the canal or the wires of the power lines, but never pausing to think that the whole economy of this country, the living of its people, depend an them. Block the canal, cut the wires, blow up the power plants, and you have a new Canada of poverty, privation, and peasantry. If you wanted to take a map and thrust a pin into the most vital point in Canada, I suppose you could do no better than to place it at Queenston, where all the ganglia of the national body meet in final concentration of energy.

This is the creation of man through government. This is the prodigious child of the Ontario Hydro, owned by the taxpayers, a huge experiment in socialism in a territory which would be horrified at the word. Call it public ownership and it is accepted as a natural and reasonable scheme. Call it socialism and people will not understand you. The name does not matter. The Hydro, a public undertaking, the obvious assumption of an inevitable monopoly by the state, has been a complete success, has provided cheap power to the factories, cheap electricity to the homes. The housewife of this region, like the industrialists, is the envy of all others throughout the nation.

This Queenston power house may be taken by the thoughtful man as a symbol of Canada's industrial development....

Move but a mile from the [Niagara] river and you are out of the reach of industry and in an ancient land. That is what charms the person from the city or from the raw country of the West – the loving care of these fields, the contented smile of old brick houses, the stone walls overgrown with creepers, the venerable orchards, the little rivers, and the bridges of field stone....

Some of the little towns are almost as perfect, with picture-book streets arched by trees, with dozing stone houses and old men sleeping in the sun. But come near the ganglia of commerce and once more you are plunged into ugliness....

Through many a nursery-rhyme town we drove that day and through the suppurating sores of modern industry, the slums growing like rank water weeds beside the canal, the horrid factory towns that mean wealth for the nation and poverty for the inhabitants. All of them were heralded on the highway as usual by a rash of billboards, those painted whores of the written word that should be kept where they belong, in restricted areas....

Even if you knew every town and road in the wedge you would still not know Ontario. Up to Hudson's Bay it sweeps and to the edge of the prairies, an empty land of rocks and woods and so much water, so many lakes and rivers, that you could almost paddle a canoe from one end of it to the other. Parks, camping places, resorts are strewn lavishly over it and I judge by the local press that every citizen of the province at one time or another has caught a twenty-pound fish and held it before a camera.

Thousand Islands sprinkled black upon the river, Bay of Quinte, lush Ottawa Valley, clean Georgian Bay, Stratford on a local Avon, in loyal imitation of the poet's birthplace, even to swans (kept in a barn in winter), Dionne Quintuplets, the prolific lakes of Haliburton and Muskoka, Algonquin Park, the little canals and locks where a dozing lock keeper will let your boat through, endless leagues of glittering water, rounded rocks and twisted pine, hot and pungent under the sun-even this is only the beginning of Ontario.

These are pleasant lands, made for men's homes and holidays, but to the west glooms the dark, somber shore of Lake Superior, the pinched, cold towns at its ragged edge, the steel mills of the Soo, and those ghastly, eyeless monuments of concrete, the round grain elevators of Fort William, where the prairie wheat is loaded on the lake boats. Farther north again, on into wilderness as wild as when the Frenchmen first saw it, where Indians yet travel by canoe and carry their young on papoose boards – even here the industry of Ontario does not pause. In the fabulous horseshoe of the Precambrian Shield, left by a fortunate convulsion when the earth crust was liquid, men have found minerals, built towns, piled up fortunes, bred millionaires, enriched distant cities, bought newspapers, sucked up the immigration of Europe, merged races, ravened through the wilderness with their lonely railways and drawn riches even from these endless barrens of glacial rocks and tiny trees.

Wild country and beautiful, but never home again to the westerner. Once he has seen the Rockies, once he has lived among the deep canyons and shattered peaks, the sheer size and savage roughness of British Columbia, all this seems lovely but never wild enough. Where are the mountains? Always in his subconscious he is searching for them, expecting to see them over the next hill, but there are more hills only, and the growth of hardwoods, which he does not know at home. No stark, parched beauty here, of dry belt and fearful cliff shape and open range, no seashore and salt smell.

The transplanted native of Ontario may sigh, but he knows that he can never go back again.

(Hutchison, *The Unknown Country,* 1942, 132–54)

6 WOOD, WIND, AND WATER, NOVA SCOTIA, REGIONALISM

☞ While discussing the economic ups and downs of Nova Scotia, Hutchison also writes about the four major economic regions of Canada, "compartments" as he calls them, examining how the country functions and how the Maritimes fit into this national economic system. Hutchison reflects that because of the strong north-south pull of

geography and economics in North America there would be no need
for the existence of Canada without one overpowering political reason
– "the construction of a nation." In comparing the regions he stresses
the significance of the tariff in favouring one section of the country
against all the others. In order for the country to survive economically, compromises have always had to be made among the four rival
economic regions and the Atlantic seaboard "has generally received the
smallest share." Nova Scotia is a land of tradition and character and
Hutchison notes the deep roots of people in their communities. ⌐

The stern character of these people is plainly written on their peninsula.
It is written in glistening little towns beside every cove, in white houses
shining on every windy rock, in men's tight, grooved faces. On the basic
rock stratum of the country is laid a gritty deposit out of Scotland, and
over it, weathering it, furrowing it, blows the clean sea wind, and every
house, every man and woman is encrusted with sea salt.

Poor country, and proud, with the fierce pride of the Scot. Once
it knew wealth, in the days of sail, when its fleets sailed every sea,
entered every port, and were the fourth of the world's merchant carriers – the great age of wood, wind, and water, alas, all too short. Since
that age died, poverty has never left here for long, but Nova Scotia
has not surrendered to poverty. It has not sunk down, hopeless and
apathetic, like the slums of cities and the sad ruins of farming towns
out West. The shore accepts poverty as a natural state and has learned
to live with it, decently and unashamed. It keeps its clothes patched, its
shoes shined, its plain, square houses painted, and every face glistens
with soap and water.

They are a long way from the rest of Canada, all the three Maritime
Provinces of Nova Scotia, New Brunswick, and Prince Edward Island.
Gaudet asked me if I came from Upper Canada – Ontario's old colonial
name, forgotten by its own people these fifty years. Upper Canada is
almost like another country to these folk, separated from them by a
thousand miles of wilderness.

What a strange and brittle structure it is, the economy of Canada,
when you come to see its distant extremity thus, at first hand! This eastern region has no fundamental economic connection with Canada at
all. It is, as nature and geography laid it out, much more a part of New
England than of Canada, but the Loyalists, fleeing from the Revolution,
made it British. This was not easy. To get the steel, coal, and fish of this
eastern shore into the central, populated areas of Canada, the nation

must pay bonuses and subventions and favorable freight rates, or the Maritimes, shut off by tariffs from their natural market in New England, could not live at all.

This region is but one of four great compartments that make up Canada. The second is the central area of Ontario and Quebec, where Canada has concentrated its manufacturers behind a tariff wall, and the people living there, guaranteed the internal market, battening on the rural parts of the country through high, protected prices, must support their poor relations like the Maritimes by sharing a small part of their artificial earnings. In bad times the central area also must bonus the third compartment, the plains that lie from the Great Lakes to the Rockies, that live on one export crop, wheat, and cannot be protected by the tariff; but the bonus is never enough to keep the prairies much above the starvation line when the world wheat market is closed by tariffs or wars. The fourth compartment lies west of the Rockies, in a region which also lives on foreign markets but has resources varied enough to survive, so far, any national tariff policy or any world collapse.

Standing here on this Atlantic Coast, amid clean, proud poverty, you can see how delicate is the balance between these four regions, how unnatural and precarious the economic organization of Canada – an attempt to make goods move across mountain barriers, leagues of lonely plains and empty forests. No economic rhyme or reason in it, or in the economic organization of the continent at large, when an imaginary forty-ninth parallel of latitude can stop the goods traveling as nature and geography intended, northward and southward. No economic reason for the economy of Canada, but an overpowering political reason – the construction of a nation. That project has succeeded in defiance of geography and economics. All politics in Canada, all the unconscious toil of its people, the sectional differences, tariff elections, struggles between provincial governments, have been nothing but an attempt to maintain some kind of compromise and balance between the four rival economic regions, between those that want tariff protection, the home market, and those that want world markets for raw products, and cheap manufactured goods for themselves.

Against all the natural tugs of trade, all the stresses of financial interest, the thing has worked; has made Canada, with less than 1 per cent of the world's population, the fourth exporter, the sixth nation in total trade, eighth in industry though thirtieth in number of inhabitants; has given Canada, next to the United States, the highest living standard and per capita income.

More than any other important nation, Canada is built on the world market, earns 30 per cent of its income from exports, prospers on its ability to specialize in the production of its special products like wheat, newsprint, lumber, minerals, fish and their sale mostly to the United States and Britain. The slightest loss in these sales produces a devastating effect on what is probably the most vulnerable economy in the world; and in a world permanently consigned to self-containment and trade restriction, Canada would have to adopt an unthinkably low standard of living.

For all its outward resemblance, the economy of Canada is far different from that of its neighbor, which depends for over 90 per cent of its business on its own market. Canada, as a royal commission reported, with a graphic touch never before achieved by such a body, is like a small man sitting in a big poker game among rich men – if he wins, his profits in relation to his capital are large, but if he loses he may be cleaned out.

So our Canadian economy has grown, not by considered plan but day by day, with constant shifts and changes, into a roughly balanced whole which works surprisingly well in a sane, trading world – an economy in which, incidentally, the United States has risked nearly four billion dollars, about a third of its total foreign investments. Now we look at the thing which grew by itself, by the urgent, human needs of men who wanted to live together as an independent nation, in their own way, and we speak of it as our economic system, as if we had created it by deliberate design.

In such a compromise no equality of wealth as between the four compartments has been possible. This eastern seaboard has generally received the smallest share. A trading world, with sailing ships, brought the Maritimes their only real era of prosperity, when their ports were crammed, their fleets ranged the world, and every cove echoed to the sound of the shipbuilder's hammer. Since the American market was almost closed by tariffs, the Maritimes' chief export, so the saying goes, has been its young men, seeking jobs in the United States or in other parts of Canada that have profited more under the great Canadian compromise....

To a Canadian who has not seen it before it is, indeed, another country. You feel it the moment you enter Digby for the first time – preferably not by bus from the south, but by ferry steamer out of St. John, across the Bay of Fundy. From the heaving bay you slide suddenly into Digby Gut, a long narrow channel with bare walls of rock on either side, where the tattered fishermen's houses cling like barnacles, and a few pitiful fields are carved out of the naked cliffs. The Gut opens suddenly into a kind of inland lake, placid and comfortable, ringed with forest. No wonder Champlain and his companions, amazed at this friendly haven, decided to make Canada's first settlement here along this pleasant shore. But it was a false beginning and they moved to Quebec.

Now Digby looks pure Scottish. You see it from the boat at first like a picture cunningly arranged, according to the laws of design, a Hollywood set for a fishing village, with a perfection of white houses scattered like dice on the hillside, among puffs of green foliage, and a long church spire in precisely the right spot. As the boat eases into the wharf, the picture falls apart, and there are only houses, a few brick buildings, and an old church. The composition, so complete at a distance, has broken up, like many other of life's anticipations.

But there is a fine, fish-smelling Scottish activity about Digby, the busy wharves, the cargoes of dried cod ready for shipment, the well-scrubbed people, the clean little town, the scallop boats starting out for Fundy, the tangle of rigging and masts by the shore, the swoop and dart of the white gulls everywhere and a sea vigor in the air, making you feel all at once a pleasure in living – making you forget what sort of world lies beyond the Gut, where the big ships are loading in St. John for the Battle of the Atlantic....

... men from Nova Scotia pushed out across all Canada and into the United States. There are as many of them in New England as there are left in Nova Scotia. They are always adaptable, generally competent, invariably thrifty. In the national politics of Canada, in the big business of Montreal, in the cities of the west, they have always been leaders and usually bosses.

Such people gave Nova Scotia more character, more variation, more local differences than any part of English-speaking Canada. You would have to write a large book merely to list the different towns of Nova Scotia and their special characteristics, their ideas, prejudices, and mores. These things can grow only in a country where settlement was early and far apart, where men of one village seldom saw those of another, and these things disappear in the newer country of the west where settlement came suddenly in an age of communication and uniformity.

Nova Scotia thus is the most storied, the most deeply grooved part of British Canada and the greatest respecter of family, clan, and local tradition. An old Nova Scotian can tell you the history of every family for miles around and, in an almost pathetic fashion, he will take pride in the local celebrity. The Nova Scotian statesman, even though politics here is hard, bitter, and often ruthless, invariably is surrounded by a certain aura of distinction, whereas the cabinet minister from Winnipeg or Saskatoon will hardly get his name into the newspapers.

These people, like the French-Canadians, have lived long in this land, but more important, they expect to remain here all their lives, while most Canadians, like most Americans, live only in the hope of moving as soon as possible to a better street, a better apartment, a larger town. Run-down, they call the Maritimes, a little gone-to-seed, some of its best blood lost through the continual emigration of its strongest sons. There is, no doubt, some truth in this rather glib diagnosis, but the real wonder is that in a country so poor, cut off from all its natural markets in New England, isolated from the markets of its own nation, people still have been able to live, to support good homes, to maintain some of the best universities in America, to preserve a true culture and a living way of their own choice.

(Hutchison, *The Unknown Country*, 1942, 183–201)

7 FUNDY'S CHILDREN, NEW BRUNSWICK, PRINCE EDWARD ISLAND, GASPÉ

⌖ Rivers, forests, and wonderful place names resonate for Hutchison in New Brunswick. But he does not really come to grips with that province, or with Prince Edward Island. He describes Percé Rock in the Gaspé Peninsula, but Nova Scotia had already stolen much of what he had to say about the geography of the Atlantic seaboard. ⌖

The Saint John River has always been the spinal cord of New Brunswick's life since the first days when everybody traveled on chuffing little steamboats and old Captain Sam Peabody used to bring up the freight, the passengers, and the news, stopping with a blast of his whistle at every farmer's wharf....

[Hutchison travels by bus.] All along the road the little farms run down the river, and every mile or two, like a friendly traffic policeman in a broad white hat and red coat, stands a little river lighthouse. Now and then there are minute ferries that will carry you to the opposite bank if you blow a horn, hung conveniently for the purpose. Every few miles stands a village with church steeple piercing the forest of the river bank – lean steeples unlike the gay, glistening spires and domes of Quebec, quiet, drab villages, with English faces and no laughing eyes or red lips like the French villages on the St. Lawrence. Back of the villages roll the low New Brunswick hills, with the pink vapor-puff of new birch twigs hanging over them like a mist, waiting for the first leaves.

A land of little trees, as we measure them in Canada, but these forests, stretching in dark tangle from the Bay of Fundy to the St. Lawrence, have kept the people of New Brunswick. Swarms of logs, wallowing down the rivers in the spring drives, little mills puffing in the backwoods, spars, for ships in the old days, planks for the great wooden fleets of the Maritimes, pulp for the modern paper mills – wood has always been the great crop of this country, while the cultivated farms stretch only in thin, frail fingers up the narrow valley. Woods, and wooden houses, and faded wooden churches and little wooden villages beside some little wooded stream – this is what you always remember of New Brunswick.

They are poor here, as poor as in Nova Scotia, and the towns often wear little paint on their faces, but they have bred a hard race of men, who, spreading throughout Canada, have succeeded richly. To the United States also they have exported many of their strongest sons, who could not find enough to do at home....

This is old country with dozing villages, covered bridges, and old tales ... It is a country of pinched and winding valleys like Matapedia, where the ripe autumn fields are walled in by fiery forests of maple, burning in harmless flame of color to the tops of the little mountains. It is the country of the world's most fantastic, mouth-twisting names.

Just try to pronounce Kou-chi-bou-guac, Washa-de-moak, Kennebeca-sis, Madawaska, Missaguash – Indian, beyond the white man's tongue, and probably beyond my spelling....

Just quaint Indian names you may call them, but to me they have always seemed much more. They seem to mark a kind of secret understanding among all New Brunswickers, as if they were the pass words of a tribal unity which forever sets them apart, by secret vows, from the rest of Canada. Wherever he goes the New Brunswicker takes something of New Brunswick with him, treasures it, boasts of it, hangs on to it. His strange place names are the symbol of a fierce, tenacious grip upon this old land....

North and east, and cuddling into the shoulder of New Brunswick and Nova Scotia, lies Prince Edward Island, Canada's tiniest province, a single speck of garden in the sea. The inhabitants – like all island folk, with a character of their own – say it is the only truly civilized spot in America, where, in the pleasant farms and quiet villages, there is still time to live....

North again and across the Bay of Chaleur (Cartier's Bay of Heat)
you are in French Canada on the Gaspé Peninsula, Quebec's round nose,
forever scenting the Atlantic. Gaspé is a country of its own, French with
an Irish mixture, where life has depended on the unfailing harvest of cod
since Cartier planted among the wondering Indians the first white man's
cross in Canada, and the French fishermen sailed here to take their salted
cargoes home again across the ocean....

Gaspé has been rediscovered – fortunately or unfortunately as you
view these things – the white villages have been pronounced picturesque
by artists, the fisher-folk have been found charmingly primitive, and the
attentions of the tourists eventually will make Gaspé primp itself and
paint its cheeks and develop a self-conscious perfection.

Nothing, however, save the elements can touch the astounding and
heroic spectacle of Percy Rock, the French Isle Percé, the pierced rock
that Cartier saw beside the shore – a sheer hunk of naked stone, richly
colored in soft reds, yellows, and greens, wallowing a few yards from the
beach, like the hulk of a ruined ship, like a stranded whale, with a hole
through it, blinking like a wild eye. Beside it, long broken from the main
body, stands a single obelisk in the water.

(Hutchison, *The Unknown Country*, 1942, 235–44)

8 THE MEN IN SHEEPSKIN COATS, MANITOBA, ETHNIC GROUPS

☞ George Parkin and Rogers, writing in the period of great immigration to the prairies before the First World War, were concerned about
the society the immigrants might create. Now, writing in 1941, we have
Hutchison's impressions of the immigrants and the landscapes they
have made. ☜

[Just north of] Winnipeg, on the east bank of the Red River, and opposite the original Scottish settlements, we could imagine we were in a
foreign country. Bulbous church domes and twisted spires rose above
the little poplar woods, the architecture of Byzantium, brought by long
and tortuous passage into the prairies of Canada. The squat log houses
were covered with white plaster and the doors and window frames were
painted blue or red. Exactly the same houses glisten white beside the
Danube as you drive down through the flocks of geese to Budapest.

There were glimpses here by the Red River – the white plastered
houses, the church domes and cupolas, the women in scarlet kerchiefs

and shapeless skirts – that could be moved bodily into central Europe and no one would know they had ever been away from it. A few of the more successful Ukrainian farmers had torn down their plastered houses or used them for barns, building new houses of Canadian style – universally hideous. They were beginning to learn the ways of the country.

In the railway station of Winnipeg you can still see the immigrants occasionally, their belongings done up in blankets and bed quilts, their children clustered around the women like scared chickens, but not many of them now.

In the spring of 1892 the station master of Winnipeg beheld two bearded men in woolly sheepskin coats who tried to speak to him, but could utter no word of English. They were Ivan Pilipiniski and Vasil Leynak. They got jobs on a farm and in the autumn they disappeared. They had spied out the ground for their friends in Galicia and presently they returned with hundreds more like them. The great trek had started.

Forty years ago the stations from Montreal to the Rockies were crammed with these people – Sir Clifford Sifton's tide of settlement that built the prairies. The Men in Sheepskin Coats, as Sifton called them. For a time they would become the chief political and economic fact of Canada.

All over Europe Sifton searched them out and brought them here, regardless of blood or tradition. On the lonely sweep of the prairies they would cultivate the ground, said Sifton, raise crops, enrich Canada, and breed a new Canadian race. Time and soil and weather would wear down by erosion their separate characteristics and shape them to this country....

[Hutchison gives recent census figures for the major ethnic groups in Canada, listed in numerical order: French, English, Scottish, Irish, German, Scandinavian, Ukrainian, Hebrew, Dutch, Polish, Indian and Eskimo, Italian, Chinese, Japanese.] The melting of these elements in the crucible of Canada is not as rapid as might be supposed. The French are confined mostly to Quebec, though they have spread lately into northern Ontario, New Brunswick, and the prairies. Of the other continental European stocks, 60 per cent are on the prairies, living often in their own communities – little isolated clots of foreign blood, not readily absorbed. Yet so widespread is the penetration of these strains that you will come upon a Ukrainian church, with mosquelike dome, on the hill above the Niagara shelf. You will find Russian peasants chanting their hymns by a wild river in the Canadian Rockies, a German family putting down its winter barrel of pigs' knuckles and sauerkraut in Kitchener, Ontario, an old Chinese vegetable grower smoking his opium in the Dry Belt of British Columbia.

A Canadian Mosaic, John Murray Gibbon called this mixture of bloods, in his fine study of our people. Most Canadians do not attempt to understand these other races. They are peasants laboring by the road-side, or a Uke kitchen maid to do the heavy work of the household, or that perennial nuisance, the naked Doukhobor, or the Oriental Problem. Only a few men like Gibbon have troubled to investigate these strange, inarticulate, shy people, have encouraged them to develop their own native arts and handicrafts, their music and dances, to enrich the Mosaic of Canada....

(Hutchison, *The Unknown Country*, 1942, 275–7)

9 DROUGHT AND GLUT, SASKATCHEWAN, THE PRAIRIES

☞ Hutchison ponders the problem of marketing wheat faced by prairie farmers. In the 1930s the prairies were devastated by drought; in 1941 there is another concern, as Canada industrializes during another world-wide war – what will happen to the prairie economy, given its dependence on agricultural exports. Here we see the vulnerabilities of a resource-based economy. Hutchison concentrates on farming in Sas-katchewan and Alberta is hardly mentioned. ☜

[Hutchison describes prairie agriculture in wartime.] ... From the begin-ning it had been a delicate balance, the constant struggle between the protectionist cities of the east and the trading farmers of the west. Grad-ually the farmers had been losing out, until the protected cities had to bonus them so that they could still live and pay high, protected prices.

The war has undermined the balance still further. By industrializing Canada it has concentrated economic power, political power, and popu-lation more than ever in the manufacturing areas. It has shifted the whole fulcrum of Canadian life eastward. It has built a new vested interest in the principle of protection on top of the old interest. It has created new factories and new towns which will want to sell manufactured goods, not wheat, after the war, which will want to control the Canadian prairie market more than ever when the war machinery must turn to peacetime goods. The position of the farmer, like the position of those fishermen in Nova Scotia, is weakened daily as Canada becomes less of an agri-cultural, more of an industrial nation, with all the problems, sores, and social strains of industrialism.

Hearn [a prairie farmer near Regina] is not alone in his alarm. In the head offices of the farmers' wheat pool in Regina the best minds of the wheat industry are desperately worried also. They see the prairies losing ground in the economic struggle and the political struggle. They know, as the puzzled men in Parliament know, that there is no cure for the prairies, no solution, no hope, no way of avoiding a slump in population, the collapse of towns, the decline of cities, the abandonment of farms, unless there is a return of world trade and foreign markets.

So today the prairie waits, with bulging barns and elevators, for the day when it can seed again as the Lord intended. Deep in the souls of these people is a strange love, of their grim land that makes them loath to leave it – the love of distance, sweep, and elbow room, the love of the rich soil between their fingers and under their plows, the pull of loneliness and the far horizon.

Here is a bitter sight for Canadians crossing the prairies. The land turns like a vast platter as the train speeds across it – in winter white and cold, with men in sheepskin coats driving in box sleighs and shivering on the station platform; in spring, black and glistening with the dark water of melting snow; in summer, green with the first wheat sprouts; in the autumn, burning yellow, when the stooks lie in endless pattern and the threshing machines belch chaff into the wind.

Good land. The best in the world, Hearn said, ...

The prairies have other sources of income besides wheat. They have coarse grains, cattle, hogs, dairying. In southern Alberta they have an oil industry sufficient to supply most of their needs. In the north they are opening up mines. A fifth of their income is derived from manufacturing, a remarkable growth in the last twenty years. The war has given the prairie cities even an air of prosperity with soldiers everywhere, and the flying fields of the British Commonwealth Air Training Plan.

There is room yet for more diversification of crops, more self-containment; better management, and better use of the land in place of "wheat mining." But if the prairies produce more of other crops, they will only offer new competition for the farmers of the east and of British Columbia, who already are drowned in surplus and have not received even the bonuses of the prairie farmer. No matter how the prairie economy is changed, no matter how crops are changed, the only real hope of maintaining the present population and the present position of the prairies in Canada is the return of the wheat market.

This is wheat land. This is the crop that nature intended most of it to grow. It is the only crop that much of it will 'grow. An economic world, seeking cheap costs and greater wealth, would grow much of its wheat here.

Perhaps the decline is permanent and much of the land must go back into pasture or be left, abandoned and empty. Perhaps Canada must reverse the process of forty years and move many of the people out of the prairies. No one dares to face it. Governments pause and argue, and deal in figures and theories and statistics, and utter patriotic slogans, and wait for the war to end and the return of an economic world.

(Hutchison, *The Unknown Country*, 1942, 302–7)

10 THE PROMISED LAND, BRITISH COLUMBIA

☞ British Columbia is home, a land whose various landscapes Hutchison can smell. It is a fresh land that has long stimulated feelings of freedom and inner satisfaction. Now, finally there is a realization of constraints, but always there is wilderness. ☞

Let me come to British Columbia in the spring, in the lush first days of April. Let me go to bed in the frozen prairies and wake among the green maple leaves, the swelling catkins, the uncurling ferns, and the blossom of old orchards beside the railway. Or blindfold me and stand me on the rear platform of the train and I will tell you, by the smell and the very feel of the air, when we pass through Golden and Revelstoke, when we reach the sagebrush country of Kamloops, when we are breathing the brave stone smell of the Fraser canyon and the meadow airs of the Chilliwack Valley. Every station and siding, every brook and field and little farm I would surely recognize by instinct, though I were blind. This is our own incomparable land.

Better still, let me steal in by night, lying, sleepless, on a lower berth, watching the moonlight skim the Thompson, the velvet hills of the Dry Belt, the lights of lonely farm houses, the bands of cattle staring at the passing spectacle of the train, and the mare with her new foal gazing from the meadow. Let me lie there and see the billows of smoke playing among the stone cliffs, and the dark, calm mass of forests and the awful bulk of the canyon at Hell's Gate.

Then, as dawn breaks, the canyon widens suddenly and there are the fields of the Pacific coast, deep green, rank, overgrown, and succulent, each with its own mountain in the corner. There are the wild currant blossoms dripping red and smelling of all the Aprils of the ages, the fierce growth of bracken, the white plumes of elderberry, and everywhere the hungry forest, marching back, with scouts of fern and alder, with shock troops of fir and hemlock, upon the settler's clearing. There in the broadening river are the great rafts of reddish cedar, the sea gulls roosting on them with wise and ancient look. There at last is the ocean and the unreal, flat shape of ships, the smell of the salt water, and the mountains dropping into it at a single leap.

Wild and upheaved, and forever changing, forever new, is this land. What hopes our fathers had for it! This was a land fit for men to live in, not just to struggle and exist in – men who had bleached in the prairie suns and frozen in the prairie winters, men who had stifled in the crowded, used-up air of eastern cities and the old world, men who wanted to be alone and free....

... [British Columbia is] a land different from any in Canada, larger, wilder, as if it belonged to a different continent....

... life is good in British Columbia and unlike the life of the prairies or the east – so unlike it – that, crossing the Rockies, you are in a new country, as if you had crossed a national frontier. Everyone feels it, even the stranger, feels the change of outlook, tempo, and attitude. What makes it so, I do not know. The size of everything, I suspect, the bulk of mountains; the space of valleys, the far glimpses of land and sea, the lakes and rivers, all cast in gigantic mold. They make a man feel bigger, more free, as if he had come out of a crowded room.

We cannot go back to our old homes east of the mountains. In our hearts we never recross that barrier.

From the beginning, when they debated the advisability of joining the United States, British Columbians have been part of Canada in constitution, in law, in the written word, but not much in the spirit. From the beginning it was the land of men who wanted to get away from everything, to start afresh, to be on their own. Only now does British Columbia begin to feel the pressure of the outside world, the regimentation of modern life, the dead weight of convention, the facts of hard economics, and the responsibilities of Canada. This thrust of men who were determined to be alone and free has paused for the first time. The British Columbia which was a magic dream for us all is fading into the light of common day.

Yet there is much of it still left, despite the dead growth of cities. There is untouched wilderness larger than half a dozen American states. There is sanctuary always close at hand if you seek it. The land is so upturned by mountains, so cut by river and lake, so heaved up, as if a hand had stirred it suddenly before it cooled, that a man can be lost to his fellows in a hundred yards and the world's armies could be hidden in a few leagues of valley or forest. There is the witchery of it – the endless variety, changing with every turn in the road, with almost every valley and hill. Always there is something lost behind the ranges and men must seek it out.

British Columbia starts with the Rockies, and even they, hardly changing through the ages, are always different. So often I have threaded them by train and automobile, and they never seem the same....

(Hutchison, *The Unknown Country*, 1942, 312–16)

11 THE LOTUS EATERS, VANCOUVER ISLAND

☞ The west coast: a land where humans can create a congenial – and beautiful – landscape. ☞

[Vancouver Island] This land is rough yet, with fence lines untrimmed, stumps yet to be blown, houses yet to be painted. Give us time. It takes more than one generation to make a farm here. Give us a thousand years, as they have had in England, and we will make this landscape more beautiful than England's, for we have not only the makings of the foreground, the soil, the growth, the sea, the English climate, but we have as well a background of mountains and glaciers. In time it will be another England and another Switzerland combined, but long after we have gone. In our lifetime it will always be wild, and men's clearings mere footsteps in the forest....

A few miles from the logging camps, the donkey engines, the railways, the devastation, you will come upon such pleasant and quiet spots as Comox, like an English town beside the sea, and the blue sweep of Comox Bay, with glaciers behind it, lovelier than the lakes of Italy. To see it in the dawn is to look at an ocean as still as an oil painting, and as vivid.

(Hutchison, *The Unknown Country*, 1942, 345–50)

12 CARIBOO ROAD, INTERIOR BRITISH COLUMBIA

☞ Earlier Hutchison described the St. Lawrence and Saint John Rivers, rivers on which local civilizations had been built. The Fraser River too has its impact on people. On the way to the Cariboo in the dry interior of British Columbia, Hutchison describes the furious Fraser River, a great fissure and a route through mountains. The Cariboo was the kind of country Hutchison had known for some years as a child, although farther south in the interior. He visits a friend in the Cariboo, a land of special meaning for the people who live here – and for Hutchison. ⌒

[On the way to the Cariboo Country.] Perhaps the canyon of the Fraser is not beautiful, like the gracious river that drains the eastern half of Canada. The Fraser is too furious, stark, and lonely for mere beauty. It is angry with the scowl of black hills and the welter of riven stone. It is melancholy with perpetual shadows and gouged with fearful wrinkles. Through this dark canyon forever bores the river, deepening its trench, boiling, swirling in brown and frenzied tide, raging at every jut of rock, cutting down cliffs and tearing at the thin islands of stone that lie in it like the funneled shapes of battleships. Forever it moves and churns with steady power and sure purpose, a roar deep in its throat. It is jealous even of the single wind-blown pine tree at its edge, and of the frail light that gleams through the darkness, and of men's presence here.

The St. Lawrence is the friend and servant of man. The Fraser is forever hostile and beyond taming. No man can stand on the cliff and look down at the brown line of the river, or stand beside the vast swirl and look up at the chaos of the hills, without fear and loneliness. Men's villages at the canyon's edge will all disappear some day, an incident in this million years of struggle between stone and water. All men, all men's civilizations are but a moment in this contest – a brief gold rush, soon to ebb again....

Past Lillooet the dawn broke out of a pale eastward streak. Suddenly, almost in a moment, the flat hills took on shape, bulk, and dimension and seemed to rush at us-no longer the tortured mountains of the canyon but the rounded clay hills and rolling range of the Dry Belt. It was the Cariboo, and it was the autumn of the uplands. The poplar trees seemed to boil like yellow paint far across the hills, just before the fall of the leaves.

... Here [in the Cariboo] was a man who had learned the satisfaction of land and space and had never known, in this stillness, the loneliness of cities.

(Hutchison, *The Unknown Country*, 1942, 355–7, 360)

8

Bruce Hutchison, *Canada, Tomorrow's Giant*, 1957

☞ Fifteen years after completing *The Unknown Country*, Hutchison made another, somewhat more, extended journey across Canada and again wrote an account of what he observed in *Canada, Tomorrow's Giant*, published in 1957. He travelled 20,000 miles, mostly by car, except for train and ferry in Newfoundland, which had federated with Canada in 1949. If sharing the northern part of the continent with the United States was an underlying motif of *The Unknown Country*, in *Tomorrow's Giant* it was the industrial expansion, really a revolution, which Canada began to undergo in the Second World War and that continued strongly into the 1950s. In Hutchison's discussion of every region he uses a few words, with essentially the same meaning, to refer to the rapid changes in the country: phrases such as "the great Canadian boom," "a sudden material revolution," "economic revolution," "revolution of the machine," and "Canadian revolution." The last phrase especially occurs again and again. In truth, Hutchison is essentially rediscovering the major Canadian regions of *The Unknown Country*, providing further rich impressions of their characteristics, adding to but not replacing his earlier interpretations. In this volume Newfoundland has been included and there are much fuller discussions of the Canadian Shield and Alberta. However, Hutchison did not visit the Canadian North.

A second theme is never far from Hutchison's mind – Canada's relationship with the United States. Shortly into his first chapter he expresses the relationship this way:

"over the whole nation from the 49th parallel to the pole, hung the historic question mark: could a nation conceived in anger against its neighbor, born in defiance of American power, of geography and economics, dedicated to the proposition that the continent must hold two great powers, friendly but forever separate – could such a nation long endure?" (Hutchison, *Tomorrow's Giant*, 1957, 9)

As I have done in *The Unknown Country*, the descriptions of all major urban centres in this volume have been placed in the next chapter. ☞

I THE MISTY ISLAND, NEWFOUNDLAND

☞ Newfoundland and Labrador joined Canada on 31 March 1949, and Hutchison reports on his first visit to the new province. He attempts to find out how Newfoundlanders have accepted becoming Canadians and, in keeping with the theme of the book, wants to assess how their noted fishery, based on cod, wood, oars, and wind, is adapting to the new technology of trawlers. He cannot, of course, anticipate the tragedy of the killing of the cod fishery by the end of the twentieth century, but the impact of the machine age on the Island is apparent.

Immigrants inevitably experience a shock in adopting their new country. Unexpectedly, through a Newfoundland outport woman's sense of wonder in beholding her new country in a few worn Canadian landscape postcards she had collected, Hutchison glimpses the profound emotion that Newfoundlanders were experiencing in joining Canada. ☞

... [Hutchison visits an outport on Conception Bay, north of St. John's] The flat-topped houses of Bauline had been fastened like the nest of some monstrous sea bird to the base of a naked cliff. No discernible street, only a rough track, wriggled between the houses, and nothing moved on the cramped sea-shelf but a few sheep and two lean cows. The little church and, beside it, the newly painted school told their story of these people's struggle for religion and learning. A shaft of cut stone held the names of twenty-five men from the fifty-two families of Bauline who had died in two world wars for Newfoundland and the British Empire – not for Canada. Beyond this scant acre of man's possession stretched six thousand miles of coastline, the solid ice, the solitary island, and the misty sea.

No such scene or people could be found anywhere else in Canada....

... here in Bauline there was no sign of spring. The fishermen huddled about their smoky stove and watched their old enemy, the ice. Then I remembered that Newfoundland was not Canada, except by yesterday's legal marriage of convenience, that in every other sense this remained foreign soil and its people strangers to us; remembered, too, that the union with Canada had been a shotgun marriage, with the United States as a silent spectator, perhaps a disappointed suitor in the long struggle to divide the continent....

... Throughout its four centuries of separate life the oldest white man's life in America north of the Spanish colonies – Newfoundland has felt little contact with Canada. Until a few years ago it found little welcome among Canadians. Its business was concentrated in Britain, the United States, the Mediterranean, the Caribbean, and South America. Its mind was concentrated on its own island, that oddly shaped doorknocker hanging from the eastern gateway of the continent....

The machine age is outdating the crude trap spread close to shore by hand. The big boats known as draggers are dredging the distant sea floor with power scoops. The drying flakes which used to cure the entire hand-made catch in the sun are being replaced by factories, salt cod by processed fish sticks to suit the modern housewife. Behind the shoreline, in the forests, the mines and larger towns, half a million Newfoundland-ers, owning vast, undeveloped riches, are beginning at last to exploit them in modern industries of many sorts. Still, the inshore fishermen, the eighteenth generation in their craft, cling to the only skills they know.

On the beach of Bauline the captain showed me the last two boats left in a port which once supported fifty, a crude winch to drag them from the water, and the eight-hundred pound killicks of long, thin stones tied to wooden crosses that serve as anchors.

These men had everything they needed and asked only a few hun-dred dollars of annual income. They seemed unaware that their living standard, as reckoned by economists, was about one third of the North American average. What economist could reckon the true standard of their life? It is to be reckoned only in contentment, memories, adven-tures, laughter, and the lonely freedom of the sea....

... The Newfoundlander is himself in a hundred ways, too subtle to be identified, but instantly felt by the stranger.

As a stranger from Canada I thought I perceived that Newfoundland-ers were more simple, in the literal meaning of the word, than most Canadians and far less sophisticated than most Americans. They have yet to feel the smartness, speed, tension, and fury of the mainland. They have not yet received the doubtful glories of a high living standard, nor the North American disillusionment which accompanies it. They therefore possess a patience, a dogged outward cheerfulness, and, I suspect, an inner contentment deeper than ours.

United by poverty and common peril, they have amassed their own philosophy of endurance, devised their own amusements, thought their own thoughts, written their own robust folklore, sung their own songs, and shared a kind of family jest.

If they have yet to see the full rewards of the machine age, now dawning, they have not suffered the North American blight of uniformity. Almost every native of Newfoundland remains a character, often an eccentric, Dickensian character, unpolished and untamable.

Though less educated, these people are more articulate than any Canadian outside Quebec; as articulate, indeed, as Americans, because lonely men must talk, and they talk ceaselessly.

More religious than most of us, they still affirm superstitions, ghosts, and legends that we lost long ago.

Their interests have always stretched abroad, but they remain the most provincial folk in Canada, their minds centered on the only land they know.

In short, four and a half centuries of separation and a century without immigration have made them Newfoundlanders and nothing else, a cohesive and recognizable race, a true nationality, and, by every definition, a people.

To me it seemed that, in acquiring Newfoundland, Canada had acquired in these people an asset far more important than the strategic northern gateway to the continent or certain raw resources....

[Waiting in the anteroom to Premier Joseph Smallwood's office, Hutchison observes people also there to see the Premier.] Among those visitors I met a women who unconsciously proclaimed the future of Newfoundland and the larger future of Canada. She was of middle age, a housewife from a poor home in some distant outport, and she had dressed for the great occasion in a new frock.

Now she sat upright on the edge of her chair, nervous at the prospect of meeting her hero. The whole story of her people, the four and a half centuries of struggle, poverty, and endurance, could be read in that woman's look. But she said nothing until I ventured to remark on the unseasonable weather. Whereupon, as my accent doubtless betrayed me as a mainlander, the floodgates of her life opened to release its contents of suffering, hope, and discovery.

The suffering was written on her lined cheeks, the hope in her eager eyes, and the discovery, oddly enough, on some colored postcards. These frayed exhibits from her handbag, more profound in their meaning than any government document, pictured in crude hues the cities of Canada, Niagara Falls, the prairies, the forest of the Pacific Coast. Had I actually seen these things? I said I had often seen them. She looked at me as at a visitor from Mars.

Someday, she added timidly, after her five sons had grown up, she would save a little money and see the mainland before she died. Then, uttering her discovery, she touched my hand and whispered: "We're all Canadians now, you know. It's our own country, every bit of it. Yes, it belongs to every last one of us. My, what a thing to think about!"

A thing to think about. How the presence of Canada had touched the mind of this woman, what improbable chemistry had been at work in some grubby outport, by what accident she had perceived the nation and accepted it as her own, I could not guess. Yet here and nowhere else on the island I thought I had encountered that inward spark and fragment of a dream which alone made Canada from the beginning and someday will join Newfoundland to it....

... [Later, a reflective Hutchison travels across Newfoundland by train, heading back to the mainland.] And suddenly I remembered that woman with her picture postcards, her valid Canadian passports. She at least, and perhaps many other unknown Newfoundlanders, had perceived Canada through the mist of the Atlantic and the centuries. Like all her people, like the fishermen in the twine loft [at Bauline], she was just entering the slow racial experience of Canadians from the beginning.

(Hutchison, *Tomorrow's Giant*, 1957, 8–33)

2 THE KINGDOM OF JOE HOWE, NOVA SCOTIA

☞ Volume 2 of British historian Arnold Toynbee's ten-volume *A Study of History* discusses humankind's relationship with the natural environment. Basically the volume analyses Toynbee's famous concept of "Challenge-and-Response." In one of his many examples he argues that the law of diminishing returns already evident in Maine's severe environment is revealed even more strongly continuing northward: "New Brunswick and Nova Scotia, which occupy the mainland between Maine and the Gulf of St. Lawrence, are the least prosperous or progressive provinces of the Dominion of Canada with the exception of the northeastern neighbour, Prince Edward Island." (Toynbee, Vol. 2, 2nd edition, 1935, 296.) Hutchison counterattacks Toynbee's belief that Nova Scotia's difficult environment is bound to hold its people back by substituting "standard of thought" for "standard of living" and praising the learning and thinking of Nova Scotians. In Captain Angus Walters, Hutchison finds his definition of Nova Scotia: "We're a strivin' people." ⌒

... [While in Halifax Hutchison had been musing about Joseph Howe, Nova Scotia's great nineteenth century statesman.] For ... fragmentary rumors from the past had started me thinking of the present – specifically of Professor Arnold Toynbee, the eminent English historian, who, disposing of the world's various civilizations like a man judging handicrafts, prize cattle, or pickles at a country fair, cites Nova Scotia as a classic example of inevitable defeat.

The Challenge of environment, in Toynbee's celebrated phrase, has proved too much for Nova Scotia's Response, and hence this province, like the northern New England states, must remain one of the "least prosperous and progressive areas in America," its civilization arrested, stunted, and forever doomed to inferiority by a niggard land and a misplaced people.

Was there anything, I wondered, in Toynbee's Olympian dictum? Before the day was finished, I concluded, with respect, that there was little or nothing in it....

Inevitably, Nova Scotia has lagged behind richer provinces in what we are pleased to call our standard of living, but what about its standard of life, especially its standard of thought?

I wished that Professor Toynbee could have been with me in the streets, offices, and homes of Halifax while I explored this question. He would have found here more ideas, more argument, more learning and clear thinking in one day than most Canadian cities can supply in a month. These people, as I should have known but didn't, as the Toynbees of the world have yet to understand, were always compelled to think hard if they were to survive. Their thoughts emerged in an illustrious role of national leaders, in perpetual civic debate, in the Howe legend, in the earthy wisdom of Judge Haliburton's immortal Sam Slick, and – let us never forget it – in the essential Atlantic ingredient of Confederation.

If these exhibits do not impress him, let the theorist of historic Challenge and Response sit for one evening under the fluted ceilings and molded cornices of some old Halifax home, let him listen to the casual talk of the dinner table, and he will encounter minds as up-to-date, active, and practical as any that made the great Canadian boom out of easy materials to the westward, together with a certain serenity, balance, and reverence for good things, good men, and good living that most Canadians have yet to learn.

He will find a sense of past time providing a sense of proportion in a hurried, disordered present. The standard of living, as measured by the Dominion Bureau of Statistics, may be relatively low. I suspected, after a few days in Nova Scotia, that the standard of life was perhaps the highest in Canada. In those terms, at least, Response was meeting Challenge.

The long struggle has left its mark. It has created a folk instantly distinguishable among the Canadian creaturehood. What most distinguished these people, it seemed to me, was their awareness of living in a poor land, of being the family's poor relation, of knowing, as few Canadians know, that life must be hard.

This makes a thrifty, unpretentious, but – because all of them must struggle together – a kindly and generous folk. They have a family feeling and next-door neighborliness almost lost in our richer communities. They resist better than most of us the conformity of the mass age. They are filled with a quiet pride and a pawky humor, the gift of Scotland, emerging in the silent chuckle, the mad tale, and the Scottish crack too wise to be called a wisecrack. They hate ostentation, support no Cadillac set, and, in the original meaning of that corrupted word, are well-bred....

... [Hutchison meets] Captain Angus Walters, the most famous seaman left in Nova Scotia and once skipper of the peerless *Bluenose,* a name to set the Canadian fancy tingling.

Strangely enough, we found Captain Walters in the steam and tin clatter of a dairy. He was hurling milk cans around, answering customers on the telephone, and talking in an accent compounded of England, Scotland, and Germany. The spirit of old Lunenburg seemed incarnate in a squat, powerful figure and a face grooved deep by Atlantic weather. Home was the sailor, home from sea, and right glad of it, he told me. This agile little man had mastered the sea, but, as he thought, the sea had turned against him and all his kind. How was that? ...

The day of the schooner, the dory, and the net was passing, and Captain Walters wanted none of the new day. "Why," he shouted in sudden fury, "the big draggers drag and rile the bottom like harrows, churnin' up the fish in' grounds and ruinin' the fish of all the sea. That's the story of it."

His fierce old eyes peered from under the dairyman's incongruous peaked cap to make sure I understood his larger meaning. After a pause the seaman who had penetrated the ultimate mystery unknown to any landsman said a curious thing: "There's in the sea everything there is on land – ah, more, far more than you can imagine. What is it? It's life, that's what. And now we're spoilin' it all. That's the story of it."

Why had he chosen, of all things, a dairy in his old age? Because without work he would die in six months. And, uttering the old faith of Lunenburg, he added: "We're a strivin' people."

A striving people. It occurred to me that the life of Nova Scotia needed no better definition.

Yet there was something rather sad in the Captain's confession that he never went near the wharves any more, this master of shipmasters. All the ships and the sails and the men he knew were gone. The intimate partnership of man, weather, ship, and fish had ended in an age of engines, factories, and processed fish sticks. A great thing had perished, or at least had changed beyond this man's recognition. Yes, but he had seen the mystery. He had mastered the sea, and he was still striving. That was the story of it.

From Lunenburg we set out in search of Peggy's Cove, which everyone has seen in a hundred familiar paintings and photographs. It was a long search in a maze of twisting roads designed by a mad engineer, and, at first sight, the famous Cove was hardly worth our trouble.

The painted glimpse of Arcady and the photographer's deceptive angle shots turned out to be nothing more than a narrow gash in a shore of solid stone, not much larger than a good-sized washtub, a surrounding chaos of boulders strewn broadcast like a giant's dice, a dozen listing houses, some wharves on rotted stilts, and a few battered fish boats. But we soon discovered something more important than scenery at Peggy's Cove.

A boy of some sixteen years was standing at the head of the cramped harbor, and his legs could almost span it. He had been grappling since dawn with his native environment, offering his own unconscious Response to Toynbee's brutal Challenge, and he had come home bearing one lobster from his homemade pot. With a man's pride the boy showed us his catch and said hopefully that he might get two or three more lobsters on the evening tide.

Oh, yes, things were mighty good at Peggy's Cove these days. Why, his grandmother could remember when only three houses stood here, and now his brother owned a truck, secondhand but still running fine. The land was thin and poor, but you could grow potatoes on beds of seaweed if you knew how. His father had a cow and moved it inland if the weather turned bad. "Oh, it's pretty, sir," he ventured, "when the waves come in a good fifty feet high over the rocks."

The lank figure in oilskins, the grinning young face against the rim of that stone inferno, and the pounding surf behind him would have made a picture for any painter. It seemed to me the humble portrait of a race. Yet all the thousand painters and photographers who have captured the mere outer quaintness of Peggy's Cove have somehow missed its meaning. So, perhaps, has Toynbee, the historian.

(Hutchison, *Tomorrow's Giant*, 1957, 40–54)

3 THE TOY CONTINENT, PRINCE EDWARD ISLAND

☞ Dubbing it a "Toy Continent," Hutchison considers Prince Edward Island to be "a state of mind," detached from the mainland "by a much wider void of thought" rather than by mere water.. Scale, stewardship of the land, and living within its means are vital elements to understand life in the province. In *The Unknown Country* Hutchison stressed that Vancouver Island was a landscape in the early stages of being created by its inhabitants: in Prince Edward Island Hutchison feels this has been accomplished. ☜

... [Hutchison had talked with various people on Prince Edward Island.] Everything, I gathered, grew better and bigger on The Island.

It was not until we reached a shore glowing like bronze in the sunset that I began to see the truth of these modest claims and to guess the nature of the miracle. For it is miraculous, all right, this tiny particle of land which seems to have been washed down by the St. Lawrence and anchored precariously in its Gulf – miraculous enough in geography, but still more unlikely in its human content.

The stranger will need a little time to discover why The Island's life is unique among all the regions of America. The reporter will not find here any "angle" for his story, since The Island has been polished smooth by more than three centuries of expert lapidary craftsmanship. But the scholar cannot confuse the Island race with any other. It has contracted out of the world's tumult, has refused to play the noisy charade of these times, and stands, by choice and necessity, alone.

No traveler, however insensitive, can fail to see, as soon as he has landed, that The Island is not merely a speck of soil detached from the mainland by water, but a state of mind detached by a much wider void of thought. This is a Lilliputian continent, physically and spiritually, and it is quite unimpressed by the larger continent beside it.

At first sight The Island denies all its portraits. The photographers and painters have long tried to convey this picture, and all have failed. Where most scenery disappoints your expectations, The Island exceeds them in a certain subtle fashion impossible to fix on film or canvas.

Impossible, I suppose, because the thing lacks all reality, evades the beholder like some shred of childhood memory, and, though inhabited by a thrifty and not very imaginative folk, somehow manages to create the brittle enchantment of a fairy tale.

You can hardly drive half a mile before you are wondering when you will wake up. This surely can be no part of America or of the contemporary world. It must be an optical illusion cunningly arranged to deceive the stranger, a conjurer's genial trick. Actually it is all the result of long and plodding toil by a people who may not have known exactly what they were doing, but have ended with a man-made miracle in miniature.

The terrain, alternately tonsured in cultivation and curled in foliage; the precise mosaic of reddish fields, each geometrically cut by a narrow wood lot of green; the gentle roll of the earth carrying inland the roll of the sea; the high-roofed and gabled houses, all as white, angular, and prim as genteel spinsters in crinoline; the fat crimson barns and over-stuffed cattle; even the farmer himself, the boy fishing with his willow stick in some quiet pond, and the lobster boats asleep in a shady cove are arranged like elaborate toys of paint and cardboard.

There is nothing like this anywhere else in America – a valentine of some two thousand square miles. To find an equal orderliness and minute design you must go to England and Europe, where men have long nursed, pampered, and worshipped their earth. Even there you will not find an exact replica. The Islanders imitate no one and defy imitators.

No fence, building, stone, tree, or blade of grass is out of place. Best of all – that is The Island's true secret – no human being is out of place either.

This smallest Canadian province has learned the partnership of man and earth as no other province or State of the Union has yet begun to learn it, undoubtedly because The Island is so small and manageable. If this is not perfection, it is the nearest equivalent that any Canadians have ever attained so far....

... Its area and wealth strictly limited, The Island, like Nova Scotia and New Brunswick, has always exported its citizens to other provinces and could never afford immigration. But Dr. MacKinnon [an historian at Prince of Wales College] thinks that the varied racial origins of Scots, English, Irish, and French, in that numerical order, have prevented a monotony of character. A casual visitor can see at least that The Island is full of nonconforming and lively characters.

It is true, nevertheless, that an insular geography has produced an insular mind, as limited and tidy as the soil around it. The Island may not have a large view of Canadian affairs, but it sees the thing at hand with peculiar clarity. It may not view the nation through a telescope, but its local microscope is a fine instrument.

These people cannot give the nation leadership, and have provided no political ideas or any statesman of note. Instead, they offer an example of thrift and management lacking in richer provinces, of alliance between man and environment, of skilled concentration on indigenous resources, of specialized production and the elimination of waste; above all, an example of sane living which a prodigal, hurried, and increasingly neurotic nation badly needs.

If The Islanders lack glamour, so called, they also lack illusions. They have the old virtues that go with simple life and long residence in one place. They are realists and they are friendly. Still, there must be some latent poetry in them – their little kingdom is as neatly put together as a sonnet.

(Hutchison, *Tomorrow's Giant*, 1957, 62–73)

4 THE LAND OF PETER EMBERLEY, NEW BRUNSWICK

☞ Peter Emberley, an obscure New Brunswick logger, is a mythic figure who incarnates the province's great logging activities of the past, and folk songs have been written about him. Despite long exploitation of forest resources, the province's attractive topography remains and New Brunswick has some of the most pleasant landscapes for living in Canada. Inhabitants are reconciled to a poor economy, but economic changes are coming. Hutchison's informants insist that Acadian culture is different from Quebecois culture. Of central importance in the life of New Brunswick is the cordial relationship of Acadians and English-speaking New Brunswickers, an example for Canada. ☜

This country was designed by nature as a cradle of contentment. Its gently rolling landscape, fair to the eye, soothing to the soul, is different from any other in Canada – not rugged enough to be called grand and appalling like the western mountains, not wild enough to be called spectacular, yet too wild and solitary to be tamed or spoiled. It is friendly to man and wholly feminine, the true motherland of the clan.

When we drove out of Fredericton, the swelling bosom of the [St. John] river was printed with the sun's red gules, and its shoulders were modestly decked in a lace of green. Spring had come at one stride, lighted the maples with the flame of scarlet bud, spangled the hills with white stars of blossom, set the birch moving in ghostly dance, and thawed out the crooked old limbs of the pines that once possessed the entire valley.

There are larger rivers in Canada than the St. John, none lovelier, and no other inhabited river so free of man's disfiguring spoor. Having lately seen the Rhine, we thought that it must have been very like this, long ago, before man populated and scarred it.

There were scars here, too, after man had cut the old pine forest, but new growth has covered them, except on the plateau around Gagetown. There the atomic age has inflicted a new scar.

As we passed by an old farming community, army workmen were removing the last of the farmers' houses and barns to prepare a vast training ground for Canadian troops.... Another struggle, the struggle for the world, had moved all the way from the Rhine of Europe to the remote Rhine of Canada....

(Hutchison, *Canada: Tomorrow's Giant*, 96–97)

... [Change is affecting the St. John River.] The economic revolution has marched in frontal attack upon most of the other provinces. It has crept slowly, almost silently into the narrow valleys of New Brunswick, and it is coming to stay. The professors [at the University of New Brunswick] and some of the province's leading politicians told me of the huge hydro-power scheme on the upper St. John, which of itself will largely transform the provincial economy, of new mineral discoveries in the north, and of other sure omens of the revolution....

(Hutchison, *Canada: Tomorrow's Giant*, 93–94)

These people may claim, almost with an inverted pride, to inhabit the poorest province per capita in Canada, next to the new province of Newfoundland and the tiny garden of Prince Edward Island, but poverty and joint memories of the great age have knit them into a clan, almost a secret society and arcanum within the nation....

... [Hutchison imagines that he and a Loyalist friend are having lunch with Captain James Murray, who in 1758 expelled the last Acadians from the Miramichi Valley.] He [i.e. Murray] would have learned [of] the total failure of his mission. He would have learned, among other things, that the Acadians, surviving every attempt to dislodge them, will soon turn New Brunswick into Canada's second predominantly French-speaking province.

I supposed that it would be dangerous to question my host, the descendant of a United Empire Loyalist family from New England, about such painful matters. But the question must be asked. Bracing myself for an explosion of Loyalist anger, I finally ventured to inquire how he would enjoy living as a member of an English-speaking minority. To my amazement, he was not angry at that prospect. He was not even alarmed.

The ethnic shift, the new age, and the most promising racial experiment in America were natural, he said, inevitable, and, to him, entirely agreeable. As a businessman he had found reliable associates among the French Canadians, and good friends with much to teach their neighbors of British stock. In another generation, he hoped, both races would be bilingual, as they should be, and still more friendly.

That reply was almost unbelievable to a Canadian from any province whose speech is predominantly English or French. Imagine what Ontario would say if it heard that it must soon face a French-Canadian majority, or how Quebec would regard the opposite prospect! My host's statement could hardly come from any English-speaking Canadian except a New Brunswicker. The clan might be secretive, it might regret the passage of the great age, but it was preparing itself for a greater.

How was it, I asked, that this community of two evenly balanced races had escaped the long and ugly racial tensions of Upper and Lower Canada that became Ontario and Quebec?

"We had something," my host explained, "that they didn't have. We had time. The thing has happened gradually, you see. We were never organized at the beginning in two separate blocs of race like Ontario and Quebec. We were always mixed up together, and race never became much of an issue with us. Each side had time to learn that the other was all right before any real trouble broke out. Time saved us." ...

[In Fredericton, Hutchison visited an Acadian community leader] The first thing to understand, he told me, was that Acadian culture had not based itself on "nationalism" as that word is used in Quebec to denote a belligerent racial isolation. It was not belligerent because its rights of language, religion, and education were not challenged here. The Acadians felt no need to isolate themselves because they were entirely secure. They would never form a racial or even a political bloc with Quebec. True enough, many people from Quebec had moved into the forest, farm, and fishing industries of New Brunswick and formed almost solid communities of their own language, like the upriver town of Edmundston, but they were being absorbed rapidly in the Acadian culture and found no cause here to resent the dwindling English-speaking majority.

The Acadian gentleman still retained some inherited French instincts. Though he was pressed for time and due at an important official meeting, his Gallic manners compelled him to escort me on foot to the hotel. There he raised his hat in farewell and gave me a little message for all Canadians.

"Tell Canada," he said, "that New Brunswick is the crucible of a great national experiment. Tell it that the experiment is working out better here than any other place in the world. People ask what New Brunswick contributes to Canadian life. That is our real contribution. Someday the nation, and perhaps the world, will appreciate its value."

This sounded much too good to be true, so I questioned some of the English-speaking politicians in the Parliament Buildings who, I felt sure, would have different views. I was wrong. These men endorsed in every detail what the Acadian had told me. The French-speaking New Brunswickers, they said, had attracted no attention until recent years. In their labors of mere survival, they had found little time for politics, were generally poor and often ill-educated. Now they were learning fast, were insisting that their sons study English to prosper in a dual society, and were training a generation of youngsters who would soon make their names in government. Future politics, however, would not be split on racial lines, as had often happened in other provinces, simply because any durable government must seek support among both races and could not rely on either alone.

Such a hopeful and friendly racial evolution, though it directly affects only some five hundred and fifty thousand people in New Brunswick, must interest any observer of the current race-mad world....

(Hutchison, *Tomorrow's Giant*, 1957, 87–9, 94–5)

5 THE LOST PEASANT, QUEBEC

 Young people leave rural Quebec for other parts of the province and distant parts of Canada and the old people left behind feel lost. Two long-established peoples in Canada, French and British Canadians, are often in conflict, their duality only "overtopped by the Canadian land." In the meantime the "engines of industry" are changing Quebec's economy, and Quebec society is changing as well.

[Hutchison talks to a farmer at Little Pabos, southwest of Percé, on the Gaspé Peninsula.] "De land," he went on, "is too small. She's not big enough for my boys. So dey go away."

His farm had been cut up again and again and divided between the sons of some twelve generations until it could be divided no more. That division and scarcity of land, repeated on countless French Canadian farms, was the beginning of Quebec's economic upheaval and, more important, of its spiritual transformation.

"Too small," the peasant repeated. "So de boys can't stay 'ome."

The village boys have been going away for a long time. In the days of this man's father, less than one century ago, the landless sons of Quebec poured into New England, half a million of them, between 1860 and 1890, and bred there a French Canadian stock of some two millions. Now the industrial revolution offers plenty of jobs in Canada, and the young are moving to the city, are pushing beyond Quebec into Ontario, the prairies, and British Columbia, and in that movement are being themselves changed as they have already changed French Canada beyond recognition.

"Big pay up dere in de city," the peasant said. "Nice house. Big car. Frigerator. Television, too. Dat's fine t'ing for young man, eh?"

I agreed it was a fine thing, but I was thinking of something else. I was trying to imagine the ceaseless wanderlust, the restless energy and thirst for adventure, the roving instincts inherited from ancestral Norsemen in Normandy, that had first carried these people across the ocean, had sent them paddling to the edge of the Rockies and down the Mississippi to the Gulf of Mexico while men of British stock were fenced east of the Alleghenies by a thin line of French power.

These Norman people, as Hilaire Belloc once said of their mother race in France, had marched forth perpetually to be sucked homeward, having accomplished nothing but an epic. The epic of the French Canadians seemed to end with the British Conquest of 1759. Their conquerors expected at first that this handful of ruined rustics would soon lose their native qualities and accept a superior British civilization. Actually the real epic was only beginning.

In less than two hundred years the French Canadians not only have fastened their own civilization – more French in some ways than France itself – upon their Laurentian homeland, but also, growing from sixty thousand to some five millions, a third of the nation, have burst the bounds of Quebec, resumed the old westward march on the moccasin trails of their fathers, and colored the whole life of Canada. In this process they have ceased to be French in anything but tongue; they have become nothing but Canadians. If they are thus nothing but North Americans, they remain a stubborn enclave, or series of enclaves, within the life of the continent.

The peasant behind the fence doubtless knew little of this epic factually. Yet he knew it better than I, who had studied it in books. He knew it racially. The long racial memory, going back to Cartier's landfall a few miles from Little Pabos, was unbroken in this man.

"De land," he said for the third time, "is too small for de boys."

I asked him if he sometimes felt lonely for his children. He didn't answer, but his eyes searched mine for communication. He hungered, I could see, for some knowledge of the far-off, mysterious land where his sons and daughters had gone, never to return. There were yearning, hurt, and bewilderment in those old eyes. He wanted to know what was happening to his family, to the life it had once lived here, to the larger life beyond the hills, the life he would never see....

Conquered? Inferior? Weak? Why, this man and his people, the handful besieged by the whole force of the British Empire and apparently destroyed, have achieved a conquest with no recorded parallel, have given us our second heritage, the treasures of French civilization, and, for all the confusing eddies on the surface of politics, have made possible the transcontinental state. Strangers to us, yes. But they are the oldest, most deeply grained and fundamental Canadians in this land.

Our roots in the British Isles have never been cut. The roots of French Canada in France were twice cut beyond repair – by the so-called Conquest and by France's Revolution. In the rest of Canada we are still torn between history and geography. In Quebec and its suburbs geography won the struggle long ago.

That is part of the Canadian duality, but even the sovereign fact is overtopped by the Canadian land, only by the land. For the common love of this land, the dream of a separate society shared by Canadians of every race, is the national solvent, the ultimate fact. It has always united Canadians through all their quarrels, through one rebellion and many terrifying collisions. As I was soon to find in Quebec, it is now uniting them much more rapidly than most of us realize....

It may be, indeed, more troubled than most of Canadian society because here the revolution of the machine is so rapid, after its long delay, so sudden and unexpected, and cuts so deep across a settled way of life and thought.

The same revolution is under way, of course, from Newfoundland to British Columbia. In Quebec it is comparatively larger in size and almost different in kind. As nowhere else it threatens the age-old habits of a race, it touches even the religion of that race, and, since modern industry cannot be isolated, it dooms the isolation of an ancient peasant society. This abrupt change, by far the largest since the so-called Conquest, is proclaimed by every industrial smokestack beside the St. Lawrence. It issues from every machine in the factories. It clamors over every labor dispute, dominates every maneuver of politics, and is uttered by farmers over their fences.

Quebec has ceased to be a simple farm community, an island of anachronism in the sea of modern America. Its livelihood is earned mainly by the engines of an industry which must soon be one of the most productive on the continent. Two thirds of its people are urban. The quaint French Canada of yesterday lives only in a few shrinking pockets, in the tourist advertisements and the holiday diaries of schoolmarms from Boston....

[Hutchison, driving westward, leaves the Gaspé.] As suddenly as it had risen, the road rolled down the southern shoulder of the St. Lawrence Gulf, that long gash of geography, that yawning mouth of the nation which, with its river, carries the nation's cargoes halfway across the continent. The Gulf was piled deep in fog today. We could not see across it, but along this southern shore we began to see, in its latest version, the nation's oldest process.

Since Cartier explored it and Champlain seized it, man has always clung to the St. Lawrence system, fought his wars for its possession, divided it between two states, and built the continental economy around it. Here in Quebec he clings to the riverbank with special tenacity.

A double line of farms and industry marks French Canada's chief heritage, its heartland. The stark smokestacks, the towns clustered around these grimy altars of commerce, the logs in booms or mountainous pyramids, the paper streaming off the rollers, the people no longer following the plow but punching the time clock, all inform the traveler of Quebec's new age.

In economic and human terms this change is wide and deep; in geographical terms narrow and thin. The double shelf of the river was colored green by agriculture long ago. Now it is dappled by the black smudges of industry. Yet only a few miles away the land has been little altered, except for a few towns and camps, since Cartier first glimpsed it from his ship.

We drove westward against the steady eastward march of the revolution. The villages began to look more prosperous, better painted, and (I have to admit it) quaint and toylike as in the travel booklets. Their houses wore those familiar gimcrack porches of the Christmas cards, the gaudy false shutters, hipped roofs, and dormers, all designed like shelves of confectionery from the kitchen of some fanciful chef. The revolution had not touched them yet, and, one hopes, will never alter them, but it was moving this way.

At a hotel in one of these river towns the agents of the revolution could be seen reconnoitering the next advance....

This well-spoken young man [an engineer staying in the hotel] was a portent of the times. In his sort Quebec had begun to educate its own technicians and supply the native managers of the revolution. The old educational system, which consigned all scholars to the humanities and thus gave the best jobs in the new industries to English-speaking Canadians, was being overhauled at last. And high time, too, the engineer said. Actually, he assured us, the myth of his people as instinctively rural and agricultural had never been more than a myth anyway.

"We always liked the town," he explained. "Why, it took twenty years after Champlain got settled in Quebec before they cleared an acre of land. If a boy couldn't get a job in town, he took to the woods. We were town people, or *coureurs-de-bois,* or soldiers by preference. Out west you see big farms, far apart. Here the towns are close together because we're social animals and always have been. This idea that we weren't made for industry is ridiculous. We take to it like a duck to water. We're far more urban by nature than you English."

Perhaps he exaggerated, but urban civilization is packed tight along the river.... So many cities and towns that no traveler can remember their names, ... are producing, wholesale, that modern species, the industrial man, and quietly spreading the uniformity of the industrial age in a French version. How, I wondered, was the process affecting the largest and oldest force in this society?

Soon I found myself in a certain village, far from the main road, pacing the sunny, walled garden of a monastery with a monk of serene look, powerful mind, and quiet speech. Yes, he said, it was true, all too true – the country boy who moved to the city often lost touch with the Church....

"Of course," this saintly little man admitted, "the impact of the new things is very great when a society is in such sudden change. The Church may lose in numbers. But numbers are not everything, you know. Quebec is being educated. We are gaining in quality."

He volunteered a piece of information which, from such a source, astounded me: "You Protestants imagine that the Church is a monolith, a single thing, inflexible. How absurd! It is single only in a few basic doctrines. Once or twice in a century, perhaps, the Pope pronounces certain fundamentals. Apart from the articles of faith, we think as we please. Do you realize that some of the most radical social thinking in Quebec today is in the Church, in Laval University especially?"

"Oh, no, my friend, the Church is not monolithic. It is full of conflicting thoughts, what some people might even call social heresies. Why, there's more difference between me and a Jesuit, for instance, in all things but the Faith, than there is between a Methodist and a Christian Scientist. And never forget this or you'll never understand Quebec – the Church, too, is changing. Not in the Faith, of course, but in everything else. It has always grown with society. That's why it remains so strong."

(Hutchison, *Tomorrow's Giant*, 1957, 106–20)

6 THE FORTRESS, QUEBEC

☞ Quebec City is a fortress of the French Canadian mind. In probing Canada's French and English duality, Hutchison's experience and contacts as one of Canada's greatest journalists come to the fore. His comments appear to foreshadow the Royal Commission on Bilingualism and Biculturalism of 1963–70. Hutchison finds that not only the economy but also society and the Church are changing. He also refers to the massive resource developments in the Quebec portion of the Canadian Shield, but, as always, comes back to Quebec's roots on the St. Lawrence. ☞

[Quebec City] ... is not only the capital of a great province, the manager of vast natural resources, and the stronghold of a race, but also the core of its struggle with another race. The outcome of that struggle has always been the paramount question in Canadian life, and the answers – hopeful or discouraging, friendly or hostile – have always come mainly out of Quebec City.

The twin forces of the French Canadian nature have erupted repeatedly here through the medium of furious politics: on the one hand, the centrifugal force of separatism and racial mystique which tries to isolate French Canada from the nation, to keep the race pure, the culture undiluted, the Faith invulnerable, Champlain's old dream intact; on the other hand, the centripetal force which would preserve French Canada's ideals but in full co-operation, friendship, and understanding with the other race.

So the inner contest of Quebec has raged ever since Wolfe's soldiers hauled down the lilies of France, has moved through countless outward variations, has sometimes produced crises almost fatal to the national state, and has thus swelled and subsided in tidal rhythm.

The personalities, the political maneuvers, the banners and slogans have often changed. The inner contest has never changed. It is now, as it always has been, a contest between the French Canadians who see, know, and love only Quebec, and those who have seen the nation whole, have perceived Quebec's great future in a dual Canadian society and welcomed it.

The English-speaking Canadian usually forgets, underestimates, or misunderstands the separatist movements called Nationalism that threatened, in the nineteenth century, to disrupt the frail Confederation laboriously built here in Quebec City; the mystical and impossible project of an independent French Canadian state; the bitter, wrenching clash between the liberal leaders of Quebec politics and the conservative leaders of the Church....

All these men were wrong. They had been watching the side eddies, not the main current of Quebec life. The main current, in alliance with English-speaking Canadians, gave us responsible government, Confederation, and the nation we know today. Always, on that main current, the greatest figures of French Canada have been moderates working with the moderates of other provinces. Not once in all the collisions of the races has a French Canadian Nationalist ever controlled the federal politics of Quebec.

The main current may slow down, twist, or sometimes seem to reverse itself. It may be disguised by contrary movements on the surface. The anxious watcher on the shore will often be distracted by the shouts of local demagogues, by the deceptive ebullience of the French race, by racialists of English tongue, and by overlearned treatises from the pens of foreign experts. Nevertheless, the current carrying two races in a joint voyage which neither can escape still moves inexorably like the St. Lawrence.

"*Mon cher Henri,*" Laurier once said to Bourassa, "Quebec does not have opinions but only sentiments." The Nationalists have always tried to manipulate those oldest sentiments of Quebec's life and one half of its nature – the xenophobia, the sense of isolation and grievance, the resentments, the nostalgia, and the folk memory of the Conquest. In local politics, though seldom in the politics of Ottawa, this manipulation has often been successful, and has succeeded abundantly in our time. But in our time the main current has suddenly accelerated.

Is Quebec moving closer to the rest of Canada or further away? I put that question to many men, high and low, and invariably got the same reply, thus phrased by an eminent Catholic churchman: "Don't be deceived by the clamor on the surface. Anyone who has read our history knows that the relations between Quebec and English Canada are incomparably better today than they've ever been. Why, in my lifetime, and I'm not an old man, the situation has changed almost beyond belief. And remember another thing – we're French by heredity, yes. But we're molded by British institutions. Politically we're British. We use the British institutions of politics to fight for our rights. Next time there's trouble, as of course there will be, remember that if your own province were the only English-speaking Protestant community in America you'd fight for your rights, just as we do. And I dare say you'd be just as prickly about it as we are." ...

[Hutchison talks to the proprietor of a hotel in the Shield, north of Quebec City.] For many years, he said, he had been the local organizer of the ruling political party. His district, I gathered, was well and tightly organized, the government's patronage distributed where it would do the most good. When I remarked that the speeches of the Quebec Nationalists sometimes alarmed English-speaking Canada, a grin of flashing dentures appeared beneath my host's mustache.

"You don't understand," he said. "That talk is for politics. Listen to it with one ear. Listen with the other ear to the people and watch what really happens. Not like the speeches, eh? No, no, that is the horse of a new color."

He winked, pressed his finger against my chest, and added: "The people are not children any more. They know what time it is of the day. Quebec is changing."

It is changing mainly because man has mastered an alchemy which transmutes the sterile Pre-Cambrian Shield into gold.

The upland reservoir, hurling its waters to the Atlantic and Hudson Bay, holds perhaps half of Canada's potential hydro power, and of itself will nourish a major workshop of the continental economy. In Quebec the Shield also holds the iron ore of Ungava, other minerals and timber in the perfect combination of industry – a treasury beyond measurement, only a portion of it yet tapped.

Yet, when you see it, man's work has made only an occasional scratch upon the surface. Saguenay's dark gorges look as empty as when Cartier reported them gleaming with "diamants and leaves of fine gold as thicke as a man's nayle." They lead not to Cartier's Kingdom of Saguenay, but to the soaring dams of Shipsaw and the factories of Arvida that turn bauxite from Guiana into aluminum. The same spill and lash of water carries the upland logs down to the river and powers the mills to turn them into paper. Then, if you move a little way from the riverbank, the land rolls on to the north as the first Frenchmen must have seen it.

The northern farm country of Maria Chapdelaine around Lake St. John, the newly rich mining towns like Rouyn-Noranda and Val d'Or, the whole industrial complex of the Abitibi country with its spreading network of roads and railways, give Quebec a new dimension. But its life, as from the beginning, is attached to the central river, at once the stomach and the lung of its economy. The St. Lawrence digests the food of the hinterland, inhales the traffic of the Atlantic, and exhales the traffic of the Canadian interior all the way to the Great Lakes.

(Hutchison, *Tomorrow's Giant*, 1957, 128–36)

7 THE HOMELAND, ONTARIO

☞ Southern Ontario, Canada's wealthiest land, the one that benefits most from protective tariffs, is the most difficult region to portray. It is 'a loose congeries of separate civilizations.' One thing is clear: Ontario is at the centre of the industrial change that is taking place in Canada, as is evident in the area between Toronto and Niagara, where the revolution is permanently recorded as a national monument composed of a trilogy of Welland Canals built at different times. ☜

[Hutchison reflects on the hold that Ontario has on himself: the boy who moved elsewhere.] That boy is dead, though still walking about, but he does not forget. He remembers Ontario, but he cannot hope to understand it. For if Ontario is the richest, the best-known, and the most powerful region of Canada, it is also the most mysterious. Every other region has been typed, at least in caricature. Ontario has no recognizable image, accurate or inaccurate. In the national gallery its portrait is a blur.

Great machines were graving new lines in that vague, composite face as we drove up the St. Lawrence. The Seaway's monstrous ditches scarred the green meadows. Square mountains of concrete had erupted in the placid current like volcanoes. Once again, as he has been doing over and over again for more than one hundred years, man was reshaping America's central channel for his purposes....

Ontario must be getting used to violent change, for it is the true vortex of the Canadian revolution. Not many places in the world have changed so rapidly, but the changes have been uneven, chaotic, and diverse in Ontario, have only served, in fact, to prove that there is no actual entity of that name. Instead, there is a loose congeries of separate civilizations lumped together for administrative purposes. Hence the blurred portrait and the mystery.

That night we found our way to a fine old stone house on the riverbank and were welcomed by one of Canada's most famous scholars. "Never talk," said he, "about Ontario. There's no such place. There's no such thing as an Ontario person. The name is only a political, not even a geographical expression. Why, I can show you at least half a dozen typical Ontarios and as many typical Ontario breeds. They're identified, for convenience, on the map. They have one provincial government. But they're as different as Nova Scotia is from British Columbia. Ontario is just a fiction."

Nevertheless, that fiction must be explored....

[Hutchison drove to the Niagara Peninsula.] Now we were in another Ontario, another climatic belt, and the Ruhr of Canada. A year earlier we had driven exactly the same sort of road, built by Adolf Hitler, through exactly the same combination of factories and smokestacks in the middle of green fields, the same orchards and vineyards, the same process which is turning a peasantry into a proletariat – a common world-wide process, but focused and perfected here as nowhere else in Canada.

I say it is perfected because most of the swelling satellite towns of Toronto are being admirably planned, though of course the old, planless villages were much better. The new factories are as modern, comfortable, and sightly as factories can be. The urban workers, many of them recent immigrants, seem to get along well with the farmers who have tilled this land since Loyalist times.

To the old-timer of the Niagara Peninsula it is tragic, just the same, to see the hungry jaws of industry biting deeper every day into the orchards, the apple trees cut down to make way for a factory, the vineyards overrun by bungaloid subdivisions in mathematical squares....

... What is coming out of Ontario's gigantic test tube? What kind of city, what kind of society, what kind of human being?

From a hill near Welland one can see both the current symptoms of this process and a glimpse of its beginnings.

Farms, towns, factories, and smoke roll out to the northern horizon. The towers of the Niagara electrical grid dance in well-ordered ballet, with outflung arms and pirouette of steel legs. Directly below the hill lies Canada's most revealing monument, the three Welland Canals, triple autograph of the nation in stone.

Today's revolution began right here when Canadians undertook their first big construction job and bypassed the continental barricade of Niagara Falls. First they made a narrow, winding ditch and queer little locks, rising in places by seven separate steps to the mile. Then they made a wider, straighter ditch, larger locks, and higher steps. Finally they made the beeline of the present Welland Canal, a broad man-made river carrying an unbroken procession of ships, day and night.

Most of the stone walls are still in place as the masons left them in the old canals, and should last as long as Egypt's pyramids. Aeons hence, if visitors from distant planets ask what manner of folk once lived in Canada, let them look at these three ditches. They tell our story better than any written word. They could have been built only by a folk of imagination, courage, and faith hidden under a deceptive look of mere competence and thrift.

A visitor in any European town is shown the ruins of some cathedral, castle, or royal tomb. In a Canadian town the proud citizenry always showed us the new factory, the marble-faced bank, or the improved sewage system. These are our castles, cathedrals, and tombs. As a national monument I prefer the three canals. They say just about everything that needs to be said, and their message is indelible.

(Hutchison, *Tomorrow's Giant*, 1957, 147–59)

8 THE SHIELD, NORTHERN ONTARIO

☞ One of the "spirit lines of the nation," Hutchison tells us, is the stone rim between the Shield and southern Ontario farmlands. It is part of the Archaean rim that J.D. Rogers delimited. This is mining country with spots of agriculture. A different spirit resides here, a life of camps, of moving on to the next camp, and a great mixing of peoples. This distinctive pioneer land – this "empire of the Shield" – captures people. Lakehead, now Thunder Bay, is already an outpost of the prairies. Since writing *The Unknown Country* Hutchison has learned to appreciate the grain elevators of Thunder Bay – "our tribal deities." ☞

[Hutchison makes a discovery "on entering the Shield."] This harsh and naked land was called Ontario. In true distance from the various Ontarios we had already traveled, it might as well have been within the Arctic Circle. It was, in fact, within another circle, or, rather, the semi-circle of the Canadian Shield, that vast stone horseshoe which lies across two thirds of the nation, from Labrador to the Mackenzie River.

On entering the Shield, hardly a hundred miles north of Toronto, we had begun to see that not only the land but also the people had changed. The people of the Shield are of many races, by national definition. They are all one race by the definition of environment and by bent of mind.

On the other side of the Shield, men's eyes are turned southward to the central river system and, beyond it, to the United States. Once the line of the Shield is crossed – and that crossing is marked as clearly as any international boundary by the sudden eruption of rounded glacial rock – you find human life turned forever northward and bounded on the south by the awesome Pre-Cambrian dike.

North of the stone rim, human life is numerically small. Most of the Canadian people live south of the rim, about seventy per cent of them within one hundred miles of the American boundary. That pattern may shift somewhat, but not much. For the Shield is arable only in a few jagged trenches, and it can never support the population of an agricultural land. Its mining towns doubtless will always be widely separated specks on the empty Arctic slope.

At all events, the Pre-Cambrian line is decisive. Yesterday we had walked the cozy streets of Ottawa and, a few days earlier, the lush orchards of Niagara. Now we seemed to have landed on a different continent. This was no longer Ontario, whatever the map might say. It was not the real north either. More than half the girth of Canada lay beyond Cobalt. Nevertheless, we had crossed one of the sharp internal borders and spirit lines of the nation....

... Evening had come before we escaped from Cobalt and headed into the empire of the Shield.

The straight, smooth road bore no mark of man's passage in an hour's travel, save countless corpses of porcupines crushed by his wheels. A yard from the pavement the Shield, oldest solid substance on our planet, and mother of all things, rolled in mammary swelling to a hard northern horizon under a dome of gunmetal. The northern twilight, like the rock beneath it, was flecked with precious mineral. Gold dust danced in the long sunset, and the air carried the old, tantalizing Canadian smell of wild rose, acrid spruce, Balm of Gilead, and damp muskeg – a smell sweet and bitter with boyhood memory and a man's vain regrets.

Suddenly the silence was shattered by a thundering frog chorus, daylight died grudgingly with a last scarlet tear, and to the northward the lights of Kirkland Lake glowed like a false dawn. As we neared the town we could make out a red neon cross against the black fringe of the world and then the ghostly mine towers floating in the moonlight.

It was after twelve o'clock when we reached the brassy main street of Kirkland Lake, but on a Saturday night no one had yet thought of going to bed. We could hardly find a place to park our car. Every restaurant was crammed. Store windows blazed with displays of refrigerators, washing machines, electric gadgets, new automobiles, women's lingerie, evening gowns, and all the essentials of civilization, more than a hundred miles from nowhere.

The townspeople saw nothing strange in this little patch of light amid the dark void of the Shield. To us the town looked as unreal as a stage set erected half an hour ago, to be dismantled and carted away at daybreak. Of course it wasn't really a town at all, for all its solid business buildings, modern homes, and shiny new cars; it was a miners' camp.

We could not hope to sleep in the stifling cubicle of the hotel. The Diamond Drillers Convention, or some such festive company, had taken over the town and would be drilling enthusiastically with a clink of glasses until dawn at least. So we went for a walk. No one else was walking. Kirkland Lake seems to travel exclusively on wheels and boasts the ownership of more cars per head than any other place in America. Yet a block from the glaring main street we found ourselves on the lip of wilderness and limbo.

The cold northern shoulder of the earth sloped downward to the pole in a hush punctuated here and there by the tick of man's machinery, in an opaque darkness pierced by his few pale winks of light. He can bore a few miles of tunnel into the body of the Shield, smelt some fragments of its ore. His camps – called towns or even cities – leave hardly a bruise on a surface little changed since it rose from the steaming liquid of creation.

The houses of Kirkland Lake clutch the bare rock faces. The rough floor of the Shield cuts through the back yards. Sidewalks sometimes reel six feet above the road, and the road is level with the next row of roofs.

Some thrifty householders have managed to grow a tree or two, a bed of flowers, or a patch of lettuce in a square yard of soil. The rich have made a few ambitious gardens. But this town remains physically and spiritually a camp. Perhaps there can never be anything but camps upon the Shield, whatever they call themselves.

We inquired our way to the office of *The Northern Daily News* and found the editor, a blonde slip of a girl, working late. She said that, after her home town of Galt in the Ontario farm country, she had been overpowered by the glacial boulders of the Shield. Then, going home on a holiday, she had found that the south was no longer home. The north had got her. It gets everyone.

The mystery, she intimated, lived in the land and in the people. The land was the most beautiful she had ever seen, once she adjusted her urban eyes to its stern contours, and the people were the best she had ever found in Canada – generous, candid, and neighborly as no other people.

The symbols of their life, she said, were the mine towers, understandable only if you looked at them in moonlight or against the dawn. A stranger might find only ugliness in these crooked steeples of metal and wood, but after a time they began to appear beautiful in their line and angular composition, like a good painting. They were the marks of man's occupancy, his title deeds to the Shield. And down below them, deep down in the substance of the Shield, men were working day and night. That, said the girlish editor, made you think. She advised us to take a second look at the towers.

We took a second look, but to us the towers were just black exclamation marks, clumsy and ill-shaped, punctuating the bright alphabet of the stars. A sensitive girl from Galt might see in these poor wooden sheds the cathedral spires of England or the minarets of Baghdad. The men who had made them and now labored in secret runnels far below had penetrated a mystery too deep for us. We were only southern Canadians, suddenly overcome by a sky that hung in spangled ceiling over emptiness and instantly cut us down to size....

[Hutchison asked an old miner in Kirkland Lake why he didn't leave the North.] "Once you're in," he said, "you can't get out. And who wants to? Sure, the big boys in Toronto get all the gravy. They don't even come up here to see us work, not them. Might get their shoes muddy. But they miss all the fun down there. What do them pansies know about minin'? They only own the mines."

He permitted himself a bitter little laugh and stretched his hands across the table for me to see the callused palms and crushed fingers.

"That," he said, "is minin'. Fifty-three years of minin' and still broke. But, hell, it's okay. This country's only beginnin'. They haven't even scratched her yet." ...

That mighty horseshoe pressed down on more than half the nation was not what we had expected after seeing it only at night or, in daylight, from trains and airplanes.

We had pictured an unbroken and uniform sweep of badland, Christmas trees, and glassy puddles. We found the Shield varying from mile to mile as the rock welled up into little mountains, sank into swamp and muskeg, parted to hold big lakes or circular inkwells, disappeared under a fur of black spruce, and opened now and then into lush meadows for man's plow.

The fertile belt of clay, the rich fields, big barns, and sleek cattle around the dairy town of Earlton, about one hundred miles within the Shield, looked almost unbelievable after the sterile rock north and south of it. A young French Canadian farmer said most of the people hereabouts came from Quebec and were doing fine. The ancient civilization of the St. Lawrence had leap-frogged across the stone dike and prospered in this remote pocket of agriculture. Plenty more land could be cleared, this man said. Life was good and everybody friendly, also bilingual, as they should be....

To the westward a combination of minerals, timber, and water power is making a series of industrial centers in the most unlikely places. Probably nature never intended man to live here, but around the smelter town of Sudbury he has improved on her work of desolation.

The fumes of his acids, in the process of extracting most of the world's nickel, have killed every blade of vegetation, stripped the rock of its thin disguise, and produced a fair replica of hell or Hiroshima. One might be traveling, for several miles along the highway, on the surface of some dead planet. Sudbury crouches around the belching Moloch of its smelter. It rears new mountains of slag. It builds a city in a vacuum of aching stone, and looks from the distance like a casual outcrop of gray ore.

As the heat gushed out of a stone oven at a hundred degrees Fahrenheit, we staggered into a little store for a bottle of cold pop to discover, behind the counter, the stately figure of Colonel Blimp, speaking in the Colonel's accent. I suspected that this English gentleman might be oppressed by the mixed population of Sudbury, and asked him obliquely if there were many foreigners in town. He bridled at my question.

"What do you mean, foreigners?" he demanded. "This, sir, is an international city. No people are foreigners to us. They're all people."

Thus rebuked, we sped westward on a busy highway at the customary local speed of eighty miles an hour.

It was too hot to pause at Blind River, a name as magical today as Cobalt was half a century ago. This village is surrounded by perhaps the largest treasury of uranium yet discovered, and confidently expects to be a leading Canadian city....

Soon we were in a region of hill, forest, lake, and river. It is cooled by the refrigerating apparatus of Lake Huron and is perfectly designed for the camper, fisherman, and painter. Now we began to understand why those pioneer Canadian painters, the distinguished Group of Seven, had gone gently mad in such surroundings. Their reckless brush strokes seem extravagant only to those who have not beheld their model.

That night we camped beside Lake Huron, in such an amphitheater of terraced green rock, wild flowers, tufted islands, wheeling gulls, and dancing fireflies as the Group of Seven has never quite captured.

An early start brought us to Sault Ste. Marie for breakfast. The Sault is a town, to be sure, a town prettier and better built than most on a single main street several miles long, so that a businessman must take a taxi to visit his neighbor in the next office. But the Sault is something more important than a town. It is the nexus and hinge of North America. [Hutchison discusses the Sault Ste. Marie canal and canal traffic, and continues westward to present Thunder Bay via U. S. roads, because the Trans-Canada Highway north of Lake Superior was not completed until 1962.] ...

The grain elevators of Fort William and Port Arthur rise, lean and lonely, beside the indigo pool of Thunder Bay like the towers of Carcassonne. The Canadian towers seemed to us more impressive than the French. Besides, the elevators, in the simplicity of their functional design, are genuine and original, whereas self-conscious Carcassonne is an overprimped reproduction of another age.

Clarence Decatur Howe, who built these concrete columns, is usually accounted only an eminent Canadian politician and businessman. At the Lakehead he had unconsciously qualified as one of our leading artists.

His work, seen at a distance in clean vertical line, is our nearest approach to Egypt's Pyramids, England's Tower of London, or India's Taj Mahal. At any rate, it expresses exactly our grim and practical northern life. All the labor, the silence, the loneliness and stern beauty of our land broods in these gray cylinders, rank on rank astride the blue metal of the lake.

The visiting spacemen of the future will make nothing of these colossal structures, will probably ascribe their upright sproutings to a religion

which worshipped strange and savage gods. In a way those future anti-
quarians will be right. Canada worships the gods of commerce. The
engineer is its idol; the production and movement of material things are
its constant fascination. Those elevators of the Lakehead contain our
tribal deities....

... It was clear anyway that the Lakehead belonged to Ontario only by
provincial statute. Its eyes are turned to the west, where the grain comes
from. The people of southern Ontario and the people of Thunder Bay
are as unlike as Canadians can be – a settled society and an impatient
band of pioneers.

As westerners we were prejudiced in this old folk argument. We like
a breed of western men who can casually build an industrial complex
five hundred miles from anywhere, blast mountains, toss the grain of the
prairies into the conveyor belt of the Lakes, plan to make a province of
their own someday, throw up their own colossi and endow them with
spirits, while moose and bear wander into town.

Yet how minute and pathetic are all these works upon the dark infini-
tude of the Shield! Walking the busy streets of Fort William and Port
Arthur, a man feels the security of human habitation. The Shield seems
far away. From an airplane he looks down on a Lake Superior which is
no more than a bowl of dark blue porcelain flecked with white soapsuds.
The largest grain ship is smaller than a pin. The elevators have become
gray pebbles at the edge of a black ocean undulating, wave on wave, to
the Arctic.

It is quite wrong, however, to imagine, as most Canadians do, that the
Lakehead, surrounded by barren rock and squat forest, must always live
on the manufacturing and transportation industries. As we soon found,
on driving west, the stone desert of the Shield contains here a huge oasis
of agricultural land. It should become one of the nation's major farm
areas when it is cleared.

A swarthy young giant of Polish descent, whose father had cleared a
fine farm now waving in hay and grain, told us that this was the best
farm country in Canada.

We asked him if he ever grew tired of hard labor and thought perhaps
of taking a job at high wages in the industries of Fort William. "Not me,"
he said. "I'm a farmer. This is good land, and there's still miles and miles
of it to clear."

He and others like him were pushing back the forest far northward to
the edge of the Shield. We left him at his gate, a happy man, a symbolic

figure of western Canada, the portrait of the pioneer. Though the prairies lay far ahead, we knew we were already in the west.

(Hutchison, *Tomorrow's Giant*, 1957, 186–203)

9 A LITTLE SECURITY, MANITOBA

☞ "The Hub" really refers to Winnipeg, placed in the next chapter. Manitoba is a subtle civilization, distinct from the regions to east and west. The significance of the Métis is noted. Viewed as a whole Manitoba has much variety, including a seacoast and part of the Shield, but the southern part is a closely settled section of the prairies, a conservative farming area, seeking security. Contrasts between prairie towns are great: some are stark, others slumbering under trees are almost like Ontario towns. ☜

The Pre-Cambrian Shield ended as suddenly as a prison wall. Like prisoners released through a stone gateway, we entered the central plain of North America.

No stranger can fail to recognize that formidable fact of geography. It hits him straight between the eyes like a physical blow. He will not guess, however, that he has entered a distinct compartment of a plain trisected by invisible lines. This compartment is named Manitoba; it is a sovereign province, but it is much more than that. In a subtle fashion known only to the natives, it is a civilization and, by Canadian standards, an old one....

... For the Manitoba cell of the prairies, outwardly a part of the west and closely joined to Ontario by geography, is inwardly disjoined from both, is practically watertight and leakproof, even in the mass age, and Winnipeg is the hard nucleus of this cell....

... Manitoba is an old country, as age goes in Canada. Selkirk's settlers walked to the Red River from Hudson Bay, their Scottish bagpipes skirling, in 1812. They found that the Métis, mixed offspring of French Canadian *voyageurs* and Indian women, already had built a society, almost a nation, around the river junction. A Manitoba character had been established seventy years before the C.P.R. crawled westward out of the Shield.

When the railway brought its first passengers to settle on the prairies, they were of solid rural Ontario stock, not adventurous immigrants, discontented folk, and often radicals from Europe or the United States like most of the settlers farther west. They were established Canadians of unalterably conservative mind. They made Manitoba perhaps the most conservative province in Canada except Quebec....

... most Canadians think of Manitoba as a field of grain beside a railway track. And even as we watched the dying glimmer on the lake [Lake Manitoba], we remembered that most of Manitoba – the forest, the rivers, the lakes innumerable, the mining towns, the stony Shield, and the Bay – still lay far to the northward. There such projects as a huge new nickel refinery are giving this farm province a broad industrial base.

But one need travel only a few miles from Winnipeg to leave every trace of civilization far behind. [From the city Hutchison took a short boat trip up the Red River] ... and in half an hour were lost on a minor Amazon .... On each bank stood an impervious jungle, unmarked by any trail, untouched by an ax. The sky was a mere slit of blue. We suffered from acute claustrophobia not five miles from the corner of Main and Portage and not half a mile from the plowed prairies.

Then we drove southwest of Winnipeg and beheld the flat plains heave, like a squall at sea, into the Pembina Hills, sink into lush valleys of grass, and end in a chain of unsuspected lakes. Americans from Dakota were joyfully catching a hideous sort of fish under the impression that they had penetrated the farthest wild west.

The railway traveler sees only the dismal villages of the main line, the whistle stops around a wooden grain elevator, a skating rink, and a garage. In southern Manitoba many charming towns sit astride some nameless stream, snore peacefully under the shade of great trees, and look almost like the blessed towns of Ontario.

Despite all his machinery and household conveniences, the life of the average farmer in this country is still hard. Of itself it explains the current change in the politics and thoughtways of the prairies, the decline of the old laissez-faire economics that once flourished here, the emergence of collectivism in the grain industry.

We stopped one night for supper in a farm kitchen and found it replete with all the electrical gadgets, plumbing, and chromium furniture of a modern city house. But the woman who cooked the supper was not a city woman (she made better pickles and pies, for one thing), and the wizened man in mechanic's overalls could never be anything but a farmer.

"All we want," he said, "is a little security, same as folks in town. But no. The town folks want security for themselves, and they tell us to take whatever the market says and be damned to us. They get paid regular. We're supposed to gamble."

He was not a radical or a socialist. He belonged to perhaps the most conservative group of Canadians in Canada's most conservative province. He was, in fact, a small capitalist – "too small," he said wryly – but he and his kind were determined to get a fairer share of the nation's income as the labor unions had got it in the towns, and to get it regularly.

His wife compelled us to eat a third piece of pie and sent us off with a big jar of her pickles. The farmer went back to his barn and began to reassemble his tractor. He had another hour of daylight and didn't intend to waste it....

We drove through Portage, whose main street, the end of the old wagon road from Winnipeg, is wide enough to carry the traffic of New York, reached the solid, well-groomed streets of Brandon, crossed the deep canyon of the Assiniboine, and drove north over the plains toward one of nature's wildest aberrations.

Ahead of us a perpendicular cliff burst from the prairie like a single mountain, perhaps an extinct volcano. Presently we were climbing a steep road through a forest of evergreens. At the summit we looked out upon a misplaced chunk of the Rockies, a long lake of clear water, a woodland glade, and, within it, a herd of sulky buffalo.

Such is Riding Mountain National Park, the most improbable park in Canada. Here the prairies, undulating eastward from the mountains, make a sheer drop, a single dizzy step down to the level of Lake Manitoba. From the eastern flank of this queer eruption we could see the farmland all around neatly squared in tints of violent green and yellow, exactly like the interior of France as painted by Van Gogh.

(Hutchison, Tomorrow's Giant, 1957, 206–19)

10 THE BIG FARM, SASKATCHEWAN

☞ Hutchison knows Saskatchewan as a land of individualistic farmers; how then has it become the home of socialism in Canada? The answer lies in the community cooperation needed during pioneer times in a land transformed "almost overnight from a frontier to a farm." ☞

In crossing the western political boundary of Manitoba, the traveler supposedly is crossing also a line of ideology. He has entered the only large-sized political unit of North America which calls itself socialist and has repeatedly elected governments of that label. But at the first sight of Saskatchewan in the dawn our eyes were too filled and our minds too staggered for mere political speculation. If this was like no other land in Canada, what exactly distinguished it?

Size, of course – size unbroken, unimaginable, overpowering in a soundless void. You can see farther here than anywhere else in the nation, breathe deeper, and, we began to think, feel better. Size on this scale might even expand the dimensions of the human being. That was only a stranger's conjecture then. As we soon discovered, it happened to be true....

At any rate, it was in Regina that the fertile womb of the great North American depression bore Canada's first socialist party in 1933 and the Manifesto of the Co-operative Commonwealth Federation, which promised an imaginary socialist state but was watered down, two decades later, because a capitalist state had meanwhile been changed into something else entirely and seemed to be working very well.

It was in this legislative building that the first Canadian socialist government took office in 1944, but its theoretical socialism soon melted under the rays of the Canadian boom.

How, the traveler may well ask, did socialism first gain office in this most improbable corner of America, by the votes of the fiercely individualistic farmers of Saskatchewan? ...

[A distinguished socialist gives Hutchison the answer.] My friend smiled tolerantly. Couldn't I understand that socialism was only a modern label for a process under way here since the first plow reached Saskatchewan, a process quite different from the early settlement of other provinces?

Those older provinces had been settled slowly by a few pioneers in primitive times, before Macdonald built his transcontinental railway. Here in Saskatchewan the railway had suddenly dumped a horde of settlers, many of them immigrants from Europe, upon raw and hostile earth.

They had no money, houses, plowed land, or knowledge of the frontier. In a common dilemma they found that a man could not survive here when Saskatchewan must be changed almost overnight from a frontier to a farm. Every man needed his neighbor's help to raise a barn, dig a well, thresh a crop, or fight a prairie fire.

Learning that need not by theory but by hard experience, every man became a co-operator; co-operation produced the farmers' huge co-operative wheat pools and then collective marketing. Finally old-fashioned co-operation devised a new label. It emerged in a new doctrine called, or miscalled, socialism, and in such things as a government power line down an isolated side road.

That, my socialist friend assured me, was the whole meaning of socialism in Saskatchewan. A few government-owned industries of little account and a handful of real socialists could be called socialism only in a headline or a political speech. The existing system, if it could be termed a system, was only the expression of a way of life established long ago by environment. It was not an ideology but an instinct.

That man was right, I think, in saying that if the Cooperative Commonwealth Federation of the Regina Manifesto had been elected only in Saskatchewan and failed of election in every other province, it had been in fact an extraordinary success. Its ideas, appropriated by the great political parties, had infiltrated, colored, and altered the whole society of Canada.

In Saskatchewan social change has been more profound than in most provinces. A government expert gave me such a bewildering mass of figures, such a detailed accounting of new oil wells and refineries, gas pipelines, mines, America's largest uranium reserves, forests, and expanding industries of all sorts that I forgot all the details and saw only a vague picture of Saskatchewan, the great grain province, becoming an industrial province, a rural people deserting the farm for the city, a population rising after ten years of decline.

The smattering of theoretical socialism looked pretty thin upon the surface of the industrial boom, especially when the government was ardently wooing the investments of wicked capitalists....

[Hutchison also learns about modern capital-intensive wheat farming.]

After hearing the government's explanation of its policies, I set out to learn how they suited the farmers. Soon I was sitting in a cool shed of machinery, far off on the edge of the Regina Plains.

The man who sat beside me there, on a monstrous new swathing machine, looked strangely unlike a farmer. He wore a Panama hat, somewhat battered but obviously expensive, an immaculate white shirt, khaki trousers of excellent cut, and shoes fit for a drawing-room. Yet he had just come from his fields, where he was working literally day and night to plant the sodden acres as they dried out.

His tanned face, set in lines of serenity, might have been the face of a successful businessman or an academic. Actually he was both. In the summer he managed the complex business of his farm and in winter he often lectured to the university students of Saskatoon. But he remained a dirt farmer by choice and a portent of agriculture's new age.

When he had finished his college education, he said, the farm of four-teen hundred acres required the labor of twenty-five men at harvest time and twenty-two horses. Now he and one hired man sowed the whole crop and reaped it. The big horse barn was empty, the machinery shed full of gadgets worth a substantial fortune.

Why, I asked, did a man of his sort choose to farm though he could live comfortably and practice a learned profession in the city? He turned on me a bantering smile. "Because," he said, "I like it."

He had found no life so interesting as the life of his own farm, nothing to equal the glory of these Regina Plains. We went outside and looked across a country as flat and smooth as a well-laid floor. On three sides a faint blur separated sky from earth. On the east an idle finger of smoke pointed down at Regina, which lay below the horizon line, like a ship far out at sea. Only the top of a grain elevator, the ship's turret, was visible behind the curve of the world.

Even a mountain man like me could see the fascination of this naked distance and understand why a recent English visitor to the farm had sat out all night alone to watch the stars and the dawn. But what was the fascination of farm work?

"I suppose," the farmer replied, "it's the new challenge every year. I mean the job of raising a crop on this dry land and beating the weather. That, believe me, takes a lot of doing."

A lot of doing on a dry land. Not long ago this man had rowed in a boat five miles around his flooded fields and, with luck and labor, day and night, he had managed to sow six hundred acres as the water subsided.

"You see," he explained, "this country's so dry most of the time that you can't even get water in a well."

He had to haul domestic water in a tank truck from the outskirts of Regina; he saved every drop of rain from the roof of his house and pumped more water from a dugout near by to irrigate his grove of trees, lawns, and flowers.

I inquired about his current crop, and his answer struck me as final definition of prairie life: "Oh, we always have a crop at this time of year." There might be none, of course, by autumn, but it was useless to worry.

My inquiries about socialism only amused him. Not one farmer in ten, he said, was opposed to the collective marketing of grain, and not one in a thousand was a socialist. ·

I risked one last question: what was the use of his education in this style of life? He thought about it for a moment and said he guessed edu-cation gave him a deeper interest in the scientific processes of agriculture.

That was only half an answer. The other half could not be put into words. This man and his kind are totally involved, physically and spiritually, in the greater process of the earth, of growth, harvest, weather, and fundamental things of which politics, in Regina or anywhere else, are only pale shadows.

The farmer went back to his fields, where he would work most of the night, with headlights, to drill the last possible grain of seed into the soil while there was yet time for it to mature before autumn frost.

(Hutchison, *Tomorrow's Giant*, 1957, 224–33)

11 THE BIG DREAMERS, ALBERTA

▹ In Alberta Hutchison finds a land of spaciousness, buoyancy, and adventurous mavericks. Rogers noted the connection with the United States and Hutchison stresses this as well. ◁

We drove north to High River, knowing its fame (no Canadian town is more famous) but not its contents. These began to reveal themselves as we entered the office of *The Times* and discovered Mrs. Hughena McCorquodale, so far the greatest discovery of our travels.

She was simultaneously reading proofs, answering a telephone, and rolling a cigarette. I use the word "rolling" in a loose sense, as loose as Mrs. McCorquodale's handiwork. For in truth, after forty-five years' vain experiment and much coaching from expert cowboy rollers, she builds her smokes like birds' nests blown and tattered by Alberta's Chinook wind.

They and their maker have become one of High River's many legends, well worthy of Bob Edwards's town and, like the newspaper which made his reputation throughout Canada, an Eye-Opener. Naturally, in such a storied place, we had called first on Edwards's successor because she represents in her insatiable appetite for life, her reckless romanticism, shameless nostalgia, and corrosive wit – a fundamental strain of Alberta's nature. The lady facing me across the littered desk was an unrepentant maverick in Canada's maverick province.

She looked up from her work to warn us sharply that there was someone we must see right away if we wished to understand her country. "Wait a minute," she said, "till I finish these damnable proofs."

You will note that she said "damnable." She didn't say "damn" or the more fastidious "damned." She said "damnable" because she is a stickler for accuracy in everything except her gruesome and bulging parcels of tobacco.

Observing our interest in that native landmark, she added: "Oh, yes, we all look crazy here. It's the altitude. It's Alberta. But you'll get used to us."

There was no need to reassure me. I had fallen in love with her at first sight, with her town and her country. Despite age and white hair, Mrs. McCorquodale was still a beautiful woman, but I didn't know then that she was also a character waiting, quite unconsciously, for a novel to grow about her, probably from the pen of her celebrated literary neighbor, Bill Mitchell.

Meanwhile she led us down the street to one of western Canada's most notable and least noted men....

When [Billy] Henry, a boy from Perthshire, came to High River over seventy years ago, southern Alberta was reputed the toughest region of the North American frontier. Not long before that the American whisky-traders of Fort Whoop-Up had debauched several Indian nations, Sitting Bull and his warriors had fled here after their victory of the Little Big Horn, and a handful of Northwest Mounted Police had tamed these desperate fugitives without firing a shot.

Now, at the age of eighty-nine, Henry was alone in his tiny house, his wife gone and all the partners of the old Whoop-Up Trail hardly remembered in the province made by their hands.

Henry remembered. How could he forget the great days, the open range, the Indians, the cattlemen, the herds moving across the American border? This migration fixed upon Alberta a special quality of mind, a certain spaciousness and buoyancy, the instinct of the gambler, which still tinctures life today. Henry was the spirit of the great days incarnate.

"Ah, well," he said in his Scottish accent, "it wasn't like the movies, you know, and the books. They were big men, but they were kind. Never tough."

He groped for the right word to describe his vanished company and added: "They dreamed big."

They dreamed big. The old man's eyes glistened with moisture at the memory. Yes, they dreamed big and lived, on their boundless, unfenced acres, a life that the world will never see again.

"Oh, sure," Henry mused, "they'd come into High River on a Saturday night shooting off their guns and making a bit of noise. I've seen the dust popping all over the street from their bullets. But it meant nothing."

"They were," he repeated, "kind men. Make no mistake, though. They meant what they said. If they warned you off their range, it was their last warning. And if a stranger came up from the States in a hurry, you asked no questions. What had happened to him down there was his business." ...

[Harold Long, legendary editor of the *Lethbridge Herald*, explains Alberta's personality to Hutchison.] The adventurous, gambling spirit of Alberta had arrived here, he said, with the original American whisky-traders, and soon afterward with the American cattlemen. On that first sedimentary layer the later waves of immigration from the States, eastern Canada, and Europe had deposited new layers of varied and often heretical ideas. (Less than half of southern Alberta's people are of Canadian stock.) But Long was inclined to think that the climate must be the greatest human fact of all.

He went on to boast that the climate was the most violent in the world. If the weather took to Chinooking, the temperature could rise by eighty degrees in a few hours. Hail might dent or puncture the roof of an automobile. Why, a year ago he had driven to Calgary on a hot June day and returned next morning behind a snowplow.

Such climatic violence, he thought, produced a certain violence of the human mind always clearly visible in Alberta's maverick politics and in the strange financial doctrine hopefully named Social Credit. Anyway, Alberta had produced in Long a great Canadian editor and in Lethbridge a fine town.

The abundant wealth of this countryside grew directly out of the earth, once water was applied. Only a few years ago several acres of bunch grass were needed to support a single beef animal. East of Lethbridge we found ourselves on a baked and withered range and then in the vast irrigated garden around the canning plants and sugar factories of Taber. Half a million acres sprouted peas, corn, beets, and other vegetables, all set in geometric lines.

We drove west again toward the Rockies and noted some further evidence of Alberta's varied life. The magnificent Mormon temple at Cardston; the Hutterite communities of bearded men in black shirts and women in billowing petticoats; the occasional cowpuncher on that obsolete machine, the horse; the pumps and pipes of the oil fields; the thin shimmer of Waterton Lake like a tear in the wrinkled eyes of the mountains; above all, the sunshine, the cloudless sky cut by nothing but the mountains' white teeth, the intoxication of the clean upland air –

these things all shouted the wealth, beauty, and inherent excitement of this land.

(Hutchison, *Tomorrow's Giant,* 1957, 245–58)

12 THE LONG DAY, ALBERTA, PEACE RIVER COUNTRY

☞ The words "Peace River Country" conjure up a final frontier of good farming land within Canada. On the northern margins of agriculture, in summer this is a land of the long day. It is a land on the edge, of fresh spirit, as farmers and townsmen in Alberta build a new community. ☞

[Hutchison arrives in the Peace River Country.] The protective dike of badlands ends at the gateway of High Prairie and a fertile plain begins. We had entered a distant annex of Alberta, the last farming frontier and possibly the most interesting region in Canada. It is an old region in our brief national history. Once it was decisive in continental affairs. It led the first Canadians to the western sea and their possession of the Pacific coast. Yet it had been peopled only yesterday, and it still felt the strong pulse beat of youth.

Here, in fact, was the final reproduction of a Canadian experience which had started three centuries before on the banks of the St. Lawrence. There will be no experience of this exact sort in America again. Hence, the settlers now subduing the northern wilds, as their ancestors subdued the south, are justified in using capital letters and naming their land the Peace River Country. It is almost a country, and may someday be a province. At any rate, it is unique.

That fact was intimated in a sudden flash. We rounded a blind corner toward nightfall to confront a staggering sight.

Below us, in its green trench, the Peace River shone like a braid of gold about six inches wide, and unraveled through winding coils to the northward. A swarm of black islands, no larger than waterfowl, swam in the current. Some white specks on the bank must be a town....

Peace River town had escaped the day's rain. It lay under a brown dust, but fine gold dust hung above the river. A brave and noisy little street told us at once that this town was no part of the Canada we had traveled from Newfoundland to the Rockies.

It looked at first like a pioneers' encampment, a bivouac on the route of march, a temporary spark of life on the outer edge of things. Except

for the automobiles solidly ranked by the sidewalk, Peace River seemed
to live like a town of western Canada's beginnings, in a time lag of fifty
years. But it is here to stay....

A good dinner fortified us for a walk about the town. It had a strident,
cheerful, neighborly air, and evidently contained a variety of races.

Some of the farmers, who arrived in muddy trucks, had unmistakable
Slavic faces and accents. Others spoke in French. A huddle of women
before an undertaker's parlor lamented their own tragedy in a strange
tongue. The undertaker – he wore an incongruous black coat and striped
gray trousers soothed these customers as best he could in the English
language, and they disappeared, like Ruth, into the alien corn.

Upstream a little way, the road petered out between some new bun-
galows and gardens of evening-scented flowers. There we watched the
sunset casually ignite both land and water in solstitial explosion.

No one could observe this crimson pageantry without guessing why
the Peace River people are fascinated by their Country and worship it
as a religion. It lacks the conventional beauty of the Maritimes, the St.
Lawrence, or the Rockies. Much of it is drab, and some of it ugly. In total
it has a grandeur of its own, a haunting quality of size and emptiness;
above all, the sense of virginity, of life in its salad days.

(Hutchison, *Tomorrow's Giant*, 1957, 267–69)

13 THE TRAIL'S END AND THE BIG TREES, BRITISH
COLUMBIA

☞ Hutchison makes a special effort to capture the life of British Columbia and its place in Canada. It is a province he knows intimately
and loves. In some ways what he has to say about this "land of lavish
dimensions" eerily reflects what he had to say about Prince Edward
Island, "The Toy Continent," because, though opposites in almost every
way, each has been a world unto its own. British Columbia, we are
told, long has had "a special quality of mind." There has always been
the gamble for opportunity in a land of vast potential resources, not
just in a few local spots but, as George Parkin discerned earlier, across
a whole immense province. From this land, so big, varied, rich, and
beautiful it has been difficult until recently to see Canada as a whole.
Hutchison travelled often and widely within British Columbia, and
his impressions of a few of its great contrasting regions – the compartments as he calls them – are a bit of a jumble. The Fraser has had a
special role in conveying people to the Pacific Ocean, and Hutchison,

feeling deep emotion, draws a contrast between the wet coastal land at the mouth of the Fraser and the Dry Belt up river in the interior, a plateau land where distance is not shut out. Hutchison ends his long journey on Vancouver Island, land he had known since boyhood. The Canadian revolution has reached this far, but there is hope. ☞

[Hutchison heads home, driving across British Columbia starting from the Peace River Country.] At the dismal village of Vanderhoof, almost exactly in the center of the province, we paused to reorient ourselves. That is never easy in British Columbia, for it is fractured, as no other province is, as by a convulsion of nature, by one sledgehammer blow; is split into at least ten main compartments and countless minor cells whose separate pockets of human life are strangers to one another....

Half of British Columbia, almost uninhabited, stretched north of us. To the west lay a lovely land that we had traveled many times before, a land of green valleys, mountains, lakes, and rivers, the storied hamlet of Hazelton beside the azure pyramid of Rocher de Boule, the decaying totem poles of Kispiox, the canyons of the Bulkley, and the gorge of the Skeena, leading to the port of Prince Rupert.

Not far from Vanderhoof the Nechako River had been dammed off from the Fraser and now flowed directly to the sea through a tunnel to spin turbines deep within a mountain at the aluminum plant of Kemano. The lakes of Tweedsmuir Park, east of the Coast Range, were rising to drown their timbered shores and swell into a new reservoir which nature had directed eastward and man had turned westward by a short-cut. Nowhere had Canada's revolution effected more rapid changes in the original substance of the continent....

Today Prince George was fairly bursting with population and civic pride, was becoming the capital and entrepôt of a virgin empire from here to the Yukon, but a few old-timers longed for the freedom, the poverty, the hope of wealth, and the gamble of the lost frontier. Though they used no such words, they knew, as I did, that British Columbia was paying for its boom with the loss of a special quality of mind, a spiritual climate, an inner tone which once distinguished it from all other provinces.

Its people necessarily were unique in Canada. They were the only Canadians who had penetrated the final barrier on the westward march. They had gone as far as man could go. Sealed off not only from Canada but also from one another in their mountain labyrinth, they were subtly united by their sense of separateness and their joint secret, the secret of British Columbia.

No mountain range could stay them. No land could satisfy their hunger until their feet were set upon the last margin of the continent. Now they stood at trail's end and shared a mystery. They alone had beheld the western sea and a world around them too big for their imagination, too beautiful for language, perhaps too rich for their own good. After that discovery they never looked back.

Once past the Rockies, they possessed the fairest or, at any rate, the most varied land in Canada, and they regarded it almost as a sovereign state, themselves as a chosen people. Their separate patriotism soon became the infatuation of a love affair – at times noble, at others mean and stupid, but always guileless, honest, and passionate.

As they lived in successive spasms of boom, from the boom of gold in Cariboo to the boom of timber on the coast, they came to expect, as their natural right, a superior place in Confederation. By any material measurement they achieved it.

If they were more provincial, self-centered, and selfish than any other Canadians, their character was redeemed by a wild generosity among themselves, a largeness of view (so long as that view went no farther east than the Rockies), by a certain boyish credulity, by boundless expectations, and, most of all, by a boisterous, out-of-door life close to the earth, the forest, and the mountain.

They hardly understood the nation or their part in it. They never produced a national idea or statesman of importance, but they were faithful to their own ways, built their own civilization, worshipped their own land, and reared a miracle of sorts in its image. The lavish dimensions of their environment expanded their spirit while its size, beauty, and wealth blinded them to the still larger facts of Canada. In short, they were primarily British Columbians, and Canadians incidentally.

That pioneer British Columbia, as one could see even in Prince George, is being re-educated, tamed, and rubbed smooth by the massive influx of Canadians from other provinces, the conforming pressures of industry, and the sudden awareness of Canada. In the last quarter-century or so, no earlier, British Columbia has truly joined the nation.

That is a gain of inestimable value to the nation. Yet there is a loss, too. A loss of color, eccentricity, and grandeur, …

… the Fraser, … is the central artery and economic aorta of western Canada, through which the nation's lifestream is pumped from the interior heartland to the coast.

This river, and its almost identical twin, the Columbia – both shaped like a clumsy letter S – alone impress some visible pattern on the chaotic geography of British Columbia. From his first arrival here thousands of years ago man's life followed that pattern and traveled the two rivers until airplanes could leap over the successive ranges of north-south mountains and the narrow intervening valleys.

Fraser reached the sea on the current of his river. The gold rush of the late eighteen-fifties retraced his steps to sift the river's sand bars and to build beside them the incredible Cariboo Road. Canada's first transcontinental railway, the Canadian Pacific, used this one practical breach in the Coast Range. But a stranger may travel a good hundred miles eastward from Vancouver today without realizing what has happened to the original road and to its builders, who, without suspecting it, were building a transcontinental state and, by a frail dike, were halting the northward surge of Manifest Destiny.

The broad Fraser delta on Vancouver's outskirts, with its green patchwork of dairy farms, looks much like the farm land of Quebec or Ontario, except for the high mountains around it, or perhaps more like Switzerland, except for its greater sweep....

[Starting with the Fraser River, Hutchison contrasts mountain, coastal and interior plateau landscapes.] ... And everywhere along the canyon you can hear the voice that spoke to the first men, the growl, the hiss and thunder of liquid force imprisoned here and yearning for the sea.

Look down upon this scoured and riven trench, the mad river, the ceaseless slides of rock and vegetation, the spark of light from some lonely shack, the momentary flash of a great train burrowing like a glowworm through limbo – then, if you are a British Columbian, you can imagine the many passengers of this last Canadian journey to the west, the Indians, the miners, the road-builders, the railway-builders, and now – the whole constricted tide of the nation's business.

Suddenly, after the river has made its right-angle northward turn at Hope, geography, vegetation, climate, and human life all change together.

The Pacific jungle of fir, cedar, and hemlock thins into red-barked pine, black spruce, and stunted juniper. The dank coastal reek is cut by the stinging medicinal whiff of sagebrush, the tantalizing scent of syringa and alfalfa, the rough emanation of parched clay and hot stone, the clean smell of new haystacks, horses, cattle, log barns, and saddle leather. Soon the mountains begin to fall by successive steps into round, kneaded hills of bunch grass. And coastal man, with his life of cities, business, and fury, is replaced by interior man, who lives, quiet and remote, upon the land, as his fathers lived before him. This is the Dry Belt, another freakish pocket in the rumpled garment of British Columbia....

The great days are finished here, as everywhere, but the Cariboo plateau is still the only place where the size of British Columbia can be
glimpsed, where distance is not shut out and the next valley hidden by
mountain or forest.

A soggy, lethargic coastal man like me fills his lungs with this dry
upland air, regains his youth, and seems to need no sleep at night. After
the metallic clamor of cities, his ears are soothed by the sound of gurgling
irrigation ditches, of rivers murmuring in the night, of bawling herds,
horses' hoofs on a muddy road, wind shredded through pine needles,
and fire crackling in a drum stove.

The Cariboo breed, impregnated with the flavor and history of this
land, is different from any other breed in Canada, but it is changing, and
the land is changing, too, as both feel the first tremors of progress....

[Hutchison reaches the Okanagan.] There all sensible Canadians
hope to retire someday, grow apples, and live happily ever afterward.
The Okanagan's endless miles of orchard, frothing in spring blossom
or reeling under the crimson weight of autumn, its three big towns, its
snug houses, trim gardens, and air of affluence are all the work of men;
for only half a century ago this was a bunch-grass range, inhabited by a
few cattle.

In a province which can plow perhaps one per cent of its land, the
Okanagan is a priceless piece of real estate. Still, the enchantment of
the valley, known by hearsay all over the nation, is not to be found
in its orchards, its towns, or even in the chameleon lakes that change,
minute by minute, from blue to green to purple. Man's real achievement
here is a perfect compromise between rustic and urban environment. A
distinct method of life is so far uncorrupted. No blasphemer questions
an indigenous religion and its ruddy local god named MacIntosh Red. It
must be an agnostic of the wilder sort who questions the presence of a
sea serpent named Ogopogo in Okanagan Lake.

[Even Vancouver Island has been affected by the Canadian revolution: logging has produced a devastated landscape, in an area near the
Pacific coast that Hutchison knew as a boy.] At last we were coming to
the end of the travels that began on the Atlantic coast. The lonely lake
was crammed with log booms, the shore fouled with the litter of a saw-
mill. The hills had turned brown under the latest devastation. But in the
middle of this havoc an old sanctuary remained intact....

Beside the ravaged brook, as everywhere, it was bootless to lament the
Canadian revolution. But I had my memories, and I wished to confirm
them before I left this spot forever.

Certain relics must still survive near by to record the old days. As a boy I could stand between three cedars, the smallest ten feet in diameter, and touch all of them with my hands. Now I found their stumps staring blankly at the sun. They would be here for centuries yet, long after a new forest had risen to conceal their nakedness.

The new forest! I knelt down to examine the earth beneath the slash, the fireweed, the sword ferns, and the first brave shoots of alder. And there I beheld – microscopic but larger by far than all man's works – the first and last fact of the Pacific coast. A seedling of fir, two inches high, held up proudly on its tip a bud, purple and shiny as a jewel.

(Hutchison, *Tomorrow's Giant*, 1957, 288–99, 324–25)

9

Bruce Hutchison, Major Canadian Cities, *The Unknown Country*, 1942, and *Canada Tomorrows's Giant*, 1957

⌐ Many Canadian cities are described in both *The Unknown Country* and in *Canada Tomorrow's Giant*, and for some parts of Canada the urban sections comprise a substantial part of the description and interpretation of the regions discussed. Gathering Hutchison's observations on major Canadian cities into one chapter, as I do here, makes it easier to compare his views on different cities and highlights his urban insights. Also, bringing his 1941 and 1956 impressions of particular cities together enriches Hutchison's observations and more readily reveals changes in the cities and in his ideas. As a minimum Hutchison always tries to find at least one distinctive quality for each city, and his impressions get quite personal. In almost every city he does two essential things to get to know the place: he walks the streets and talks to citizens. Quickly and candidly he responds to both the ugly and the beautiful, and attempts to get to the essence of a city's being and its role in the region and country. In the larger cities there are references to slums. In the 1940s, Canada had barely recovered from the 1930s depression and the drought years in the West, and even in the 1950s urban planning was just getting well underway in Canada and social support services were still being developed, so poor and miserable districts were very evident within cities.

In these vignettes of cities the role of people in creating the geography of a country becomes very evident. Usually it is through the numerous people he meets in cities that Hutchison explains how the region and the country function, but, paradoxically, he never says anything about how a city itself functions as a municipality. This is a matter of scale. By usually saying very positive things about a city's role within a region he counteracts the often harsh things he may write about its appearance or its climate. Indeed, in his imaginative way, Hutchison usually paints a glowing, mythic picture of a city's role in creating a region and the country.

Most of the larger cities are described in both volumes, but a few centres not covered in *The Unknown Country* appear in *Canada Tomorrow's Giant,* and others that received long analyses in the first volume are written up only briefly in the second. The descriptions of the cities are organized going across the country from the Atlantic coast to the Pacific. The chapter headings are taken from Hutchison's two books, to make it easier to refer back to the appropriate regional excerpts, and the dates in the headings are for the years that Hutchison was doing his field work, 1941 and 1956 respectively. ☞

I THE MISTY ISLAND, ST. JOHN'S, NEWFOUNDLAND, 1956

☞ Hutchison senses the authentic ancient roots of St. John's in the amalgam of sea, wood, and stone that has grown on the rock that is Newfoundland. St. John's is a capital, cosmopolitan, a base for the Portuguese fishing fleet, and a supply centre for outports. ☞

No city could have looked more foreign to a mainland Canadian than this dark lichen growth crawling up the sea rocks; no spectacle more unlikely than the ice-coated harbor, a shiny bathtub of white porcelain, full of a child's toy ships.

St. John's is foreign to all mainlanders in history, architecture, and spirit, and far older than any white man's habitation in Canada or the United States. Foreign and unique.

There may be touches of an English port along its busy wharves, memories of Devon in its tangled rigging, a whiff of London in some walled garden, a crooked street, or the Gothic cathedral. Yet this agglomerate of sea, stone, and wood is not derivative. It is original and indigenous, built by native craftsmen to a native design as the authentic capital of an authentic nationality, the ancient fortress of a seagoing race. The sea more than the land has shaped and colored it, has penetrated every cranny and aching bone of the town with storm, fog, salt, fish smell, and memories.

This place is bleak and ugly, I suppose, by the usual definition. Its tiers of square wooden houses (built overnight after the last of three total conflagrations) have been packed together cheek by jowl. Most of them are antiquated, shabby, and identical in every line. The business streets, for all their bustling traffic and modern goods, have still a dingy Victorian look.

But stand off a little way, stand on Signal Hill above the narrow canyon of the harbor gate, and observe St. John's whole. Its ugliness, like the ugly face of an old friend, turns into a wrinkled, scarred, and timeless beauty, the beauty of character, suffering, toil, and human adventure beside the calm and awful beauty of the sea.

On this May morning St. John's waited, in a murk of fog and coal smoke, for a northeast wind to change and clear the harbor. Newfoundland's genial summer could not be many days off.

The skipper of a chunky schooner, heavily laden with gasoline drums, lumber, and two automobiles for the outports, stared at the swirling haze and cursed the "damn hice." Two big freighters lay helpless at their iron buoys. A crowd of longshoremen, garbed like the longshoremen of Liverpool or Southampton in long, clumsy overcoats, shivered idly in the lee of a brick wall.

Near by, her bow thrust almost into the main street, the white Portuguese ship *Maria Celeste* glistened by an alien shore like an exiled ray of Mediterranean sun. Her decks sprouted a gay flower bed of crimson, brown, and yellow sails on her fifty dories. The squat sailors, in berets, sweaters, and wooden-soled sea boots, mended their nets on the wharf, spoke only among themselves, and hummed some song from home. Their ship, like countless European ships through the centuries, had been fishing on the Grand Banks and had found sanctuary in the old haven of the North Atlantic.

Water Street, only a few yards away – a fisherman's trail long before the feet of Canadians or Americans touched the soil of the mainland – ignored the Portuguese. It had grown used to foreigners, and seemed to have pressing affairs.

It was absurd, of course, to expect that any business street in America would be different from another. Still, Water Street, bursting with traffic and crowded with businessmen in the universal business uniform, rather disappointed us at first. After we had walked its full length, the smell of ships and cod, the cold sniff of ice, the clutching fingers of the fog, assured us that St. John's did not belong to the mainland. It stood alone on its island, lost that day in Atlantic cloud banks. No ship could enter or leave its harbor. No plane could reach its airport. The people bustled about their business, but essentially they were marooned in mid-ocean like the original Newfoundlanders who awaited here the first sail of springtime, long ago.

Only a mainlander could feel the loneliness and piercing cold of St. John's. The natives knew that a belated spring would arrive tomorrow or next day, sweep the ice from the harbor overnight, free the fishing fleet, and open the Atlantic gate. The town was cheerful in anticipation of that annual release.

(Hutchison, *Canada Tomorrow's Giant*, 1957, 28–30)

2 SAILORS' TOWN, HALIFAX, 1941

⌒ Halifax continues to be shaped by the sea; its past is as much a part of the city as the present. Hutchison observes it as it has come to life in the fight to protect Great Britain against Hitler. ⌒

... [Halifax] has a Georgian look of square old brown stone houses and fanlight windows, and narrow Georgian streets, and neat little squares and parks laid out with the stiff precision of a Georgian nosegay, and fine old churches, where eminent worshipers used to sit in long coats and skin-tight pants, graciously accepting God into the very best society....

... Halifax in its outdoor setting is one of the most beautiful cities of men, and in business hours, one of the world's busiest ports. In the broad shelter of Bedford Basin the great convoys of war ride at anchor, waiting to slip through the narrow sea gates into the Atlantic – more ships than you have ever seen in one place before, with crews of almost every language. Among the merchantmen move the lean little Canadian destroyers, herding them, barking at them like sheep dogs,

When the St. Lawrence freezes, and Quebec and Montreal are closed with ice, Halifax, with its neighbor, St. John, must handle Canada's Atlantic exports, and winter is always a rushing time down here. When war came in 1939 Halifax found itself the most vital shipping port in the British Commonwealth. Into Halifax, by rail and ship, poured the goods of war from all over America, on their way to the siege of Britain. The streets were soon crowded with soldiers, ready to embark for overseas. Every barrack, every shed and hall they could find was crammed with Canadian sailors in training for a new navy, started after the war began. In Admiralty House, that spacious Georgian mansion, set in its little park, you found in the mess the young officers who, next morning, would take the convoys out to sea, and a good many of them would not come back again. So crowded was Halifax with the bustle, the goods, and the litter of war that you could hardly find a vacant room to sleep in.

Of a sudden the old Georgian has awakened from her doze beside the sea and perhaps she will never find time to sleep again....

Some parts of Halifax are run-down and dingy, after years of genteel poverty, but the gentility does remain. None of the blaring crudity of our western cities is there, none of the push and salesmanship, but a kind of sober, trim, cheerful life which, though it is essentially North American out of New England, makes you think of life in a faded mansion on the coast of old England. That, I suppose, is only fancy, and the merchant of Halifax would not know what you were talking about; nor the modern politician, though he makes his laws in the weathered grandeur of Province House, which certainly does not belong to this age.

Most Canadian cities spread a blight across their outskirts, but the country around Halifax is strangely unspoiled. The shoreline of bare rock still clutches somehow the lop-sided pine trees....

Always the sea has been the central fact of the city's life. Always the ships of sail, of steam, and of war have sailed in and out of Bedford Basin, and the Citadel has smiled down at them impartially. Fleets beyond number have anchored there from the beginning – ...

Always Halifax has lived with the sea. It is a sailors' town with the air of the navy about it. The Canadian Navy is yet small, but has been growing at an astonishing rate, and most of it is in Halifax. Its young officers give the society of the town a certain breeziness, as the sailors keep the streets gay and the girls a-flutter.... Having found its sea legs, Canada will never be without a navy again. Halifax will always be a sailors' town.

(Hutchison, *The Unknown Country*, 1942, 211–17)

3 THE KINGDOM OF JOE HOWE, HALIFAX, 1956

☞ Solidly built, compact, facing Europe on one side, the rest of Canada on the other, Halifax is a self-assured city, a welcoming mature community. ☜

[Hutchison inspects Halifax on foot.] I had not walked long before I began to realize, as I had never realized on former visits, that here, in this unlikely place, the civilization of Canada had built a civic masterpiece.

Only the peculiar virtues, crotchets, and glorious lunacy of the British Isles, above all, the granitic instinct and stern whimsy of Scotland, could conceive this museum piece of square Georgian architecture, combine it with the soaring Gothic of Edinburgh, use it to house Canada's first responsible government, and go on to invent a private myth more durable than any public institution.

The outside of Halifax is deceptive, and more deceptive still the outside of its people....

The Georgian look is only stone-deep. I had just begun to penetrate it, after walking three blocks through the jumble of Barrington Street, when, by a minor transcontinental accident, I encountered a youth of my acquaintance from Vancouver. He was gazing at the tower of St. Paul's – cunningly painted in 1750 to look like stone because the new hamlet could afford nothing better than wooden boards cut in New England – and he was catching his own vision of an unknown country.

This boy from the Pacific coast had been bred in a prodigal society of brash and perpetual boom. In the quiet of the Dalhousie law school he had found a new kind of life. It had amazed him, as it amazes all western visitors to the Maritime provinces. The people of Halifax, he said, had first asked his politics and religion (still matters of importance in the Maritimes) and then, careless of his heresies and ignorance, had taken him to their homes and hearts.

He tried to explain his discovery, found no words to fit it, and could only say: "These are the best people in Canada. They've got something we never had – what, exactly, I don't know, but it makes you warm. You hear that everybody wants to leave this town and go west and get rich. Me, I'm going to stay. You can really live here."

I left that boy to ponder his first glimpse of a nation infinitely diverse, ...

(Hutchison, *Canada Tomorrow's Giant*, 1957, 37–8)

4 THE TOY CONTINENT, CHARLOTTETOWN, 1956

☞ A small seaside city, Charlottetown becomes a magical mystery. Being a capital, even of a tiny province, gives a sense of gravitas and occasion. ☜

Charlottetown, rising on the far side of a placid bay, was obviously no suburb of Canada, of America, or of England. Seen in the distance, it looked purely European, perhaps a port in Normandy, a stray morsel of the Channel coast, a lost fraction of France under the twin towers of a Latin basilica; or it might be a stage setting by a classical designer for some royal masque at Versailles.

That illusion of Europe was rudely broken as soon as we reached the busy streets of Charlottetown on a Saturday evening, an evening

of special celebration. Seen up close, the Provincial Building of square
Georgian cut, the churches of rusted rock and Gothic line, the gardens
behind mossy walls, are a mellow mixture of England and Scotland.
The clapboard houses, the modern stores, and the people's accent are
unmistakably Canadian. Nevertheless, if not foreign, the town is unreal.

It was particularly unreal that night to us who had just come from the
frozen coast of Newfoundland and the smoke of the Cape Breton coal
fields. Of course I cannot convey this air of unreality, the sensation of
leaving a familiar world and emerging upon the pages of a child's picture
book. I only affirm that Charlottetown, swimming in foliage and moonlight, almost incorporeal in the mystery of dark shadows and ancient
stone, and suddenly haunted by a faint ghost of music, was no part of
the life I had ever seen before, was not a few miles but at least a century
from the mainland.

                    (Hutchison, *Canada Tomorrow's Giant*, 1957, 64)

5 FUNDY'S CHILDREN, SAINT JOHN, 1941

☞ Saint John would have been happier if Hutchison had essentially
overlooked it, as he did Prince Edward Island on this journey. This is a
harsh picture: the town is seen from the outside, with no local informant to help Hutchison understand a seemingly closed-in city. This
urban portrait stands out as the only negative one in the book. Fifteen
years later Hutchison did a mea culpa. ☜

The city of St. John at the river mouth is a rare study in ugliness. It is
ugly with the fascination of a person who is too ugly to be plain, too
unusual to be dull. It has the fine, hard, deep-lined ugliness of an old
Scotsman, with courage and shrewdness and strength in every line of
it.... This Canadian city on the Bay of Fundy is a town from Scotland
moved stone by stone, spire by spire, street by street, across the ocean.
It is Greenock rising in its trim tiers of stone from the seashore. It is a
minor Dundee upon the Firth.

St. John is as hard as any Scottish town, its flat, glum face made of
brick and stone upon a round and barren hill. Like the Scottish towns
that bore it, St. John clings to the sea, crowds against the beach and the
slippery sea rocks, lives by the sea's bounty and asks nothing better –
asks neither beauty nor vegetation, nor any soft delights of land. Up to
the ends of the streets, beside stone quays like the quays of a Scottish

herring village, the ravenous tide of Fundy creeps, brown and urgent, driving the sea gulls before it, lifting up the little ships that lie drunkenly on the mud, washing up to the very doorsteps of the houses.

Only a few green spires of churches, as dour as the frown of John Knox, break the line of stone upon St. John's naked hill. Only by a large public square and an ancient burial ground on the hill's hump does St. John admit the need of recreation, for its life is in the harbor, in the fleets of merchant ships, in the little freighters and fishing craft. There is no time for amusement, for decoration, for the earth. The sea is waiting at the door and the tide is rising.

Walking these stark streets at night, you have the feeling that the crowds of boys and girls, the soldiers in uniform, the sailors, are trying desperately, under a little speck of incandescence here and there, at a movie theater or a soda fountain, to overcome the settled melancholy of the place – a few moments stolen from the dark clutch of the city, saved from the scowl of this granite face. As I strolled through the town I came upon an old man, ragged and bearded, sitting on the curb and playing a fiddle. He wore a sign which said: "Blind, but happy." Perhaps you would be happier in St. John if you were blind.

But in the morning early, when I walked up the hill, across the square, and down the solemn streets of stone and brick houses, each cheek by cheek, but cold and sexless as a tombstone – just then, and for a brief moment, St. John seemed to relax and smile. As the sun rose it caught the windows and they gleamed suddenly, like sparkling eyes, a sly quick smile, the smile of a Scotsman with his joke. Then, as suddenly, the light died in the city's eyes, as if it were ashamed of being caught in a moment of weakness. Yet out at sea, when I got to the street end, the sun still shone on the glistening sides of liners and on the rusty bellies of old freighters that prepared to sail into the Battle of the Atlantic, and everywhere was bustle and cheerful sound, the noisy but well-ordered speed of a great world port of war. Only on the sea is St. John truly itself.

(Hutchison, *The Unknown Country*, 1942, 239–40)

6 THE LAND OF PETER EMBERLEY, SAINT JOHN, 1956

☞ Saint John is a gritty port city that has seen better days, especially since Halifax eclipsed it. Hutchison skillfully attempts to make up for criticizing Saint John in *The Unknown Country*; abashed though he may be, his conversion does not come easily. ☞

A daring impostor, it appeared, had written a book about Canada under my name some dozen years ago and described Saint John as homely, grimy, and forlorn. Of course I indignantly disclaimed all responsibility for this slander. With a little effort, I almost believed my denial. For any man who cannot see the beauty of this place must have no sense of line, contour, or composition. He must be blind to form and color, deaf to the music of the sea. Let no such man be trusted.

Saint John, the mate of female Fredericton, is male, muscular, and hard. Best of all, it has managed to retain in man's work the natural scheme of a granite coast. Native stone bursts through the floor of the streets to remind the inhabitants of their origins. All the buildings and disjointed towers seem to be merely the jagged upthrusts and careless top stories of the continental shelf. The town is anchored deep and immovable in the enduring stuff of the planet.

Where the builders could not afford stone, even their wooden houses, leaning together for support like aged men around a fire, possess a kind of tragic symmetry which always fascinates painters and is best captured in the water-colors of a native artist, Mr. Jack Humphrey.

The Atlantic gales have boomed ceaselessly up this harbor, but they could never dislodge the first French fort of Charles de la Tour, the British settlement of Parrtown, and the city built by the timber boom. They have washed Saint John's face in salt spray, gouged its cheeks, and given it a seaman's shrewd, narrow gleam. It squints at the sea with the stone wrinkles of time. What goes on behind those steady eyes?

A stranger cannot hope to analyze a civic character so old, wise, and reticent, but I began to suspect, after talking to its citizens in ancient parlors and modern offices, that Saint John, like Halifax, is split between the nostalgia of the old and the impatient energies of the young.

A city which was once the fourth shipping port of the world and has seen other ports on both Canadian coasts far outstrip it in business must feel a bitter disappointment not easily disguised. The wistfulness of genteel poverty lies heavy here like the sea fog and makes the old cling for compensation to a lavish past of wealth, boundless hope, political fury, and sometimes riot.

What other bustling Canadian city of fifty thousand people would keep the Loyalists' graveyard, a valuable piece of real estate, green and pampered among its business buildings? ....

The Loyalist legend, born when the refugee ships dumped their human cargoes on the beach of Parrtown, is fading out, but its mark will never be erased so long as the buildings sprawl in Victorian corpulence, the streets still climb and curve across the naked hills of granite, and men can smell the ocean and see the ships at their doors.

Though wistfulness is a discernible flavor in Saint John, so is the smoky smell of labor. The sigh of the old is almost drowned by the impatient shout of the young. This town is commonly accounted one of the dullest in the nation, especially by Canadians who have never seen it, but its intellectual life is suddenly quickening. It has produced some excellent writers, painters, sculptors, and craftsmen, and they find their inspiration right here at home.

(Hutchison, *Canada Tomorrow's Giant*, 1957, 97–9)

7 THE HOME TOWN, FREDERICTON, 1941

☞ Hutchison reveals his love for the enclosing comfort and haven of the small North American town, created before the automobile, deliberately going about its business under an enveloping canopy of trees. In his journey across Canada he does not often stay in such towns, so he embraces Fredericton all the more heartily. It happens to be a capital, but it is the way of life that Fredericton represents within North America that touches Hutchison. ☜

… This little capital of New Brunswick is an old man, very poor, very respectable and intelligent, United Empire Loyalist to the core, blinking in the sun, shouting out suddenly that it will have its rights and then going to sleep again; for really it does not want its rights. It only asks to be left alone at the river edge. It doesn't want a new age and a new barbarism to disturb its reverie.

The new age and new barbarism have not disturbed it. The twentieth century has not yet discovered it. Time somehow has missed it altogether, until you might say that this is the last surviving Home Town of America, uncorrupted and innocent as your grandmother, rocking on her porch chair.

You can only compare it to some of the little towns of England. If you stand at the end of the main street, in the well-treed cathedral yard, you will think you are in Gray's Stoke Poges, or in Burford, or in the churchyard at Stratford, by the Avon, where Shakespeare's bones lie, with the commoners', under the church floor. The Fredericton cathedral is a perfect reproduction of an old Norman church, with gaunt tower, clean-cut walls, and plain buttresses, almost lost among the foliage of great elms – an English church, built by men of English blood, out of long practice and a deep, well-hidden mysticism. The churchyard, as only the mystical English can make it, is the most pleasant and cheerful spot in town.

But Fredericton is not English. It is pure North. American. It has brought the architecture, the furniture, the flavor of New England in its trek from the Thirteen Colonies after the Revolution, and it is still the kind of North American town that Emerson lived in. He or Hawthorne or Longfellow or Thoreau would have been perfectly at home here and, if smuggled in somehow today, blindfolded, would hardly know that their age had died. Yet English still because all these things came from England originally, from a little exile England in America.

Fredericton is the unmarred and unscratched relic, the perfect museum piece, and with that final rarity in our time, a complete unconsciousness of itself, for it has never been discovered, extolled, or exploited by the traveler.... It is the Home Town as it should be, where men can sit and dream, as they must have dreamed in the Athens of Pericles.

Fredericton lies on a gentle flat by the stream which bore the first settlers up here from the sea.... the land was good and the river a clear highway to the ocean. No wonder either that it was chosen as the capital of the province of New Brunswick, for it was quiet, thoughtful, far from the centers of corruption, a good place for sound legislation.

Now, in summer, it is lost in meditation and in a soft tangle of verdure. Every street is lined with trees, every back alley and every yard. The trees are more precious to these people than gold, and when caterpillars started to devour them a few years ago the whole town rose up, levied new taxes, bought a gigantic pumping machine, and sprayed the invaders to extinction. Life to a man in Fredericton without the elms above him is unthinkable....

Ah, Fredericton! That spot where Time lost his way and halted and could not rouse himself to move on – ...

(Hutchison, *The Unknown Country*, 1942, 222–4)

8 THE LAND OF PETER EMBERLEY, FREDERICTON AND MONCTON, 1956

☞ Fredericton and Moncton provide contrasts. Fredericton has grown since 1941 and Hutchison sets out to find whether the friendly small capital on a gentle stretch of the Saint John River retains its placid character. He decides that in essence it has, although he notes a dangerous indicator of change. Moncton has assumed significance: commercially because of its central location in the Maritimes, culturally as a centre for the Acadian people. ⌒

In the dozen years since we had seen it last, Fredericton had changed distressingly on the surface. How deep did the change go?

Sharp spires still pierced a cloud of spring foliage and floated upside-down in the river. The current of the St. John moved in majestic strides ...

[Fredericton is] the loveliest town in Canada, so perfect in every line, its ingredients so subtly mixed and matured to such ripeness, that no stone, brick, or board in all its singular anatomy should ever be changed and no vandal finger should be allowed to rub a speck from its mellow patina. A town, in short, or rather the imagined image and daydream of a town where a shady veranda, a girl, a guitar, and a moon on the river might rescue a man from this rude age and return him to the innocency of his youth when all the world was young.

Or was it conceivable that Fredericton might become just another normal town and lose its character in a nation that has no characters to spare? We set out on an early morning walk and found everything apparently in order.

The velvet turf of the Loyalists' graveyard lay undisturbed in the middle of the business district. The Parliament Buildings, their absurd dome shaped like King George Ill's nightcap, remained as homely and yet as beautiful as ever. The original Audubon prints – one of the last two complete sets in existence, as we were told, and Fredericton's most valuable possession – reposed securely in the fireproof vault of the archives. The brown clapboard house of Bliss Carman, Canada's greatest poet and leader of New Brunswick's humble Renaissance, was in good repair.

Down the street that monstrous golden hand on a church steeple still pointed its gilt forefinger to heaven in a gesture of eternity. The English cathedral presided with Gothic grin and silent elegy over Gray's imitation English churchyard. The university meditated, unruffled, on the hill. The painted iron dolphins gamboled in their fountain. A solid roof of green, on the soaring pillars of the Loyalists' trees, covered the whole town, leakproof.

But superficially Fredericton was changing faster than any other community in the Maritimes. It had become a little city of twenty thousand people. It was swelling up and down the riverbank; it had built a luxurious hotel (named for Beaverbrook, of course) out of its own capital; replaced the rabbit warren of *The Gleaner's* editorial office and

its Dickensian inmates with a newspaper of three daily editions; and, as
the final proof of its new opulence, had produced a formidable parking
problem. A parking problem in Fredericton! ...

[Hutchison visits Moncton.] They used to call this second city of New
Brunswick simply The Bend. It had nothing to distinguish it except the
bore of the Petitcodiac River, which rushes inland like a minor tidal wave,
exactly on the minute, so that you can set your watch by its arrival. Then
Moncton became the main railway junction of the Maritimes, then a
thriving business city, and then the unofficial capital of the Acadian race.

A community unlike any other in the nation, because it is evenly divided between two races and virtually bilingual, Moncton may be called
the inner crucible of the New Brunswick experiment. The contents of
the crucible are significant mainly because they are outwardly invisible.
An English-speaking Canadian will not find Moncton a French city, like
the cities of Quebec. A French-speaking Canadian from Quebec will
not find it English. It is purely Canadian, the pivot and symbol of the
nation's dual culture. So well is the experiment succeeding that the stranger is unaware of it.

(Hutchison, *Canada Tomorrow's Giant*, 1957, 90–2, 100)

9 MOTHER OF CANADA, AND THE ROCK, QUEBEC CITY, 1941

☞ "Mother of Canada" is a hymn celebrating Quebec City's role in
Canada as a mate of the St. Lawrence River. Together river and city
symbolize the country since the arrival of the French. But that is Canada conceived as North Atlantic history and geography; neither the
North Pacific or Arctic roots of Canada are mentioned. In the second
excerpt Quebec City is "The Rock." Hutchison knows this city of "two
worlds" through the soles of his boots and the eyes of history, walking
up and down Quebec City, observing its streets, buildings and people
from various angles. He uses urban landscapes to compare French and
English Canadians in a city to which he has deep emotional attachment. The italics are in the original. ☜

Mother of Canada
*City of Quebec they call you, as if stones and mortar and a name
could hold that urgent spirit! Fair and lovely and quaint, the strangers have called you, but who save your children can know you,
Mother of Canada! Who save your sons shall know the meaning of*

the smile on your wrinkled face, the touch of your aged hand, they who have gladly died for you, from the Long Sault to Vimy Ridge?

From your womb came we all, came every man who, calls himself Canadian, came this whole nation of Canada, from sea to sea. And you have watched your children grow, how patiently, how long! What sons have nursed at your unfailing breast to learn wisdom and courage and the love of this land, to fight the savage, to plow the earth and build railways and rear up other cities of another tongue, to sail across the sea and fly in alien skies that you might still live here, in your old way!

How long have you watched the River, who was your mate from the beginning! Watched him, with leaping heart, bring the ships from France in the spring, when you were hungry and sick and betrayed; watched him, with dim, longing eyes, as he carried the last sail away in the dying autumn; watched, unafraid, the enemy fleets of Kirke and Phips and Walker, and the last English fleet of Wolfe, who was to take you, but never to possess you. War the River brought you, and siege and bombardment and pestilence, yet he was your mate and you loved him. Always the River lay beside you in ceaseless rise and fall of tide, and you clung to him for life....

... How many different times and things and men you have known ... the top-hatted, stuffy days of Confederation when the Canadian nation was built here within your gates; and now the days of your comfortable old age, when you have become a legend, a name, and a monument, and strangers, knowing no better, call you quaint.

Still you are our Mother. Still you watch the river bearing his tides of ships and men and events ceaselessly up and down – your ancient mate, the St. Lawrence. Now behind you are new sounds, the sounds of men marching and drilling and flying in your skies. Deep sounds, rumbling in factories, woods, mines, and fields, the sounds of your nation coming of age. Your work bears at last its full fruit. Your sons are grown to manhood now. You have waited long for them and now they are ready. Oh, Mother, can you hear?

(Hutchison, *The Unknown Country*, 1942, 21–3

The Rock

On Maitre Abraham's field the modern Canada, the nation of two races, had begun. The battlefield is a good starting place for your own march upon Quebec.

Enter it, like Montcalm in his last hours, through the St. Louis Gate
– not the original but rebuilt with broad arch and tower on the original
plan – walk down St. Louis Road and the Grand Allee, and you will
know at once, though you have seen all the cities of the world, that
you have seen none exactly like this. Any tourist pamphlet will recite
its names, streets, monuments, buildings, legends, views; and Monsieur
Carrel, in his well-known guidebook, has drained the English dictionary
quite dry of adjectives and grafted them to the French idiom in a truly
astounding fashion. But no one, so far as I know, has ever caught the
peculiar essence of Quebec, which falls into no recognizable category,
being of two worlds.

Even Kipling could mutter only a few clipped phrases of astonishment, and novelists failed more dismally than soldiers in their attempts
to capture Quebec. Probably because there is no place in the New World,
at least, to which it can be precisely compared. Boston, perhaps, holds
as much history, but Boston is an aged spinster, growing fat with good
living, virtue triumphant but to lovelife unknown. Quebec, though older,
is French and no spinster, has known life, lived it and relished it all and
still looks out with bright, knowing eyes from the rock.

Quebec has that rare thing known in Europe, but almost unknown
in America – the perfection of planning which comes of no plan, which
has grown like a plant unfolding, street by street, stone by stone, planless and perfect. You would change no stone of it, from the obese English citadel on the peak of Cape Diamond to the meanest house in
Lower Town....

Quebec must be seen in all weathers and seasons. Its streets must be
trudged in sunshine and in snow – when the first grass is breaking green
on the slopes of the Citadel, when the maple trees are scarlet along the
cliffs, when it is all buried deep in white winter. And then it is no use trying to put it into words any more than five centuries of poets could catch
the peculiar and subtle rhythm of London, and every man is astounded,
even now, to discover this new and nameless thing for himself.

Only in a few places – in an English cathedral, perhaps, or in an old
Paris street, or in a forgotten white village by the Danube – is it possible
to capture the pungent flavor of enduring life; of individual men's lives
left somehow in the stones that they have shaped, the streets they have
laid, the houses they have built, so that it can be sensed and breathed,
communicating itself, as one living man to another – so that you may
know the touch of their vanished hands by the touch of their enduring
stone, the cast of their mind by the things they have made, the look of

their eyes by some sudden glimpse of a ruined wall or an old garden. In all America, Quebec alone holds this ultimate magic....

Half of it lies on a flat beside the river – the Lower Town by law of gravity and by law of social caste. Half of it lies on the tableland above – the Upper Town, where the Upper Classes have always lived. Winding, panting little streets toil up the cliffs to join the two-streets of oldest Europe and not of America – and to the sheer cliffs cling strange buildings as if they had fallen from the top and paused halfway down, wedged in the rock. Over all, always, from every angle, day and night, looms the dark shape of the rock, rising suddenly out of the river, with the round walls of the Citadel ringing its head like a dull crown – English, stolid as a steak-and-kidney pudding....

The inner heart of Quebec has always been the square ... where Champlain stands in heroic bronze, doffing his hat, on the site of his old chateau....

Across the square, facing Champlain, is the English cathedral, so English with its square unornamented body, its pointed steeple, that Wren should have built it, for the design was evidently stolen from him. All the basic differences in the two races are here, fixed in the stone of the English church and of the French churches all about it – the glum, unsmiling look of the English, who hide the most sentimental nature in the world under a concerted national look of solidity, building their churches like their faces, permitting only a few carved wrinkles of respectable amusement, an occasional cautious chuckle in Gothic; and the French, whose laughter is hewn in marble, whose plump and comfortable bodies bulge out in fat, spangled towers, whose tripping tongue and bubbling accent are captured for a moment in the richness of jeweled altars, vaulted roofs, and painted ceilings.

From the square you stroll down the winding street, cut into the rock of the cliff, past the little park, where, in a hotel now gone, the nation of Canada emerged in written constitution (the work of a few bearded men in frock coats), and near by a family of sleepy antique cannons loll, with open mouths over the ramparts. Then, by further curves and steep, cobbled hills, you reach Lower Town. It is there, in these narrow streets, where children play and good wives gossip, and storekeepers argue, that you feel the absurdity of Quebec.

Absurd, I mean, that people should walk these streets in modern clothing or, worse, drive through them in automobiles....

From Lower Town, from its canyons, gulfs, and gorges, you can look up at the living stone of the cliff that thrusts itself through the streets, overhangs the houses, and is as clean, untouched, and virginal in the middle of the city as on the day when Cartier first saw it. It is something like the up-ended rock of Edinburgh, but Edinburgh is Scottish, with lean, tightlipped old castle, standing alone. This is all French and as friendly as a sidewalk cafe. But do not inquire too deeply. On the bluffs above you is such a welter of spires, roofs, pinnacles, steeples, walls, monuments, and statues as only a guide book can distinguish – such a jumble of stone and mortar and labor that I never attempt to learn the names of its pieces, but am content to wander among them, aimlessly, as through a wood....

I walked back to town by the narrow streets but substantial houses of Upper Town – respectable, stern houses, cheek by jowl, flush with the pavement, shuttered and mysterious, with the French touch of little courtyards, the English flavor of walled gardens. It is all clean, compact, solid, a city where a man expects to remain, to live his life out in the same house, while all America moves on and on, leaving behind a wake of slums....

It is the houses, not the monuments, squares, and public buildings that hold the life of Quebec, that intangible thing by which you may know a city (and there are not half a dozen in America), a living organism made of memories and joint toil and common suffering. But it must forever escape the stranger so that, looking at the shuttered window, the bolted door, he can only sense it, like a distant perfume, like the sound of voices behind a garden gate, forever closed to him.

(Hutchison, *The Unknown Country*, 1942, 27–40)

10 THE FORTRESS, QUEBEC CITY, 1956

☞ Quebec City is "The Fortress," central to French Canadian culture within North America. But as well, the city is an ancestral gateway for all Canadians. It is that emotional symbolization and impact that concerns Hutchison, and it is almost incidentally that he remarks that it is "America's most spectacular city." ☞

The Rock of Quebec, slanting black across the St. Lawrence, was the primary fortress of America for nearly two hundred years, the focal point and strategic hinge of the continent. Many men have stood there watching the river and its freight of human events. From the rock, Champlain and his garrison watched the descent of that first hungry winter and then the sails of the first English fleet. Here Frontenac defied the second fleet from New England, Montcalm heard the last fleet announce the doom of New France, Carleton saved Canada from the American Revolution, and, in our time, Churchill and Roosevelt planned the world's largest war.

The rock has always been held by giants. Though it is no longer a military center, it remains a fortress. It is the spiritual fortress of a great people. Any man standing on the rock sees with his eyes the noblest sight in Canada and, with his imagination, the tragedy and triumph of the French Canadian race. It has lived from the beginning, and still lives, under siege....

[Quebec] always deceives the visitor from English-speaking Canada unless he is a very clever or a very dull man. The clever man sees through the facade of America's most spectacular city and suspects the turmoil behind it. The dull man sees nothing beyond the spectacle contrived for tourists. An average Anglo-Saxon (always as naive and romantic at heart as the Latin is cold and logical) finds his judgment melting before nature's lavish work and man's reckless architecture upon the riverbank.

No Canadian is worthy of the name if he can sail up the river and, as he catches his first glimpse of the rock and its towers athwart the western sky, feel no constriction of the throat and sudden dampness of the eye. Such a man is not fit to be called a Canadian. If he is not embraced at once, as in the arms of a dark enchantress, and dazzled by a pair of ageless eyes, he is not fit, whatever his nationality, to be called a man.

(Hutchison, *Canada Tomorrow's Giant*, 1957, 124–6)

11 VILLE MARIE, MONTREAL, 1941

☞ Hutchison knows Montreal in the last glorious years of the railway era, when the railway station still is the epicentre of meeting and interaction. In Montreal he perceives a "metropolitan attitude," urban "glamour," and "the acceptance of the city as a natural way of life." Time and again in this volume Hutchison compares other Canadian urban centres to Montreal. To him Montreal is the one true city in Canada, cosmopolitan, urbane, knowing, very accepting of individualistic behaviour, and somewhat wicked. This is where the men lived who created the transportation systems essential to building Canada. Utilizing Montreal's matchless location on the St. Lawrence and Ottawa Rivers, they gave the city its commercial and industrial start, and developed confidence in exerting power. Hutchison recognizes the labouring classes on which the wealth of the city was built, but says little about the relations of the French and British in Montreal,

although he gives much attention to that relationship in a wider
Canadian context elsewhere in the book. ☞

Montreal is the second French city of the world, much too large for the
country behind it, swarming with over a million people out of Canada's
entire eleven millions, far gone in the dropsical American disease of size,
and its urgent skyscrapers, like weeds in a garden, are crushing out the
last relics of a great and noble history.

Quebec, though thirty-four years older, is spry, bright-eyed, fascinat-
ing, unmistakably the grand dame. Montreal is losing her figure, tries to
hide it under diamonds, fur coats, and rouge, and she appears in public
with a shaven poodle on a leash, escorted by a stout gentleman who
owns a railway, some banks, and an indifferent digestion.

But Montreal is still as much the metropolis of Canada as New York
is of the United States – not by size alone, but by consent, by tradition,
force, history, and sheer character. Everybody goes to Montreal. Through
the Windsor Station, as through the Grand Central, flow all the tides of
the world, and in the old Windsor Hotel, which somehow has refused to
be hurried, you eventually meet everyone.

The money of Canada has drained for three centuries into Montreal.
The toil of farmers on the prairies, of trappers up north, of lumberjacks
in the New Brunswick woods, of fishermen on the West Coast has built
up here our only great city, with a great city's daily habits; our chief
accumulation of wealth, rich living, and true metropolitan attitude; the
city's cast of mind and, you might say – if the word had not been seduced
and bedeviled in the advertising columns – its glamour. Montreal is one
of the half dozen cities in America that can be compared with the sea-
soned and settled cities of Europe, the rest being only small towns with
growing pains.

You pass the shuttered houses of Quebec and dream of old fashioned
gallantry and forgotten loves. You pass the ostentatious houses of Montreal and glimpse visions of modern riches, butlers, maids, flunkies. You
see the master class, an overstuffed but genteel luxury, something like
that of Park Avenue and Long Island, but with an entirely different flavor, a certain added elegance and floridity which is French.

You are likely to forget, in your wonderment, where all this came
from. It came out of the labor of millions of poor Canadians, far from
Montreal, by a cunning arrangement of geography and economics, and
it lives, this splendid life of Westmount and Mount Royal, on top of a
teeming slum, as luxury does everywhere....

Montreal ... manages to stand out against the American tide a little better than most places. It is, to begin with, a unique habitation, sprouting out of an island in the middle of the St. Lawrence, with a lush green mountain in the middle of it....

... At first sight the dark chimneyed sweep of the city on the river fiat, with the broad glint of the river, the thin line of bridges, and the Green Mountains of Vermont faint to the south, is like the appearance of many other American cities.

Then you notice the upthrust of church spires everywhere, the green copper domes and frail steeples, through the billows of green foliage. Montreal is different because it has architecture, and most of it the work of the Catholic Church. Only a few North American cities have any concerted scheme of architecture; Montreal is rich and prodigal with it, has statues at every corner, noble buildings on every street, like an old European city but, still hugging its mountain, it has never quite lost touch with the forest that Maisonneuve found there long ago....

The true flavor of Montreal is to be found not in relics but in the swarming streets, from the spacious, tree-lined boulevards of the West End down to the slums of the East. In the west, on Sherbrooke Street, beside the sleepy campus of McGill – a real street, like a minor "Champs," like a little Vienna Ring, where most of the thoroughfares of America are mere gashes between brick and stone – it is all English. Everywhere there are fine old stone houses, mellow now, a little tired, that used to shelter a life of friendly, slightly stuffy formality in top hats, whiskers, and wide skirts, moving by summer in carriages, by winter in jingling sleighs.

When you cross that formidable boundary, garish, brawling St. Lawrence Street, you have entered another country. Here the inhabitants are all French-Canadian, living in the metropolis and not making a very good job of it. Here the French-Canadian's original genius for communal living in the village is drowned by numbers, by cheap, mean streets and gaudy arcades, by noise and filth, but you can still get a French meal there, as good as in Paris. It is the slum of any great city, our universal vice of accumulation, but the French-Canadian has given it a certain extra barbarity....

Near by you walk down St. James Street on tiptoe, for it is the Wall Street of Canada (cursed by every backwoods orator from Gaspé to Okanagan), the headquarters of our great corporations, the strong box of our wealth. After listening to the orators in the sticks you expect to see molten gold flowing in the gutters and rich men in carriages running over the children of the poor. It is rather disappointing to find nothing but a few better-dressed gentlemen and the flat dome of the Bank of Montreal....

Yes, there is something about Montreal, a feeling that we do not have in our other Canadian cities – city manners, the acceptance of the city as a natural home and way of life, where most other cities are only villages trying to ape New York. There is something here which, for lack of a better name, must be called elegance with a touch of wickedness; for beneath all the culture, the refinement, and luxury is not only poverty but an organized underworld of vice and crime, with politics not as bold as in some American cities, but worse than anything Canada has ever known....

The kind snow of winter suddenly covers all the ugly memories and sights of Montreal, and it becomes a dream city then, as fine as Budapest or Munich or Brussels, with all its domes, steeples, squares, trees, and crowded bronze statues crusted with white.

In Dominion Square on such a night, with the fat, frosted French dome of St. James on one side, the Gothic, tight-lipped lines of the English church glistening white on the other side, you sense suddenly how men have built here on this island, through the centuries, a complicated structure of luxury, ease, religion, and civilization against the devastation of the Canadian winter – and built it with a sense of the good and the beautiful.

Don't look behind at the skyscrapers crowding the square now, look straight ahead at the snow, the sleigh bells, the glimpse of a beautiful woman in furs, the glitter of lights in the Windsor, the rich people drinking wine in the dining room, the teeming night life of cafe and club and the encircling cold. This, you think, must be like St. Petersburg before the Revolution – a certain glittering sinfulness and sophistication, which makes us simple western Canadians feel very young, innocent, and gauche.

Montreal! The rolling, thunderous sound of it has always meant for us Canadians life and riches and lovely women, money and power and masterful men. Moréal, the sweeter French version, has meant for us the city, the metropolis, the gaiety, the splendor that we could never hope to know back home.

The mustard seeds scattered by Maisonneuve on the rich island soil have grown indeed, producing rankest weeds, but some lavish flowers.

(Hutchison, *The Unknown Country*, 1942, 64–76)

12 THE FORTRESS, MONTREAL, 1956

☞ Hutchison is very much aware that Montreal, as a commercial centre, is still "the Canadian metropolis of a metropolitan age," but the city is much more to him: it is "a civilization, a state of mind," a place of wonderment, a special place in Canada. Here he reinforces his earlier feeling for Montreal, but in truth he reveals more about himself than adding much to what he said previously about the city. ☞

... One hot evening, we saw the final autograph of the [industrial and social] revolution scrawled across the sky by the smoke and lights of Montreal.

How fertile was that "grain of mustard seed" planted here by Maisonneuve when he founded, at the base of Mount Royal, his Ville Marie and dedicated it to the Virgin! And how quickly Montreal lost her own virginity!

An immortal trollop with a heart of gold, this city has been called – always a mistress, never a wife – or a metropolitan wen and parasitic growth forever swelling across its island and ravening through the farm-lands on the river's bank. Nouns and adjectives all wither in this colossal presence. It is simply Montreal, a civilization, a state of mind, and the only true city in Canada, beside which all others, however large, are only grown-up towns or camps of steel and concrete.

Yes, a city not by the mere measurement of size, not by its proud title of the second French-speaking community in the world, but by the meas-urement of time, wealth, diversity, and urban instinct, its violent clash of slum and mansion, its men of secret power in mahogany boardrooms, its middle class in endless vistas of ugly houses, its proletariat swarming through the unspeakable rabbit warrens of the east end. All this amor-phous jumble somehow has been welded together in a single organism. That is Montreal, and its very name sounds like the thunder of its streets, the gurgle of its two rivers.

Here is an island joined to the mainland by many bridges and yet forever an island in the life of Canada, spiritually separate and alone. The nation's life flows past and washes the island, but cannot erode it. So it has flowed through the nation's jugular since 1642, and from the flood Montreal takes what it wants at pleasure. As it once exchanged fur for French coin, it now transforms the toil of unknown men throughout the hinterland all the way to the Pacific into the products of its factories, into the profits of its counting houses, into its own wealth or poverty.

Montreal, the sleek entrepreneur and greedy broker of our economy, is crapulous, they say, with vice and crime. It is continually reforming and always unreformed. Maybe so, but most of its inhabitants, far more than one million people, have never entered a night club, met *les filles,* or made a dishonest dollar.

In short, for all its virtues and vices, all its shocking contrast of money and destitution, all its legendry, fable and fact, this is the heart of Quebec's revolution, the Canadian metropolis of a metropolitan age.

Though I have seen it many times, Montreal always fills me anew with the horror, the admiration, and the envy of a country boy seeing his first city in all its wickedness. A walk of half an hour will take you from some hideous night spot, awriggle with nudes on a Sunday night, to the splendid avenue of trees on Sherbrooke Street, the quiet campus of McGill University, and then past the stone houses of the rich to the top of Mount Royal, whence, like Cartier, you can see the island moated by its rivers and laced loosely to the shore by its bridges.

(Hutchison, *Canada Tomorrow's Giant*, 1957, 136–7)

13 THREE O'CLOCK OTTAWA TIME, OTTAWA, 1941

☞ Hutchison titles this chapter "Three O'Clock Ottawa Time" because that is question time in the House of Commons, when members of Parliament ask government leaders questions on behalf of Canadian citizens. Hutchison views Ottawa as a nascent national capital. It is an Ontario town that happens to be the centre of Canadian government, with splendid parliament buildings, and does have the potential to become a "nobler capital." ☞

... Ottawa is probably the most unsophisticated capital in the world. It is only Bytown grown up a little – the old lumber village which was selected for a capital because they couldn't agree on any established city. Though a deputy minister's wife may consider herself a trifle above the wife of an assistant deputy and not know the wife of a mere clerk, though the pretensions of a few snobs in Rockcliffe may startle the crude westerner, Ottawa on the whole is neighborly, folksy, essentially simple, a place where you could see the first citizen of the nation strolling with his aged dog, the leader of the opposition getting a shave at the corner, and the governor of the Bank of Canada at a movie. As for mystery, outside of the inner circle itself there is no secret in Ottawa for more than twenty-four hours. The place is a sounding board, a whispering gallery, a natural echoing cave. A rumor started in the parliamentary lobbies at three o'clock will be heard at every dinner table in town by evening. Always Ottawa is drenched in rumor, but not the mighty rumor of London or Washington, just the gossip of the neighbors who happen to live in the capital.

Ottawa is growing slowly but surely into the physical stature of a world capital. Alas, how much better it might have been planned! Here was an almost perfect site – a high, well-treed bank beside a broad river which cascades over a noble waterfall. Budapest was built on almost the identical formation and became a spectacle in fairyland. Instead, Ottawa's falls have been harnessed and lost in dingy power houses, and the north bank of the river is blighted with the industries of Hull, in Quebec, from whose match factory emerges, if the wind is blowing from that quarter, a queer, rather pleasant smell of sulphur. But if you can ignore the industries and look across the river from Hull to the high bank on the Ontario side, you will see a group of Gothic buildings which, in total effect, far surpass those of Westminster itself – the soaring pinnacle of the Center Block, the crazy, windblown turrets of the East and West Blocks, the wondrous flying buttresses of the old library, all mixed together in a lovely tangle, and yet a perfect design of stone and spires, rising out of a green surge of maple trees....

The city of Ottawa clusters around the towered hill of Parliament like a medieval town around its castle. It is an old town as these things are reckoned in Canada, its streets are narrow, and its original buildings drab. They are constantly improving it, however, have built a fine system of driveways and flowering boulevards along the Rideau Canal, carved out grassy parks, started to cut a broad mall from the hill southward, and maintained with jealous care the great trees along its streets....

One usually thinks of Ottawa in the winter when Parliament opens and the Hill is deep in snow and heavy with intrigue. But when Parliament has gone home, Ottawa becomes a leafy Ontario town again, happy beside its river. On a summer evening the sun sinks behind the tangled towers, glints on the populous bronze statues, and makes magic among the carvings of the stone walls. Only a few old men and whispering lovers sit on the benches and the birds are singing their evening song in the elms. Then it is good to be in Ottawa, to meditate on the men who have worked here for Canada, to picture Macdonald climbing these steps beside you, and Laurier strolling these shady streets. It is good to think of the nobler capital which will yet rise here.

(Hutchison, *The Unknown Country*, 1942, 102–5)

14 THE CLIFF, OTTAWA, 1956

☞ In 1956, Hutchison presents a much more emotional picture of
Ottawa than he did fifteen years earlier, as he reflects how much the
"sinewy lines" of the central tower of the parliament buildings "have
caught by chance the harsh beauty, the distance, the loneliness, and the
human struggle of our land." He remains highly critical of the city but
still believes it can "become a worthy capital, unlike any other in the
world." ☜

Ottawa should be approached from the north side of its river, preferably
by a detour through the winding, mossy ways of the Gatineau Valley.
They led us to the old, familiar tangle of gray towers afloat in a green
mist. But every road in Canada, every trail through forest, prairie, and
tundra, leads at last to Ottawa. Every traveler who hopes to understand
the nation must come here.

For Ottawa, with all its faults and disguises, its smiling face and incessant hidden war, its endless adventure and blind groping that men call
politics, is the nation's brain – not its heart, mind you, but its brain,
radiating impulses, wise or foolish, to every nerve and muscle of the
half-continent.

Inevitably we came back, as so many times before, to the falls of Chaudière, where Champlain propitiated the Indian gods with an offering of
tobacco, to the sheer cliff on which his successors built a capital before
they built a nation, to the abiding enigma of that nation's life....

We crossed the river on its death-trap bridge, entered perhaps the
worst-managed traffic in Canada, and drove up to the Hill....

In any season since I first saw it as a scared cub reporter nearly forty
years ago, the central tower [of the Parliament buildings] makes me
pause a moment in humility; not because it is an original masterpiece
of architecture – it is, in fact, a Gothic imitation from Europe, a remote
offspring of Big Ben's tower by the Thames – but because its sinewy lines
have caught by chance the harsh beauty, the distance, the loneliness, and
the human struggle of our land. And as I stood before this sharp arrow
aimed at the sun, the carillon bells chimed out suddenly in triumphant
peal. A silent nation had found its voice....

There are, of course, two Ottawas – the cosy, rather provincial Ontario
town built by Colonel By on the river cliff and the separate kingdom of
the Hill.

When Queen Victoria selected Ottawa for the capital of an unborn nation, hardly yet a gleam in Macdonald's eye, she had not seen this site and never would see it.

When Goldwin Smith, that prophet of ineluctable Canadian-American amalgamation, announced that Ottawa was a "sub-Arctic lumber village converted by royal mandate into a political cockpit," he (and most Englishmen) did not foresee either the present nation or its capital....

Later on, when Laurier remarked that "it is hard to say anything good" of Ottawa and that "it is not a handsome city and does not appear destined to become one," he could not imagine the Ontario town now spread miles beyond his Sandy Hill, the majestic Chateau named for him, the mansions of Rockcliffe, the spacious driveways, the prime minister's stately residence, the still finer city planned for the future.

To be sure, the dingy defile of Sparks Street and the other streets of business remain much as Laurier knew them. His own ugly house is preserved intact, with all its litter of Victorian horrors, as a monument to his heir, Mackenzie King. The industrial skyline and smoke of Hull, across the river, mar the whole civic design. Some surviving slums still crawl to the edge of Parliament Hill.

But if the architects and town-planners are allowed to complete their work; if the projected green belt is preserved on the city's rim; if new avenues are driven from the Hill through the business section (one fancies the encrusted old gentlemen of the Rideau Club gently lifted, chairs and all, by steamshovel, the American ambassador respectfully removed from Wellington Street and deposited elsewhere); if Ottawa has the time, money, and imagination, it will become a worthy capital, unlike any other in the world.

(Hutchison, *Canada Tomorrow's Giant*, 1957, 169–72)

15 THE WEDGE, TORONTO, 1941

☞ Hutchison catches the complexity of Toronto. Already in the 1940s he sees financial dominance passing from Montreal to Toronto. It is a city that is simultaneously parochial and connected across the Atlantic to Britain, and now has to become a true national centre in culture and finance. That is where the confusion in understanding the city arises: it has attained metropolitan power without having had the maturing experience of developing and using its power to further the growth of all parts of Canada. Self-confidence in creating a great country was built up by politicians and railway builders in Ottawa and Montreal, whereas Toronto has inherited something it has not built and has not yet grown into its new role. Hutchison's strong, visceral, reaction to Toronto is surprising; in essence the city represents the protectionist industrial wedge of southern Ontario, even willing to help poor neighbouring regions in order to protect its sheltered tariff position. ⌒

To any Canadian from a distance, Toronto, Ontario's capital and metropolis, is almost an alien city. He may well feel more at home in Boston or San Francisco. "One of the worst blue-devil haunts on the face of the earth!" cried John Galt, the Scottish immigrant poet, in the days of the Family Compact. "The City of Toronto has more grasping, greedy, unctuous people in it than any other city in the world!" shouts Ralph Maybank, of Winnipeg, in the Parliament of Canada today. These are fearful words out of desperate mouths – too fearful, too desperate.

Toronto is a great and gracious city, second only to Montreal in size (getting on for a million people); and the remains of York, except for a few earthworks, barracks, and rusty cannons, have been engulfed in stone and mortar. By the lake shore the streets are old and narrow but they turn to noble avenues as the city marches ever northward. There Toronto has spacious parks, fine homes, modern skyscrapers, an illustrious university. If there is a Canadian culture in the strict sense, this probably is its center. Here books are published, and national magazines. Here writers and artists work. Here Banting made insulin. Here, too, the financial headquarters of Canada are fast centering, in place of their old capital at Montreal. In Toronto most of the larger commercial organizations of the country maintain their central offices.

Still, to many Canadians it retains the old name given to it by jealous neighbors long ago. It is Hog Town – Hog Town one supposes, because it fattened on the rest of the surrounding country through a protective tariff, at the expense of other towns and whole provinces. An unfair name for any city, but Toronto is certainly a queer place, an exhibit which no student of Canada can afford to overlook.

It comes out of our deep past and uncertain present. It is the United Empire Loyalist town of York grown up and, perhaps, the Family Compact in a twentieth-century incarnation. That fine old Loyalist stock is the foundation of modern Toronto and one of the three great influences which merge in its strange character.

That part of Toronto which comes of this stout breed often remains more British than Britain, more loyal than the King. It brought with it from the revolting Thirteen Colonies, a prejudice against the United States and this, among some natives, has never died. There is still a hard kernel of people here who have not outgrown the War of 1812 or the Rebellion of 1837. It is not without significance that not until a few years ago was a statue raised in Toronto to William Lyon Mackenzie, the Rebel, and then only at the side of the legislative buildings, as if Toronto were rather ashamed of him.

Here the Colonial Mind, that curious vestigial organ which no longer functions but often can ache, still manages to exist without nourishment and without reason or use. Out of Toronto occasionally comes such a bleat of colonialism and inferiority complex, such a desire to be in chains again, such a moan for the world that has gone, as no other North American can understand. This is sometimes miscalled Imperialism. Actually, it is pure nostalgia. But it is not to be confused with something better which makes the young men of Toronto rush to the colors whenever war breaks out – a considered belief in the British Commonwealth of Nations. In the wails of a few people who are afraid to grow up, this finer sentiment is often misunderstood among Canadians, which is a pity.

It should not be forgotten either that out of Toronto has come some bold Canadian national thinking and more influence towards co-operation with the United States than the public yet knows. Still, Toryism, old-fashioned nineteenth-century Imperialism, and Family Compactism still form one of the three basic strains in this Toronto character.

The second is Ontario's attitude towards Quebec. To the French race, its aspirations, character, and religion, Ontario considers itself the necessary counterbalance. At times this feeling becomes plain race prejudice, blue-devil worship in the worst form. Orange Lodges parading down the streets with King William on a white horse, clerics screeching against the Pope in obscure Toronto churches, frenzied editorial howls in the *Telegram* have been the outward manifestations of this anti-French feeling, which ebbs and flows perpetually.

The third factor in this character is purely economic. Central Ontario, the great wedge, with Toronto in the middle of it, has been built on the principle of isolation, on the basis of economic self-containment, in the shelter of a high tariff. It cannot conceive of life without this protection. It cannot imagine how its great industries could survive if they had to compete on equal terms with the richer, more economical industries of the United States. Ontario has to cling to what it owns, to fight down all attempts to remove its tariff wall, to drive its wedge ever deeper into the economy of Canada, if necessary to bonus its poor neighbors so that they will accept the high price of Ontario goods.

That is why the wedge is a separate community of its own, far more than a physical island. It is an economic and spiritual island. That is why Toronto must be the most insular city of its size anywhere, the largest small town in the world. That, too, is part of the old prejudice against Americans – a secret fear of American goods. But the final paradox lies in the fact that of all Canadian cities Toronto is the most American in appearance, in organization, and in daily habits.

I do not pretend to understand Toronto. All students of Canada have tried to plumb these depths, but all, so far as I know, have failed. The views of outsiders must be weighed, against their prejudice, distance from the place, and envy. The fact remains, however, that Toronto is a city apart, and the Canadian from other places stifles here. He finds Toronto people busy with their own local affairs and not interested in his, and much of the content of the newspapers, the largest in Canada, are a mystery to him.

He finds an odd stuffiness and exaggerated respectability (or so it seems to him), a strait-jacket regularity of behavior, a deep-blue conventionalism, and not merely the lack of the free and easy life as we know it out West but, worse, the lack of a desire for it, the knowledge of its possibility. He finds also a piety here which annoys him (perhaps because he is not so virtuous himself) and in every Canadian's mind the symbol of Toronto, the accepted caricature, is a gentleman in a top hat walking to church on Sunday with a Bible under his arm, and frowning at the neighbor who is cutting the grass. Few cut the grass in Toronto on Sunday. Toronto the Good, we call it, and that is the sneer of the tough boy who doesn't like Sunday school.

(Hutchison, *The Unknown Country*, 1942, 133–6)

16 THE HOMELAND, TORONTO, 1956

☞ Toronto remains a conundrum: a furiously expanding overgrown town of many elements, changing quickly as it becomes Canada's central ethnic melting pot. It is true many changes have occurred, but still Hutchison recognizes only one true Canadian city, Montreal, as he told us when he discussed that city. But he has hopes for Toronto. ☞

... we were now approaching the hub of modern Ontario. Toward evening a smudge of smoke appeared against the sunset. There could be no more doubt about it. We confronted the awful presence of Toronto.

Every Canadian traveler and visiting fireman thinks he knows Toronto, and usually dismisses it with a sigh or a 'sneer. In fact, no one really knows it, not even its own inhabitants. For Toronto has grown past all knowledge and boasts that it is growing faster than any other city in the world. It has become, like the province around it, a series of diverse elements loosely knitted together by stitches of steel and concrete, articulated by the first Canadian subway, glued by the adhesive of business, but not yet fused like its only rival, Montreal.

There are as many Torontos, I suppose, as the numerous Ontarios that feed its divided body – a Toronto of old-timers saddened by the jungle of skyscrapers around their tranquil homes, of newcomers dazzled by their first glimpse of Babylon; a staid provincial capital of Toronto at Queen's Park; a financial capital of brassy tycoons in Bay Street; a capital of learning at Canada's largest university; a Toronto of churchgoers, organized crime, and commercialized vice; a Toronto of writers, artists, musicians, and scholars nurturing that tender little plant called Canadian Culture; a Toronto of old Loyalist stock, who founded muddy York long ago and retained its muddy prejudices; a dozen Torontos of foreign stocks speaking their own languages, eating their own diets, and thinking their own thoughts in Canada's central melting-pot.

York was a village in a swamp beside Lake Ontario. Toronto, York's successor, was a town of fixed customs and cohesive mind. The several Torontos of our time compose neither a village nor a town, and have yet to become a city. They are a series of communities in shifting combination, continual flux, and perpetual expansion.

Yet great things have happened here. When William Lyon Mackenzie, a furious little creature in flaming red wig and three overcoats, led his mob of country bumpkins to the barricades of Gallows Hill in the Rebellion of 1837 and fled to sanctuary in the United States, he had unconsciously altered the history of the world. But Toronto is too busy nowadays to remember that its comic-opera revolution doomed the existing British Empire governed from London and, by a century of experiment, finally issued in the Commonwealth of independent nations. If that curious structure can be said to have any birthplace, it is this sprawling, ill-jointed civic colossus by the lake....

In all the endless suburban checkerboards, where a man can hardly find his own house among ten thousand others of identical design, how many Torontonians know the story of the ruined Rebel, whose treason was expunged and family honor restored by his grandson, Mackenzie King? ·

How many can remember even yesterday's familiar caricature of Toronto – the spinster lady in Victorian lace who abhorred drink, Sunday sports, and the morals of her French neighbor down the St. Lawrence? She is gone, or retired into some obscure mansion with blinds tightly drawn. Her voice may grumble sometimes in the morning's *Globe and Mail,* but it is lost in the afternoon screams of *The Star* and *The Telegram,* the new voices of a Toronto in birth but not yet born, and all the more shrill and positive because they are so uncertain.

Still, if Toronto sucks into its insatiable maw, through the gullet of the Lakes, half the nation's farmstuffs, minerals, timber, oil, and water power, and uses them to nourish a distended and dropsical body, its mind is nourished by new people with new ideas from every corner of Canada and from many foreign lands. It is slowly building a second Canadian city. The shiny smugness, the well-fed, aldermanic look, and the self-infatuation that so repel strangers will disappear in time. A folk who could invent the Commonwealth in the swamp of York can surely invent something better than this overgrown country town and second-class New York.

(Hutchison, *Canada Tomorrow's Giant,* 1957, 151–3)

17 THE FRONTIERSMAN, WINNIPEG, 1941

☞ When Hutchison visits a city that symbolizes some aspect of Canadian development he does not begrudge space, and for Winnipeg, as he for Quebec and Montreal, he provides a history of the city and surrounding region in the context of the nation. Winnipeg is a gateway city: people flowed through it to the prairie, the grain trade shaped it, and the city still has a feeling for the soil. Hutchison, however, mainly views Winnipeg through the impact of a great Canadian, John W. Dafoe, editor of the *Winnipeg Free Press.* In particular, Hutchison recognizes Winnipeg's unmatched association through the grain-trade with what is happening in the rest of the world. Winnipeg's grasp of the world outside Canada, and the illuminating ideas on Canada of an exemplary editor, are what interest Hutchison, not, for example, the great ethnic mixing in the city, which he barely mentions. There is a hint of George Parkin's breadth of international vision in Hutchison's remarks on Canada, the Second World War, and the country's future responsibilities. ⌒

John W. Dafoe, editor of the *Winnipeg Free Press,* is the greatest Canadian of his time.... [The record of his life] is so largely the record of his time, [that it] must be examined by everyone who wants to understand Canada, where it came from and where it is going in the world....
... [Winnipeg] was the ideal place for him. Winnipeg largely gave him his character. His character has largely made the mental climate of Winnipeg. To understand either, you must investigate both, and both are worth investigation.
Winnipeg lies alone on the empty prairie, thrusting itself suddenly out of the flat plains like a mirage. Being isolated, it has developed its own ways, its own thoughts, and its own looks, free from the monotony of multitudes. Winnipeg is still the West and far more western than the cities further westward. Despite its size and physical structure it is, in spirit, the frontier. Its inhabitants come out of the western soil, out of immigration, hardship, loneliness, and the hope of riches. They are frontier folk and many of them remember the buffalo herds....
At last the railway came to the plains, then the surge of settlement, the grain sprouting from the Lakes to the Rockies, and Winnipeg the center of it all – Main Street churned into deep mud by horse and wagon, Portage Avenue still the trail westward to Portage, and the young journalist, Dafoe, picking ice out of the water barrel in his kitchen every morning.
Some old men and women still alive remember most of this history. Their square houses of warm yellow stone stand along the Red River, north of Winnipeg, hard by the massive walls, gates, and buildings of Lower Fort Garry. Their Scottish kirks stand there also with the stern look brought from Scotland, ...
A great story, the Scottish origins of Winnipeg, overlaid now by the deep strata of immigration from Europe, by the hordes of whiskered men who had never seen the Hebrides. Yet the flavor of old Winnipeg remains, and the attitude of the settler in a new land – the expectation of continuing growth, the willingness to gamble, the confidence of wealth. Why, this town has gambled through its grain exchange on every crop, on every season's rain and sunshine and hail, on every passing storm. Its richest men have watched the clouds in the morning and the look of the sunset, smelled rain in the sky, brooded over the reports of moisture, and staked their fortunes on the thousand miles of rippling yellow wheat stalks.

Winnipeg has never lost its grasp of the plow, its feeling for the soil, for weather, and for freedom. But it has reached out, selling its grain the world over, and it has had to think about the business of other countries, to ponder a drought in the Argentine, the Russian crop, the prospects in Hungary. Winnipeg, the frontier town, having world-wide interests, is the least provincial spot in Canada. It has a better grasp of national and world affairs than any Canadian city, except Ottawa, because it has to market its product everywhere.

You can sense this combination of the old west and broad modern ideas as soon as you reach the place. Whenever I land in Winnipeg, though it is usually forty below zero and a blizzard whipping down Main Street, I can feel a warm surge of friendliness and a sudden uplift of the spirit. These people, lost in their immense prairies, forced to make their own amusement and think their own thoughts, have a vigor about them, of the body and the mind, which makes a coastal Canadian feel frail and flabby. They have made their own culture also, of music, dramatics, and art, in the fashion of their fathers in old Fort Garry, because they had to. They have taken the bald-headed prairie and made parks and planted trees and reared up business buildings, fine homes, and a notable university....

... Winnipeg has seen boom and depression as sudden as the failure of a crop or the decline of a foreign market and is used to evil fortunes. Some authorities will argue today that the depression of the world's wheat industry limits the city to its present size or less. Perhaps it may, but the spirit of Winnipeg is the true hope of Canada – the forward look, the broad, world-wide feeling, the pioneer spirit, the willingness to gamble.

It is no accident, therefore, that Canada's best thinking in the last twenty years has come out of such a place. Out of it came Dafoe, and probably he could not have flourished anywhere else. It was he who gave direction and point to this thinking and persistently forced it by persuasion, by eloquence, and by argument, upon the Canadian people.

So wide is this man's range, traveling in person and by pen from London, Paris, and Geneva into the smallest prairie hamlet, walking with kings and never losing the common touch of Main Street, that his ideas are the common property of the nation, a large part of our current stock in trade. Any ideas on public affairs which, by chance, have found their way into this book, are very likely his, but he will not miss them, having plenty more....

Canada will never lapse again into the position of nationhood at home and a colony in world affairs. Never again will this country take its foreign policy, complete and beyond question, from London. The folly of refusing to accept responsibility, to make commitments, only to find that we have responsibility and commitments everywhere, has been burned into the Canadian soul by the second world war. Never again, having feared actual attack for the first time in its life, will Canada leave itself without defenses on both oceans.

The war has remade Canada economically and industrially. It has built a stronger nation than we ever thought possible in our time. Greatly led, Canada can play its great part in the next peace, as the hinge between the democracies which will have to shoulder, whether they want to or not, the load of a ruined world. No man will have done more than Dafoe to prepare Canada for its manifest destiny.

(Hutchison, *The Unknown Country*, 1942, 249–67)

18 THE HUB, WINNIPEG, 1956

☞ Old cities that once dominated a region and then decline are sometimes easier to understand geographically than cities that prosper quietly. As Hutchison puts it: "Winnipeg's former sovereignty has decayed." Winnipeg and the grain-trade are surrogates for discussing greater government regulation in economic affairs, what Hutchison terms a switch from individualistic to collective behaviour. It is a city where he once worked, and he recognizes its historical connections with the land, its rivers, and the first inhabitants of the area, something that is being renewed in the twenty-first century. Unparalleled international awareness may exist in Winnipeg because of the grain-trade, yet at the same time, because of its geographical situation, "alone in the terrifying vacuum of the plains," it has had to build Canada's strongest community. The national significance of a native son is recognized: Hutchison visits St. Boniface and the grave of Louis Riel. ☜

… At last we had reached the hub and crossroads of Canada, the beating pulse, the very heart, halfway between the oceans.

But Winnipeg had changed. By the estimate of the oldtimers, it had deteriorated.

The change was not apparent in the city's affluent exterior, the wide noisy canyon of Portage Avenue, the spreading suburbs, the well-kept, thrifty, and peculiarly boyish look which has always illuminated this place and its people. Nevertheless, a fundamental shift had altered the economic, political, and, more important, the mental gravity of the central plain. Winnipeg no longer ruled it from the lakes to the mountains. John Wesley Dafoe was gone....

In those days he and his newspaper represented a solid, concentrated, and potent force in the nation's affairs. They spoke for the entire west from its undisputed capital of Winnipeg. They stood for the old-fashioned Liberalism of the Manchester School, the simple, farm-based democracy of Jefferson, the economics of Adam Smith, the distrust of centralized government and mass mind, the theory of the sacred, individual person.

Now Dafoe was gone, and his era with him. Its ideals of individualism had been replaced by the seemingly new and actually age-old ideal of collectivism and big government. The Sanhedrin [Dafoe's privy council of knowledgeable Winnipeg business and professional men] was dissolved. Winnipeg had become the capital of Manitoba only. The prairie citadel of ideas had fallen before the mass march....

Still, if Winnipeg's former sovereignty has decayed, I find it on every visit a bigger, busier, richer city than ever. It is still our strongest and most coherent Canadian community. It is filled with our liveliest folk.

This I can say with a fine impartiality, since I detest the outside look, the flat terrain and cruel climate of Winnipeg, but respect its soul just this side idolatry....

Winnipeg cannot belong to anyone, can never be understood by anyone or perhaps endured by anyone except its natives, an exclusive brotherhood....

{Hutchison takes a] good look at town which had long been [his] second home....

The lavish width and reckless pedestrians of Portage Avenue; the run-down look of lower Main Street, whose day has passed; the City Hall, that incomparable masterpiece of pinnacled and leering ugliness; the parliament buildings in whimsied mixture of miscellaneous architectures and topped by the Golden Boy, a civic idol; the pot-bellied curve of Wellington Crescent and its double line of rich men's castles, many shaped like high-class penitentiaries; the older streets of broken mansions beside some new business block; the trees laboriously planted and faithfully tended in garden and boulevard until only a few spires prick the green ceiling of summer; the savage winter winds around the Fort Garry Hotel and the sparrows roosting for warmth on the light bulbs of the porte-cochere; the roomy park where they grow bananas and tropical blooms in a vast conservatory while the demented blizzards dance out of Hudson Bay – all these things were as familiar to me as my own back yard.

I also knew a little of the North End, on the wrong side of the C.P.R. tracks, an enclave of foreign languages, almost a separate city, and the oldest Canadian melting-pot....

In short, I knew Winnipeg to be our strongest community because it is alone in the terrifying vacuum of the plains, must think its own thoughts, invent its own pleasures, and do its own work. Surrounded by a waterless sea, it builds its own island, battens down against the perpetual storms of cold, heat, and river flood, flashes from its lighthouse an indomitable ray of courage, and, in a voice never quiet day or night, shouts its defiance at the darkness of midcontinent.

But it is for natives only. Not many Canadians are strong enough to sustain its climate or its pace....

Human life here duplicates the restless weather which has become the pride of Winnipeg and the jest of the nation. Only natives can keep track of all the teeming people's enterprises, the indigenous ballet, the symphony orchestra, the clubs, societies, charities, celebrations, campaigns, concerts, theatricals, athletics, and so much debate, local politics, and bewildering civic adventure that the visitor reels out of town, exhausted after one week-end.

Considering its circumstances, Winnipeg must be accounted the most prodigious growth in Canada. Prodigious and altogether different in kind from any other Canadian community. It is not glamorous and sinful like Montreal, nor obese and smug like Toronto, nor scenic, brassy, and *nouveau-riche* like Vancouver. It has no glamour, no scenery. It is too busy for sin. It moves too rapidly to grow obese, and must struggle too hard ever to become smug. It is too old to be *nouveau-riche* and, besides, it lacks the means.

Winnipeg is closer than any other Canadian city to the earth, to harvest and common things. The civilization at the junction of the Red and the Assiniboine is flavored with the strong juices of early Canada, but it contains a hidden paradox.

Though it stands alone, it has become our least provincial city with the single exception of Montreal. Compelled to mind its own business and build a metropolis out of Red River mud, it shaped itself to fit the wide world. Collecting the prairie grain and selling it at the far ends of the earth, Winnipeg must know, in the ordinary course of business, what crops are ripening, what markets fluctuating, what governments rising or falling everywhere.

Moreover, many of its people came from those far places, and Winnipeg has taken a daunting race problem in its stride. It welcomes immigrants into its professions, appoints a Ukrainian to is provincial cabinet, a Jew to its courts. Precisely because it is so conscious of race, it abhors racial discrimination.

Go to Montreal, Toronto, or Vancouver and you will hear men talk of money, minerals, timber, oil, gas, transportation, and factories. Go to Winnipeg and you will hear them talk of grain, moisture, frost, hail, rust, foreign markets, and foreign politics.

A businessman here may never have lifted a pitchfork, but he knows how grain grows. He knows that the livelihood of the prairies hangs on a thin margin, a few inches of rain, a few degrees of temperature, a few days more or less of growing weather. He is, indeed, a farmer in *absentia*, and his character, molded by these natural forces, makes the character of Winnipeg....

This story is written legibly at the nexus of the two rivers. The old days are more palpable here than in any other Canadian town since Winnipeg is closer to them in spirit. Here the dullest man can see, as pictured in Whittier's verse, "the smoke of the hunting lodges of the wild Assiniboine" and hear, from the great basilica across the Red, "the bells of the Holy City, the bells of St. Boniface." ...

... Across the river the towers of the basilica identify an older French Canadian sub-island within the island of Winnipeg.

I walked across the bridge to St. Boniface, a town of French speech, a distant suburb of Quebec, and stood for a moment observing the gravestone of Riel. After his second rebellion in Saskatchewan and his execution in Regina, his friends brought his body home in a freight car and on his grave planted a ring of lilac bushes. Not many people pause to note the resting-place of a man whose death, by turning the French Canadian race against a Conservative government, altered the whole political history of the nation. Yet the rebel, martyr, or madman of the west could say truthfully to the jurors at his trial: "I know that, through the grace of God, I am the founder of Manitoba."

(Hutchison, *Canada Tomorrow's Giant*, 1957, 206–14)

19 THE BIG FARM, REGINA, 1956

☞ Hutchison senses that Regina is of one piece with its province and hinterland: people from the Big Farm, the wheat growing area around Regina, feel comfortable in Regina because it thrives or suffers along with the region around it. He too feels at home here; the link with the land is strong, and Hutchison always responds to that. ✐

... No one ever received a chilly reception in Regina even at forty below zero, a common winter temperature. This town's heart is an unfailing furnace. It keeps the human temperature thermostatically controlled the year around, at exactly the right level, for resident and visitor alike. And it is no hyperbole, it is a simple, statistical fact, to say that Regina is our most successful Canadian town.

Other western towns faced the same terrible climate, but they were built with nature's aid. Winnipeg, Saskatoon, and Edmonton, for instance, found navigable rivers at their doors, the original highways of travel. Calgary had the warming Chinook wind and, at no extra charge, the backdrop of the Rockies for decoration. Regina had nothing but a Pile of Bones to fasten its earliest name, as a buffalo-hunters' camp, on the mapless prairie.

It is entirely man-made. It is built against nature's clear intent and ferocious opposition. Man has won that long contest. After flattening his town under the tornado of 1912, nature withdrew, defeated. Man cleared away those ruins and made a habitation perfectly suited to his needs, physical, spiritual, and even, perhaps, political. I call that success.

Wide business streets and clean-cut buildings declare Regina's youth, prosperity, and unlimited expectation. A shady square of trees and flowers in the middle of the business district suggests a rare civic sense of proportion, an instinct of communal beauty.

Near by, a causeway arches across a little prairie creek, cunningly dammed and widened until it looks like a miniature Thames. An art gallery and museum of fine, simple lines smiles with stone dignity upon a park of blossom that man has learned to grow in this harsh weather. Finally, a swamp has been enlarged into a lake of clean water and reflects, like a mirror, the chaste body of the legislative building and its formal gardens, a corner of King Louis's garden at Versailles.

These are the title deeds of Regina's success. If they are artificial, they are by no means unnatural or temporary. The concrete bulk of grain elevators and a thick spiderweb of railway lines around them anchor Regina in the reality of the plains.

Wandering about the streets on a Saturday night, we felt at home for the first time since we began our journey. Regina has a warm, intimate, homelike quality. It seems to belong, as few towns do, to its people, to the farm lads with tanned faces and big hands in town for an evening's fun, to the comfortably stout farm women in their best clothes, to the immigrants with fierce whiskers, to all that potent mixture of peoples, histories, and accents who are making a new breed on the prairies.

In the streets, cafés, and spacious park there is none of the hurry, impatience, and stuffiness of a city. There is still the relaxed, neighborly spirit of the village common and the country store and the first furrow ever plowed across the Saskatchewan soil. Regina is still young in heart. May it never become a city.

Such a town could be built by the ordinary skill of men's hands even on this worst of all possible sites. Something more than skill and the hope of profit was required to build the community within the town.

A first hint of mysterious inner elements appears in the palatial, almost unbelievable grandeur of the government offices. They might be occupied by socialist governments; they were designed to house the kings of the earth, the dynasts of the Saskatchewan farm.

These corridors, galleries, apartments, and chasms of marble must surely be the work of an unusual race. It disregards climate, economics, and every rational calculation to raise up here, in proud defiance, its testament to a boundless hope. As I had suspected, the dimensions of geography expand the dimensions of men's minds.

(Hutchison, *Canada Tomorrow's Giant*, 1957, 226–8)

20 THE BIG DREAMERS, CALGARY AND EDMONTON, 1956

⌒ Hutchison approached Calgary, as he had approached Toronto, in a state of apprehension. A new, high-spirited city, happily coping with fresh enterprise, overwhelms the old cow town. The foundations of a new Alberta and further dreams, founded on an "invisible caldron of oil and gas," are being laid in Calgary, spurred on by American oilmen. However, the city won't hold still for Hutchison's scrutiny as a new personality is being forged within the larger Canadian context.

Obsessed with growth, Edmonton, Hutchison feels, has not made as much of its physical setting as it should. A gateway city, Edmonton is self-confident in its geographical situation and the economic dreams of northwestern Canada.

In Alberta Hutchison spent much time in the cattle country at High River, and I have the impression he did not leave enough time to walk the streets of Calgary and Edmonton and talk with their inhabitants, to get a fuller insight into their early lives, as he did in other Canadian cities. ⌒

It was now time to creep up on Calgary. As we approached it between a double rank of garish motels, I felt like the logger in the old American tale who said he was going to Bangor, Maine, to get drunk and, oh, how he dreaded it.

Calgary has always bewildered me. Since my last visit it had become more bewildering than ever; far larger, too, richer and more extroverted. It is the beamish boy of fortune, the wonder child of the west, the temple of the world's greatest Stampede, the inner shrine of the Alberta myth, the unbroken colt among Canadian towns, and our wildest maverick.

It was built, like Rome, on many hills, and is cut by its own Tiber, the Bow, and the Bow's child, the Elbow. Another Rome, superior to the original, could have been reared on this plump flank of the Rockies, but Calgary is no Rome, in body or in mind.

Its body sprawls, undulant and sensual, in the sun. Its mind is the mind of an overgrown cowtown. (I say that with no disrespect, for I can think of nothing better than a cowtown and a race of cowmen.)

The jolly aberration of these urban dwellers – they wear cowboy hats on every ceremonial occasion and like to think themselves true western characters, though they have never felt a saddle between their soft thighs – is refreshing, guileless, and valuable in a prosaic nation.

No one can be here half a day without feeling invigorated, young, and rich. This is the town of youth eternal, and it revels in youth's strength, folly, uncertainty, and glory. All the adventures of the great days have issued here in a town of lofty buildings, crowded streets, and homemade millionaires.

Thus, you will find a rich man's Cadillac parked before a store which sells secondhand saddles, broken bridles, and rusty spurs – the reality and the myth. The bellboy in the hotel will ask for market tips on the latest oil stocks and offer you some of his own. If you enter one of the new skyscrapers and the office of an oil tycoon, you will think you are in New York or Hollywood....

... In their oil-and-gas industry they have revolutionized Alberta's finances, its society, and its mind, turning it into a second Texas.

Now they are undertaking to tap the world's largest known supply of oil in the Athabaska tar sands up north. And they are only beginning to make Alberta Canada's largest source of fuel, power, and, perhaps, wealth.

Calgary may be, as its residents affirm, the most American town of our most American province. Three separate waves of American immigration have rolled up here to pause at the foothills. The first came on horseback some seventy years ago. The second came by railway in the real-estate boom of 1912. The third arrived after the last war by Cadillac, on visitors' permits, to bore for oil.

This latest influx is so large, friendly, and rich that some early Calgarians – a fine old buckskin aristocracy – wonder if the original spirit of the place can survive.

We spent an evening of civic lamentation among these folk on an eminence once known as American Hill, then renamed Mount Royal, to assert Canadian autonomy, and given such patriot street names as Frontenac, Montcalm, Levis, and Carleton.

Alas, said our hosts, the Americans were capturing the hill again. They lived mostly among themselves in a foreign enclave, regarded their stay here as a brief tour of foreign duty, and yearned for home. Some thirty thousand American visitors to Alberta, most of them in Calgary, had drastically changed the town's ways, raised wage scales, filled the shops with luxury goods far beyond Canadians' means, and set a dizzy social pace that Canadians could not hope to equal.

We drove north across some of America's fairest farmland and over the invisible caldron of oil and gas beneath it. Nothing marked that treasure except a few drilling rigs, some shiny tanks, and those birdlike pumps whose beaks peck rhythmically at the ground. Ahead of us the towers of Edmonton's oil refineries and chemical plants stood out suddenly like the funnels and spars of a navy at anchor.

Edmonton is a fine town, but how much finer it could have been and never will be! It bestrides the deep trough of the North Saskatchewan on a site exactly like that of Budapest, which it does not otherwise resemble. That, of course, is not Edmonton's fault but the fault of North American civilization.

Making all allowances, the people of Edmonton could have done better on the majestic gulch of their river. They could have raised on its brink more than the single tower of the Macdonald Hotel and the pompous, fussy little domes of the Parliament Buildings, now overshadowed and dwarfed by some ghastly public buildings of glass and green bathroom tiles.

Nothing seems to matter here if it represents growth. For growth is Edmonton's pride, joy, and, an outsider may suspect, its mortal danger. Once the wealth of oil, gas, farm, forest, and coal mine, from central Alberta all the way to the Arctic, has been sucked into this entrepôt by railway, road, airplane, and pipeline, Edmonton will be the largest city between the Great Lakes and the Rockies. Unless it changes its ways, Edmonton will never be a beautiful city.

But it has its glimpses. The bridges hang like gossamer across the canyon. Every house has a brief summer garden of a brilliant hue known only in the north. The university stands above the river on a broad campus. The river, a few miles from town, churns through a ravine of rock, clay, and forest not yet spoiled by the march of subdivisions....

... In all Canada there is no other town so pleasantly egocentric, so certain of Providence's special dispensation, so childishly happy about everything, so well aware of its own perfection. It is the self-worshipping Narcissus of the nation. Yet a friendly town, inhabited by generous folk who overwhelm you with hospitality and the statistics of growth.

(Hutchison, *Canada Tomorrow's Giant*, 1957, 259–62)

21 THE PROMISED LAND, VANCOUVER, 1941

☞ Vancouver is subject to an irresistible urban growth force, based on an exploitive resource economy that humans must work hard to control and guide. Hutchison recognizes that because of geography and economics "Vancouver was bound to succeed," and he says this dispassionately without a shred of boosterism. He contrasts Vancouver's exceptionally beautiful physical setting with the city that humans have actually built: though he voices despair, he sees a "noble opportunity" as well. Self-centred as Vancouver may be, with abundant wealth, it has also been a good city for the ordinary man. ☞

Among the cities of the world that I have seen, Vancouver has easily the best setting. Men who have seen more than I generally agree. That Vancouver itself has never been worthy of its setting is the fault of our haste, our fury, and our appetite. In a thousand years, perhaps, there will be a city good enough for this site, but hardly before.

You come into Vancouver along a broad arm of the sea, which probably was once the mouth of the Fraser. Between Burrard Inlet on the north and the present three-tongued channel of the river to the south, Vancouver sits upon an ancient delta, heaped up high by the prehistoric river and once deep in rank forest. Across the inlet the North Shore Mountains seem as close as stage scenery, leaping suddenly out of the water, in mottled blue and green, until they turn white, like old men, at the top. Always the mountains rise up flat and unreal at the end of every main street and lie in deep reflection upon the water of the harbor. There the ships come from China and Japan, from all the oceans of the world, the white liners, the rusty freighters lurching along like revelers out of a bar, the ferryboats, as pretty and fresh as girls on a beach.

Into the harbor thrusts the green nose of Stanley Park. It was one of the few sensible things done in our youth, the preservation of this sweep of timber in the center of a large city, with its beaches, rocks, and cliffs, undefiled. Five minutes from Granville Street and you are in the virgin forest, if you want solitude, or in gardens of flowers, pleasant lawns, and little lakes. When you see the size of the original trees, the solid wall of underbrush, the dismal jungle, you wonder how Vancouver could ever have been cleared, how men could have found room here to live or even pitch a tent. Many men in Vancouver today, and not so very old either, can remember when most of the city was the same kind of wilderness, with no path through it....

... Since it was Gas Town, a sawmill beside the salt chuck, since the earlier day when Captain Vancouver sailed up here and met the Spaniards off Point Grey and left his name on all this territory, the town has grown furiously, tumultuously, recklessly, the greatest boom town in Canada.

Back from the harbor it pushed, street by street, not pausing even to blast out the stumps, building its skyscrapers a few yards from the original wooden shacks. You may turn off Granville or Hastings Street today and, in two blocks, find yourself among run-down wooden slums that belong to a frontier town. You may step out of the unspoiled verdure of the park and find across the street the dilapidated hot-dog stands that belong to some cow town on the prairies.

Slowly the brawling boom town grows up, builds great homes and gardens, lays out parks everywhere, plants new trees to replace the old forests, clears its beaches, yearns after architecture, and wonders whether the square matchbox of the new City Hall is truly beautiful.

From the day when Captain Vancouver found that the Straits of Juan de Fuca were not a river mouth, as Cook supposed, and, following them, discovered the Fraser and Burrard Inlet, Vancouver was bound to be great. Geography and economics had conspired to lay their fingers upon this spot beside the sea. It was the western end of the natural pass through the coast mountains. It was the mouth of the river. It had to be the end of the railway. It had to drain out the products of the whole hinterland back to the Rockies and beyond. Into its safe harbor must come the Pacific ships, and the Panama Canal would bring it close, by competitive shipping cost, to Europe. It could not help becoming, if it had wanted to, Canada's third city, as it may ultimately become one of the great cities of the world.

Vancouver has lived by the legend of continual growth and feels ill if it is not in a constant state of expansion. The North American disease of proliferation and giantism has become chronic here and seems like normal health. Size, population, business appear as the end and supreme object of civic life. Already Vancouver holds half of British Columbia's people – a top-heavy and dropsical arrangement, but Vancouver never suspects that. It is always getting ready to move into a larger house, a better street. It is always thrusting new streets and miles of new houses into the second-growth that the loggers left a few years ago.

Lumbering, mining, fishing, agriculture, all come to focus here and build upon the back of the producer the parasitical growth which is the substance of all cities....

Vancouver, living on its hinterland and dominating British Columbia, has set the tone of British Columbia's thinking. This part of Canada has never paused to conserve, to question, to doubt the future. When a royal commission of experts warns it that its prosperity is thin and brittle, being built on foreign markets and on resources now used up at an appalling rate, no one pays the least attention. Hew down the forest, dig up the precious spots of agricultural lands between the mountains, gamble on the latest mining strike, scour the fisheries, build big houses, expand and make money – there is the spirit of youth everywhere, and Vancouver is young.

None of the elegance of Montreal is here, none of the stability of the Maritime aristocracy, and little of Winnipeg's broad view. Still, life in Vancouver has been better for the ordinary man than in any large Canadian city, than in most cities anywhere.

Climate alone, the mild green winters (you get used to rain and fog) draw Canadians to it from all over the country and, in bad times, fill it every autumn with the jobless off the freight cars. In the cool summers every man can have a garden, can bask on a beach or sail a boat. There is outdoor sport for everyone. Young folks leave the Vancouver gardens in bloom and swarm up the North Shore Mountains to ski. Old men bowl in the park or play endless outdoor checkers on a twenty-foot checkerboard, meditating each move by the hour. In the summer evenings Vancouver strolls in the park to listen to band concerts. An public services are of the best. Houses are cheap to build, living costs low, wages high. Vancouver still manages somehow to keep many of

the advantages of the small town. It is, in fact, a boisterous small town
growing out of its clothes.

Vancouver has always thought of little but Vancouver....

It will change, ... and very fast. In fifty years it will be as different
from the present city as the present city is from Gas Town. In a thousand
years one would like to come back and see what men have done with
this unique site, this noble opportunity. They could build here the finest
city ever inhabited by our species.

(Hutchison, *The Unknown Country*, 1942, 319–26)

22 THE BIG TREES, VANCOUVER, 1956

☞ Humans and the forest environment are linked in British Columbia,
as Emily Carr reminds us. The forests that grew where Vancouver
stands have been stripped, but gardens save the city's soul. Hutchison
recognizes the booms that have created wealth in British Columbia,
riches reflected and concentrated in Vancouver. Powerful businesses
and unions exist, much as Parkin foresaw, but Hutchison also notes
the leavening effect of university education and the arts on this brash
materialistic frontier society. ☞

No other city in Canada, I thought, and few in the world, had been
planted in such a setting, between mountain, sea, and forest. To be
sure, the setting had been heavily overlaid by man's toil and folly, but
around the wharves the seagulls still screamed, the smell of wood and
sap and salt spiced the autumn air, and a high tide brought whispers of
the Pacific and the gorgeous East, as when the first white men saw this
shore. Captain George Vancouver had found it good. He had not foreseen the improbable monument to be built here in his honor.

Yet there was something strange and alarming about Vancouver's
city and its people. What? I tried, though a prejudiced coastal man, to
consider the question impartially as a stranger, but only a coastal man
would ask it or understand the answer....

... I could not keep my eyes off her – this distillate of jungle and ocean,
this mixture of beauty and ugliness, this ever spreading fungus of wealth
and slums, this woodland clearing where man has heaped up overnight
the brassiest, loveliest, craziest of all Canadian towns, and now worships
his inferior masterpiece in childlike wonder, fierce greed, and a sure conviction of superiority.

Well, I looked at her, I imagined for a moment what men could have made here to match nature's masterpiece, and I was tempted to weep....

Lawren Harris, publicly a genius of the painter's art and privately a philosopher, took me and my questions in hand and led the way to the Vancouver Art Gallery without a word of explanation. None was needed.

The walls of the gallery were covered by the paintings of the late Emily Carr, whom I remembered in Victoria, fifty years ago, as a dumpy old maid of quick temper and sharp tongue.

She had captured, as no one else has ever captured, the primal fact of the Pacific coast. She had invented almost a new art form to illuminate the dark tide of vegetation pouring from the mountains to the shore.

There, on canvas, was the force of geography, climate, and steaming growth which had conditioned men's outdoor life from the beginning and, by its terrible presence, had shaped his spirit.

I saw at once what Harris meant, and it answered my question. Coastal men, or most of them, had severed the human roots growing in this forest soil for more than a century. They still live on the forest, but are no longer of it. They have retired into imagined urban security, forgotten their beginnings, and, as Miss Carr seemed to be saying, have lost their way.

But the works of the dead Victorian spinster (so poor that she painted some of her best pictures on cheap, perishable wrapping paper) remind the urban creature that the primal fact of the coast remains. The forest stands at every Vancouver street end. Butchered, it always rises again. Indestructible, it awaits the day of man's departure, when it will repossess its own.

Everywhere in Vancouver, beyond the business district, the forest asserts its title deeds and imposes its green caveat on men's work. The trees of the immense park stand virgin and untamed as some of them have stood for a thousand years. Beside the newest skyscraper a solid cedar stump registers, in death, a life far longer and more secure than man's.

The gardener, if he neglects his garden for a single season, will find it surging up in alder, maple, or the first filaments of the conifers. Every new residential area is soon covered by an umbrella of dense foliage. Leave it unpruned for half a century or less, and Vancouver will be lost, like Sleeping Beauty, in impervious tangle....

Though it will resent the compliment, Vancouver must be judged an unusually innocent city, despite its contrary reputation. It has wealth, but is too young to have acquired sophistication. It is too successful, too busy in its own business, and too self-adoring to pay much heed to Canada at large, and it customarily goes to the United States for its holidays.

To tell the truth, Vancouver is not a city at all. Like every other Canadian community except Montreal, it is an overgrown town; or, rather, in Vancouver's case, an overgrown camp, repeatedly enlarged by a series of frontier booms until boom is taken as normal, as these people's reward, under a just Providence, for their wisdom in coming here....

The doubtful phenomenon known as progress has been too fast to permit sensible civic planning, with the result that hovels abut on business streets; Hastings and its skyscrapers run suddenly into Skid Row; Granville and Burrard soar on majestic bridges over a manufacturing area whose smoke ascends into the leafy English boulevards and the rich men's mansions of Shaughnessy Heights.

Two generations back, the inhabitants of Vancouver were clearing homesteads in the forest, breaking the earth, and diking the islands of the Fraser's estuary. Even a generation back these were an outdoor people, a pioneer and essentially primitive people. Their town was ruled by men who themselves had felt axes, plowhandles, miners' picks, and ships' rigging in their hands.

Now it is ruled by the softer sons of the pioneers. Hereditary wealth, extracted raw from forest, mine, and sea, enables young men who otherwise would be drapers' assistants or apprentice undertakers to own their fathers' fortunes, command great corporations, manipulate politics, and spend the winter in Honolulu.

All this happened in many parts of Canada, but perhaps nowhere else so rapidly, enthusiastically, and crudely as in Vancouver. The ruling class thus lacks the patina and manners of Montreal's elite, the thinner shine of Toronto, and the sober thrift of Winnipeg. For all purposes of political, economic, and social power, no other major Canadian city is so *nouveau riche* as Vancouver, so self-centered and isolated from the nation. None is so completely conditioned by its easy environment, its genial climate, and that legend of ceaseless sunshine which a winter of almost ceaseless rain and frequent London fog can never destroy.

Such environment, climate, and legend produce able and imaginative businessmen, powerful labor unions, organized crime, and vulgar politics. They have never produced a single statesman of first rank, or second.

Nevertheless, better things are growing in Vancouver. Its real thinking and its hope are to be found on the Peninsula of Point Grey. There the University of British Columbia's campus looks south across the oily

Fraser, north to the white fiord of Howe Sound, and makes any other campus in Canada appear cramped and mean.

The site is not very important. The university's greatness resides in its teachers, in the successive crops of students who have manned British Columbia's industries and leavened the lump of a frontier society, in the scientists, poets, artists, and heretics. These men and women, you might almost say, have started a counterrevolution against the revolution of machinery and wealth.

(Hutchison, *Canada Tomorrow's Giant*, 1957, 308–13)

23 THE LOTUS EATERS, VICTORIA, 1941

⌒ Hutchison admits he cannot be objective about Victoria, his home in this land of "the Lotus Eaters." Victoria is an English outpost, founded in the days of the Empire, and it still is, he says, becoming Canadian. People from many varied places continue to arrive (refugees according to Hutchison), and it has become a tolerant place, respectful of difference. Victoria, he believes, is where most Canadians hope to end their days ⌒

To be frank, I am unable to write about Victoria, British Columbia, with that same judicious poise and lack of enthusiasm which has marked these pages so far. I fell in love with her long ago, as a boy. This puppy love has only grown with the years into the settled attachment of old age and long daily companionship. I am but one of many. Even with a toughened traveler like Kipling it was love at first sight, and, "sighing like furnace," he added a reckless prose poem to the long chant of her praises.

No one who has entered the Inner Harbor of Victoria, so far as the official records show, has ever wanted to leave again. It is the normal, accepted ambition of most Canadians to spend their last days here. This is the island where Ulysses met the sirens. This is the land of the Lotus Eaters, and many of those original inhabitants are still here....

It took some time [after Confederation] to make Victoria part of Canada. The process is far from complete yet. From the earliest times it was an English outpost, with an English naval base near by at Esquimalt, with English people finding here, in the warm climate of the Japan Current, a perfect replica of Devonshire or Cornwall, finding the surroundings; vegetation, and even the giant oak trees that they had known at home. It was far from the cities, the people, and the problems of Canada, nearer to London in spirit than to Montreal.

Victoria became an English town in happy exile. It had none of Quebec's history, Montreal's wealth, the push of Winnipeg, nor the appetite of its young neighbor, Vancouver, which has always appeared here as a parvenu....

... Early life in Victoria must have been the final perfection of country life everywhere. Hearing of it, the English headed towards it by pure instinct and, for a little time, made it their own. Not for long.

The legend of the English town still persists but, like so many things, Victoria has outlived its legend. It has become modern. It has even recognized its own quaintness, which is fatal, and sold it to the tourists, who have never seen the original....

Victoria does move more slowly than most cities in America, I suppose ... So they laugh at us, they write jokes about us, but everybody in Canada would like to live here, in this almost winterless climate. Perhaps they will in time, judging by the sudden growth of building, which threatens to drown out the old Victoria altogether. We feel now like the Romans when the barbarian hordes swarmed in to sack their city.

Do not judge Victoria by its front door, by the old warehouses and dilapidated docks that stand by the harbor edge on the site of the original fort. To us they have grown familiar and rather dear with age. Disregard also the stark grain elevator which is the tombstone marking the grave of our old hope of becoming an industrial city. Look rather to the right, at the lawns of the Parliament Building, with its green dome and a golden Captain Vancouver glistening atop it. Look at the broad rose gardens and ivy walls of the Empress Hotel, like an enlarged country house, beside the water. Drive up through Beacon Hill Park, where the swans live, among the old homes of Rockland Avenue, or along the seafront to the Uplands, and then into the country.

In no other human community, I make bold to say, will such gardens be found, such multitudes of flowers, such rockeries spouting color from the mossy native rocks, so many people who insist on living amid beauty and are marvelously skilled and learned in the culture of plants.... There are finer gardens and bigger homes in many places, and architecture to go with them, but hardly such a concentrated devotion to the earth....

Yet it is a sad, undeniable fact, contrary to the belief of the whole Canadian nation, that men work in this paradise, and that the early Victorians die out, with a last sputter of protest in the *Colonist*. You may find a few bronzed gentlemen and elderly ladies with long long, handsome English faces, still riding bicycles.... But the distinct civilization of Victoria certainly is perishing, the thing born in the wilderness when English life had to take root here, grow strong, or die. A rich and valuable strain is going out of the Canadian breed.

Something new is taking its place. Instead of an English culture, as the outside world supposes, we are developing here a strange combination of the naive and the sophisticated. To Victoria have come refugees from all the countries of the earth – from England again, from eastern Canada, from the United States, from Europe, from the Orient. You can find here, in some obscure house by the sea, unknown to his neighbors, a retired rubber planter, a richer trader from Shanghai, a forgotten Hollywood actor, an American millionaire, a Czech physician, British admirals and knights to burn. This has made Victoria one of the most tolerant and easy-going places on earth. Nobody cares what you say, what you think or, least of all, what you wear. (We are probably the worst-dressed place on the continent, another cause for rejoicing.) But Victoria is a rich city, despite its lack of industry. It has the provincial government payroll and it has the money of its retired men, so that it is able to support stores, hotels, and generally a way of life more luxurious than those of any comparable Canadian city. Man for man, it is probably the wealthiest place in Canada, its people the best kept, its poverty the least.

(Hutchison, *The Unknown Country*, 1942, 332–8)

24 THE BIG TREES, VICTORIA, 1956

☞ Victoria may have a quaint façade for tourists, but it is false. Hutchison felt at home in Regina, and that city's essence of community, of earth and people intimately linked, shines through in this his home city as well. Victoria's true quality, and the example it provides other parts of Canada, is that of sanity, expressed in a collective vision of beauty in the numerous gardens, and of living in sympathy with the natural environment. People who retire here soon acquire that same sanity. ☜

[Finally, Hutchison arrives home.] A Victoria medical man – he could not claim to be a Victorian, of course, since he had lived here a scant twenty years stood beside us on the deck, and at this sight of home his eyes filled. He blew his nose violently and apologized for an unseemly show of emotion. "I just can't help it," he said.

Being a Victorian, even a mid-Victorian, I understood. We are all affected in the same way. I cannot tell you why, for the setting of Victoria does not compare with the first glimpse of Vancouver or Quebec, and man has not improved it much. The harbor is only an enlarged dishpan, smeared on the north side by the grime of industry but ornamented on east and south by the fat-domed legislative buildings, the Causeway; and the Empress Hotel amid acres of lawn and roses. Only a native could fail to see that Victoria started to make an immaculate portal and abandoned the job, half done.

However, if you keep your eyes fixed on the better half, the introduction to Victoria is startling in its precise, miniature design. It was all contrived by man since Douglas founded his fort beside this harbor in 1843.

The site was strategic but not promising. Douglas faced a sweep of barren rock, a ravine of stinking tidal mud, and the cedar huts of an Indian village.

Even today, though the ravine has been filled and crowned by the Causeway and the splendid hotel, no one but a native would call the business district of Victoria anything but commonplace and rather drab. The main streets are distinguished chiefly by flower baskets hung from every lamp post to titillate the tourists and by a few human relics who totter about, like stage props, in English tweeds.

Yet somehow Victoria has created not only real beauty, outside the business district, but a synthetic, profitable myth of quaintness, eccentricity, and charm well known throughout the world and sold over and over again to unsuspecting visitors. If this is a feat of commercial genius, something more than the profit motive is at work....

A reality lies behind the commercial facade, and it is too deep for commerce or explanation. No stranger will guess it; no Victorian will reveal it....

The secret is to be found not in the myth but in the reality of the earth and the people. These people know how to live and, more than any other urban Canadians, they live close to the earth; so close, indeed, that they usually vegetate in middle life, mellow in their autumn, and quietly go to seed – not before they have performed their own special prodigy.

I call it special and prodigious because I have never seen in America, or even in England, anything to match the gardens and gardeners of Victoria. Gardening here is not merely a skill, hobby, or cult as in Vancouver. It is outwardly a pictorial art and is spread, without a single break, across a rumpled canvas of some twenty square miles. Inwardly it is a philosophy, almost a religion, and always a passion.

The gardener, whether he tends a city lot or the stupendous ravines of the Butchart Gardens, must be a mechanic, an artist, a botanist, and a believer. Other Canadians may cultivate flowers; the Victorian worships them, nurses them with scientific care, exhibits them in fierce annual competition, debates them at weekly meetings, imports their seeds from the ends of the earth, and, by his labors, usually on his knees in prayer, has acquired a collective vision of beauty, a civic intimation of immortality.

Victoria has given the nation little else in modern times, but this town of apparent lunatics has taught a profound lesson of sanity. The nation can use it. Nevertheless, Victoria's original human growth, mostly out of seeds from England, is steadily retreating before a new growth out of Canada.

The Victoria I knew fifty years ago was indeed a Bit of England, superficially at least. It was managed by an aristocracy of English birth, dress, manners, and accent, yet not truly English, much less Canadian, for that unique species had become purely Victorian, and its mind never reached beyond its island.

Now, despite all the tourist propaganda, this town is purely Canadian. It is ruled by natives who grew up as Canadians and by newcomers from the foreign nation of Canada who are skeptical of quaintness, scornful of the myth, and determined to make a metropolis even though they lack any industrial base or large payroll except the provincial government's civil service. The North American illusion that size is the measurement of worth and happiness has penetrated even this last stronghold of sanity....

Governor Douglas's fort within a two-by-four stockade, the camp of the Cariboo gold rush, the village by the stinking mud flats, have swelled five miles north, east, and west and seem likely to cover most of the verduous Saanich Peninsula before long. However, if Victoria is growing like any other Canadian town, and faster than most, growth here has a subtle ingredient of its own.

Newcomers do not recognize this quality or resent it as mere dullness. Then, before they know what is happening to them, the most progressive young businessmen, the most impatient boosters and Philistines, the retired tycoons from Toronto, or the stolid farmers from the prairies – all that influx of Canadians in search of a final haven – begin to acquire the secret of this place through their pores and soon fall helpless under the spell. They become Victorians. No other town will satisfy them again. Having crossed that Rubicon, the Gulf of Georgia, they have passed the point of no return.

(Hutchison, *Canada Tomorrow's Giant*, 1957, 315–18)

10

Thomas R. Berger, *Northern Frontier – Northern Homeland, The Report of the Mackenzie Valley Pipeline Inquiry*, 1977

☞ In 1974 the Government of Canada established a one-person Royal Commission to study the advisability of constructing a gas pipeline from northern Alaska across northern Yukon and up the Mackenzie River valley to Alberta. Thomas Berger (1933–), a British Columbia lawyer and judge, was appointed commissioner. In *Northern Frontier – Northern Homeland: The Report of the Mackenzie Valley Pipeline Inquiry,* Judge Berger recognizes that the indigenous people of Northern Canada must have a central role in making decisions on northern resource development. The report is a call for a Canadian awakening. Of course it was known that indigenous people lived in the North and that outside culture and government policies were affecting them drastically, but the procedures followed in Judge Berger's inquiry, especially the emphasis placed on consulting northerners, particularly aboriginals, made it clear to the rest of the Canadian people that the North was a homeland to these people and northern residents must be given a voice. The report effectively reveals the arrogant – and appalling – takeover of First Nations and Inuit peoples' homelands and resources by Europeans from the time they began to arrive in North America. The consultative process Berger adopted in carrying out his mandate, and the eloquent language he used to emphasize that basic rights must be respected, were as important as the report's recommendation that a pipeline along the Yukon Arctic coast be permanently banned and a ten-year moratorium imposed on building a Mackenzie valley pipeline while native lands claims were settled. It took until the first decade of the twenty-first century for renewed negotiations to build a pipeline to be resumed, and this time Northern residents are full participants.

Berger's report is a good counterbalance not only to R.C. Wallace's resource-oriented interpretation of the North published in 1930 but also to the limited attention given to the North by the other authors considered here. Joseph Bouchette, it must be said, and this also holds for J.D. Rogers, began their books with the North. Bouchette does allow the words "savages" and "barbarians" to creep into his discussion of the Far North, people he very clearly considered to be the "Other." Elsewhere in his book, however, he accepts that Indians are well settled in Upper and Lower Canada and are continuing members of society. Rogers barely acknowledges the presence of indigenous people in northern Canada but recognizes their importance in the early history of New France. In New Brunswick, Rogers tells us, indigenous peoples foreshadowed Europeans in establishing major routes, and in Newfoundland he recognizes their importance and that the interior was their homeland. Neither Bouchette nor Rogers discusses indigenous peoples fully in their own right: they are always seen in relationship to Europeans, and this colours the discussion. Harold Innis has little to say on First Nations peoples, and Bruce Hutchison rarely mentions them, although in his work on British Columbia, in passages not included in this volume, he discusses Indians in northern British Columbia more sympathetically. ☞

I THE NORTH

a) *Northern Frontier, Northern Homeland*

☞ Berger defines the different relations that might develop between northern and southern Canada if there is massive energy development and discusses the implications this would have for northern Canada. Canadian attitudes and policies regarding the North "will tell us what kind of a people we are." He emphasizes that northern people live in harmony with the natural environment. ☞

This Inquiry was appointed to consider the social, environmental and economic impact of a gas pipeline and an energy corridor across our northern territories, across a land where four races of people – Indian, Inuit, Metis and white – live, and where seven languages are spoken. The Inquiry was also empowered to recommend terms and conditions that ought to be imposed to protect the people of the North, their environment, and their economy, if the pipeline were to be built.

Today, we realize more fully what was always implicit in the Inquiry's mandate: this is not simply a debate about a gas pipeline and an energy corridor, it is a debate about the future of the North and its peoples.

There are two distinct views of the North: one as frontier, the other as homeland.

We look upon the North as our last frontier. It is natural for us to think of developing it, of subduing the land and extracting its resources to fuel Canada's industry and heat our homes. Our whole inclination is to think of expanding our industrial machine to the limit of our country's frontiers. In this view, the construction of a gas pipeline is seen as the next advance in a series of frontier advances that have been intimately bound up with Canadian history. But the native people say the North is their homeland. They have lived there for thousands of years. They claim it is their and, and they believe they have a right to say what its future ought to be.

The question whether a pipeline shall be built has become the occasion for the joining of these issues.

In the past, Canada has been defined by its frontiers. In the words of Kenneth McNaught:

From the time of the earliest records Canada has been part of a frontier, just as in her own growth she has fostered frontiers. The struggle of men and of metropolitan centres to extend and control those frontiers, as well as to improve life behind them, lies at the heart of Canadian history – and geography determined many of the conditions of that struggle. [*The Pelican History of Canada*, p. 7]

H. A. Innis insisted that it was Canadian geography and Canadian frontiers that made possible and defined the existence of the country. The nation's lines of transportation and communications were based on the St. Lawrence River, the Great Lakes and western waterways. French and British dependence on fish, fur, timber and wheat influenced the course of Canadian history, one staple after another drawing the nation from one frontier to the next. Innis refuted the notion that Canada's economy is simply a series of projections northward from the economic heartland of North America.

The French, the fur trade, British institutions – these have all played a part from the earliest times in the development of a separate community in the northern half of the continent. But it is a northern tradition that in large measure makes Canada distinct from the United States today.

We share a mass culture with the United States, but it is Canada that has – and always has had – a distinct northern geography and a special concern with the North.

What happens in the North, moreover, will be of great importance to the future of our country; it will tell us what kind of a country Canada is; it will tell us what kind of a people we are. In the past, we have thought of the history of our country as a progression from one frontier to the next. Such, in the main, has been the story of white occupation and settlement of North America. But as the retreating frontier has been occupied and settled, the native people living there have become subservient, their lives moulded to the patterns of another culture.

We think of ourselves as a northern people. We may at last have begun to realize that we have something to learn from the people who for centuries have lived in the North, the people who never sought to alter their environment, but rather to live in harmony with it. This Inquiry has given all Canadians an opportunity to listen to the voices on the frontier.

In the past at each frontier we have encountered the native people. The St. Lawrence Valley was the homeland of the Huron and the Iroquois – they were overwhelmed; the West was the homeland of the Cree they were displaced; the Pacific Coast was the homeland of the Salish – they were dispossessed. Now, we are told that the North is the homeland of the Dene, the Inuit and the Metis. Today in the North we confront the questions that have confronted Canadians before – questions from which we must not now turn away.

Should the future of the North be determined by the South? The question can, of course, be answered by saying that since 1867 the Government of Canada has had responsibility for the welfare of the native people, and that since 1870 it has had jurisdiction over the Northwest. This is to say that Ottawa is sovereign, and has the power to dispose of the North as it wills. But the Government of Canada has not been satisfied to make such an answer, and has established this Inquiry to make it plain that the goals, aspirations and preferences of the northern peoples should be fully explored before any decision is taken.

The choice we make will decide whether the North is to be primarily a frontier for industry or a homeland for its peoples. We shall have the choice only once. Any attempt to beg the question that now faces us, to suggest that a choice has already been made or need never be made will be an inexcusable evasion of responsibility.

The issues we face are profound ones, going beyond the ideological conflicts that have occupied the world for so long, conflicts over who

should run the industrial machine, and who should reap the benefits.
Now we are being asked: How much energy does it take to run the
industrial machine? Where must the energy come from? Where is the
machine going? And what happens to the people who live in the path of
the machine?

It may be that, in the national interest, the gas pipeline and the
energy corridor should be built. It may be that they should not. But
we owe to the peoples of the North, and to future generations, a careful consideration of the consequences before we go ahead with such
projects. This report is an attempt to set out what those consequences
will be....

b) Northern Peoples

☞ The aboriginal history of the North is long and has many facets,
resulting in complex social systems in Indian, Inuit, and Metis societies. ☜

The North is the homeland of a complex of indigenous cultures. We
in the South may speak airily of "native people," and thereby convey
the impression that there is a single culture, a single social system that
occupies the vast arctic and sub-arctic terrain. But the term "native"
is an inheritance from the European colonists, who usually regarded
the original inhabitants of the lands they sought to subdue and settle,
as a single group unified by "primitive" customs, and by their political
relationship to the colonial powers themselves. In this way, the term
"native" obscures essential differences between the cultures encountered
in the course of European expansion.

The landscapes of the North have been shaped only marginally by
the activities of man. The northern peoples have always been hunters
and gatherers, and most have lived with a high degree of mobility. Small
groups travelled over large areas, hunting and gathering what they
needed, but without altering the environment itself. It is not always easy
to remember, as one flies over the unbroken boreal forest, the tundra,
or the sea ice, that the Canadian North has been inhabited for many
thousands of years. The populations that have used this great area were
never large by European standards, but their skills as travellers and
hunters made it possible for them to occupy virtually all of the land.
Extremely slow rates of northern plant growth and of decay mean that
it is possible to see almost everywhere in the North signs, of ancient

occupation – old house remains, tent rings, fire-cracked rocks – and for archaeologists to find, on or close to the surface, a wealth of artifacts and other evidence to show the richness, diversity and wide extent of northern aboriginal society.

In the North, there are not just "native peoples," but a network of social systems. The Indians of the Mackenzie Valley and Western Arctic, are part of the Athabascan language and culture group. They are separated into the Kutchin (or Loucheux), Hare, Slavey, Dogrib and Chipewyan. The Athabascan people are one of the most widely dispersed groups of Indians in North America. In addition to the Indians of the North-west Territories and the Northern Yukon, they include the Koyukon and Tanana of Alaska, the Tutchone of the Southern Yukon, the Beaver and Carrier of British Columbia, the Navaho and Apache of the Southwest United States, and still other in California and Oregon. All these Indians, with whatever dialectical variation in their languages, regard themselves as *the people*. To the Slavey, they are the *Dene*, to the Navaho *Dine;* in Kutchin the word is *Dindjie;* in Apache it is *Nde*. Today, in the North, the Indian people collectively call themselves the *Dene*.

The native peoples of the Western Arctic also include the Eskimos or, as they are now widely known, the Inuit; they occupy part of the Mackenzie Delta and the shores of the Beaufort Sea. Although all of the Inuit, from Siberia to eastern Greenland, speak closely related dialects if the same language, regionally there are differences in technology and social organization that even today complicate anthropological generalizations about them. Certainly the Inuit themselves perceive major differences between their various groups: the Inuvialuit of the Delta see themselves as distinct from the Copper Eskimos, who are their neighbours to the east; and the Copper Eskimos – or Qurdlurturmiut – emphasize that they are unlike the Netsilik, the Aivilik or the Igloolik people, who live still farther east. And, within each of these broad groups, there are yet finer divisions and distinctions that reflect different patterns of land use and are represented by changes in dialect and in hunting techniques.

This brief elaboration of social systems may seem to lie at the periphery of this Inquiry, but it indicates that the Dene and the Inuit – as well as the Metis, to whom I shall return – are distinct peoples in history. They have common interests in relation to the proposed Mackenzie Valley pipeline, and they therefore share many concerns. But the intensity of their feelings, no less than the vigour with which they are now expressing their hopes and fears, reflect historical and cultural depths that cannot be comprehended by the term "native." The North has become our frontier during the past few decades; it has been a homeland of the Dene and Inuit peoples for many thousands of years.

(Berger, *Northern Frontier – Northern Homeland*, 1977, 1–6)

2 CULTURAL IMPACT

⊂ The cultural interaction between indigenous peoples and Euro-Canadians is viewed historically. In the context of contrasting beliefs about the proper use of the land, Berger considers the cultural impact of fur trade, mission, and government activities on Northern societies, suggesting that Euro-Canadian eyes were blinkered with respect to native cultures and that Euro-Canadians had a sense of mission about changing and re-shaping natives. Yet the native cultures did not die. Berger makes the important point that southern Canadians should place themselves in the shoes of a native person to understand the impact of this cultural assault. ⊂

Cultural Impact: A Retrospective

EARLY VIEWS OF THE NORTH

Before considering the economic and social impact that the pipeline and the energy corridor will have, we should examine the history of the cultural impact of white civilization upon the native people of the North. The relations between the dominant society and the native society, and the history of that relationship from the earliest times to the present, should be borne in mind: they condition our attitudes to native people, and theirs towards us.

When the first Europeans came to North America, they brought with them a set of attitudes and values that were quite different from those of the original peoples of the continent. At the heart of the difference was land. To white Europeans, the land was a resource waiting to be settled and cultivated. They believed that it was a form of private property, and that private property was linked to political responsibility. This political theory about land was coupled with religious and economic assumptions. Europeans believed that the conditions for civilized existence could be satisfied only through the practice of the Christian religion and cultivation of the land. As an early missionary phrased it, "Those who come to Christ turn to agriculture."

To the Europeans, the native people's use of the land, based upon hunting and gathering, was extravagant in extent and irreligious in nature. But to the native people, the land was sacred, the source of life and sustenance, not a commodity to be bought and sold.

Chief Justice John Marshall of the Supreme Court of the United States, writing in 1823, described the attitudes of the Europeans in this way:

> On the discovery of this immense continent, the great nations of Europe were eager to appropriate to themselves so much of it as they could respectively acquire. Its vast extent offered an ample field to the ambition and enterprise of all; and the character and religion of its inhabitants afforded an apology for considering them as a people over whom the superior genius of Europe might claim an ascendency. The potentates of the old world found no difficulty in convincing themselves that they made ample compensation to the inhabitants of the new, by bestowing on them civilization and Christianity, in exchange for unlimited independence. [Johnson v. McIntosh (1823) 21 U.S. 543, 572J]

It was to be the white man's mission not only to tame the land and bring it under cultivation, but also to tame the native people and bring them within the pale of civilization. This sense of mission has remained the dominant theme in the history of white-native relations.

In Northern Canada, even though the possibilities for agriculture were virtually non-existent in comparison with the prairie lands, the white man's purpose was the same: to subdue the North and its people. In the old days that meant bringing furs to market; nowadays it means bringing minerals, oil and gas to market. At all times it has meant bringing the northern native people within white religious, educational and economic institutions. We sought to detach the native population from cultural habits and beliefs that were thought to be inimical to the priorities of white civilization. This process of cultural transformation has proceeded so far that in the North today many white people – and some native people, too – believe that native culture is dying. Yet the preponderance of evidence presented to this Inquiry indicates beyond any doubt that the culture of the native people is still a vital force in their lives. It informs their view of themselves, of the world about them and of the dominant white society.

Euro-Canadian society has refused to take native culture seriously. European institutions, values and use of land were seen as the basis of culture. Native institutions, values and language were rejected, ignored or misunderstood and – given the native people's use of the land – the Europeans had no difficulty in supposing that native people possessed no real culture at all. Education was perceived as the most effective instrument of cultural change; so, educational systems were introduced that were intended to provide the native people with a useful and meaningful cultural inheritance, since their own ancestors had left them none.

The assumptions implicit in all of this are several. Native religion had to be replaced; native customs had to be rejected; native uses of the land could not, once the fur trade had been superseded by the search for minerals, oil and gas, be regarded as socially important or economically significant.

This moral onslaught has had profound consequences throughout Canada. Yet, since the coming of the white man, the native people of the North have clung to their own beliefs, their own ideas of themselves, of who they are and where they came from, and have revealed a self-consciousness that is much more than retrospective. They have shown a determination to have something to say about their lives and their future. This determination has been repeatedly expressed to the Inquiry.

THE FUR AND MISSION ERA

The penetration of European values in the North has been felt for nearly two centuries. In the early days of the fur and mission era, the native people were able to participate in the fur trade with comparatively little disruption to many of their patterns of social and economic organization, and with little change to their basic cultural values. For most of the year they still lived off the land, travelling in small groups of families in the semi-nomadic tradition of hunting and gathering peoples. Their aboriginal cycle of seasonal activity was modified to include visits to the trading post and mission to sell their furs, to buy tea, sugar, flour and guns, and to go to church.

Father Felician Labat, the priest at Fort Good Hope, tracing a century of history through the diary of the mission told the Inquiry about life during the fur and mission era:

The trading post of Good Hope was deserted during the winter
months. Christmas and Easter would see a good many of [the
Dene] back in the Fort for a few days, but soon after New Year they
would go back to their winter camps. Then it would be the spring

hunt, when beavers would start to come out of their houses and travel down the many rivers. Summer would bring nearly everyone back into Fort Good Hope.... The people lived close to nature, and their life pattern followed the pattern of nature. Winter and spring were times for working, when transportation into the heart of the lands was easier. Summer, on the other hand, was a bit of a holiday, with drums echoing for days and days. That life pattern remained unchanged until recently, when white people started to come down this way in greater numbers. [(Library and Archives Canada, Mackenzie Valley Pipeline Inquiry Records), C1873ff.]

Even though contact with white civilization, the Hudson's Bay Company and, in later years, the RCMP was intermittent, its impact was pervasive. White society dictated the places and terms of exchange, took care to ensure that its rituals (social as well as religious and political) took precedence in any contact between native and white, and provided a system of incentives that was irresistible. Political, religious and commercial power over the lives of the native people came to reside in the triumvirate of policeman, priest and Hudson's Bay store manager.

Behind these agents at the frontier lay the power of the metropolis as a whole, a power that was glimpsed occasionally when a ship, a plane flew overhead, or a law court with judge and jury came to hold court. White people in the North were powerful because of what they did, the goods they dispensed, and all that they represented. Their power became entrenched during the fur and mission era in the Mackenzie Valley and the Western Arctic.

Although the fur and mission era ended 20 years ago, the RCMP, Church and Hudson's Bay Company still possess considerable authority in the North, but their authority is no longer exclusive. Government has proliferated. The mining industry and the oil and gas industry have arrived. And these new authorities – governmental and industrial – possess a power that transcends the old order: a power to alter the northern landscape and to extinguish the culture of its people.

But make no mistake: the process of transformation has in a sense been continuous. With the fur trade, many native northerners became dependent on the technology and on some of the staples of the South, and this dependence gave outsiders a power quite out of proportion to their number. Although at that time many white people in the North needed the help of native people and had to learn local skills, they none the less controlled northern society – or were seen to do so. The authority of traditional leadership was greatly weakened. The power and influence of traders, missionaries and policemen were noticed by many early observers of the northern scene. No less an authority than Diamond Jenness believed that, "The new barter economy – furs in exchange for the goods of civilization" had caused great harm to the Inuit, and indeed had made them "economically its slaves."

But the native people did not always see it that way. They felt – and still feel – that they gained materially from the fur trade, even if at the same time they became dependent upon and subordinate to outsiders. The material culture of the fur trade did, in fact, become the basis of what is now regarded as the traditional life of the native people – and this is so throughout the Canadian North. It is not surprising that the fur trade era, dependent as it was on traditional skills and a blending of technology with aboriginal ways, often seems to have been a better time, for it was a time when life still had a coherence and purpose consistent with native values and life on the land. Today, when Indian and Eskimo people speak of the traditional way of life, they are not referring to an unremembered aboriginal past, but to the fur and mission era. Most of today's adults in the Mackenzie Valley and the Western Arctic were raised in it and remember it vividly.

THE GOVERNMENT PRESENCE

The traditional way of life, based on the fur trade, lasted until about 20 years ago. As native people became increasingly dependent on trade goods and staples, so their economic well-being became increasingly tied to the fortunes of the fur market. It was the long depression in the price of fur in the years after the Second World War that led to the collapse of the northern fur economy in the 1950s. When the fur market failed, the federal government had to come to the aid of the native people.

It was at this time that the welfare state – made its appearance in the North. Family allowances and old age pensions were paid to native northerners. Nursing stations and schools were built; then housing was supplied. All these things were provided by the federal government, which soon had a pervasive influence on the life of every native person. It offered what few parents anywhere would ever refuse – food, medicine and education for their children. Northern natives entered a system whose object – wholly benign in intent – was to reorder their daily lives.

In 1953 there were between 250 and 300 federal employees in the Northwest Territories. Today the Government of Canada (including its crown corporations) and the Government of the Northwest Territories have almost 5,000 employees there. What we are now observing in the North is a determination by native people to wrest from the government control of their daily lives.

THE GROWTH OF SETTLEMENTS

Federal policy in the North since the late 1950s has proceeded on the assumption that the traditional way of life was dying, and that native people had no alternative but the adoption of the white man's way. The short-run solution to the northern crisis was the provision of health and welfare measures. The long-run solution was the education of native people to enable them to enter the wage economy.

The native people who were still living in the bush and on the barrens had to live in the settlements if they were to receive the benefits of the new dispensation, and if their children were to attend school. Doubtless, the promise of greater comfort and ease made the move to settlements seem more attractive; but evidence given at the Inquiry reveals that many people do not remember the move as entirely voluntary. Many were given to understand that they would not receive family allowances if their children were not attending school. At the same time, the children in school were being taught a curriculum that bore no relation to their parents' way of life or to the traditions of their people.

What occurred on the Nahanni River exemplifies much of what happened as settlements grew. In the past the Dene did not live at Nahanni Butte but in camps along the Nahanni River. The government brought them all into Nahanni Butte so that their children could be taught at the school the government had established there. Nahanni Butte, though a beautiful place with an awesome view, is not a particularly good location for hunting, fishing or trapping. Neither the establishment of the school nor the arrangement of the school year and the curriculum – much less the location of the settlement itself – was planned in consultation with the native people.

The establishment of new government facilities in the settlements made available a few permanent and some casual jobs, especially in summer. Typically, these jobs were at the lowest level, such as janitor and labourer. Thus a hunter of repute, a man who might be highly esteemed in the traditional order, joined the new order on the lowest rung. Yet so depressed was the traditional economy that even the lowest paid native wage-earner lived with more security and comfort than most hunters and trappers. For those who wanted to continue living off the land, welfare was sometimes the only means of financing the purchase of ammunition and equipment. Whereas traders had previously extended credit to make sure families stayed on the land, now some administrators preferred the hunters to stay around the settlement to look for casual work rather than to give them welfare so they could go out hunting. Hence wage labour often came to be seen as antithetical to traditional life.

The building of the DEW Line [Distant Early Warning Line, built during the Cold War] accelerated this process in the Western Arctic. The DEW Line offered stores and medical facilities where there had been none. Many Inuit, such as those from Paulatuk, came to live in the shadow of the DEW Line stations. These sites had been chosen for strategic and military purposes, but they were often in areas without sufficient fish and game to sustain the native people.

When the people first moved into the settlements, they lived in tents or log cabins. The government, at the urging of those in the South who were disturbed by the plight of native northerners, decided that settlements should be modernized and new housing provided. These new communities were laid out to be convenient for services, such as sewage disposal systems, that were often never installed.

Along with the introduction of health, welfare, education and housing programs came new political models. Municipal government, derived from Southern Canada, was chosen as the institution for local government in the native communities. We ignored the traditional decision-making process of the native people, whereby community consensus is the index of approved action. Today in the Northwest Territories many native people sit on municipal councils, but the councils deal with matters such as water supply and garbage disposal, which the native people do not consider as vital to their future as the management of game, fish and fur, the education of their children, and their land claims. This is not to gainsay the usefulness of local government in the Northwest Territories. It is merely to remark that native people regard these local institutions as secondary to the achievement of their main goals. Their existence has not diminished in any way the growing native desire for self-determination.

Northern needs were defined by the government, or by Canadians concerned about northern natives. Programs were conceived and implemented in response to the sensibilities of southern public servants. And because few were able to find out how native people really lived or what they wanted, much less to heed what they said, many government programs were conceived and implemented in error.

This is not to depreciate the benefits that government has brought to the native people in the North. It is easy to discount these benefits now, but the attraction they held for the native people, and the need the people quickly felt for them, soon became apparent. Today housing, health services, schools and welfare are all made available by the government, and the native people have been continually and forcefully reminded of the advantages to themselves and their children of accepting these things.

As northern settlements have grown, white compounds have become established within them. In many places it is no exaggeration to speak of southern enclaves occupied by whites who have no links with the native population, but are there to administer the programs of the Government of Canada and the Government of the Northwest Territories. Many native witnesses expressed the resentment they feel toward the white people within their communities who have large houses, clean running water and flush toilets, while they have none of these amenities.

It is important to recognize the speed with which these changes have came about: some of the children who were barn in tents or log cabins and were raised in the bush or on the barrens, have gone to school; they now live in settlements and have entered the wage economy – all in just a few years.

THE WAGE ECONOMY

Wage employment and the greater availability of cash have had an impact an native culture. Much of the income earned by native people is, of course, used to buy provisions and equipment, such as snowmobiles, guns and traps. In this way, wage employment serves to reinforce the native economy and the native culture. But much of the cash that is earned is not so used, and this has had consequences that have been destructive and divisive.

Wage employment has, within the past decade or so, been important chiefly in the larger centres – Inuvik, Hay River, Fort Simpson, Yellowknife. Even in these places wage employment has created possibilities for men who wish to improve their hunting gear, and has encouraged the flow of consumer durables and processed foods into many families. But this has also meant that many native people have taken – at least temporarily – a place an the lowest rungs of the pay and status ladder. Because the number of such participants has grown considerably in recent years, and because there are persistent and increasing pressures on virtually everyone to participate in the wage economy, the cultural and social ramifications have been very wide.

THE IMPORTANCE OF THE LAND

There have always been indigenous peoples on the frontier of western civilization. The process of encroachment upon their lands and their way of life is inseparable from the process of pushing back the frontier. In the North, the process of detaching the native people from their traditional lands and their traditional ways has been abetted by the fact that fur trappers are at the mercy of the marketplace. There is no organized marketing system for their furs, no minimum price, no guaranteed return. Thus the fur economy is denied the support we accord to primary producers in the South. Nor is it comparable in any way to the network of capital subsidies, tax incentives and depreciation allowances that we offer to the non-renewable resource extraction industry in the North.

To most white Canadians, hunting and trapping are not regarded as either economically viable or desirable. The image that these activities bring to mind includes the attributes of ruggedness, skill and endurance; but they are essentially regarded as irrelevant to the important pursuits that distinguish the industrial way of life. This is an attitude that many white northerners hold in common with southerners. But the relationship of the northern native to the land is still the foundation of his own sense of identity. It is on the land that he recovers a sense of who he is. Again and again I have been told of the sense of achievement that comes with hunting, trapping and fishing with making a living from the land.

Much has been written about the capacity of the native people to wrest a living from the country in which they live. Only to the southerner does their land seem inhospitable; to the native people it offers a living. In every village of the Mackenzie Valley and the Western Arctic there are people who use, and feel they depend on, the land.... .

Other people in Canada who live in rural and isolated settlements are having their lives changed by the impact of industrial development. White people who lived to some extent off the land by hunting, fishing and trapping, and whose wants were few, have been drawn into the path of industrial development. Their own rural way of life has been discarded under pressure from the metropolis. But we should remember that white people in rural Canada have generally shared the economic and political traditions that have led to the growth of the metropolis. The challenge the metropolis represents to their self-esteem is not as great as it is for the native peoples. Although the impact of rapid change on their communities and on family ties is often quite severe, there are possibilities for translating some of these traditions and values into an urban and metropolitan context. Few such possibilities exist for the native people of the North.

SOME IMPLICATIONS OF THE PIPELINE

In the days of the fur trade, the native people were essential. In the North today, the native people are not essential to the oil and gas industry, and they know it. The outside world may need the North's oil and gas resources, but it does not need the native people to obtain those resources. Outsiders know exactly what they want and exactly how to get it, and they need no local help. Now they can travel anywhere with tractors, trucks, airplanes and helicopters. They can keep themselves warm, sheltered, clothed and fed by bringing in everything they need from outside. They have, or claim to have, all the knowledge, techniques and equipment necessary to explore and drill for gas and oil, and to take them out of the country. They can bring all the labour they need from outside. The native people are not necessary to any of this work.

The attitude of many white people toward the North and native northerners is a thinly veiled evolutionary determinism: there will be greater industrial development in which the fittest will survive; the native people should not protest, but should rather prepare themselves for the challenge that this development will present. It is inevitable that their villages should cease to be native villages, for in this scheme, native villages are synonymous with regressive holdouts. "Progress" will create white towns, and the native people will have to become like whites if they are to survive. But this kind of determinism is a continuation of the worst features of northern history: southerners are once again insisting that a particular mode of life is the one and only way to social, economic and even moral well-being.

We must put ourselves in the shoes of a native person to understand the frustration and fury that such an attitude engenders in him. If the history of the native people of the North teaches us anything, it is that these people, who have been subjected to a massive assault on their culture and identity, are still determined to be themselves. In my consideration

of the impact of the pipeline, insofar as it bears on the predicament of
northern native people, I will return often to the historical influences on
the present situation.

(Berger, *Northern Frontier – Northern Homeland*, 1977, 85–9)

3 ECONOMIC IMPACT

⌒ The Canadian North's first major economic interaction with the outside commercial world was through the fur trade. Other outside economic forces entered and became magnified over the twentieth century.
Innis, as we have seen, wrote that the completion of Canadian Pacific
Railway in 1885 was a landmark in the spread of Western civilization
over the northern half of North America, and Hutchison stated that the
Canadian industrial revolution was changing the country. Such revolu-
tions reached the North in various stages as new technologies, labour
economics, and life styles were imposed on its land and society. How
then could viable northern societies survive? Barely. The transition
from an earlier way of life, on which native self-respect depends, to a
way of life that is less meaningful and offers non-permanent employment can be demoralizing, with disastrous social consequences. Forms
of economic development must be found that "accord with native values and preferences." Priority must be given to achieving a sustainable
native economy before disruptive, crisis-producing large-scale industrial activities are introduced. ⌒

Discussion of the northern economy is always bedevilled by two related
problems. In the first place, the relationships between social, cultural
and economic problems of the native people are so intimate and intricate
that it is not possible to separate the narrowly economic from the more
broadly social. It is impossible, for example, to assess the problems of
employment and unemployment in the North in isolation from the kinds
of lives that the native people want to lead, or without regard to the
present condition of their culture... .

The second and more serious problem is the quality of the statistical
information that is available. Louis St-Laurent once remarked that, for a
long time, Canada had seemed to govern its North in a state of absence
of mind. Although he was referring to the 1930s and 1940s, his judgment may cast some light on the situation today. Despite the expenditure
of millions of dollars and the efforts of thousands of public servants,

data on some crucial aspects of northern economic life are either simplistic or are not to be found at all... .

The absence of data is, of course, an indirect consequence of policy. We have been committed to the view that the economic future of the North lay in large-scale industrial development. We have at times even persuaded the native people of this. We have generated, especially in northern business, an atmosphere of expectancy about industrial development. Although there has always been a native economy in the North, instead of trying to strengthen it, we have, for a decade or more, followed policies by which it could only be weakened or even destroyed. We have believed in industrial development and depreciated the indigenous economic base. Indeed, people who have tried to earn a living by depending on that base have often been regarded as unemployed.

The consequences of federal policy priorities in the past go beyond the problem of inadequate statistics. The development of the non-renewable resources of a region can bring serious pressures to bear on its population: people who try to continue to live on the renewable resources experience relative poverty, and may be faced with the loss of a productive way of life. Gradually more and more people give up one kind of work, and therefore relinquish the way of life associated with it, in favour of another kind of work and life. Where this has happened, they often feel they had very little choice in the matter. If the neglected sector of the economy represents a preferred or culturally important way of life, if it is a means of self-identification and a source of self-respect, then the devaluation of that way of life can have widespread and dismaying consequences. These consequences are exacerbated if the industrialized economy offers rewards that are only short-term.

Long ago, the native people of the North developed an economy based on the seasonal harvesting of renewable resources, which was for centuries the sole basis of their livelihood. That economy is still a vital part of their livelihood today, but the growth of industries based on non-renewable resources has created an imbalance in the northern economy as a whole. The traditional or native economy has come to be associated with relative poverty and deprivation. To the extent that a person tries to live off the land, he must often accept a low income and, in relation to the values of the white world, a lower social status than those who do not. Because success in hunting, fishing and trapping are the hallmarks of traditional native values, this imbalance may all too easily undermine the native people's whole way of life.

In this chapter, I shall refer to the total intrusive effect of the industrial economy on native society. By this process, the native people are pushed and pulled into the industrial system. The process, which is caused by several economic and social factors that will be spelled out, begins with the depreciation of a way of life and ends with the demoralization of a whole people. If a pipeline is built and an energy corridor established before the present severe imbalance in the northern economy is redressed, its intrusive effects will be total.

I do not mean to suggest that native people will not want to participate in the opportunities for employment that industrial development will create. Some native people already work alongside workers from the South. Many native people have taken advantage of opportunities for wage employment on a limited or seasonal basis to obtain the cash they need to equip or reequip themselves for traditional pursuits. But when the native people are made to feel they have no choice other than the industrial system, when they have no control over entering it or leaving it, when wage labour becomes the strongest, the most compelling, and finally the only option, then the disruptive effects of large-scale, rapid development can only proliferate. Eventually the intrusion of the industrial system is complete, and the consequences for the native people disastrous.

Southern views of "development" and "progress" have resulted in distorted data on unemployment; consequently, many nonrenewable resource projects have been at least partially justified on the grounds that they would create jobs for the native people. Government subsidies have been sought and obtained because it seemed appropriate for government to help solve the unemployment problem. But the fact is that large-scale projects based on non-renewable resources have rarely provided permanent employment for any significant number of native people. Even in its own terms, therefore, the policy of the past two decades has not been a success, and there is abundant reason to doubt that a pipeline would or could provide meaningful and on-going employment to many native people of the Mackenzie Valley and the Western Arctic.

It is important to understand the main point of this chapter. The failure so far of large-scale industrial projects to provide permanent wage employment for large numbers of native people has led to expressions of indignation by government spokesmen and by native people. But the real danger of such developments will not be their continued failure to provide employment to the native people, but the highly intrusive effects they may have on native society and the native economy. The real failure of the past lies in a persistent refusal to recognize, and therefore to strengthen, the native economy and native skills. This failure is evidenced by our tendency, perhaps our compulsion, to adopt solutions that are technologically complex. We, as members of an industrial society, find it difficult, perhaps impossible, to resist technological challenge. Technology and development have become virtually synonymous to us. In the North new technology or technology-for-its-own-sake may sometimes inhibit solutions. It seems easier to ship prefabricated housing units from the South than to build log cabins from local materials. When that kind of thing happens, local skills rust or remain undeveloped.

The real economic problems in the North will be solved only when we accept the view that the Dene, Inuit and Metis themselves expressed so often to the Inquiry. We must look at forms of economic development that really do accord with native values and preferences. If the kinds of things that native people now want are taken seriously, we shall cease to regard large-scale frontier industrial development as a panacea for the economic ills of the North.

This consideration of economic impact leads inexorably to the conclusion that the interests of native people are in conflict with those of large-scale industrial developers. In the short run, the strengthening of the native economy in the Mackenzie Valley and Western Arctic should take first priority; otherwise its very foundations will be undermined by the intrusive effects of pipeline construction. But, once the native economy has been strengthened, the Mackenzie Valley corridor could be developed as a pipeline right-of-way. Only by this means can we ensure that these interests will not be in conflict in the long run as well as in the short run.

In the end, it is the native people who will have to live with the economy that is developed in the North; their interests must, therefore, be kept very clearly in mind. I do not mean by this that the white business community, or any economic interest in the Mackenzie Valley or the Western Arctic, should simply be ignored.... But we must face the fact that where interests conflict, and only one choice can be made, priorities must be set.

If we build the pipeline now, the native people's own land-based economy will be further weakened or even destroyed, and many of them will be drawn into the industrial system against their will. They strongly oppose this prospect. We must recognize now that if we remain indifferent to their opposition, that indifference will bring yet more severe deformation of the native economy, serious social disarray, and a cluster of pathologies that will, taken together, constitute the final assault on the original peoples of the North.

(Berger, *Northern Frontier – Northern Homeland*, 1977, 115–16)

Index